2

Chile Handbook

Published by Footprint Handbooks
6 Riverside Court
Lower Bristol Road
Bath BA2 3DZ. England
T +44 (0)1225 469141
F +44 (0)1225 469461
Email discover@footprintbooks.com
Web www.footprintbooks.com

ISBN 1 900949 28 8
ISSN 1363-741X
CIP DATA: A catalogue record for this book
is available from the British Library

In USA, published by
Passport Books, a division of
NTC/Contemporary Publishing Group
4255 West Touhy Avenue, Lincolnwood
(Chicago), Illinois 60712-1975, USA
T 847 679 5500 F 847 679 2494
Email NTCPUB2@AOL.COM

ISBN 0-8442-2127-9
Library of Congress Catalog Card Number
on file

© Footprint Handbooks Ltd 1999
Second edition

Credits

Series editor
Patrick Dawson
Editorial
Senior editor: Sarah Thorowgood
Editor: Jo Williams
Maps: Jo Williams
Production
Pre-press Manager: Jo Morgan
Typesetting: Richard Ponsford,
Emma Bryers and Bookcraft Ltd
Maps: Robert Lunn, Claire Benison,
Alasdair Dawson and Kevin Feeney
Proof reading: Tim Heybyrne, John Work
and Howard David

Design
Mytton Williams

Photography & drawings
Front cover: Impact Photos
Back cover: Robert Harding Picture
Library
Inside colour section: Trip Photo Library,
Pictures Colour Library, Tony Stone
Images, South American Pictures, Impact
Photos, Eye Ubiquitous Images Colour
Library

Printed and bound
in Italy by LEGOPRINT

Chile

Footprint

Handbook

Charlie Nurse

Latin America series editor: Ben Box

"I can see how puzzling a country can be that starts at the frozen South Pole and stretches upwards to salt mines and deserts where it hasn't rained for eons."

Pablo Neruda, *Memoirs*

Contents

Left: *penitentes at Guataquina Pass on the Chile/Argentina frontier.*

Right: Santiago, Virgen del San Cristóbal.

A foot in the door

Highlights

Chile, with its unique shape, over 4,000 kilometres from north to south and under 100 kilometres from east to west, has something for everyone: deserts, snowy wastes, glacial lakes, volcanoes, forests, vineyards, lively cities, peaceful islands. The problem is what to choose? Since most travellers start from Santiago, the capital, do you go north or south or both?

The Santiago region The bustling city of Santiago is likely to be your first destination if you arrive by air. Nearby on the coast is the port of Valparaíso, which sprawls back from the port over a range of hills climbed by funicular railways. With its superb views, Valparaíso is one of the most attractive cities in the country.

Parcque Nacional Lauca Lauca, in the far north on the Bolivian border, is one of Chile's most outstanding national parks. Ringed by snow capped volcanoes and renowned for its birdlife, most of the park is a high plain where guanaco, vicuñas and llamas graze.

San Pedro de Atacama The Atacama desert, one of the driest deserts on earth, and the small town of San Pedro have become popular destinations. You can watch the sun set over the lunar landscape of the Valle de la Luna and watch it rise again over the geysers of El Tatio. Nearby is the Salar de Atacama, the third largest expanse of salt flats in the world. San Pedro is also home to one of Chile's finest archaeological museums, preserving artefacts of the ancient Atacama civilisations

The Lake District This region, 700-1,000 kilometres south of Santiago, offers so much that you could easily spend weeks here. Apart from the twelve great lakes there are many smaller ones, most of them overlooked by snow capped volcanoes. The port of Valdivia is one of Chile's most lovely cities and around Lago Llanquihue, the largest of the lakes, are the German-looking towns of Frutillar and Puerto Varas, a reminder that this was a centre of German settlement. From Puerto Montt, at the southern end of the region, you can cross to Bariloche in Argentina by boat across Lago Todos Los Santos, one of the most beautiful and inaccessible lakes in the region.

Chiloé To get the special feel of this large island to the south of the Lake District you need to slow down. Easily reached from Puerto Montt, the island can be explored from a base such as Castro or Chonchi: ferries connect with the smaller off-shore islands which are ideal for a complete escape.

The Camino Austral Built in the 1980s, this gravel track offers one of Chile's great journeys. It runs south from Puerto Montt for over 1,000 kilometres through a wonderful landscape of forests and lakes, rushing rivers and waterfalls.

Voyages in the Southern Ocean Puerto Montt, at the southern end of the Lake District, is the departure point for two unforgettable voyages The ferry Puerto Edén spends four days weaving through the islands and channels to reach Puerto Natales, the stepping off point for the famous Parque Nacional Torres del Paine. Other vessels visit the beautiful San Rafael Glacier, north of Puerto Natales, which sheds giant icebergs into the Laguna San Rafael.

Easter Island Lying in the middle of the Pacific Ocean, 3,790 kilometres west of the South American mainland, this unique island is easily reached by air from Santiago. It is now generally accepted that the island was colonised by Polynesians, who were responsible for carving the moai, the huge stone figures which make the island famous. Easter Island can easily be explored in a couple of days by bike or motorbike

Left: Valparaíso, Ascensor Artillería, one of 16 funicular railways which climb the steep hills around the port.
Below: Salt flats near San Pedro de Atacama at sunset.

Centre: Valle de la Luna, near San Pedro de Atacama.
Left: A huaso, or Chilean cowboy at work at a Cattle market, Temuco in the Lake District.
Overleaf: Easter Island, Moais at Tongariki.

Right: Parque
Nacional Torres del
Paine.
Below: Lago Pehoe
and the Paine massif
in the Parque
Nacional Torres del
Paine.

Above: Hostería Las
Torres in the Parque
Nacional Torres del
Paine. *Right*:
Whitewater kayaker
in action down the
Biobío River in the
Central Valley.

Wilderness park at the end of the world

Everyone should see Parque Nacional Torres del Paine at least once in their lives. Situated in the far south this is one of the great national parks of the American continent, well worth the long journey even if you are forced to fly there and miss many of the delights *en route*. To the west of the park is a great ice-cap, the third largest on earth: from here glaciers drop into deep lakes of many different colours. At its heart is the Paine *massif* with its three great volcanic plugs forming the famous towers which give the park its name. Despite lying so far south, the park's microclimate supports subtropical plants, though they have to put up with changes in the weather every few hours (or minutes). In summer (December-February) the park is carpeted with flowers, but perhaps the park is even more attractive in spring and autumn when you will also have the advantage of missing the crowds who visit the park each January, the local summer holiday month.

Torres del Paine is great trekking country. Roads run through the lower, southern parts of the park, where there are a few hotels, but the only way to see most of Paine is on foot. Energetic travellers spend five days walking *El Circuito* (the Circuit), a route round the far side of the Paine *massif* and back alongside the magnificent Glaciar Grey. There are shorter walks for the less intrepid, or for those whose visit coincides with bad weather when the Circuit may be closed. Though there are *refugios* (shelters) the real *aficionados* take camping gear.

Adventure Sports

Chile might have been designed for adventure sports enthusiasts. The main population centres are no more than a few hours by bus from the Andes: its 4,000 kilometre length provide opportunities to practice a wide range of adventure activities throughout the year. In winter (July-August), for example, when activities in the far south are restricted, there are climbing opportunities in the far north while the ski-season is also at its height around Santiago.

Beaches, often deserted except at weekends and in high summer (January), can be found along the whole length of the country's Pacific coastline. Many of the lakes in the Lake District are suitable for watersports and there are over 20 rivers between Santiago and Tierra del Fuego which are suitable for rafting. The best waters for sea-kayaking are also in the south: around the smaller islands off eastern Chiloé or near Hornopirén at the northern end of the Camino Austral. Although Chile's international ski resorts all lie near Santiago, there are also ski slopes further south: these are often more relaxed and friendly and they have the additional advantage of being cheaper. The great length of the Andes also provide extensive and varied opportunities for climbing including the hundreds of volcanoes, ranging from the high altitude peak of Parinacota in the Parque Nacional Lauca in the far north to the much lower cones in the Lake District and along the Camino Austral.

The most popular centre for adventure sports is undoubtedly the small town of Pucón in the Lake District: situated on a the edge of a lake and at the foot of an active volcano, it caters to all tastes: you can climb the volcano, go rafting on the nearby rivers, trek or mountain bike in the nearby Parque Nacional Huerquehue and go waterskiing, windsurfing and sailing on the lake. Though Pucón sells itself on its volcano and adventure sports, there are other less well-known bases in the Lake District. Cycling is an ideal way to explore the less accessible parts of the region and mountain bikes are readily available for hire in most towns.

Left: Bottles of salsa
and spices in the
marketplace. **Below:**
Concha y toro
vineyard.

Centre: A Pescadería,
or fish stall, near the
port of Angelmó,
Puerto Montt, in the
Lake District.
Right: Fruit stall in
Puerto Montt, the
Lake District.
Overleaf: 17th
century adobe church,
Iglesia San Pedro, in
San Pedro de
Atacama.

Food and drink

Not surprisingly for a country with such a long coastline, seafood and fish forms an important part of Chilean cuisine, eaten, in most coastal towns, in small restaurants near the harbour. Usually the fish market is nearby as well. Eat here and you can be sure that the food on your plate has not been frozen and transported: lunch is the morning's catch. From Arica in the far north to Chiloé in the south, this is the place to eat. These small restaurants often seat only ten customers, so you get a good look at other people's plates and your food is cooked within metres of your table. There is often lively competition for custom between the owners: expect to be approached if you are just idly wandering by.

Eating Seafood Chilean style

Though Santiago is inland, one of the most popular lunch places for travellers is the fish restaurants of the capital. It may be difficult to imagine yourself on the beach when you are in the middle of the capital, but the old market shelters small fish and seafood restaurants where you can give it a try.

Probably the most famous Chilean seafood cuisine is curantos. A regional dish from the island of Chiloé and the southern Lake District, curantos is a kind of stew of meat, fish, seafood, potato bread and other ingredients. Despite the rather odd combination of ingredients, curantos is delicious but you should make sure you are hungry before you accept the invitation to sit down as it is served in large quantities.

Though curantos is served throughout Chiloé, one of the best places to try it is in the port of Angelmó, just west of Puerto Montt. Here there are dozens of little fish restaurants selling curantos and other fish and seafood dishes. Some of the more modern places overlook the harbour; on the right day you can see the ferry *Puerto Edén*, loading or unloading before her journey south to Puerto Natales.

Back from the water's edge, near the market with its stalls of fruit and vegetables and (inevitably) fish, there are other restaurants, less sparklingly new but just as good, even if they lack the view. What you really need to wash down your curantos is a drop of cold Chilean white wine, but you will have to ask for te frío blanco (cold white tea) since wine cannot, apparently, be sold openly for legal reasons.

Lovers of wine will know Chile's increasing fame as a producer of fine wines. Though the historic heart of the wine industry is the Maipo valley near Santiago, some wine is produced as far north as the Elqui valley, near the attractive neo-colonial city of La Serena, and as far south as the Río Bobío, at the northern edge of the Lake District. The Elqui valley is also the home of *pisco*, a strong spirit distilled from grapes. Visits can be made to many of the *bodegas* (wineries) and Chilean wines can be sampled throughout the country.

Vineyards

Essentials

2

Essentials

Planning your trip

In common with the practice established by the *South American Handbook* this
volume makes no attempt to be prescriptive. Tastes in travel vary as in everything else.
This is particularly important in light of the great variety of attractions available in
Chile. There are, however, a number of places which stand out as the most popular
destinations for travellers.

Any list of such destinations would have to include Chilean Patagonia, notably the
Torres del Paine Parque Nacional, one of the great parks of the world. Almost as
popular, and at the other end of the country, is the small oasis town of San Pedro del
Atacama, a centre for excursions to geysers, saltflats and mountains. Lying between
the two, and easily accessible, is the island of Chiloé. Although often likened to Ireland,
it is more evocative of a bygone age, before the advent of modern commercial
agriculture. The Lake District, just north of Chiloé, is a major attraction for both
Chileans and foreign travellers: lakes, volcanoes, forests, rivers and waterfalls offer
some of the most picturesque scenery in the country.

Chile is, however, much richer for the tourist than this list of highlights suggests.
Less visited, but still popular options exist: the northern city of La Serena is one of the
most attractive in the country; the main port, Valparaíso, has a special feel and is close
to beaches which, if popular at weekends in summer, are deserted at other times; the
Parque Nacional Lauca, situated in the far north, offers volcanoes, saltflats and a richly
varied birdlife all at high altitude; Santiago, the capital, though hardly among the most
beautiful cities in the world, has one of the most varied cultural scenes in South
America and is close to ski resorts, beaches and fine walking country; the northern
cities of Arica and Iquique are centres for excursions into the Atacama desert.

Alternative attractions abound: Lago Lanalhue and the Sierra de Nahuelbuta, south
of Concepción, receive far fewer visitors than the lakes further south and offer varied
scenery, good facilities and a range of activities; the Camino Austral, perhaps best
travelled by mountain bike, is sparsely inhabited but rapidly opening up to tourism
and the lakes round Coyhaique are a good alternative to those of the Lake District;
some of the coastal resorts west of the Central Valley have miles of sand and few
visitors. A final suggestion is Easter Island with its unique archaeology but easily
reached from Santiago by plane.

The variety for which Chile is famous offers the visitor a superb range of choice, but
getting the most from your visit requires a little advanced planning. Apart from the
length of time at your disposal, two other factors are likely to influence your travel
plans, namely your point of entry into the country and the time of year. Both of these
are related to Chile's unique geography which rules out circular routes within the
country, forcing you to choose between going north or south, and which gives rise to
contrasting climatic conditions in different parts of the country.

Travellers arriving by air usually arrive at Santiago and are immediately presented
with the dilemma of whether to travel north or south, or both. Those arriving from
neighbouring Argentina and Bolivia usually do so by one of seven routes, all of which
can be recommended. These are, from north to south: overland from Tacna in Peru to
Arica; along the international highway from La Paz, Bolivia to Arica; the train journey
from Bolivia to Calama; by road from Mendoza in Argentina through the international
tunnel to Santiago; by bus and boat to Puerto Montt from Bariloche; the Patagonian
road route from El Calafate to Puerto Natales; the road and ferry crossings from Tierra
del Fuego to Punta Arenas. Naturally if you enter in the far north or the far south, your
choice of direction is simpler.

Even if your point of arrival is Santiago imaginative planning will help to reduce the
need to retrace your steps to a minimum. One of the consequences of Chile's
geography is that most of the country is linked by one road, the Pan-American

Highway, marked on maps as Route 5, which runs from the Peruvian frontier to the south of the island of Chiloé. This is paved throughout its length and dual carriageway for almost the entire stretch south from Santiago to Chillán. Some of the most popular destinations in Chile lie to the south of the southern city of Puerto Montt. Travelling to this part of the country requires careful planning especially if you are short of time. Though much of the mainland to the south of Puerto Montt can be reached by the Camino Austral, a gravel road marked on maps as Route 7, bus services on this are less reliable than elsewhere in the country and there is no direct overland route from here to the far south. The only overland routes to the far south are through Argentina; the alternatives are by sea from Puerto Montt and by air. Several ferry services provide vital links in this region, notably those linking Chiloé with Puerto Montt and Chaitén, for the Camino Austral, Puerto Montt with Puerto Chacabuco (and Coyhaique) and Puerto Montt with Puerto Natales in the far south. The longer ferry routes are very busy in the high season and reservations are essential.

Travellers with very limited time to spare should consider flying. Chile's national airline, LanChile, offers a domestic air pass which is extremely good value, but which has to be bought at the same time as an international ticket. While air travel can also offer fantastic views stretching from the Andes to the sea, the disadvantage, of course, is that it reduces the amount of local colour you experience compared to overland travel. Irrespective, however, of where you choose to go and how you choose to get there, do not try to do too much: Chile is a great place to experience so slow down and give yourself time to experience one of the most diverse countries on earth.

The South If time is limited you may want to focus on the southern part of the country which features many of the top attractions. A two week visit to the south could include a few days in the Lake District, where there are many options, followed by two or three days in Chiloé and four days in the far south, relying mainly on air travel especially for the long trip from Puerto Montt and Punta Arenas. Travellers with more time could easily add another two weeks in the south, spending extra time in the Lake District, perhaps including a boat trip across the lakes to Bariloche, and adding a journey down the Camino Austral to Coyhaique and a boat trip, either between Puerto Montt and Puerto Natales or to visit Laguna San Rafael.

The North Most visitors to northern Chile include the oasis town of San Pedro de Atacama in their itinerary, but a brief visit to the north could also include a few days in the Parque Nacional Lauca, reached by bus from Arica, and a stopover in La Serena. Although the long distance involved would once again mean relying heavily on air travel, some bus journeys would be required and would give the traveller a good impression of the Atacama Desert.

Other options While the above suggestions include the most popular destinations for visitors to Chile, other options abound. Those with an interest in museums and/or big city nightlife could spend a few days in Santiago, though the experience is much more pleasant in spring or autumn than in the extreme heat of summer. The old port of Valparaíso, an easy day trip from Santiago, is well worth a visit and a few days could easily be spent at some of the beach resorts near the city. Much of the rest of Chile's long coastline is dotted with beaches: depending on the season, you could include a few days at one or more of these, whether along the northern coast, in the Central Valley or in the Lake District. The Central Valley itself, passed over by most travellers, is particularly interesting if you want to understand rural and small town life in Chile: a fertile region, it will be of particular interest to wine lovers. Travellers should also remember that a visit to Chile is also a good opportunity to visit Easter Island and/or the Juan Fernández Islands, both which can be reached relatively easily and cheaply by air from Santiago.

When planning your trip you should also take into account the time of year. In high **When to go** summer (January-February) most options are open to you, though you may find the northern cities uncomfortably hot and the Parque Nacional Lauca can experience heavy rain at this time of year. In summer many destinations will be busy especially in the far south and bus fares and hotel prices are higher. During the winter months of June, July and August many services in the south of the country are closed and transport links reduced, but the north is a good option at this time and the skiing season is in full swing. Probably the ideal seasons are spring (October-November) and autumn (March-April) when many facilities in the south are open but less crowded and temperatures in the northern and central regions are lower.

Everybody has their own list. Obviously what you take depends on where you are **What to take** planning to go, what you are planning to do and what your budget is. Those items most often mentioned over the years by travellers include the following: air cushions for slatted seats, inflatable travel pillow for neck support, strong shoes (and remember that footwear over 9½ English size, or 42 European size, is difficult to obtain), a small first-aid kit and handbook, fully waterproof top clothing, waterproof treatment for leather footwear, wax earplugs (which are almost impossible to find outside large cities) and airline-type eye mask to help you sleep in noisy and poorly curtained hotel rooms, sandals (rubber-thong Japanese-type or other – can be worn in showers to avoid athlete's foot), a polyethylene sheet two by one metres to cover possibly infested beds and shelter your luggage, polyethylene bags of varying sizes (up to heavy duty rubbish bag size) with ties, a toilet bag you can tie round your waist, if you use an electric shaver, take a rechargeable type, a sheet sleeping-bag and pillow-case, a one and a half to two metre piece of 100 percent cotton can be used as a towel, a bedsheet, beach towel, makeshift curtain and wrap; a straw hat which can be rolled or flattened and reconstituted after 15 minutes soaking in water, a clothes line, a nailbrush (useful for scrubbing dirt off clothes as well as off oneself), a vacuum flask, a water bottle, a small dual-voltage immersion heater, a small dual-voltage (or battery-driven) electric fan, a light nylon waterproof shopping bag, a universal bath-and basin-plug of the flanged type that will fit any waste-pipe (or improvise one from a sheet of thick rubber), string, velcro, electrical insulating tape, large penknife preferably with tin and bottle openers, scissors and corkscrew – the famous Swiss Army range has been repeatedly recommended (for knife sharpening, go to a butcher's shop), alarm clock or watch, candle, torch (flashlight) – especially one that will clip on to a pocket or belt, pocket mirror, pocket calculator, an adaptor and flex to enable you to take power from an electric light socket (the Edison screw type is the most commonly used). Remember not to throw away spent batteries containing mercury or cadmium; take them home to be disposed of, or recycled properly.

Useful medicaments are given in **Health**, page 59; to these might be added some lip salve with sun protection, and pre-moistened wipes (such as Wet Ones). Always carry toilet paper. Dental floss can be used for backpack repairs, in addition to its original purpose. **Never** carry firearms. Their possession could land you in serious trouble.

Specialist tour operators *South American Experience*, 47 Causton Street, Pimlico, **Tours & tour** London SW1P 4AT, T0171-9765511, F0171-9766908. Apart from booking flights and **operators** accommodation, also offer tailor-made trips. *Passage to South America*, Fovant Mews, 12 Noyna Road, London SW17 7PH, T0181-7678989. Wide range of tailor-made packages throughout the region including the lost kingdom of the Incas. *Journey Latin America*, 14-16 Devonshire Road, Chiswick, London W4 2HD, T0181-7473108. Long established company running escorted tours throughout the region. They also offer a wide range of flight options. *Hayes & Jarvis*, 152 King Street, London W6 0QU, T0181-2227844. Long established operator. Offers tailor-made itineraries as well as

Essentials

packages. *Ladatco Tours*, 2220 Coral Way, Miami, Florida 33145, USA, T USA 305-8548422, F USA 305-2850504. Run 'themed' explorer tours based around the Incas, mysticism etc. *Austral Tours*, 120 Wilton Road, London SW1V 1JZ, T0171-2335384, F0171-2335385. *Last Frontiers*, Swan House, High Street, Long Crendon, Buckinghamshire, HP18 9AF, T01844-208405. *South American Explorers Club*, 126 Indian Creek Road, Ithaca, New York 14850, USA, T USA 607-2770488, F USA 607-2776122. *Trailfinders*, 48 Earl's Court Road, London W8 6EJ, T0171-9383366. *STA Travel*, Priory House, 6 Wrights Lane, London W8 6TA, T0171-9384711. *Cox & Kings Travel*, St James Court, 45 Buckingham Gate, London, T0171-8735001. *Discover Chile Tours*, 7325 Flagler St, Miami, Florida 33144. T(local) (305) 2665827, F(305)2662801, T toll-free 1-800-826-4845, tours@discover-chile.com, www.discover-chile.com. *Myths and Mountains*, Incline Village, NV, USA, T800-6706984/7775-8325454, travel@mythsandmountains.com, www.mythsandmountains.com. Educational tour operator offering cultural, wildlife and environmental trips.

Specialist
interest travel

Adventure tourism Chile might have been designed for adventure tourism. The main population centres are not more than a few hours' drive away from the *Cordillera*: its great length provides an extremely diverse terrain and enables visitors and Chileans alike to practise a wide range of adventure activities throughout the year. In the high summer month of January, for instance, when Parinacota volcano in the north is shrouded in cloud, the Torres del Paine in Patagonia enjoy their main season and the ski slopes in the centre of the country are ideal for mountain biking.

The infrastructure for what might be termed 'soft' adventure tourism, such as a half-day's rafting on a Grade 3 river (quite a thrill), or a day spent climbing a volcano and returning to your nearby hotel, is quite good. Agencies in centres such as Pucón, Puerto Varas and Puerto Montt organize combinations of activities, many for one day but some for longer durations. Santiago is also well placed for short trips, especially to the ski resorts nearby. Some of the world's top rafting and fishing is also easily accessible.

'Tougher' adventure tourism, such as camping at high altitudes, in the unforgiving Atacama Desert, on the inhospitable Patagonian Ice Cap, or even off the recently built Camino Austral, is also possible, though it is often difficult to obtain information, particularly on high grade mountaineering. Chile offers boundless opportunities for well equipped independent adventure: the best way to see the Atacama Desert is in your own or rented four-wheel drive vehicle and a mountain bike is still the best form of transport on the Camino Austral. It is important to check the experience of agencies offering expeditions to remote areas.

Among the organizations involved in adventure tourism several deserve special mention:

CATA (Consejo de Autoregulación de Aventura), Arzobispo Casanova 3, Providencia, Santiago, T7358034,

Chilean national parks

Chile has an extensive system of protected natural areas, covering seven million hectares in all. These areas are divided into national parks, forest reserves, natural monuments and natural sanctuaries, but these distinctions are of little importance for the visitor. Most of these areas have public access and details of the majority are given in the text. Camping areas are usually clearly designated, especially in the major natural areas, and wild camping is discouraged and frequently banned.

The first forest reserve was the Reserva Forestal Malleco, created in 1907, and the first national park was the Parque Nacional Vicente Pérez Rosales, founded in 1926. The expansion of the system has been based not just on the desire to preserve natural resources which may be under threat, but also on giving access for the public to areas of outstanding beauty.

All of these protected areas are managed by Conaf (the Corporación Nacional Forestal), a dependency of the Ministry of Agriculture which also has responsibility for forestry development. The address of Conaf's head office in Santiago is given below. It maintains an office in each of the regions of the country and kiosks in some natural areas and other locations. It publishes an illustrated guide to the parks and maps of the major protected areas which can be obtained from its head office and from some regional offices, the addresses of which are given in the text. As well as the book mentioned in the **Adventure Tourism** section, Conaf publishes a useful little book on native trees, Arboles nativas de Chile, Guía de Reconocimiento, by Claudio Donoso Zegers (1983).

F7772375 is a new organization formed by the more reputable agencies to try (with mixed success) to regulate adventure tourism to ensure safety and exclude 'cowboy' operators. It works closely with Conaf.

Conaf (Corporación Nacional Forestal), Presidente Bulnes 291, piso 1, Santiago, T02-3900126/3900125, regulates adventure activities within the national parks, following CATA's written guidelines on matters such as the experience required of guides, types of activity provided, size of groups and safety requirements. It also publishes a number of leaflets and has documents and maps about the national park system that can be consulted or photocopied in its Santiago office, but these are not very useful for walking.

Sernatur has a separate section specializing in providing information on adventure tourism and ecotourism located within its head office in Santiago: Av Providencia 1550 (Casilla 14082), T02-2361416, TxSERNA CL 240137.

Essentials

Further reading *Una Aventura Navegando Los Canales del Sur de Chile* by Alberto Mantellero is a guide to sailing the southern coast, with maps; also available is *Regata*, a monthly sailing magazine. Climbers will find *Cumbres de Chile*, two books with accompanying tapes, each covering 20 peaks, of interest. The first part of a five-year project to cover 100 peaks, they have also appeared in parts in *El Mercurio. The High Andes*, by John Biggar (Castle Douglas, Kirkudbrightshire: Andes, 1996), contains three chapters with information on Chilean peaks. Conaf, see above, has published *Guía de Parques Nacionales y Otras Areas Silvestres Protegidas de Chile*, US$12, a very useful guide to the main parks containing information on access, camping sites, flora and fauna; *Chile Forestal* is a monthly magazine published by Conaf with articles on the parks and ecological issues. On the Camino Austral, see *Cuentos de la Carretera Austral* by René Peri Fagerstrom.

Climbing There are four distinct terrains for climbing in Chile: each poses different problems.

Rock climbing is not organized on a national basis, though *ENAM* (Escuela Nacional de Montaña de Santiago) runs courses in rock climbing as well as ice climbing. Adventure tourism agencies are just beginning to offer rock climbing activities. The three granite towers in the **Parque Nacional Torres del Paine** are the best known and most difficult climbs, but they are in such demand that a climbing fee is levied, the only place where this occurs in Chile. On the shores of **Lago Todos Los Santos** there are very high cliffs (800 metres) at the eastern end and at Cerro Picada (800 metres) on the northwest shore.

Chile has high mountains such as **Tupungato** and **Ojos del Salado** which rival the Argentine peak of Aconcagua for climbing. Like the latter they pose few technical difficulties but the weather can be vicious and the altitude should be taken very seriously. Moreover, Ojos del Salado is not easily accessible.

By contrast some of the most important high altitude ice climbs are easily reached from Santiago: the **Loma Larga** and **Plomo** massifs are two to three hours drive from the capital. The *Federación de Andinismo* can advise on the better known and more difficult climbs such as El Plomo, El Altar and El Morado, though it is less useful for information of mountains further afield and its offices are often closed.

Volcanoes provide the fourth type of climbing. There are hundreds to choose from, ranging from the high altitude **Parinacota** in the far north and remote **Licancábur** on the Bolivian frontier to the chain of much lower cones in the Lake District and along the Camino Austral. Some of these, such as **Puntiagudo** and **Corcovado** with their distinctive plugs are difficult climbs. The easiest and most popular are **Villarrica** and **Osorno**, though Conaf rightly controls access to these because the crevasses are hazardous. Osorno, with its seracs and ice caves is a more attractive climb, but Villarrica has the dubious advantage of being more active and hiring guides is much cheaper.

Permission must be obtained from the *Dirección de Fronteras y Límites*, p 5, Ministerio de Relaciones Exteriores, Bandera 52, Santiago, T6714210, F6971909, to climb some mountains in frontier areas, notably Ojos del Salado and Parinacota. Preferably apply three months in advance; Chilean embassies abroad can help.

Mountain rescue services are provided by the *Cuerpo de Socorro Andino*, based in Santiago but with rescue groups in popular climbing areas: if organizing a climb register with them, often at the entry control to the mountain and with the local *carabineros*. Away from the popular areas you are on your own, which can also be one of Chile's main attractions.

Information *Federación de Andinismo de Chile*, Almte Simpson 77A, Santiago, T2220888, F2226285, in theory open daily but frequently closed especially in January/February (high season), has a small museum (1100-1330, 1700-2000, free) and library (weekdays except Wednesday 1930-2100). The shop in the foyer sells climbing guides and equipment and is often open when the office is closed. *Escuela*

Nacional de Montaña (ENAM), at same address, T2220799, holds seminars and conferences on climbing, runs rock and ice climbing courses and qualification courses for guides in Santiago and elsewhere. Also administers the *Carnet de La Federación de Chile*, a climbing card which is often required to climb mountains especially where Conaf control access. The *carnet* can be renewed through Conaf offices.

Trekking Chile offers limitless possibilities for both short and long treks in vastly differing landscapes: a one-day hike to the **Valle de la Luna** near San Pedro de Atacama is half a continent away from the famous circuit of the **Parque Nacional Torres del Paine**. Over 1,000 kilometres of new hiking opportunities have been opened up by the building of the Camino Austral, though the heavy rainfall in this area can be a drawback.

Within the national parks there are often short two to three hours signposted nature trails, starting from a visitor's centre, where, in season, there are sometimes lectures, usually only in Spanish, on flora and fauna and other highlights of the park.

Skiing Chile's major international ski resorts lie in the Andes near Santiago and are described in the text.

Most skiing elsewhere is on volcanoes to the south of Santiago, although back-country ski-mountaineering is quite possible on the volcanoes of the northern *altiplano*; guide essential, expertise required. The larger resorts in the south are Termas de Chillán, Villarrica/Pucón and Antillanca, 400 kilometres, 750 kilometres and 900 kilometres from Santiago respectively, all of which have accommodation on or near the slopes. There are, however, alternatives to these: many suitable volcanoes close to towns have a small base lodge and a lift which functions at weekends or peak periods. Here prices tend to be very reasonable and basic equipment rental is usually possible in the nearest town. Hitching is often the only form of transport though determined questioning in the nearest town may put you in touch with the local *Club Andino* through whom it is sometimes possible to arrange transport. After all the effort to reach the snow, the atmosphere is happy-go-lucky and the outback skiing is great. Examples of these tiny resorts are Antuco, Llaima and Lonquimay, but don't be limited to these: ask locally.

In the southern resorts skiing is for the laid-back and adventurous only. Snow conditions tend to become more spring-like and slushy the further south you go. Lift systems are not the most modern, fast or well maintained, piste preparation is mediocre and the weather is often more rainy than snowy. Despite all these disadvantages skiing on top of an active volcano looking down onto five huge lakes, as is the case at Villarrica/Pucón, is truly a memory which will last a lifetime.

Mountain biking Cheap mountain bikes, of variable quality, are manufactured in Chile. Mountain biking is a popular activity, particularly on descents from the Continental Divide and from *refugios* on volcanoes such as Antillanca and Osorno. Touring the length of the Camino Austral by mountain bike is also popular.

Parapenting and hang gliding Aerial sports are usually organized in Santiago, although there is a parapenting centre at the Antillanca ski resort.

Canyoning The southern bank of the Río Petrohué offers many fantastic canyons for climbing. Nearby *Aquamotion* have fixed rope ladders in the canyon of the Río Leon, 30 minutes by boat from Petrohué on the southern shore of Lago Todos Los Santos.

Rafting and kayaking Over 20 rivers between Santiago and Tierra del Fuego are excellent for white water rafting. Apart from the Maipo, which is the most easily accessible from Santiago, the main ones are the Cachapoal, Teno, Claro, Maule and

Biobío; the Trancura, Fuy, Bueno, Rahue and Petrohué; the Yelcho, Futaleufú; Corcovado, Palena and Baker and the Serrano and Tyndall.

Some of these rivers run through spectacular mountain scenery: one of the most beautiful is the Río Petrohué, which flows between the Osorno and Calbuco volcanoes and has lush temperate rainforest along its banks. The Río Biobío, Chile's most famous river for rafting is in decline: one dam has already been built and the completion of a second, due in 1997, will mark the end of a great rafting river. Some expert rafters have long maintained that the Biobío was, in any case, inferior to the Río Futaleufú. This river, east of Chaitén, will inevitably become known as one of the great Grade 5 rafting rivers in the world.

Rafting is generally well organized and equipment usually of high quality. Access to the headwaters of most rivers is easy. Many agencies, particularly in Santiago, Pucón and Puerto Varas, offer half-day trips to Grade 3 rivers for beginners, US$40-69 per person. Rafts should ideally carry six people and certainly no more than seven plus guide.

The most attractive waters for sea kayaking are around the islands off eastern Chiloé or around Hornopirén, just off the northernmost section of the Camino Austral in the fjords of the sheltered Gulf of Ancud. The highlight for lake kayaking is the annual open competition on Lago Llanquihue, involving five stages totalling 310 kilometres around the lake shore. Kayaks can be hired from *Oceanic*, Santiago (F2325539) and *Kayak Equipment*, San Vicente de Paul 5831, La Reina, Santiago (T/F2775288) and *Canoas Tours*, Rosario 1305, Puerto Varas (T233587). Courses are available at the *Chiloé Sea Kayaking Centre* near Dalcahue and are bookable through *Altué Expeditions* in Santiago.

There are regattas on Llago Llanquihue every Saturday, racing Lasers, Vagabonds and catamarans, organized by a group of local sailors known as the Northwest fleet. Other water sports, such as diving and surfing, are generally practised in northern Chile.

See box **Sailing and yachting** Sailing, both wind and motor powered, is becoming increasingly popular as the Chilean economy continues to expand. Protected harbours, yacht clubs and racing fleets can be found at most sizeable coastal towns from Arica southwards. Lagos Villarrica and Llanquihue are particularly popular for sports sailing and windsurfing: there are weekly regattas on both lakes and more important annual regattas. The biggest regatta is the biennial event in January (even years) from Puerto Montt around the coast of Chiloé.

The best ocean sailing is in the relatively sheltered waters from Puerto Montt south via the Archipiélago de los Chonos to Cape Horn. You should allow at least a week to begin to do justice to Chiloé and the islands off its eastern shore. Three weeks or more are required to reach the glaciers of Laguna San Rafael.

Chartering A variety of sail and power boats can be chartered from *MDS Charters* in Puerto Montt (address under Puerto Montt). Most charters are skippered: unusually good sailing credentials are required for a bareboat charter. For the really adventurous a dozen or more sailing yachts are based in Ushuaia/Puerto Williams: these are blue water sailing yachts doing charters to Cape Horn and Antarctica. They advertise in sailing magazines and are often booked a year in advance.

Yacht Facilities There are three travel lifts in Valdivia, among them a 35-tonne lift and complete yacht repair facility at the modern Awolplast boatyard. The Valdivia yacht club often has slips available. At Puerto Montt Marina del Sur is a brand new marina with 65 slips, showers and laundry: a new hydraulic lift was scheduled for operation by early 1997 and a tidal grid (with 25 foot tides) is also available. Budget minded sailors can pick up a mooring at the Club Náutico. South of Puerto Montt there are no marina facilities. Complete re-provisioning can be carried out in Puerto Montt, Castro, Puerto Aisén, Puerto Natales and Ushuaia; odds and ends can be obtained at Melinka and Puerto Aguirre, but fuel and other supplies are virtually unobtainable between Puerto Aguirre and Puerto Natales.

Sailing through the southern channels

The real Mecca for cruising boats is along the coast from Puerto Montt to Cape Horn via Chiloé, among the islands of the Archipiélago de los Chonos and further south through the channels of Patagonia. There is probably no better way to see this stunningly spectacular and remote part of South America than by yacht during the summer months. It is largely undiscovered as a cruising ground: few foreign yachts pass through these channels in any one season.

These archipelagos provide some of the finest and most challenging sailing in the world. In general the navigation and the weather conditions become more difficult as you go south. At the very tip of this 1,600 kilometre long stretch of islands and glacier-backed fjords is, of course, the sailor's supreme challenge, western Tierra del Fuego and Cape Horn. Anyone who can take their boat this far south is already among a hardy but slowly growing band of experts, some of whom now cross the formidable Drake Straits south of the Cape, normally in January or February, to cruise to Antarctica.

For lesser mortals a much friendlier region lies just south of Puerto Montt, at approximately 42°S, a region dotted with populated islands which, with their hedged patchworks of pasture, wheat and potato fields, look like Western England or Maine a century ago. The sailing, especially in January-March, is tough but sporty rather than dangerous. These

waters, shown on charts as the Gulf of Ancud and the Gulf of Corcovado, are completely protected by Chiloé from the giant swells of the southern Pacific. The weather is at best unsettled and even the fishermen and farmers frequently get it wrong. Strong winds can suddenly die to a flat calm, burning sun may be wiped out by squalls of rain and even hail. That's summer. Winter is Scottish.

Tides of six to eight metres mean strong rips; shoals are frequent, but usually well marked on charts, 'usually' meaning that special care is needed around the smallest islands, especially on the mainland side. It's rare to be out of sight of land and you mostly know where you are to within 100 metres or so even without electronics.

The best harbours are, from north to south, Quemchi, Mechuque, Quehui, Castro, Queilén and Quellón. Fuel for outboard motors is usually available at Quemchi, Castro, Chonchi and Queilén. Water generally has to be brought aboard in jerry cans filled from a friendly householder's kitchen tap. Connections to shore electricity do not exist and, indeed, the smaller islands only have power themselves for an hour or two at night. The larger islands have at least a couple of general stores but much better to stock up in Puerto Montt or Castro. The same applies for recharging batteries.

Robert and Caroline Ely of the Yacht Elyxir (Seattle, USA).

Essentials

Navigation The yachting season runs from November to March in these southern waters. South of 45S the weather is significantly worse than at corresponding latitudes in Europe and North America. Weather forecasts are provided by the Chilean Navy and are updated twice daily: they are broadcast over HF radio by voice and weatherfax map. Their accuracy is quite good considering the massive unstable low pressure systems which regularly roll in off the Southern Ocean. Complete chart portfolios are stocked at the Navy administration offices in Puerto Montt and Puerto Williams. Individual charts cost US$23 each and are generally superior to the US charts. A high quality colour chart atlas containing 28 centimetres by 43 centimetres reductions of the entire Chile chart portfolio was published in 1997.

Fishing The lakes and rivers of Regions IX (Araucanía), X (Los Lagos) and XI (Aisén) offer great opportunities for fishing, especially trout (rainbow, brown and fario) and salmon (coho and chinook). The season runs from 15 November to the first Sunday in

Competition calendar

January

Chiloé/Puerto Montt Regatta (every two years, next 2000)

International Rally of Kayaking, Lago Llanquihue, 310 kilometres, five stages

Regatta, Lago Villarrica; Pentathlon, Lago Todos Los Santos/Petrohué

January/February

International Triathlon, Pucón

February

International windsurfing contest (slalom and speed categories), Lago Llanquihue, incorporating a rafting, canoeing and

kayaking competition on Río Petrohué. Rafting Open, Pucón, beginners and experts categories

April

International Mountain Bike Competition, Antillanca

September

Horseracing on beach in Parque National Chiloé (Chepu sector) and kayaking and canoeing races on Río Chepu

October

International Surfing Competition, Pichilemu.

May except on Lago Llanquihue where it starts on 15 September. A licence is required whether for one day or a longer period: licences are usually obtained from the local Municipalidad, though some tourist offices also sell them. There are so many waters that overfishing is generally not a problem though probably the most exciting possibilities lie along the Camino Austral. Organized fly fishing with a guide can be expensive: trolling and spinning are the more widely practised methods.

Sea fishing is popular between Puerto Saavedra in the IX Region (Araucanía) and Maullín in the X Region (Los Lagos): the main centres are Mehuín, the Valdivia coast from Niebla to Curiñanco, Maicolpue, Llico and Maullín itself where salmon may be caught in the sea.

The Lake District is popular for trout fishing. Both rainbow and fario trout are found in all the major lakes; the largest fish are found in Lago Llanquihue, while Lago Todos Los Santos, on which very few boats are permitted, is noted for quantity. Salmon fishing is particularly popular with visitors from Europe and North America. Apart from the main lakes, Lago Maihue and Lagunas El Toro, El Encanto and Paraíso (all in the Parque Nacional Puyehue) have been recommended. In the southern Lake District the main rivers for salmon fishing include the ríos Pescado, Petrohué, Puelo, Maullín and, on Chiloé, the Chepu and Pudeto.

The greatest fishing area in Chile lies along the Camino Austral: Lago Yelcho and the Ríos Futaleufú and Palena are important areas for fly fishing, while further south the rivers and lakes around Coyhaique offer some of the best fishing in the world.

Santiago and Valparaíso residents fish at the mountain resort of Río Blanco.

Fishing equipment: *Pesca Mundo Caza*, Benavente y M Rodríguez, Puerto Montt; *Winkler Deportes*, Antonio Varas 841, Puerto Montt; *Lagollan*, San José 315, Puerto Varas.

Useful information: for details on licences and local conditions, contact the Asociación de Pesca y Caza, or Sernap, San Antonio 427, piso 8, Santiago, open Monday-Friday 0900-1400. Check with Sernatur on closed seasons.

Horseriding   Mountain horse treks are organized in Santiago. South of Concepción there is more of an equine culture than further north. One of the best places for hiring and riding horses is along the west coast of Chiloé. Expect to pay US$5 per hour.

Finding out more
See also embassies and consulates box page 32
Those seeking information before leaving home are advised to contact the Commercial Department of the nearest Embassy of Chile, called Pro Chile (eg London, 12 Devonshire Street, London W1N 2DS, T0171-5806392, F0171-2551848). The Tourism Promotion Corporation of Chile is at Antonio Bellet 77, Oficina 602,

Providencia, Santiago, T2350105, F2362166. In the Netherlands, the office is at Siemenwei 63, 4464 BX, Goes, T31-113270096, F113-613610, addewit@pi.net.

On the Internet, there are a great many sites about Chile which surfers may wish to explore, but note that you may have to weed out the sites related to chile peppers. Three useful sites specifically on Chile are: www.chile.cl/; www.prochile.cl/; www.chileinfo.com/. Two sites of general interest on Latin America are The Latin American Travel Advisor (see below) and *El Planeta Platica: Eco Travels in Latin America*, edited by Ron Mader, http://www.txinfinet.com/mader/ ecotravel/schools/ schools.html.

The Latin American Travel Advisor offers a travel information service including a comprehensive quarterly newsletter (free sample available), country reports sent by email or fax, and a wide selection of travel maps. These provide up to date and reliable information on conditions for travel in Chile as well as for 16 other countries in Central and South America. Individual travel planning assistance is also offered to subscribers. Credit card payment is required for fax or mail orders. Contact PO Box 17-17-908, Quito, Ecuador; USA and Canada toll-free F888-2159511, International F593-2562566, lata@pi.pro.ec, http://www.amerispan.com/lata/.

Before you travel

Documents   A passport valid for at least six months and tourist card only are required for entry by all foreigners except citizens of Guyana, Haiti, Kuwait, all African countries apart from South Africa, Cuba and some ex-Communist countries, who require visas. It is imperative to check visa requirements before travel. These details were correct in July 1999 according to the Chilean Consul in London, but regulations change frequently. National identity cards are sufficient for entry by citizens of Argentina, Brazil, Colombia, Paraguay, and Uruguay.

Getting in

Tourist cards are valid for 90 days, except for nationals of Belize and Greece where their validity is 60 days; they can be obtained from immigration offices at major land frontiers and Chilean airports; you must surrender your tourist card on departure and it is essential that you keep it safe. An onward ticket is officially required but is rarely asked for. Nationals of Australia are required to pay US$30 on entry: nationals of USA are charged US$45 on entry, and those of Canada are charged US$55. Ninety day extensions (costing US$100) are obtained from the Ministerio del Interior (Extranjeria) in Santiago or from any local Gobernación office, but the procedure is complex and includes proof of funds; then you have to go to Investigaciones for an international record check. If you wish to stay longer than 180 days as a tourist, it is easier to make a short trip into Argentina, or Peru if near Arica, and return with a new tourist card, rather than to apply for a visa, which involves a great deal of paperwork. Tourist card holders are not allowed to change their status to enable them to stay on in employment or as students: to do this you need a visa, obtained from a Chilean consulate. On arrival you may be asked where you are staying in Chile.

Visas   Very few nationalities need consular visas to visit Chile. Those that do are New Zealand, Guyana, Haiti, Kuwait, Cuba and some African and former Communist countries. The normal length of stay permitted for tourists is 90 days.

For some nationalities a visa will be granted within 24 hours upon production of an onward ticket, for others, such as Guyana, authorization must be obtained from Chile. A charge is made, but it varies from country to country. Note that to travel overland to or from the Far South and Tierra del Fuego a multiple entry visa is essential since the Argentine-Chilean border is crossed more than once (it is advisable to get a multiple entry visa before arriving, rather than trying to change a single entry visa once in Chile). A student card is sometimes useful for obtaining discounts on buses, etc.

Essentials

Essentials

Chilean officials are very document-minded. You should always carry your passport in a safe place about your person, or if not going far, leave it in the hotel safe. If staying for several weeks, it is worthwhile registering at your embassy or consulate. Then, if your passport is stolen, the process of replacing it is simplified and speeded up. Keeping photocopies of essential documents, including your flight ticket, and some additional passport sized photographs, is recommended.

Remember that it is your responsibility to ensure that your passport is stamped in and out when you cross frontiers. The absence of entry and exit stamps can cause serious difficulties: seek out the proper immigration offices if the stamping process is not carried out as you cross. Do not lose your entry card; replacing one causes a lot of trouble, and possibly expense. Citizens of countries which oblige visitors to have a visa can expect more delays and problems at border crossings.

Students If planning to study in Chile for a long period it is essential to get a student visa in advance: you obtain this by contacting a Chilean consulate (you will be asked for proof of affiliation to a Chilean university). Student cards can be obtained from Providencia 2594, Local 421 and cost US$8, photo and proof of status required.

If you are in full-time education you will be entitled to an International Student Identity Card, which is distributed by student travel offices and travel agencies in 77 countries. The ISIC gives you special prices on all forms of transport (air, sea, rail etc), and access to a variety of other concessions and services. If you need to find the location of your nearest ISIC office contact: The ISIC Association, Box 9048, 1000 Copenhagen, Denmark T+45-33939303.

Identity and membership cards Membership cards of British, European and US motoring organizations have been found useful for discounts off hotel charges, car rentals, maps, towing charges, etc. Student cards must carry a photograph if they are to be of any use in Latin America for discounts. If you describe yourself as a student on your tourist card you may be able to get discounts, even if you haven't a student card. Business people should carry a good supply of visiting cards, which are essential for good business relations in Latin America.

Duty free and export allowance 500 cigarettes, 100 cigars, 500 grams of tobacco, three bottles of liquor, and all articles of personal use, including vehicles, radios, portable tape recorders, cameras, personal computers, and similar items. Fruit, vegetables, meat, flowers and milk products may not be imported.

NB There are internal customs checks for all travellers going south on leaving Region I in the far north (ie for duty-free goods from the Zofri free zone in Iquique).

Before you travel make sure the medical insurance you take out is adequate. Have a check up with your doctor, if necessary, and arrange your immunizations well in advance. Try ringing a specialist travel clinic if your own doctor is unfamiliar with health in the region. No vaccinations are demanded by immigration officials in Chile, but you would do well to be protected by vaccination against typhoid, polio, tetanus and hepatitis A, if you are living rough or spending time in rural areas. There is no malaria in Chile. *Health*

Money

The unit is the peso, its sign is $. Notes are for 500, 1,000, 2,000, 5,000, 10,000 and 20,000 pesos and coins for 1, 5, 10, 50 and 100 pesos. Official exchange rates are quoted in *El Mercurio* and *El Economista*. Rates tend to be worse in the far north and far south of the country. *Currency*
For recent exchange rates, see box page 34

Essentials

Embassies and consulates

Argentina, San Martin 439, Piso 9, Buenos Aires, T54-11-43946582, F54-11-43280434.

Australia, 10 Culgoa Circuit, O'Malley Act 2606, PO Box 69, Canberra, T61-6-62862430, F61-6-62861289.

Austria, Lugeck 1/3/9, Vienna 1010, T43-1-5129208, F43-1-5129208.

Belgium, 40 Rue Montoyer, 1040 Brussels, T32-2-2801620, F32-2-2801481.

Brazil, Ses-Avda Des Nacoes, Lote 11, CEP 70.407-900, Brasília, T55-61-2265198, F55-61-2255478.

Canada, 50 O'Connor Street, Suite 1413, Ottawa, Ontario K1P 6L2, F1-613-2354402, echile@globalx.net.

Colombia, Calle 100 Nro 11 B-44, Apartado Aereo 90061, Santa Fe de Bogotá, T57-1-2147990, F57-1-6193863.

Costa Rica, Del Automercado Los Yoses, 50 Mts Este y 225 Mts Norte, Blvd Dent, A Postal 10102, T506-2241702, F506-2537016.

Czech Republic, U Vorliku 623/4, 16000 Prague 6, T420-2-24315064, F40-2-24316069, Tx1212464.

Denmark, Kastelsvej 15, 3 2100, Copenhagen, T45-35261535, F45-31384201, chiledk@inet.uni-c.dk.

Dominican Republic, Avenida Anacaona No 11, Mirador del Sur, Santo Domingo, T1-809-5327800/5308441, F1-809-5308310.

Ecuador, Juan Pablo Sanz 3617 y Amazonas, 4 Piso, Edificio Xerox, Quito, T593-2-256947, F593-2-258348.

Egypt El-Asmak Building, Isaleh Ayoub Street, 7th floor, Apt 74, Zamalek, Cairo, T20-2-3408446, F20-2-3403716.

El Salvador, Pasaje Bellavista 121, 9 Calle Poniente, Colonia Escalón, T503-2634285, F503-2634308.

Finland, Erottajankatu 11-0130 Helsinki, T358-9-611699, F358-9-611377.

France, 64 Bd de la Tour Maubourg, 75007 Paris, T33-1-47054661, F33-1-47054661.

Germany, Leipziger Strasse 63, 10117 Berlin, T49-30-2044990, F49-30-20444312.

Greece, Vassilisis Sofias 25, 2º Piso, 10674 Athens, T30-1-7252574, F30-1-7252536.

Guatemala, 14 Calle 15-21, Zona 13, Casilla 643, Ciudad de Guatemala, T502-2-3321149, F502-2-3348276.

Honduras, Edificio Interamericano, Piso 6 Blvd Morazán, Colonia Los Castaòos, Tegucigalpa, T504-2324095, F504-2328853.

Hungary, Jozsefhegyi Ut 28-30, F/7, 1025 Budapest, T36-1-2120060, F36-1-2120059.

Indonesia, Bina Mulia I Building 7th Floor, JL Rasuna Said, Kav 10, Kuningan, Jakarta, T62-21-5201131, F62-21-5202005.

Israel, Havakook No 7, Tel Aviv, T972-3-6020129, F972-3-5662133.

Italy, Via PO No 23, 00198 Roma, T39-6-8841449, F39-6-8412348.

Japan, Nihon Seimei Akabanebashi Bldg 8F, 3-1-14 Shiba, Minato-ku, Tokyo 105, T81-3-34527561, F81-3-34524457.

Lebanon, Nouvelle Naccache 2º

Exchange **ATM** In cities the easiest way to obtain cash is by using automatic telling machines (ATMs). These are situated at the major banks and often in other locations especially the larger supermarkets. ATMs operate under the sign Redbanc; both Cirrus (Mastercard) and Plus (Visa) are accepted. Transactions up to US$250 are accepted.

Credit Cards Visa, Mastercard and Diners' Club are readily accepted (*Bancard*, the local card, is affiliated to both Mastercard and Visa) but American Express is less useful. Credit card use does not usually incur a commission or higher charge in Chile, but in parts of Argentina commission of 10 percent is often charged. In shops identification is usually necessary to use credit cards. In case of loss or theft of your card make sure that you carry the phone numbers necessary to report it. Some travellers have reported problems with their credit cards being frozen by their bank as soon as a charge from a foreign country is incurred. To avoid this problem, notify your bank before departure that you will be making charges in Chile (and other countries). To avoid charges from your bank top up your credit card account with sufficient cash before departure.

Bifurcation après La Belle Antique avant le car, Beirut, T961-1-418670, F961-1-418672.

Malaysia, Wisma Selangor Dredging West Block 8th floor, 142-C Jalan Ampang, T60-3-2616203, F60-3-2622219.

Mexico, Goldsmith 38, Oficina 106, Colonia Polanco, CP 11560, Mexico DF, T52-5-2804462, F52-5-2808085.

Netherlands, Mauritskade 51, 2514 HG, The Hague, T31-70-3639884, F31-70-3616227.

New Zealand, 1-3 Willeston St, Axon House 7th Floor, PO Box 3861, Wellington, T64-4-4716270, F64-4-4725324, embchile@ihug.co.nz.

Nicaragua, Edif Julia, Piso 2, Carretera Sur, AP 4541, Telcor Central, Managua, T505-2-665684 F505-2-660181.

Norway, Meltzers Gate 5, 0257 Oslo, T47-22445496, F47-22442421.

Panama, Edif Banco De Boston, Piso 11, Elvira Mendez y Via España, Panama, T507-2621375, F507-2635530.

Paraguay, Guido Spano 1687 Casi Juan B Motta, Asuncion, T595-21-600671, F595-21-662755.

Peru, Avda Javier Prado Oeste 790, San Isidro, Lima, T51-1-2212817, F51-1-2212816.

Poland, Ul Staroscinska 1b Oficinas 2 y 3, 02-516, Warsaw, T48-22-6469963, F48-2-6462610.

Portugal, Avda Miguel Bombarda 5-1000, Lisbon, T351-1-3148054, F351-1-3150909.

Romania, Boulevard Ana Ipatescu No 8, Sector 1, Bucarest, T40-1-2103805, F40-1-3123621.

Singapore, 105 Cecil St 25-00, The Octagon Building, Singapore, T65-2238577, F65-2250677.

South Africa, Campus Centre (Volkskas Bank Building) 5th floor, Burnett & Hilda St, Pretoria, T27-12-3421511, F27-12-3421658.

Spain, Rafel Calvo 18–5° D, 28010 Madrid, T34-91-3190763, F34-1-3193278.

Sweden Vasagatan No 36, Stockholm, F446-8-6531188, cgestose@swipnet.se.

Switzerland, Eigerplatz 5, 12 Piso, 3007 Berne, T41-31-3717050, F41-31-3720025.

Syria, 45 Rue Al-Rashid, Mohajirin, Damascus, T963-11-3338443, F963-11-3331563.

Thailand, 15 Sukhumvit Soi 61, Prakanong, Bangkok 10110, T66-2-3918443, F66-2-3918380.

UK, 12 Devonshire Street, London, W1N 2DS, T44-171-5801023, F44-171-4365204.

Uruguay, Calle Andes 1365, Piso 1, Montevideo, T598-2-9082223/9082616, F598-2-9021649.

US, 1732 Massachusetts Ave NW, Washington DC 20036, T1202-7851746, F1202-8875579.

Venezuela, Av Venezuela, Edifcio Venezuela, Piso 3, Oficina 31, El Rosal, Caracas, T58-2-9531485, F58-2-9531501.

The Former Republic of Yugoslavia, Cakorska No 3, 11000 Belgrade, T38-11-3670403, F381-11-3670404.

Travellers' Cheques These are accepted at reasonable rates if exchanging them for pesos, though rates are better in Santiago than in most other places and this has become more difficult in most towns apart from Arica, Antofagasta and Puerto Montt. Travellers' cheques can be changed into dollars in Santiago, but is much more difficult elsewhere: check if a commission is charged as this practice seems to vary.

Cash US dollars are widely accepted by banks and *casas de cambio*, but rarely by shops and other establishments apart from hotels. Before changing check whether any commission is charged. Do not take other currencies as these are not generally accepted. If crossing to Argentina take some low value US dollar bills: the Argentine peso is par with the dollar and dollars are widely accepted. Dollar bills are often scrutinized carefully and rejected if torn or marked in any way.

Essentials

☞ *Bank exchange rates: October 1999*

US$1	531	DM1	295
UK£1	887	Dutch guilder 1	261
Aus $1	342	French franc 1	88
Can $1	356	Spanish peseta 100	347
NZ $1	270	Italian lira 1,000	298
Yen 100	505		

Casas de Cambio In many cities and towns changing cash and/or travellers' cheques is simpler and quicker at *casas de cambio* (exchange shops). Exchange rates are not necessarily better than banks and may be worse, so shop around.

Transferring money Money can be transferred between banks. A recommended method is, before leaving, to find out which local bank is correspondent to your bank at home, then when you need funds, telex your own bank and ask them to telex the money to the local bank (confirming by fax). Give exact information to your bank of the routing number of the receiving bank. Funds can be received within 48 banking hours. Western Union for money transfers T02-6968807.

Cost of living Food is reasonable, but food prices vary tremendously. Santiago tends to be more expensive for food and accommodation than other parts of Chile. Slide film is very expensive, much cheaper in Bolivia.

In July 1999 *South American Experience* in London was recommending that travellers to South America take a minimum budget of US$25 per day for basic accommodation and food, plus US$25 for every 1,000 kilometres of overland travel planned. You should note that Chile is more expensive than the average for South America, although it is cheaper than Argentina. Cheap accommodation in Santiago costs over US$12 per person while north and south of the capital rates are US$6-10 per person. Breakfast in hotels, if not included in price, is about US$2 (instant coffee, roll with ham or cheese, and jam). *Alojamiento* in private houses (bed, breakfast and often use of kitchen) costs US$7-10 per person (bargaining may be possible). Southern Chile is more expensive between 15 December and 15 March.

Travelling with children

Chile is a good place for travelling with children as there are few health risks and children are very popular. Travel with children can bring you into closer contact with Latin American families and, generally, presents no special problems, in fact the path is often smoother for family groups. Officials tend to be more amenable where children are concerned and they are pleased if your child knows a little Spanish. Moreover, even thieves and pickpockets seem to have some of the traditional respect for families, and may leave you alone because of it!

Note, however, that a lot of time can be spent waiting for buses, trains, and especially for aeroplanes. On bus journeys, if the children are good at amusing themselves, or can readily sleep while travelling, the problems can be considerably reduced. If your child is of an early reading age, take reading material with you as it is difficult, and expensive to find. A bag of, say 30 pieces, of Duplo or Lego can keep young children occupied for hours. Travel on trains, while not as fast or at times as comfortable as buses, allows more scope for moving about. Some trains provide tables between seats, so that games can be played. Beware of doors left open for ventilation especially if air conditioning is not working. There is little point in taking a baby buggy as the roads are usually very rough away from town centres.

Food can be a problem if the children are not adaptable. It is easier to take biscuits,
drinks, bread etc with you on longer trips than to rely on meal stops where the food
may not be to taste. Avocados are safe, easy to eat and nutritious; they can be fed to
babies as young as six months and most older children like them. A small immersion
heater and jug for making hot drinks is invaluable.

On all long-distance buses you pay for each seat, and there are no half-fares if children
occupy a seat. For shorter trips it is cheaper, if less comfortable, to seat small children on
your knee. Often there are spare seats which children can occupy after tickets have been
collected. In city and local excursion buses, small children generally do not pay a fare, but
are not entitled to a seat when paying customers are standing. On sightseeing tours you
should *always* bargain for a family rate – often children can go free.

All civil airlines charge half for children under 12. Note that a child travelling free on
a long excursion is not always covered by the operator's travel insurance; it is advisable
to pay a small premium to arrange cover.

In all hotels, try to negotiate family rates. If charges are per person, always insist that
two children will occupy one bed only, therefore counting as one tariff. If rates are per
bed, the same applies. In either case you can almost always get a reduced rate at
cheaper hotels. Occasionally when travelling with a child you will be refused a room in
a hotel that is 'unsuitable'.

Getting there

Air

From Europe To Santiago: British Airways from London via Rio or São Paulo (three
times a week); Air France from Paris (three per week); from Madrid LanChile and Iberia
(four a week each); KLM from Amsterdam (three), Lufthansa (three) and LanChile from
Frankfurt (four a week), Alitalia from Rome (two) and Aeroflot from Moscow (two).
Connections from Europe can be in Buenos Aires.

From North America American Airlines fly daily from Miami direct. LanChile also
has daily flights from Miami. Also from Miami, United flies daily, and AeroPerú via Lima.
From New York, United and LanChile. From Los Angeles there are flights with LanChile
via Mexico City and Lima, Lacsa via Mexico City, San José and Lima, and Mexicana via
Mexico City and Bogotá. From Dallas with American. From other US cities, connect
with LanChile flights in Miami, New York or Los Angeles. From Canada, take Canadian
Airlines International to São Paulo from Toronto, or LanChile from Vancouver to Los
Angeles and then make onward connections with LanChile.

Transpacific routes LanChile flies once or twice a week, depending on season,
between Tahiti (making connections from Japan, Australia and New Zealand) and
Santiago; they stop over at Easter Island. Air New Zealand and LanChile have a
co-sharing agreement on weekly flights between Auckland, Sydney and Santiago. For
excursion fares between Australia/New Zealand and Chile, the stopovers at Easter
Island now carry a surcharge of about US$125.

Within Latin America To/from Buenos Aires (about 75 per week) by LanChile,
Aerolíneas Argentinas, Air France, Alitalia, KLM, Swissair, American, or Avianca (many
depart at the same time, check carefully); from Mendoza by LanChile. From Montevideo
(eight per week) by LanChile and Pluna; from Asunción four days a week with Lapsa;
from Rio de Janeiro with British Airways (once) and Iberia direct (four a week), LanChile,

or Varig via São Paulo; from São Paulo non-stop by LanChile, Varig, British Airways; from La Paz five per week by Lloyd Aéreo Boliviano (LAB) and daily with LanChile (LAB also from Cochabamba and Santa Cruz, LanChile three a week from Santa Cruz); from Caracas, LanChile and Viasa; from Lima (23 per week) by Aero-Perú, Lacsa, United and LanChile; from Bogotá (12) by Avianca, Mexicana and LanChile; from Ecuador, LanChile, Tame and Saeta non-stop from Guayaquil (Saeta and Tame's flights start in Quito). To Arica and Iquique, from La Paz and Santa Cruz by LAB and LanChile.

General tips Airlines will only allow a certain weight of luggage without a surcharge; this is normally 30 kilos for first class and 20 kilos for business and economy classes, but these limits are often not strictly enforced when it is known that the plane is not going to be full. On some flights from the UK via Paris special outbound concessions are offered (by Iberia, Viasa, Air France, Avianca) of a two-piece allowance up to 32 kilos, but you may need to request this. Passengers seeking a larger baggage allowance can route via the US, but with certain exceptions, the fares are slightly higher using this route. On the other hand, weight limits for internal flights are often lower; best to enquire beforehand.

Prices and discounts 1. It is generally cheaper to fly from London rather than a point in Europe to Latin American destinations; fares vary from airline to airline, destination to destination and according to time of year. Check with an agency for the best deal for when you wish to travel.

2. Most airlines offer discounted fares of one sort or another on scheduled flights. These are not offered by the airlines direct to the public, but through agencies who specialize in this type of fare. In UK, these include *Journey Latin America*, 12-13 Heathfield Terrace, Chiswick, London W4 4JE (T0181-7478315). *Trailfinders*, 48 Earl's Court Road, London W8 6EJ (T0171-9383366). *South American Experience*, 47 Causton Street, Pimlico, London SW1P 4AT (T0171-9765511). *Last Frontiers*, Fleet Marston Farm, Aylesbury, Buckinghamshire, HP18 0PZ (T01296-658650). *Passage to South America*, Fovant Mews, 12 Noyna Road, London SW17 7PH (T0181-7678989). *STA Travel*, Priory House, 6 Wrights Lane, London W8 6TA (T0171-9384711). *Cox & Kings Travel*, St James Court, 45 Buckingham Gate, London (T0171-8735001). *Hayes & Jarvis*, 152 King Street, London W6 0QU (T0181-2227844). *Austral Tours*, 20 Upper Tachbrook St, London SW1V 1SH (T0171-2335384).

In the US: *Ladatco Tours*, 2220 Coral Way, Miami, Florida 33156 (T USA 305-8548422).

The very busy seasons are 7 December-15 January and 10 July-10 September. If you intend travelling during those times, book as far ahead as possible. Between February-May and September-November special offers may be available.

3.   Other fares fall into three groups, and are all on scheduled services:

Excursion (return) fares with restricted validity eg five to 90 days. Carriers are introducing flexibility into these tickets, permitting a change of dates on payment of a fee.

Yearly fares: these may be bought on a one way or return basis. Some airlines require a specified return date, changeable upon payment of a fee. To leave the return completely open is possible for an extra fee. You must fix the route (some of the cheapest flexible fares now have six months' validity).

Student (or under 26) fares   Do not assume that student tickets are the cheapest; though they are often very flexible, they are usually more expensive than A or B above. Some airlines are flexible on the age limit, others strict. One way and returns available, or 'Open Jaws', see below. **NB** If you foresee returning home at a busy time, such as Christmas or August, a booking is advisable on any type of open return ticket.

4.   For people intending to travel a linear route and return from a different point from that which they entered, there are 'Open Jaw' fares, which are available on student, yearly, or excursion fares.

5.   Many of these fares require a change of plane at an intermediate point, and a stopover may be permitted, or even obligatory, depending on schedules. Simply because a flight stops at a given airport does not mean you can break your journey there – the airline must have traffic rights to pick up or set down passengers between points A and B before it will be permitted. This is where dealing with a specialized agency (like Journey Latin America) will really pay dividends. On multi-stop itineraries, the specialized agencies can often save clients hundreds of pounds.

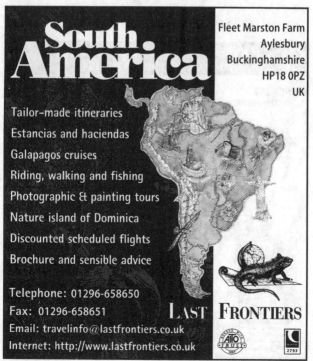

6. Although it's a little more complicated, it's possible to sell tickets in London for travel originating in Latin America at substantially cheaper fares than those available locally. This is useful for the traveller who doesn't know where he or she will end up, or who plans to travel for more than a year. Because of high local taxes a one way ticket from Latin America is more expensive than a one way in the other direction, so it's always best to buy a return. Taxes are calculated as a percentage of the full IATA fare; on a discounted fare the tax can therefore make up as much as 30-50 percent of the price.

7. Travellers starting their journey in continental Europe may try: Uniclam-Voyages, 63 rue Monsieur-le Prince, 75006 Paris, for charters. The Swiss company, Balair (owned by Swissair) has regular charter flights to South America. For cheap flights in Switzerland, Globetrotter Travel Service, Renweg, 8001 Zürich, has been recommended. Also try Nouvelles Frontières, Paris, T1-41415858; Hajo Siewer Jet Tours, Martinstr 39, 57462 Olpe, Germany, T02761-924120. The German magazine *Reisefieber* is useful.

8. If you buy discounted air tickets *always* check the reservation with the airline concerned to make sure the flight still exists. Also remember the IATA airlines' schedules change in March and October each year, so if you're going to be away a long time it's best to leave return flight coupons open.

In addition, check whether you are entitled to any refund or re-issued ticket if you lose, or have stolen, a discounted air ticket. Some airlines require the repurchase of a ticket before you can apply for a refund, which will not be given until after the validity of the original ticket has expired. The Iberia group and Air France, for example, operate this costly system. Travel insurance in some cases covers lost tickets.

9. Note that some South American carriers change departure times of short-haul or domestic flights at short notice and, in some instances, schedules shown in the computers of transatlantic carriers differ from those actually flown by smaller, local

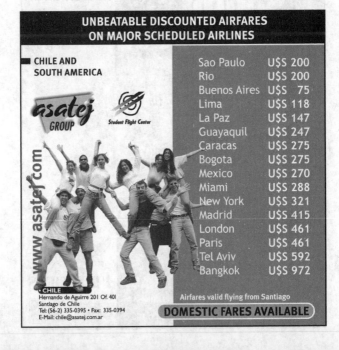

carriers. If you book, and reconfirm, both your transatlantic and onward sectors through your transatlantic carrier you may find that your travel plans have been based on out-of-date information. The surest solution is to reconfirm your outward flight in an office of the onward carrier itself.

Overland from neighbouring countries By land: good roads connect Santiago with Mendoza, and Osorno and Puerto Montt with Bariloche, in Argentina. There is also a good road between Arica and La Paz, Bolivia. Less good road connections north and south of Santiago are described in the main text. Other routes are poor. Note that any of the passes across the Andes to Argentina can be blocked by snow from April onwards. Chile and Peru are linked by a road between Arica and Tacna.

Chile is linked with its neighbours by two **railway** lines but passenger services operate on only one of these, from Calama to Uyuni and Oruro in Bolivia.

Sea

Enquiries regarding passages should be made through agencies in your own country, or through John Alton of Strand Cruise and Travel Centre, Charing Cross Shopping Concourse, The Strand, London WC2N 4HZ, T0171-8366363, F0171-4970078. Also in London: The Cruise People, 88 York Street, W1H 1DP, T0171-7232450 (reservations 0800-526313). In Switzerland, contact Wagner Frachtschiffreisen, Stadlerstrasse 48, CH-8404 Winterthur, T052-2421442, F2421487. In the USA, contact Freighter World Cruises, 180 South Lake Ave, Pasadena, CA 91101, T818-4493106, or Traveltips Cruise and Freighter Travel Association, 163-07 Depot Road, PO Box 188, Flushing, NY 11358, T800-8728584.

Touching down

Airport information

The Aeropuerto Arturo Merino Benitez, which handles both international and domestic flights, is located 26 kilometres northwest of the centre of Santiago at Pudahuel. There are separate terminals for domestic and international flights. In the international terminal there is a *casa de cambio* for changing money near the baggage reclaim area. Procedures at customs (*aduana*) quick and efficient. Outside customs there are kiosks for bus and taxi companies serving Santiago as well as car hire companies but passengers are approached by people offering taxi and bus services as they emerge from the customs area.

Transport into
Santiago

Airport buses Frequent bus services between the airport and the city centre are operated by two companies: *Tour Express* Moneda 1529, T7617380, airport T6019573/6019621, every 10-15 minutes during daytime, first from centre 0530, last from airport 0030, US$2.50; *Centropuerto*, T6019883/6958058, first from centre 0600, last from airport 2230, US$1.50 return tickets are cheaper than two singles. These buses leave from outside international and domestic terminals; in the city centre from Moneda y San Martín, with stops at Plaza Los Héroes (near the yellow Linea 2 metro sign), Estación Central and Terminal Santiago. (Do not confuse these buses with the bus marked *Aeropuerto* which stops two kilometres short of the airport.)

Airport minibuses Minibus services between the airport and hotels/other addresses in the city are operated by four companies which have offices in the airport: *Transfer*, T7777707, *Delfos* T6011111, *Turismo Bar-C* and *Navett*, T6956868. These charge US$5 to/from the city centre, US$7 to/from Las Condes. For transport to the airport book the previous day.

Touching down

Business hours *Banks: 0900-1400, but closed on Saturday.* **Government offices:** *1000-1230 (the public is admitted for a few hours only).* **Businesses:** *0830-1230, 1400-1800 (Monday to Friday).* **Shops** *(Santiago): 1030-1930, but 0930-1330 Saturday.*

Official time *GMT minus 4 hours; minus 3 hours in summer. Clocks change from mid-September or October to early March.* **Voltage** *220 volts AC, 50 cycles.* **Weights & measures** *The metric system is obligatory but the quintal of 46 kilos (101.4 lb) is used.*

Essentials

Airport taxis   There is a taxi office inside the international terminal. Taxi to/from centre US$17, to/from Providencia US$20. Agree fare beforehand.

Airport facilities   Facilities in the international terminal include banks (with ATMs), fast food outlets, a Sernatur tourist information office which offers an accommodation booking service and several car hire offices. Left luggage US$2.50 per item per day. The domestic terminal also has banks, a casa de cambio, a few expensive shops and an expensive bar and restaurant.

Airlines check-in time for international flights is two hours, one hour for domestic flights. Some airlines, including *Aerolíneas Argentinas* will perform check-in at their offices in the city the previous day, after which they require you to be at the airport 45 minutes only before departure. Remember that airlines require you to reconfirm bookings on international flights 72 hours in advance. Taxis to the airport are cheaper if flagged down in the street rather than booked by phone or from a hotel. International terminal information T6901900/6018758; flight information T6763149/6763297.

Airport departure information

Airport departure tax   7,500 pesos, or US$18.25 for international flights; US$9 for domestic flights (credit cards not accepted). There is a tourist tax on single air fares of two percent, and one percent on return fares beginning or ending in Chile; also a sales tax of five percent on all transport within Chile.

   Entry tax   US citizens are charged an entry tax of US$45, Canadian citizens US$55, Australian citizens US$30.

The national secretariat of tourism, *Sernatur*, has offices throughout the country (addresses are given in the text). The head office is at Av Providencia 1550, Santiago, T2362420, F2518469. City offices provide town maps, leaflets and much useful information. See **Further reading**, page 66, and the **Adventure tourism**, page 22 for useful organizations and their publications. Ancient Forest International, Box 1850, Redway, CA 95560, T/F707-3233015, USA, can be contacted regarding Chilean forests. For general information on travel in the region, see the **Latin American Travel Advisor**, page 29.

Tourist information

Rules, customs and etiquette

Warm sunny days and cool nights are usual during most of the year except in the far south where the climate is like that of Scotland. Ordinary European medium-weight clothing can be worn during the winter (June to mid-September). Light clothing is best for summer (December to March), but men do not wear white tropical suits.

   Chileans are very fashion conscious. How you dress is mostly how people will judge you. Dress well though conservatively: practical travel clothing makes you stick out as a foreigner. Buying clothing locally can help you to look less like a tourist. A medium

Clothing

weight shawl with some wool content is recommended for women: it can double as pillow, light blanket, bathrobe or sunscreen as required. For men, a smart jacket can be very useful.

Courtesy Remember that politeness – even a little ceremoniousness – is much appreciated. In this connection professional or business cards are useful. Men should always remove any headgear and say "con permiso" when entering offices, and be prepared to shake hands; always say "Buenos días" (until midday) or "Buenas tardes" and wait for a reply before proceeding further. Always remember that the traveller from abroad has enjoyed greater advantages in life than most Chilean minor officials, and should be friendly and courteous in consequence. Never be impatient; do not criticize situations in public: the officials may know more English than you think and they can certainly interpret gestures and facial expressions. In commercial transactions (buying a meal, goods in a shop, etc) politeness should be accompanied by firmness, and always ask the price first.

Politeness should also be extended to street traders; saying "No, gracias" with a smile is better than an arrogant dismissal. Whether you give money to beggars is a personal matter, but your decision should be influenced by whether a person is begging out of need or trying to cash in on the tourist trail. In the former case, local people giving may provide an indication. Giving money to children is a separate issue, upon which most agree: don't do it. There are occasions where giving away food in a restaurant may be appropriate, but first inform yourself of local practice.

Tipping Ten percent in restaurants and a few pesos in bars and soda fountains. Railway and airport porters: US$0.50 a piece of luggage. Cloakroom attendants and cinema usherettes: US$0.20. Taxi drivers are not tipped.

Prohibitions **Law enforcement** There are several types of police. *Carabineros* (green uniforms) handle all tasks except immigration. *Investigaciones* (in civilian dress), are the detective police who deal with everything except traffic. *Policia Internacional*, a division of Investigaciones, handle immigration. **You should never offer an official a bribe**.

Responsible It is often assumed that tourism only has an adverse impact on the environment and
tourism local communities at the more excessive end of the travel industry, as seen along the Spanish coast or in Bali. However travellers can have an impact, no matter how few in number they may be, especially in areas 'off the beaten track' where local people may be unused to their conventions or lifestyles and where natural environments may be very sensitive.

In recent years legislation to protect the environment has been introduced in most countries; in some cases this can have a direct bearing on the activities of travellers. The establishment of national parks and other protected areas, for example, involves the creation of rules and guidelines for visitors; these should always be followed, as should legislation on the use of natural resources (especially wildlife). Chile, along with most European countries, the US and Canada, is a signatory of the Convention on International Trade in Endangered Species (CITES), which aims to control the trade in live specimens of endangered plants and animals as well as 'recognizable parts or derivatives' of protected species. The full list of protected species varies from country to country, so if you feel the need to purchase trinkets and souvenirs derived from wildlife, it would be prudent to check whether they are protected. Importing products derived from CITES protected species into a country which is a signatory of the agreement can lead to heavy fines, confiscation of goods and even imprisonment. Information on the status of legislation and protective measures can be obtained from Traffic International, UK office T01223-277427, traffic@wcmc.org.uk.

Safety

Chile is generally a safe country to visit, although like all major cities, Santiago and Valparaíso do have a crime problem especially in the centre, where the following suggestions are particularly applicable. Keep all documents secure; hide your main cash supply in different places or under your clothes: extra pockets sewn inside shirts and trousers, pockets closed with a zip or safety pin, moneybelts (best worn below the waist rather than outside or at it or around the neck), neck or leg pouches, a thin chain for attaching a purse to your bag or under your clothes and elasticated support bandages for keeping money and cheques above the elbow or below the knee have been repeatedly recommended (the last by John Hatt in *The Tropical Traveller*). Keep cameras in bags, preferably with a chain or wire in the strap to defeat the slasher, or briefcases; take spare spectacles (eyeglasses); don't wear expensive wrist watches or jewellery. If you wear a shoulder bag in a market, carry it in front of you. A backpack should be lockable at its base.

Look out for tricks intended to distract your attention or separate you from your possessions. One common ruse in large city centres is 'the mustard trick': the victim is sprayed with mustard, ketchup or some other substance, apparently accidentally, and an accomplice offers sympathy and helps to clean your jacket, removing your wallet at the same time.

Be wary of plainclothes police; insist on seeing identification and on going to the police station by main roads. Do not hand over your identification, or money – which police should not need to see anyway, until you are at the station. On no account take them directly back to your lodgings. Be even more suspicious if the police officer seeks confirmation of status from a passer-by. If someone tries to extract a bribe from you, insist on a receipt. If attacked, remember your assailants may well be armed, and try not to resist.

It is best, if you can trust your hotel, to leave any valuables you don't need in the safe deposit there when sightseeing locally. Always keep an inventory of what you have deposited. If you lose valuables, always report to the police and note details of the report for insurance purposes.

Travelling alone The following hints have mainly been supplied by women, but most apply to any single traveller. When you set out, err on the side of caution until your instincts have adjusted to the customs of a new culture. If, as a single woman, you can befriend a local woman, you will learn much more about the country you are visiting. Unless actively avoiding foreigners like yourself, don't go too far from the beaten track; there is a very definite 'gringo trail' which you can join, or follow, if seeking company. This can be helpful when looking for safe accommodation, especially if arriving after dark (which is best avoided). Remember that for a single woman a taxi at night can be as dangerous as wandering around on her own. At borders dress as smartly as possible. Travelling by train is a good way to meet locals, but buses are much easier for a person alone; on major routes your seat is often reserved and your luggage can usually be locked in the hold. It is easier for men to take the friendliness of locals at face value; women may be subject to much unwanted attention. To help minimize this, do not wear suggestive clothing and, advises Alex Rossi of Jawa Timur, Indonesia, do not flirt. By wearing a wedding ring, carrying a photograph of your 'husband' and 'children', and saying that your "husband" is close at hand, you may dissuade an aspiring suitor. If politeness fails, do not feel bad about showing offence and departing. When accepting a social invitation, make sure that someone knows the address and the time you left. Ask if you can bring a friend (even if you do not intend to do so). A good rule is always to act with confidence, as though you know where you are going, even if you do not. Someone who looks lost is more likely to attract unwanted attention.

Where to stay

See inside front cover for hotel price grades

Essentials

In most parts of Chile accommodation is plentiful and finding a room to suit your budget should not present major problems except during the summer holiday month of January when space can be scarce especially in the more popular holiday venues of the south and during the Independence Day holidays in the middle of September.

Top class hotels are available in Santiago and in most major cities, but elsewhere choice is usually more limited. Many establishments are described by names other than 'hotel': *hosterías* tend to be in rural areas and may have many of the facilities of a hotel; the terms *hostal*, *residencial* and *hospedaje* usually refer to a small family-run establishment with limited facilities and services. A *motel*, especially if it is situated on the outskirts of a city, is likely to be a short-stay establishment unless it is described as a *motel turístico*: usually the name or sign outside will indicate what type it is. In parts of the country, especially in the south, many families offer accommodation; often this is advertised by a sign in the window. In these towns people often meet buses to offer accommodation.

Prices quoted in the accommodation listings are for two people sharing a double room; usually (unless otherwise stated) with a bathroom (shower and toilet). Single rooms can be difficult to find and can be almost as expensive as double rooms. Accommodation, as with everything else, is more expensive in Santiago than in most other parts of the country. Prices also tend to be higher the further south you go as well as in some northern cities such as Antofagasta. In tourist areas, prices are higher in the high season (January/February, plus any local festivity), but off-season you can often bargain for a lower price, though you will usually have to be staying for two or more days to be successful: ask politely for a discount (*descuento*).

On hotel bills service charges are usually 10 per cent. Value Added Tax (known as IVA) at 18 per cent is charged on hotel bills and should be included in any price quoted in pesos. Whether VAT is charged on meals and other services on the bill seems to depend on the policy of the management. VAT and service charges do not apply in cheaper establishments. The government waives the VAT charge for hotel bills paid in dollars (cash or travellers' cheques) but only for hotels which have an agreement (*convenio*) with the government on this. As a result larger hotels (but few other establishments) can offer you much lower tariffs if you pay in dollars than those advertised in pesos.

Naturally you should establish clearly in advance what is being included in the price rather than relying on prices posted or services claimed on notices in the reception area. Many hotels have restaurants serving lunch and dinner; few budget places have this facility. Many places offer breakfast, though this usually consists of instant coffee or tea and bread. An increasing number of cheaper establishments offer kitchen facilities, but if you are relying on these you should check them out first. Most establishments will not allow you to wash and dry clothes in your room, but some offer facilities for you to do your own laundry. Many hotels have parking facilities, though in large cities this may be a few blocks from the hotel itself. Motorcycle parking is widely available.

Advice and suggestions The cheapest and often the nastiest hotels are often situated around bus terminals. If you arrive late and are just passing through they may be okay. Better quality accommodation is often, but not always, found near the main plaza. Taxi and bus drivers are sometimes useful sources of information about accommodation, but, especially in tourist centres, they may also try to take you to a place where they know they will get a commission.

Reception areas in hotels can be very misleading, so it is a very good idea to see the room before booking. Hoteliers often try to offload their least desirable rooms first. If you are shown a dark room without a window, ask if they have rooms with a window. In large cities the choice may be between an inside room without a window and a room with a window over a noisy street but often you will find that the choice is not so stark. Many middle range establishments have two or more categories of room: with private bathroom (*con baño privado*) and without (*con baño común*) so it is often worth asking whether there is anything cheaper than the price initially quoted.

Toilets Many hotels, restaurants and bars have inadequate water supplies. **Almost without exception used toilet paper should not be flushed down the pan, but placed in the receptacle provided**. This applies even in quite expensive hotels. Failing to observe this custom will block the pan or drain, a considerable health risk. If you are concerned about the hygiene of the facility, put paper on the seat. Carry toilet paper with you as cheaper establishments as well as restaurants, bars, etc frequently do not supply it.

Camping is easy but no longer cheap at official sites. A common practice is to charge US$10 for up to five people, with no reductions for fewer than five. 'Camping Gaz International' stoves are recommended, since green replaceable cylinders are available in Santiago (white gas – *benzina blanca* – is available in hardware shops; for good value try the *Sodimac* or *Tricot* chains of DIY stores). Copec run a network of 33 'Rutacentros' along Ruta 5 which have showers, cafeterias and offer camping. Free camping is available at many filling stations. Campsites are very busy in January and February. *Turistel* publish an annual guide which lists campsites. | Camping

There are youth hostels throughout Chile; average cost about US$5-8 per person. Although some hostels are open only from January to the end of February, many operate all year round. The Hostelling International card is usually readily accepted. In summer they are usually crowded and noisy, with only floor space available. A Chilean YHA card costs US$5. An additional stamp costing US$4 enables you to use the card in Argentina, Uruguay and Brazil. Hostelling International card costs US$15. These can be obtained from the Asociación Chilena de Albergues Turísticos Juveniles (ACHATJ), Hernando de Aguirre 201, Oficina 602, T2333220/2343233, achatj@ hostelling.co.cl, together with a useful guidebook of all youth hostels in Chile, *Guía Turística de los Albergues Juveniles*. In summer there are makeshift hostels in many Chilean towns, usually in the main schools. | Youth hostels

Getting around

LanChile (who also own Ladeco) and the smaller airline Avant fly between Santiago and major cities. Several smaller airlines serve the south. Details of most flights are given in the text. For the best views of the Andes try to sit on the left flying south and the right flying north. | *Air*
See pages 531-535 for maps of main routes through Chile

Visit Chile Airpass LanChile sells a Visit Chile Airpass which can be used on all LanChile routes within Chile with the exception of Easter Island. The Airpass can only be purchased abroad and can only be purchased at the same time as a transatlantic ticket to Chile. The airpass is valid for one month from the use of the first coupon. Minimum three coupons, maximum six coupons. If bought with a LanChile transatlantic flight the airpass costs US$50 per coupon (Easter Island US$525). If bought with a transatlantic flight with another carrier the pass costs US$350 for the first three coupons plus US$80 for each additional coupon (Easter Island US$898). There are no discounts on airpass prices for children apart from those aged under two and not occupying a seat who travel free. Reservations should be made well in | *You have to confirm domestic flights at least 24 hrs before departure* advance since many flights are fully booked. Flight dates can be altered without penalty, but route changes incur a penalty of US$30 per change. There is no increase in the number of coupons is permitted but booked destinations can be left out. LanChile also sell a **Mercosur Airpass,** duration also one month, which covers air travel within the Mercosur area (Argentina, Brazil, Chile, Paraguay and Uruguay) but does not include Easter Island.

NB Book several months in advance for flights to Easter Island in January and February. Check with the airlines for matrimonial, student and other discounts. Both LanChile and Ladeco sell out-price tickets with up to 50 percent off either as part of special promotions or to standby passengers, though the availability of standby fares is often denied. Note that with some fares it is as cheap to fly long distance as take a *salón cama* bus, especially with Avant, whose fares are usually considerably lower than LanChile or Ladeco.

Chile, major domestic air routes

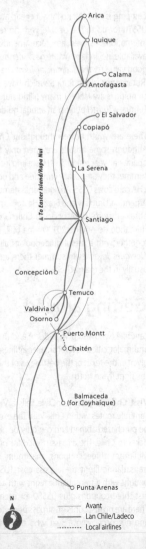

Train There are 4,470 kilometres of line, of which most are state owned. Most of the privately owned 2,130 kilometres of line are in the northern deserts where only one line, from Calama to Uyuni, Oruro and La Paz (Bolivia) carries passengers. In the south and centre of the country passenger services have become steadily more restricted. The main passenger service runs south from Santiago to Temuco, though in 1999-2000 this is likely to terminate at Chillán. There are also suburban passenger trains around Santiago and inland from Valparaíso. The Ferrocarriles del Estado publish an annual *Guía Turística*, available in various languages from the larger stations.

Trains in Chile are moderately priced, and not as slow as in other Andean countries, but dining car food is expensive. There is a 15 percent discount on return tickets and a 10 percent discount for senior citizens aged 60 or over. There is a railway information office at O'Higgins 853, at the end of the arcade, Santiago, for all lines except the Calama/Antofagasta to Bolivia. English is spoken.

Road About a half of the 79,593 kilometres of roads can be used the year round, though a large proportion of them is unimproved and about 11,145 kilometres are paved. Many other roads are described as *ripio* (gravel and/or stones). Speeds on these are usually slower. The region round the capital and the Central Valley are the best served.

Bus fares in Chile

The following is intended to provide an idea of single bus fares from Santiago. Fares given are for standard services; other services such as salón cama *and* semi cama *are more expensive. Lower fares than those shown are often available, especially at the last minute, but much higher fares are charged in summer (January-February) and during the independence celebrations in September. Prices quoted are in dollars.*

Northbound		**Southbound**	
La Serena	12-18	Talca	6-8
Copiapó	20-23	Temuco	10-15
Antofagasta	36-41	Valdivia	12-18
Iquique	47-49	Puerto Montt	13-19
Arica	47-53	Ancud	20-25
		Castro	21-29

Bus Buses are frequent and on the whole good. Apart from holiday times, there is little problem getting a seat on a long-distance bus. *Salón-cama* services run between main cities; TurBus and Tramaca are highly recommended. Generally avoid back seats near the toilet due to smell and disruption of passing passengers. *Salón-cama* means 25 seats, *semi-cama* means 34 and *Salón-ejecutivo* means 44 seats. Stops are infrequent. Prices are highest between December-March and fares from Santiago double during the Independence celebrations in September. Since there is lots of competition between bus companies, fares may be bargained lower, particularly just before departure. Students and holders of Hostelling International cards may get discounts, which varies in amount, but these are not usually available in high season. Most bus companies will carry bicycles, but may ask for payment; on TurBus payment is mandatory.

Taxis & colectivos Taxis usually have meters and can be engaged either in the street or by phoning, though they tend to be more expensive when booked from a hotel. Agree beforehand on fares for long journeys out of city centres or for special excursions. A 50 percent surcharge is applied after 2100 and on Sunday. Taxi drivers may not know the location of streets away from city centres. There is no need to give a tip unless some extra service is performed. *Colectivos* (collective taxis) which operate on fixed routes (identified by numbers and destinations) are a good way of getting about cities. *Colectivos* have fixed charges, which increase at night and weekends and which are usually advertised in the front windscreen. They are flagged down on the street corner (in some cities such as Puerto Montt there are signs). It is best to take small change as the driver takes money and offers change while driving. *Colectivos* also operate on some interurban routes, leaving from a set point when full. On interurban routes they compete favourably with buses for speed but not for comfort.

Motoring **Documents** Always carry your passport and driving licence. According to the Chilean Ley de Tránsito, foreign drivers need only have their national driver's licence, but in the north especially, the carabineros will only accept an international driver's licence. To avoid problems, obtain one before leaving home. Car drivers also require a *Relaciones de pasajeros* document, available at borders, and must present the original registration document of their vehicle, as must motorcyclists. In the case of a car registered in someone else's name, carry a notarized letter of authorization. Car drivers should have all their papers in order and to hand since there are frequent checks, but fewer in the south. Carabineros are strict about speed limits: Turistel maps mark police posts, make sure you are not speeding when you pass them.

Essentials

According to the RAC in the UK there are three recognized documents for taking a vehicle into South America: a *carnet de passages* issued by the Fedération Internationale de l'Automobile (FIA – Paris), a *carnet de passages* issued by the Alliance Internationale de Tourisme (AIT-Geneva), and the *Libreta de Pasos por Aduana* issued by the Federación Interamericana de Touring y Automóvil Clubs (FITAC). Officially, any one of these three is required for Chile, but in practice, none is asked for. The *libreta*, a 10-page book of three-part passes for customs, should be available from any South American automobile club member of FITAC; cost seems to be US$200, half refundable. The *carnet de passages* is available only in the country where the vehicle is registered. In the UK it can be obtained from the RAC and the AA either bank indemnity or insurance indemnity, half of the premium refundable value of the vehicle and countries to be visited required). In the USA the AAA seems not to issue the *carnet*, although the HQ in Washington DC may give advice. It is available from the Canadian Automobile Association (1775 Courtwood Crescent, Ottawa, K2C 3JZ, T613-2267631, F613-2257383) from whom full details may be obtained.

Insurance for the vehicle is obligatory and can be bought at borders. It is getting increasingly difficult to insure against accident, damage or theft in the country of origin. It is very expensive to insure against accident and theft, especially as you should take into account the value of the car increased by duties calculated in real (ie non devaluing) terms. If the car is stolen or written off you will be required to pay very high import duty on its value. Get the legal minimum cover, not expensive, as soon as you can, because if you should be involved in an accident and are uninsured, your car could be confiscated. If anyone is hurt, do not pick them up (you may become liable). Seek assistance from the nearest police station or hospital if you are able to do so.

Further reading on page 66 gives more details of maps and guide books

Information and maps Members of foreign motoring organizations may join the Automóvil Club de Chile, Av Vitacura 8620, Santiago, T2125702, F2295295 (US$58 per three months) and obtain hotel discounts. Road maps are available at the Santiago headquarters, or other regional offices. Several individual maps provide greater detail than the Club's road atlas. The *Turistel* guides (see **Further reading**, page 66) are very useful for roads and town plans, but not all distances are exact. The description *ripio* (gravel) usually requires high clearance; *buen ripio* should be OK for ordinary cars.

Fuel Gasoline (sold in litres) costs the equivalent of US$2.40 a gallon; it becomes more expensive the further north and further south you go. Unleaded fuel, 93 octane, is available at many service stations in the major cities. Unleaded 95 and 97 octane are less common. Diesel fuel is widely available. Service stations are frequently reluctant to accept credit cards. Often when they advertise that they accept credit cards, they refuse to do so: always ask beforehand. When driving in the south (on the Camino Austral particularly), and in the desert north, always top up your fuel tank and carry spare fuel. Car hire companies may not have fuel cans. These are obtainable from some supermarkets but not from service stations. The standard of facilities in service stations is generally good.

Preparation Preparing your own car for the journey is largely a matter of common sense: obviously any part that is not in first class condition should be replaced. It's well worth installing extra heavy-duty shock absorbers (such as Spax or Koni) before starting out, because a long trip on rough roads in a heavily laden car will give heavy wear. Tyres need to be hard-wearing (avoid steel belt). Fit tubes on 'tubeless' tyres, since air plugs for tubeless tyres are hard to find, and if you bend the rim on a pothole, the tyre will not hold air. Take spare tubes, and an extra spare tyre. For car and motorcycle tyres try Calle Serranos 32, Santiago, reported to be the best stock in South America. Also take spare plugs, fanbelts, radiator hoses and headlamp bulbs; even though local equivalents can easily be found in cities, it is wise to take spares for those occasions late at night or in remote areas when you might need them. You can also change the fanbelt after a stretch of long, hot driving to prevent wear (eg after 15,000 kilometres/10,000 miles). If your vehicle has more than one fanbelt, always replace them all at the same time (make sure you have the necessary tools if doing it yourself). If your car has sophisticated electrics, spare 'black boxes' for the ignition and fuel injection are advisable, plus a spare voltage regulator or the appropriate diodes for the alternator, and elements for the fuel, air and oil filters if these are not a common type. (Some drivers take a spare alternator of the correct amperage, especially if the regulator is incorporated into the alternator.) Dirty fuel is a frequent problem, so be prepared to change filters more often than you would at home: in a diesel car you will need to check the sediment bowl often, too. An extra in-line fuel filter is a good idea if feasible (although harder to find, metal canister type is preferable to plastic), and for travel on dusty roads an oil bath air filter is best for a diesel car. For driving on gravel (*ripio*) roads, especially the Camino Austral, a good windscreen protector should be fitted: primitive versions are often of wire mesh. It is wise to carry a spade, jumper cables, tow rope and an air pump. Fit tow hooks to both sides of the vehicle frame. A 12 volt neon light for camping and repairs will be invaluable. Spare fuel containers should be steel and not plastic, and a siphon pipe is essential for those places where fuel is sold out of the drum. Take a 10 litre water container for self and vehicle. In Santiago car parts available from many shops on Calle 10 de Julio.

Security Apart from the mechanical aspects, spare no ingenuity in making your car secure. Use heavy chain and padlocks to chain doors shut, fit security catches on windows, remove interior window winders (so that a hand reaching in from a forced vent cannot open the window). All these will help, but none is foolproof. Anything on the outside – wing mirrors, spot lamps, motifs etc – may be stolen too. Wheels should be secured by locking nuts. Try never to leave the car unattended except in a locked garage or guarded parking space. Remove all belongings and leave the empty glove compartment open when the car is unattended. Also lock the clutch or accelerator to the steering wheel with a heavy, obvious chain or lock. Street children will generally protect your car fiercely in exchange for a tip. Be sure to note down key numbers and carry spares of the most important ones (but don't keep all spares inside the vehicle).

Driving at night is not recommended; be especially careful on major roads into and out of cities in the early evening because people tend to cross the highway without warning.

Car hire is an increasingly popular way of travelling in Chile, although it tends to reduce your contact with local people. Many agencies, both local and international, operate in Chile. Vehicles may be rented by the day, the week or the month, with or without unlimited mileage. Rates quoted do not normally include insurance or 18 percent VAT. Make sure you know what the insurance covers, in particular third party insurance. Often this is only likely to cover small bumps and scratches. Ask about extra cover for a further premium. If you are in a major accident and your insurance is inadequate, your stay in Chile may well be prolonged beyond its intended end. A small car, with unlimited mileage costs about US$500 a week in high season, a pick-up much more. In some areas rates are much lower off-season. (At peak holiday times, eg Independence celebrations, car hire is very difficult.) Shop around, there is much competition. Note that the Automóvil Club de Chile has a car hire agency (with discounts for members or affiliates) and that the office may not be at the same place as the Club's regional delegation. **NB** If intending to leave the country in a hired car, you must obtain an authorization from the hire company, otherwise you will be turned back at the frontier. When leaving Chile this is exchanged for a quadruple form, one part of which is surrendered at each border control. If you plan to leave more than once you will need to photocopy the authorization.

Car hire

Motorcycling People are generally very amicable to motorcyclists and you can make many friends by returning friendship to those who show an interest in you.

The machine It should be off road capable: a good choice would be the BMW R80/100/GS for its rugged and simple design and reliable shaft drive, but a Kawasaki KLR 650s, Honda Transalp/Dominator, or the ubiquitous Yamaha XT600 Tenere would also be suitable. A road bike can go most places an off road bike can go at the cost of greater effort.

Preparations Fit heavy duty front fork springs and the best quality rebuildable shock absorber you can afford (Ohlins, White Power). Fit lockable luggage such as Krausers (reinforced luggage frames) or make some detachable aluminium panniers. Fit a tank bag and tank panniers for better weight distribution. A large capacity fuel tank (Acerbis), +300 mile/480 kilometres range is essential if going off the beaten track. A washable air filter is a good idea (K&N), also fuel filters, fueltap rubber seals and smaller jets for high altitude Andean motoring. A good set of trails-type tyres as well as a high mudguard are useful. Get to know the bike before you go, ask the dealers in your country what goes wrong with it and arrange a link whereby you can get parts flown out to you. If riding a chain driven bike, a fully enclosed chaincase is useful. A hefty bash plate/sump guard is invaluable.

Spares Reduce service intervals by half if driving in severe conditions. A spare rear tyre is useful but you can buy modern tyres (see under **Motoring** above). Take oil filters, fork and shock seals, tubes, a good manual, spare cables (taped into position), a plug cap and spare plug lead. A spare electronic ignition is a good idea, try and buy a second-hand one and make arrangements to have parts sent out to you. A first class tool kit is a must and if riding a bike with a chain then a spare set of sprockets and an 'o' ring chain should be carried. Spare brake and clutch levers should also be taken as these break easily in a fall. Parts are few and far between, but mechanics are skilled at making do and can usually repair things. Castrol oil can be bought everywhere and relied upon.

Take a puncture repair kit and tyre levers. Find out about any weak spots on the bike and improve them. Get the book for international dealer coverage from your manufacturer, but don't rely on it. They frequently have few or no parts for modern, large machinery.

For motorcyclists the following shops in Santiago have been recommended: *Calvín y Calvín*, Av Las Condes 8038, T2243434, run by Winston Calvín, friendly, helpful, speaks English, knows about necessary paperwork for buying bikes, Honda and Yamaha parts and service; *Solo Moto*, Vitacura 2760, T2311178, English spoken, service and parts for Honda and Yamaha; *Moto Service*, Vitacura 2715, new and second-hand Honda and Yamaha dealer; *Guillermo de Freitas Rojas* (Willy), C Félix Mendelson, 4740-Santiago, T5211853, excellent BMW mechanic; *Miebacc*, Doble Almeda 1040, Nunoa, T2237533, for BMW parts and service. Mechanics, etc outside Santiago are given in the text.

Clothes and equipment A tough waterproof jacket, comfortable strong boots, gloves and a helmet with which you can use glass goggles (Halycon) which will not scratch and wear out like a plastic visor. The best quality tent and camping gear that you can afford and a petrol stove which runs on bike fuel is helpful.

Security Try not to leave a fully laden bike on its own. An Abus D or chain will keep the bike secure. A cheap alarm gives you peace of mind if you leave the bike outside a hotel at night. Most hotels will allow you to take the bike inside. Look for hotels that have a courtyard or more secure parking and never leave luggage on the bike overnight or whilst unattended.

Documents Passport, International Driving Licence, bike registration document are necessary. Riders fare much better with a *carnet de passages* than without it.

At first glance a bicycle may not appear to be the most obvious vehicle for a major journey, but given ample time and reasonable energy it most certainly is the best. It can be ridden, carried by almost every form of transport from an aeroplane to a canoe, and can even be lifted across one's shoulders over short distances. Cyclists can be the envy of travellers using more orthodox transport, since they can travel at their own pace, explore more remote regions and meet people who are not normally in contact with tourists.

Choosing a bicycle The choice of bicycle depends on the type and length of expedition being undertaken and on the terrain and road surfaces likely to be encountered. Unless you are planning to restrict your journey almost exclusively on paved roads – when a high quality touring bike such as a Dawes Super Galaxy would probably suffice – a mountain bike is strongly recommended. The good quality ones (and the cast iron rule is **never** to skimp on quality) are incredibly tough and rugged, with low gear ratios for difficult terrain, wide tyres with plenty of tread for good road-holding, cantilever brakes, and a low centre of gravity for improved stability. Although imported spares are available in the larger cities, locally manufactured parts are of a lower quality and rarely last. Buy everything you possibly can before you leave home.

Bicycle equipment A small but comprehensive tool kit (to include chain rivet and crank removers, a spoke key and possibly a block remover), a spare tyre and inner tubes, a puncture repair kit with plenty of extra patches and glue, a set of brake blocks, brake and gear cables and all types of nuts and bolts, at least 12 spokes (best taped to the chain stay), a light oil for the chain (eg Finish-Line Teflon Dry-Lube), tube of waterproof grease, a pump secured by a pump lock, a Blackburn parking block (a most invaluable accessory, cheap and virtually weightless), a cyclometer, a loud bell, and a secure lock and chain. *Richard's Bicycle Book* makes useful reading for even the most mechanically minded.

Luggage and equipment Strong and waterproof front and back panniers are a must. When packed these are likely to be heavy and should be carried on the strongest racks available. Poor quality racks have ruined many a journey for they take incredible strain on unpaved roads. A top bag cum rucksack (eg Carradice) makes a good addition for use on and off the bike. A Cannondale front bag is good for maps, camera, compass, altimeter, notebook and small tape-recorder. (Other recommended panniers are Ortlieb – front and back – which is waterpoof and almost 'sandproof', Mac-Pac, Madden and Karimoor.) 'Gaffa' tape is excellent for protecting vulnerable parts of panniers and for carrying out all manner of repairs.

All equipment and clothes should be packed in plastic bags to give extra protection against dust and rain. (Also protect all documents, etc carried close to the body from sweat.) Always take the minimum clothing. It's better to buy extra items en route when you find you need them. Generally it is best to carry several layers of thin light clothes than fewer heavy, bulky ones. Always keep one set of dry clothes, including long trousers, to put on at the end of the day. The incredibly light, strong, waterproof and wind resistant goretex jacket and overtrousers are invaluable. Training shoes can be used for both cycling and walking.

Useful tips Wind, not hills, is the enemy of the cyclist. Try to make the best use of the times of day when there is little; mornings tend to be best but there is no steadfast rule. Take care to avoid dehydration, by drinking regularly. In northern Chile, where supplies of water are scarce between towns, be sure to carry an ample supply. For food, carry the staples (sugar, salt, dried milk, tea, coffee, porridge oats, raisins, dried soups, etc) and supplement these with whatever local foods can be found in the markets. Give your bicycle a thorough daily check for loose nuts or bolts or bearings. See that all parts run smoothly. A good chain should last 2,000 miles, 3,200 kilometres or more but be sure to keep it as clean as possible – an old toothbrush is good for this – and to oil it lightly from time to time. Remember that thieves are attracted to towns and cities, so when sight-seeing, try to leave your bicycle with someone such as a café owner or a priest. Country people tend to be more honest and are usually friendly and very inquisitive. However, don't take unnecessary risks; always see that your bicycle is secure (most hotels will allow bikes to be kept in rooms). In more remote regions dogs can be '; carry a stick or some small stones to frighten them off. Traffic on the Pan-American Highway, particularly around Santiago, can be a nightmare; it is usually far more rewarding to keep to the smaller roads if they exist. Most towns have a bicycle shop of some description, but it is best to do your own repairs and adjustments whenever possible.

The Expedition Advisory Centre, administered by the Royal Geographical Society, 1, Kensington Gore, London SW7 2AR has published a useful monograph entitled *Bicycle Expeditions*, by Paul Vickers, (1990) which is available direct from the Centre. (In the UK there is also the Cyclist's Touring Club, CTC, Cotterell House, 69 Meadrow, Godalming, Surrey, GU7 3HS, T01483-417217, cycling@ctc.org.uk for touring, and technical information.)

Most cyclists agree that the main danger comes from other traffic. A rearview mirror has been frequently recommended to forewarn you of vehicles which are too close behind. You also need to watch out for oncoming, overtaking vehicles, unstable loads on trucks, protruding loads etc. Make yourself conspicuous by wearing bright clothing and a helmet.

Hitchhiking Hitchhiking is relatively easy and safe, but in some regions especially in the south traffic is sparse.

Boat Shipping information is given in the text under Santiago and all the relevant southern ports. Local newspapers are useful for all transport schedules.

Keeping in touch

Language
See also the inside back cover for a list of useful words and phrases

Though English is understood in many major hotels, tour agencies and airline offices (especially in Santiago), travellers are strongly advised to learn some Spanish before setting out. The local pronunciation of Spanish, very quick and lilting, with final syllables cut off, can present difficulties to the foreigner.

Postal services Postal services are efficient. Airmail takes three to four days from the UK. Seamail takes eight to 12 weeks. There is a daily airmail service to Europe. Poste restante only holds mail for 30 days, then returns it to sender. The *Lista de Correo* in the Central Post Office in Santiago is good and efficiently organized, but letters are kept separately for men and women so envelopes should be marked Sr or Sra/Srta. Rates: letters to Europe/North America US$1.20, aerogrammes US$0.75. To register a letter costs US$0.75. Surface mail rates for parcels to Europe: less than one kilo US$14; one to three kilos US$18; 10 kilos US$30.

Telephone services National and international calls have been opened up for competition. There are eight main companies (known as *carriers)* offering competing rates, which are widely advertised. Though this sounds confusing, it is simple to operate and does mean that

Spanish pronounciation

Essentials

The stress in a Spanish word conforms to one of three rules: 1) if the word ends in a vowel, or in **n** or **s**, the accent falls on the penultimate syllable (ventana, ventanas); 2) if the word ends in a consonant other than **n** or **s**, the accent falls on the last syllable (hablar); 3) if the word is to be stressed on a syllable contrary to either of the above rules, the acute accent on the relevant vowel indicates where the stress is to be placed (pantal**ó**n, met**á**fora). Note that adverbs such as cuando, 'when', take an accent when used interrogatively: ¿cuándo?, 'when?'

Vowels: **a** not quite as short as in English 'cat'; **e** as in English 'pay', but shorter in a syllable ending in a consonant; **i** as in English 'seek'; **o** as in English 'shop', but more like 'pope' when the vowel ends a syllable; **u** as in English 'food'; after 'q' and in 'gue', 'gui', u is unpronounced; in 'güe' and 'güi' it is pronounced; **y** when a vowel, pronounced like 'i'; when a semiconsonant or consonant, it is pronounced like English 'yes'; **ai**, **ay** as in English 'ride'; **ei**, **ey** as in English 'they'; **oi**, **oy** as in English 'toy'

Unless listed below **consonants** can be pronounced in Spanish as they are in English. **b**, **v** their sound is interchangeable and is a cross between the English 'b' and 'v', except at the beginning of a word or after 'm' or 'n' when it is like English 'b'; **c** like English 'k', except before 'e' or 'i' when it is as the 's' in English 'sip'; **g** before 'e' and 'i' it is the same as j; **h** when on its own, never pronounced; **j** as the 'ch' in the Scottish 'loch'; **ll** as the 'g' in English 'beige'; sometimes as the 'lli' in 'million'; **ñ** as the 'ni' in English 'onion'; **rr** trilled much more strongly than in English; **x** depending on its location, pronounced as in English 'fox', or 'sip', or like 'gs'; **z** as the 's' in English 'sip'.

See also inside back cover for a list of useful words & phrases

domestic and international phone rates are not excessively high. Callers choose companies by dialling an access code before the city code, see box on page 54. For international calls you dial the company code, then 0, then the country code. International calls are cheap. Ask which carrier has the best links with the country you wish to call (eg for making collect calls); for instance CTC is good for phoning Germany.

To call collect/reverse charges (*cobro revertido*) on international calls using CTC dial 800800+0+country code or using Entel 800360+0+country code.

Telephone boxes can be used to make local and long-distance calls, for making collect calls and receiving calls. Although it is possible to make international calls from these phones, in practice it may be easier to go to a company office. Telephone boxes have been programmed to direct calls via one carrier: to make a local call, simply dial the number you require and pay the rate charged by the carrier who owns the booth, US$0.20-0.30 per minute. To make an inter-urban call, dial '0' plus the area code (DDD) and the number; if you wish to select a carrier, dial its code, then the area code (leaving out '0'), then the number. The area codes given in the text include '0'; omit this if selecting a carrier. To make an international call from a carrier's booth without choosing a different company, dial '00' before the country code. Yellow phones accept only 50 peso coins. Blue phones accept pre-paid phone cards costing 5,000 pesos (*tarjeta telefónica*); available from kiosks. On phone cards, only the time of the call is charged rather than the normal three minutes minimum. There are special phones for long-distance domestic calls which accept Mastercard and Visa credit cards. Entel has strategically-placed, self-dialling phones, which are white. Users press a button and are instantly connected with the operator from their own country.

To send a fax abroad costs US$4-5 per sheet, depending on the company. There is also a charge for receiving a fax. VTR also operate telex services. Amex Card holders can often use telex facilities at Amex offices free of charge.

Essentials

 Access codes: for national and international phone calls

Entel 123	Chilesat 171
CTC Mundo 188	Bell South Chile 181
CNT (Telefónica del Sur – in south) 121	Isutel 155
VTR 120	Transam 113

Media **Newspapers** Santiago daily papers *El Mercurio* (centre-right), *La Nación* (liberal-left), *La Segunda*, *La Tercera*, *La Quarta*, *Las Ultimas Noticias* and *La Hora*. Both *El Mercurio* and *La Tercera* have special travel supplements in their Sunday editions. *News Review*, a weekly in English (which includes the *Guardian Weekly*) is published on Fridays, US$1.35, on sale at selected kiosks; address: Casilla 151/9, Santiago, T2361423/24, F2362293; newsrevi@mcl.cl.

Weekly magazines *Hoy*, *Qué Pasa*, *Ercilla*, *Rocinante* (art, culture, society), rocinante@ctreuna.cl. Monthly: *Rutas* (official organ, Automobile Association).

Radio World Band Radio South America has more local and community radio stations than practically anywhere else in the world; a shortwave (world band) radio offers a practical means to brush up on the language, sample popular culture and absorb some of the richly varied regional music. International broadcasters such as the BBC World Service, the Voice of America, Boston (Mass)-based Monitor Radio International (operated by *Christian Science Monitor*) and the Quito-based Evangelical station, HCJB, keep the traveller abreast of news and events, in both English and Spanish.

Compact or miniature portables are recommended, with digital tuning and a full range of shortwave bands, as well as FM, long and medium wave. Detailed advice on radio models (£150 for a decent one) and wavelengths can be found in the annual publication, *Passport to World Band Radio* (Box 300, Penn's Park, PA 18943, USA). Details of local stations is listed in *World TV and Radio Handbook* (WTRH), PO Box 9027, 1006 AA Amsterdam, The Netherlands, US$19.95. Both of these, free wavelength guides and selected radio sets are available from the BBC World Service Bookshop, Bush House Arcade, Bush House, Strand, London WC2B 4PH, UK, T0171-2572576.

Television TV channels include TVUC (Universidad Católica) on Channel 13, the leading station; TVN (government operated) on Channel 7; Megavisión (private) on Channel 9 and La Red (private) on Channel 4.

Internet cafés These can be found in most cities and any towns. Addresses are given in the text. Email is widely available.

Food and drink

Food The main meals are breakfast (*desayuno*), lunch (*almuerzo*) and dinner (*cena*). Lunch is eaten at about 1300 and dinner after 2100. *Las Onces* (literally elevenses) is the name given to a snack usually including tea, served at around 1700. Cocktails are served after 1900. Breakfast usually consists of bread, butter and jam, served with coffee or tea. By law restaurants have to serve a cheaper fixed price meal at lunch time; this is often called *la colación* or *el menu*. It may not be referred to on the menu, which (confusingly) is called *la carta*. When ordering from the menu note that vegetables, other than potatoes, are not usually included in the price quoted for main dishes. Waiters are referred to as *garzón* and never, as in some other parts of South America, as *mozo*.

Empanadas de pino

Although other fillings are used nowadays for empanadas, the traditional filling is pino, a mixture of meat, onions, and spices. Most Chilean families have their own recipes: this one was kindly supplied by Manuel and Ximena Fernández.

Ingredients (to make 20 empanadas)

Pastry: 1 kilogram flour; 125 grams margarine, butter or lard; 1 level spoonful salt; cold water.

Filling: 600 grams meat, chopped into small pieces (or lean minced meat); 2 large onions; 4 or 5 teaspoons cooking oil; teaspoon each of cumin, black pepper and chilli powder; 1 teaspoon paprika; 3 cloves garlic, finely chopped; salt to taste; 4 hard boiled eggs; 1 teaspoon flour; 20 black olives; 40 raisins.

Methods

Pastry: in a bowl mix the flour and margarine, add salt (dissolved in ½ a cup water), gradually add more water to make soft but consistent pastry and leave it for at least 1 hour, then knead it for 10 minutes, before replacing it in the bowl and leaving it covered with a clean cloth.

Filling: heat the cooking oil in a large frying pan or pot, then add the onion and fry for about 8 minutes. Add spices and salt, then fry for 2 minutes. Add meat and fry for 15 minutes, stirring continuously, until the onions are crystal-like and softly cooked. Add the flour, lower the heat and simmer for 5 minutes. Leave the mixture overnight. Shell the eggs and cut each lengthwise into 5 pieces.

Making the empanadas:

Divide the pastry into 20 pieces, then roll each piece into a thin round shape. On one "hemisphere" of each piece of pastry place the following: 1 piece of egg; one heaped teaspoon of the filling; 2 raisins and 1 olive. Carefully paint the rim of each piece of pastry with water, then fold the empty "hemisphere" over to enclose the filling; press the rim down. You should now have a semicircular turnover: paint the outer rim again with water and fold it again towards the centre of the empanada.

Bake the empanadas in a preheated oven (200°C). After about 5 minutes reduce the heat to 150°C and bake for a further 14 minutes until the empanadas are nicely browned. To improve their appearance paint the empanadas with a thin coat of cold water as soon as you remove them from the oven.

Serve hot with Chilean red wine.

Essentials

Although there are vegetarian restaurants in major cities, vegetarians will find that their choice of food is severely restricted especially in smaller towns and away from tourist areas. Vegetarians should be prepared to explain which foods they cannot eat, rather than saying 'Soy vegetariano' (I'm a vegetarian) or 'No como carne' (I don't eat meat). Vegetarians may be advised to look for accommodation which offers cooking facilities.

Cuisine All the necessary ingredients for good cuisine can be found in Chile. The long coastline provides abundant supplies of high quality fish and shellfish. The benign Mediterranean climate of the central regions is perfect for growing a wide variety of fruit and vegetables. The semi-tropical climate of northern Chile supplies mangos, papayas, lúcumas and chirimoyas, delicious tropical fruits used extensively in local dishes and drinks. The lush grasslands of the south are ideal for dairy and beef farming as well as for growing apples, plums and cherries. Local markets in most parts of the country are full of beautiful fruit and vegetables at very reasonable prices.

Although Chilean cuisine is mostly rooted in the Spanish tradition, it has also been influenced by the German, Italian and other immigrant groups who have settled in the country. Each new wave of immigrants introduced new ideas and combinations of ingredients and flavours. The pastry making skills of the Germans have produced 'onces Alemanas', a kind of high tea with kuchen, fruit tarts and gateaux. The original 'pan de Pascua', a traditional Christmas fruit loaf also derives from Germany.

Essentials

👉 *Pisco Sour*

*Most Chileans have their own recipe for
this famous drink: this one was kindly
supplied by Jaime Baez.*

    Ingredients *for 450 millilitres of
pisco sour: 200 millilitres refrigerated 30°
pisco; 150 millilitres lemon juice; 2
teaspoons granulated sugar; ½ teaspoon
egg white.*

    Method: *Put all the ingredients in*

*liquidizer and mix for a few seconds,
until the sugar is well dissolved, then
place in refrigerator until cold.*

    NB *What is important in making
pisco sour is the balance between the
ingredients; once the mixing is done you
can add extra sugar, pisco or lemon to
taste. The egg white is purely for
presentation.*

Of all the quality ingredients available, perhaps the most outstanding is the seafood, usually eaten at fish restaurants on the coast. Although there are good fish restaurants in Santiago, the fish restaurants in the popular coastal resorts in the Bay of Valparaíso, are popular with families from the capital, especially in summer when the heat of the interior can be intense. There are some excellent seafood restaurants along the 35 kilometres coastline of the Bay, stretching from Playa Ancha to Concón.

Most of these seafood restaurants receive their supplies of fish and shellfish from local fishing boats which land their catch every morning in the *caletas* or fishing ports. If you have the courage to bargain you may be able to pick up some delicious, fresh fish from the boats or from the stalls along the harbour at good prices. The most popular fish are *merluza* (hake), better known in Viña del Mar as *pescada, congrio* (conger), *corvina (bass), lenguado* (sole) and *albacora* (sword fish). *Merluza*, which is usually fried, is an inexpensive fish, found in ordinary restaurants. *Congrio* is a very popular quality fish, particularly delicious served as *caldillo de congrio*, a soup containing a large *congrio* steak. *Albacora* is a delicious fish, available mainly in quality restaurants. *Ceviche*, fish marinated in lemon juice, is usually made with *corvina*.

A wide selection of shellfish is also available especially around Valparaíso. Look out for *choros* (mussels), *ostiones* (scallops), *ostras* (oysters) and *erizos* (sea-urchins). However the most characteristic products of this area are the delicious *machas, picorocos* and *locos* which are only found in these seas. *Machas a la parmesana* are *machas* prepared in their shells with a parmesan cheese sauce, grilled and served as a starter, or as a canapé with *pisco sour*. *Picorocos* (giant barnacles), which are normally boiled or steamed in white wine, are grotesque but have a very intense taste: it may be very disconcerting to be presented with a plate containing a rock with feathery fins but it is well worth taking up the challenge of eating it. *Locos* are the most popular Chilean mollusc, but because of overexploitation its fishing is frequently banned (*en veda*): the ban is lifted periodically, but only for a few days at a time. This situation has led to an extensive illegal trade, both nationally and internationally, with *locos* being exported illegally to parts of Asia where they are eaten as a substitute for a local mollusc. The main crustaceans are *jaiva* (crab), *langosta* (lobster) and the local *centolla*, an exquisite king crab from the waters of the south.

Packages of dried seaweed, particularly *cochayuyo* which looks like a leathery thong, can be seen for sale along coastal roads. Both *cochayuyo* and *luche*, are made into a cheap, nutritious stew with vegetables and eaten with potatoes or rice. Until recently salmon was available only in the south where the rivers and lakes are full of 'wild' salmon that has escaped from farms. It is now farmed extensively in the south and can be found on menus in many parts of the country. In Puerto Montt and nearby Angelmó seafood is abundant and cheap: try the famous *curanto*, a stew of shellfish, pork, chicken and other ingredients.

Among the many snacks sold in Chile, the most famous are *empanadas*, traditionally made with meat and onions. The quality of *empanadas* on sale varies:

many are full of onions rather than meat and many places offer *empanadas* filled with seafood or cheese which may be better value. Sandwiches are fairly substantial: typical examples are the *chacarero* which contains thinly sliced steak and salad; *barros luco*, with steak and grilled cheese; and *barros jarpa* with grilled cheese and ham. *Completos*, one of the most popular snacks, betray the German influence on everyday food: though very similar to hot dogs, they are ideally served with plenty of extras, mustard, avocado, choukrut, tomatoes and mayonnaise or any combination of these.

For the cuisine section, grateful thanks to Dereck Foster, *Buenos Aires Herald*.

The *South American Handbook* adds: a very typical Chilean dish is *cazuela de ave*, a nutritious stew containing large pieces of chicken, potatoes, rice, and maybe onions, and green peppers; best if served on the second day. *Valdiviano* is another stew, common in the south, consisting of beef, onion, sliced potatoes and eggs. *Pastel de choclo* is a casserole of meat and onions with olives, topped with polenta, baked in an earthenware bowl. *Humitas* are mashed sweetcorn mixed with butter and spices and baked in sweetcorn leaves. *Prieta* is a blood sausage stuffed with cabbage leaves. A normal *parrillada* or *asado* is a giant mixed grill (including sliced udder) served from a charcoal brazier. The *pichanga* is similar but smaller and without the brazier. *Bistek a lo pobre* (a poor man's steak) can be just the opposite: it is a steak topped by a fried egg, mashed potatoes, onions and salad. A *paila* can take many forms (the *paila* is simply a kind of dish), but the commonest are made of eggs or seafood. *Paila Chonchi* is a kind of bouillabaisse, but has more flavour, more body, more ingredients.

Drink

Coffee is generally instant except in expresso bars including popular chains of cafés such as *Café Haiti, Café Brasil* and *Dino*, found in major cities. Elsewhere specify *café-café, expresso*. The soluble tea should be avoided, but tea bags are widely available. If you order '*café*', or *té, con leche*', it will come with all milk; to have just a little milk in either, you must specify that. After a meal, instead of coffee, try an *agüita* – hot water in which herbs such as mint, or aromatics such as lemon peel, have been steeped. There is a wide variety, available in sachets, and they are very refreshing.

The local wines are very good; the best are from the central areas. The bottled wines are graded, in increasing excellence, as *gran vino, vino especial* and *vino reservado*. Champagne-style wines are also cheap and good. A small deposit is charged on most wine bottles. In supermarkets and shops, wine is also sold in litre cartons. Beer is quite good and cheap; the draught lager known as Schop is good; also try *Cristal Pilsener* or *Royal Guard* in the central regions, *Kunstmann* around Valdivia, and *Escudo Austral* and *Polar* in the south. *Malta*, a dark beer, is recommended for those wanting a British-type beer. European-style lager is brewed by HBH, company which began life in Temuco and which has bars in Santiago.

For more on wine, see page 522

The most famous spirits is *pisco*, usually drunk with lemon or lime juice as *pisco sour* (see box and page 56). Good gin is produced. Reasonably good brandy, *anís* and crème de menthe are all bottled in Chile. *Manzanilla* is a local liqueur, made from *licor de oro* (like Galliano); *crema de cacao*, especially Mitjans, has been recommended. Two popular drinks are *vaina*, a mixture of sherry, egg and sugar and *cola de mono*, a mixture of *aguardiente*, coffee, milk and vanilla served very cold at Christmas. *Chicha* is any form of alcoholic drink made from fruit; *chicha cocida* is three-day-old fermented grape juice boiled to reduce its volume and then bottled with a tablespoonful of honey. Cider (*chicha de manzana*) is popular in the south. *Chicha fresca* is plain apple juice. *Mote con huesillo*, made from wheat hominy and dried peaches, is very refreshing in summer.

Shopping

There is an excellent variety of handicrafts: woodwork, pottery, copperware, leatherwork, Indian woven goods including rugs and ponchos in the south. However, many of the goods sold in main handicraft markets are from elsewhere in South America, in some cases with the country of origin labels cut off, VAT is 18 percent.

Holidays and festivals

1 January: New Year's Day
Easter: Holy Week (two days)
1 May: Labour Day
21 May: Navy Day
15 August: Assumption
First Monday in September: Day of National Unity
18, 19 September: Independence Days
12 October: Columbus Day
1 November: All Saints Day
8 December: Immaculate Conception
25 December: Christmas Day.

Health

For anyone travelling overseas, health is a key consideration. With the following advice and precautions you should keep as healthy as you do at home. Most visitors return home having experienced no problems at all apart from some travellers' diarrhoea. The health risks depend to a large extent on where and how you travel. There are clear health differences in the risks faced by the business traveller, who stays in international class hotels in large cities, the backpacker trekking from country to country and the tourist who heads for the beach. There are no hard and fast rules to follow; you will often have to make your own judgment on the healthiness or otherwise of your surroundings. There are English (or other foreign language) speaking doctors in most major cities who have particular experience in dealing with locally occurring diseases. Your embassy representative will often be able to give you the name of local reputable doctors and most of the better hotels have a doctor on standby. If you do fall ill and cannot find a recommended doctor, try the Outpatient Department of a hospital – private hospitals are usually less crowded and offer a more acceptable standard of care to foreigners.

Before travelling

Take out medical insurance. Make sure it covers all eventualities especially evacuation to your home country by a medically equipped plane, if necessary. You should have a dental check up, obtain a spare glasses prescription, a spare oral contraceptive prescription (or enough pills to last) and, if you suffer from a chronic illness (such as diabetes, high blood pressure, ear or sinus troubles, cardio-pulmonary disease or nervous disorder) arrange for a check up with your doctor, who can at the same time provide you with a letter explaining the details of your disability in English and if possible Spanish. If you are on regular medication, make sure you have enough to cover the period of your travel.

Health checklist

Sunglasses *Ones designed for intense sunlight*

Earplugs *For sleeping on aeroplanes and in noisy hotels*

Suntan cream *With a high protection factor, especially if travelling to the far south*

Insect repellent *Containing DET for preference*

Tablets *For travel sickness*

Tampons

Condoms

Contraceptives

Water sterilizing tablets

Anti-infective ointment *eg Cetrimide*

Dusting powder *For feet etc containing fungicide*

Antacid tablets *For indigestion*

Sachets of rehydration salts *Plus anti-diarrhoea preparations*

Painkillers *Such as Paracetamol or Aspirin*

Antibiotics *For diarrhoea etc*

First Aid kit *Small pack containing a few sterile syringes and needles and disposable gloves. The risk of catching hepatitis etc from a dirty needle used for injection is negligible, but some may be reassured by carrying their own supplies – available from camping shops and airport shops.*

Essentials

More preparation is probably necessary for babies and children than for an adult and perhaps a little more care should be taken when travelling to remote areas where health services are more basic This is because children can be become more rapidly ill than adults (on the other hand they often recover more quickly). Diarrhoea and vomiting are the most common problems, so take the usual precautions, but more intensively. Breastfeeding is best and most convenient for babies, but powdered milk is generally available and so are baby foods. Papaya, bananas and avocados are all nutritious and can be cleanly prepared.

Children

The treatment of diarrhoea is the same for adults, except that it should start earlier and be continued with more persistence. Children get dehydrated very quickly in hot countries and can become drowsy and uncooperative unless cajoled to drink water or juice plus salts. Upper respiratory infections, such as colds, catarrh and middle ear infections are also common and if your child suffers from these normally take some antibiotics against the possibility. Outer ear infections after swimming are also common and antibiotic eardrops will help. Wet wipes are always useful and sometimes difficult to find as, in some places, are disposable nappies.

There is very little control on the sale of drugs and medicines. You can buy any and every drug in pharmacies without a prescription. Be wary of this because pharmacists can be poorly trained and might sell you drugs that are unsuitable, dangerous or old. Many drugs and medicines are manufactured under licence from American or European companies, so the trade names may be familiar to you. This means you do not have to carry a whole chest of medicines with you, but remember that the shelf life of some items, especially vaccines and antibiotics, is markedly reduced in hot conditions. Buy your supplies at the better outlets where there are refrigerators, even though they are more expensive and check the expiry date of all preparations you buy. Immigration officials occasionally confiscate scheduled drugs (Lomotil is an example) if they are not accompanied by a doctor's prescription.

Medicines & what to take

Vaccination against the following diseases is recommended:

Vaccination & immunization

Typhoid This is a disease spread by the insanitary preparation of food. A number of new vaccines against this condition are now available; the older TAB and monovalent typhoid vaccines are being phased out. The newer, eg Typhim Vi, cause less side effects, but are expensive. For those who do not like injections, there are now oral vaccines.

Infectious Hepatitis This is less of a problem for travellers than it used to be because of the development of two extremely effective vaccines against the A and B form of the disease. A combined hepatitis A and B vaccine covers both diseases.

Other vaccinations Might be considered in the case of epidemics eg meningitis. There is an effective vaccination against rabies which should be considered by all travellers, especially those going through remote areas or if there is a particular occupational risk, eg for zoologists or veterinarians.

Further information Further information on health risks abroad, vaccinations etc may be available from a local travel clinic. If you wish to take specific drugs with you such as antibiotics these are best prescribed by your own doctor. Beware, however, that not all doctors can be experts on the health problems of remote countries. More detailed or more up-to-date information than local doctors can provide are available from various sources. In the UK there are hospital departments specializing in tropical and subtropical diseases in London, Liverpool, Birmingham and Glasgow. In the USA the local Public Health Services can give such information and information is available centrally from the Centre for Disease Control (CDC) in Atlanta, T404-3324559.

There are additional computerized databases which can be assessed for destination-specific up-to-the-minute information. In the UK there is MASTA (Medical Advisory Service to Travellers Abroad), T0171-6314408, F0171-4365389, Tx8953473 and Travax (Glasgow, T0141-9467120, ext 247). Other information on medical problems overseas can be obtained from the book by Dawood, Richard (Editor) (1992) *Travellers' Health: How to stay healthy abroad*, Oxford University Press 1992, £7.99. We strongly recommend this revised and updated edition, especially to the intrepid traveller heading for the more out of the way places. General advice is also available in the UK in *Health Information for Overseas Travel* published by the Department of Health and available from HMSO, and *International Travel and Health* published by WHO, Geneva.

Staying healthy

Intestinal upsets Although the thought of catching a stomach bug worries visitors to Latin America, this is much less of a problem in Chile. Travellers' diarrhoea and vomiting is due, most of the time, to food poisoning, usually passed on by the insanitary habits of food handlers. As a general rule the cleaner your surroundings and the smarter the restaurant, the less likely you are to suffer. Drinking water is rarely the culprit. Sea water or river water is more likely to be contaminated by sewage and so swimming in such dilute effluent can also be a cause.

Foods to avoid Uncooked, undercooked, partially cooked or reheated meat, fish, eggs, raw vegetables and salads, especially when they have been left out exposed to flies. Stick to fresh food that has been cooked from raw just before eating and make sure you peel fruit yourself. Wash and dry your hands before eating – disposable wet-wipe tissues are useful for this.

Shellfish eaten raw are risky and at certain times of the year some fish and shellfish concentrate toxins from their environment and cause various kinds of food poisoning. See in particular the warning about *marea roja* under Punta Arenas. **Heat treated milk** (UHT) pasteurized or sterilized is available in Chile, as is pasteurized cheese. On the whole matured or processed cheeses are safer than the fresh varieties and fresh unpasteurized milk from whatever animal can be a source of food poisoning germs, tuberculosis and brucellosis. This applies equally to icecream, yoghurt and cheese made from unpasteurized milk, so avoid these homemade products – the factory made ones are probably safer.

Tap water is generally safe in most places in Chile (but see the warning under San Pedro de Atacama). Stream water, if you are in the countryside, can be contaminated by communities living higher in the mountains. Filtered or bottled water is usually available and safe.

Identifying the causes Infection with various organisms can give rise to travellers' diarrhoea. They may be viruses, bacteria, eg Escherichia coli (probably the most common cause worldwide), protozoal (such as amoebas and giardia), salmonella and cholera. The diarrhoea may come on suddenly or rather slowly. It may or may not be accompanied by vomiting or by severe abdominal pain and the passage of blood or mucus when it is called dysentery.

How do you know which type you have caught and how to treat it?
If you can time the onset of the diarrhoea to the minute ('acute') then it is probably due to a virus or a bacterium and/or the onset of dysentery. The treatment in addition to rehydration is Ciprofloxacin 500 milligrammes every 12 hours; the drug is now widely available and there are many similar ones.

If the diarrhoea comes on slowly or intermittently ('sub-acute') then it is more likely to be protozoal, ie caused by an amoeba or giardia. Antibiotics such a Ciprofloxacin will have little effect. These cases are best treated by a doctor as is any outbreak of diarrhoea continuing for more than three days. Sometimes blood is passed in ameobic dysentery and for this you should certainly seek medical help. If this is not available then the best treatment is probably Tinidazole (Fasigyn) one tablet four times a day for three days. If there are severe stomach cramps, the following drugs may help but are not very useful in the management of acute diarrhoea: Loperamide (Imodium) and Diphenoxylate with Atropine (Lomotil). They should not be given to children.

Any kind of diarrhoea, whether or not accompanied by vomiting, responds well to the replacement of water and salts, taken as frequent small sips, of some kind of rehydration solution. There are proprietary preparations consisting of sachets of powder which you dissolve in boiled water or you can make your own by adding half a teaspoonful of salt (three and a half grammes) and four tablespoonsful of sugar (40 grammes) to a litre of boiled water.

Thus the linchpins of treatment for diarrhoea are rest, fluid and salt replacement, antibiotics such as Ciprofloxacin for the bacterial types and special diagnostic tests and medical treatment for the amoeba and giardia infections. Salmonella infections and cholera, although rare, can be devastating diseases and it would be wise to get to a hospital as soon as possible if these were suspected.

Fasting, peculiar diets and the consumption of large quantities of yoghurt have not been found useful in calming travellers' diarrhoea or in rehabilitating inflamed bowels. Oral rehydration has on the other hand, especially in children, been a life saving technique and should always be practised, whatever other treatment you use. As there is some evidence that alcohol and milk might prolong diarrhoea they should be avoided during and immediately after an attack.

Diarrhoea occurring day after day for long periods of time (chronic diarrhoea) is notoriously resistent to amateur attempts at treatment and again warrants proper diagnostic tests (most towns with reasonable sized hospitals have laboratories for stool samples). There are ways of preventing travellers' diarrhoea for short periods of time by taking antibiotics, but this is not a foolproof technique and should not be used other than in exceptional circumstances. Doxycycline is possibly the best drug. Some preventatives such as Enterovioform can have serious side effects if taken for long periods.

Paradoxically **constipation** is also common, probably induced by dietary change, inadequate fluid intake in hot places and long bus journeys. Simple laxatives are useful in the short-term and bulky foods such as maize, beans and plenty of fruit are also useful.

High altitude   Travelling to high altitudes can cause medical problems, all of which can be prevented if care is taken. In Chile, these problems are mainly encountered when visiting the Parque Nacional Lauca in the far north, especially on day trips from Arica.

On reaching heights above about 3,000 metres, heart pounding and shortness of breath, especially on exertion are a normal response to the lack of oxygen in the air. A condition called acute mountain sickness (*soroche* in South America) can also affect visitors. It is more likely to affect those who ascend rapidly, eg by plane and those who over-exert themselves (teenagers for example). Soroche takes a few hours or days to come on and presents with a bad headache, extreme tiredness, sometimes dizziness, loss of appetite and frequently nausea and vomiting. Insomnia is common and is often associated with a suffocating feeling when lying in bed. Keen observers may note their breathing tends to wax and wane at night and their face tends to be puffy in the mornings – this is all part of the syndrome. Anyone can get this condition and past experience is not always a good guide.

The treatment of acute mountain sickness is simple – rest, painkillers, (preferably not aspirin based) for the headache and anti sickness pills for vomiting. Oxygen is actually not much help, except at very high altitude. Various local panaceas – Coramina glucosada, Effortil, Micoren are popular and *mate de coca* (an infusion of coca leaves widely available and perfectly legal) will alleviate some of the symptoms. See box, page 233.

To **prevent** the condition: on arrival at places over 3,000 metres have a few hours rest in a chair and avoid alcohol, cigarettes and heavy food. If the symptoms are severe and prolonged, it is best to descend to a lower altitude and to reascend slowly or in stages. If this is impossible because of shortage of time or if you are going so high that acute mountain sickness is very likely, then the drug Acetazolamide (Diamox) can be used as a preventative and continued during the ascent. There is good evidence of the value of this drug in the prevention of soroche, but some people do experience peculiar side effects. The usual dose is 500 milligrammes of the slow release preparation each night, starting the night before ascending above 3,000 metres.

Watch out for **sunburn** at high altitude. The ultraviolet rays are extremely powerful. The air is also excessively dry at high altitude and you might find that your skin dries out and the inside of your nose becomes crusted. Use a moisturiser for the skin and some vaseline wiped into the nostrils. Some people find contact lenses irritate because of the dry air. It is unwise to ascend to high altitude if you are pregnant, especially in the first three months, or if you have a history of heart, lung or blood disease, including sickle cell.

A more unusual condition can affect mountaineers who ascend rapidly to high altitude – **acute pulmonary oedema**. Residents at altitude sometimes experience this when returning to the mountains from time spent at the coast. This condition is often preceded by acute mountain sickness and comes on quite rapidly with severe breathlessness, noisy breathing, cough, blueness of the lips and frothing at the mouth. Anybody who develops this must be brought down as soon as possible, given oxygen and taken to hospital.

A rapid descent from high places will make sinus problems and middle ear infections worse and might make your teeth ache. Lastly, don't fly to altitude within 24 hours of scuba diving. You might suffer from 'the bends'.

Parts of Chile are extremely hot and dry, mainly in the north. Full acclimatization to **Heat & cold** high temperatures takes about two weeks. During this period it is normal to feel a bit apathetic, especially if the relative humidity is high. Drink plenty of water, use salt on your food and avoid extreme exertion. Tepid showers are more cooling than hot or cold ones.

The burning power of the sun, especially at high altitude, is phenomenal. Always wear a wide brimmed hat and use some form of suncream lotion on untanned skin. Normal temperate zone suntan lotions (protection factor up to seven) are not much good; you need to use the types designed specifically for the tropics or for mountaineers or skiers with protection factors up to 15 or above. Glare from the sun can cause conjunctivitis, so wear sunglasses especially on beaches, where high protection factor sunscreen should also be used.

Remember that, especially at high altitude, there can be a large and sudden drop in temperature between sun and shade and between night and day, so dress accordingly. Warm jackets or woollens are essential after dark at high altitude. Loose cotton is still the best material when the weather is hot. It can also be extremely cold and wet the further south you go, so take appropriate clothing. In the south and at high altitude the ultra-violet rays of the sun are particularly strong, so do not forget your hat and sun protection cream.

These are mostly more of a nuisance than a serious hazard and if you try, you can **Insects** prevent yourself entirely from being bitten. Sleep off the ground and use a mosquito net or some kind of insecticide.

You can also use insect repellents, most of which are effective against a wide range of pests. The most common and effective is diethyl metatoluamide (DET). DET liquid is best for arms and face (care around eyes and with spectacles – DET dissolves plastic). Aerosol spray is good for clothes and ankles and liquid DET can be dissolved in water and used to impregnate cotton clothes and mosquito nets. Some repellents now contain DET and Permethrin, insecticide. Impregnated wrist and ankle bands can also be useful.

If you are bitten or stung, itching may be relieved by cool baths, antihistamine tablets (care with alcohol or driving) or mild corticosteroid creams, eg. hydrocortisone (great care: never use if any hint of infection). Careful scratching of all your bites once a day can be surprisingly effective. Calamine lotion and cream have limited effectiveness and antihistamine creams are not recommended – they can cause allergies themselves.

Bites which become infected should be treated with a local antiseptic or antibiotic cream such as Cetrimide, as should any infected sores or scratches.

This virus, transmitted by mice, produces haemorrhaging and lung problems: some **Hanta virus** estimate that 50 percent of those infected in the Americas have died as a result. There is no known vaccine; the faster medical attention is obtained the more likely recovery will occur. The virus is contracted either by breathing air contaminated by the excrement, urine or saliva of infected field mice or by eating food contaminated in this way. It can also be contracted by handling infected field mice or as a result of a bite. Early symptoms are similar to those of 'flu: fever, headache, aching limbs, vomiting. These are followed by high temperature and difficulty in breathing. Guidelines issued by the Chilean Ministry of Health advise people on measures to avoid attracting mice into their homes, for example by storing food in sealed containers and by disposing of rubbish properly. The virus is not resistant to the heat of the sun, detergents or disinfectants. While the risk to most travellers is minimal, you should avoid staying in accommodation which is dirty or using dirty and badly maintained campsites. If camping you should use a tent with a proper floor. Most of the cases in Chile have

Essentials

occurred in the Lake District; there have also been cases in the Argentine Lake District. It is present in country areas across much of the south between Concepción and Coyhaique.

Prickly heat A very common intensely itchy rash, prickly heat is avoided by frequent washing and by wearing loose clothing. It is cured by allowing skin to dry off through use of powder and spending two nights in an airconditioned hotel!

Athletes Foot This and other fungal skin infections are best treated with Tolnaftate or Clotrimazole.

Other risks and more serious diseases

Rabies Rabies is endemic throughout Latin America, so avoid dogs that are behaving strangely and cover your toes at night from the vampire bats, which also carry the disease. If you are bitten by a domestic or wild animal, do not leave things to chance: scrub the wound with soap and water and/or disinfectant, try to have the animal captured (within limits) or at least determine its ownership, where possible, and seek medical assistance at once. The course of treatment depends on whether you have already been satisfactorily vaccinated against rabies. If you have, then some further doses of vaccine are all that is required. Human diploid vaccine is the best, but expensive: other, older kinds of vaccine, such as that derived from duck embryos may be the only types available. These are effective, much cheaper and interchangeable generally with the human derived types. If not already vaccinated then anti rabies serum (immunoglobulin) may be required in addition. It is important to finish the course of treatment whether the animal survives or not.

AIDS AIDS (locally *SIDA*) is increasing but is not wholly confined to the well known high risk sections of the population, ie homosexual men, intravenous drug abusers and children of infected mothers. Heterosexual transmission is now the dominant mode and so the main risk to travellers is from casual sex. The same precautions should be taken as with any sexually transmitted disease. The Aids virus (HIV) can be passed by unsterilized needles which have been previously used to inject an HIV positive patient, but the risk of this is negligible. It would, however, be sensible to check that needles have been properly sterilized or disposable needles have been used. If you wish to take your own disposable needles, be prepared to explain what they are for. The risk of receiving a blood transfusion with blood infected with the HIV virus is greater than from dirty needles because of the amount of fluid exchanged. Supplies of blood for transfusion should now be screened for HIV in all reputable hospitals, so again the risk is very small indeed. Catching the AIDS virus does not always produce an illness in itself (although it may do). The only way to be sure if you feel you have been put at risk is to have a blood test for HIV antibodies on your return to a place where there are reliable laboratory facilities. Test results only become positive some three months after the virus has been contracted.

Infectious Hepatitis (Jaundice) The main symptoms are pains in the stomach, lack of appetite, lassitude and yellowness of the eyes and skin. Medically speaking there are two main types. The less serious, but more common is Hepatitis A for which the best protection os the careful preparation of food, the avoidance of contaminated drinking water and scrupulous attention to toilet hygiene. The other, more serious, version is Hepatitis B which is acquired usually as a sexually transmitted disease or by blood transfusions. It can less commonly be transmitted by injections with unclean needles and possibly by insect bites. The symptoms are the same as for Hepatitis A. The incubation period is much longer (up to six months compared with six weeks) and there are more likely to be complications.

Hepatitis A can be protected against with gamma globulin. It should be obtained from a reputable source and is certainly useful for travellers who intend to live rough. You should have a shot before leaving and have it repeated every six months. The dose of gamma globulin depends on the concentration of the particular preparation used, so the manufacturer's advice should be taken. The injection should be given as close as possible to your departure and as the dose depends on the likely time you are to spend in potentially affected areas, the manufacturer's instructions should be followed. Gamma globulin has really been superseded now by a proper vaccination against Hepatitis A (Havrix) which gives immunity lasting up to 10 years. After that boosters are required. Havrix monodose is now widely available as is Junior Havrix. The vaccination has negligible side effects and is extremely effective. Gamma globulin injections can be a bit painful, but it is much cheaper than Havrix and may be more available in some places.

Hepatitis B can be effectively prevented by a specific vaccine (Engerix) – three shots over six months before travelling. If you have had jaundice in the past it would be worthwhile having a blood test to see if you are immune to either of these two types, because this might avoid the necessity and costs of vaccination or gamma globulin. There are other kinds of viral hepatitis (C, E etc) which are fairly similar to A and B, but vaccines are not available as yet.

Snake bite

This is a very rare event indeed for travellers to Chile. If you are unlucky (or careless) enough to be bitten by a venomous snake, spider, scorpion or sea creature, try to identify the creature, but do not put yourself in further danger. Snake bites in particular are very frightening, but in fact rarely poisonous – even venomous snakes bite without injecting venom. What you might expect if bitten are: fright, swelling, pain and bruising around the bite and soreness of the regional lymph glands, perhaps nausea, vomiting and a fever. Signs of serious poisoning would be the following symptoms: numbness and tingling of the face, muscular spasms, convulsions, shortness of breath and bleeding. Victims should be got to a hospital or a doctor without delay. Commercial snake bite and scorpion kits are available, but usually only useful for the specific type of snake or scorpion for which they are designed. Most serum has to be given intravenously so it is not much good equipping yourself with it unless you are used to making injections into veins. It is best to rely on local practice in these cases, because the particular creatures will be known about locally and appropriate treatment can be given.

Treatment of snake bite Reassure and comfort the victim frequently. Immobilize the limb by a bandage or a splint or by getting the person to lie still. Do not slash the bite area and try to suck out the poison because this sort of heroism does more harm than good. If you know how to use a tourniquet in these circumstances, you will not need this advice. If you are not experienced do not apply a tourniquet.

Chagas' Disease (South American Trypano-somiasis)

This is a chronic disease, very rarely caught by travellers and difficult to treat. It is transmitted by the simultaneous biting and excreting of the Reduvid bug, also known as the Vinchuca or Barbeiro. Somewhat resembling a small cockroach, this nocturnal bug lives in poor adobe houses with dirt floors often frequented by opossums. If you cannot avoid such accommodation, sleep off the floor with a candle lit, use a mosquito net, keep as much of your skin covered as possible, use DET repellent or a spray insecticide. If you are bitten overnight (the bites are painless) do not scratch them, but wash thoroughly with soap and water.

Dangerous animals

Apart from mosquitos the most dangerous animals are men, be they bandits or behind steering wheels. Think carefully about violent confrontations and wear a seat belt if you are lucky enough to have one available to you.

Essentials

When you return home Remember to take your antimalarial tablets for six weeks after leaving the malarial area. If you have had attacks of diarrhoea it is worth having a stool specimen tested in case you have picked up amoebas. If you have been living rough, blood tests may be worthwhile to detect worms and other parasites. If you have been exposed to bilharzia (*schistosomiasis*) by swimming in lakes etc, have a blood test when you get home, but leave it for six weeks because the test is slow to become positive. Report any untoward symptoms to your doctor and tell the doctor exactly where you have been and, if you know, what the likelihood of disease is to which you were exposed.

The above information has been compiled for us by Dr David Snashall, who is presently Senior Lecturer in Occupational Health at the United Medical Schools of Guy's and St Thomas' Hospitals in London and Chief Medical Adviser to the British Foreign and Commonwealth Office. He has travelled extensively in Central and South America, worked in Peru and in East Africa and keeps in close touch with developments in preventative and tropical medicine.

Further reading

Maps & guide books The best guide book to Chile published in the country is *Turistel*, published annually in three parts, *Norte*, *Centro*, and *Sur*, as well as a separate volume listing campsites. The series is sponsored by the CTC telephone company, and contains detailed information and a wealth of maps covering the whole country and neighbouring tourist centres in Argentina (eg Mendoza, San Martín de los Andes, Bariloche), in Spanish only. Each volume costs around US$15, but buying the whole set is better value; they are available from bookshops and from newspaper kiosks in the centre of Santiago. The publisher is Turiscom, Av Santa Maria 0120, Providencia, Santiago, T3658800, F3658801, turiscom@chilesat.net. Sernatur publishes a *Guía Turística*/Tourist Guide in Spanish and English, good maps, useful text, free.

A good map of Santiago is the *Plano de Santiago*, published annually by Publiguías, Av Santa María 0792, Providencia, Santiago; this contains sectional maps of the city and a street index. Publiguías also publish a *Guía Comercial y Profesional de Providencia*. A series of maps of the major tourist areas is published by Mapas JLM, Gral del Canto 105 T/F2364808; these are sold at newpaper kiosks and elsewhere. Geophysical and topographical maps (US$11) are available from **Instituto Geográfico Militar**, at the main office Dieciocho 369, T6987278, open 0900-1800 Monday-Friday (0800–1400 January/February). The Instituto Geográfico has published a *Guía Caminera*, with roads and city plans (available only at IGM offices, not 100 percent accurate). The Biblioteca Nacional, Moneda 650, has an excellent collection of IGM maps, sections of which can be photocopied, particularly useful for climbing.

Conaf (see **Tourist offices**, page 105) publishes a series of illustrated booklets in Spanish/English on Chilean trees, shrubs and flowers, recommended, as well as **Juventud, Turismo y Naturaleza**, which lists national parks, their facilities and the flora and fauna of each. Bird-lovers will appreciate *Guía de Campo de Las Aves de Chile*, by B Araya and G Millie.

A recommended series of general maps is that published by *International Travel Maps* (ITM), 345 West Broadway, Vancouver BC, V5Y 1P8, Canada, T604-8793621, F604-8794521, compiled with historical notes, by the late Kevin Healey.

Chile's recent history is examined in S Collier and W F Sater, *A History of Chile 1808-1994* (Cambridge University Press, 1996) while M H Spooner's *Soldiers In A Narrow Land* (University of California Press, 1994) is a readable account of the Pinochet dictatorship by a North American journalist resident in the country at the time. Among travellers, Bruce Chatwin's *In Patagonia* (Pan 1977) is a classic for those visiting the far south, though Chatwin is heavily criticized by John Pilkington in *An Englishman In Patagonia* (Century 1991); also worth reading on the south is *In Darwin's Wake* by John Campbell (Sheridan House 1997). Rosie Swale in *Back to Cape Horn* (Glasgow: Fontana, 1988) describes her epic horse ride the length of Chile; Sara Wheeler recounts her journey through Chile in *Travels in a Thin Country* (London: Little, Brown and Co, 1994). John Hickman, a former British Ambassador to Chile, analyzes Chile's history in *News from the End of Earth: A Portrait of Chile* (Hurst, 1998), with an emphasis on the 1970s to the present.

Jan Read's *The Wines of Chile* (Mitchell Beazley, 1994) is a gazetteer of the vineyards and wineries, ideal for the discerning specialist. *Patagonia*, by Claudio Almarza V (Punta Arenas: GeoPatagonia) is a book of photographs, with text, on the region.

Further reading on activities and **adventure tourism** is given on page 24. See **Literature**, page 510, and **Arts and crafts**, page 504, for many other suggestions for further reading. The latter mentions information on the Mapuche; more can be found, within the entire American Indian context, in *Return of the Indian: Conquest and Revival in the Americas*, by Phillip Wearne (London: Cassell/Latin America Bureau, 1996).

The South American Explorer, the journal of the *South American Explorers Club*, regularly publishes articles on Chile (126 Indian Creek Road, Ithaca, New York 14850, USA). Issues 22 (August 1989) and 31 (May 1992) both had features on Easter Island. Other titles on Easter Island will be found in that chapter.

Other suggestions

Essentials

The Santiago Region

The Santiago Region

This bustling capital city of over five million people is the first experience of Chile for many travellers. Like most South American capitals it is a city of contrasts sprawling around the old city centre, which lies just south of the Río Mapocho. To the east, running towards the foothills of the Andes, are affluent modern areas such as Alto de las Condes; to the west and south are poorer neighbourhoods. Though Santiago is unlikely to be the highlight of your trip to Chile, it does warrant a visit. Here, for example, you can see the best museums in the country, eat in restaurants which could grace any capital in the world and find music and nightlife to suit almost any taste. The contrast with the lifestyle in the outlying areas of the country is stark; if you want to understand the country you are visiting, Santiago is a must.

Like many large cities, Santiago has a problem with pollution, especially in the winter months of July and August. These months are, however, the high season for skiing; east of the city there are six of the best ski resorts in South America, all within easy reach. In summer the city empties as people head for the coastal resorts around Viña del Mar and Valparaíso or further afield. Spring is perhaps the best time for a visit, though autumn too has its attractions; the area south of the city is perhaps the best wine-producing area in the country, and autumn, when the grapes are being harvested, is a particularly good time to visit the vineyards.

Background

Geography

This region can be divided into three; to the east are the peaks of the Andes; to the west is the Coastal Range and between is the Central Valley, much of which is between 600 and 1,000 metres above sea level. On the eastern edge of the Central Valley lies the city of Santiago, its suburbs spreading east into the foothills of the Andes.

Some of the highest peaks in the Andes lie in this region; over the border in Argentina, Aconcagua, the highest mountain in the world outside Asia, rises to 6,964 metres. Chilean peaks above 6,000 metres include Marmolejo (6,108 metres), Juncal (6,060 metres), Nevado El Plomo (6,050 metres) and Tupungato (6,570 metres). There is a mantle of snow on the mountains: at Aconcagua it begins at 4,300 metres. The lower slopes are covered with dense forests. Between the forest and the snowline there are alpine pastures; during the summer cattle are driven up to these pastures to graze. The coastal range is lower here than in the northern desert but still reaches over 2,000 metres.

Three river systems flow west from the Andes across the Central Valley, cutting their way through the Coastal Range through narrow gorges. In the north the Río Aconcagua, which rises in Argentina, flows into the sea north of

The Santiago region

Valparaíso. Further south the Río Maipo flows south of Santiago, reaching the Pacific near San Antonio; its most important tributary is the Río Mapocho, the river on which Santiago is situated.

Over 40 percent of the people of Chile live in this comparatively small area. The population density of the area around Santiago is over 300 per square kilometres, though it is much lower in the valleys around Los Andes.

Santiago

Attractively situated in the Central Valley, Santiago has grown to become the fifth largest city in South America. It is a bustling modern city, the political, economic and financial capital of Chile.

Population: almost 5 million
Altitude: 600m
Phone code: 02
Colour map 3, grid B3

The Santiago Region

Over 50 percent of the country's manufacturing industry is located here. It is a major communications centre, home to the country's major newspapers and its television stations. With the country's main international airport nearby at Pudahuel, it is a major entry point for visitors to Chile.

The city is crossed from east to west by the Río Mapocho, which passes through an artificial stone channel, 40 metres wide, spanned by several bridges. The magnificent chain of the Andes, with its snow-capped peaks, is in full view for much of the year, rain and pollution permitting.

As in most cities of its size, traffic and pollution are major problems: driving in the city is restricted according to licence plate numbers (prohibited registration numbers are published in the press each day).

Ins and outs

International and domestic flights arrive at the Aeropuerto Arturo Merino Benitez at Pudahuel, 26 km northwest of the city centre. If you are arriving by bus there are 4 bus terminals, all located close to each other, just west of the city centre and not far from the train station. The train station and bus terminals are all situated along the Avenida O'Higgins, the main east-west avenue through the city and within easy reach of Line 1 of the city metro.

Getting there
For more detailed information, see Transport, page 97

Note that the city's main avenue, Avenida O'Higgins, is generally referred to as the Alameda and that Plaza Baquedano, one of the city's main squares, is usually called Plaza Italia. Most of the more expensive accommodation is situated in the city centre or further east in the neighbourhoods of Providencia and Las Condes. Most budget accommodation is located in the city centre or further west in the vicinity of the bus terminals. Although parts of the centre can be conveniently explored on foot, you will need to master the city's transport system, which is, on the whole, well organised, even if crowded and slow in peak periods.

Getting around
See page 74 for a map of Santiago metro

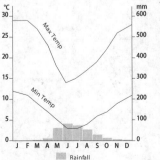
Climate: Santiago

Like all large cities, Santiago has problems of theft. Pickpockets and bagsnatchers, who are often well-dressed, operate especially on the Metro, around the Plaza de Armas as well as around the restaurants in Bellavista. The Cerro Santa Lucía area is said to be dangerous even in daytime.

Security

Climate   The Santiago area enjoys a Mediterranean climate, with long dry summers and day-time temperatures rising to over 30°C. Rainfall is heaviest in autumn and winter: long spells of rain are uncommon, storms being heavy and brief. Snowfall is rare, though frost is not uncommon. There is usually less wind in spring and autumn, making smog a more serious problem over the city (forecast levels of smog are published in the daily papers). Pollution levels vary; the old 'city centre' is usually worst affected than the more modern eastern areas around Las Condes. Pollution is usually at its worst in July, exacerbated by the lack of wind, and by the wet and cold. It is lightest in September/October and after rainfall.

History

Santiago was founded by Pedro de Valdivia in 1541 on the site of a small indigenous settlement between the southern bank of the Río Mapocho and the Santa Lucía hill. During the colonial period it was only one of several Spanish administrative and cultural centres; also important were Concepción to the south and La Serena in the north. Nevertheless by 1647 there were 12 churches in the city, but of these only San Francisco (1618) survived the earthquake of that year. A further earthquake destroyed most of the city in 1730.

Following independence the city became more important; in the 1870s under the *Intendente* Benjamín Vicuña MacKenna, an urban plan was drafted, the Santa Lucía hill was made into a public park and the first trams were introduced. As the city grew at the end of the 19th century the Chilean élite, wealthy from mining and shipping, built their mansions west of the centre around Calle Dieciocho. Expansion east towards Providencia began in 1895. In the 20th century, like most Latin American capital cities, Santiago has spread

Santiago metro

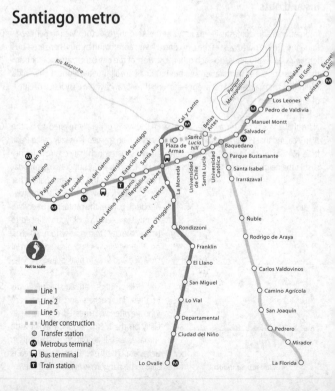

Line 1
Line 2
Line 5
Under construction
○ Transfer station
Ⓜ Metrobus terminal
🚏 Bus terminal
🇹 Train station

rapidly, especially since the 1950s, with the more affluent moving east into new neighbourhhods in the foothills of the Andes and with new poorer neighbour-hoods being established to the west of the centre.

Sights

The centre of the old city lies between the Río Mapocho and Avenida O'Higgins. From the **Plaza Baquedano** in the east of the city's central area, the Mapocho flows to the northwest and Avenida O'Higgins runs to the south-west. From Plaza Baquedano, Calle Merced runs due west to the **Plaza de Armas**, the heart of the city which lies five blocks south of the Mapocho.

On the eastern and southern sides of the Plaza de Armas there are arcades with shops; on the northern side is the Post Office and the Municipalidad; and on the western side the Cathedral and the archbishop's palace. The **Cathedral**, much rebuilt, contains a recumbent statue in wood of San Francisco Javier, and the chandelier which lit the first meetings of Congress after independence; it also houses an interesting museum of religious art and historical pieces. In the **Palacio de la Real Audiencia**, on the northern side is the Museo Histórico Nacional (see **Museums**, below). A block west of the Cathedral is the **former Congress** building now occupied by the Ministry of Foreign Affairs (the new Congress building is in Valparaíso). Nearby are the law courts. At Calle Merced 864, a few metres east of the Plaza de Armas, is the **Casa Colorada**, built in 1769, the home of the Governor in colonial days and then of Mateo de Toro, first President of Chile. It is now the Museum of the History of Santiago. From the Plaza de Armas Paseo Ahumada, a pedestrianized street lined with cafés runs south to Avenida O'Higgins four blocks away, crossing Calle Huérfanos, which is also pedestrianized.

Four blocks north of the Plaza de Armas is the interesting **Mercado Central**, at 21 de Mayo y San Pablo. The building faces the Parque Venezuela, on which is the Cal y Canto metro station, the northern terminus of Line 2, and, at its western end, the former **Mapocho Railway Station**, now a cultural centre. If you head east from Mapocho station, along the river, you pass through the Parque Forestal (see page 78), before coming back to Plaza Baquedano.

Avenida O'Higgins runs through the heart of the city for over three kilometres. It is 100 metres wide, and ornamented with gardens and statuary: the most notable are the equestrian statues of generals O'Higgins and San Martín; the statue of the Chilean historian Benjamín Vicuña MacKenna who, as mayor of Santiago, beautified Cerro Santa Lucía (see **Parks and gardens** below); and the great monument in honour of the battle of Concepción in 1879.

The eastern end of the Alameda is at Plaza Baquedano, where there is a statue of Gen Baquedano and the Tomb of the Unknown Soldier. From here the Alameda skirts, on the right, Cerro Santa Lucía, and on the left, the Catho-lic University. Beyond the hill the Alameda goes past the neo-classical **Biblioteca Nacional** on the right, which also contains the national archives. Beyond, on the left, between Calle San Francisco and Calle Londres, is the old-est church in Santiago: the red-walled church and monastery of **San Francisco** (1618). Inside is the small statue of the Virgin which Valdivia carried on his saddlebow when he rode from Peru to Chile. Near the church cloisters is the Museo de Arte Colonial. South of San Francisco is the Barrio París-Londres, built in 1923-29, now restored and pedestrianized. Two blocks north of the Alameda on Calle Agustinas is the **Teatro Municipal**. A little further west along the Alameda, is the **Universidad de Chile**; the **Club de la Unión**, an

Around the Plaza de Armas

Along the Alameda

The Santiago Region

Paris, Madrid and Seville?

"Santiago, 'most notable and most loyal,' is a mixture of Paris, Madrid and Seville. It is far ahead of Spanish towns in its electric tramways, broad avenues and brisk movement. But the larger houses are all characteristically Spanish. They are built around a central court or patio, which is usually open to the sky above and full of flowers and graceful shrubs. Very often there are sparkling fountains and statuary

also. In fact, through the great gateway of a large Santiago house the most delicious little views of water, flowers and greenery can be gathered in passing. This gateway has heavy wooden doors, carefully locked at night; the windows opening on the street are usually heavily barred, which is by no means a useless precaution".

'Chile', by Scott Eliot, quoted in GR Knock, Spanish America, London 1925.

exclusive social club founded in 1864, is almost opposite (the current building dates from 1925). Nearby, on Calle Nueva York is the **Bolsa de Comercio** (public viewing of the trading is permitted; passport essential).

One block further west there are three plazas: the Plaza de la Libertad to the north of the Alameda, the Plaza Bulnes in the centre, and the Plaza del Libertador O'Higgins to the south. To the north of the Plaza de la Libertad, hemmed in by the skyscrapers of the Centro Cívico, is the **Palacio de la Moneda** (1805), the Presidential Palace containing historic relics, paintings and sculpture, and the elaborate Salón Rojo used for official receptions (guided visits only with written permission from the Dirección Administrativa – three weeks' notice required). Although the Moneda was damaged by air attacks during the military coup of 11 September 1973 it has been fully restored. In front of the Palace is the statue of former President Arturo Alessandri Palma. (Ceremonial changing of the guard every other day, 1000). Four blocks south of the Plaza del Libertador O'Higgins is a park, Parque Almagro, notable for the **Iglesia de los Sacramentinos**, a gothic church loosely designed in imitation of a church in Montmartre in Paris.

The Alameda continues westwards to the **Planetarium** (Avenida O'Higgins 3349, T7762624, US$5) and, opposite it on the southern side, the railway station (Estación Central or Estación Alameda). On Avenida Matucana, running north from here, is the very popular **Parque Quinta Normal** (see page 78). About six blocks west of the Estación Central are the major bus terminals.

Lastarria & Bellavista

Between the Parque Forestal, Plaza Baquedano and the Alameda is the **Lastarria** neighbourhood (Universidad Católica metro). For those interested in antique furniture, objets d'art and old books, the area is worth a visit, especially the **Plaza Mulato Gil de Castro** (Calle Lastarria 305). Occasional shows are put on in the square, on which are the Museo Arqueológico de Santiago in a restored house, a bookshop (*Librería Latinoamericana*), handicraft and antique shops, an art gallery, the Instituto de Arte Contemporáneo and the *Pergola de la Plaza* restaurant. Nearby, on Calle Lastarria, are the **Jardín Lastarria**, a cul-de-sac of craft and antique shops (No 293), *Gutenberg, Lafourcade y Cía*, an antiquarian bookseller (No 307), the Ciné Biógrafo (No 131) and, at the corner with Calle Merced, the Instituto Chileno-Francés (see page 101).

The **Bellavista** district, on the north bank of the Río Mapocho from Plaza Baquedano at the foot of **Cerro San Cristóbal** (see page 79), is the main focus of nightlife in the old city. Around Calle Pío Nono are restaurants and cafés, theatres, entertainments, art galleries and craft shops, especially those selling lapis lazuli.

East of Plaza Baquedano, the main east-west axis of the city becomes **Avenida** **Providencia**
Providencia which heads out towards the residential areas, including Las
Condes, at the eastern and upper levels of the city. It passes through the neighbourhood of Providencia, a modern area of shops, offices and restaurants
around Pedro de Valdivia and Los Leones metro stations; the national offices
of Sernatur, the national tourist board, are located here. At Metro Tobalaba it
becomes Avenida Apoquindo.

Parks and gardens

Near the heart of the city, bounded by Calle Merced to the north, Avenida **Cerro Santa**
O'Higgins to the south, calles Santa Lucía and Subercaseaux, is a cone of rock **Lucía**
rising steeply to a height of 70 metres called Cerro Santa Lucía. It can be scaled
from the Caupolicán esplanade, on which, high on a rock, stands a statue of
that Mapuche leader, but the ascent from the northern side of the hill, where
there is an equestrian statue of Diego de Almagro, is easier. There are striking
views of the city from the top, reached by a series of stairs, where there is a fortress, the Batería Hidalgo (the platform of which is its only colonial survival –
the building is closed). On clear days you can see across to the Andes; even on
smoggy days, the view of the sunset is good; the Cerro closes at 2100. It is best
to descend the eastern side, to see the small Plaza Pedro Valdivia with its waterfalls and statue of Valdivia. The area is famous, at night, for its gay community.
At all times travellers should beware of thieves here.

The Santiago Region

Santiago orientation

Related maps
A West of the centre,
page 86

B Centre, page 78

C Bellavista, page 80

D Providencia, page 84

E Las Condes, page 88

Parque O'Higgins This lies about 10 blocks south of Avenida O'Higgins. It has a small lake, playing fields, tennis courts, swimming pool (open from 5 December), an open-air stage for local songs and dances, a discothèque, the racecourse of the Club Hípico, an amusement park, *Fantasilandia* (■ *adults US$9, children US$7, unlimited rides, open at weekends only in winter, and not when raining*), kite-flying contests on Sunday, and a group of about 20 good, typical, restaurants, some craft shops, the Museo del Huaso, an aquarium and a small insect and shellfish museum at El Pueblito. Cars are not allowed in the Parque. It is reached by Metro Line 2 to Parque O'Higgins station or by bus from Parque Baquedano via Avenida MacKenna and Avenida Matta.

Parque Quinta Normal Situated north of the Estación Central on Av Matucana y D Portales, the Quinta Normal was founded as a botanical garden in 1830. It contains four museums, details of which are given below.

Parque Forestal This lies due north of Santa Lucía hill and immediately south of the Mapocho. The Museo Nacional de Bellas Artes is in the wooded grounds and is an extraordinary example of neo-classical architecture, details below.

Centre

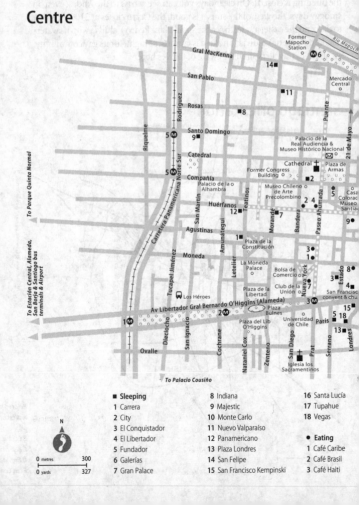

■ **Sleeping**
1 Carrera
2 City
3 El Conquistador
4 El Libertador
5 Fundador
6 Galerías
7 Gran Palace
8 Indiana
9 Majestic
10 Monte Carlo
11 Nuevo Valparaíso
12 Panamericano
13 Plaza Londres
14 San Felipe
15 San Francisco Kempinski
16 Santa Lucía
17 Tupahue
18 Vegas

● **Eating**
1 Café Caribe
2 Café Brasil
3 Café Haiti

Also known as Parque Gran Bretaña, this lies east of Plaza Baquedano and is perhaps the most beautiful park in Santiago. The Museo Tajamares del Mapocho is here, see page 83.

Parque Balmaceda

The sharp, conical hill of **San Cristóbal**, forming the Parque Metropolitano, to the northeast of the city, is the largest and most interesting of the city's parks and, on a clear day (rare) provides excellent views over the city and across to the Andes. There are two sectors, sector Cumber on Cerro San Cristóbal and, further east, sector Tupahue. There are two entrances: west from Pío Nono in Bellavista and east from Pedro de Valdivia Norte. ■ *Daily 0900-2100, vehicles, US$3.* On Cerro Cumbre (300 metres) stands a colossal statue of the Virgin, which is floodlit at night; beside it is the astronomical observatory of the Catholic University which can be visited on application to the observatory's director. Near the Bellavista entrance is the **Jardín Zoológico**, which has an excellent collection of animals which are well-cared for. ■ *Tuesday-Friday 1000-1300, 1500-1800, Saturday, Sunday and holidays 1000-1800, US$3.*

Parque Metropolitano

Further east in the Tupahue sector there are terraces, gardens, and paths; in one building there is a good, expensive restaurant (*Camino Real*, T2321758) with a splendid view from the terrace, especially at night, and an **Enoteca**, or exhibition of Chilean wines from a range of vineyards. You can taste one of the six 'wines of the day', US$2 per glass, and buy if you like, though prices are higher than in shops. Nearby is the Casa de la Cultura which has art exhibitions and free concerts at midday on Sunday. There are two good swimming pools: one at Tupahue (US$9); the other, Antilen (US$12) has a fine panoramic view over the city; it can be reached from the road that branches off north from below the Enoteca. East of Tupahue are the Botanical Gardens, with a collection of Chilean native plants, guided tours available. ■ *Daily 0900-1800.*

Access By **funicular**: every few minutes to Cerro San Cristóbal from Plaza Caupolicán at the northern end of Calle Pío Nono, 1000-1900 Monday-Friday, 1000-2000 Saturday and Sunday (closed for lunch 1330-1430), US$2. By **teleférico** from Estación Oasis, Avenida Pedro de Valdivia Norte via Tupahue to San Cristóbal near the funicular's upper station, 1030-1900 at weekends, 1500-1830 weekdays, US$3. A combined funicular/teleférico ticket is US$4. An open bus operated by the *teleférico* company runs to San Cristóbal and Tupahue from the Bellavista entrance with the same

The Santiago Region

Map labels:
Cervantes
Av Recoleta
Av López de Bello
Patronato
Dardignac
Bellavista
Av Santa María
Parque Forestal
Miraflores
Museo Nacional de Bellas Artes
Mosqueto
José M de la Barra
Monjitas
MacIver
Merced
Museo Iglesia de la Merced
•6
atro nicipal
Cerro Santa Lucía
Subercaseaux
10 Padre Luis de Valdivio
To Providencia, Bellavista & Las Condes
Biblioteca Nacional
Ⓜ4
Guayacil
Marcoleta
del Campo
Santa Rosa
San Isidro
Quito
Carmen

4 Café Santos
5 Chez Henry
6 Da Carla
7 El 27 de Nueva York
8 El Naturista
9 El Vegetariano
10 Lung Fung

Ⓜ **Metro Stations**
1 Los Héroes
2 Moneda
3 Universidad de Chile
4 Santa Lucía
5 Santa Ana (2 entrances)
6 Cal y Canto

schedule as the *teleférico* itself. The *teleférico* does not operate in winter; to reach Tupahue take the funicular or a taxi either from the Bellavista entrance (much cheaper from inside the park as taxis entering the park have to pay entrance fee), or from Metro Pedro de Valdivia. Alternatively you could walk from Metro Pedro de Valvivia, 1 kilometre.

Cementerio General Situated in the *barrio* of La Recoleta, just north of the city centre, this cemetery contains the mausoleums of most of the great figures in Chilean history and the arts, including Violetta Parra, Victor Jara and Salvador Allende. There is also an impressive monument to the victims of the 1973-90 military government; their names, ages and dates of detention or disappearance are listed in two sections: those who disappeared and those executed for political reasons. The cemetery can be reached by any Recoleta bus from Calle Miraflores.

Museums

Centre *Almost all museums are closed on Monday and on 1 November* **Museo Histórico Nacional**, Plaza de Armas 951, in the former Palacio de la Real Audiencia, covers the period from the Conquest until 1925. ■ *US$1, free on Sundays. Tuesday-Sunday, 1000-1730.*

Bellavista

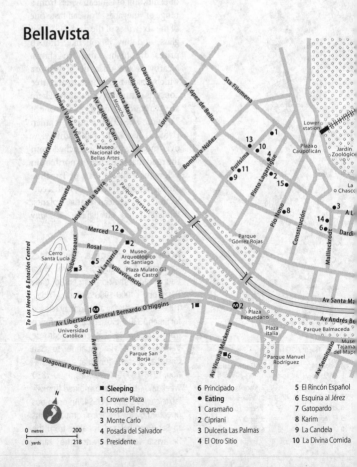

	■ Sleeping	6 Principado	5 El Rincón Español
	1 Crowne Plaza	● Eating	6 Esquina al Jérez
	2 Hostal Del Parque	1 Caramaño	7 Gatopardo
	3 Monte Carlo	2 Cipriani	8 Karim
	4 Posada del Salvador	3 Dulcería Las Palmas	9 La Candela
	5 Presidente	4 El Otro Sitio	10 La Divina Comida

0 metres 200
0 yards 218

Museo de Santiago, Casa Colorada, Merced 860, covers the history of Santiago from the Conquest to modern times, with excellent displays and models, and guided tours. ■ *US$2, students free. Booklet, US$0.35. Tuesday-Saturday, 1000-1800, Sunday and holidays, 1000-1300.*

Museo Chileno de Arte Precolombino, Bandera 361, in the former Real Aduana, has a representative exhibition of objects from the pre-Columbian cultures of Central America and the Andean region, highly recommended. ■ *US$4, students free, Sundays free. Booklet, US$0.35. Tuesday-Saturday 1000-1800. Sunday 1000-1400.*

Museo Iglesia de la Merced, MacIver 341, houses a colonial religious art and archaeological collection from Easter Island. ■ *US$1. Tuesday-Friday 1000-1300, 1500-1800, Saturday 1000-1300.*

Museo de Arte Sagrado, is located in the Cathedral. ■ *Free. Monday and Friday only, 0930-1230, 1530-1830.*

Museo de Arte Colonial, Londres 4, beside Iglesia San Francisco, has displays of religious art. One room has 54 paintings of the life of St Francis; in the cloisters is a room containing Gabriela Mistral's Nobel Prize medal; also a collection of locks. ■ *US$1. Tuesday-Saturday 1000-1800, Sunday 1000-1400.*

Palacio de la Alhambra, Compañía 1340 y Amunátegui, is a national monument sponsored by the Society of Arts; it stages exhibitions of paintings as well as having a permanent display. ■ *T80875. Monday-Friday 1100-1300, 1700-1900.*

Biblioteca Nacional, Moneda 650, has temporary exhibitions of books, book illustrations, documents, posters. ■ *Free. Monday-Friday 1000-1400, 1530-1830, Saturday 1000-1400.*

Palacio Cousiño, Calle Dieciocho 438, five blocks south of the Alameda, is a large mansion in French rococo style with a superb Italian marble staircase. The upper storey was damaged by fire in 1968. Note the family monogram on the curtains, mirrors and doors. Owned by the Municipalidad, it is used for official receptions but is open as a museum. See also box on page 82. ■ *US$3. Guided tours only, in Spanish, English and Portuguese, visitors have to wear cloth bootees to protect the floors. Tuesday-Friday 0930-1330, 1430-1700, Saturday, Sunday and holidays 0930-1330.*

Virgen
Cumbre station (teleférico)
Upper station (funicular)
Parque Metropolitano

Sofía Concha
Arz Casanova
M Concha
Bellavista
To Providencia & Las Condes

Av Providencia
Av Salvador
Gral Salvo
Av José M Infante
Av Eleodoro Yáñez

1 La Tasca Mediterránea
2 Les Assasins
3 Mosaique
4 San Fruttuoso
5 Venezia

Ⓜ Metro Stations
1 Universidad Católica
2 Baquedano
3 El Salvador

╫╫╫ Funicular railway

The Santiago Region

The Santiago Region

From coal to wine: The Cousiño dynasty

A small group of families have dominated much of Chilean history since independence, their surnames often recurring as politicians, writers and entrepreneurs. One of the most important of these in the 19th century was the Cousiño family with its interests ranging from mining to vineyards. Matías Cousiño (1810-63), the founder of the family's fortunes, began his working life in Copiapó where he helped build the Caldera to Copiapó railway (1848) and became chief assistant to the silver magnate, Carlos Goyenechea. After the deaths of his first wife and Goyenechea, Matías Cousiño married Goyenechea's widow, becoming one of the wealthiest men in Chile. The family fortune was secured when Luis, Matías Cousiño's only son by his first marraige, later married the only daughter of Goyenechea, Isadora.

Matías Cousiño later played an active role in politics and was elected to Congress, but it is as the founder of the first major coal mine in Chile at Lota in 1852 that he is best remembered. Lota became the biggest coal mine in Chile and, until the entry of US capital into the copper industry, the Compañia Minera de Lota was the largest company in the country, largely due to the efforts of 4 generations of the family. After Matías's death, Luis and Isadora extended the family's firtunes and founded the country's leading newspaper, El Mercurio. Luis's son, Carlos, founded the first cement

company in Chile and built the first hydroelectric plant. In the 1880s the family pioneered plantation forestry and modern porcelain and glass manufacture.

Mindful of the need to announce their wealth to the world, Luis and Isadora hired a French architect to design the Palacio Cousiño in Santaigo. Luis died of tubercolosis in 1873 aged 38 leaving Isadora, a widow at the age of 37, to oversee its completion. Furnished with tapestries, antiques and pictures imported from France, the palace startled Santiago society with its great luxury and its advanced technology, including its own electricity generators and the first lifts in the country. Isadora's other great project was the famous park in Lota: here overlooking the mine and the town whose workers had contributed so much to the family fortunes, she oversaw the cultivation of plants from all over the world.

One of Luis's other achievements was the transformation of the family's vineyards, Cousiño Macul, on the eastern outskirts of Santiago and among the oldest in the country, which had been purchesed by Matías in 1856. Luis imnported cuttings from France and engaged French architects to design cellars to the best contemporary standards. It is, however, said that Isadora never permitted the serving of anything but French wine in the Palacio Cousiño. It was perhaps fitting that her death, in 1899, occurred in Paris.

Museo de la Solidaridad, Virginia Opazo 38 (Metro República), houses a collection of over 400 art works produced by Chilean and foreign artists in support of the Unidad Popular government and in opposition to the Pinochet dictatorship. Artists include Alexander Calder, Joan Miró, Oswaldo Guayasamin and Roberto Matta. There are also videos of interviews (in Spanish) with survivors of the 1973 coup. ■ *T6971033, Monday-Friday 1100-1800.*

Parque Quinta Normal   **Museo Nacional de Historia Natural**, housing exhibitions on zoology, botany, mineralogy, anthropology, ethnography and aeology. ■ *US$1. Tuesday-Sunday 1000-1745.*

Museo Ferroviario, contains 13 steam engines built between 1884 and 1953 including a rare surviving Kitson-Meyer. ■ *US$1.50, free to those over 60, photography permit, US$2.50. Tuesday-Friday, 1000-1215, 1400-1700, Saturday, Sunday and holidays, 1100-1330, 1500-1830.*

Museo Ciencia y Tecnología. ■ *US$1.50. Same hours as Museo Ferroviario.*

Museo Artequín, is nearby on Avenida Portales in the Chilean pavilion built for the 1889 Paris International Exhibition, containing prints of famous paintings and activities and explanations of the techniques of the great masters. Recommended. ■ *US$1.25. Daily 1000-1800.*

Museo Arqueológico de Santiago, in Plaza Mulato Gil de Castro, Lastarria 307, has temporary exhibitions of Chilean archaeology, anthropology and pre-Columbian art. ■ *Free. Monday-Friday 1030-1400, 1530-1900, Saturday, 1030-1400.*

Museo Nacional de Bellas Artes, in the Parque Forestal, has a large display of Chilean and foreign painting and sculpture; contemporary art exhibitions are held several times a year. ■ *US$1. Tuesday-Saturday 1000-1800, Sunday and holidays 1100-1800.* In the west wing of the building is the **Museo de Arte Contemporáneo**. ■ *US$1.*

La Chascona, is the house of the poet Pablo Neruda and now headquarters of the Fundación Pablo Neruda. This is really three houses, built on a steep hillside and separated by gardens. ■ *F Márquez de la Plata 0192, T7778741, US$2.50 guided visits only, English guides can be booked (see page 137). Daily except Monday, 1000-1300, 1500-1800.*

Museo Tajamares del Mapocho, Parque Balmaceda, Av Providencia 222, has an exhibition of the 17th and 18th century walls built to protect the city from flooding by the river, and of the subsequent canalization. Also houses temporary exhibitions. ■ *Tuesday-Saturday 1000-1800, Sunday 1000-1330.*

Museo Benjamín Vicuña MacKenna, Av V MacKenna 94, records the life and works of the 19th century Chilean historian and biographer who became one of Santiago's most important mayors. It also has occasional exhibitions.

Museo del Huaso, houses a small, interesting collection of criollo clothing and tools. ■ *Free. Tuesday-Friday 1000-1300, 1430-1715, Saturday, Sunday and holidays 1000-1800.*

Acuario Municipal at Local 9. ■ *Small charge. Tuesday-Friday 1000-2000 (till 2100 Saturday, Sunday, holidays).*

Museo de Insectos y Caracoles, Local 12, has a collection of insects and shellfish. ■ *Same hours as the aquarium but open till 2200 at weekends and holidays.*

Museo de la Escuela Militar, Los Militares 4500, Las Condes, has displays on Bernardo O'Higgins, the Conquest and the Pacific War. ■ *Monday-Friday 1500-1800.*

Museo Ralli, Sotomayor 4110, Vitacura, has a collection of works by modern European and Latin American artists, including Dali, Chagall, Bacon and Miró. ■ *Free. Tuesday-Sunday 1100-1700.*

Museo de Artes Decorativas, Casas de Lo Matta, Av Presidente Kennedy 9350, Vitacura, is a beautiful museum containing Don Hernán Garcés Silva's bequest to the nation: antique silverplate from South America and Europe, 17th-18th century Spanish colonial and European furniture, 15th century Book of Hours, housed in an 18th century country mansion. ■ *Tuesday-Friday 1000-1300, 1430-1730, Saturday 1100-1800. Guided tours Tuesday-Friday 1000-1330, 1500-1800. Guided tours available; by bus, take Intercomunal No 4 from Mapocho station, or take a taxi; in either case ask to be let out at Casas lo Matta.*

Museo Aeronáutico, Camino a Melipilla 5100, Cerrillos Airport, has displays on space exploration, and is worth a visit. ■ *Tuesday-Sunday 1000-1700, free.*

Lastarria & Bellavista

Parque O'Higgins

Other museums

The Santiago Region

Excursions

Maipú is a suburb 10 kilometres southwest of Santiago where a monument marks the site of the Battle of the Maipú, 5 April 1818, which resulted in the final defeat of the Spanish royalist forces in mainland Chile. Nearby is the interesting **National Votive Temple of Maipú**, of fine modern architecture and stained glass; ■ *Daily 0800-2100, also daily mass at 1830, 1730 Saturday, 1000-1400, 1600-2000 Sunday and religious holidays.* The **Museo del Carmen**, attached, which contains carriages, furniture, clothing and other colonial and later items is also interesting. ■ *Saturday 1600-2000, Sunday and holidays, 1100-1400, 1600-2000. Getting there: bus from Teatinos y O'Higgins, 45 minutes.*

Essentials

Sleeping
■ *on maps*
pages 78, 80, 86 and 88
Price codes:
see inside front cover

Check if breakfast and 18% tax is included in the price quoted (if foreigners pay in US$ cash or with US$ travellers' cheques, the 18% VAT should not be charged; if you pay by credit card, there is often a 10% surcharge). There is very little good accommodation under US$20 per person.

Expensive hotels

Providencia L1 *Park Plaza*, Ricardo Lyon 207, T2336363, F2336668. Good. **L1** *Torremayor*, Ricardo Lyon 322, T2342000, F2343779. Clean, modern, good service, good location. **L2** *Aloha*, Francisco Noguera 146, T2332230/7, F2332494. Helpful,

Providencia

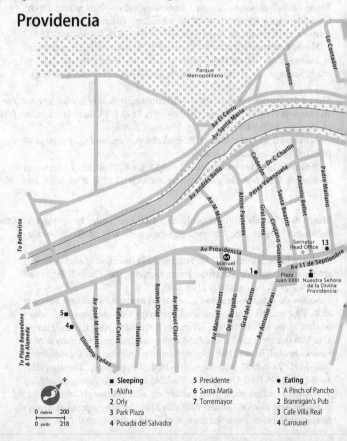

■ Sleeping
1 Aloha
2 Orly
3 Park Plaza
4 Posada del Salvador
5 Presidente
6 Santa María
7 Torremayor

● Eating
1 A Pinch of Pancho
2 Brannigan's Pub
3 Cafe Villa Real
4 Carousel

0 metres 200
0 yards 218

good restaurant. **L2** *Orly*, Pedro de Valdivia 27, metro Pedro de Valdivia, T2328225, small, comfortable, has apartments for rent on Juana de Arco. Good. US$70 a day (reductions may be possible), also smaller and cheaper rooms. **L2** *Presidente*, Eliodoro Yáñez 867, almost at Providencia, T2358015, F2359148. Good value and good location. **L1** *Sheraton San Cristóbal*, Santa María 1742, T2335000, F2236656. Best in town, good restaurant, good buffet lunch, and all facilities. Also *Sheraton Towers*. Slightly cheaper. **L3** *Santa María*, Santa María 2050, T2326614, F2316287. Excellent, friendly, small, good breakfast, other meals good value. Highly recommended. **A2** *Posada del Salvador*, Eliodoro Yáñez 893, T2359450, F2518697. Metro Salvador, with bath. **A2** *Lyon*, Ricardo Lyon 1525, T2257732, F2258697, with breakfast, small, intimate, good value, also has annex B with breakfast.

Las Condes **L1** *Hyatt Regency Santiago*, Av Kennedy 4601, T2181234, F2182279. Superb, beautifully decorated, large outdoor pool, gymnasium, Thai restaurant. Highly recommended. **L1** *Radisson Royal*, Av Vitacura 2610, T2036001, F2036003, 5-star. **L2** *Montebianco*, Isidora Goyenechea 2911, T2330427, F2330420. Small, smart motel. **L2** *Parinacota*, Av Apoquindo 5142, T2466109, F2205386. 4-star, small, all services, no pool. **L3** *Manquehue*, Esteban Dell'Orto 6615, T/F2128862. Very good with new wing and new pool. **A1** *Santa Magdalena Apartments*, office: Helvecia 244, Las Condes, T3746875/6, http://www.santamagdalena.cl, info@santamagdalena.cl. Apartment rental 1 block from metro stations, a/c.

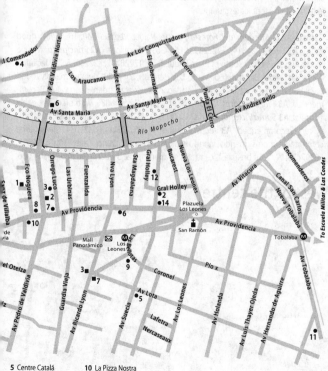

The Santiago Region

5 Centre Catalá
6 Copelia
7 El Huerto
8 Gatsby
9 La Mía Pappa

10 La Pizza Nostra
11 L'Ermitage
12 Mr Ed
13 Phone Box Pub
14 Red Pub

Centre L1 *Carrera*, Teatinos 180, T6982011, F6721083. Art-deco lobby, slightly faded grandeur, rooftop pool and restaurant (good buffet lunch), outstanding. **L1** *Crowne Plaza*, O'Higgins 136, T6381042, F6336015. All facilities, spacious, a/c (book through travel agent for better rates). **L1** *Fundador*, Paseo Serrano 34, T/F6322566. Helpful, good value, charming staff. **L1** *Galerías*, San Antonio 65, T6384011, F6395240, large rooms, good breakfast. **L1** *San Francisco Kempinski*, O'Higgins 816, T6393832, F6397826. Lufthansa affiliated, excellent breakfast, large rooms, Lan Chile office in basement, comfortable. **A1** *El Conquistador*, Miguel Cruchaga 920, T/F6965599. **L2** *Hostal del Parque*, Merced 294, opposite Parque Forestal, T6392694, F6392754. Comfortable, quiet, friendly. Recommended. **L3** *Tupahue*, San Antonio 477, T6383810, F6395240. Comfortable. **A2** *City*, Compañía 1063, T6954526, F6956775. Run down, theft reported. **A2** *Conde de Anzúrez*, Av República 25, T6996368, F6718376. Metro República, convenient for airport, central station and bus terminals, clean, helpful, safe, luggage stored. **A2** *Ducado*, Agustinas 1990, T6969384/672-6739, F6951271. With breakfast. Clean, quiet at back. Secure parking. Recommended. **A2** *Gran Palace*, Huérfanos 1178, T6712551, F6951095. Overpriced, good restaurant. **A2** *Libertador*, O'Higgins 853, T6394212, F6337128. Helpful, stores luggage, good restaurant, bar, roof-top pool. Recommended. **A2** *Majestic*, Santo Domingo 1526, T6958366, F6974051. With breakfast, pool, Indian restaurant, English spoken. Recommended. **A2** *Monte Carlo*, Subercaseaux 209, T6339905, F6335577. At foot of Santa Lucía, modern, restaurant, stores luggage. Recommended. **A2** *Panamericano*, Teatinos 320 y Huérfanos, T6723060, F6964992. Comfortable, serves popular business lunch between 1230 and 1530. **A2** *Santa Lucía*, San Antonio 327 y Huérfanos, piso 4, T6398201. Garage 2 blocks away, clean, comfortable, good, small, quiet restaurant.

Mid-price hotels **Centre A2** *El Marqués del Forestal*, Ismael Valdés Vergara 740, T6333462, good value. **A2** *Lira*, Lira 314, T2222492, F6343637. Excellent. **A2** *Principado*, Vicuña MacKenna 30, 1 block south of Plaza Baquedano, T2228142, F2226065. Full facilities. **A2** *Tokyo*, Almte Barroso 160, Metro Los Héroes, T6984500. Helpful, friendly, good breakfast, manager speaks English and Japanese, lovely garden, good value. Recommended. **A3** *Plaza Londres*, Londres 75, T6333320, F6640086, with breakfast, cable TV, quiet. **A3** *Santa Victoria*, Vicuña MacKenna 435, T6345753. Quiet, small, safe, family run. Recommended. **A3** *Vegas*, Londres 49, T6322514, F6325084. Clean, large comfortable rooms, friendly, good breakfast. **B** *Hostal Quito*, Quito 36, T6399918, F6397470. Without breakfast, central, also apartments. **B** *Hostal Vía Real*, Marín 066,

West of the centre

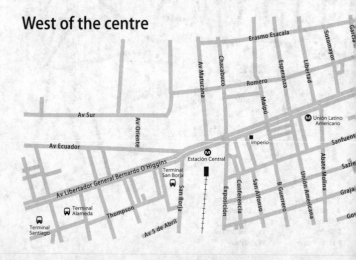

The Santiago Region

T6354676, F6354678. Charming, friendly, helpful, small, laundry. Recommended. **B** *Hostal Río Amazonas*, Rosas 2234, T6984092, F6719013, with breakfast and bath, good value. **B** *Imperio*, O'Higgins 2876, T6897774, F6892916, with breakfast, parking, convenient for bus terminals, gloomy. **B** *Du Maurier*, Moneda 1510, quiet. Recommended. **C** *Res Alemana*, República 220 (no sign), T/F6712388, Residencial.Alemana@usa.net. Metro República, with bath, **D** without, clean, with breakfast, pleasant patio, central, heating on request, good cheap meals available, Recommended. **C** *París*, Calle París 813, T6640921, F6394037. With bath, quiet, clean, good meeting place, good value, luggage store. Recommended. **C** *Res Londres*, Londres 54, T/F6382215. Near San Francisco Church, former mansion, large old-fashioned rooms and furniture, few singles, no heating, English spoken, very popular. Recommended.

Providencia C *Hostal Parada*, Grau Flores 168, T4606640. Spacious, clean.

Centre C *España*, Morandé 510, T696-6066. With bath, hot water, clean, run down. **D** *Res del Norte*, Catedral 2207, T6969251. Without bath, with breakfast, friendly, safe, clean, large rooms, credit cards accepted. **D** pp *San Patricio*, Catedral 2235, T6954800. With bath, **E** pp without, with breakfast, clean, safe, friendly, good value. **D** *Maury*, Tarapacá 1112, T6725859, F6970786. Without bath, clean, friendly, safe, meals, English and French spoken; **D** *Santo Domingo*, Santo Domingo 735. With bath **E** without, cleanish, basic, gloomy. **E** *Indiana* (no sign), Rosas 1339, T714251. Very basic, kitchen facilities. **E** pp *Nuevo Valparaíso*, Morandé y San Pablo, T6715698. Simple, central, erratic hot water, poor beds, safe, basic, use of kitchen (no utensils), cable TV, popular, good meeting place. **E** pp *Olicar*, San Pablo 1265. Cooking facilities, quiet, clean.

Cheaper hotels

West of the centre near Metro República C *Alojamiento Diario*, Salvador Sanfuentes 2258 (no sign), T6992938. With bath, **E** pp dormitory accommodation. Kitchen facilities. **D** *Res Mery*, Pasaje República 36, off 0-100 block of República, T6968883. Big green building down an alley, hot showers, quiet, good value. Recommended. **E** pp *Letelier*, Cumming 97, without breakfast, also Spanish classes. **E** pp *Res Vicky*, Sazie 2107, T6963772. Kitchen and laundry

facilities, good dormitory accommodation, good beds. **E** pp *SCS Habitat*, San Vicente 1798, T6833732, English spoken, helpful and informative. Recommended. On north side of Alameda opposite bus terminals. **F** pp Federico Scoto 130, T7799364. Use of phone and fax, good meals, cooking facilities, hot water, large rooms, clean, good meeting place. Recommended. **E** pp Huérfanos 2842, T6814537. Kitchen, laundry, dormitory accommodation.

Providencia C *Res Providencia*, Vicuna MacKenna 92B, T2220533 (Metro Baquedano), with bath, quiet. **C** *Res Manuel Montt*, M. Montt 628, T2358048 (Metro Manuel Montt), kitchen and laundry facilities, garden, meals.

Morandé, Gral MacKenna, San Martín and San Pablo are in the red light district

North of the Plaza de Armas near Mapocho Station Several on Gral MacKenna 1200 block, all very basic, including **D** *San Felipe*, No 1248, T6714598. Cheap laundry service, kitchen, noisy (2nd floor quieter), luggage stored, cable TV. Recommended. **E** *Res Sur*, Ruiz Tagle 055, T7765533. Clean, meals available. Same owner has *Bernal*, Bernal del Mercado, T7762679. Good. **D** *Res Wilson*, Jota Beche 225, T7764073.

Staying with families
Travellers can find good accommodation in comfortable family guesthouses through *Amigos de Todo el Mundo*, Av Pdte Bulnes, Paseo, 285, dept 201, Casilla 52861 Correo Central, T6726525, F6981474, run by Sr Arturo Navarrete, prices from US$16 with

Las Condes

■ Sleeping	● Eating	
1 Hyatt Regency santiago	1 Delmónico	3 Route 66
2 Montebianco	2 Praga	4 Shoo Gun

0 metres 100
0 yards 109

breakfast, other meals extra, monthly rates available, also transport to/from airport. Recommended. *Marilú Cerda*, Rafael Cañas 246 C, Providencia, T2355302, F3639154, tradesic@intermedia.cl and *Urania Cerda*, Boccaccio 60, Las Condes, T2102922, F3639154. Both offer bed and breakfast (**C** pp), comfortable, no credit cards, friendly, good beds, English and French spoken. Warmly recommended. **D** *Cecelia Parada*, Llico 968, T5229947, F5216328. One block from Metro Departamental, laundry service, gardens, quiet. **D** pp *Rodrigo Sauvageot*, Gorbea 1992, dpto 113, T6722119. With breakfast, reservation essential. **E** pp *Sra Lucía*, Catedral 1029, piso 10, dept 1001, T6963832. Central, friendly, safe, cooking facilities, basic. **E** pp *Sra Marta*, Amengual 035, Alameda Alt 4.400, T7797592. (Metro Ecuador), good, hospitable, kitchen facilities, motorcycle parking.

See the classified ads in *El Mercurio*, flats, homes and family *pensiones* are listed by district, or in *El Rastro* (weekly), or try the notice board at the tourist office. In furnished apartments, if you want a phone you may have to provide an *aval*, or guarantor, to prove you will pay the bill, or else a huge deposit will be asked for. Estate agents handle apartments, but often charge half of the first month's rent as commission, while a month's rent in advance and 1 month's deposit are required. Recommended apartments are *Edificio San Rafael*, Miraflores 264, T6330289, F2225629. US$30 a day single, US$46 a day double, minimum 3 days, longer periods discounted. Staying with a family is an economical and interesting option for a few months. *Tempo Rent*, Santa Magdalena 116, T2311608, F3340374, tempo.rent@chilnet.cl. Nancy Lombardo, MacIver 175, oficina 42, T6382009; F6330210, offers apartments with 1, 2 or 3 bedrooms, fully furnished.

Longer stay sleeping

The Chilean Youth Hostel association, the *Asociación Chilena de Albergues Turisticas Juveniles* (ACHATJ) has its offices at Hernando de Aguirre 201, oficina 602, T2333220/2343233, achatj@hostelling.co.cl. (Worth getting a list of YH addresses around the country as these change.) Hostels in the capital include **E** pp Cienfuegos 151, T6718532 (5 minutes from metro Los Héroes), modern, clean, satellite TV, no cooking facilities, cafeteria, laundry facilities, parking, unwelcoming. **E** pp *Res Gloria*, Almte Latorre 447, T6988315. Metro Toesca, clean, popular, meals, difficult to use kitchen.

Youth hostels

'Wild' camping on the Farellones road near the river or south of Santiago near Puente Alto. At Km 25 south of city on Panamericana, Esso garage offers only a vacant lot near highway. Excellent facilities about 70 km from Santiago at Laguna de Aculeo, called *Club Camping Maki*. Includes electricity, cold water, swimming pool, boat mooring, restaurant, but only available to members of

Camping

Centro Comercial Lo Castillo

2 Av Vitacura
El Coigue
El Colgue
Las Nieves
Las Nipas
atico
Ciruelillo
Los Laureles
El Clonqui
El Pangue
Los Coligues
Los Quiltes
Las Quiltes
Av Américo Vespucio
La Luma
3

1

Av Circunvalación Américo Vespucio
Cerro Colorado
Los Talaveras
Artilleros
Los Cadetes
Los Estandartes
Yungay
Av Presidente Riesco

Escuela Militar

Ⓜ1
Los Militares
1Ⓜ
Av Apoquindo
Luis Rodríguez
Puerta del Sol
ía

Ⓜ Metro stations
1 Escuela Militar 3 El Golf
2 Alcántara 4 Tobalaba

certain organizations. An alternative site is *El Castaño* camping (with casino), 1 km away, on edge of lake. Very friendly, café sells fruit, eggs, milk, bread and kerosene, good fishing, no showers, water from handpump.

Eating
● *on maps*
pages 80, 84 and 88

Luxury hotels have computerized information on the more expensive restaurants, particularly useful if you are not sure what to eat.

Centre *Chez Henry*, on Plaza de Armas. Expensive restaurant and delicatessen. Also has a delicatessen at O'Higgins 847. Highly recommended. *Faisan d'Or* on Plaza de Armas. Good *pastel de choclo*, pleasant place to have a drink and watch the world go by. *Torres*, O'Higgins 1570. Traditional bar/restaurant, good atmosphere, live music at weekends. *Mermoz*, Huérfanos 1048. Good for lunches. *Bar Nacional No 1*, Huérfanos 1151 and *Bar Nacional No 2*, Bandera 317. Good restaurants, popular, local specialities. *Omar Khayyam*, Peru 570. Arab specialities. *Guimas*, Huérfanos y Teatinos. Good, reasonable prices, good value *almuerzo*. *Bar Central*, San Pablo 1063. Popular, noisy, good specialities, good value. Recommended. *Fra Diavolo*, París 836 (near *Res Londres*). Lunches only, excellent food and service, popular. *Bar-restaurant Inés de Suárez*, Morandé 558. Cheap. *El Lagar de Don Quijote*, Morandé y Catedral. Bar/restaurant, parrilladas, good wines, popular, good. *Congreso*, Catedral 1221. Similar to *Don Quijote*. Popular at lunchtime. *Círculo de Periodistas*, Amunátegui 31, piso 2. Unwelcoming entrance, good value lunches. Recommended. *El 27 de Nueva York*, Nueva York 27. International cuisine, pricey, good. *Savory Tres*, Ahumada 327. Good. *Los Ricos Pobres*, Brasil 373. *Nuria*, Agustinas y MacIver. Wide selection. *Da Carla*, MacIver 577. Italian food, good, expensive. *San Marco*, 2 doors away. Better still. *Les Assassins*, Merced 297. French, very good. Highly recommended. *L'Omelette*, Agustinas. Good. Closes 2100. Some of the best and most popular seafood restaurants are to be found in the Mercado Central (by Cal y Canto metro; lunches only), or at the Vega Central market on the opposite bank of the Mapocho. Cheap lunches are served in a large underground *comedor Pavo Real*, Estado 33 (just off O'Higgins), self-service, good value, US$5.

Oriental: *Ostras Azocar*, Bulnes 37, good seafood but pricey. Good Indian restaurant inside *Hotel Majestic*, Santo Domingo 1526. *Guo Fung*, Moneda 1549. Elegant location. Recommended. *Lung Fung*, Agustinas 715. Delicious food, pricey, large cage in the centre with noisy parrots. *Bella China*, Compania 2280, large portions. *Pai Fu*, Santa Rosa 101. Good. *Kam Thu*, Santo Domingo 771. Near San Antonio. Large helpings, all Chinese.

Lastarria and Bellavista **Lastarria**: *La Pergola de la Plaza* in Plaza Mulato Gil de Castro. *Gatopardo*, Lastarria 192. Good value. Highly recommended. *Café Universitario*, Alameda 395 y Subercaseaux (near Sta Lucía). Good, cheap *almuerzos*, lively at night, separate room for lovers of rock videos, very pleasant. *El Rincón Español*, just off Rosal. Spanish, good, reasonably priced, try the paella. Next door is *El Bar Escondida*, a small but pleasant bar.

Many restaurants/bars on **Pío Nono** including: *Venezia*, Pío Nono y Lopez de Bello. Huge servings, good value. *Eladio*, No 251. Argentine cuisine, good steaks. *Los Ladrillos*, No 350. Popular, lively. *Cafetería La Nona*, No 99. Real coffee, good empanadas, fresh fruit juices. Recommended. *Karim*, No 127. Arab and international cuisine, shish kebabs, good fish dishes, reasonably priced, pleasant ambience. *El Antojo Gaugin*, No 69. Good *brochetas a la plancha*, pricey.

On Pinto Lagarrigue: *Nuevo Cipriani*, No 195. Italian, elegant atmosphere, US$25-30, top class. *Picoroco*, No 123. Good seafood.

On López de Bello: *El Otro Sitio*, No 53. Peruvian, excellent food, elegant not cheap. **On Purísima**: *Caramaño*, No 257. Good seafood, reasonably priced, ring doorbell. Recommended. *Capricho Español*, No 65. Good Spanish menu. *Le Coq au*

Vin, No 0110. French, excellent cuisine, reasonably priced. Recommended. *Las Mañanitas*, No 131. Mexican, sometimes with live music. *Pica Isidro*, Purísima 269. Seafood specialities, good, inexpensive. *La Divina Comida*, No 93. Italian with 3 rooms – Heaven, Hell and Purgatory. Highly recommended. *Libro Café Mediterraneo*, next door. Popular with students, lively, not expensive. *Cava de Dardignac*, Dardignac 0190. Portuguese cuisine with live fado music at night. *La Tasca Mediterránea*, Dominica 35, extensive menu including fish, seafood, pricey but good value, good food. Recommended.

On Mallinckrodt: *La Esquina al Jérez*, No 102. Excellent Spanish. *San Fruttuoso*, No 180. Italian. Recommended.

Providencia On Av Providencia: *Lomit's*, No 1980. Good. *Gatsby*, No 1984. American food, as-much-as-you-can-eat buffet and lunch/dinner, snack bar open till 2400, tables outside in warm weather, good.

Italian: *La Pizza Nostra*, Av Las Condes 6757. Pizzas and good Italian food, real coffee, pricey. Also at Av Providencia 1975 and Luis Thayer Ojeda 019. *da Renato*, Mardoqueo Fernández 138. (Metro Los Leones). Good. *La Mía Pappa*, Las Bellotas 267, also at 11 de Septiembre 1351 and Vitacura 8927. Good value. Very popular lunches. *Valerio*, Apoquindo 4300, also Coronel Pereira 139. Smart, good wines, not cheap.

French: *Carousel*, Los Conquistadores 1972. Fine cuisine, expensive. *L'Ermitage*, Tobalaba 477. Celebrated, not cheap. *El Giratorio*, 11 de Septiembre 2250, piso 16. Good food eaten while the whole city rotates outside your window. Recommended. *Au Bon Pain*, 11 de Septiembre 2263. 'The French bakery café', salads, sandwiches, real coffee, also at Miraflores 235, El Bosque Norte 0181 and elsewhere.

Oriental: *Bin-Xiang*, M Montt 155, Chinese. *Mikado*, Bilbao 1933. *Jardín de Bambú*, Salvador 1827. Vietnamese. *Oriental*, M Montt 584. One of the best Chinese in Santiago.

Others: *A Pinch of Pancho*, Gral del Canto 45. Seafood and fish specialities, very good. *El Rincón Brasileiro*, M Montt 116. *Salvaje*, Av Providencia 1177. Excellent international menu, open-air seating, good value lunches. Warmly recommended. *Centre Catalá*, Av Suecia 428 near Lota. Good, reasonably priced. *Carousel*, Los Conquistadores 1972. French, very good, nice garden, over US$20. *Eladio*, 11 de Septiembre 2250, piso 5, reasonably priced, good meat dishes.

Las Condes Oriental: *Sakura*, Vitacura 4111. Japanese. *Shoo Gun*, Enrique Foster Norte 172. Japanese. *Benyarong*, Américo Vespucio Norte 2970. Thai. *Taj Mahal*, Isadora Goyenechea 3215 (Metro El Golf), T2323606. Indian, expensive but excellent.

Seafood: *Mare Nostrum*, La Concepción 281. *Puerto Marisko*, Isadora Goyenechea 3471, good.

On Vitacura: *Delmónico*, No 3379. Excellent, reasonably priced. *El Madroñal*, No 2911, T2336312. Excellent, Spanish cuisine, one of the best restaurants in town, booking essential. *Praga*, No 3917. Czech. *Jabri*, No 6477. Arab cuisine.

On Isadora Goyenechea: *München*, No 204. German. Recommended. *Pinpilinpausha*, No 2900. Good. *La Cascade*, No 2930, French, long established, closed Sundays.

On El Bosque Norte: La Estancia, No 058, another branch at 11 de Septiembre 2250. *El Club*, No 0380 (approximately). Popular, good value (US$15-20). *Coco Loco*, No 0215. Fish, seafood, good.

On Av Las Condes: *La Querencia*, No 14980. A bit cheaper, both good. *Santa Fe*, No 10690. *Tex-Mex*, with *T'Quila Bar* next door. Excellent margaritas.

Others: *La Tasca de Altamar*, Noruega y Linneo. Good seafood, reasonably priced. *Route 66*, Alonso de Córdova 4357. North American, closed Sundays.

Many first class restaurants, including grills, Chilean cuisine (often with music), French cuisine and Chinese. This area tends to be more expensive than central restaurants

The Santiago Region

The Santiago Region

Restaurants with a floor show **Centre**: *Los Adobes del Argomedo*, Argomedo 411 y Lira. Good Chilean food, floor show (Monday-Saturday) includes cueca dancing, salsa and folk. *El Villorio*, San Antonio 676, T6335605. Meat specialities. **Providencia**: *Circulo Libanes*, Santa María 1880, T2332688. *García Lorca*, Guardia Vieja 109, T2339677. Spanish cuisine. **Bellavista**: *Cipriani*, Ernesto Pinto Lagarrigue 195, T7350630. Italian food. *La Esquina al Jerez*, Mallinckrodt 102, T7354122. Spanish cuisine. *Sibaritas*, Mallinckrodt 184, T7771470. International menu. *Eladio*, Pio Nono 241, T7773337. Meat dishes.

Eating on a budget Budget travellers should make the *almuerzo* their main meal. For cheap meals in the evening try the *fuentes de soda* and *schoperias* scattered around the centre. Cheap lunches are served in the casino of the Universidad de Chile, Blanco Encalada 2186, next to Parque O'Higgins, Monday-Friday 1215-1415, except January-March.

Vegetarian restaurants *El Huerto*, Orrego Luco 054, Providencia, T2332690. Recommended. Open daily, live music Friday and Saturday evenings, varied menu, very good but not cheap, popular. *El Viejo Verde*, López de Bello 94, Bellavista. *El Naturista*, Moneda 846, excellent, closes 2100. *El Vegetariano*, Huerfanos 827, Local 18. *Unicornio*, Plaza Lyon, Local 49. Natural Green, Huerfanos 1188, T3609689, also at Puente 689, Local 314.

Snacks and ice cream Several good places on Av Providencia includes *Copelia*, No 2211. *Bravissimo*, No 1406. *El Toldo Azul*, No 1936.

Cafés, bars & nightclubs
Note that almost all hotel bars are closed on Sunday

Cafés and bars For good coffee try *Café Haití*, *Café Brasil* and *Café Caribe*, all on Paseo Ahumada and elsewhere in centre and in Providencia. Some of the best beer in Santiago can be found at *HBH bars*, Irarrázaval 3126 in the centre and at Gral Holley 124, Providencia.

Centre: *Café Paula*. Several branches, eg Estado at entrance to Galería España, excellent coffee and cake, good breakfast, also on San Antonio opposite the Teatro Municipal. *Café Colonia*, Maclver 133. Splendid variety of cakes, pastries and pies, fashionable and pricey. Recommended. *Café Santos*, Huérfanos 830, Av Providencia 2236 and other branches. Popular for excellent 'onces' (afternoon tea). *Bon Bon Oriental*, Merced 345. Superb Turkish coffee, savouries and cakes. *Tip-Top Galetas*. Recommended for freshly baked biscuits, branches throughout the city.

Bellavista and Lastarrria: *Café de la Dulcería Las Palmas*, López de Bello 190. Good pastries and lunches. Several on Purísima 100-200, including *La Candela*, No 129. Evening meals, Chilean folk song performances on Friday and Saturday evenings. *El Biógrafo*, Villavicencio 398. Informal atmosphere, open for lunch and dinner. Recommended.

Providencia: many on Av Providencia including *Phone Box Pub*, No 1670, T496627. *El Café del Patio*, next door. Real coffee, vegetarian food, popular with students. *Salón de Té Tavelli*, Drugstore precinct, No 2124. *Golden Bell Inn*, Hernando Aguirre 27. Popular with expatriates. *Flannigans*, Encomenderos 83, Irish pub with Guinness. Many other good bars nearby on Av Suecia including *Mr Ed*, No 1552; *Brannigan Pub*, No 35. Good beer, live jazz, lively. *Red Pub*, No 29. *Café Mistral*, C Arzobispo 0635, T7776173, owned by French mountain-climber, free climbing wall, internet services.

Las Condes: *Country Village*, Av Las Condes 10680. Open Monday-Saturday from 2000, Sunday from lunch onwards, live music Friday and Saturday. Further east on Av Las Condes at Paseo San Damián are several popular bar-restaurants including *Tequila*. *Morena Pizza and Dance Bar*, No 0120. Nice dance floor, good sound system, live music at weekends, happy hour before 2200.

Nightclubs Listings are given in *El Mercurio*. Clubs in Bellavista are cheaper and more down market generally than those in Providencia. *Peña Nano Parra*, San Isidro 57. Good folk club, cheap. *Emmanuelle*, Andrés Bello 2857. Shows at 0100 and 0300. *Maeva*, Andrés Bello 2863.

Some of the restaurants and cafés which have shows are given above

Discotheques *Gente*, Av Apoquindo 4900. *Heaven*, Recoleta 345. Thursday, Friday, Saturday 2330-0500, entry US$14 per person. *Enigma*, Av Las Condes 9179. *Las Uracas*, Vitacura 9254, US$15 but free before 2300 if you eat there. *Club Tucán Salsoteca*, Pedro de Valdivia 1783. Caters to lovers of Brazilian rhythms. *Caribbean*, López de Bello 40. Reggae. *Bogart*, López de Bello 34. Rock. See also *Moreno Dance Bar* (under **Bars** above). Many more, mainly in the Providencia and Las Condes areas.

Cinemas Seats cost US$4-6 with reductions on Wednesday (elsewhere in the country the day varies). Some cinemas offer discounts to students and over 60s (proof required). 'Ciné Arte' (quality foreign films) is very popular and a number of cinemas specialize in this type of film: *El Biógrafo*, Lastarria 181. *Alameda Cultural Centre*, Av Providencia 927. *Casa de Extensión Universidad Católica*, Av B O'Higgins 390, T2221157. *Espaciocal*, Goyenechea y Vitacura. *Tobalaba*, Av Providencia 2563, and others, full details are given in the press. *Cine Arte Normandie*, Tarapacá 1181, T6972979. Varied programme, altered frequently, films at 1530, 1830 and 2130 daily, students half price Try also *Goethe Institut* (address below). There are large multi-screen complexes in the Parque Aranco and Alto de Las Condes shopping malls.

Entertainment

The Santiago Region

Theatres *Teatro Municipal*, Agustinas y San Antonio, stages international opera, concerts by the Orquesta Filarmónica de Santiago, and the Ballet de Santiago, throughout the year; on Tuesday at 2100 there are free operatic concerts in the Salón Claudio Arrau; tickets range from US$8 for a very large choral group with a symphony orchestra, and US$10 for the cheapest seats at the ballet, to US$80 for the most expensive opera seats. Some cheap seats are often sold on the day of concerts. *Teatro Universidad de Chile*, Plaza Baquedano, is the home of the Orquesta y Coro Sinfónica de Chile and the Ballet Nacional de Chile.

Free classical concerts are sometimes given in San Francisco church in summer; arrive early for a seat.

There are a great number of theatres which stage plays in Spanish, either in the original language or translations, eg *La Comedia*, Merced 349, *Abril*, Huérfanos 786, *Camilo Henríquez*, Amunátegui 31, *Centro Arrayán*, Las Condes 14891, *El Galpón de los Leones*, Av Los Leones 238, *El Conventillo*, Bellavista 173. Four others, the *Opera*, Huérfanos, *California*, Irarrázaval 1546, *Humoresque*, San Ignacio 1249 and *Picaresque*, Recoleta 345, show mostly Folies Bergères-type revues. *Santiago Stage* is an English-speaking amateur drama group. Outdoor rock concerts are held at the *Estadio Nacional*, Av Unión Latino Americana (metro of same name), at the *Teatro Teletón*, Rosas 325 (excellent sound system), and elsewhere. Events are listed in *El Mercurio* and *La Epoca*. The most comprehensive listings appear in *El Mercurio's Wikén* magazine on Friday.

Bicycles For parts and repairs *Importadora Caupolicán*, San Diego 863, T6972765, F6961937. Wide range, helpful. Ask for Nelson Díaz 'a walking encyclopaedia' on bikes. *Luis Cabalin*, Coquimbó 1114, T6984193, good for maintenance and repairs.

Sports

Bowling *Bowling Center*, Av Apoquindo 5012.

Cricket Saturday in summer at Club Príncipe de Gales, Las Arañas 1901 (bus from Tobalaba metro).

Football in Chile

Whilst Chilean football may not enjoy the worldwide recognition given to Argentina and the mighty Brazil, there is no doubt that Chileans follow 'the beautiful game' with as much pride and passion as their illustrious neighbours and have produced several world-class players: modern heroes include Iván Zamorano and the supremely talented Marcelo Salas, known affectionately as 'El Matador' (The Killer).

Football arrived in Chile towards the end of the 19th century, courtesy, as in much of South America, of the British. The role of British workers, employed in the construction of the railway system, is reflected in the names of several of the leading teams, notably Santiago Wanderers (who are based in Viña del Mar!) and Everton. The game's popularity grew rapidly; by the 1940s most large towns boasted their own team and stadium. In 1962, Chile's importance as a soccer nation was recognised internationally when she hosted the World Cup.

The season starts in March and runs through the winter to November. The national league consists of a First Division and two Second Divisions, one northern, one southern. However, most of the support (and money) goes to the big three clubs, all based in Santiago: Universidad de Chile (known as La U), Colo-Colo and Universidad Católica, the team favoured by the wealthy of Santiago. The greatest rivalry is between La U and Colo-Colo, who are also known as Los Indios (their strip carries an image of the great Mapuche leader after whom they were named). The most fervent supporters of the former are known as los de abajo (the underdogs), while those of the former are called la garra blanca (the white claw). The 1998 champions were Colo-Colo who beat La U by one point.

A visit to a match, especially if it is either a clasico (local derby) or an international game, is an unforgettable experience. Watching football is still very much a family affair and the supporters dance, sing and wave their team colours beneath a nonstop rain of confetti, fireworks and coloured smoke. Tickets cost around US$5. If you decide to visit the Estadio Nacional, the home of La U where international matches are played, find a seat high up on the terraces and you will be able to watch the sun set over the mountains around Santiago.

by Maggie Wilkinson

Football The 3 biggest clubs in Santiago are *Colo Colo* who play at the Estadio Monumental (reached by any bus to Puente Alto; tickets from Cienfuegos 41, T6883244), *Universidad de Chile* (Campo de Departes, Nunoa, T2392793) who play at the Estadio Nacional (Av Grecia 2001, T2388102), and *Universidad Católica* who play at San Carlos de Apoquindo, reached by bus from Metro Escuela Militar, tickets from Andrés Bello 2782, Providencia, T2312777).

Gymnasium *Sesame*, Los Leones 2384, with pool, aerobics. Highly recommended. *Gimnasio Alicia Franché*, Moneda 1481, T6961681. Aerobics and fitness classes (women only). Another at Huérfanos 1313, T6711562.

Racecourses *Club Hípico*, Blanco Encalada 2540, racing every Sunday and every other Wednesday afternoon (moves to Viña del Mar, January-March), worthwhile even if only to watch dusk fall over the Andes, entry to main stand US$8, card of up to 18 races. Also at the Hipódromo Chile every Saturday afternoon; pari-mutuel betting.

Running The Hash House Harriers hold runs every other week; information through the British Embassy and Consulate.

Skiing and climbing The two main climbing areas near Santiago are the Grupo Loma Larga near the Cajón del Maipo and the Grupo Plomo near the ski resort of La Parva. For details of climbing in these areas, see pages 107 and 110. For ski resorts in the Santiago area see page 106. *Club Andino de Chile*, Enrique Foster 29. Ski club (open 1900-2100 on Monday and Friday). *Federación de Andinismo de Chile*, Almte Simpson 77A (T2220888, F2226285). Open daily. (See **Climbing** in **Adventure tourism**, page 24.) It has the addresses of all the mountaineering clubs in the country and has a mountaineering school. *Club Alemán Andino*, El Arrayán 2735, T2425453. Open Tuesday and Friday, 1800-2000, May-June. Equipment hire is much cheaper in Santiago than in ski resorts. Sunglasses are essential. **Skiing and climbing equipment**: *Mountain Service*, Ebro 2805, Las Condes (Metro Tobalaba) T2429723. English spoken, tents, stoves, clothing, equipment rental. Recommended. *Panda Deportes*, Paseo Las Palmas 2217 (Metro Los Leones), T2321840.

For detailed information on skiing near Santiago see pages 106-108. Transport to the 4 ski resorts of Farellones, El Colorado, La Parva and Valle Nevado is operated by *Skitotal*, Av Apoquindo 4900, oficina 40-42, T2463344, F2064078, who also rent equipment, organize accommodation, lessons. English, German spoken.

Sports clubs *Ñuñoa*, T2237846. With swimming pool, tennis courts and school. *Chess Club*, Alameda O'Higgins 898. Monday-Saturday 1800, lively.

Swimming pools *Tupahue* (large pool with cafés, entry US$9; two for the price of one on Wednesdays) and *Antilen*, US$12 both on Cerro San Cristóbal. Open daily in summer except Monday 1000-1500 (closed April-October). There are two pools in the Parque O'Higgins (one for children), summer only, T5569612, US$4. Olympic pool in Parque Araucano (near Parque Arauco Shopping Centre, closest Metro Escuela Militar), open Tuesday-Saturday 0900-1900 November-March.

Tai Chi Tai Chi & other martial arts: Raul Tou-Tin, Irarrázaval 1971, T2048082.

Tennis *Santiago Tennis Club*; also, *Club de Tenís Jaime Fillol*, Rancho Melnichi, Par 4.

During **November** there is a free art fair in the Parque Forestal on the banks of the Río **Festivals** Mapocho, lasting a fortnight. In **October** or **November** there are a sumptuous flower show and an annual agricultural and industrial show (known as *Fisa*) in Parque Cerrillos. Religious festivals and ceremonies continue throughout **Holy Week**, when a priest ritually washes the feet of 12 men. The image of the Virgen del Carmen (patron of the Armed Forces) is carried through the streets by cadets on **16 July**.

Handicrafts *El Almacén Campesino*, Purísima 303, Bellavista, cooperative association in **Shopping** an attractive colonial building, sells handicrafts from all over Chile, including attractive Mapuche weavings, wood carvings, pottery (best bought in Pomaire, 50 km away, see page 105) and beautiful wrought copper and bronze. Prices are similar to those in shops in Temuco. Ask about shipping. *Prisma de los Andes*, Santo Domingo 1690 (Metro Santa Ana), T6730540, a women's social project, sells distinctive high quality textiles made in the organization's co-operative workshops (which can be visited). The gemstone lapis lazuli can be found in a few expensive shops in Bellavista but is cheaper in the arcades on south side of the Plaza de Armas and in the *Centro Artesanal Santa Lucía* (Santa Lucía metro, south exit) which also has a wide variety of woollen goods, jewellery, etc. Try also *Marita Gil* Los Misioneros 1991, Pedro de Valdivia Norte, T 2326853, F 2322520. A cheaper craft market is next to the bridge of Pio Nono in Bellavista, best at weekends. *Amitié*, Av Ricardo León y Av Providencia (Metro Los Leones). *Dauvin Artesanía Fina*, Providencia 2169, Local 69 (Metro Los Leones) have also been recommended. *H Stern* jewellery shops are located at the *San Cristóbal Sheraton, Hyatt Regency* and *Carrera* hotels, and at the International

The Santiago Region

Airport. *Cema-Chile* (Centro de Madres), Portugal 351 and at Universidad de Chile metro stop, *Manos Chilensis*, Portugal 373, *Artesanías de Chile*, Varas 475, *Artesanía Popular Chilena*, Av Providencia 2322 (near Los Leones metro), and *Artesanía Chilena*, Estado 337, have a good selection of handicrafts. *Talleres Solidarios*, de la Barra 456, small selection. Antique stores in Plaza Mulato Gil de Castro and elsewhere on Lastarria (Merced end).

Beside and behind the Iglesia de los Dominicos, on Av Nueva Apoquindo 9085, is *Los Graneros del Alba*, or *El Pueblo de Artesanos*, open daily except Monday, 1130-1900. All types of ware on sale, classes given in some shops, interesting. *Restaurant El Granero* is here. To get there, take a No 326 or 327 bus from Av Providencia, marked 'Camino del Alba'. Get out at the children's playground at the junction of Apoquindo y Camino del Alba, at the foot of the hill leading up to the church, and walk up.

Markets *Mercado Central*, between Puente y 21 de Mayo by the Río Mapocho (Cal y Canto metro) is excellent but quite expensive; there is a cheaper market, the *Vega Central*, on the opposite bank of the river. There are other craft markets in an alleyway, 1 block south of Av O'Higgins between A Prat and San Diego, as well as on the 600 to 800 blocks of Santo Domingo (includes pieces from neighbouring countries) and at Pío Nono y Av Santa María, Bellavista. The shopping arcade at the Central Station is good value, likewise the street market outside. Cheap clothes shops in the city, eg on Bandera esp 600 block, are good for winter clothes for travellers, often secondhand (look for sign Ropa Europea). The flea market at Franklin y Santa Rosa on Saturday and Sunday morning, is the largest and cheapest flea market in the city (Chileans say that if there was a market for souls someone would be selling them off at cost price in Franklin). There is a good outside fruit market at Puente 815, by *Frutería Martínez*. There is an antique fair on Sunday (1000-1400) in the summer and a Fiesta de Quasimodo on the first Sunday after Easter at Lo Barnechea, 30 minutes by bus from Santiago.

Shopping malls There are 2 large shopping centres east of the centre in Las Condes: Parque Arauco, on Av Kennedy, north of Metro Escuela Militar; and the larger and more modern Centro Comercial Alto Las Condes, further east on Av Kennedy, open 1000-2200.

Book prices are very high compared with Europe, even for second-hand books

Bookshops *Librería Albers*, Vitacura 5648, Las Condes, T2185371, F2181458, and 11 de Septiembre 2671, Providencia, T2327499 (Spanish, English and German – good selection, cheaper than most, helpful, also German and Swiss newspapers). *Librería Catalonia*, Huérfanos 669. *Feria Chilena del Libro*, Huérfanos 623, and in Drugstore precinct, Providencia 2124. *Librería Inglesa*, Huérfanos 669, local 11, and Pedro de Valdivia 47, Providencia, T2319970, good selection of English books, sells the *South American Handbook*. *South American Way*, Av Apoquindo 6856, Las Condes, T2118078, sells books in English. There are many bookshops in the Pedro de Valdivia area on Av Providencia. Second-hand English books from *Librería El Patio*, Av Providencia 1652 (Metro Pedro de Valdivia), expensive, exchange for best deal. Also, from Henry at Metro station Los Leones, and *Books*, next to *Phone Box Pub*, in the patio at Av Providencia 1670 (the artist's shop in same precinct sells attractive cards). Much better value but with a smaller selection are the bookshops on the shopping mall at Av Providencia 1114-1120. There are several second-hand book kiosks on San Diego between Eleuterio Ramirez and Condor, 4 blocks south of Plaza Bulnes, next to the Iglesia de los Sacramentinos. *Librairie Française*, books and newspapers, Estado 337. *Apostrophes*, Merced 324, specialize in French publications including literature. As well as the antiquarian bookshop mentioned above in the Lastarria district, there are other good antiquarian bookshops on Merced around the corner from Lastarria, eg *América del Sur Librería Editorial*, No 306, *Libros Antiguos El Cid*, No 344. Many stalls on Paseo Ahumada/Huérfanos sell overseas newspapers and journals.

Camera repairs and film *Harry Müller*, Ahumada 312, Oficina 402. Not cheap but good and fairly quick. Recommended. Speaks German and English. For Minolta and Canon repairs, *TecFo*, Nueva York 52, piso 2, T6952969. Recommended. Many developers on Ahumada offer 24-hour service of varying quality (some develop, but do not mount, slides, slow service). *Tecnofoto*, Ahumada 131, piso 7, Oficina 719, T6725004. Recommended as quick and efficient. *Prontofoto*, Ahumada 264, T6721981. Good quality developing and printing. *Moretto*, Merced 753. Recommended as cheap and good. *Black Box*, Pérez Valenzuela 1503 (Metro Manuel Montt). Highly recommended. For camera batteries and other spares try *Fotocenter*, Ahumada y Huérfanos. *Carmen Pérez Gúzman*, MacIver 148, good quality, helpful, some English spoken.

Camping equipment Standard camping gas cartridges can be bought at *Fabri Gas*, Bandera y Santo Domingo, or *Unisport*, Av Providencia 2503. Other equipment for camper-vans from *Bertonati Hnos*, Manuel Montt 2385. **Tent repairs**: *Juan Soto*, Silva Vildosola 890, Paradero 1, Gran Avenida, San Miguel, Santiago, T5558329. Camping goods from *Club Andino* and *Federación de Andinismo* (see page 95); expensive because these articles are imported. *Patagonia*, Helvecia 210, Providencia, T3351796 (Tobalaba metro), good range of clothing and equipment. *Outdoors & Travel*, Encomeneros 206, Las Condes, T 3357104, for wide range of imports and locally made goods. For packs also try Sr Espinosa, San Martín 835. Repair of camping stoves at *Casa Italiana*, Tarapacá 1120. For second-hand equipment try Luz Emperatriz Sanhuela Quiroz, Portal de León, Loc 14, Providencia 2198 (Metro Los Leones).

Local Bus: yellow buses serve the whole city: they show destination on the front as well as the fare (US$0.40). Blue buses, known as Metrobuses, run from metro terminals to outlying parts of the city.

Metro: line 1 of the underground railway system runs west-east between San Pablo and Escuela Militar, under the Alameda, Line 2 runs north-south from Cal y Canto to Lo Ovalle. The connecting station is Los Héroes. Line 5 runs north-south from Baquedano on Line 1 to La Florida and work is under way to extend it northeast from Baquedano to meet Line 2 at Santa Ana. The trains are fast, quiet, and very full. The first train is at 0630 (Monday-Saturday), 0800 (Sunday and holidays), the last about 2245. Fares vary according to time of journey; there are 3 charging periods: high 0715-0900, 1800-1900, US$0.45; medium 0900-1800, 1930-2100 and weekends, US$0.40; low 0630-0715, 2100-2230, US$0.25. The simplest solution is to buy a *boleto valor*, US$4.50; a charge card from which the appropriate fare is deducted. Metrobus services (blue buses, fare US$0.30) connect the metro stations of Lo Ovalle, San Pablo, Las Rejas, Pilar del Granso, Cal y Canto, Salvador and Escuela Militar with outlying parts of Gran Santiago.

Taxi: taxis (black with yellow roofs) are abundant, and not expensive, with a minimum charge of US$0.60, plus US$0.12 per 200m. Taxi drivers are permitted to charge more at night, but in the daytime check that the meter is set to day rates. Taxis are more expensive at bus terminals and from taxi ranks outside hotels – best to walk a block and flag down a cruising taxi. Avoid taxis with more than 1 person in them especially at night. For journeys outside the city arrange the charge beforehand. The private taxi service which operates from the bottom level of *Hotel Carrera* has been recommended (same rates as city taxis), as has Radio Taxis Andes Pacífico, T2253064/2888; similarly Rigoberto Contreras, T6381042, ext 4215, but rates above those of city taxis.

Colectivo: collective taxis, which operate on fixed routes between the centre and the suburbs, are a convenient form of transport. They carry destination signs and route numbers. US$0.75, higher fares at night.

Transport
See also ins and outs, page 73

See map on page 74

The Santiago Region

> **Only posing officer!**
>
> On 4 March 1997, London's Financial Times reported "Chilean Police stopped 49 motorists in Santiago for using cellular phones while driving, only to find that a third were pretending to talk on fake phones."

Car hire: prices vary a lot so shop around first. Hertz, Avis, Budget and others available from airport. *Hertz*, Costanera Andrés Bello 1469, T2359666, F2360252, and airport, T6019262/6010477, at Hotel Hyatt T2455936. Has a good network in Chile and cars are in good condition. *Avis* at La Concepción 334, T495757. Poor service reported. *Seelmann*, Antonio Varas 1472, oficina 156, T2252138, F2853222. *ANSA*, Eliodora Yañez 1198, T2510256, F2510425. *Dollar*, Málaga 115, oficina 913, Localiol, T2456175/2280943 and airport, T/F6018656. *Full Famas*, Bilboa 2942, T3430664, F3430667. *Automóvil Club de Chile* car rental, Marchant Pereira 122, Providencia, T2744167/6261. Discount for members and members of associated motoring organizations. A credit card is usually asked for when renting a vehicle. Tax of 18% is charged but usually not included in price quoted. If possible book a car in advance. Remember that in the capital driving is restricted according to licence plate numbers; look for notices in the street and newspapers.

Motorcycle: small BMW workshop, Av San Camilo 185, Sr Marco Canales. BMW car dealer *Frederic*, Av Portugal, has some spares. Also tyre shops in this area. BMW riders can also seek help from the *carabineros* who ride BMW machines and have a workshop with good mechanics at Av Rivera 2003.

Bicycle: *Aricel*, Manuel Montt 933, Providencia, T2744952. Several other spare parts dealers on C San Diego 800 and 900 blocks.

Long distance Air: for details on the Aeropuerto Arturo Merino Benitez, see above under **Touching Down**, page 40. For domestic flights from Santiago see under relevant destinations.

Bus: there are frequent, and good, interurban buses to all parts of Chile. Check if student rates are available (even for non-students), or reductions for travelling same day as purchase of ticket; it is worth bargaining over prices, especially shortly before departure and out of the summer season. Also take a look at the buses before buying the tickets (there are big differences in quality among bus companies); ask about the on-board services, many companies offer drinks for sale, or free, and luxury buses have meals and wine, colour videos, headphones. Reclining seats are common and there are also *salón cama* sleeper buses. Fares from/to the capital are given in the text. On Friday evening, when night departures are getting ready to go, the terminals are murder.

Bus terminals: there are 4 terminals, all located close to each other near the city centre: *Terminal Alameda*, which has a modern extension with a shopping centre called Mall Parque Estación, O'Higgins 3712 (Metro Universidad de Santiago). This has the best left luggage facilities in the city. All Tur Bus and Pullman Bus services arrive and depart from here. *Terminal Santiago*, O'Higgins 3878, 1 block west of Terminal Alameda (Metro Universidad de Santiago) and sometimes referred to as the 'Terminal del Sur'. This terminal is used by services to and from the south as well as Valparaíso and Viña del Mar and international services. *Terminal San Borja*, O'Higgins y San Borja, T block west of Estación Central, 3 blocks east of Terminal Alameda (Metro Estación Central). There are separate sections for local buses including some services to Valparaíso and Viña del Mar and for buses to northern Chile. Booking offices are arranged according to destination. The entrance is, inconveniently, through a shopping centre. *Terminal Los Héroes*, on Tucapel Jiménez, just south of Av O'Higgins (Metro Los Héroes). Some services to the northern and southern destinations leave from here as well as some buses for Argentina. Note also that some long distance bus services also call at **Las Torres de Tajamar**, which is much more convenient if you are planning to stay in Providencia. Tur Bus also has a booking office in the centre at Bulnes 96, T6973541.

International buses: **Short distance**: there are frequent services through the Cristo Redentor tunnel to **Mendoza** in Argentina, 6-7 hours, US$20, many companies, departures around 0800, 1200 and 1600, touts approach you in Terminal Santiago. Also Tur Bus services from the Terminal Alameda. There are *colectivos* from the Terminal Santiago and from the 800/900 blocks of Morandé (Chi-Ar taxi company, Morandé 890. Recommended. Chile-Bus, Morandé 838; Cordillera Nevada, Morandé 870, T6984716), US$25, 5 hours, shorter waiting time at customs.

Long distance: to **Buenos Aires**, US$65, 22 hours (TAC and Ahumada recommended); to **Montevideo**, most involving a change in Mendoza, eg Tas Choapa, 27 hours, including meals; to **Córdoba** direct, US$32, 18 hours, several companies including Tur Bus, Tas Choapa and TAC (El Rapido not recommended); to **San Juan**, TAC, Tas Choapa, US$20; to **Bogotá** US$200, 7 days; to **Caracas** (Tuesday and Friday 0900) US$230; to **Lima**, Ormeño, 51 hours, US$90, it is cheaper to take a bus to Arica, a *colectivo* to Tacna (US$4), then bus to Lima. To **São Paulo** and **Rio de Janeiro**, eg Chilebus, Tuesday, Thursday, Saturday, US$100, 52 hours; to **Asunción**, 4 a week, 28 hours, US$75; to **Guayaquil** and **Quito**. Tramaca, runs a *combinación* service which links with the train from Calama to **Uyuni** and **Oruro** in Bolivia.

Trains: there are no passenger trains to northern Chile, Valparaíso or Vína del Mar. The line runs south to Rancagua, San Fernando, Curicó, Talca, Linares, Parral and Chillán, thereafter services go to **Concepción** and **Temuco**. Schedules change with the seasons, so you must check timetables before planning a journey. See under destinations for fares and notes on schedules. *Expreso* services do not have sleepers; some *rápidos* do (in summer *rápidos* are booked up a week in advance). *Dormitorio* carriages were built in Germany in the 1930s, bunks (comfortable) lie parallel to rails, US-Pullman-style (washrooms at each end, one with shower-bath – often cold water only); an attendant for each car; bar car shows 3 films – no cost but you must purchase a drink ticket in advance. There is also a newer, *Gran Dormitorio* sleeping car (1984), with private toilet and shower, US$10 extra for 2. Recommended. Also a car-transporter service to Chillán and Temuco. Trains are still fairly cheap and generally very punctual, although 1st class is generally more expensive than buses; meals are good though expensive. Cycles can be carried but check in advance. There are family and senior citizen discounts. No student discounts. Trains can be cold and draughty in winter and spring. There are also frequent local *Metrotren* services south to Rancagua. Booking offices: Alameda O'Higgins 853 in Galería Hotel Libertador, Local 21, T6322801, Monday-Friday 0830-1900, Saturday 0900-1300; or Metro Escuela Militar, Galería Sur, Local 25, T2282983, Monday-Friday 0830-1900, Saturday 0900-1300; Estación Central, open till 2230, T6895718/6891682. Left luggage office at Estación Central.

A steam train runs tourist services between Santiago and Los Andes, a 5-hour journey, T6985536 for details.

Hitchhiking: to Valparaíso, take Metro to Pajaritos and walk 5 minutes to west – no difficulty. Alternatively, take bus 'Renca Panamericana' from MacIver y Monjitas. To hitch south, take Buses del Paine from outside the Terminal San Borja as far as possible on the highway to the toll area, about US$1, 75 minutes. To hitch north not easy but

All trains leave from Estación Central at Alameda O'Higgins 3322

take blue Metrobus marked 'Til-Til' (frequent departures from near the Mercado Central as far as the toll bridge (*peaje*), 40 minutes, US$1), then hitch from just beyond the toll-bridge. To Buenos Aires (and Brazil) take a bus to Los Andes, then go to Copec station on the outskirts (most trucks travel overnight).

Shipping: *Navimag*, Av El Bosque Norte 0440, T2035030, F2035025. For services from Puerto Montt to Puerto Natales and vice versa. *Transmarchilay*, Agustinas 715, Oficina 403, T/F6335959. For services between Chiloé and the mainland and ferry routes on the Camino Austral. *M/n Skorpios*: Augusto Leguía Norte 118, Las Condes, T2311030, F2322269 for luxury cruise out of Puerto Montt to Laguna San Rafael. Transmarchilay also sail to the Laguna San Rafael in summer. *Patagonia Connection SA*, Fidel Oteíza 1921, Oficina 1006, Providencia (Metro Pedro de Valdivia), T2256489, F2748111, for services Puerto Montt-Coyhaique/Puerto Chacabuco-Laguna San Rafael.

Check shipping schedules with shipping lines rather than Sernatur.

Directory **Airline offices** LanChile, sales office: Agustinas 640, Torre Interamericana, T600-6004000 and several other offices, including 1 in the Centro Comercial Alto Las Condes. *Ladeco*, Huérfanos 607, T3331694 and Pedro de Valdivia 2286, T3347569. *Aerovías DAP*, Luis Thayer Ojeda 0180, oficina 1304, Providencia, T3349672, F3345843. *British Airways*, Isidora Goyenechea 2934, Oficina 302, T2329560, airport F6018571/2. *Air France*, Alcantara 44, piso 6, Las Condes, T3620140, F3620362. *Aerolíneas Argentinas*, Moneda 756, T6395001. *Varig*, Miraflores 156, piso 4, T6320922. Moneda, T6395976. *Aero Perú*, Fidel Oteiza 1953, piso 5, T2742033. *Iberia*, Bandera 206, piso 8, T6714510. *KLM*, San Sebastián 2839, Oficina 202, T2330011 (sales), T2330991 (reservations). *South African Airlines*, Santa Magdalena 75, Oficina 411, T3353272. *Avant*, Luis Thayer Ojeda 0140, T/F3639030, F2324283 and Santa Magdalena 75, T3353560, F2324283, airport 6010770. *Viasa*, Tenderini 82, piso 6, T6393922. *LAB* and *Ecuatoriana*, Moneda 1170, T6951290. *LACSA*, Dr Barros Borgoño 105, piso 2, T6951290. *Aeroflot*, Guardia Vieja 255, Oficina 1008, T3310244. *LAPSA*, Moneda 970, piso 13, T6301679. *Swissair*, Barros Errázuriz 1954, Oficina 1104, T2442888. *Lufthansa*, Moneda 970, piso 16, T6301000.

Banks, open from 0900 to 1400, but closed on Saturday

Banks Official daily exchange rates are published in *El Mercurio* and *La Nación*. Some *casas de cambio* reduce their rates slightly when banks are closed. *Banco de Chile*, Ahumada 251. Demands the minimum of formalities, but may charge commission. *Citibank*, Av Providencia 2653 and branches elsewhere in the city. *American Express*, Andrés Bello 2711, piso 9, T3506700 (Metro Tobalaba) (Turismo Cocha, Av El Bosque Norte 0430, T2301000, Providencia, for travel information and mail collection). No commission, poor rates (better to change TCs into dollars – no limit – and then into pesos elsewhere). Thomas Cook/Mastercard agent, *Turismo Tajamar*, Orrego Luco 023, T3368000. For Cirrus ATMs go to Banco Santander and Banco de Santiago and other banks with Redbanc sign. Visa at *Corp Banca*, Huérfanos y Bandera, but beware hidden costs in 'conversion rate', and *Banco Santander*, Av Providencia y Pedro de Valdivia. No commission. For stolen or lost Visa cards go to *Transbank*, Huérfanos 770, piso 10. *Casas de Cambio* (exchange houses) in the centre are mainly situated on Agustinas and Huérfanos. *Exprinter*, Bombero Osso 1053. Good rates, low commission, *cambios*. *Inter*, Andrés de Fuenzalida 47, Providencia. *Cambios Andino*, Ocho, Agustinas 1062. *Afex*, Moneda 1140. Good rates for TCs. *Intermundi*, Moneda 896. *Alfa*, Agustinas 1052, *Cambios Manquehue*, Huérfanos 1160, Local 5 (Galeria Alessandri). In Providencia several around Av Pedro de Valdivia, eg at Gral Holley 66. Good rates. *Casa de Cambio Blancas*, opposite *Hotel Orly* on Pedro de Valdivia, and *Mojakar*, Pedro de Valdivia 072. *Bataex*, Pedro de Valdivia 042 Guínazu, Pedro de Valdivia 048. *Cambios Azul*, Galeria Las Palmas 2209, Local 034, Av Pedro de Valdivia. All major currencies can be bought or or sold. Some *casas de cambio* in the centre open Sat morning (but check first). Most *casas de cambio* charge 3% commission to change TCs into dollars. Unless you are feeling adventurous avoid street money changers (particularly common on Ahumada and Agustinas): they will usually ask you to accompany them to a *Casa de Cambio* or somewhere more obscure. Rates for such transactions are no better and the passing of forged notes and muggings are reported.

Communications Telephones: *Compañía de Teléfonos de Chile*, Moneda 1151. Closed Sun. International phone calls also from: *Entel*, Huérfanos 1133. Mon-Fri 0830-2200, Sat 0900-2030, Sun 0900-1400, calls cheaper 1400-2200, fax upstairs. Fax also available at CTC offices, eg *Mall*

Panorámico, 11 de Septiembre, 3rd level (phone booths are on level 1). There are also CTC phone offices at some metro stations including *La Moneda*, *Escuela Militar*, *Tobalaba*, *Universidad de Chile* and *Pedro de Valdivia* for local, long-distance and international calls. There are also phone boxes in the street from which overseas calls can be made. International telex service, Bandera 168. **Post Office:** Plaza de Armas (0800-1900), poste restante well organized (though only kept for 30 days), passport essential, list of letters and parcels received in the hall of central Post Office (one list for men, another for women, indicate Sr or Sra/Srita on envelope). Also has philatelic section, 0900-1630, and small stamp museum (ask to see it). Other offices at Moneda 1155 and on Av Providencia, next to Sernatur. If sending a parcel, the contents must first be checked at the Post Office. Paper, tape etc on sale. Open Mon-Fri 0800-1900, Sat 0800-1400. **Internet Access:** *Café Internet*, Gen Holley 170, Providencia, T2314207 (US$7.50 per hour). *Café Virtual*, O'Higgins 145, T6386846, www.cafe-virtual.cl, cybercafe, good food. *ES Computación*, Salvador Sanfuentes 2352, T6887395, nine@ctc.internet.cl (Metro Republica), US$6 per hour.

Cultural centres *Instituto Chileno Británico de Cultura*, Santa Lucía 124, T6382156. 0930-1900, except 1330-1900 Mon, and 0930-1600 Fri, has English papers in library (also in Providencia, Darío Urzúa 1933, and Las Condes, Renato Sánchez 4369), runs language courses. *British Chamber of Commerce*, Av Suecia 155-C, Providencia, Casilla 536, T2314366. *British Council*, Av Eliodoro Yáñez 832, near Providencia, T2234622. The British community maintains the *British Commonwealth Society* (old people's home etc), Av Alessandri 557, T2238807, and the interdenominational Santiago Community Church, at Av Holanda 151 (Metro Tobalaba), Providencia, which holds services every Sun at 1045. *Instituto Chileno Francés de Cultura*, Merced 298, T6398433. In a beautiful house. *Instituto Chileno Alemán de Cultura*, Goethe-Institut, Esmeralda 650, T6383185. *German Chamber of Commerce*, Ahumada 131. *Instituto Chileno de Cultura Hispánica*, Providencia 927. *Instituto Chileno Italiano de Cultura*, Triana 843. *Instituto Chileno Israeli de Cultura*, Moneda 812, oficina 613. *Instituto Chileno Japonés de Cultura*, Providencia 2653, oficina 1902. *Instituto Chileno Norteamericano de Cultura*, Moneda 1467, T6963215. Good for US periodicals, cheap films on Fri. Also runs language courses and free Spanish/English language exchange hours (known as Happy Hours) which are a good way of meeting people. (Ask also about Mundo Club which organizes excursions and social events.) *Instituto Cultural del Banco del Estado de Chile*, Alameda 123. Regular exhibitions of paintings, concerts, theatrical performances. *Instituto Cultural de Providencia*, Av 11 de Septiembre 1995 (Metro Pedro de Valdivia). Art exhibitions, concerts, theatre. *Instituto Cultural Las Condes*, Av Apoquindo 6570, near beginning of Av Las Condes. Also with art exhibitions, concerts, lectures, etc.

Embassies and consulates Embassies: *Argentina*, Miraflores 285, T6331076. *Australia*, Gertrudis Echeñique 420, T2285065. 0900-1200. *Austria*, Barros Errázuriz 1968, piso 3. *Belgium*, Av Providencia 2653, depto 1104, T2321071. *Bolivia*, Av Santa María 2796, T2328180 (Metro Los Leones). Open 0930-1400. *Brazil*, Alonso Ovalle 1665, piso 15, T6982347. *Denmark*, Jacques Cazotte 5531, Vitacura T2185949, Mon-Fri 0800-1700. *Finland*, 11 de Septiembre 1480, Oficina 73, T2360107. *France*, Condell 65, T2251030. *Germany*, Agustinas 785, piso 7 y 8, T6335031. *Israel*, San Sebastian 2812, T2461570. *Italy*, Ramón Diaz 1270, T2259439. *Japan*, Av Ricardo Lyon 520, T2321307. *Netherlands*, Las Violetas 2368, T2236825. Open 0900-1200. *New Zealand*, Av Isadora Goyenechea 3516, Las Condes, T2314204. *Norway*, San Sebastian 2839, T2342888. *Spain*, Av Providencia 1979, piso 4, T2040239. *Panama*, Del Inca 5901, T2208286. Open 1000-1330. *Peru*, Av Andrés Bello 1751, T2326275 (Metro Pedro de Valdivia). *South Africa*, Av 11 de Septiembre 2353, Edif San Román, piso 16, T2312862. *Sweden*, 11 de Septiembre 2353, Torre San Ramón, piso 4, Providencia, T2312733, F2324188. *Switzerland*, Av Vespucio Sur 100, piso 14 (Metro Escuela Militar), T2322693. Open 1000-1200 (Metro Tobalaba). *UK*, El Bosque Norte 0125 (Metro Tobalaba), Casilla 72-D, T2313737, F2319771. Will hold letters, open 0900-1200. *USA*, Av Andrés Bello 2800, T2322600, F3303710.

Consulates Contact the embassies except for the following: *Argentina*, Vicuña MacKenna 41, T2226947, F2226853. Australians need letter from their embassy to get an Argentinian visa here, open 0900-1400 (visa US$25, free for US citizens), if you need a visa for Argentina, get it here or in the consulates in Concepción, Puerto Montt or Punta Arenas, there are no facilities at the borders. *United States*, T710133. Merced 230 (visa obtainable here). *Brazil*, MacIver 225, piso 15. Mon-Fri 1000-1300, US$10 (visa takes 2 days). Take: passport, 2 photos, ticket into and out of Brazil, photocopy of first 2 pages of passport, tickets, credit card and Chilean tourist card. *Paraguay*, Huérfanos 886, Oficina 514, T6394640. Open 0900-1300 (2 photos and copy of 1st page of passport required for visa).

The Santiago Region

Hospitals and medical services Emergency Pharmacy: Portugal 155, T382439. **Hospitals:** emergency hospital at Marcoleta 377 costs US$60. If you need to get to a hospital, it is better to take a taxi than wait for an ambulance. For yellow fever vaccination and others (but not cholera), *Hospital San Salvador*, J M Infante 551, T2256441. Mon-Thur 0800-1300, 1330-1645; Fri 0800-1300, 1330-1545. Also *Vaccinatoria Internacional*, *Hospital Luis Calvo*, MacKenna, Antonio Varas 360. *Clínica Central*, San Isidro 231, T2221953. Open 24 hrs, German spoken. *Clínica Alemana*, Vitacura 5951, Las Condes. German and English spoken (bus 344 from centre). Cheapest hospital is the public *Hospital de Urgencia*, Portugal 125, from US$125. **Physician:** *Dr Sergio Maylis*, T2320853. 1430-1900. **Dentist:** *Antonio Yazigi*, Vitacura 3082, Apto 33, T2087962/2085040. English spoken. Recommended. *Dr Torres*, Av Providencia 2330, Depto 23. Excellent, speaks English.

See also box **Language schools** *Top Language Services*, Huérfanos 886, oficina 1107, T/F6390321, offers Spanish in groups and individually, accommodation organized. *Escuela de Idiomas Violeta Parra*, Ernesto Pinto Lagarrigue 362A, Recoleta-Barrio Bellavista, T/F7358240, vioparra@chilesat.net. Courses aimed at budget travellers, information programme on social issues, arranges accommodation and visits to local organizations and national parks. *Carolina Carvajal*, T/F381000, ccarvajal@interactiva.cl. Spanish taught to individuals and small groups, intensive/business courses offered. *AmeriSpan Unlimited* has an affiliated school in Santiago, details from PO Box 40513, Philadelphia, PA 19106, USA, T2159854522/8008796640, F2159854524, info@amerispan.com. Many private teachers, includes Carolina Carvajal, Miraflores 113, depto 26, T3810000. Highly recommended. Patricia Vargas Vives, José Manuel Infante 100, oficina 308, Providencia, T2442283. Qualified and experienced (US$12.50 per hr). Lucía Araya Arévalo, Puerto Chico 8062, Villa Los Puertos, Pudahuel, T2360531 (after 1800). Speaks German and English. *Pacifica*, Guillermo Acuña 2884, Providencia, T2055129, F3437802, pacifica@netline.cl, arrange accommodation with families and courses either in language schools or with private teachers, minimum 1 month, US$70 fee.

Laundry Cheapest wet-wash in the centre is probably *Lavandería Lola*, Av Ricardo Cumming y Monedo. Very busy so get there before 1100, US$4.50 per load. Other wet-wash places in the

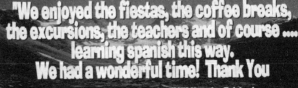

English language teaching: no longer a gold mine

An increasing number of private language institutes offer English language classes. Many of the difficulties involved in teaching in these are highlighted by Russell Trounce, a teacher in Santiago:

"Most of these institutes are small and new but they have no classes for teachers. If they do have classes they pay woeful salaries, and you can easily be replaced because there are so many teachers seeking work. If you arrive in Santiago these days expecting to pick up easy work teaching English, then you may easily be disappointed. In addition, the institutes are becoming more fussy and require native speakers with experience, teachers who are clean-cut and well-dressed, and teachers who have residency, or are at least prepared to stay 6 months. The major institutes won't even look at foreigners who are illegal. Beware of some institutes who take 20%

income tax off your wages (10% is normal). The pay is poor: if you wish to be paid between US$2.50 and US$3 after tax per hour then go for it. Santiago is now an expensive city to live in and US$3 won't buy you a decent meal. I would warn travellers not to come here with too many illusions about teaching English: it takes time to establish yourself as a foreigner and you have to be extremely patient."

Work permits can only be obtained by teachers themselves, not by the institutes. We have also received reports of more unscrupulous institutes employing teachers with 90-day tourist visas and 'discovering' as this expires that the teacher is not entitled to work, at which point it is difficult to obtain unpaid wages. English language teachers seeking work should apply in mid-February/early March with a full CV and photo.

centre: at Agustinas 1532, also *Nataly*, another at Bandera 572, at Catedral y Amunátegui and *Lava Fácil*, Huérfanos 1750. Mon-Sat 0900-2000, US$4 per load. There are plenty of dry-cleaners, eg Merced 494. Nearby, just south of Metro Universidad Católica there are several, including *American Washer*, Portugal 71, Torre 7, local 4. US$3, open 0900-2100 including Sun, can leave washing and collect it later, also at Monjitas 650. Wet wash laundries in Providencia including *Marva*, Carlos Antúñez 1823 (Metro Pedro de Valdivia), wash and dry US$8; Av Providencia 1039, full load, wet wash, US$5, 3 hrs. *Laverap*, Av Providencia 1600 block, Manuel Montt 67. At the corner of Providencia and Dr Luis Middleton there are several self-service dry cleaners (Metro Pedro de Valdivia, 11 de Septiembre exit).

Places of worship *American Presbyterian Church*, Iglesia San Marcos, Av Manquehue Norte 1320, Los Hualtatas. Service in English Sun 0915. *Anglican Church*, Holanda 151. Service 1030. *Synagogues*, Tarapacá 870, T393872, and Las Hortensias 9322, T2338868.

Tour companies and travel agents *Wagons-Lits Cook*, Carmencita, Providencia, T2330820. Recommended. *Turismo Cocha* (American Express representatives with mail service), Av El Bosque Norte 0430, Casilla 191035, Providencia, Metro Tobalaba, T2301000. *Passtours*, Huérfanos 886, Oficina 1110, T6393232, F6331498. Many languages spoken, helpful. Recommended. *VMP Ltda*, Huérfanos 1160, Local 19, T/F6967829, for all services. Many languages spoken, helpful. Recommended. *Selectours*, Agencia de Viajes, Las Urbinas 95, Providencia, T2520201/3342637, F2342838. *All Travels*, Huérfanos 1160, local 10, T6964348. Good for flight tickets. *Asatej Student Flight Centre*, Hernando de Aguirre 201, Oficina 401, T3350395, F3350394, chile@asatej.com.ar. For cheap flights and youth travel, also tours, car rental, ISIC cards, medical insurance and hotels. *Patagonia Connection SA*, Fidel Oteíza 1921, Oficina 1006, Providencia (Metro Pedro de Valdivia), T2256489, F2748111, info@patagoniaconnex.cl. For cruises to Patagonia. *Eurotur*, Huérfanos 1160, local 13. For cheap air tickets to Europe. *Blanco*, Pedro de Valdivia near Av Providencia. Good for flight information and exchange. *Rapa-Nui*, Huérfanos 1160. Specializes in trips to Easter Island. *Turismo Grace*, Victoria Subercaseaux 381, T6933740. Good service. **For local tours:** *Ace Turismo*, O'Higgins 949, T6960391. City tour, US$12 for ½ day. *Maysa*, Paseo Ahumada 6, Of 43, T/F6964468. Good tours of wine bodegas and Valparaíso, US$35. *Nicole Aventuras,* T/F2256155, Cell8241277, avenic@gmx.net, http://www. fis.puc.cl/~gtarrach/avenic. Excursions in Santiago region, including wildlife and glacier tours.

For adventure tours and trekking: *Sportstours*, Teatinos 330, piso 10, T6968832/6983058. German-run, helpful, 5 day trips to Antarctica (offices also at Hotels *Carrera*, and *San Cristóbal*). *Altue Expediciones*, Encomenderos 83 piso 2, Las Condes, T2321103/2332964, F2336799, altue@entelchile.net. For wilderness trips including tour of Patagonia and sea-kayaking in Chiloé. Climbing and adventure tours in the Lake District and elsewhere: *Antu Aventuras*, Casilla 24, Santiago, T2712767, Tx440019, RECAL CZ. *Azimut 360*, Arzobispo Casanova 3, Providencia, T7358034, F7772375, azimut@reuna.cl, http://www.azimut.cl. Low prices. Adventure and eco tourism throughout Chile, Aconagua base camp services and mountaineering expeditions. Highly recommended. *Mountain Service*, Paseo Las Palmas, 2209 (Metro Los Leones) T2330913. Recommended for climbing trips. *Racies*, Plaza Corregidor Zañartu 761. Cultural tours, including Robinson Crusoe Island and Antarctica, T/F6382904. *Turismo Grant*, Huérfanos 863, Oficina 516, T6395524. Helpful, English spoken. *Patagonia Chile*, Constitución 172, Bellavista, T351871. Offer mountain trips, river rafting, trekking. *Turismo Cabo de Hornos*, Agustinas 814, Of 706, T6338481, F6338486. For DAP flights and Tierra del Fuego/Antártica tours. *Andina del Sud*, Bombero Ossa 1010, piso 3, Of 301, T6971010, F6965121. For tours in the Lake District. Ask at *Hotel Maury*, address above, for tours with Fernández (Tony), who speaks English, riding, rafting and barbecue, US$50 per person. Recommended. For skiing in the Santiago area see above, page 95. *Turismo Joven*, Av Suecia Norte 0125, T2329946, F3343008, turjoven@mailent.rdc.cl. Youth travel services for young people and students for travel, studies, leisure with links in Latin America and worldwide.

Tourist offices *Servicio Nacional de Turismo* (Sernatur – the national tourist board), Av Providencia 1550 (Casilla 14082), T2361416, TxSERNA CL 240137. Between metros Manuel Montt and Pedro de Valdivia, next to Providencia Municipal Library. Open Mon-Fri 0900-1900, Sat 0900-1300. English and German spoken. Maps (road map US$1.50), brochures and posters are available. Good notice board. Ask for the free booklet, *Paseos en Santiago* (City Walks in Santiago), which is very useful for those with time to explore on foot. Kiosk on Ahumada near Agustinas (erratic opening times). Information office also at the airport, open 0900-2100 daily. Municipal Tourist Board, Casa Colorada, Merced 860, T336700/330723, offers walking tours of the city, Wed

The Santiago Region

1500, or from kiosk on Paseo Ahumada. **NB** Many tourist offices outside Santiago are closed in winter, so stock up on information here. Excellent road maps (US$2.50) and information may be obtained from the ***Automóvil Club de Chile***, Vitacura 8620, T2125702/3/4, F2295295 (Metro Pedro de Valdivia then bus to Vitacura, or a US$6 taxi ride from the centre), which also gives discounts to members of affiliated motoring organizations; open Mon-Fri 0845-1815, Sat 0900-1300, very helpful. **Further reading**, page 66 contains more information on maps and guide books. *Conaf* (Corporación Nacional Forestal), Presidente Bulnes 291, piso 1, T3900126/3900125, publishes a number of leaflets and has documents and maps about the national park system that can be consulted or photocopied (not very useful for walking). *CODEFF* (Comité Nacional Pro-Defensa de la Fauna y Flora), Bilboa 691, Providencia, T2510262, can also provide information on environmental questions.

Useful addresses Immigration: *Ministerio del Interior*, *Extranjería* section, Moneda 1342. Mon-Fri 0830-1530, arrive early to queue, extension of tourist card US$100. **Policia Internacional:** for lost tourist cards, etc, Santo Domingo y MacIver.

Day trips outside Santiago

Pomaire

A small town 65 kilometres west of Santiago, Pomaire is famous for its ceramic work. Pottery can be bought and the artists can be observed at work. The area is rich in clay and the town is noted for its cider in the apple season (*chicha de uva*, for its three strengths: *dulce, medio* and *fuerte*) and Chilean dishes; highly recommended. *Restaurant San Antonio*, is welcoming and has good food and service.

Altitude: 220m
Colour map 3, grid B3

From Santiago take the Melipilla bus from C San Borja behind Estación Central metro station, every few minutes, US$1 each way, Rutabus 78 goes on the motorway, 1 hour, other buses via Talagante take 1 hour 25 minutes (alight at side road to Pomaire, 2-3 km from town, *colectivos* every 10-15 minutes – these buses are easier to take than the infrequent, direct buses); en route, delicious *pastel de choclo* can be obtained at *Restaurant Mi Ranchito*.

Transport

Visits to vineyards

The Maipo Valley is considered by many experts to be the best-wine producing area of Chile. Several vineyards in the Santiago area can be visited.

Cousiño-Macul, Av Quilin on the eastern outskirts of the city, offers tours Monday-Friday, phone first T2382855.

Concha y Toro at Pirque, near Puente Alto, 40 kilometres south of Santiago, T8503168, give short tours (Spanish, English, French, German, Portuguese), Monday-Saturday and Sunday pm, free entry, wines US$1 per glass. Take 'La Puntilla' bus from Metro O'Higgins, one hour, US$1, asking to be dropped at Concha, or *colectivo* from Plaza Baquedano, US$2.50. (Travel agents in Santiago charge US$30 for this trip.)

The *Undurraga* vineyard at Santa Ana, southwest of Santiago, T8172346, also permits visits but with prior reservation only, 0930-1200, 1400-1600 on weekdays (tours given by the owner-manager, Pedro Undurraga). Take a Melipilla bus (but not Rutabus 78) from the Terminal San Borja to the entrance.

Viña Santa Carolina, Rodrigo de Araya 1341, in Nuñoa, offers tours at weekends.

Viña Santa Rita, Padre Hurtado 0695, Alto Jahuel, 30 kilometres south of Santiago, T8214211, good tour. Take Buin-Maipo bus from Metro Los Héroes, US$1, to Buin, then *colectivo* to Alto Jahuel.

Visits to haciendas

See under **Excursions**, San Fernando, for **Los Lingues**, page 248.

Ski resorts

Colour map 3, grid B3 There are six main ski resorts near Santiago, four of them around the mountain village of Farellones, 32 kilometres east of the capital. All have modern lift systems, international ski schools, rental shops, lodges, mountain restaurants and first aid facilities. The season runs from June to September/October, weather permitting, although some resorts have equipment for making artificial snow. Altitude sickness can be a problem, especially at Valle Nevado and Portillo: avoid over exertion on the first day or two.

Farellones The first ski resort built in Chile is situated on the slopes of Cerro Colorado at
It offers beautiful views 2,470 metres and is reached by road in under 90 minutes. Now it is more of a ser-
for 30 km across 10 vice centre for the three other resorts, but it provides affordable accommoda-
Andean peaks and tion, has a good beginners area and is connected by lift to El Colorado. Perhaps
incredible sunsets the most popular resort for residents of Santiago, it is busy at weekends; it has several large restaurants. Daily ski-lift ticket, US$30; a combined ticket for all four resorts is also available, US$40-50 depending on season. One day excursions are available from Santiago, US$5; enquire Ski Club Chile, Goyenechea Candelaria 4750, Vitacura (north of Los Leones Golf Club), T2117341.

Sleeping **A1** *Motel Tupungato*, Candelaria Goyenechea 4750, Santiago, T2182216. **A3** pp *Refugio Club Alemán Andino* (address under **Skiing & Climbing**, page 95). Hospitable, good food. **A1** *Posada de Farellones*, T2013704. Highly recommended. **L3** *La Cornisa*, T2207581, half board.

El Colorado Eight kilometres further up Cerro Colorado along a very circuitous road, El Colorado has a large but expensive ski lodge at the base, offering all facilities, and a mountain restaurant higher up. There are nine lifts giving access to a large intermediate ski area with some steeper slopes. *La Cornisa* and *Cono Este* are two of the few bump runs in Chile. This is a good centre for learning to ski. Lift ticket US$37.

Sleeping **L3** *Colorado Apart Hotel* (Av Apoquindo 4900, Oficina 43, Santiago, T2460660, F2461447). **L2** *Edificio Los Ciervos* and *Edificio Monteblanco*, in Santiago, San Antonio 486, Oficina 151, T2335501, F2316965.

The Santiago Region

Climbing opportunities in the Grupo Plomo

Situated northeast of Santiago, this group lies near the ski resort of La Parva. The main peaks are La Parva itself (4,070 metres), El Plomo (5,430 metres), Paloma (4,930 metres) and El Altar (5,222 metres). El Plomo is not particularly difficult and is often used as an acclimatization climb before tackling Aconcagua or Ojos del Salado. It was the southernmost Inca sacrificial peak and the ruins near the summit are in good condition. Allow three to four days, ice axe and crampons essential. El Altar is one of the hardest climbs in Chile; particularly difficult is the rarely scaled south face, grade 5.9 on loose rock.

La Parva Situated nearby at 2,816 metres, La Parva is the upper class Santiago weekend resort with 12 lifts, 0900-1730. Accommodation is in a chalet village and there are some good bars in high season. Although the runs vary, providing good intermediate to advanced skiing, skiers face a double fall-line. Not suitable for beginners. Connections with Valle Nevado are good. Lift ticket, US$40; equipment rental, US$10-15 depending on quality.

In summer, this is a good walking area: a good trail leads to the base of Cerro El Plomo which can be climbed.

Sleeping L2 *Condominio Nueva Parva*. Good hotel and restaurant, reservations in Santiago: Roger de Flor 2911, T2121363, F2208510. 3 other restaurants.

Valle Nevado Sixteen kilometres from Farellones, Valle Nevado is owned by Spie Batignolles of France and was the site of the 1993 Pan American winter games. It offers the most modern ski facilities in Chile. "One has to imagine a deluxe hotel complex high up in the mountains with nothing else around" (Josselyn van der Pol and Leandro Yáñez). Although not to everyone's taste, it is highly regarded and efficient. There are 25 runs accessed by eight lifts. The runs are well prepared and are suitable for intermediate level skiers and beginners. There is a ski school and excellent heliskiing is offered. Lift ticket US$30 weekdays, US$42 weekends.

Sleeping L1 *Valle Nevado*, T2060027, F2080695. *Puerta del Sol*, T6980103, F2080695. *Condominium Mirador del Inca*, T6980103 (Santiago 2060027), 6 restaurants. *Casa Valle Nevado*, Gertrudis Echeñique 441, T2060027, F2288888.

Transport Buses from Santiago to Farellones, El Colorado, La Parva and Valle Nevado are run in the ski season by Ski Total, Av Apoquindo 4900, Edificio Omnium, oficinas 40-42, T2463344, F2064078 and leaves from outside their offices, 4 blocks from Escuela Militar Metro, daily at 0830, essential to book in advance, US$13.50. It is easy to hitch from the junction of Av Las Condes/El Camino Farellones (YPF petrol station in the middle): take a Barnechea bus from C Merced.

Portillo Situated at 2,855 metres, Portillo lies 145 kilometres north of Santiago and 62 east of Los Andes near the customs post on the route to Argentina. One of Chile's best-known resorts, Portillo lies near the Laguna del Inca, five and a half kilometres long and one and a half kilometres wide; this lake, at an altitude of 2,835 metres, has no outlet, is frozen over in winter, and its depth is not known. It is surrounded on three sides by accessible mountain slopes. From *Tío Bob's* there are magnificent views of the lake and surrounding area and condors may be spotted from the terrace. The runs are varied and well prepared, connected by 12 lifts, two of which open up the off-piste areas. This is an excellent family resort, with highly regarded ski school, and there are some gentle slopes for beginners near the hotel. The major skiing events are in August and September. Cheap packages can be arranged at the beginning and out of season. Lift ticket US$35, equipment hire US$22.

There are boats for fishing in the lake; but beware the afternoon winds, which often make the homeward pull three or four times as long as the outward pull. Out of season this is another good area for walking, but get detailed maps before setting out. Mules can be hired for stupendous expeditions to the glacier at the head of the valley or to the Cerro Juncal, to the pass in the west side of the valley.

Sleeping **L2** *Hotel Portillo*. Cinema, nightclub, swimming pool, sauna and medical service, on the shore of Laguna del Inca. Accommodation ranges from lakefront suites, full board, fabulous views, to family apartments, to bunk rooms without or with bath (much cheaper, from C up), parking charges even if you go for a meal, self-service lunch, open all year, minibus to Santiago US$50 each. Reservations, Roger de Flor 2911, T2313411, F2317164, Tx440372 PORTICZ, Santiago. **L3** *Hostería Alborada*, includes all meals, tax and service. During Ski Week (last in September), about double normal rate, all inclusive. Reservations, Agencia Tour Avión, Agustinas 1062, Santiago, T726184, or C Navarro 264, San Felipe, T101-R. Cheaper accommodation can be found in Los Andes but the road is liable to closure due to snow.

Eating Cheaper than the hotels are *Restaurant La Posada* opposite *Hotel Portillo*, open evenings and weekends only. Also *Restaurant Los Libertadores* at the customs station 1 km away.

Transport Except in bad weather, Portillo is easily reached by taking any bus from Santiago or Los Andes to Mendoza; you may have to hitch back (best done from the Chilean *aduana*).

Lagunillas Lagunillas lies 67 kilometres southeast of Santiago in the Cajón del Maipo, 17 kilometres east of San José de Maipo (see page 110 for transport to San José de Maipo). Accommodation in the lodges of the Club Andino de Chile (bookings may be made at Ahumada 47, Santiago). Tow fee US$20; lift ticket US$25; long T-bar and poma lifts; easy field. Being lower than the other resorts, its season is shorter, but it is also cheaper.

Santuario de la Naturaleza Yerba Loca

Situated 45 kilometres northeast of Santiago and reached by Route G21 (paved) towards Farellones, this park was founded in 1973. It covers 39,000 hectares of the valley of the Río Yerba Loca ranging in altitude between 900 and 5,500 metres. Park administration is at Villa Paulina, four kilometres north of Route G21, reached by a dirt road. From here a four hour walk leads north to Casa de Piedra Carvajal, which offers fine views. Further north are two hanging glaciers, La Paloma and El Altar.

Wildlife Native tree species include the mountain olive. Birdlife includes eagles and condors.

Park essentials Open September to April (Entry US$3). No accommodation or transport. Maps and information available from Conaf in Santiago.

Termas de Colina

Situated 43 kilometres north of Santiago, this is an attractive, popular spa in the mountains. **L3** *Hotel Termas de Colina*, T8441408, has modern, thermal baths (US$20), beautiful swimming pool (closed Friday) US$8, formal restaurant; facilities open to public, crowded at weekends. ■ *Getting there: take a bus from Cal y Canto metro station to the town of Colina (hourly in summer only, 40 minutes), then another to the military base one and a half kilometres from town. From here a rough road leads through beautiful countryside six kilometres; last return bus at 1900. On the walk to the hotel do not take photos or even show your camera when passing the military base. Taxi from Colina to the hotel, US$6.*

Altitude 915m
Colour map 3, grid B3

The small towns in the Aconcagua Valley to the north – San Felipe, Jahuel and Los Andes – are described in the section **From Santiago to Argentina**, page 111.

Reserva Nacional Río Clarillo

Forty five kilometres south of Santiago, this park is reached by paved road via San Bernardo and Pirque. This park covers 10,185 hectares and is situated in the precordillera at between 850 and 3,000 metres. ■ *Administration at entrance, two kilometres southeast of El Principal. Open all year.*

Colour map 3, grid B3

Bus from Puente Alto to El Principal, US$2.50, 1 hour.

Transport

Cajón del Maipo

Southeast of Santiago, in the Upper Maipo valley (Cajón del Maipo) are a number of resorts easily reached from the capital by a road which runs east from Puente Alto via Las Vizcachas, where the most important motor racing circuit in Chile is located, and **San José de Maipo**. About 10 kilometres east of Las Vizcachas is the **Restaurant El Calipso**, reputed to be one of the best restaurants in the country. The mountain town of **Melocotón** is six kilometres south of San José de Maipo, and **San Alfonso**, four kilometres on. The walk from San Alfonso to the *Cascada de las Animas* is pleasant; ask permission to cross the bridge at the campsite (see below) as private land is crossed.

Cajón del Maipo

The Santiago Region

Climbing opportunities in the Grupo Loma Larga

This massif, located around 100 kilometres southeast of Santiago, lies just north of the Parque Nacional El Morado and is reached via Baños Morales. The main peaks are El Morado (5,060 metres), Meson Alto (5,297 metres), San Francisco (4,940 metres), Arenas (4,400 metres), the Mirador del Diablo and Cerro Unión. Cerro Morado, on the northern edge of the national park, is one of the most difficult climbs in Chile; the south face climb to the southern summit (5,000 metres) is particularly arduous involving 1,000 metres of vertical climbing, grade 9, on rock and ice.

Sleeping & eating **San José** E *Alojamento Inesita*, Comercio 301. Good. **Melocotón** B *Millahue*, T/F8899006. **San Alfonso** B *Posada Los Ciervos*, T8611587. With breakfast, **A** full board, good. **C** *Res España*. Clean, comfortable, restaurant. Also others. Campsite at the *Comunidad Cascada de las Animas*, T2517506. Also rents cabins (**C** for 4, hot water, cooking equipment etc) sauna, horseriding.

Restaurant El Campito, Camino al Volcán 1841. Very good.

Transport Buses leave Santiago from Metro Parque O'Higgins, Av Norte-Sur, or west side of Plaza Ercilla, every 30 minutes to San José, US$2, 2 hours.

The road continues up the valley and divides 14 kilometres southeast of **San Alfonso**. One branch forks northeast and runs via Embalse El Yeso to **Termas del Plomo**, Km 33, thermal baths with no infrastructure, very poor road (four-wheel drive essential). The other branch continues and climbs the valley of the Río Volcán. At **El Volcán** (1,400 metres), 21 kilometres from San Alfonso, there are astounding views, but little else (the village was wiped away in a landslide). **NB** If visiting this area or continuing further up the mountain, be prepared for military checks: passport and car registration numbers may be taken. From El Volcán the road (very poor condition) runs 14 kilometres east to **Lo Valdés**, a good base for mountain excursions. Nearby are warm natural baths at **Baños Morales**. ■ *Open from October, US$2.* Twelve kilometres further east up the mountain is **Baños Colina** (not to be confused with Termas de Colina, see above); hot thermal springs, free, horses for hire. This area is popular at weekends and holiday times, but is otherwise deserted.

Sleeping & eating **Lo Valdés** B pp *Refugio Alemán Lo Valdés*, T2207610. Stone-built chalet accommodation, full board, own generator, good food. Recommended.

Baños Morales D *Pensión Díaz*, T8611496. Friendly, good food, the only place to stay open all year round, very friendly. Highly recommended. **C** pp *Refugio Baños Morales*. Full board, hot water. **D** pp *Res Los Chicos Malos*, T2885380. Comfortable, fresh bread, good meals. Free campsite. **Baños Colina**: **D** pp *Res El Tambo*. Full board, restaurant, also camping. No shops so take food (try local goats cheese).

Transport **Bus** 3 companies from Metro Parque O'Higgins, to **El Volcán** every 30 minutes (US$2) and to **Baños Morales** daily in January/February, weekends only in March and October-December, at 0700, US$3, 3 hours, returns at 1800; buy return on arrival to ensure seat back. Between Baños Morales and Baños Colinas you may be able to arrange a lift on one of the tour buses which run in summer. Between April and September there is no public transport beyond San José. On weekdays hitching from San José is possible on quarry tracks.

Situated north of Baños Morales, the park covers an area of 3,000 hectares of the valley of the Río Morales, including the peaks of El Morado (5,060 metres) and El Mirador del Morado (4,320 metres), and El Morado glacier. ■ *Administration near the entrance, just north of Baños Morales. Park open October-April. Entry US$2.*

Parque Nacional El Morado

From Santiago to Argentina

The route across the Andes via Los Andes and the Redentor tunnel is one of the major crossings to Argentina. Before travelling check on weather and road conditions beyond Los Andes. For buses on this route see **International Buses**, page 99.

Route 5 runs north of Santiago through the rich Aconcagua Valley, known as the Vale of Chile. The road forks at the Santuario de Santa Teresa, the west branch going to San Felipe, the east branch going to Los Andes and Mendoza.

San Felipe

The capital of Aconcagua Province, San Felipe is an agricultural and mining centre with an agreeable climate. Part of the Inca highway has recently been discovered in the city; previously, no traces had been found further south than La Serena. **Curimón**, three kilometres southeast of San Felipe, is the site of the Convento de Santa Rosa de Viterbo (1727) which has a small museum attached. A paved road (13 kilometres) runs north from San Felipe to the old town of **Putaendo**; in its church there is an 18th century baroque statue of Christ.

Population: 42,000
Altitude: 635m
Phone code: 034
96 km N of Santiago
128 km NE of Valparaíso
Colour map 3, grid A3

A3 *Hostería San Felipe*, Merced 204, T510508, F513356.

Sleeping

Situated high in the Cordillera, Termas de Jahuel lies 18 kilometres by road northeast of San Felipe. The mountain scenery includes a distant view of Aconcagua. **L2** *Termas de Jahuel*, T511240 or Santiago 393-810, has a thermal pool and tennis courts.

Termas de Jahuel
Altitude: 1,190m

Los Andes to Mendoza (Argentina)

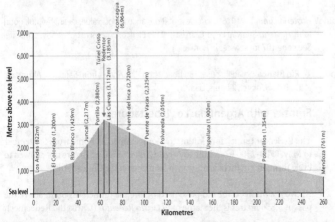

Los Andes

Population: 30,500
Altitude: 730m
Phone code: 034
77 km N of Santiago
Colour map 3, grid B3

Sixteen kilometres southeast of San Felipe, Los Andes is situated in a wealthy agricultural, fruit farming and wine-producing area, but is also the site of a large car assembly plant. It is a good place for escaping from Santiago and a convenient base for skiing at nearby Portillo. There are monuments to José de San Martín and Bernardo O'Higgins in the Plaza de Armas, and a monument to the Clark brothers, who built the Transandine Railway to Mendoza (now disused). Good views from El Cerro de la Virgen, reached by a trail from the municipal picnic ground on Independencia (one hour). There is a museum **Museo Arqueológico de los Andes**, on O'Higgins y Santa Teresa. ■ *US$1, 1030-1300, 1500-1830.*

Sleeping **A1** *Baños El Corazón*, at San Esteban 2 km north of Los Andes, T421371. With full board, use of swimming pool but thermal baths extra, take bus San Esteban/El Cariño (US$0.50). **A3** *Plaza*, Esmeralda 367, T421929. Good but restaurant expensive. **D** *Central*, Esmeralda 278, T421275. Reasonable and very friendly (excellent bakery opposite, try the *empanadas*). **D** *Alameda*, Argentina 576, T422403. Without bath, clean. **F** pp *Res Maruja*, Rancagua 182. Cheap, clean. **E** pp *Estación*, Rodríguez 389, T421026, without breakfast. Cheap restaurant. **F** *Valparaíso*, Sarmiento 160. Clean.

Transport **Bus** Terminal is 1 block east of the Plaza de Armas. To Mendoza (Argentina) Tas Choapa, Fenix Pullman Norte, Cata and Ahumada. (Any of these will drop passengers off for Portillo, US$6.) **Hitchhiking** Over the Andes this is possible on trucks from Aduana building in Los Andes.

Directory **Banks** ATMs at banks on the Plaza de Armas. *Cambio Inter* at *Plaza Hotel*. Good rates, changes TCs. **Communications** Telephones: *CTC*, O'Higgins 405. **Useful addresses** *Automovil Club de Chile*, Chacabuco 33, T422790.

East of Los Andes

The road to Argentina follows the Aconcagua valley for 34 kilometres until it reaches the village of **Río Blanco** (1,370 metres), where the Ríos Blanco and Juncal meet to form the Río Aconcagua. There is a fish hatchery with small botanical garden at the entrance to the Andina copper mine. East of Río Blanco the road climbs until Juncal where it zigzags steeply through a series of 29 hairpin bends at the top of which is the ski resort of Portillo, see page 107-108.

Sleeping *Hostería Luna*, T421026, 4 km west of Río Blanco. Good value, clean, helpful, good food. *Hostería Guardia Vieja*, 8 km east of Río Blanco. Expensive but untidy, campsite. See page 107 for services in Portillo.

Transport **To Río Blanco** Saladillo buses run hourly from Los Andes; from Santiago, Ahumada, at 1930 daily, direct, 2 hours, US$2.

Frontier with Argentina: Los Libertadores

The Redentor tunnel, four kilometres long, is open 24 hours from September to May, 0700-2300 from June to August, toll US$3. Cyclists are not allowed to cycle through but there is no-one to stop you on the Chilean side.

Above the tunnel is the old pass, used before the tunnel was built; above the pass at 3,854 metres is the statue of *El Cristo Redentor* (Christ the Redeemer), which was erected jointly by Chile and Argentina in 1904 to commemorate King Edward VII's decision in the boundary dispute of 1902. It is completely dwarfed by the landscape. The old road over the pass is in a very poor state, especially on the Chilean side, and is liable to be blocked by snow even in summer. When weather conditions permit, the statue can be reached on foot from **Las Cuevas**, a modern settlement on the Argentine side (four and a half hours up, two down). There are also 12-hour excursions to the statue from Mendoza.

In Chile The Chilean border post is at Portillo. Bus and car passengers are dealt with separately. There may be long delays during searches for fruit, meat and vegetables, which may not be imported into Chile. Remove all camera film from your luggage as hand luggage is not X-rayed.

Customs & immigration

Casa de Cambio in customs building in Portillo.

Exchange

In Argentina Ingeniero Roque Carranza, 13 kilometres from the tunnel.

Customs & immigration

Just beyond Argentine customs and immigration is **Puente del Inca**, a sports resort named after the natural bridge which crosses the Río Mendoza. The bridge, apparently formed by sulphur-bearing hot springs, is 19 metres high, has a span of 21 metres and is 27 metres wide. At the resort are *Hostería Puente del Inca* and *Residencial Vieja Estación* (much cheaper), as well as camping, transport to Mendoza and information and access for climbing **Aconcagua** (6,959 metres), the highest mountain peak on earth outside Asia.

Into Argentina

Seventeen kilometres further east is **Punta de Vacas**, from where there is a good view of Tupungato (6,550 metres). The only town of any size between the frontier and Mendoza is **Uspallata** with hotels and transport links, from where two roads lead to Mendoza: the paved, southern branch of Route 7, via Porterillos and Cacheuta, and the unpaved, northern branch via Villavicencio.

The Santiago Region

Valparaíso and Viña del Mar

4

Valparaíso and Viña del Mar

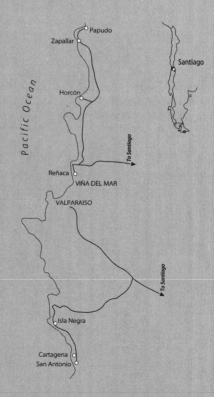

The coastal strip west of Santiago, stretching 130 kilometres from the Río Petorca in the north to the Río Maipo in the south, includes two major cities, Valparaíso and Viña del Mar and a string of 24 other resorts, easily visited from Santiago. This proximity to the capital and a favourable climate make this the country's most popular coastal resort area attracting large numbers of Chileans and visiting Argentines.

Midway along the coast is Viña del Mar, one of the most famous resorts in South America. In many respects more interesting, however, is the nearby city of Valparaíso, Chile's most important port: sprawling back from a broad bay, Valparaíso offers wonderful views over the Pacific for those who climb its steep hills or take one of the aged funicular railways which are one of its features. Among the smaller resorts north of Viña del Mar are Papudo and Zapallar, both exclusive retreats in the early 20th century. South of Valaparaíso, towards the mouth of the Río Maipo, are a number of other centres, including Algarrobo, perhaps the most affluent resort along this coast, and Isla Negra, a village famous as the site of Pablo Neruda's home, which is increasingly popular for day trips from Santiago.

Background

History

This was one of the earliest areas settled by the Spanish, the lands being assigned to prominent conquistadores during the 16th century. For most of the colonial period this region was an important exporter of wheat and other foodstuffs to Peru. During the 19th century Valparaíso rose to become one of the most important ports on the Pacific coast of South America, but there were few other large centres of population along this coastline until the 1880s when the fashion for holidaying near the sea spread from southern Europe. Viña del Mar was established in 1880 and several other resorts followed between 1880 and 1900: Algarrobo, Cartagena, Las Cruces, Zapallar and Papudo, all owing part of their popularity to the building of railway lines linking them to the capital. Although the influence of European resorts can still be seen in some of the buildings, especially in Viña del Mar and Zapallar, most of the older buildings have not withstood earthquakes and bulldozers.

Valparaíso & Viña del Mar

Neruda on Valparaíso

"The hills of Valparaíso decided to dislodge their inhabitants, to let go of the houses on top, to let them dangle from cliffs that are red with clay, yellow with gold thimble flowers, and a fleeting green with wild vegetation. But houses and people clung to the heights, writhing, digging in, worrying, their hearts set on staying up there, hanging on, tooth and nail, to each cliff. The port is a tug-of-war between the sea and nature, untamed on the cordilleras. But it was man who won the battle little by little. The hills, and the sea's abundance gave the city a pattern, making it uniform, not like a barracks, but with the variety of spring, its clashing colours, its resonant bustle. The houses became colours: a blend of amaranth and yellow, crimson and cobalt, green and purple."

Pablo Neruda, Memoirs, Penguin, 1978.

Geography

This area is one of the major economic centres of the country and its third most important industrial area. Valparaíso and San Antonio are major ports, between them handling much of the country's trade. Other facilities include an oil terminal and copper refinery at Quintero, an oil refinery at Concón and important chemical industries in Viña del Mar. The region is also a major producer of agricultural products, particularly soft fruit such as grapes and peaches. Its population is over 90 percent urban.

Climate

This coastline enjoys a Mediterranean-style climate; the cold sea currents and coastal winds produce much more moderate temperatures than in Santiago and the central valley. Rainfall is moderate in winter and the summers are dry.

Valparaíso

The capital of Región V, Valparaíso, is the principal port of Chile and an important naval base. With the building of the new Congress building in the 1980s, it is also the seat of the Chilean parliament. The city is situated on the shores of a sweeping bay and over a crescent of seven hills behind. Seen from the ocean, it presents a majestic panorama: a great circle of hills is backed by the snow-capped peaks of the distant Cordillera.

Population: 274,228
Phone code: 032
90 km W of Santiago
Colour map 3, grid B2

History

Founded in 1542, Valparaíso became, in the colonial period, a small port used for trade with Peru. It was raided by pirates and corsairs, including Drake, at least seven times during the colonial era. The city prospered from independence more than any other Chilean town. It was used in the 19th century by commercial agents from Europe and the US as their trading base in the southern Pacific, and became a major international banking

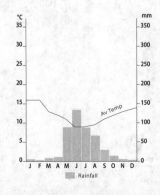

Climate:
Valparaíso

(right margin, vertical text) Valparaíso and Viña del Mar

centre as well as the key port for shipping between the northern Pacific and Cape Horn. Its decline was the result of two factors: the development of steam ships which stopped instead for coaling at Punta Arenas and Concepción and the opening of the Panama Canal in 1914. Since then it has declined further owing to the development of a container port in San Antonio, the shift of banks to Santiago and the move of the middle classes to nearby Viña del Mar.

Little of the city's colonial past survived the pirates, tempests, fires and earthquakes of the period, but a remnant of the old colonial city can be found in the hollow known as El Puerto, grouped round the low-built stucco church of La Matriz. Most of the principal buildings date from after the devastating earthquake of 1906 (further serious earthquakes occurred in July 1971 and in March 1985), though some impression of its 19th century glory can be gained from the banking area of the lower town and from the mansions of wealthy merchants.

Sights

There are two completely different cities. The lower part, known as **El Plan**, is the business centre, with fine office buildings on narrow streets strung along the edge of the bay. Above, covering the hills, or 'cerros', is a fantastic agglomeration of fine mansions, tattered houses and shacks, scrambled in oriental confusion along the narrow back streets. Superb views over the bay are offered from most of the *cerros*. The lower and upper cities are connected by steep

Valparaíso

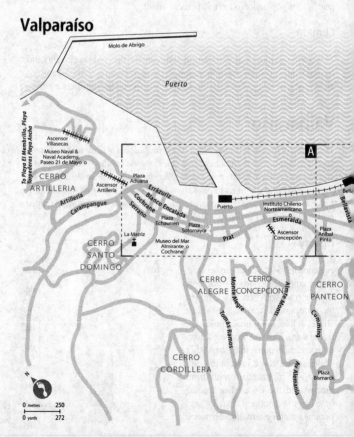

winding roads, flights of steps and 16 *ascensores* or funicular railways dating from the period 1880-1914. The most unusual of these is **Ascensor Polanco** (entrance from Calle Simpson, off Avenida Argentina a few blocks southeast of the bus terminal), which is in two sections, the first of which is a 160 metre horizontal tunnel through the rock, the second a vertical lift to the summit on which there is a *mirador*, or viewpoint. Note that the lower entrance is in a slum area which is unsafe: do not go alone and do not take valuables.

The old heart of the city is the **Plaza Sotomayor**, dominated by the former **Intendencia** (Government House), now used as the Regional Naval Headquarters. Opposite is a fine monument to the 'Heroes of the Battle of Iquique' (see page 268). The passenger quay is one block away (handicraft shops on quay are expensive and poor quality) and nearby is the railway station, from which passenger services run on the metropolitan line to Viña del Mar and Limache. In the evening the station is a gathering place for chess players; join in if your Spanish and chess are up to it. The harbour is worth a visit on Saturday mornings to watch the fishing vessels unload their catch. Tell the gatekeeper you want to buy fish or you may be refused entry. The streets of El Puerto run on either side from Plaza Sotomayor. Calle Serrano runs northwest for two blocks to the Plaza Echaurren, near which stands the church of **La Matriz**, built in 1842 on the site of the first church in the city. Further northwest, along Bustamante, lies the Plaza Aduana from where there is an *ascensor* to the bold hill of **Cerro Artillería**, crowned by the huge Naval Academy and a park.

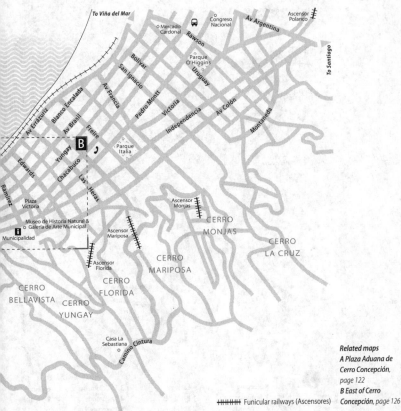

Related maps
A *Plaza Aduana de Cerro Concepción*, page 122
B *East of Cerro Concepción*, page 126

╫╫╫╫ Funicular railways (Ascensores)

Valparaíso and Viña del Mar

Southeast of Plaza Sotomayor calles Prat, Cochrane and Esmeralda run through the old banking and commercial centre to Plaza Aníbal Pinto, around which are several of the city's oldest bars. Further east is the Plaza de la Victoria with the Plaza Simon Bolívar just north and the Cathedral on its east side; south of the Plaza on Cerro Bellavista is the **Museo al Cielo Abierto** (see box on page 123). East of Plaza de la Victoria, reached by following Pedro Montt, is Plaza O'Higgins, which is dominated by the imposing new **Congreso Nacional**.

To the west of **Cerro Artillería** the Avenida **Playa Ancha** runs to a stadium, seating 20,000 people, on Cerro Playa Ancha. Avenida Altamirano runs along the coast at the foot of Cerro Playa Ancha to **Las Torpederas**, a picturesque bathing beach. The **Faro de Punta Angeles**, on a promontory just beyond Las Torpederas, was the first lighthouse on the west coast; you can get a permit to go up. On another high point on the other side of the city is the **Mirador de O'Higgins**, the spot where the Supreme Dictator exclaimed, on seeing Cochrane's liberating squadron: "On those four craft depends the destiny of America".

The New Year is celebrated by a superb 40 minute firework display on the bay, which is best seen from the *cerros*. The locals take supper and champagne to celebrate from vantage points around the bay.

Plaza Aduana to Cerro Concepción

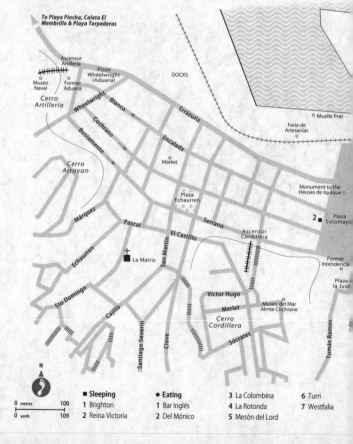

El Museo al Cielo Abierto

Opened in 1992, this open air museum was the result of an initiative of the Universidad Católica de Valparaíso. Seventeen of Chile's leading contemporary artists were invited to present sketches for the large-scale murals which can be seen on the outside walls of buildings on Cerro Bellavista. The circuit starts at the foot of a steep flight of steps leading up from Calle Aldunate, one block south of Plaza Victoria. Murals can be seen at regular intervals as you climb to Pasaje Guimera. A further climb brings you to the top of Ascensor Espiritú Santo. Another series of murals appears as you continue along Calle Rudolph and then along Calle Ferrari which runs back down to Calle Aldunate. Look out in particular for the large (six metres by three metres) mural by Chile's most famous contemporary artist Roberto Matta, situated just before you reach the Ascensor Espiritú Santo; a typical example of his later work with sharp-toothed gape-jawed monsters hurtling through space. The walk is delightful in itself. Though the other artists may be less well known internationally, this unusual collection should not be missed.

Simon Watson Taylor.

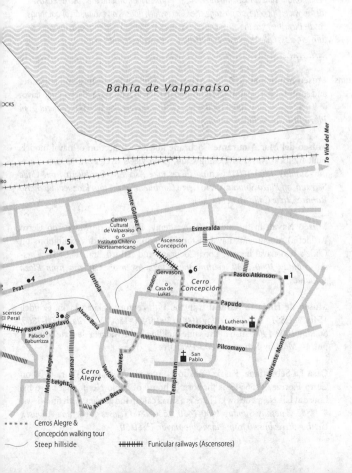

Bahía de Valparaíso

To Viña del Mar

Centro Cultural de Valparaíso

Esmeralda

Instituto Chileno Norteamericano

Ascensor Concepción

7 ● 1 ● 5 ●

Gervasoni

● 6

Paseo Atkinson

■ 1

Prat ● 4

Urriola

Paseo

Casa de Lukas

Cerro Concepción

Papudo

scensor El Peral

3 ●

Alvaro Besa

Paseo Yugoslavo

Lutheran ✝

Concepción Abtao

Palacio Baburrizza

Ventola

Galvez

Pilcomayo

San Pablo ✝

Monte Alegre

Miramar

Cerro Alegre

Leighton

Alvaro Besa

Templeman

Almirante Montt

- - - - - Cerros Alegre & Concepción walking tour

〜 Steep hillside

╫╫╫╫╫ Funicular railways (Ascensores)

A walking tour of Cerros Alegre and Concepción

This is one of the best ways to view Valparaíso. From the Plaza de la Justicia a narrow passage (marked Museo de Bellas Artes) leads south to Ascensor El Peral. At the top end of the Ascensor, turn left along Paseo Yugoslavo which offers superb views over the bay. On your right on the corner of Monte Alegre is the Palacio Baburrizza, formerly the residence of the nitrate barons, Ottorino Zanelli and Pascual Baburrizza, now housing the Museo de Bellas Artes.

The red and white mansion further along Monte Alegre on your left is now the Art Faculty of the University of Playa Ancha. At the end of the block turn left into Calle Leighton to reach a fork in the road, over which towers an unusual building, four storeys high and three metres wide. Opposite is a passage, the Pasaje Bavestrello; at the other end of this turn left, cross Calle Urriola and climb the steps into Pasaje Galves. Take the first passage on your right (Pasaje Templeman) and you will emerge into Calle Templeman. About 50 metres along this is the Anglican church of San Pablo, built in 1858. From here follow Templeman one block northeast, turn onto Calle Abtao and you will reach the Iglesia Luterano (1897) from the base of which there are fine views over the Cerros. From the east end of the church follow Paseo Atkinson round (more fine views) and then turn right into Calle Papudo and right again into Calle Templeman. At the northeast end of Templeman is the Paseo Gervasoni, from where you can return to the lower city via the Ascensor Concepción. Before doing this, however, take a look around the Casa de Lukas, which houses an exhibition of paintings of Valparaíso and cartoons, the work of Renzo Peccenino Lukas.

Museums **Museo Municipal de Bellas Artes**, with Chilean landscapes and seascapes and some modern paintings, is housed in Palacio Baburizza, Paseo Yugoslavo. ■ *Tuesday-Sunday 1000-1800. Free. Getting there: take Ascensor El Peral from Plaza Justicia, off Plaza Sotomayor.*

Museo del Mar Almirante Cochrane houses a collection of naval models built by local Naval Modelling Club, good views over port. ■ *Free. Tuesday-Sunday 1000-1800. Getting there: take Ascensor Cordillera from Calle Serrano, off Plaza Sotomayor, to Cerro Cordillera; at the top, Plazuela Eleuterio Ramírez, take Calle Merlet to the left.*

Museo Naval, in the old Naval Academy, Paseo 21 de Mayo (on Cerro Artillería), documents naval history 1810-80, and includes exhibitions on Chile's two naval heroes, Lord Cochrane and Arturo Prat. ■ *US$1. Tuesday-Sunday 1000-1730. Getting there: take Ascensor Artillería from Plaza Aduana.*

Museo de Historia Natural is in the 19th-century Palacio Lyon, Condell 1546. ■ *US$1. Tuesday-Friday 1000-1300, 1400-1800, Saturday 1000-1800, Sunday 1000-1400.* Also in the same building is the **Galería de Arte Municipal.** ■ *Monday-Saturday, 1000-1900, free.*

Casa La Sebastiana, Pasaje Collado 1, Avenida Alemania, Altura 6900 on Cerro Florida, T256606, is the former house of Pablo Neruda (see also his house at Isla Negra below). There is a small café in the garden, with fine views. ■ *US$3. Tuesday-Sunday 1030-1430, 1530-1800 (closes 1700 June-August). Getting there: bus 40 from Plaza Sotomayor, US$0.50.*

Lord Cochrane

Lord Thomas Alexander Cochrane (1775-1860), born into a Scottish aristocratic family, began his career in the British navy during the Napoleonic Wars, rising rapidly as an officer, fighting a duel with a French officer in Malta and later being captured by the French and ransomed. He was elected to Parliament in 1806 as MP for Honiton and in 1807 as MP for Westminster. Although he had never been on good terms with his naval superiors, his use of the House of Commons to accuse the naval commander, Lord Gambier, of incompetence, led to his downfall. Gambier was court-martialled and acquitted; Cochrane was retired on half-pay and spent the next three years exposing corruption and abuses in the navy. His links with a financial scandal in 1814 provided his enemies with an opportunity for revenge: he was dismissed from the navy, expelled from Parliament and sentenced to 12 months' imprisonment (he escaped and was recaptured).

Recruited for the armed forces by the Chilean agent in London, he quickly became friendly with O'Higgins and was put in command of the new republic's navy, a few ill-equipped vessels which relied on foreign adventurers for
experienced sailors. With this fleet Cochrane harassed the Spanish-held ports along the Chilean coast; his audacious storming of the fortresses of Corral, San Carlos and Amargos led to the capture of the key Spanish base of Valdivia. Later that year Cochrane transported San Martin's troops along the Pacific coast to invade Peru, but his relations with San Martin were poor and he became very critical of the latter's cautious strategy. Afterwards he continued to attack Spanish shipping in the Pacific, in 1822 sailing as far north as Mexico.

In 1823 the new government of Brazil appointed him to head its navy in the struggle for independence from Portugal. Once again leading a motley collection of boats manned largely by foreigners, Cochrane drove a Portuguese fleet from Bahia and pursued it back to Portugal. In 1825 he fell out with the Brazilian government and returned to Britain. Two years later he volunteered to help the Greeks in their struggle for independence from Turkey. He was reinstated in the British navy in 1832, was promoted to Rear-Admiral and spent much of the rest of his life promoting developments in the use of steam power in shipping.

Casa Mistral, Avenida Gran Bretaña y Amunatega, Playa Ancha, has an exhibition dedicated to life and work of Gabriela Mistral. ■ *Tuesday-Sunday 1000-1330, 1530-1930.*

Tours Launches run trips in summer around the harbour from Muelle Prat, 30 minutes, US$2, to Playa Las Torpederas and to Viña del Mar; beware that groups of foreign tourists are liable to be overcharged. Other boats can be hired for fishing. **NB** Don't photograph naval ships or installations.

The **Camino Cintura** (Avenida Alemania) is the only road which connects all the hills above Valparaíso; it affords constantly changing views, perhaps the best being from Plaza Bismarck. No 9 'Central Placeres' bus gives a fine scenic drive over the hills to the port. Bus 'Mar Verde' (O) which runs from Viña del Mar along Av Argentina near the bus terminal to Plaza Aduana.

Excursions

Reserva Nacional Peñuelas covers 9,260 hectares surrounding the artificial Lago Peñuelas. The park, which is covered by pine and eucalyptus forest, is situated southeast of Valparaíso near the main road to Santiago (Route 68). Access is permitted for walking and fishing. Administration is at the park

Valparaíso and Viña del Mar

entrance, about 30 kilometres from Valparaíso, 95 kilometres from Santiago. ■ *US$2, buses between Valparaíso and Santiago pass the entrance.*

Laguna Verde, 18 kilometres south of Valparaíso, is a picturesque bay for picnics, reached by a two hour dusty walk over the hills. There is **E** per person *Posada Cruz del Sur*, also camping, *Camping Los Olivos* with good facilities, well run and friendly. ■ *Bus No 6, marked 'Laguna Verde' from Victoria y Rancagua, hourly.*

Essentials

Sleeping
■ *on maps page 122 and below*
Price codes: see inside front cover

A2 *Brighton*, Paseo Arkinson 151, Cerro Concepción, T/F223513, comfortable, excellent restaurant, glorious views, café. **A2** *Puerta de Alcalá*, Pasaje Pirámide 524, T/F227478, 3-star, restaurant, very good value. **B** *Casablanca*, Victoria 2449, T234036, F219915, charming, lovely rooms. Recommended. **B** *Lancaster*, Chacabuco 2362. With bath and breakfast, clean, parking, comfortable. **C** *Prat*, Condell 1443, T253081. Comfortable rooms, central, good restaurant with good value *almuerzo*. Under same management is **C** *Condell Pasaje*, Pirámide 557, T212788. Similar. **C** *Reina Victoria*, Plaza Sotomayor 190, T212203. **D** on top floors, without bath, with breakfast, poor beds, run down, overpriced.

East of Cerro Concepción

To Viña del Mar

■ Sleeping	● Eating	4 Club Español
1 Condell	1 Bogarín	5 Club Valparaíso
2 Prat	2 Cinzano	6 Pau San
3 Puerta de Alcalá	3 Club Alemán	7 Riquet

0 metres 100
0 yards 109

D *Hostal Kolping*, Vergara y Independencia, T216306, F230352, without bath, pleasant, quiet, good value. **D-E** pp *Austral*, Las Heras 622, T257034, without breakfast, kitchen facilities, central. **D-E** pp *Res Eliana*, Av Brasil 2146, T250954, large old house, without breakfast. Recommended. **D-E** pp *Sr Juan Carrasco*, Abtas 668, Cerro Concepción, T210737. **E** *Enzo and Martina Tesser*, Av Quebrada Verde 192, Playa Ancha, T288873. Lovely building, fine views, with breakfast, German spoken. Highly recommended (reached by bus 1). **E** *Garden*, Serrano 501, T252776. Friendly, large rooms, gloomy, in rough area, us of kitchen. **E** pp *María Pizarro*, Chacabuco 2340, Casa No 2, T230791. Clean, lovely rooms, central, quiet, kitchen. Highly recommended. Also her neighbour, *Elena Escobar*, Chacabuco 2340, Casa No 7, T214193, same price. Recommended. **E** *Res Dinamarca*, Dinamarca 539, T259189 (from Plazuela Ecuador – just south of Condell y Bellavista – take any micro marked 'Cárcel'; or climb 10 minutes up Av Ecuador). With breakfast, clean, good value, parking, not near restaurants. **E** *Res Lily*, Blanco Encalada 866, T255995, 2 blocks from Plaza Sotomayor, clean, gloomy. **E** pp *Res El Rincon*, Blanco Encalada 1146, 4 piso, depto 6, T594027, good vlaue. **E** pp *Res Latino*, Independencia 2312, T235840. **E** pp *Sra Silvia*, Pje La Quinta 70, Av Argentina, 3 blocks from Congress, T216592. Clean, quiet, kitchen facilities. Recommended. Youth hostel office at Edwards 695, piso 3, will extend membership; nearest hostel in Viña del Mar.

·········· Route around Museo
    Al Cielo Abierto

╫╫╫╫╫ Funicular railways (Ascensores)

Eating
● *on maps page 122 and left*

Tentazione, Pedro Montt 2484. Good, cheap. *La Parrilla de Pepe*, Pedro Montt 1872. Good food, pricey, live music at weekends. *Del Mónico*, Prat 669. Good seafood, good value lunches, expensive à la carte. *La Rotonda*, Prat 701. Good food. Two traditional bar/restaurants on Plaza Aníbal Pinto are: *Riquet*, comfortable, expensive, good coffee and breakfast. Recommended; *Cinzano*, founded 1896, relaxed atmosphere, live music and dancing to 0400 at weekends, popular. *Bar Inglés*, Cochrane 851 (entrance also on Blanco Encalada). Good food and drink, traditional, not cheap. Recommended. There are lots of little *comedores* on the second floor of the central market, large portions, cheap, closed evenings. Around the market there are also lots of cheap lunch restaurants, specializing in seafood including *Los Porteños*, Valdivia 169, very good. At Caleta Membrillo, 2 km northwest of Plaza Sotomayor there are several good fish restaurants including *Club Social de Pescadores*, Altamirano 1480. Good. Opposite are *San Pedro*, shabby but friendly, and *El Membrillo*, more expensive. Other good places for lunch: *Aquísi*, Cochrane 846. Cheap, busy, self-service. *Nahuel*, Donoso 1498. Popular, cheap. *Mesón del Lord*, Cochrane 859. *Bambú*, Pudeto 450. Vegetarian, good. *Ave Cesár*, P Montt 1776. Fast food, good. *Club*

Valparaíso, Condell 1190, piso 10. International cuisine, expensive. *Marco Polo*, Pedro Montt y Gen Cruz. Delicious cakes, good Italian, good value *almuerzo*. *La Colombina*, Pasaje Apolo 91, Cerro Alegre. Fish and seafood, good wines, fine views. Recommended. Also owns *Apolo 77* tour agency (see below). *Club Alemán*, O'Higgins y Bellavista. Good German food, not cheap. *Club Español*, Brasil 1589. Fine Spanish cuisine, elegant surroundings. *Club Peruano*, Victoria 2324. Peruvian. *Sancho Panza*, Yungay 2250. Parrillada. Many Chinese including: *Pekin*, Pudeto 422; *Tun Sun*, Victoria 2361; *Pau San*, Independencia 1766. *Winnipeg*, in Centro Cultural de Valparaíso, Esmerelda 1083, good food, well stocked bar.

Cafés and bars *Westfalia*, Cochrane 847. Coffee, breakfasts, vegetarian lunches. *Café do Brasil*, Condell 1342. Excellent coffee, juices, sandwiches. *Bogarín*, Plaza Victoria. Great juices, sandwiches. Good bars at *Cinzano* and *Bar Ingles* (see above), in **Hotel Brighton** (wonderful views) and in Centro Cultural Valparaíso. *Turri*, Templemann 147, on Cerro Concepción, T259198. Good food and service, expensive, wonderful views, lovely place. *Café Arte*, at the top of the Ascensor Artilleria.

Entertainment *Proa Al Canaveral*, Errázuriz 304. Good seafood restaurant downstairs, pleasant bar upstairs with dancing from 0100, poetry reading on Thursday. Many popular bars on Subida Ecuador, some with live music and small entry charge.

Discotheques *Cosmonova*, Pedro Montt 1195; *Escape*, in Galeria of Hotel Prat, subsuelo; *Gioko*, Las Heras 304. *Hadobar Pub*, Plaza Anibal Pinto 1175, Latin and rock, every night except Thursday.

Shopping There is a large flea market around Plaza O'Higgins on Saturday and Sunday mornings. **Bookshop** *Librería Universitaria*, Esmeralda 1132. Good selection of regional history; many others.

Transport **Local Taxi**: more expensive than Santiago. *Colectivos*, which pick up and set down passengers anywhere en route, operate along the same routes as buses and offer a cheap and quick form of transport. **Bus** Buses and modern electric buses, US$0.35 within city limits. **Ascensores**: US$0.25.

Car hire *Match Viña*, Las Heras 428, T259429. *Rutamar*, Errázunz 646, T256981. *Bert Rent A Car*, Francia 362, T254842.

Train Regular service on Merval, the Valparaíso metropolitan line between Valparaíso, Viña del Mar, Quilpué and Limache, to Viña del Mar every 15-30 minutes, US$0.50, 15 minute journey. *El Porteño* tourist train (sometimes with steam locomotive) runs on Sunday, 1 January-28 February and on most public holidays.

Long distance Shipping: for shipping services from Valparaíso to the Juan Fernández Islands, see the **The Chilean Pacific Islands** chapter.

Bus: Terminal Pedro Montt y Rawson, 1 block from Av Argentina; plenty of buses between terminal and Plaza Sotomayor. Excellent and frequent service to **Viña del Mar**, 25 minutes, US$0.45 from Plaza Aduana, passing along Av Errázuriz; *colectivos* to Viña US$0.50. To **Santiago**, 2 hours, shop around, frequent (book on Saturday to return to the capital on Sunday); to **Chillán**, US$10, 8 hours; to **Concepción**, 11 hours, US$12; to **Puerto Montt**, 17 hours, US$18; to **La Serena**, 8 hours, US$10; to **Calama**, US$35; to **Arica**, US$40, Fénix *salón cama* service, US$50. To **Argentina**: to **Mendoza**, 4 companies, 6-7 hours, US$25; to **Córdoba**, US$40.

Motoring: Route 68, the main road to Santiago, passes through 2 tunnels, toll of US$3.25 paid at the first which is 51 km southeast of Valparaíso, but this can be avoided by turning off onto the old road over the mountains about 1 km before the tunnel; the toll is unavoidable on the return journey. There is another toll further east, 56 km west of Santiago.

Hitchhiking: To Santiago is easy from the service station on Av Argentina.

Directory

Airline offices *American*, Esmeralda 940, oficina 61, T257777. *Avant* Blanco Encalada 838, T255889, F257867. *Continental*, Pje Ross 149, oficina 205, T745600. *Iberia*, Blanco Encalada 838, piso 2, T256009. *Air France*, Cochrane 667, oficina 603, T213249. *United*, Urriola 87, piso 3, T216569. *LanChile*, Esmeralda 1048, T251441. *Ladeco*, Esmeralda 973, T216355. **Banks** Banks open 0900 to 1400, but closed on Sat. Good rates at *Banco de Santiago*, Prat 816, and *Banco de Crédito e Inversiones*, Cochrane 820. *Exprinter*, Prat 887 (the building with the clocktower at junction with Cochrane). Good rates, no commission on TCs, open Mon-Fri 0930-1400, 1500-1800. *Inter Cambios*, Errázuriz esq Plaza Sotomayor. Good rates. *Gema Tour*, Esmeralda 940. *New York*, Prat 659. Good rates for cash. *Ascami*, Esmeralda 940. *Andino*, Esmeralda 970. *Prat*, Prat 847. When *cambios* are closed, street changers operate outside *Inter Cambios*. **Communications Post office:** Plaza Sotomayor. **Telecommunications:** *VTR Telecommunications*, Cochrane 825. *CTC*, Esmeralda 940 or Pedro Montt 2023. *Entel*, Condell 1491. **Cultural centres** *Centro Cultural de Valparaíso*, Esmeralda 1083, T216953. Open daily 1400-2000, exhibitions, concerts, theatre and other activities. Also has Restaurant Winnipeg (see above). *Instituto Chileno-Norteamericano*, Esmeralda 1069. Shows foreign films. **Consulates** *Argentina*, Donoso 1052, T217154. *Bolivia*, Prat 827, piso 12, T213494. *Ecuador*, Blanco Encalada 1623, oficina 1704, T222167. *Spain*, Brasil 1589, piso 2, T214466. *Guatemala*, Brasil 1199, Local 4, T255214. *Panama*, Plaza Vergara 172, oficina 307, T/F697466. *Peru*, Blanco Encalada 1215, oficina 1402, T253403. **Hospitals & medical services** Dentist: *Dr Walther Meeden Bella*, Condell 1530, Depto 44, T212233. **Laundry** *Las Heras 554*. Good and cheap. **Security** Robbery is increasingly common in El Puerto and around the *ascensores*, especially on Cerro Santo Domingo. Beware of the mustard trick (see **Safety** under **Essentials**). **Tour companies & travel agencies** *Apolo 77*, Pasaje Apolo 60C, Cerro Alegre, T592446, F235126. Colombin@CTCReuna.cl, offer city tours on foot and by bus as well as railway trips between Baron and Puerto stations in a restored 1930s carriage, minimum 20 passengers. **Tourist offices** In the Municipalidad building, Condell 1490, Oficina 102. Open Mon-Fri 0830-1400, 1530-1730. Kiosks at bus terminal (good map available), helpful, open 0900-1300, 1530-1930 (closed Thur, Mar-Nov), Muelle Prat, open Nov-March 1030-1430, 1600-2000, and in Plaza Victoria, open 1030-1300, 1430-2000 Nov-Mar. **Useful addresses** YMCA *(Asociación Cristiana de Jóvenes)*, Blanco Encalada 1117. YWCA *(Asociación Cristiana Feminina)*, Blanco 967. *Valparaíso Seamen's Institute*, Blanco Encalada 394.

From Valparaíso to Argentina

Route 62 runs through Viña del Mar, climbs out of the bay and goes through **Quilpué**, Km 16, 1½ kilometres east of El Retiro, a popular inland resort with medicinal springs and a municipal zoo. It crosses a range of hills and reaches the Aconcagua Valley at **Limache**, a sleepy market town, 40 kilometres from Valparaíso (*Population* 22,511). Route 62 joins Route 60 just before **Quillota** (*Population* 54,000; *Altitude* 130 metres), a fruit growing centre (**B** *Balneario El Edén*, five kilometres north, cabins for rent, up to six people, very good restaurant in an old estate building, T311963, F312342, good swimming), continuing to La Calera, Km 88, where it joins the Pan-American Highway; turn southeast and east for Llaillay, San Felipe, Los Andes and the Redentor tunnel to Mendoza.

Situated north of Olmué (eight kilometres east of Limache), the park covers 8,000 hectares and includes Cerro La Campana (1,828 metres) which Darwin climbed in 1836 and Cerro El Roble (2,200 metres). There are extensive views from the top of these hills, but there are a number of difficult ascents; visitors without climbing experience should seek advice or take a guide. Take food and drink.

Parque Nacional La Campana

Wildlife Much of the park is covered by native woodland. Near Ocoa there are areas of Chilean palms (*kankán*), now found in natural woodlands in only two locations in Chile, see box on page 130.

The Chilean wine palm

Once widespread in those parts of the country with a Mediterranean-type climate, the Chilean wine palm (Jubea chilensis) or kankán was thought ugly by Darwin because of the curious bottle-like appearance of its grey trunk which is much thicker in the middle than at the base or top. In Darwin's day its sweet sap was consumed as a delicacy, being felled in *such a way that the trunk fell downhill while the stump remained vertical, thereby holding the sap in the trunk. Sections would then be cut off as needed and the sickly sweet sap was always on tap. It grew so widely that Darwin reported counting several hundred thousand on one estate before giving up.*

  Jane Norwich

Getting there   There are 3 entrances: at Granizo, 5 km east of Olmué (local bus from Limache to the entrance); at Cajón Grande, reached by unpaved road which turns off the Olmué-Granizo road; at Palmar de Ocoa to the north reached by unpaved road (10 km) leading off the Pan-American Highway between Hijuelas and Llaillay. There is no public transport to this part of the park.

Viña del Mar

Population: 304,203
Phone code: 032
Colour map 3, grid B2

Nine kilometres northeast of Valparaíso via Route 68 which runs along a narrow belt between the shore and precipitous cliffs, is Viña del Mar, one of South America's leading seaside resorts.

Six kilometres further north along the coast is the more exclusive resort of **Reñaca**, reached by bus No 9 from Calle 2 Norte.

Sights

The older part is situated on the banks of a creek, the Marga Marga, which is crossed by bridges. Around Plaza Vergara and the smaller Plaza Sucre to its south are the **Teatro Municipal** (1930) and the exclusive **Club de Viña**, built in 1910. The municipally owned **Quinta Vergara**, formerly the residence of the shipping entrepreneur Francisco Alvarez, lies two blocks south. The grounds are superb and include a double avenue of palm trees. The **Palacio Vergara**, in the gardens, houses the Museo de Bellas Artes and the Academia de Bellas Artes. Part of the grounds is a children's playground, and there is an outdoor auditorium where concerts and ballet are performed in the summer months; in February an international song festival is held here, tickets from the Municipalidad.

  Further west on a headland overlooking the sea is **Cerro Castillo**, the president's summer palace; its gardens can be visited. Just north, on the other side of the Marga Marga, is the **Casino**, built in the 1930s and set in beautiful gardens. ■ *US$6, jacket and tie for men required, open all year.*

  North are the main beaches, Acapulco and Las Salinas, but south of Cerro Castillo is Caleta Abarca, also popular. Beaches may be closed due to pollution. The coastal route north to Reñaca provides lovely views over the sea. East of the centre is the **Valparaíso Sporting Club** with a racecourse and playing fields. North of here in the hills are the Granadilla Golf Club and a large artificial lake, the **Laguna Sausalito**, which has an excellent tourist complex with swimming pools, boating, tennis courts, sandy beaches, water skiing, restaurants. ■ *US$2.50, children under 11, US$1.75.* Nearby is the Estadio Sausalito, home to Everton soccer club. Getting there: take colectivo No 19 from Calle Viana.

Museo de la Cultura del Mar, in the Castillo Wulff, on the coast near Cerro
Castillo, contains a collection on the life and work of the novelist and maritime
historian, Salvador Reyes. ■ *Tuesday-Saturday 1000-1300, 1430-1800,
Sunday 1000-1400.* **Museo de Bellas Artes** is in the Palacio Vergara.
■ *US$0.50. Tuesday-Sunday 100-1400, 1500-1800.* **Palacio Rioja**, Quillota
214, was built in 1906 by a prominent local family and is now used for official
municipal receptions. The ground floor is preserved in its original state.
■ *Tuesday-Sunday, 1000-1400, 1500-1800. Recommended.* **Museo Sociedad
Fonk**, Calle 4 Norte 784, is an archaeological museum, with objects from
Easter Island and the Chilean mainland displayed, including Mapuche silver.
■ *US$1. Tuesday-Friday 1000-1800, Saturday-Sunday 1000-1400.* **Centro
Cultural**, Libertad 250, holds regular exhibitions.

Excursions

Jardín Botánico Nacional This was formerly the estate of the nitrate magnate Pascual Baburizza and is now administered by Conaf which lies eight kilometres southeast of the city. Covering 405 hectares, it contains over 3,000
species from all over the world and a collection of Chilean cacti but the species
are not labelled. ■ *US$1. Getting there: take bus 20 from Plaza Vergara.*

Essentials

There are a great many more places to stay in addition to those listed here, including **Sleeping**
private accommodation (**E**). Out of season furnished apartments can be rented ■ *on map page 132*
through agencies (with commission). In season it is cheaper to stay in Valparaíso and *Price codes:*
commute to the beaches around Viña. *see inside front cover*
There are many hotels in
L3 *Albamar*, San Martín 419, T975274, F970720. Tastefully decorated. **L3** *Alcázar*, *L3-A3 range, some*
Alvarez 646, T685112, F884245, good restaurant, 4 star. **L3** *Miramar*, Caleta Abarca, *with beach*
T62677, F2-6713165, 5 stars. **L3** *San Martín*, San Martín 667, T689191, F689195.
L2 *José Francisco Vergara*, Dr von Schroeders 367, T626022, F660474. Has *cabañas*
for up to 5. **A3** *Cap Ducal*, Marina 51, T626655, F665478, old mansion charm, good
restaurant. **A3** *Andalue*, 6 Poniente 124, T684147, F684148, with breakfast, central,
recommended. **A3** *Offenbacher Hof*, Balmaceda 102, T621483, F662432. Clean,
friendly. Recommended. **A3** *Petit Palace*, Paseo Valle 387, T663134. Small rooms,
good, central, quiet. **A3** *Quinta Vergara*, Errázuriz 690, T685073. Clean, friendly, large
rooms, beautiful gardens. Recommended. **A2** *Español*, Plaza Vergara 191, T/F685145,
large rooms, run down.

B *Alejandra*, 2 Poniente 440, T974404. With shower and breakfast (**C** in low season). **B** *Balia*, von Schroeders 36, T976307, F680724, parking, overpriced. **B** *Res Victoria*, Valparaíso 40, T977370. Without bath, with breakfast, clean, central. **C** *El Escorial*,
2 places: one at 5 Poniente 114, the other at 5 Poniente 441, T975266. With breakfast,
shared bath, clean, central. **C** *Res France*, Montaña 743, T685976. Clean, safe, helpful.
C *Res Helen Misch*, 1 Poniente 239, T971565, F972135. **C** *Res Magallanes*, Arlegui 555,
T685101. With breakfast, clean, mixed reports. **C** *Res Remanso*, Av Valparaíso 217,
T689057, without bath, with breakfast. **C** *Res Villarica*, Arlegui 172, T942807. Good,
friendly, without bath.

D *Res Agua Santa*, Agua Santa 34. Basic, hot shower. **D** pp *Res Blanchart*, Valparaíso
82A, T974949. Clean, with breakfast, hot water, good service. **D** *Res Capric*, von Schroeder
39, T978295. With bath and breakfast, TV. **D** *Res Caribe*, Von Schroeders 46, T976191, with
bath, small rooms. **D** *Res de Casia*, Von Schroeders 151, T971861. **D** *Res Tajamar*, Alvarez
884, T882134. Opposite railway station, old-fashioned, central, huge rooms, full of character. **E** pp *Res Victoria*, Agua Santa 36. **E** pp *Res Patricia*, Agua Santa 48.

Camping *Camping Reñaca*, Santa Luisa 401, east of centre, expensive, dirty, also *cabañas*. *Reñaca Center*, in town centre on river bank, T833207, good facilities, US$30 per site.

Youth hostels **E** pp *Res La Montaña*, Agua Santa 153, T622230. Hostelling International discount, with breakfast, other meals available, dingy, dirty bathroom, no cooking facilities, also family rooms. **E** pp *Lady Kinnaird Hostal*, 1 Oriente 1096, T975413. YWCA, central, friendly, English spoken, women only. Recommended. See also *Residencial Capric* above.

Reñaca A3 *Cabañas Don Francisco*, Torreblanca 75, T834802, helpful. **A3** *Montecarlo*, V. MacKenna 136, T830397, very modern, comfortable. Several motels. Accommodation here is much cheaper out of season.

Eating **Hotels** *Cap Ducal*. Seafood, expensive. *Colonial*, at Hotel Español. **Others** Raul, Valparaíso 533. Live music. *Casino Chico*, Valparaíso y von Schroeders. Fish, seafood. *Machitún Ruca*, San Martín 529. Excellent. *Pizzería Mama Mía*, San Martín 435. Good, reasonably priced. *Armandita*, San Martín 501. *Parrilla*. Large portions, good service. *El Encuentro*, San Martín y 6 Norte. Fish, very good. *Las Gaviotas*, 14 Norte 1248. Chilean meat dishes, not expensive, live music. Many restaurants on Av Valparaíso, try in the Galerías (arcades), eg *Café Big Ben*, No 469. Good coffee, good food. *Alster*, No 225. Expensive. *Samoiedo*, No 637, *Confitería*, grill and restaurant. *Pau San*, Quinta 122. Chinese. *Africa*, No 324. Extraordinary façade, very good. Several pleasant restaurants and cafés along the renovated Muelle Vergara including *La Mía Pappa*. Italian, good lunches and evening buffets. Kumei, Valparaíso between Von Schroeders and Ecuador, best set lunches in town, wide selection, not expensive. *La Piccola Italiana*, 14 Norte 1340. The *Escuela de Hotelería y Turismo*, on the road to Valparaíso,

Viña del Mar

Sleeping ■	6 Español	Eating ●
1 Albamar	7 José Francisco Vergara	1 Africa
2 Balia	8 Miramar	2 Armandita
3 Blanchart	9 Offenbacher Hof	3 Café Alster
4 Cap Ducal	10 Res Magallanes	4 Café Samoiedo
5 Capric	11 San Martin	5 Casino Chico

T625799, has a good fixed price lunch menu. *Flavia*, 6 Poniente 121, good Italian food, good service, good desserts and wine selection. **Vegetarian**: *Punto Verde*, Arlegui 346, Local A.

   Reñaca *El Pancho*, Av Borgoño 16180. Excellent seafood and service; *Rincón Marino*, Av Borgoño 17120. Good seafood, pricey. *Hotel Oceanic*, Av Borgoño, T830006. Very good, expensive. *El Ciervo*, Av Central y Segunda, bar/cafe, live music in evenings. Recommended.

Cinemas *Cine Arte*, Plaza Vergara 42. **Discotheques** Several including *Twister*, Av Borgoño; *Neverland* and *Cocodrilo*, south of town; *Kamikaze*, east of town. | **Entertainment**

El Roto, **20 January**, in homage to the workers and peasants of Chile. | **Festivals**

Market At intersection of Av Sporting and river, Wednesday and Saturday. | **Shopping**

Local Car hire: *Euro Rent-A-Car*, in *Hotel O'Higgins*, clean cars, efficient. *Hertz*, Quillota 766, T971625/6389918. **Car Mechanic**: Luis Vallejos, 13 Norte 1228. Recommended. | **Transport**

Long distance Air: Ladeco Santiago-Viña del Mar (to naval airfield near Concón), several daily, US$15.

   Train: Services on the Valparaíso Metropolitan line (Merval) stop at Viña (details under Valparaíso).

   Bus: terminal 2 blocks east of Plaza Vergara at Av Valparaíso y Quilpué. To **Santiago**, US$3-4, 2 hours, frequent, many companies, heavily booked in advance for travel on Sunday afternoons, at other times some buses pick up passengers opposite the train station; to **La Serena**, 6 daily, 8 hours, US$10, to **Antofagasta**, 20 hours, US$35, to **Temuco**, 12 hours, US$14, to **Mendoza** (Argentina) CATA, US$16, 8 hours, daily 0830.

Airline offices *Avant*, Ecuador 127, T695405, F695240. **Banks** Many *casas de cambio* on Arlegui including *Afex*, No 641 (open 0900-1400 Sat). *Cambio Norte*, No 610. *Cambio Andino*, No 644. Also in the tourist office. **Communications** Telephone: *CTC*, Valparaíso 628. *Global Telecommunications/Entel*, 15 Norte 961. Internet Access: Av Valparaíso 196, T690529. **Cultural centres** *Instituto Chileno-Británico de Cultura*, 3 Norte 824, T971061. *Instituto Chileno – Norteamericano de Cultura*, 2 Oriente 335, T/F686191. *Casa Italia* (cultural centre, consulate, restaurant), Alvarez 398. *Instituto Chileno – Aleman de Cultura Goethe Haus*, Alvarez 2950, T/F677249. *Instituto Chileno-Francés de Cultura*, Alvarez 314, T685908. **Embassies & consulates** United Kingdom, Libertad 919, oficina 51, T685211, 0900-1300. **Places of worship** St Peter's (Anglican) and Union (Presbyterian) churches have English language services on Sun mornings. **Tourist offices** *Sernatur*, Valparaíso 507, Of 303, T882285. Municipal office on the corner of Plaza Vergara. Arrangements may be made at the municipal tourist office for renting private homes in the summer season. *Automóvil Club de Chile*, 1 Norte 901, T689509. | **Directory**

Resorts north of Viña del Mar

North of Viña del Mar the coast road runs through Las Salinas, a popular beach between two towering crags, Reñaca and Cochoa, where there is a large sea lion colony 100 metres offshore, to Concón. There is also a much faster inland road, between Viña del Mar and Concón.

Concón

Colour map 3, grid B2 Situated 18 kilometres north of Viña del Mar, Concón lies on the southern shore of a bay at the mouth of the Río Aconcagua. A series of beaches stretch along the bay between Caleta Higuerilla at the western end and La Boca at the eastern end. An oil refinery (not visible from the beaches) causes occasional pollution.

Sleeping **L3** *Hostería Edelweiss*, Av Borgoño 19200, T814043, F903600. Modern *cabañas*, clean, comfortable, sea views, including breakfast, excellent food in attached restaurant, German spoken. Recommended. Several motels. **A2** *Concón*, T814212, F813855. **A2** *Internacional Playa Amarilla*, T811915, F814042. **C** *Cabañas Los Romeros*, T813671. **C** *Cabañas Rio Mar*, T/F814644. **Camping** *Matagua*, 3 km north, T811415, well equipped but very expensive, also *cabañas*.

Eating Look out for good seafood empanadas at bars. In **Caleta Higuerilla** *Vista al Mar*, *Both Caleta Higuerilla* Av Borgoño 21270, T812221. Good fish restaurant, good value. *Don Chico*, Av *and La Boca are* Borgoño 21410. Good seafood. In **La Boca** *Carla*, excellent, cheap. Several others *renowned for their* nearby. Also recommended is *Mirador Cochoa*, Av Borgoño 17205. Good, pricey, 3 *restaurants* km north of Renacá.

Quintero

Population: 16,000 Another 23 kilometres north of Concón, Quintero is a fishing town situated on *Colour map 3, grid B2* a rocky peninsula with lots of small beaches. On the north shore of the bay at Las Ventanas are a power station and copper processing plant.

Sleeping **A2** *Yachting Club*, Luis Acevedo 1736, T/F931557. **B** *Isla de Capri*, 21 de Mayo 1299, T930939. Pleasant, sea views. **C** *Monaco*, 21 de Mayo 1530, T930939. Run down but interesting, good views. Lots of *residenciales*.

Horcón

Colour map 3, grid A2 Set back in a cove surrounded by cliffs, Horcón, also known locally as Horcones, is a pleasant small village, mainly of wooden houses. On the beach cheap and unusual jewellery and trinkets are sold. Seafood lunches with the catch of the day, sold at any number of stalls on the seafront, are recommended. It is best avoided in January-February when it is packed out. Drinking alcohol on the beach is forbidden – and enforced by the *carabineros*.

Sleeping & **B** *El Ancla*. *Cabañas*, pleasant. **B-C** *Cabañas Arancibia*, T796169. With bath, **D** with- **eating** out, pleasant gardens, good food, friendly. Recommended. Also rooms in private houses. No campsite but camping possible at private houses.
   Santa Clara, try the *chupe de mariscos* and *pastel de jaivas*. Recommended. *El Ancla* recommended. *Reina Victoria*. Cheap, good.

Parapente Aventura, T09-233-0349, parapent@cix.cl, offer paragliding, US$70 per **Sports** flight, and paragliding courses, US$500.

Maitencillo, 19 kilometres north of Las Ventanas, consisting mainly of cha- *Population: 1,200* lets, has a wonderful long beach. Just to the south is the tourist complex of Marbella, which has a hotel, conference centre, restaurants, golf course, tennis courts, pools. There is **A3** *Cabañas Hermansen* and several other hotels.

Zapallar

A fashionable resort with a lovely beach, Zapallar lies 33 kilometres north of *Population: 2,200* Las Ventanas. A hint of its former glory is given by a number of fine mansions *Colour map 3, grid A2* along Avenida Zapallar. At Cachagua, three kilometres south, a colony of penguins on an island may be viewed from the northern end of the beach, take binoculars.

L3 *Isla Seca*, T741224, F741228. Small, pool, good restaurant. **A1** *César*, T741259. **Sleeping &** Very nice but expensive. **B** *Hostal Villa Real*, large rooms, with breakfast. Recom- **eating** mended. Good, reasonably priced food in *Restaurant César* (different management *Accommodation is very* from hotel), on seafront. No *residenciales*, no campsite. *expensive especially in the centre where it is very sparse*

Papudo

Ten kilometres further north, is this site of a naval battle in November 1865 in *Population: 2,500* which the Chilean vessel *Esmeralda* captured the Spanish ship *Covadonga*. *Colour map 3, grid A2* Following the arrival of the railway Papudo rivalled Viña del Mar as a fashionable resort in the 1920s but it has long since declined. Among the buildings surviving from that period is the Casa Rawlings, now the *Casa de la Cultura*. There are two fine beaches, which are empty except at weekends in summer and weekdays at holiday times.

A *Carande*, Chorrillos 89, T791103, F791118, best. **A2** *D' Peppino*, No 609, T791108. **Sleeping** **A2** *Moderno*, F Concha 150, T711496. **C** pp *Armandini*, F Concha 525, full board. **C** *Res Donde Tito*, Chorrillos 149, T791096, with breakfast. **D** *Res Valencia*, Chorrillos 107. **D** *Res La Plaza*, Chorrillos 119. Many more.

Bus From Valparaíso and Viña del Mar: To **Concón** bus 9 or 10 (from Av Libertad **Transport** between 2 and 3 Norte in Viña), US$0.50; to **Quintero** and **Horcón**, Sol del Pacífico, every 30 minutes, US$1, 2 hours; to **Zapallar** and **Papudo**, Sol del Pacífico, 4 a day (2 before 0800, 2 after 1600), US$3.

Resorts south of Valparaíso

This cluster of resorts stretches along the coast from the mouth of the Río Maipo north towards Valparaíso. Although road links with the latter are poor, there are two good routes from Santiago, one leading from the main Santiago-Valparaíso highway to Algarrobo and the other, Route 78, direct to San Antonio.

San Antonio

Population: 74,742
Phone code: 035
112 km S of Valparaíso
113 km to Santiago
Colour map 3, grid B2

Situated near the mouth of the Río Maipo, San Antonio is a container port and commercial centre for this part of the coast. It has a fishing port and fishmeal plants and is the terminal for the export of copper brought by rail from the large mine at El Teniente, near Rancagua. The town was badly damaged by the 1985 earthquake. There is a museum, the **Museo Municipal de Ciencias Naturales y Arqueología.** ■ *Av Barros Luco. Monday-Friday 0900-1300, 1500-1900.*

Nearby to the south are two resorts: **Llolleo** (four kilometres), famous for the treatment of heart diseases, and seven kilometres further **Rocas de Santo Domingo**, the most attractive and exclusive resort in this area with 20 kilometres of beaches and a golf course; even in high season it is not very crowded.

Sleeping **San Antonio** **B** *Jockey Club*, 21 de Mayo 202, T211777, F212922. Best, good views, restaurant. **D** *Colonial*, Pedro Montt 196. **Llolleo D** pp *Oriente*, Inmaculada Concepción 50, T32188. *Res El Castillo*, Providencia 253, T373821. **Santo Domingo A3** *Rocas de Santo Domingo*, La Ronda 130, T444356, F444494. No cheap accommodation – try Llolleo.

Transport **Bus** To **Valparaíso**, Pullman Bus, every 45 minutes until 2000, US$2; to **Santiago**, Pullman Bus, every 20 minutes, US$2.

Cartagena

Population: 10,318
Colour map 3, grid B2

Eight kilometres north of San Antonio, Cartagena is the biggest resort on this part of the coast. In the early years of this century it was a fashionable summer retreat for the wealthy of Santiago; a number of mansions, notably the *Castillo Foster* overlooking the bay, survive. The centre lies around the Plaza de Armas, situated on top of the hill. To the south is the picturesque Playa Chica, overlooked by many of the older hotels and restaurants; to the north is the Playa Larga. Between the two a promenade runs below the cliffs; high above hang old houses, some in disrepair but offering spectacular views. Cartagena is a very popular resort in summer, but out of season especially it is a good centre for visiting nearby resorts; there are many hotels and bus connections are good.

Sleeping **C** *Biarritz*, Playa Chica, T450476. **D** *La Bahía*, Playa Chica, T31246. **D** pp *Res Carmona*, Playa Chica, T450485. Small rooms, basic, clean, good value. **D** *Violeta*, Condell 140, T234093, swimming pool, good views. **E** pp *El Estribo*, just off Plaza de Armas, with breakfast, basic, cheap *comedor*.

North of Cartagena

The road to Algarrobo runs north along the coast through several small resorts including **Las Cruces**, **El Tabo** and **El Quisco**, a small fishing port with two beautiful white beaches (crowded during Chilean holidays). Just south of Las Cruces is **Laguna El Peral**, a nature reserve which protects a wide range of

••

The Poet and the Sea

The Sea

The Pacific Ocean was overflowing the
borders of the map. There was no place to
put it. It was so large, wild and blue that it
didn't fit anywhere. That's why it was left in
front of my window.
The humanists worried about the little men
it devoured over the years.
They did not count.
Not even that galleon, laden with cinnamon
and pepper that perfumed it as it went
down.
No
Not even the explorers' ship – fragile as a

cradle dashed to pieces in the abyss –
which keeled over with its starving
men.
No
In the ocean, a man dissolves like a bar
of salt.
And the water doesn't know it.

Pablo Neruda (The House in the Sand,
Prose Poems by Pablo Neruda,
translated by Dennis Maloney and
Clark M Zlotchew; Minneapolis:
Milkweed, 1990, page 19).

••

aquatic birds including black-necked swans. ■ *September-April 0900-1400,
1500-1800 daily; May-August 0900-1300, 1400-1800 daily.*

Las Cruces C *La Posada*, T21280. With bath and breakfast, good birdwatching. **El
Tabo** C *Hotel El Tabo*, T33719. Good, and *Motel El Tabo*, T212719. Next door
(overfull in January-February), 2 cheap and basic campsites. **El Quisco** (accommodation generally expensive) **A3** *Motel Barlovento*, T471030, 3-star. *Residenciales*
100-200m from beach in **C** range, for example *Res Oriental*, T471662. With breakfast,
good, clean, hot water. **D** pp *Cabañas del Irlandés Volador*, Aguirre 277, T473464.
D *Cabañas Pozo Azul*, Capricornio 234, T471401. Southeast of town, quiet. **D** *Res
Julia*, Aguirre 0210, T471546. Very clean, quiet, good value. Recommended. Several
on Dubournais (main street) including **C** *Gran Italia*, No 413, T/F481631, good beds,
pool, recommended; **D** *El Quisco*, No 166, T481923. With breakfast, clean, open weekends only, with excellent seafood restaurant.

Sleeping (margin)

Isla Negra

Four kilometres south of El Quisco in the village of Isla Negra is the beautifully
restored **Museo-Casa Pablo Neruda**. Bought by Neruda in 1939 this house,
overlooking the sea, was his writing retreat in his later years. It contains
artefacts gathered by Neruda from all over the world. ■ *Guided tours in Spanish, English or French, (see also Neruda's Santiago house, La Chascona, page 83,
and La Sebastiana, page 124), Tuesday-Sunday 1015-1230, 1500-1800, in summer 1000-1745, US$3, students US$1.50, T035-461284 for opening hours or to
book English guide (US$5).*

Colour map 3, grid B2 (margin)

The celebrated 1994 film **Il Postino** was based on Antonio Skármeta's novel
Ardiente Paciencia, which is set in Isla Negra during the last years of Neruda's
life. Skármeta himself adapted the book for the cinema in 1983, but after the
1994 success the novel was retitled *El Cartero de Neruda* (*Neruda's Postman*).

B *Hostería Santa Elena*, T213439. Beautiful building and location, restaurant, some
rooms damp and gloomy. **E** pp *Casa Azul*, Av Santa Luisa, T461154, with breakfast,
kitchen and living room, English spoken, camping. Recommended.

Sleeping (margin)

Transport **Bus** From Santiago: Pullman Bus service from Terminal Alameda, frequent in summer, US$8 return; also regular services by Robles and other companies from Terminal Sur. Tours from Santiago, departing at 0900 from Plaza de Armas (Compañia y Ahumada), cost US$23.75 and include seaside resorts, T232-2574.

Algarrobo

Colour map 3, grid B2 North of Cartagena by 29 kilometres, Algarrobo is the largest resort north of Cartagena and the most chic, with its large houses, yacht club and marina. Its shallow waters and sheltered bay ensures that sea temperatures here are much warmer than at most other resorts in central Chile. Conveniently located for Santiago, it was, in the 1960s, the retreat of politicians – both Salvador Allende and Eduardo Frei had summer residences here. From Playa Canelo there are good views of pelicans and boobies in a seabird colony on an offshore island (no entry). In summer there are boat tours round the island from the jetty.

Sleeping **A3** *Costa Sur*, Alessandri 2156, T481151, F2-7795944. **C** *Uribe*, behind *Costa Sur*, T481035. Pleasant, quiet. **C** *Res Vera*, Alessandri 1521, T481131. With breakfast, good. **E** pp *Res San José*, Av Principal 1598, T481131. Basic, no hot water.

Transport **Bus** To Santiago, Pullman Bus, every 20 minutes, 2 hours, US$3, stopping in Cartagena and the resorts along the coast (but not San Antonio). Services to San Antonio by *Empresa de Buses San Antonio* (frequent, last bus around 2000) and Empresa Robles.

From Santiago to La Serena

5

From Santiago to La Serena

This region stretches from Santiago to the fertile Elqui Valley, nearly 500 kilometres further north. Much of this region is frequently overlooked by travellers from overseas, though the coastal resorts are popular with Chileans. The largest resort is the attractive city of La Serena, a good place to break the long bus journey north and the usual centre for visiting the Elqui Valley. This attractive oasis is one of the world's most important astronomical centres, with four observatories, including one built especially for visitors.

South of La Serena are Andacollo, a little mining town and a great pilgrimage centre, and the small city of Ovalle. Although of little interest in itself, it is a base for several excursions in this area, including to the Parque Nacional Fray Jorge, a temperate rainforest which survives in this dry region due to the sea mists that hang almost constantly over its hills.

Background

History

Archaeological finds indicate that the river valleys were inhabited at an early stage in prehistory; among the later peoples were the Diaguitas who crossed the Andes around 900 AD and settled throughout the area.

Soon after the arrival of the Spanish and the foundation of Santiago, Pedro de Valdivia attempted to secure control over northern Chile by founding La Serena in 1544. Throughout the colonial period, La Serena dominated the rest of the region; although small, it was the only city in the north and its leading families had close ties to the main Spanish landowners in the other valleys. After independence the area became an important mining zone, producing large amounts of silver, copper and gold.

Geography

Stretching north from the Río Aconcagua to the Río Elqui, this area is a transitional zone between the fertile heartland and the northern deserts. North of the Aconcagua the Andes and the coastal *cordillera* merge and are crossed by river valleys separated by mountain ridges. North of La Ligua, the Pan-American Highway mainly follows the coastline, which is relatively flat, passing many beautiful coves, alternatively rocky and sandy, with good surf, though the water is very cold. The valleys of the main rivers, the Choapa, Limarí and Elqui, are green oases; the land is intensively farmed using irrigation to produce fruit and vegetables. Elsewhere the vegetation is characteristic of semidesert (dry scrub and cactus), except in those areas where sea mists provide sufficient moisture to support temperate rainforest.

Climate

Rainfall is rare and occurs only in winter. Temperatures are relatively stable, with little seasonal variation, especially on the coast where the average temperature is 14°C, morning mists are common and humidity is high; the interior is dry, with temperatures averaging 16-17°.

Economy

Despite the dry climate agriculture is important, employing over a third of the labour force. Much of the region's industry is linked to its agricultural produce, notably the distilling of *pisco* from grapes. There are large fish-meal and processing plants in Coquimbo. Mining is also important: among the major mines are El Indio, inland from La Serena, the biggest gold producer in Chile as well as a source of copper and El Romeral, north of La Serena, the most important iron ore deposit in the country. Quartz and the precious stone lapis lazuli are also mined.

North to the Elqui Valley

See page 229 for service stations between Santiago and the Peruvian border *The first stretch of the Pan-American Highway from Santiago is inland through green valleys with rich blue clover and wild artichokes. North of La Ligua it follows the coast.*

Los Vilos

Situated 216 kilometres north of Santiago, Los Vilos is a former mineral port, now a small seaside resort. Offshore are two islands reached by frequent launches: Isla de Los Huevos, situated in the bay, and, five kilometres south, Isla de Los Lobos where there is a colony of seals. **Pichidangui**, 26 kilometres

Population: 9,422
Phone code: 053
Colour map 3, grid A2

From Santiago to La Serena

south, is a popular resort on a rocky peninsula with a beautiful beach to the north. **Los Molles**, 10 kilometres south of Pichidangui, is a fishing village where many wealthy residents of Santiago have their summer homes. Nearby are the Puguén blow holes (entry US$1, free off-season) and the Piscina Los Molles, a natural swimming pool.

Sleeping **Los Vilos** **C** *Lord Willow*, Hostería 1444, T541037. Overlooking beach and harbour, with breakfast and bath, pleasant, parking, weekend disco next door. **D** *Bellavista*, Rengo 20, T541073. With breakfast, without bath, hot water, clean. **F** pp *Res Angelica*, Caupolicán 627. Central, warm water, restaurant attached, expensive camping (US$13 per site). The *American Motel* is right on the highway, Km 224, T541020, and is a convenient stopping place between Viña del Mar or Santiago and La Serena, expensive but good value.

    Pichidangui *Motel El Bosque*, El Bosque s/n, T541182. Recommended. **B** *Motel Pichidangui*, Francis Drake s/n, T594010. Swimming pool. **C** *Puquen*, 2 Poniente s/n. Attractive, good value. Various other hotels and *pensiones* in every price range.

    Los Molles *Cabañas Los Molles*, F791787. *Cabañas Lourdes*, T Santiago 5589778.

    Camping Los Vilos *Campomar*, near centre, F541049, **F** pp, also *cabañas*. **Pichidangui** *El Bosque de Pichidangui*, T531030, **E** per site. *Bahía Marina de Pichidangui*, T531120, sports facilities, *cabañas*.

Eating **Los Vilos** *Restaurant Costanera*. Good views over ocean, good meals, expensive. Restaurants in Pichindangui tend to be pricey although there is a food shop. *Alisio*, Caupolicán 298. Seafood and fish, good value.

Transport **Bus** Only 1 bus daily Pichidangui-Santiago, but north-south buses (for example Inca Bus) on the Highway pass Los Vilos and Pichidangui.

Illapel

Population: 18,900
Altitude: 350m
Phone code: 053
Colour map 3, grid A3

Situated inland 59 kilometres northeast of Los Vilos, Illapel lies in the valley of the Río Choapa 287 kilometres north of Santiago. Founded on its present site in 1788, it is a commercial centre for the valley. There is a small archaeological museum in the Casa de la Cultura, just off the Plaza de Armas.

Excursions To **Reserva Nacional Las Chinchillas**, 15 kilometres north along a good dirt road. The reserve covers 4,229 hectares and protects the last remaining colony of chinchillas in this region. The chinchillas and six related species can be viewed from behind two-way mirrors. Entry US$3. Accommodation is available, **D** per person, with kitchen facilities and there is a campsite, US$4 per person.

Sleeping Several on Ignacio Silva including **C** *Domingo Ortíz de Rozas*, No 241, T/F522127, 3-star. *Alemán*, No 45, T522511. *Alameda*, No 20, T522355. *Diaguitas*, Constitución 276, T/F522587. *Londres*, Mackenna 21, T211906.

Ovalle

Situated inland in the valley of the Río Limarí, a fruit, sheep-rearing, and mining district, the town is famous for its talabarterías (leather workshops) and for its products made of locally mined lapis lazuli.

Population: 53,000
Altitude: 200m
Phone code: 053
412 km N of Santiago
Colour map 2, grid C1

Market days are Monday, Wednesday, Friday and Saturday, till 1600; the market, *feria modelo*, is on Benavente. **Museo del Limarí**, Independencia 329, has displays of petroglyphs and a good collection of Diaguita ceramics and other artefacts. ■ *Tuesday-Sunday 1000-1600.*

Embalse La Paloma, the largest reservoir in Chile, is 26 kilometres southeast. On the northern shore is the small town of **Monte Patria** (*Population*: 4,000) with a pisco distillery which can be visited. Nearby accommodation is available at the *Hotel Hacienda Juntas*, **A3**, which stands in 90 hectares of vineyards, spectacular views, swimming pool.

Excursions

Monumento Nacional Valle del Encanto, about 22 kilometres southwest of Ovalle, is one of the most important archaeological sites in northern Chile. Artefacts from hunting peoples from over 2,000 years ago have been found but the most visible remains date from the Molle culture (700 AD). There are over 30 petroglyphs as well as great boulders, distributed in six sites. Camping facilities. ■ *US$1. Monday-Friday 0815-1300, 1500-1900 (2000 in summer), Saturday 0900-1300, 1500-1800, Sunday 1000-1300. Getting there: no local bus service; you must take a long distance bus and ask to be dropped off – five kilometres walk to the valley; flag down a bus to return.*

To **Termas de Socos**, situated 35 kilometres southwest of Ovalle on the Pan-American Highway. There are fine thermal springs (entrance US$5), a good hotel (**A2**, T Ovalle 621373, Casilla 323) and a campsite (US$10 per tent, but bargain) nearby. Bus US$2.

Essentials

D *Res Bristol*, Araucano 224. Pleasant spacious building, restaurant. **On Libertad D** *Francia*, No 231, T620828. Pleasant, friendly, restaurant. **D** *Roxy*, No 155, T620080. Constant hot water, clean, friendly, patio, *comedor*. Highly recommended. **E** *Venecia*, No 261, T620968. Clean, safe, friendly. Recommended. **E** *Res Socos*, Socos 22, T624157. Clean, quiet, family run. Recommended. For cheaper accommodation try **G** *Res Lolita*, Independencia 274, without bath, **F** with, basic, short-stay. Several other cheap *residenciales* in Calle Socos (short stay). *Gran*, V Mackenna 210, T621084, F624122. *Turismo*, Victorio 295, T623536.

Sleeping
■ *on map page 146*
Price codes:
see inside front cover

Club Social, V MacKenna 400 block. Excellent fish dishes though pricey. *Club Social Arabe*, Arauco 255. Spacious glass-domed premises, limited selection of Arab dishes, good but not cheap. *El Quijote*, Arauco 294. Intimate atmosphere, good seafood, inexpensive. Good value *almuerzos* at

Eating
● *on map page 146*

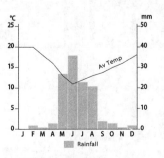

°C / mm

Av Temp

J F M A M J J A S O N D
▨ Rainfall

Climate: Ovalle

From Santiago to La Serena

Casino La Bomba, Aguirre 364, run by fire brigade, *Bavaria*, V MacKenna 161. For drinks and snacks try *Café Caribe Express*, V MacKenna 241. *Yum Yum*, V MacKenna 21. Good, cheap, lively. *D'Oscar Bar*, Plaza de Armas. *Pastelería Josti*, Libertad 427. *Club Comercial*, Aguirre 244 (on plaza). Open Sunday.

Shopping For articles made of lapis lazuli try Sr Wellington Vega Alfaro at kiosk on Plaza de Armas, 1000-1400, 1600-2100; his workshop, on the northern outskirts, is difficult to reach without transport, T620797.

Transport Buses to **Santiago**, several, 6½ hours, US$7; to **La Serena**, 12 a day, 1½ hours, US$2; to **Antofagasta**, US$20.

Directory **Tourist offices** Kiosk on the Plaza de Armas. *Automóvil Club de Chile*, Libertad 144, T620011. Very helpful, overnight parking.

Longer excursions from Ovalle

Parque Nacional Fray Jorge This park, a UNESCO Biosphere Reserve, covers 9,959 hectares and contains original temperate rainforests which contrast with the otherwise barren surroundings. Receiving no more than 113 millimetres of rain a year, the forests survive because of the almost constant fog and mist covering the hills. This is the result of the discharge of the warm waters of the Río Limarí into the cold waters of the Pacific.

Getting there Situated 90 kilometres west of Ovalle and 110 kilometres south of La Serena at the mouth of the Río Limarí, the park is reached by a dirt road leading off the Pan-American Highway. The entrance and administration are at Km 18, from where it is 10 kilometres further to the summit of the coastal hills (known as the Altos de Talinay) which rise to 667 metres.

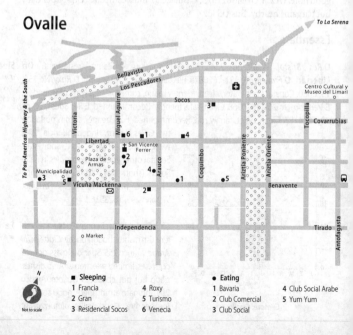

Ovalle

■ **Sleeping**		● **Eating**	
1 Francia	4 Roxy	1 Bavaria	4 Club Social Arabe
2 Gran	5 Turismo	2 Club Comercial	5 Yum Yum
3 Residencial Socos	6 Venecia	3 Club Social	

Not to scale

The price of gold

Though the economy of northern Chile is dominated by mining, it is an entirely large-scale operation. Andacollo offers probably the only opportunity in Chile to see small-scale gold mining in operation, though your chances may depend on whether the world price of gold makes it worthwhile for the miners to extract and process the ore.

The independent gold miners' ore is processed in two types of small mills. The larger independent miners use the trapiche, which consists of two heavy vertical wheels in a container half filled with water. As the ore is ground between the wheels, the gold dust sticks to mercury which is spread on the sides of the container. The other type of mill, the maray, resembles a large mortar and pestle and is hand driven. Both the trapiche and the maray are rented by the miner to process their own ore, the rent being paid as a share of the ore. The best time to see miners processing ore is probably on a Friday as the miners need the gold for the weekend.

Francine Audet and Jean Laforest,
Quebec, Canada

Park essentials Entry US$4. Open Saturday, Sunday and public holidays only, entry 0830-1600, last departure 1800. Visits are closely controlled owing to risk of fire. Basic accommodation is available in an old hacienda. There are two campsites, one of which is at the administration centre, T053-620058. Waterproof clothing essential. Scientific groups may obtain permission to visit from The Director, Conaf, Cordóvez 281, La Serena, T211124. Getting there: round trip in taxi from Ovalle, US$30, Abel Olivares Rivera, T053-620352. Recommended.

Some 47 kilometres northeast of Ovalle at an altitude of 1,350 metres, this park contains petrified tree trunks and archaeological remains, including a vast cave, comparable to the Cueva Milodón outside Puerto Natales, with remnants of ancient roof paintings. Gigantic rock formations can be seen on the surrounding mountains. ■ *US$3. 0800-1200, 1400-1700. Getting there: The park is reached by an unpaved and winding road which runs from Ovalle through to Vicuña (see below). Daily bus from Ovalle to Hurtado passes the turn off (to San Pedro) about 42 kilometres from the city. From here it is three kilometres to the park and about two kilometres further to sites of interest.*

Monumento Natural Pichasca

Andacollo

The good road inland between Ovalle and La Serena makes an interesting contrast to Ruta 5, the Pan-American Highway, with a fine pass and occasional views of snowcapped Andes across cacti-covered plains and semi-desert mountain ranges. Sixty one kilometres north of Ovalle a side road runs 44 kilometres southeast, with the last 20 kilometres being very bad, to **Andacollo**.

Population: 10,216
Altitude: 1,050m
Colour map 2, grid C1

Situated in a gorge 53 kilometres south of La Serena, Andacollo has been a mining centre since before the arrival of the Spanish (see box on page 147). Ruins of mines and waste tips dot the area. Two large mines, one copper and one gold, still operate

Around Ovalle

To La Serena

44 — Andacollo

Monumento Natural Pichasca

To La Serena & the North

61

Parque Nacional Fray Jorge
18

37 — Valle del Encanto
17 — Ovalle
45

2 — Termas de Socos

To Santiago

To Hurtado & Vicuña

N

Distance in km

From Santiago to La Serena

and there are many independent mines and *trapiches*, small processing plants, which can be visited. Andacollo, however, is more famous as one of the great pilgrimage sites in Chile. In the enormous **Basilica** (1893), 45 metres high and with a capacity of 10,000, is the miraculous Virgen del Rosario de Andacollo. Nearby is the **Templo Antiguo**, smaller and dating from 1789. There is a museum, **Museo de Andacollo**, which is open daily 0900-1300, 1500-1830. There are no hotels, but some *pensiones*. During the festival private houses rent beds and some let you pay for a shower.

Festivals The *Fiesta Grande* from **23-27 December** (most important day December 26) attracts 150,000 pilgrims from northern Chile. The ritual dances date from a pre-Spanish past. Transport is available from La Serena and Ovalle but 'purists' walk (torch and good walking shoes essential). Two villages are passed on the route, which starts on the paved highway, then goes along a railway track and lastly up a steep, dusty hill. There is also a smaller festival, the *Fiesta Chica* on the first Sunday of **October**.

Transport **Bus** From **Ovalle** colectivo, US$2.40; bus, US$1.70. From La Serena, yellow colectivos run from C Domeyko.

Directory **Tourist office** on the Plaza de Armas, can arrange tours to the Basilica and to mining operations.

The Elqui Valley

Coquimbo

Population: 122,000
Phone code: 051
Colour map 2, grid C1

Eighty four kilometres north of Ovalle and on the same bay as La Serena, Coquimbo is a port of considerable importance. It has one of the best harbours on the coast and several major fish-processing plants. The city is strung along the north shore of a peninsula. Most of the commercial life is centred on three streets which run between the port and the steep hillside on which are perched many of the poorer houses. On the south shore of the peninsula lies the suburb of Guayacán, with an iron-ore loading port, a steel church designed by Eiffel and an English cemetery. In 1981 heavy rain uncovered 39 ancient burials of humans and llamas which had been sacrificed. A small museum has been built in the Plaza Gabriela Mistral to exhibit these.

Coquimbo was used during the colonial period as a port for La Serena, attracting a lot of attention from English pirates including Francis Drake, who visited in 1578. A statue to Drake was erected in the city in 1998. Legends of buried treasure at Bahía la Herradura de Guayacán persist. From these small beginnings Coquimbo grew into a city in the 19th century, when it and the separate centre of Guayacán became important in the processing of copper. By 1854 there were two large copper foundries in Coquimbo and in 1858 the largest foundry in the world was built in Guayacán.

Nearby is **La Herradura**, two and a half kilometres from Coquimbo which has the best beaches. Also nearby is a resort complex called *Las Tacas*, with beach, swimming pool, tennis, flats, *apart-hotel*, etc. At **Totoralillo** (*Population: 3,350*), 12 kilometres south, there are good beaches, ideal for swimming.

Sleeping
■ *on map*
Price codes:
see inside front cover
Accommodation is
cheaper than La Serena

B *Lig*, Aldunate 1577, T311171. Comfortable, friendly, overpriced, near bus terminal. **B** *Prat*, Bilbao y Aldunate, T311845. Comfortable, pleasant. **B** *Punta del Este*, Videla 170, T312768. Nice rooms. **C** *Iberia*, Bandera 206, Piso 8, T312141, with bath, **D** without. Friendly. Recommended. Several hotels in La Herradura, including **C** *La Herradura*, Costanera 200, T321320. **Camping** *Camping La Herradura*, T312084.

Lots of good fish restaurants including *Sal y Pimienta del Capitán Denny*, Aldunate **Eating**
769, one of the best, pleasant, old fashioned, mainly fish, US$12-20 per person. *La* ● *on map*
Picada, Costanera near statue of O'Higgins. Excellent, pricey. *Crucero*, Valera. Excellent. *La Barca*, Ríos y Varela. Modest but good. *La Bahía*, Pinto 1465. Excellent, good value. Several good seafood restaurants at the municipal market, Melgarejo entre Bilbao y Borgoño (*El Callejón*. Recommended). *Mai Lai Fan*, Av Ossandón 1. Excellent Chinese. Recommended.

Bus Terminal at Varela y Garriga. To **La Serena**, every few minutes, US$0.30. To **Transport**
Guanaqueros, US$0.80, 45 minutes, and to **Tongoy**, US$1, 1 hour, with Ruta Costera, frequency varies according to day (more on Sunday) and season. *Colectivos* to Guanaqueros US$1.40; to Tongoy US$1.70.

Communications Telephones: *CTC*, Aldunate 1633. **Tourist offices** Kiosk in Plaza de Armas **Directory**
(open summer only).

Resorts south of Coquimbo

Guanaqueros, 37 kilometres south, is a fishing village on the southern coast of *Population: 1,200*
a large bay, east of the village is a 10 kilometre long beach. There is the clean *Phone code: 051*
and simple **D** *La Bahía* or **C** *Cabañas Bahia Club*, T395818, with kitchens are *Colour map 2, grid C1*
on the waterfront. Recommended. Camping *Oasis* on the beach, US$8 per site

From Santiago to La Serena

Coquimbo

0 metres 200	■ **Sleeping**		● **Eating**
0 yards 218	1 Iberia	3 Prat	1 La Bahía
	2 Lig	4 Punta del Este	2 Sol y Pimienta del Capitán Denny

To Guayacán, La Herradura & Santiago

Tongoy
Population: 3,350
Phone code: 051
Colour map 2, grid C1

Fifty kilometres south is an old fishing port occupying the whole of a small peninsula. It is now a rapidly growing resort and well worth a visit: the Playa Grande to the south is 14 kilometres long; the Playa Socos to the north is four kilometres in length.

Sleeping
A1-B *Yachting Club*, Costanera 20, T391154. Good. **A2** *Panorámico*, Mirador 455, T391944. Includes breakfast, all rooms with view of bay and fishing boats, excellent, clean, friendly. *Samay*, Mirador 770, T391355. **E** *Plaza*, on main square, T391184. Several basic *residenciales*. *Hostería Tongoy*, Av Costanera 10, T391203. F391900. **E** *Res La Bahía*, Urmeneta Sur 95, T391244.

Eating
Try the *marisquerías* near the fishing port, excellent value. *Restaurant El Buque*, Puesto 17 on seafront, near fishing harbour. Fish and meat with superb sauces, good service. Highly recommended.

La Serena

Population: 120,000
Phone code: 051
473 km N of Santiago
Colour map 2, grid C1

Twelve kilometres north of Coquimbo, La Serena is the capital of Región IV. Built on a hillside two kilometres inland from the Bahía de Coquimbo, it is an attractive city of white buildings in neo-colonial style. It has rapidly become a major tourist centre with extensive modern development on the reclaimed marshlands between the city centre and the beach.

History

La Serena was founded by Juan de Bohón, aide to Pedro de Valdivia, in 1544, destroyed by Diaguita Indians in 1546 and rebuilt by Francisco de Aguirre in 1549. The city was sacked by the English pirate Sharpe in 1680. In the colonial period it was the main staging-post on the route north to Peru; many of the religious orders built churches and convents here providing accommodation for their members. In the 19th century the city grew prosperous from copper-mining; the neoclassical mansions of successful entrepreneurs from this period can still be seen. The characteristic neo-colonial style architecture of the centre dates from the 1950s when the city was remodelled.

Sights

Around the attractive Plaza de Armas are most of the official buildings, including the Post Office, the **Cathedral**, built in 1844 and featuring a carillon which plays every hour, and the **Casa González Videla**, the great man's residence from 1927 to 1977, which now houses the Museo Histórico Regional , see below. There are 29 other churches, several of which have unusual towers. **San Francisco**, Balmaceda y de La Barra, built 1586-1627, has a baroque façade and faces a small plaza with arcades. **Santo Domingo**, half a block southwest of the Plaza de Armas, built 1755 with a clock tower dating from 1912, is fronted by a small garden with statues of sea lions. **San Augustín**, Cantournet y Rengifo, originally a Jesuit church, dates from 1755 but has been heavily modified.

Opposite San Augustín at Cienfuegos y Cantournet is **La Recova**, the market, which includes a large display of handicrafts and, upstairs, several good restaurants. One block west of the Plaza de Armas is the **Parque Pedro de Valdivia**, with the **Parque Japonés** just south of it. ■ *US$1.25. Daily 1000-2000.*

González Videla and the Plan Serena

The present-day layout and architectural style have their origins in the 'Plan Serena' drawn up in 1948 on the orders of Gabriel González Videla, a native of the city. Born in 1898 González Videla was a lawyer, diplomat and Radical party politician who was elected President of Chile in 1946 as a result of deal with the Communist and Liberal parties. Once elected, he claimed to have discovered a left-wing plot, outlawed the Communist party and had many of its members imprisoned. The poet Pablo Neruda, a member of the Communist party, was understandably scathing, describing him as 'an irresponsible and frivolous clown' and 'a contemptible creature' with 'an insignificant but twisted mind'. It should be added that it was González Videla's government which gave the vote to women.

Eager to leave his mark on his native city, González Videla ordered the drafting of an urban plan. Under this, Avenida Francisco de Aguirre was modernized and the Pedro de Valdivia gardens, west of the city, were built. All new buildings in the centre were to be in Californian colonial style, though his regulation has since been modified permitting the construction of some modern buildings.

Av Francisco de Aguirre, a pleasant boulevard lined with statues and known as the **Alameda**, runs from the centre to the coast, terminating at the **Faro Monumental**, a neo-colonial mock-castle (entry US$0.50). A string of beaches stretch from here to Peñuelas, six kilometres south, linked by the Avenida del Mar. Many apartment blocks, hotels, *cabañas* and restaurants have been built along this part of the bay.

Museo Histórico Regional in the Casa González Videla on the Plaza de Armas, **Museums** including several rooms on the man's life. ■ *US$1. Tuesday-Saturday 0900-1300, 1600-1900, Sunday 1000-1300. Ticket also valid for Museo Arqueológico.*

Museo Arqueológico, Cordóvez y Cienfuegos, outstanding collection of Diaguita and Molle Indian exhibits, especially of attractively decorated pottery. Poor labelling of items. ■ *US$1. Tuesday-Saturday 0900-1300, 1600-1900, Sunday 1000-1300.*

Museo De Arte Religiosa, in the San Francisco church, which includes the funeral mask of Gabriela Mistral.

Museo Mineralógico in the University of La Serena, A Muñoz between Benavente and Infante (for geologists). ■ *Free. Monday-Friday 0930-1200.*

Route 5 from La Serena to Coquimbo is lined with cheaper accommodation, from hotels to *cabañas*, and restaurants. There are also hotels and other types of accommodation along Av del Mar. There are no buses along this road, but it's only 500 metres off Route 5.

L3 *Costa Real*, Av de Aguirre 170, T221010, F221122, 5-star, restaurant, bar, pool, conference centre. **L3** *Francisco de Aguirre*, Córdovez 210, T/F222991. With breakfast, shower, good rooms, reasonable restaurant. **L3** *Hostería La Serena*, Av de Aguirre 0660, T225745, F222459. Large pool, sports facilities. **L3** *Mediterráneo*, Cienfuegos 509, Casilla 212, T225838, F225837. Includes good breakfast. Recommended.

A3 *El Escorial I*, Colón 617, T224793, F221433, good. **A3** *Pucará*, Balmaceda 319, T211966, F211933, with bath and breakfast, modern, clean, quiet. **A2** *Berlín*, Córdovez 535, T222927, F223575. Clean, safe, efficient. Recommended. **A2** *Casablanca*, Vicuña 414, T213070, F212062, 3-star. **A1** *Los Balcones de Alcalá*, Av de Aguirre 452, T225999, F211800. Comfortable, clean, TV. **A1** *Los Balcones de Aragón*, Cienfuegos 289, T225724.

Sleeping
■ *on map page 152*
Price codes:
see inside front cover
Accommodation in town centre is expensive.
The tourist office in the bus terminal is helpful and has accommodation information

From Santiago to La Serena

B *Hostal Croata* Cienfuegos 248, T/F224997. With bath, **C** without, with breakfast, laundry facilities, cable TV, patio, hospitable. Recommended. **B** *Londres*, Córdovez 550, T214673. With bath, **C** without, restaurant, old fashioned. **C** *Alameda*, Av de Aguirre 450, T213052. Run down, clean and comfortable. **C** *Brasilia*, Brasil 555, T225248. Friendly, small rooms, overpriced. **C** *El Pacifico*, E de la Barra 252, T225674. Quiet. **C** *Hostal Santo Domingo*, Andres Bello 1067, T212718. With breakfast. Highly recommended. **C** *Lido*, Matta 547, T213073. Hot water, clean, friendly. **C** *Res Suiza*, Cienfuegos 250, T216092. With bath and breakfast, good beds, excellent value. Highly recommended. **C-D** *Res La Japonesita*, Muñoz 218, T213039. With breakfast.

D *Casona de Cantournet*, Cantournet 815, T217162. With bath, huge rooms in old mansion, comfortable. **D** *Edith González*, Los Carrera 885, T221941, with bath, **E** without. Cooking and laundry facilities. Recommended. **D** *El Cobre*, Colón y Matta, T221457. Large rooms, clean. **D** *Res Chile*, Matta 561, T211694. Basic, without bath, small rooms, clean, hot water morning only, overpriced. **D** *Res El Loa*, O'Higgins 362, T210304. Without bath, with breakfast, good inexpensive home cooking, friendly, good value. **D** *Res Petit*, de la Barra 586, T212536. Hot water. **D** *Rosa Canto*, Cantournet 976, T213954. Kitchen, comfortable, family run, good value. Recommended. **D** *San Juan*, Balmaceda 827. Clean, central.

La Serena

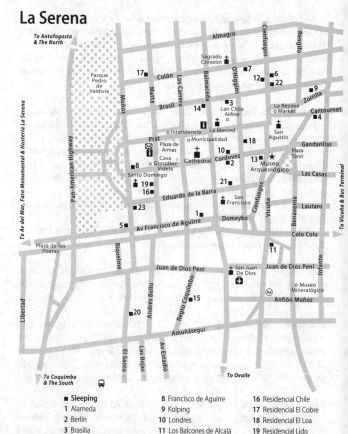

■ **Sleeping**

1 Alameda	8 Francisco de Aguirre	16 Residencial Chile
2 Berlín	9 Kolping	17 Residencial El Cobre
3 Brasilia	10 Londres	18 Residencial El Loa
4 Casablanca	11 Los Balcones de Alcalá	19 Residencial Lido
5 Costa Real	12 Los Balcones de Aragón	20 Residencial Lorena Carvajal
6 Croata	13 Mediterráneo	21 Residencial Petit
7 El Escorial I	14 Pucará	22 Res Suiza
	15 Residencial Ana Jofre	23 Viña del Mar

Not to scale

The Buccaneers of the Chilean coast

Sir Francis Drake was one of the first Europeans to commit piracy along the west coast of South America but his example was soon widely followed. By the second half of the 17th century free-booting renegades from all parts of the world, but particularly the English, French and Dutch, were roaming the South Seas preying on Spanish coastal towns and shipping in the hope of getting rich quick.

Basil Ringrose has a special place amongst these desperadoes because he left a fascinating first-hand account of his activities. Towards the end of 1679 he set out, under the command of a Captain Sharp, to take and plunder what Ringrose describes as the 'vastly rich town of Arica'. On finding the Spanish defence of Arica too strong to overcome, however, they had to continue south to nearby Hilo where they managed to land and occupy the sugar factory. The besieged Spaniards agreed to supply Ringrose and his comrades 'four score of beeves' on condition they didn't burn the sugar factory to the ground. After several days of waiting for the 'beeves' to arrive the pirates began to smell a rat and decided to burn

the factory down regardless and retreated to their ship. It was as well they did because they had no sooner re-embarked than they saw 300 Spanish horseman advancing on their encampment. But Ringrose was still impressed by Hilo, describing it as 'a valley very pleasant being all over set with figs, olives, oranges, lemons, and lime trees, and many other fruits agreeable to the palate'. What Ringrose most remembered Hilo for, however, was its 'good chocolate' of which they 'had plundered some small quantity'.

After the double disappointment of Arica and Hilo the pirates continued south to the Bay of Coquimbo where they discovered the city of La Serena, 'most excellent and delicate, and far beyond what we could expect in so remote a place'. Ringrose was particularly impressed by the town's seven churches which he and his companions hoped to loot, but again news of their activities preceded them and the Spaniards had already removed the churches' treasures. Instead they 'found strawberries as big as walnuts and very delicious to the taste'.

Nigel Pickford

E pp *Amuñategui 315*, with bath, kitchen facilities, patio, good beds. Recommended. **E** Adolfo Ballas 1418, T223735. **E** pp *Ana Jofré*, Rgto Coquimbo 964 (entre Pení y Amuñátegui), T222335, hostaljofre@hotmail.com. With bath and breakfast, good beds, garden, near bus terminal. Recommended. **E** pp *Celia Rivera*, Las Rojas 21, T215838. Near terminal, use of kitchen, clean, friendly. **E** pp *Gabriela Matus*, Juan de Dios Peni 636, T211407. **E** pp *Gregoria Fernández*, Andrés Bello 979A, T224400. Highly recommended. Clean, friendly, good beds, 3 blocks from terminal, excellent breakfast. Next door is **E** pp *Raquel Pereira*, Andrés Bello 979B, T222419. Dormitory accommodation, with breakfast. **E** pp *Luis Muñoz*, Brasil 720, T211619. With breakfast, good showers, nice garden, English and French spoken, helpful. Recommended. **E** pp *Maria Pizarro*, Las Rojas 18, T229282. Very welcoming, laundry facilities, camping, very helpful. Recommended. **E** pp *Res Lorena*, Cantournet 850, T223330. Quiet, pleasant. **E** *Backpacker Lodging*, El Santo 1058, T227580. Kitchen facilities, central, camping. **E** pp *Las Rojas 26*, Kitchen facilities, basic, family run, camping.

Youth Hostel E pp *Res Limmat*, Lautaro 914, T/F211373. With breakfast, central, patio, tours offered, English and German spoken, Hostelling International reduction. Recommended.

Motels and cabañas L3 *Cabañas Los Papayos*, Gonzalez Videla, Huertos 66/67, 2 km south of city (Vista Hermosa bus), T213221, much cheaper out of season, 2 bedroom cabins, pool, gardens. Recommended. **A3** *Cabañas El Palmar*, Av del Mar 5700, T247983. **A3** *Cabañas de Turismo*, Av del Mar 1000, T212453. **A3** *Canto del Agua*, Av del Mar 2200, T216630, F241767. Very good, pleasant *cabañas*, also apartments. **A3** *Hostal Del Mar*, Cuatro Esquinas 0680 (near beach), T22559. Also apartments, clean, friendly. **A3** *La Fuente*, Av del Mar 5665, T245755, F541259. Apartments, cable TV, parking, very good. Several more motels along Av del Mar. **A3** *Les Mouettes*, Av del Mar 2500, T225665, F226278. Good restaurant, includes breakfast. Recommended.

Camping Three sites south of La Serena: *Antares*, Los Pescadores 4655, Peñuelas; *Sole di Mare*, Peñuelas Vega Sur, on seafront, fully equipped; *Hipocampo*, Av del Mar, 4 km south, T214276, reached by Coquimbo bus (get off at Colegio Adventista). English spoken. Also *Maki Payi*, 153 Vegas Norte, T213628, 5 kilometres north of La Serena, near sea, friendly, also *cabañas*. Recommended.

Eating

For good fish lunches try the restaurants on the upper floor of the Recova market. The quality of restaurants, especially on Av del Mar, varies considerably; often many dishes on the menu are not available

Ciro's, Av de Aguirre 431, T213482. Old-fashioned, good lunch. Recommended. *El Cedro*, Prat 572. Arab cuisine, expensive. *La Mía Pizza*, O'Higgins 460. Italian, good value, inexpensive (branch on Av del Mar in summer). *Pastissima Limitado*, O'Higgins 663. Wide variety of pizzas, delicious pancakes, not cheap, live music and dancing at weekends. *Mai Lai Fan*, Cordóvez 740. Good Chinese, reasonably priced. *Club Social*, Córdovez 516, 1 piso. Unpretentious but excellent value. *El Minero*, Cienfuegos 360. Good fish, seafood, good value, friendly. Recommended. *D'Carlo*, Córdovez 516. Good fish, seafood, reasonably priced, good value *almuerzo*. *Donde El Guatón*, Brasil 750. Parrillada, paradise for meat eaters, expensive. *Taiwan*, Cantournet 844. Cantonese, good quality, reasonably priced. *Qahlúa*, Balmaceda 655. Good fish, seafood, popular, cheap. *Plaza Royal*, Prat 465. Light meals and snacks, pleasant. Recommended. *Bravissimo*, Balmaceda 545. Ice cream palace. *Bavaria*, E de la Barra 489. International menu. *Diavoletto*, Prat 565 and O'Higgins 531. Fast food, popular.

Cafés & bars *Café do Brasil*, Balmaceda 461. Good coffee. *Bocaccio*, Prat y Balmaceda. Good cakes, modern, smart, popular. *Café del Patio*, Prat 470, café, bar with pub (Tijuana Blues) from 2100 with live music to the early hours. On Saturday, offers The Beatles Club from 2300. Also tour agency, (see below). *Taverna Afro Son*, Balmaceda 824. Good food, drink, late night live music. Recommended. Good meeting place. *VIP*, E de la Barra 649. Popular night spot, intimate atmosphere. *Tahiti*, Córdovez 540, local 113. Real coffee, pastries. Recommended.

Entertainment **Cinema** *Cine Centenario*, Córdovez 399.
Discotheque *Pub-Discosalsa Katango*, Balmaceda 679. *Kamikaze*, Av del Mar y 4 Esquinas. (Summer only.)

Sports *Gimnasio GFU*, Amunátegui 426, T222420. *Vitalia*, Córdovez 756, T221939.

Shopping *La Recova* handicraft market, though many items imported from Peru and Bolivia. *Cema-Chile*, Los Carrera 562. *Las Brisas* supermarket, Cienfuegos y Córdovez, open 0900-2200, very good. *Rendic* supermarket, Balmaceda 561. Open 0900-2300, good.

Transport **Local Buses**: city buses US$0.25. **Taxis** *Colectivos* operate on fixed routes throughout city. City taxis US$0.75 and US$0.20 every 200m. **Car hire**: *Hertz*, Av de Aguirre 0225, T225471/226171, prices range from US$65 to US$110 per day; *Budget*, Balmaceda 850, T248200; *Daire*, Prat 645, T226933, recommended, good service; *Avis*, Av de Aguirre 068, T/F227171; *La Florida*, at airport, T225015, F215135. Cheapest is *Gala*, Huanhuali 435, T221400. **Bicycle repairs**: *Mike's Bikes*, Av de Aguirre 004, T224454. Sales, hire, repairs, English spoken, helpful. **Motorcycle spares**: *Tonino Motos*, Balmaceda 1461, T223628

Long distance Air: Aeropuerto La Florida, 5 km east of the city, T223419. Ladeco flies to **San Juan**, Argentina; summer only. To **Santiago** and **Copiapó**, Lan Chile and Avant.

Bus: terminal, El Santo y Amunátegui (about 8 blocks south of the centre). Buses daily to **Santiago**, several companies, 7-8 hours, US$15-18 (Pullman Bus, *semi cama*, US$30); to **Arica**, US$30; to **Calama**, US$23, 16 hours; to **Vallenar**, 3 hours, US$5. **Valparaíso**, 7 hours, US$10; to **Caldera**, 7 hours, US$10; to **Antofagasta**, 11-12 hours, several companies, US$20 (Flota Barrios cama US$30), and to **Iquique**, 17 hours, US$25; semi-cama US$40 to **Vicuña**, Frontera Elqui, Colo Colo y Esmeralda, frequent service, 1 hour, US$2; also colective taxis from Domeyko y Balmaceda, US$2.50; to **Pisco Elqui**, Vía Elqui, 4 a day from terminal, US$3, but other services run along Av Amunátegui outside terminal; to **Coquimbo**, bus No 8 from Av Aguirre y Cienfuegos, US$0.30, every few minutes; also *colectivos* from Av de Aguirre y Balmaceda.

Airline offices *LanChile*, E de la Barra 435-A, T221531. *Ladeco*, Córdovez 484, T225753. *Avant*,   **Directory**
Córdovez 309, T219275/6, F217267.

    Banks *Corp Banca*, O'Higgins 529, Visa. ATMs at Banco Santander, Córdovez 351; Banco Sud Americano, Córdovez 699; Banco Santiago, Balmaceda 1015; Banco de Chile, Prat 481; Banco BHIF, Prat 528; Banco BCI, Prat 614; also at the Las Brisas supermarket. **Casas de Cambio**: *Cambio Galeria Córdovez*, *Córdovez 533*. *Viajes Val*, Balmaceda 460, oficina 2 (open Sat 1100-1400). *Intercam*, E de la Barra 435, Prat 515. Changes TCs, 3 casas de cambio in the Caracol Colonial, Balmaceda 460, including *Cambio Fides*. Good rates, changes TCs (*Gira Tour*, Prat 689, basement, building closed 1400-1600). If heading north note that La Serena is the last place to change TCs before Antofagasta.

    Communications Telecommunications: long distance calls from Cordóvez 446 and La Recova market. *Entel*, Prat 571. CTC administration on Plaza de Armas sells *Turistel*. **Internet access**: *Ingservitur* (address under **Tour companies** below). The Electric Net, Domeyko 560, T212224. Students may be albe to use the University system free of charge.

    Cultural centres *Instituto Chileno-Francés de Cultura*, Cienfuegas 632, T224993. Library, French courses, films etc. *Centro Latino-Americano de Arte y Cultura*, Balmaceda 824, T229344. Offers music and dance workshops, art gallery, handicraft workshops, also *Taverna Afro Son* (see under Bars). *Nueva Acropolis*, Benavente 692, T21214. Lectures, discussions, free entry.

    Laundry *Ro-Ma*, Los Carrera 654. *Laverap*, Av de Aguirre 447. *La Universal*, Balmaceda 851, also Av de Aguirre 411 and Colón 560. *Nevada*, Los Carrera y Av de Aguirre.

    Tour companies & travel agents *San Bartolmé*, Brasil 415, T/F221992. *Gira Tour*, Prat 689, T223535. *Valle Mar*, Los Carrera 594, T213784. *Talikay Adventure Expeditions* and *Inca Travel*, both at Café del Patio (address above), both offer a range of local tours including Valle del Elqui, also trekking and climbing. *Ingservitur*, Matta 611, T/F220165, ingsvtur@ctcreuna.cl. Guided tours to Valle del Encanto, Fray Jorge, Andacollo, Isla Chañaral, Valle del Elgui and to observatories. Approximate tour prices: Valle del Elgui US$33, Parque Nacional Fray Jorge US$35, Tongoy US$30, city tour US$13. *Intijalsu Tours* Matta 621, T/F217945, intijalsu@entelchile.net, www.intijalsu. cv.cl. Specially trained guides and telescopes in a mobile observatory.

    Tourist offices Main *Sernatur* office in Edificio de Servicios Públicos (next to the Post Office on the Plaza de Armas), T225138. Open Mon-Fri 0900-1300, 1500-1730 (0830-1800 in summer). Kiosks at bus terminal (summer only) and at Balmaceda y Prat (open in theory Mon-Sat 1100-1400, 1600-1900), helpful. *Automóvil Club de Chile*, E de la Barra 435, T225279.

Observatories

The clear skies and dry atmosphere of the valleys around La Serena have led to the area becoming one of the astronomical centres of the world (see box page 156). There are four observatories. Travel agents in La Serena and Coquimbo including Ingservitur, Gira Tour and Turismo Cristóbal, receive tickets from the observatories and arrange tours to two of them, El Tololo and La Silla (to El Tololo US$22 per person), though you will need to reserve in advance, up to three to four months in holiday periods. If you can arrange tickets directly with the observatory, taxi drivers will provide transport; one recommended as cheap and good is Cecilia Cruz, T222529 (mobile 09-5510579), US$63 to La Silla.

The clear skies of northern Chile

Astronomy favours clear skies and remoteness from sources of dust or artificial light and northern Chile, with its large expanses of uninhabited desert and its dry atmosphere, has become one of the great astronomical centres of the world. In the Elqui valley alone there are no fewer than four observatories, one of them purposely built for visitors to the region. The other three were built by international organizations with important backing from Europe or the US. One, La Silla, is owned by European Southern Observatory (ESO), which is financed by the governments of Belgium, Denmark, France, Germany, Italy, The Netherlands and Sweden. There is also a small Swiss telescope on the site. The other two are El Tololo, which belongs to a consortium of US and Chilean universities, and Las Campanas, which is owned by the Carnegie Institute. All of these welcome visitors but visitors are not allowed to use the telescopes. For visitor arrangements see text. The fourth observatory, however, Mamalluca, financed partly by the Municipalidad de Vicuña and built specifically for the public, offers night-time visits and provides an opportunity to view the southern skies from the vantage point of the Elqui Valley.

Away from the Elqui the great powers of the world of astronomy continue to expand their operations in northern Chile. A new observatory was opened by ESO in March 1999 at Cerro Paranal, 120 kilometres south of Antofagasta: it includes what is claimed to be the most powerful telescope in the world, with a power equivalent to a normal telescope with a diameter of 200 metres, and capable of seeing items on the moon as small as one metre long. However, planning is now under way on an even larger project at Chajnantor, over 5,000 metres up in the Andes; this giant observatory, to include over 100 radio telescopes, is being financed by ESO along with the governments of the UK, the US and Japan.

These new developments are not without controversy, however. Construction of Cerro Paranal was held up by local landowners, who refused to renounce rights to permit mining activity on their land (which would threaten the observatory with increased dust). Eventually this forced the Chilean government to introduce new legislation to permit it to buy out the landowners.

With grateful thanks to Gerry Gilmour, Institute of Astronomy, University of Cambridge.

El Tololo Situated at 2,200 metres, 87 kilometres southeast of La Serena in the Elqui valley, 51 kilometres south of Vicuña, this belongs to Aura, an association of US and Chilean universities. It possesses the largest telescope in the southern hemisphere (diameter four metres), six others and a radio telescope. ■ *Open to visitors by permit only every Saturday 0900-1200, 1300-1600; for permits (free) write to Casilla 603, La Serena, T051-225-415, then pick your permit up before 1200 on the day before (the office is at Colina Los Pinos, on a hill behind the new University – personal applications can be made here for all three observatories). During holiday periods apply well in advance; at other times it is worth trying for a cancellation the day before. They will insist that you have private transport; you can hire a taxi, US\$33, but you will require the registration number when you book. Motorcycles are, apparently, not permitted to use the access road*

La Silla Located at 2,400 metres, 156 kilometres northeast of La Serena, this belongs to ESO (European Southern Observatory), financed by eight EU countries, and comprises 14 telescopes. ■ *Open Saturdays except in July and August, 1430-1730. Registration in advance in Santiago essential (Alonso de Córdoba 3107, Santiago, T2285006/6988757) or write to Casilla 567, La Serena, T224527. Getting there: from La Serena it is 120 kilometres north along Route 5 to the turn-off (**D** Posada La Frontera, cabañas), then another 36 kilometres.*

Pisco

The national strong spirit of Chile is pisco, a liquor made from grapes and known until the late 19th century as aguardiente de vino. Under a law of 1985 defining its demarcation, the term pisco is reserved for a spirit produced and bottled in regions III and IV and made entirely by the distillation of wine grown in these regions. Although the Elqui Valley is the heartland of the pisco industry, the climate and soil being ideally suited to the cultivation of grapes with a high sugar-content, vines for pisco are grown in the valleys of rivers throughout these two Regions, from the Río Copiapó in the north to the Río Choapa in the south.

After crushing and pressing, the juice is fermented and then distilled, before being aged four to 12 months in large oak barrels, stronger spirits spending more time in the wood: it is then diluted with water to the appropriate strength. There are four grades of strength: selección (30°); especial (35°); reservado (40°) and gran pisco (43°).

The grapes for pisco are grown by small holders, who, until the 1930s, sold their grapes to a number of private distilleries: dissatisfaction among the smallholders led to the establishment in 1931 of a co-operative, Control (full name Co-operativa Agrícola Control de Elqui Limitada) with modern equipment. Other groups of small-holders followed suit, setting up their own co-operatives are responsible for distilling 95% of all pisco: Control, based in La Serena, has 700 members; Capel (Co-operativa Agricola Pisquera de Elqui Limitada), which was established in 1942, and has 1,300 members.

Las Campanas This observatory is at 2,510 metres, 162 kilometres northeast of La Serena, 30 kilometres north of La Silla. Belonging to the Carnegie Institute, it has five telescopes and is altogether a smaller facility than the other two. ■ *Open every Saturday 1430-1730. For permit, write to Casilla 601, La Serena, T224680. Getting there: follow Route 5 to the same junction as for La Silla, take the turning for La Silla and then turn north after 14 kilometres. La Silla and Las Campanas can be reached without private transport by taking any bus towards Vallenar (two hours, US$4) getting out at the junction (desvío) and hitching from there.*

Mamalluca Situated at 1,500 metres, six kilometres north of Vicuña, this new observatory was built specifically for the public. The first telescope, diameter 30 centimetres, was donated by El Tololo. There is a multimedia centre and cafeteria. Visits daily at 2000, 2200 and 2400, US$6 plus transport US$4 per person. Booking from the office at Gabriela Mistral 260, T411352, obser_mamalluca @yahoo.com. Advance booking strongly recommended.

Vicuña and the Upper Elqui Valley

The valley of the Río Elqui is one of the most attractive oases in this part of northern Chile. There are mines, orchards, orange groves and vineyards. The road up the valley is paved as far as Varillar, 24 kilometres beyond Vicuña, the capital of the valley. Except for Vicuña, most of the tiny towns have but a single street.

The Elqui valley is the centre of pisco production: of the nine distilleries in the valley, the largest is Capel in Vicuña. Huancara, a delicious liqueur introduced by the Jesuits, is also produced in the valley. The Río Elqui is being dammed just east of the village of **El Molle**, 30 kilometres east of La Serena. When complete this project will force the relocation of five small towns in the valley.

Vicuña

Population: 7,716
Altitude: 610m
Phone code: 051
Colour map 2, grid C2

Sixty six kilometres east of La Serena, this small, clean, friendly, picturesque town was founded in 1821. On the west side of the plaza is the Municipalidad, built in 1826 and topped in 1905 by a medieval-German-style tower – the Torre Bauer – prefabricated in Germany and imported by the German-born mayor of the time. Inside the Municipalidad is a gallery of past local dignitaries. Also on the plaza are the Iglesia Parroquial, dating from 1860 and the tourist office. There are good views from Cerro La Virgen, north of town.

The distillery does not operate on Sundays

The **Capel Pisco** distillery is one and a half kilometres east, to the right of the main road; guided tours (in Spanish) are offered in December-February. ■ *Free. December-February, Monday-Saturday 0930-1200, 1430-1800, Sunday 1000-1230; March-November, Monday-Friday 0930-1200, 1430-1800, Saturday 1000-1230. No booking required.* Six kilometres north of Vicuña is the new observatory of Mamalluca; for details see above.

Museums Museo Gabriela Mistral is at Gabriela Mistral y Riquelme; next door is the house where the poet was born. ■ *US$1, students half price. Tuesday-Saturday 0900-1300, 1500-1900, Sunday 1000-1300.* **Museo Entomológico**, Calle Chacabuco, has over 3,000 insect species displayed. **Museo Histórico**, Prat, houses sections on Diáguita and Hispanic cultures. **Solar de los Madariaga**, Gabriela Mistral, is a former residence containing artefacts belonging to a prominent local family.

Sleeping
■ *on map*
Price codes:
see inside front cover

L3 *Hostería Vicuña*, Sgto Aldea 101, T411301, F411144. Swimming pool, tennis court, excellent restaurant. **A2** *Yunkai*, O'Higgins 72, T411195, F411593. *Cabañas* for 4/6 persons, pool, restaurant. **On Gabriela Mistral C** *Valle Hermoso*, No 706, T411206. Clean, comfortable, parking. Recommended. **D** *Sol del Valle*, at No 743. Hot water, TV, vineyard, restaurant. **E** *Hostal Mistral*, No 573. Large gardens, kitchen facilities. **E** *Res Moderna*, at No 718. Full board available, no hot water, nothing modern about it, but quiet, clean, very nice. **E** pp *Res Mistral*, at No 180. Restaurant, basic, hot water, clean. **D-E** *La Elquina*, O' Higgins 65, T411317. Lovely garden, laundry and kitchen facilities.

Vicuña

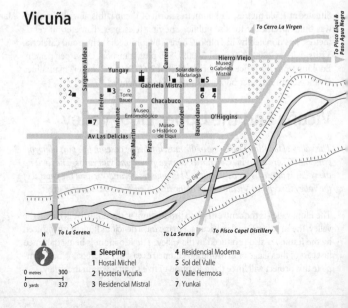

■ **Sleeping**
1 Hostal Michel
2 Hostería Vicuña
3 Residencial Mistral
4 Residencial Moderna
5 Sol del Valle
6 Valle Hermosa
7 Yunkai

0 metres 300
0 yards 327

Camping *Gabriela Mistral 152*, T09-4286158. US$4 per person, hot showers, kitchen. *Camping y Piscina Las Tinajas*, east end of Chacabuco, swimming pool, restaurant.

Mainly on Gabriela Mistral *Club Social de Elqui*, at No 435. Very good, attractive **Eating** patio, good value *almuerzo*, real coffee. *Mistral*, at No 180. Very good, popular with locals, good value *almuerzo*. *Halley*, at No 404. Good meat dishes, swimming pool (US$5 entry). *Yo Y Soledad*, No 364. Inexpensive, good value. *Pizzería Virgos*, on plaza.

Bus To **La Serena**, about 10 a day, most by Frontera Elqui, first 0800, last 1930, 1 hour, **Transport** US$2, *colectivo* from Plaza de Armas US$2.50; to **Santiago** via La Serena, Expreso Norte at 1145 and 2200; to **Pisco Elqui**, 4 a day, Vía Elqui and Frontera Elqui, 1 hour, US$2.

The Upper Elqui Valley

From Vicuña a *ripio* road runs south via Hurtado, Km 46, Pichasca, Km 85, and the Monumento Natural Pichasca to Ovalle, Km 120. The main road through the Elqui Valley continues east another 18 kilometres to **Rivadavia** where the ríos Turbio and Claro meet. Here the road divides, the main route (Route 41) winding through the mountains to the Argentine frontier at Agua Negra (see below). At Juntas there is a turning to Baños del Toro and the Mina el Indio, which can be visited only with a permit (obtainable from Compañía Minería del Indio, Baño Industrial Piñuelas, La Serena).

The other branch of the road runs through Paihuano (camping) to **Monte Grande**, where the schoolhouse that Gabriela Mistral lived and was educated by her sister is now a museum. The poet's tomb is situated one kilometre out of town. To get there, take a bus from the plaza in Vicuña. Here the road forks, one branch leading to El Colorado. Along this road are several Ashram places, some of which welcome visitors; camping allowed. **Pisco Elqui** (*Population*: 500) is situated two kilometres south of Monte Grande along the other branch of the road. It is an attractive town situated around a shady plaza with two *pisco* plants outside town. The one opposite the plaza offers free tours and tastings.

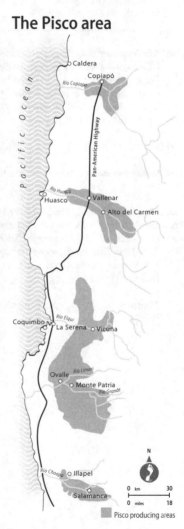

The Pisco area

From Santiago to La Serena

■ Pisco producing areas

The Elqui Valley in the words of its poet

"It is a heroic slash in the mass of mountains, but so short as to be little more than a green-banked torrent, yet small as it is one comes to love it as perfect. It contains in perfection all that man could ask of a land in which to live: light, water, wine and fruit. And what fruit! The tongue which has tasted the juice of its peaches and the mouth which has eaten of its purple figs will never seek sweetness elsewhere.

The people of the Elqui take remarkable pride in their green soil.

Whenever there is a hump, a ridge or bare patch without greenery, it is because it is naked rock. Wherever the Elquino has a little water and three inches of soil, however poor, he will cultivate something: peaches, vines or figs. That the leafy, polished vines climb only a little way up the mountainsides is because if they were planted higher, they would wither in the pitiless February sun."

Gabriela Mistral, quoted in Jan Reed, The Wines of Chile, Mitchell Beazley, 1994.

Sleeping **B** *El Tesoro del Elqui*, T/F228474. *Cabañas*, pleasant gardens, German spoken. **C** *Carillón*, A Prat s/n. Pool, also cabanas (**B**). **E** *El Elqui*. Hot shower, good restaurant. Recommended. Not always open. **E** pp *Hostería de Don Juan*. With breakfast, fine views, noisy. **Camping** *Sol de Barbosa*, T451102, **F** per site. Showers, open all year. **G** pp. *El Olivo*, T451970. Small restaurant, pool, excellent facilities. Well-stocked supermarket 1 block from the plaza.

Transport Buses to La Serena, US$3, 6 a day, via Vicuña.

Directory **Useful information** *CODEFF*, the environmental organization, has an office on the outskirts of town.

Frontier with Argentina: Paso Agua Negra Paso Agua Negra (4,775m) is reached by unpaved road from Rivadavia, 18 kilometres east of Vicuña. Chilean immigration and customs are at Juntas, 84 kilometres west of the frontier, 88 kilometres east of Vicuña. They are open 0800-1700. There is basic accommodation at Huanta (Guanta on many maps) Km 46 from Vicuña, **G**, clean, ask for Guillermo Aliaga. Huanta is the last chance to buy food.

Transport No public transport beyond Rivadavia. El Indio mine transport may give lifts to Juntas.

North of La Serena

This is a region of oasis towns separated by large expanses of desert and semidesert. From La Serena, the semidesert stretches north as far as the mining and agroindustrial centre of Copiapó, north of which the Atacama Desert begins. The main population centres are in the valleys of the ríos Huasco, Copiapó and Salado which are oases of olives and vineyards, but the most important economic activity is mining, especially around Vallenar and inland at El Salvador.

Though much of this region appears lifeless and of limited interest to visitors, the area around Vallenar is famous for the flowering of the desert following the rare occasions on which there is heavy rainfall. There are three national parks; two, the Reserva Nacional Pingüino de Humboldt and the Parque Nacional Pan de Azúcar, protect areas which are home to a wide range of marine life; the third, the Parque Nacional Tres Cruces, covers extensive areas of salt flats northeast of Copiapó. East of the Parque Nacional Tres Cruces is the Paso San Francisco, one of the highest crossings to Argentina; near the pass are some of the highest peaks in the Andes, though most are best tackled from Argentina.

Background

History

Although small groups of Spanish settlers took over the fertile lands in the Huasco and Copiapó valleys in the 16th century, no towns were founded in this area until late in the colonial period. Even the valleys were sparsely populated until the 19th century when the development of mining led to the creation of the ports of Caldera, Chañaral and Huasco, and encouraged the building of railways between the mines and the ports.

Geography

This part of the country can be divided into two: between the Río Elqui and the Río Copiapó the transitional zone continues; north of the Copiapó the Atacama desert begins. East of Copiapó the Andes divide: between the eastern range (Cordillera de Claudio Gay) and the western range (Cordillera de Domeyko) is a basin which collects the waters from the Andes but allows no escape. Here there are salt flats, the most extensive being the Salar de Pedernales. The eastern range rises to some of the highest peaks in Chile: Ojos del Salado (6,879 metres/6,864 metres – see page 171), Incahuasi (6,610 metres), Tres Cruces (6,330 metres) and San Francisco (6,020 metres). The valleys of the three main rivers, the Ríos Huasco, Copiapó and Salado, form oases in this barren landscape.

Climate

On the coast temperatures are moderated by the sea and mist is common in the mornings. Inland temperatures are higher by day and cooler by night. Rainfall is sparse and occurs in winter only. Amounts decrease as you go north: average annual rainfall in Vallenar is 64 millimetres, while in Copiapó it is 28 millimetres. Drivers should beware of high winds and blowing sand north of Copiapó.

Economy

Mining is a major economic activity: one of the largest state-owned **copper mines** is at El Salvador and over 50 percent of all Chilean iron ore is mined around Vallenar. Other minerals include gold and silver. Agriculture is mainly limited to the river valleys; the Copiapó valley is an important producer of grapes, while the lower Huasco valley is Chile's biggest olive-growing area. Fishing, centred on Caldera, and on a smaller scale, Chañaral and Huasco, is also important.

The Huasco Valley

This valley is an oasis of olive groves and vineyards. It is rugged and spectacular, dividing at Alto del Carmen, 30 kilometres east of Vallenar, into the Carmen and Tránsito valleys. There are pisco distilleries at Alto del Carmen and San Félix, which has a basic residencial. A sweet wine known as Pajarete is also produced.

Vallenar

The chief town of the Huasco valley, Vallenar was founded in 1789. Its original name was San Ambrosio de Ballenary to mark the birthplace of Ambrosio O'Higgins. The town is centred on a pleasant Plaza de Armas. **Museo del Huasco**, Sgto Aldea 742, contains historic photos and artefacts from the valley. Opposite is the northernmost Chilean palm in the country. ■ *Tuesday-Friday 1030-1230, 1530-1900; Saturday-Sunday 1000-1230, US$0.75.*

Population: 42,725
Altitude: 380m
Phone code: 051
194 km N of La Serena
Colour map 2, grid B2

North of La Serena

Excursions **Freirina**, 36 kilometres west, is easily reached by *colectivo*. Founded in 1752, Freirina was the most important town in the valley, its prosperity based upon the nearby Capote goldmine and on later discoveries of copper. On the main plaza are the Municipalidad (1870) and the Santa Rosa church (1869). There is no accommodation.

Reserva Nacional Pingüino de Humboldt on Isla Chañaral, has penguins, seals, sea lions, a great variety of seabirds and, offshore, a colony of grey dolphin. It is reached by following the Pan-American Highway to Domeyko, 51 kilometres south where an unpaved road turns west for Caleta Chañaral. Permission to visit must be sought from Conaf in Caleta Choros.

Sleeping
■ *on map*
Price codes:
see inside front cover

A2 *Hostería de Vallenar*, Ercilla 848, T614379. Excellent, pool, good breakfast, Hertz car hire office. **B** *Cecil*, Prat 1059, T614071. With bath and hot water, clean. Recommended. **B** *Hostal Camino del Rey*, Merced 943, T/F613184, clean. **C** *Vall*, Aconcagua 455, T611226. Parking. Recommended. **D** *Res La Oriental*, Serrano 720, T613889. Parking. Recommended. **D** *Viña del Mar*, Serrano 611, T611478. Clean, *comedor*, smoking disapproved of. There are several *residenciales*.

Eating *Bavaria*, restaurant. Serrano 802, cafetería, Santiago 678. Good, not cheap. *El Fogón*, Ramírez 944. For meat dishes, *almuerzo* good value. *Shanghai*, Ramírez 1267. *Pizza Il Boccato*, Plaza de Armas, good coffee, good food, not cheap. Chinese. Cheap places along south end of Av Brasil.

Transport **Bus** No bus terminal; services depart from company offices: Tur Bus, Merced 561. Pullman Bus, Serrano 551. Tas Choapa, Serrano 580. To Copiapó US$5, 2 hours; to Chañural, US$10, 5 hours.

Directory **Banks** *Corpbanca*, Prat 1070, with ATM. *Banco de Chile*, Prat 1010, with ATM. **Tourist office** Information from the Municipalidad on the Plaza de Armas.

Vallenar

To Copiapó & Route 5 North

Merced · Ramírez · Prat · Serrano · Faez · Sargento Aldea

Aconcagua · Vallejos · Ambrosio · Santiago · Brasil · Colchagua · Alonso de Ercilla · Verdaguer

Municipalidad

Pullman & Tas Choapa

Market

Museo del Huasco

To Huasco & Route 5 South to La Serena

N

0 metres 50
0 yards 55

■ **Sleeping**
1 Camino del Rey
2 Cecil
3 Hostería de Vallenar
4 Residencial Oriental
5 Vall
6 Viña del Mar

● **Eating**
1 Bavaria

The flowering of the desert

The average annual rainfall of this region declines as you travel northward: in Vallenar it is 65 mm, in Copiapó 20 mm. In most years the semidesert appears to support only bushes and cacti and these become sparser as you continue north. However, in years of heavier than usual winter rainfall, this semidesert breaks into colour as dormant seeds and bulbs germinate and produce blankets of flowers, while insects which normally hide underground emerge to enjoy the foliage.

The most recent years in which this 'flowering of the desert' (desierto florido) has occurred include 1983, 1987, 1991 and 1997. On the latter occasion a record 76 mm of rain fell in the space of 15 hours on 12 June; by July and August much of the region was covered with expanses of green; by September and October expanses of different colours could be seen in unexpected places.

Although the first traces of the desierto florido can be seen as far south as La Ligua and Los Molles, it is particularly worth seeing around Vallenar. From La Serena northwards, the Pan-American Highway is fringed with expanses of different colours: there are great stretches of violet Pata de Guanaco (Calandrinia longiscapa), yellow Corona del Fraile (Encelia canescens var oblongifolia) and blue Suspiro del Campo (Nolana paradoxa). Not all of these species can be seen at the same time: as the brief spring unfolds the colours change as new species push through to replace others.

Around Vallenar, however, the colours are more varied as different species compete to celebrate this infrequent coming of spring: the Pan-American Highway north of the city as far as Copiapó and the coastal road north of Huasco are both recommended for a prime view. For guided tours, contact Roberto Alegría, T613865, Vallenar. For information, contact the tourist office in Vallenar.

Situated at the mouth of the river, Huasco lies 56 kilometres west of Vallenar. West of the town is a terminal for loading iron ore from Algarrobal, 52 kilometres north of Vallenar. Destroyed by an earthquake in 1922, Huasco is a modern town with a large beach which is popular in summer.

Huasco
Population: 7,000

B *Hostería Huasco*, Craig y Carrera Pinto, T531026. **Camping** *Tres Playitas*, 12 km north along the coastal road. Also in Huasco near the post office, US$2 per site. *Restaurant Escorial*. Best. Cheap seafood restaurants near port.

Sleeping & eating

The Copiapó Valley

The valley of the Río Copiapó, generally regarded as the southern limit of the Atacama desert, is an oasis of farms, vineyards and orchards about 150 kilometres long.

Copiapó

The capital of Región III, Atacama, Copiapó lies 144 kilometres north of Vallenar, 60 kilometres inland. It is an important mining centre with a big mining school. Founded in 1744, Copiapó became a prosperous town after the discovery in 1832 of the third largest silver deposits in South America at Chañarcillo. The wealth from Chañarcillo formed the basis of the fortunes of several famous Chilean families and helped finance the first railway line in South America, linking Copiapó to Caldera (1851). There is a *Fiesta de la Candelaria* on the first Sunday in February

Population: 100,000
Altitude: 400m
Phone code: 052
Colour map 2, grid B2

North of La Serena

Sights Several of Copiapó's churches will appeal to lovers of religious architecture. The **Cathedral**, on Plaza Prat, dating from 1851, was designed by the William Rogers. **San Francisco**, five blocks west of the Plaza, built in 1872 (the nearby convent is from 1662), is a good example of a 19th century construction using *Pino Oregano* and Guayaquil cane. **Belén**, at Infante near Yerbas Buenas, a colonial Jesuit church, was remodelled in 1856. The **Santuario de la Candelaria**, three kilometres southeast of the centre, is the site of two churches, the older built in 1800, the other in 1922; inside the latter is the Virgen de la Candelaria, discovered in the Salar de Maricunga in 1788. The wealth of the 19th century mining families is reflected in the **Villa Viña de Cristo**, built in Italian renaissance style, 1½ kilometres north of the centre on Calle Freire. At Matta y O'Higgins there is a monument to Juan Godoy, the mule driver, who, in 1832, discovered silver at Chañarcillo. The Norris Brothers steam locomotive and carriages used in the inaugural journey between Copiapó and Caldera in 1851 can be seen at the Universidad de Atacama about two kilometres north of the centre on Calle Freire.

Museums **Museo Mineralógico**, Colipí y Rodríguez, one block east of Plaza Prat, is the best museum of its type in Chile. Many ores shown are found only in the Atacama desert. ■ *US$0.50. Monday-Friday 1000-1300, 1530-1900, Saturday 1000-1300.*.

Museo Regional del Atacama, Atacama y Rancagua, contains collections on local history, especially from the 19th century. ■ *US$1 (free on Sunday). Tuesday-Thursday 0900-1245, 1500-1915, Friday 0900-1245, 1500-1815, Saturday 1000-1245, 1500-1745, Sunday 1000-1245.*

Museo Ferroviario is in the old railway station on Calle Ramirez, west of the centre. It has photos and artefacts from the railway age.

Excursions **Centro Metalúrgico Incaico** is a largely reconstructed Inca bronze foundry, 90 kilometres up the Copiapó valley by paved road. There is no

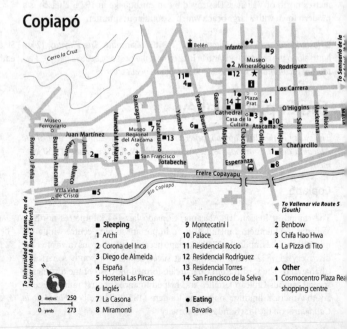

Copiapó

■ Sleeping
1 Archi
2 Corona del Inca
3 Diego de Almeida
4 España
5 Hostería Las Pircas
6 Inglés
7 La Casona
8 Miramonti
9 Montecatini I
10 Palace
11 Residencial Rocío
12 Residencial Rodríguez
13 Residencial Torres
14 San Francisco de la Selva

● Eating
1 Bavaria

2 Benbow
3 Chifa Hao Hwa
4 La Pizza di Tito

▲ Other
1 Cosmocentro Plaza Real shopping centre

The churches of Copiapó

The 'Age of Silver' which followed the discovery of Chañarcillo, has left an unmistakable if subtle mark on the architecture of Copiapó's churches. New building materials, brought in to build railway stations and bridges, were used on houses and churches. Chief among these materials was Pino Oregano: neither a pine nor from Oregon (it is native to northern California), it offered the size and strength of timber required for the new buildings. Guayaquil cane, a type of large diameter bamboo from the Ecuadorean coast, was also introduced: sliced lengthways and flattened, it made strips of light fibre which could be used to make thin walls. At the same time, builders and carpenters from Britain and the United States, attracted by

opportunies in railway and mine development, employed their skills on the new buildings of the city.

Church building in Copiapó was influenced by all these factors: architects such as the Englishman William Rogers designed churches which are generally recognized as reflecting English neoclassicism. Particularly noticeable is the design of the tower, positioned in the centre of the church and decorated with columns and wooden cornices. Built of wood and using strips of Guayaquil cane covered with clay, in an almost rainless climate, they have withstood earthquakes to become the oldest buildings in Copiapó.

accommodation in the nearby villages of Villa Hermoso, Las Juntas or Los Loros, which was the site of a clinic for pulmonary diseases at the beginning of the 20th century, attended by the rich from Santiago. ■ *Getting there: by public transport: take Casther bus, 0845, to Valle del Cerro, US$1.50, two hours and get off at Valle Hermoso (foundry is one kilometre walk from main road). Return buses pass about 1400 and 1600.*

South of Copiapó by 59 kilometres via the Pan-American Highway is a signpost for the turning to the silver mine of **Chañarcillo**, along a very poor road. Although the mine was closed in 1875, the tips are being reworked and this has destroyed much of the ruins.

L3 *Miramonti*, Freire 731, T/F210440. All facilities. **L3** *Hostería Las Pircas*, Copayapu 095, T213220, F211633. Bungalows, pool, good restaurant. **A1** *San Francisco de la Selva* Los Carrera 525, T217013, F213255. Modern cafetería/bar. **A2** *La Casona*, O'Higgins 150, T217278. Clean, friendly, tours organized. **A2** *Diego de Almeida*, Plaza Prat, T/F212075. Cable TV, good restaurant, spacious bar, pool. **A2** *Corona del Inca*, Las Heras 54, T217019, F213831. No restaurant. **A2** *Hostería Pan de Azúcar*, Freire 430, T212755, F217052. Pool **A3** *Palace*, Atacama 741, T212852. Comfortable, good breakfast, parking. **B** *El Sol*, Copiapó 550, T/F215672, with breakfast. **B** *España*, Yerbas Buenas 571, T/F217198. With breakfast. **B** *Inglés*, Atacama 337, T211286. Old-fashioned, spacious. **B** *Montecatini I*, Infante 766, T211363, F217021. Pool. **B** *Res Nuevo Chañarcillo*, Rodríguez 540, T212368. With bath, **C** without, comfortable. Recommended.

C *Res Chacabuco*, O'Higgins 921, T213428, with bath, **D** without. Near bus terminal, quiet, clean. **C** *Res Rocío*, Yerbas Buenas 581, T215360. With bath, **D** without, good value, clean, attractive patio. Recommended. **C** *Res Rodríguez*, Rodríguez 528, T212861. With bath, **D** without, basic, friendly, good *comedor*. Recommended. **D** *Archi*, Vallejos 111, T/F212983. Without bath. **D** *Res Torres*, Atacama 230, T219600. Without bath. Several cheap places, **E**, around local bus terminal.

Sleeping
■ on map
Price codes:
see inside front cover

North of La Serena

Eating
● on map page 168

La Carreta, Av Copayapu. Parrillada. expensive. *El Corsario*, Atacama 245. Good food in shaded patio, reasonably priced. Recommended. Several *chifas* (Chinese) including *Chifa Hao Hwa*, at Colipí 340 and Yerbas Buenas 334. *Benbow*, Rodríguez 543. Good value *almuerzo*, extensive menu. Recommended. *La Pizza di Tito*, Infante y Chacabuco. Pizzas with good fillings, sandwiches, not cheap. *Y Se Llama Perú*, O'Higgins 12. Genuine Peruvian cuisine, lively atmosphere, live music at night. Warmly recommended. *Willy Beer*, Maipú 386. Restaurant/bar, cheap *almuerzo*, popular with locals. *Bavaria*, Plaza Prat. Pricey restaurant upstairs, cafeteria downstairs (open 0800 for breakfast), salón de té around the corner in Los Carrera. *Tebuk*, in the Cosmocentro Plaza Real. Self service, good range, reasonably priced, good views overlooking Plaza Prat. On the northern outskirts: *Drive-In Esso*, pizzas, pastas, seafood, giant video screens, live music at weekends. Many cheap restaurants on Chacabuco around the local bus terminals.

Cafés *Café Haiti*, Cosmocentro Plaza Real 215. Real coffee, snacks, overlooks Plaza Prat, popular meeting place. *El Bramador*, Paseo Julio Aciares (part of Casa de la Cultura). Real coffee, good meeting place. Recommended.

Shopping

Cosmocentro Plaza Real, on the east side of Plaza Prat, with cafés and restaurants. On the ground floor is a good bookshop, *Andres Bello*.

Transport

Local Car hire: *Hertz*, Copayapu 173, T213522; *IQSA*, Copayapu 1233, T/F216926; *Avis*, Peña 102, T/F213966; *Budget*, Colipí 500, T218802 and at airport, T217355; *Flota Verschae*, Henriquez y Copayapu, T230012. **Cycle repairs**: *Bicicleteria Biman*, Las Carrera 998A, T217391. Sales, repairs, parts. Recommended.

Long distance Air: Chamonate Airport, 12 km north (taxi US$10). LanChile, daily to/from Santiago, also to El Salvador.

Buses: terminal 3 blocks southwest of centre on Freire y Chacabuco. To **Santiago** 12 hours; to **La Serena** 5 hours; to **Caldera** 1 hour; to **Antofagasta** US$16, 8 hours; to **Calama** US$22.

Directory

Airline offices *LanChile*, Colipí 526, T213512, airport T214360. *Ladeco*, Colipí 484, Loc 206-F, 2 piso, Cosmocentro Plaza Real. *Avant*, Colipi 510, T238926, F239546, airport T/F210481. **Banks** *Cambio Fides*, Atacama 541, Galeria Coimbra local 3, 2 piso. Mon-Fri 1000-1400, 1600-1900 (closed Sat/Sun). *Banco Concepción*. Cash advance on Visa. *Finandes*, Colipí 484. Mastercard agent. *Corp Banca*, Chacabuco 481. Visa agent. **Communications Post office:** O'Higgins 531. Open Mon-Fri 1000-1400, 1600-2000. **Telecommunications:** *Entel*, Colipí 484. *CTC*, O'Higgins 531. **Cultural centres** *Casa de la Cultura*, Plaza Prat. In a colonial-style mansion, with a gallery devoted to plastic arts; also organizes workshops. Film shows once a week. An annex houses the Café El Bramador, theatre productions and recitals. **Laundry** *Lavandería Añañucas*, Chañarcillo 612. **Tour companies & travel agents** *Azimut 360*, Arzobispo Casanova 3, Providencia, Santiago, T2-7358034, F7772375, azimut@reuna.cl, www.azimut.cl. Adventure and ecotourism, mountaineering expeditions to Ojos de Salado and Incahuasi. *Turismo Atacama*, Los Carrera 716, T/F212712. *Holovet Travel*, Infante 971, T/F217056. *Tursmo Cobre*, O'Higgins 640, T/F211072. **Tourist offices** Los Carrera 691, north side of Plaza de Armas, T212838. Helpful.

East of Copiapó to Paso San Francisco

The Argentine frontier can be crossed at Paso San Francisco (4,726 metres) which is situated just north of **Ojos del Salado**, considered to be the third highest peak in the Americas, see box. Its height is now thought to be 6,864 metres, though the Chilean IGM map gives its height as 6,879 metres. The pass can be reached from Copiapó by three roads, all poor *ripio*, and by a *ripio* road which runs south and east from Salvador. All these routes meet up near the Parque Nacional Tres Cruces (see below). The road from Salvador meets the

Climbing Ojos del Salado

Ojos del Salado is best climbed between January and March, though ascent is possible between November and April. In November, December and April it can be hit by the Invierno Boliviano, a particularly nasty weather pattern coming from the northeast. Temperatures have been known to drop to -40°C with high winds up to 150 kilometres per hour.

Access is by a road turning off the main Chile-Argentina road at Hostería Murray (burned down). Base camp for the climb is at the old Argentine frontier post (4,500 metres). There are two refugios: Refugio Atacama (four to six beds) at 5,200 metres and Refugio Tejos (better, 12 beds) at 5,700 metres. The spur to the former is not easy to find, but with a high clearance four-wheel drive vehicle you

can drive to the refugio. From the latter it is 10-12 hours climb to the summit, approx grade three. The climb is not very difficult, except the last 50 metres, which is moderate climbing on rock to the crater rim and summit. There is little or no snow: water is available at Hostería Murray but it may be advisable to carry it from Copiapó. Large quantities must be taken on the ascent. Guides and equipment can be hired in Copiapó: try Rubén E Rubilan Cortes, O'Higgins 330, T216535 and others (US$450-600).

Permits are required: obtainable free from the Dirección de Fronteras y Límites in Santiago (address page 24, or from the Municipalidad in Copiapó, which will fax Santiago).

North of La Serena

main road from Copiapó near the Salar de Maricunga, 96 kilometres east of Paso San Francisco. The other two routes from Copiapó are branches off the main one: the first forks off 10 kilometres east of the Pan-American Highway and runs south through the Quebrada San Miguel to reach the Laguna del Negro Francisco in the southernmost sector of the Parque Nacional Tres Cruces before turning north; the second runs through the Quebrada de Paipote and then through the northernmost sector of the park. Travellers taking either of these alternatives *en route* for Argentina will need to deviate north to pass through the Chilean immigration post at the Salar de Maricunga. Paso San Francisco lies 104 kilometres east of the Salar de Maricunga by a *ripio* road which runs along the southern shore of Laguna Verde, where there are thermal springs and a good campsite.

The route to Argentina via the Paso de San Francisco

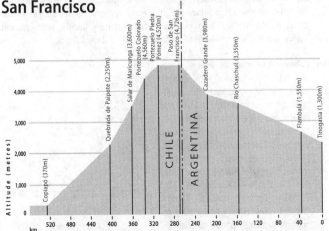

Parque Nacional Tres Cruces Extending over 59,082 hectares, this newly designated park is in three sectors: the largest part, the northern sector, includes Laguna Santa Rosa and parts of the Salar de Maricunga, an expanse of salt flats covering 8,300 hectares at 3,700 metres; the central sector includes Cerro Ciénaga Redondo (5,190 metres); the southernmost sector covers the area around Laguna del Negro Francisco, a salt lake covering 3,000 hectares at 4,200 metres. The lakes are home to some 47 bird species, including all three species of flamingos, as well as guanacos and vicuñas. There are two Conaf *refugios*, one southeast of Laguna Santa Rosa and the other southeast of Laguna del Negro Francisco. There are no public transport connections.

Frontier with Argentina

Paso San Francisco Although officially open all year, this crossing is liable to closure after snow in winter. On the Argentine side a poor road, described as "quite some washboard", continues to Tinogasta. It is suitable only for four-wheel drive vehicles.

Chilean immigration & customs Near the Salar de Maricunga, 100 km west of the frontier, open 0830-1830; US$2 per vehicle charge for crossing Saturday, Sunday and holidays.

North from Copiapó

There are two alternative routes north: west to Caldera and then north along the coast to Chañaral, 167 kilometres; and the inland route via Diego de Almagro and then west to meet the Pan-American Highway near Chañaral, 212 kilometres.

Caldera

Population: 12,000
Phone code: 052
Colour map 2, grid B2

Situated 73 kilometres northwest of Copiapó, Caldera is a port and terminal for the loading of iron ore. In the late 19th century it was a major railway engineering centre, but there are few reminders of this era; the **Iglesia de San Vicente** (1862) on the Plaza de Armas was built by English carpenters working for the railway company.

Bahía Inglesa, six kilometres south of Caldera and six kilometres west of the Pan-American Highway, is popular with Chileans for its beautiful white sandy beaches and unpolluted sea. It is very expensive and can get crowded January-February and at weekends. It was originally known as Puerto del Inglés after the visit in 1687 of the English pirate, Edward Davis.

Sleeping

Caldera A3 *Portal del Inca*, Carvallo 945, T315252. *Cabañas* with kitchen, English spoken, restaurant not bad, order breakfast on previous night. **A2** *Hostería Puerta del Sol*, Wheelwright 750, T315205. *Cabañas* with kitchen, view over bay. **B** *Costanera*, Wheelwright 543, T316007. Takes credit cards, simple rooms, friendly. **C** *Pucará*, Ossa Cerda 460, T315258. **B** *Res Fenicia*, Gallo 370, T315594. Eccentric owner. Recommended. **E** *Res Millaray*, Cousiño 331 on main plaza, friendly, good value, basic.

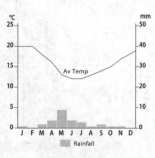

Climate: Caldera

Bahía Inglesa Very expensive in summer: cheaper to stay in Caldera. **A3** *El Coral*, Av El Morro, T315331. Also *cabañas* **C**. Overlooking sea, good seafood, open all year. **B** *Los Jardines de Bahía Inglesa*, Av Copiapó, T315359, *cabañas*. Open all year, good beds, comfortable. *Camping Bahía Inglesa*, Playa Las Machas, T315424, **B** per site. Fully equipped *cabañas* for up to 5 persons. **C** *cabañas*, Playo Paraíso, T315363, F315507, on beach, solar heating. Recommended.

Caldera *Miramar*, Gana 090, at pier. Good seafood. *El Pirón de Oro*, Cousiño 218. Good but not cheap. *Charles*, Ossa Cerda. Slow service, good seafood.   **Eating**

Bus To **Copiapó** (US$2) and **Santiago**, several daily; to **Antofagasta**, US$18, 7 hours;   **Transport** to travel north, it may be better to take a bus to **Chañaral** (Inca-bus US$2), then change. Hourly buses between Bahía Inglesa and Caldera, US$0.30; *colectivos* US$1.

The Salado Valley

The valley of the Río Salado, 130 kilometres long, is less fertile and prosperous than the Copiapó or Huasco valleys and is the last oasis south of Antofagasta.

Chañaral

This is a neglected looking town with wooden houses perched on the hillside. In its heyday it was the processing centre for ore from the nearby copper mines of El Salado and Las Animas, but it is now a base for visits to beaches and the Parque Nacional Pan de Azúcar.

*Population: 12,000
Phone code: 052
93 km N of Caldera
968 km N of Santiago.
Colour map 2, grid B2*

B *Hostería Chañaral*, Miller 268, T480055. Excellent restaurant. **C** *Mini*, San Martín   **Sleeping &** 528, T480079. Good value restaurant. **D** *Nuria*, Costanera 302. Good. **D** *Jiménez*,   **eating** Merino Jarpa 551. Without bath. Friendly, patio with lots of birds. Recommended. Restaurant good value. **E** *La Marina*, Merino Jarpa 562. Basic.
Rincón Porteño, Merino Jarpa 567. Good and inexpensive. *San Remo*, Torreblanca. Good seafood. *Restaurante de los Pescadores*, in La Caleta. Good fish, clean, cheap. Recommended.

Bus Terminal Merino Jarpa 854. Frequent services to **Antofagasta** US$14, 5 hours,   **Transport** and **Santiago**.

Banks Poor rates for cash. Nowhere to change TCs. **Tourist offices** Kiosk on the Pan-American   **Directory** Highway at south end of town (closed winter). Alternatively, try the Municipalidad.

Parque Nacional Pan de Azúcar

North of Chañaral is this park, consisting of the Isla Pan de Azúcar, home to Humboldt penguins and other sea birds, and some 43,700 hectares of coastal hills rising to 900 metres. There are beaches, which are popular at weekends in summer. A sea lion colony can be observed by following the signs marked 'loberas' from the park entrance. Fishermen near the Conaf office offer boat trips round Isla Pan de Azúcar to see the penguins, US$25, though these are sometimes visible from the mainland. **NB** There are fines for driving in 'restricted areas' of the park.

Wildlife Vegetation is mainly cacti, of which there are 26 species, nourished by frequent sea mists (*camanchaca*). After rain in some of the gullies there are tall alstroemerias of many colours. The park is home to 103 species of birds as well as guanaco and foxes.

Park essentials Two entrances: north by good secondary road from Chañaral, 28 km to Caleta Pan de Azúcar; from the Pan-American Highway 45 km north of Cañaral, along a side road 20 kilometres (road in parts deep sand and very rough, four-wheel drive essential). **Conaf** office in Caleta Pan de Azúcar, maps available; park entry US$6, camping, US$14, no showers, take all food (tap water is sold by the bottle).

Transport **Bus** Daily from opposite the library in Chañaral 0730; returns 1800, US$2.50, but check first. Taxi from Chañaral US$25, or hitch a lift from fishermen at sunrise.

El Salvador
Population: 10,437
Altitude: 2,300m
Phone code: 052
Colour map 2, grid A2

A modern town, built near one of the biggest copper mines in Chile, El Salvador lies 120 kilometres east of Chañaral in the valley of the Río Salado, reached by a road which branches off the Pan-American Highway 12 kilometres east of Chañaral. All along the valley there are people extracting metal ore from the water by building primitive settling tanks. Further east, 60 kilometres by unpaved road is the **Salar de Pedernales**, salt flats 20 kilometres in diameter and covering 30,000 hectares at an altitude of 3,350 metres where pink flamingoes can be seen. There is *Hostería El Salvador*, Potrerillos 003, T472492, *Camino del Inca*, El Tofo 333, T472311 and *Residencial Linari*, Potrerillos 705.

Transport **Air**: Lan Chile from Santiago and Copiapó. **Buses**: Pullman bus daily to Santiago.

Taltal

Population: 9,000
Phone code: 055
Colour map 2, grid A2

Situated 25 kilometres off the Pan-American Highway and 146 kilometres north of Chañaral, Taltal is the only town between Chañaral and Antofagasta, a distance of 420 kilometres. Along Avenida Prat are several wooden buildings dating from the late 19th century when Taltal prospered as a mineral port of 20,000 people, exporting nitrates from 21 mines in the area. The town is now a fishing port with a mineral processing plant. There is an archaeological museum on Avenida Prat. North by 72 kilometres is the Quebrada El Médano, a gorge with ancient rock-paintings along the upper valley walls.

Sleeping &
eating
B *Hostal del Mar*, Carrera 250, T611612, modern, comfortable. **C** *Hostería Taltal*, Esmeralda 671, T611173. Excellent restaurant, good value *almuerzo*. **C** *Verdy*, Ramírez 345, T611105. With bath. **E** without. Clean, spacious, restaurant. Recommended. Opposite is **E** *Taltal City*, Ramirez 348, T611440. Clean, without bath. **E** *San Martín*, Martínez 279, T611088, F268159. Without bath, good *almuerzo*. **E** *Viña del Mar*, Progreso 507.

Caverna, Martínez 247. Good seafood. *Club Social Taltal*, Torreblanca 162. Excellent, good value. The former club of the British community, with poker room, billiard table and ballroom.

Transport **Bus** To **Santiago** 2 a day; to **Antofagasta** Tramaca, Tur Bus and Ramos, US$5. There are many more bus services from the Pan-American Highway (taxi US$8). **Air** There is an airport, but few flights.

North of La Serena

Antofagasta, Calama and San Pedro

7

Antofagasta, Calama and San Pedro

Both Antofagasta, the largest city in northern Chile, and Calama are service centres for the mining industry which dominates this region. Both are visited mainly as stopover points. Calama is the departure point for the sole remaining passenger train service in northern Chile, to Uyuni and Oruro in Bolivia. The most popular destination in this region is, however, San Pedro de Atacama, the centre for excursions to spectacular desert landscapes such as the Valle de la Luna and the Salar de Atacama, as well as to the El Tatio Geysers. Excursions can also be made over the frontier into Bolivia to the Salar de Uyuni and to two beautiful lakes, Laguna Colorada and Laguna Verde.

Background

History

The area around San Pedro de Atacama was one of centres of the Atacameño culture, until the arrival of the Incas around 1450. After the expeditions of Diego de Almagro in 1536 and Pedro de Valdivia in 1540, the early Spanish presence in this region was limited to the sharing out of productive lands among a few Spanish settlers and the foundation of a mission in San Pedro. By the end of the colonial era the Spanish had established urban settlements only in San Pedro and Chiu Chiu. By independence most of the region became part of Bolivia, though the frontier with Chile was ill-defined. Before the War of the Pacific deprived her of this coastal territory, Bolivia formally established several towns along the coast, notably Cobija (1825), Mejillones (1841), Tocopilla (1843) and Antofagasta (1872). Nevertheless, by 1875 the total population of

Antofagasta, Calama & San Pedro

the region was under 10,000. After the War of the Pacific the territory passed to Chile; the exploitation of nitrates led to a population increase, construction of railways and ports and Antofagasta's growth into one of Chile's most important cities.

Geography

The Atacama Desert stretches 1,255 kilometres north from the Río Copiapó to the Chilean frontier with Peru. The Cordillera de la Costa, at its highest in this region (the highest peak is Cerro Vicuña, 3,114 metres), runs close to the coast, an inhospitable pink cliff face rising to a height from 600 metres to 900 metres. Below this cliff, on the edge of the Pacific is a ledge on which are situated the city of Antofagasta, several smaller towns and a road connecting them. In the eastern branch of the Andes several peaks rise to around 6,000 metres: Llullaillaco (6,739 metres), Socompa (6,051 metres), Licancábur (5,916 metres), Ollagüe (5,863 metres). The western branch of the Andes ends near Calama. In between these two ranges the Andean Depression includes several saltflats, including the Salar de Atacama and the smaller Salar de Ascotán.

Although there are small streams around San Pedro de Atacama, the only river in this part of Chile is the Río Loa, 440 kilometres long, the longest in the country. It has been dammed at Conchi to provide irrigation for several oases around Calama.

Climate

As elsewhere in northern Chile, there are major differences between the climate of the coast and that of the interior. The coast is frequently humid and cloudy; *camanchaca*, a heavy sea mist caused by the cold water of the Humboldt current, is common in the morning. In the interior the skies are clear day and night. The temperatures on the coast are fairly uniform; in the interior there is often a great difference in the temperature between day and night; the winter nights are often as cold as -10°C. Strong winds, lasting for up to a week, are common in the interior, especially, it is said, around the full moon. Between December and March there are often violent storms of rain, snow and hail in the highlands, a phenomenon known as *invierno altiplánico* (highland winter) or *invierno boliviano* (Bolivian winter).

Antofagasta, Calama & San Pedro

Nitrates

The rise and fall of the nitrate industry played an important part in opening up the northern desert areas between Iquique and Antofagasta to human settlement. In the second half of the 19th century, nitrates became important in Europe and the US as an artificial fertilizer and for making explosives. The world's only known deposits of nitrates were in the Atacama desert provinces of Antofagasta in Bolivia and Tarapacá in Peru. After the War of the Pacific, Chile gained control of all the nitrate fields, giving her a monopoly over world supply. Ownership was dominated by the British who controlled 60 percent of the industry by 1900. Taxes on the export of nitrates provided Chilean governments with around half their income for the next 40 years.

The processing of nitrates was labour intensive: at its height over 60,000 workers were employed. Using a combination of dynamite and manual labour, the workers dug the nitrate ore from the desert floor. It was then transported to nitrate plants known as oficinas, *crushed and mixed with water, allowing pure nitrates to be extracted. The mining and refining*

processes were dangerous and cost many lives, but wages were relatively high. Everything had to be brought in from outside the region, including food which was sold at the company stores using special tokens with which the workers were paid.

The development of the Haber-Bosch process, a method of producing artificial nitrates in Germany during the First World War, dealt a severe blow to the nitrate companies and many mines closed in the 1920s. New techniques were introduced by the Guggenheim company, but the world depression after 1929 led to the collapse of demand for nitrates and with it the Chilean nitrate industry. Only one mine survives today, at María Elena. Traces of the nitrate era can, however, still be seen: the mining ghost towns of Humberstone, near Iquique, and Chacabuco, north of Antofagasta, can be visited as can Baquedano, the most important junction of the nitrate railways; most of the other oficinas *are marked only by piles of rubble at the roadsides north of Antofagasta.*

Economy

Mining is the most important economic activity. The region includes large copper mines at Chuquicamata, Mantas Blancas, Escondida and La Exótica as well as new reserves at Zaldívar and El Abra and smaller-scale operations along the road between Antofagasta and Tocopilla. María Elena produce nitrates and iodine from the Salar del Miraje, while the Salar de Atacama and the Salar de Ascotán contain respectively the world's largest known deposits of lithium and borax. Fishing is a major industry: the three main ports are Antofagasta, Mejillones and Tocopilla; there are 24 fish processing plants. Other industries include the manufacture of explosives at Calama and cement at Antofagasta. Agricultural activity is limited by the lack of water and poor soils. Apart from tropical fruit production on the coast south of Antofagasta, agriculture is limited to inland areas around the Río Loa and its tributaries.

The main towns, Antofagasta and Calama, account for 87 percent of the population of the area, 98.8 percent of which is urban. Other urban centres are mining towns with few economic activities not associated with the mining companies. Life in the area is artificial. Water has to be piped for hundreds of kilometres to the cities and the mining towns from the Cordillera; all food and even all building materials have to be brought in from elsewhere.

Antofagasta

Situated on the edge of a bay, Antofagasta is the largest city in northern Chile and the fourth largest in the country. It is the capital of the Region II and is a major port for the export of copper from Chuquicamata. It is also an important commercial centre and home of two universities.

Population: 228,408
Phone code: 055
1,367 km N of Santiago
699 km S of Arica
Colour map 1, grid C1

Apart from the lack of rain, the climate is delightful; the temperature varies from 16°C in June and July to 24°C January and February, never falling below 10°C at night.

Although used as a port throughout the 1860s, Antofagasta's existence was not recognized by the Bolivian government until 1869, with the name Peñablanca. From a population at that time of about 300 it grew quickly as the terminal of the Antofagasta Nitrate and Railway Company, forerunner of the FCAB (see below).

Sights

In the main square, **Plaza Colón**, is a clock tower donated by the British community in 1910. It is a miniature of Big Ben with a carillion which produces similar sounds. Two blocks north of Plaza Colón, near the old port, is the former **Aduana**, built as the Bolivian customs house in Mejillones and moved to its current site after the War of the Pacific. Opposite are two other buildings, the former **Capitanía del Puerto** and the former **Resguardo Marítimo** (now housing DIGADER, the regional coordinating centre for sport and recreation). East of the port are the buildings of the **Antofagasta and Bolivia Railway Company** (FCAB) dating from the 1890s and beautifully restored, but still in use and difficult to visit. These include the former railway station, company offices and workers' housing. Just north of the port is the **Terminal de Pescadores**, where there are markets selling seafood, fruit and vegetables. Pelicans sit on the fish market roof and sea lions swim in the harbour. The former main plaza of the **Oficina Vergara**, a nitrate town built in 1919 and dismantled in 1978, can be seen in the campus of the University of Antofagasta, four kilometres south of the centre (bus 3 or 4). Also to the south on a hill (and reached by Bus B) are the ruins of **Huanchaca**, a Bolivian silver refinery built after 1868 and closed in 1903. From below, the ruins resemble a fortress rather than a factory.

Museo Regional de Antofagasta, in the former Aduana, Balmaceda y Bolívar, includes displays on the geology and natural history of the north, as well as sections on the War of the Pacific and the Nitrate Era. Explanations are in Spanish only. Recommended. ■ *US$1.20, children half-price. Tuesday-Saturday 1000-1300, 1530-1830, Sunday 1100-1400.*

Museums

Museo Geológico of the Universidad Católica del Norte, Av Angamos 0610, is inside the university campus. ■ *Free. Monday-Friday, 0830-1230, 1500-1800. Getting there: colectivo 3 or 33 from town centre.*

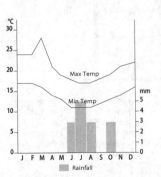

Climate: Antofagasta

Antofagasta centre

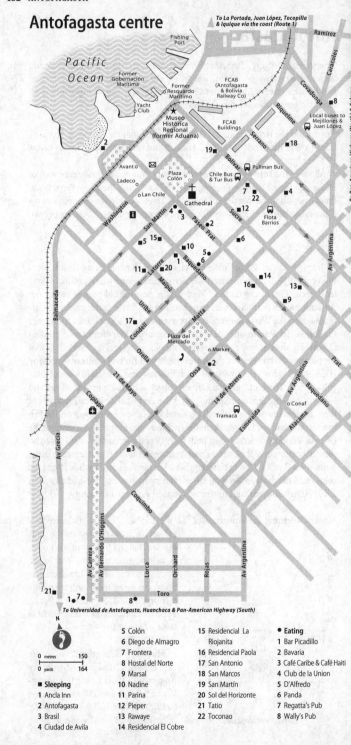

■ **Sleeping**
1 Ancla Inn
2 Antofagasta
3 Brasil
4 Ciudad de Avila

5 Colón
6 Diego de Almagro
7 Frontera
8 Hostal del Norte
9 Marsal
10 Nadine
11 Parina
12 Pieper
13 Rawaye
14 Residencial El Cobre

15 Residencial La Riojanita
16 Residencial Paola
17 San Antonio
18 San Marcos
19 San Martín
20 Sol del Horizonte
21 Tatio
22 Toconao

● **Eating**
1 Bar Picadillo
2 Bavaria
3 Café Caribe & Café Haiti
4 Club de la Union
5 D'Alfredo
6 Panda
7 Regatta's Pub
8 Wally's Pub

Excursions

La Portada, 16 kilometres north, has fantastic cliff formations which are the symbol of the Second Region. La Portada can be reached by minibuses from Latorre y Sucre (US$4 return) or any bus for Mejillones from the Terminal Centro. Taxis charge US$11. Hitching is easy. From the main road it is two kilometres to the beach which, though beautiful, is too dangerous for swimming. There is an excellent seafood restaurant, *La Portada*, and café, open lunchtime only. A number of bathing beaches are also within easy reach.

Juan López, 38 kilometres north of Antofagasta, is a windsurfers' paradise. The sea is alive with birds, including Humboldt penguins, especially opposite Isla Santa María. There are a couple of hotels: *La Rinconada*, T268502 and *Hostería Sandokan*, T692031. Buses go there at weekends in the summer only; there are also minibuses daily in summer from Latorre y Sucre. If you have your own transport, follow the road out of Juan López to the beautiful cove at Conchilla. Keep on the track to the end at Bolsico.

Baquedano, 72 kilometres northeast of Antofagasta on the Pan-American Highway), was formerly an important railway junction. Here you can see the old railway station, still used by goods trains, and a large and neglected collection of old and rusting locomotives with the grand title of Parque Histórico Ferrocarril. Take any bus heading north from Antofagasta, but you may have to hitch back.

Chacabuco, 30 kilometres north and just off the Pan-American Highway, is a large abandoned nitrate town, opened in 1924 and closed in 1938. Chacabuco was used as a concentration camp by the Pinochet government between 1973 and 1975. Workers' housing, the church, theatre, stores and the mineral plants can be visited. There is a free guided tour in Spanish. To get there, hitch or take a bus from Antofagasta towards Calama, get off at the Carmen Alto junction and walk the last four kilometres. **NB** It is essential to take water and set out early morning as you will probably be hitching back.

Essentials

L3 *Antofagasta*, Balmaceda 2575, T/F268259. Garage, pool, lovely view of port and city, good restaurant, with breakfast (discount for Automóvil Club members), beach.

A1 *Parina*, Maipú, T223354, F266396. Modern, comfortable, cable TV, restaurant, conference centre, good value. **A1** *Plaza*, Baquedano 461, T269046, F266803, pool, parking. **A2** *Ancla Inn*, Baquedano 508, T224814, F261551. TV, salon de té, pool, parking, recommended, exchange (see below), also has apartments. **A2** *Diego de Almagro*, Condell 2624, T268331, F251721. Good for the money but a bit tatty. **A2** *Nadine*, Baquedano 519, T227008, F265222. TV, bar, café, parking, etc. **A2** *Tatio*, Av Grecia 1000, T/F277602. Modern building, out of old town on the beach, good restaurant. **A3** *Marsal*, Prat 867, T268063, F221733. Modern, very comfortable, Catalan owner. Recommended. **A3** *Pieper*, Sucre 509, T266488, F266715. Clean, modern. Recommended. **A3** *San Martín*, San Martín 2781, T263503, F268159. With bath, TV, parking, clean, safe and friendly. **A3** *Sol del Horizonte*, Latorre 2450, T/F221886. Cable TV, bar, good value.

B *Colón*, San Martín 2434, T261851, F260872. With breakfast, quiet, clean. **B** *San Marcos*, Latorre 2946, T251763, F221492. Modern, comfortable, parking, avoid rooms at the back (loud music), overpriced. **C** *Brasil*, Ossa 1978, T267268. With bath, **D**

Sleeping
■ *on map*
Price codes:
see inside front cover
Cheap hotels are scarce and poor quality. The tourist office does not maintain a list of cheaper places

without, basic. **C *Ciudad de Avila***, Condell 2840, T/F221040. Very clean, TV, restaurant, excellent value. Warmly recommended. **C *Frontera***, Bolívar 558, T281219. With bath, **D** without, comfortable, good value. **C *Hostal del Norte***, Latorre 3162, T251265, F267161. With bath, **D** without, clean, comfortable, quiet. **C *Maykin***, Condell 3130, T/F259400, with bath, modern, helpful, good value. Recommended. **C *San Antonio***, Condell 2235, T268857. Clean, helpful, modern but noisy.

D *Res El Cobre*, Prat 749, T225162. Without bath, clean, dingy, unattractive. **C *Res Toconao***, Bolívar 580, T263449. Grim, overpriced. **E** pp ***Res Astor***, Condell 2955, basic, clean, parakeets which are noisy – avoid ground floor rooms. **E *Rawaye***, Sucre 762, T225399. Very basic, hot water morning only, no towels. **E *Res La Riojanita***, Baquedano 464, T226313. Basic, old-fashioned, hot water on demand, noisy.

Camping To the south on the road to Coloso are: *Las Garumas*, Km 9, T247763 ext 42. US$10 for tent (bargain for lower price out of season), US$22 for cabins (sleep 4); cold showers and beach (reservations Av Angamos 601, casilla 606); wild camping on the beach nearby. *Rucamóvil*, Km 10, T223929. Open year-round, expensive. To the north are: *La Gruta*, Km 12 and *La Rinconada*, Km 30, off road to Mejillones, between La Portada and Juan López, T261139.

Eating
● on map page 182

Club de la Unión, Prat 474, 2 piso. Excellent *almuerzo*, good service, traditional atmosphere. Recommended. ***Marina Club***, Av Ejército 0909. Good fish and seafood dishes and a view, expensive but worth it. ***Tío Jacinto***, Uribe 922. Friendly, good seafood. ***El Arriero***, Condell 2644. Good service, good set lunch otherwise pricey, live music. ***Bavaria***, Ossa 2428. Expensive restaurant with excellent meat and German specialities, cheaper cafetería downstairs, real coffee. ***D'Alfredo***, Condell 2539. Pizzas, good. ***Chicken's House Center***, Latorre 2660. Chicken, beef and daily specials, open till 2400. ***La Yugoslava***, Matta 2341. Fast food, cheap *almuerzo*, snacks. ***Limachino***, Latorre 2747. Cheap, popular with locals, welcoming, cheap *almuerzos*. ***Oliver Café Plaza***, Plaza Colón. Self-service, modern, reasonably priced. Recommended. ***Casa Vecchia***, O'Higgins 1456. Good value. ***Panda***, Condell y Baguedano. Self-service, eat all you can for US$8. Difficult to find coffee or breakfast before 0900. For real coffee: *Café Haiti*, in galeria at Prat 482. *Café Bahía*, Prat 474, and *Café Caribe*, Prat 482. Open 0900. Cafetería of *Hotel Nadine*, real coffee, pastries, ice cream. Recommended. Many eating places in the market; above the market are several good places selling seafood *almuerzos* including *El Mariscal* and *Toledo*. Good fish restaurants in *terminal pesquero centro* and at *Caleta Coloso*, 8 km south. *Chez Niko's*, Ossa 1951. Bakery, *pastelería*, good pizzas, *empanadas* and bread. *Pastelería La Palmera*, Ossa 2297. Good cakes, pastries, bread. *Chifa Pekín*, Ossa 2135, Chinese, smart, reasonable prices. *Rincón Oriental*, Washington 2432. Excellent Cantonese, pricey, 'over the top' jolly atmosphere.

Bars *Coco's Pub Bar*, Condell 2569. Open 2200-0600, giant video screen, live music, karaoke. *Bar Picadillo*, Av Grecia 1000. *Regatta's Pub*, Angamos 906. *Juan Sebastian Bar*, Balneario El Huascar. *Wally's Pub*, Toro 982. British expat-style with darts and beer, closed Sunday. *Castillo Pub*, Pasaje Carrera 884. Live music, good food with good value *almuerzo*, good fun. Recommended.

Entertainment **Discotheques** *Vox*, Comino y Coloso, popular. *Contutti*, Av Grecia 421. Latin rhythms. *Parador 63*, Baquedano 619. Disco, bar-restaurant, live shows, good value. *New Popo's*, *Extasis* and *Konigan's*, all on Av Ejército, on southern outskirts.

Theatre *Teatro Municipal*, Sucre y San Martín, T264919. Modern, state-of-the art. *Teatro Pedro de la Barra*, Condell 2495. Run by University of Antofagasta, regular programme of plays, reviews, concerts etc, high standard, details in press.

Swimming: *Balneario Municipal*, Av Ejército. **Sauna**: *Geyser*, Chillán 1245, T255278.
Genuine sauna plus Turkish bath, hydromasssage, health suite. **Tennis**: *Club de Tenis Antofagasta*, Av Angamos 906, T247756 for details of temporary membership.

29 June, **San Pedro**, patron saint of the fishermen: the saint's image is taken out by
launch to the breakwater to bless the first catch of the day. On the last weekend of
October, the foreign communities put on a joint festival on the seafront, with
national foods, dancing and music.

Galería de Arte Imagen, Uribe 485. Sells antiques including artefacts from nitrate
plants.
  Bookshops *Libreria Andres Bello*, Condell 2421. Excellent selection. *Librería
Universitaria*, Latorre 2515. Mainly technical books. Opposite is *Multilibro*, contemporary Latin American literature, also English language authors. Recommended.
  Market *Municipal market*, Matta y Uribe. Fish market is on Av Pinto. Next to it is
the Feria Modelo O'Higgins, which has excellent fruit and vegetables as well as restaurants. **Supermarkets** *Lider* on A Pinto, north of the fishing port; *Las Brisas*,
Baquedano 750, has an ATM. *Tricot*, Ossa 2450, has an ATM.

Local Car rental: *Avis*, Balmaceda 2499, T221073. *Budget*, Prat 206, T251745. *Hertz*,
Balmaceda 2492, T269043. Offer city cars and jeeps (group D, Toyota Landcruiser) and
do a special flat rate, with unlimited mileage. *Localiza*, Baguedano 300, T225370.
IQSA, Balmaceda 2575 (Hotel Antofagasta), T260177.
  Bicycle spares: Rodrigo Baez Banda, Condell 3071, also repairs. Cicles Miranda,
Matta 2795, T223867.
  Car mechanic: Andrés Ljubetic Romo, Atacama 2657, T268851. Recommended.

Long distance Air: Cerro Moreno Airport, 22 km north. Taxi to airport US$7, but
cheaper if ordered from hotel. LanChile Ladeco and Avant fly daily to Santiago,
Iquique and Arica.

Train: there are no passenger services from Antofagasta. The journey to Uyuni and
Oruro in Bolivia starts from Calama (see page 191) – tickets from Tramaca, Uribe 936
or in Calama.

Bus: buses for **Mejillones** and **Tocopilla**, operated by Barrios, Tramaca, Camus and oth- *No main terminal; each*
ers, depart from the Terminal Centro at Riquelme 513. Minibuses to Mejillones leave *company has its own*
from Latorre 2730. Bus company offices as follows: Tramaca, Uribe 936, T200124; Flota *office in town, quite*
Barrios, Condell 2782, T268559; Géminis, Latorre 3055, T251796; Fénix Pullman Norte, *some distance from the*
San Martín 2717, T263396; Incatur, Maipú 554; Turis Norte, Argentina 1155; Libac, *centre*
Argentina 1155; Pullman Bus, Latorre 2805, T262591; Chile-Bus (to Argentina and Brazil)
and Tur-Bus, Ramirez y Balmaceda, T266691. To **Santiago**, 18 hours (Flota Barrios,
US$60, *cama* including drinks and meals); 30% reduction on Inca, Tramaca, and
Géminis buses for students, but ask after you have secured a seat; many companies:
fares US$35-40, book 2 days in advance. If all seats to the capital are booked, catch a bus
to **La Serena** (11 hours, US$20, or US$33 semi cama), or **Ovalle**, US$20, and re-book. To
Valparaíso, US$35. To **Arica**, US$16 Tur-Bus, 13½ hours, Tramaca, US$18. To
Chuquicamata, US$6, frequent, 3 hours. To **Calama**, several companies, US$5, 3 hours;
to **San Pedro de Atacama**, Tur Bus direct service 0800, US$6, 4 hours or go via Calama;
to **Copiapó**, US$16; to **Iquique**, US$13, 8 hours, frequent.
  Buses to Salta and Argentina Tramaca, Wednesday 0700 via Calama, San
Pedro, Paso Sico and Jujuy US$52, student discount if you are persistent. Immigration
check at San Pedro de Atacama. Book in advance for this service, take food and as
much warm clothing as possible. There is nowhere to change Chilean pesos en route;

take small denomination dollar bills to use in Argentina. The service can be picked up in San Pedro, but book first in Calama or Antofagasta and notify bus company.

Hitchhiking If hitching to Arica or Iquique try at the beer factory a few blocks north of the fish market on Av Pinto, or the lorry park a few blocks further north. If hitching south go to the police checkpoint/restaurant/gas station La Negra, about 15 km south of the city.

Directory

Airline offices *LanChile*, Washington 2552, T265151, F222526. *Ladeco*, Washington 2589, T269170, airport T268830, F260440. *LAB*, San Martín 2399, T/F260618. *Avant*, Prat 230, T452055, F452056, airport T221059.

It is impossible to change TCs south of Antofagasta until you reach La Serena

Banks Major banks around Plaza Colón including *Corp Banca*, Visa agents. Banco Santiago and Banco BCI, all have ATMs. There are also ATMs at the Tricot and Las Brisas supermarkets. *Casas de Cambio*, Ancla, Baguedano 524. Open Mon-Fri 0900-1400, 1600-1900, Sat 0900-1400, poor rates (if closed try the ice cream shop next door). *AFEX*, Latorre 668. Open Mon-Fri 0830-2000, Sat 0830-1400, better rates for TCs than Ancla.

Communications Post Office: on Plaza Colón. 0830-1900, Sat 0900-1300. **Telephones:** *Entel Chile*, Baquedano, 753. *CTC*, Condell 2529. **Internet Access** Intitour (see below under **Tour companies**). Conecta Computación, Giacoman Galeria, Baquedano 498, oficina 22/23, conectacom@entelchile.net.

Consulates *Argentina*, M Verbal 1640, T222854. *Bolivia*, Prat 272, piso 5B, T225010. *France and Belgium*, Baquedano 299, T268669.

Cultural centres *Instituto Chileno-Norteamericano de Cultura*, Carrera 1445, T263520. *Instituto Chileno-Alemán de Cultura*, Bolívar 769, T225946. *Centro Cultural Nueva Acropolis*, Condell 2679, T222144. Talks on Wed 2100, also Tai Chi, yoga, archaeological and philosophical discussions.

Laundry *París*, Condell 2455. Laundry and dry cleaning, expensive, charges per item. *Laverap*, 14 Febrero 1802, efficient, not cheap. *Clean clothes*, G Lorca 271. *La Ideal*, Baguedano 660.

Tour companies & travel agents Many including *Intitour*, Baquedano 460, T266185, F260882, intitour@entelchile.net, English spoken. *Tatio Travel*, Washington 2513, T269144, F263532. English spoken, tours arranged for groups or individuals. Highly recommended. *Turismo Corssa*, San Martín 2781, T/F251190. Recommended. *Terra Expedition Tour*, Balmaceda 2575 (in Hotel Antofagasta), T/F223324. Alex Joseph Valenzuela Thompson, Atacama Wüstereisedienst, Apartado Postal 55, T243322, F259132. Offers to guide German speakers around the area.

Tourist offices Maipú 240, T264044. Mon-Fri 0830-1300, Mon-Thur 1500-1930, Fri 1500-1930, kiosk on Balmaceda near *Hotel Antofagasta* Mon-Fri 0930-1300, 1530-1930, Sat/Sun 0930-1300 kiosk at airport (open summer only). *Automóvil Club de Chile*, Condell 2330, T225332. **Customs agent:** Luis Piquimil Bravo, Sucre 363, oficina 28, T251789, F6385727. Excellent, fast service, efficient.

Mejillones

Population: 5,500
Phone code: 055
60 km N of Antofagasta
Colour map 1, grid C1

This little port stands on a good natural harbour protected from westerly gales by high hills. Until 1948 it was a major terminal for the export of tin and other metals from Bolivia. Remnants of that past include a number of fine wooden buildings: the Intendencia Municipal, the Casa Cultural, built in 1866, and the church, 1906, as well as the Capitanía del Puerto. Today the town lives mainly by fishing, coming alive in the evening when the fishermen prepare to set sail. The sea is very cold because of the Humboldt current. A Mediterranean-style tourist complex is planned for Mejillones Bay.

Sleeping & eating

A2 *Costa Del Sol*, M Montt 086, T621519, 4-star, new. **D** *Res Marcela*, Borgoño 150. With bath, pleasant. **F** *Res Elisabeth*, Alte Latorre 440, T621568. Friendly, basic, restaurant. No campsite, but wild camping possible on the beach.

Juanito, Las Heras 241. Excellent *almuerzo*. *Sion-Ji*, Alte Latorre 718. Chinese, good value.

Routes north from Antofagasta

There are two routes from Antofagasta north to Iquique.

Along the Pan-American Highway

The Highway continues north via Baquedano (Km 72) and Carmen Alto (Km 98), the turning to Calama. A turning 69 kilometres north of Carmen Alto leads to **Pedro de Valdivia**, a nitrate town abandoned in 1996, which has been declared a National Monument and can be visited.

From Pedro de Valdivia a road runs north, parallel to the Pan-American Highway, crossing the Salar del Mirage to **María Elena** (*Population*: 7,700; *Altitude*: 1,250 metres), the only nitrate town still functioning. The **Museo Arqueológico y Histórico** on the main plaza has exhibits on pre-hispanic cultures. ■ *US$1*. There is the run down **D** per person *Residencial Chacance*, T632749, but nicer clean rooms are around the corner; cheap meals at the *Casino Social*. Buses to Iquique take six hours, US$10.

Some 22 kilometres southeast of María Elena, part of the Pan-American Highway, is the Balneario Chacance, also known as the Parque El Loa, where bathing and camping are available on the banks of the Río Loa.

North of María Elena, the Pan-American Highway crosses the Tocopilla-Calama road 107 kilometres north of Alto Carmen. Fifteen kilometres further north there is accommodation at *Posada Los Arbolitos*, **E** per person, also *cabañas*, meals, no running water. At **Quillagua**, Km 81, there is a customs post where all vehicles heading south are searched. Situated 111 kilometres further north is the southernmost and largest section of the **Reserva Nacional Pampa del Tamarugal**; the other sections are further north, near La Tirana (see page 221) and 60 kilometres north of Pozo Almonte (see page 220).

In the southern section are the **Geoglifos de Pintados**, about 400 figures of humans, animals and geometric shapes on the hillside three kilometres west of the highway. North of the Reserve are Pozo Almonte and the turn-off for Iquique.

Along the coastal road

The coastal road, Route 1, is an attractive alternative to the Pan-American Highway. There is no fuel between Mejillones and Tocapilla. From Mejillones the road runs at the foot of 500 metre cliffs, behind which are mountains which are extensively mined for copper, often by *piquineros*, small groups of

Routes north from Antofagasta

Distance in km

self-employed miners. There are larger mines, with the biggest concentration inland of Michilla, 107 kilometres north.

Reminders of the area's mining past can be seen at several points, principally the ruins of **Cobija**, 127 kilometres north, founded by order of Simón Bolívar in 1825 as Bolivia's main port. A prosperous little town handling silver exports from Potosí, it was destroyed by an earthquake in 1868 and again by a tidal wave in 1877 before losing out to the rising port of Antofagasta. Adobe walls, the rubbish tip right above the sea and the wreckage of the port are all that remains. The haunting ruins of the port of Gatico are at Km 144. About four kilometres further north there is an amazing ransacked cemetery.

A very steep zigzag road winds up the cliffs to the mine at Mantos de la Luna about 152 kilometres north of Antofagasta. At the top there are rather dead-looking groves of giant cactus living off the sea mist which collects on the cliffs. Wildlife includes foxes, or *zorros*.

There are good, weekend beach resorts at Hornitos, 88 kilometres north of Antofagasta, and Poza Verde, 117 kilometres north.

Tocopilla
Population: 24,600
Phone code: 055
Colour map 1, grid C1

This town is 187 kilometres north of Antofagasta via the coast road, or 365 kilometres via the Pan-American Highway. It is dominated by a thermal power station, which supplies electricity to the whole of northern Chile, and by the port facilities used to unload coal and to export nitrates and iodine from María Elena and Pedro de Valdivia. There are two good beaches: Punta Blanca 12 kilometres south and Caleta Covadonga three kilometres south, which has a swimming pool. There is also fine deep sea fishing if you can find a boat and a guide.

Sleeping On 21 de Mayo: B *Atenas*, No 1448, T/F813650. Good restaurant, overpriced. **B** *Chungará*, No 1440, T811036. Overpriced. **B** *Vucina*, No 2069, T811571. Modern, good restaurant. **C** *Bolívar*, Bolívar 1332, T812783, **E** pp without bath. Modern, helpful. **C** *Casablanca*, No 2054, T813222, F813104. Friendly, helpful, good restaurant, good value. **C** *Hostal Sucre*, No 1329, T812783. **D** *Res Alvarez*, Serrano 1234, T811578. **E** *América*, Serrano 1243. Without bath, clean. **E** *Gran*, No 1460, T813175. Scruffy but clean, without bath.

Eating *Club de la Unión*, Prat 1354. Pleasant atmosphere. Good value *almuerzo*. *Bavaria*, Rodriguez 1280. Cafetería, fine sea views from veranda. *Luciano's Pizzas*, 21 de Mayo 1995. Fairly good. *Echikhouse*, 21 de Mayo 2132. Good value 4-course *almuerzo*. *Piero's Place*, 21 de Mayo 1395. Café-bar, lively, good music with video screen. Recommended. 2 Chinese restaurants: *Chifa Jok San*, 21 de Mayo 1488; *Chifa Ji Kong*, 21 de Mayo 1848. *Los Dos Leones*, 21 de Mayo 1993. Sandwiches, good value *almuerzo*, popular with locals. Good meals in restaurants of *Hotel Bolívar*, *Hotel Vucina* and *Hotel Casablanca*. Good seafood at La Caleta opposite the old wooden clock tower. At Caleta Covadonga: *Caleta Boy*, seafood. Recommended.

Transport Bus: To **Antofagasta** 8 a day, several companies including Barrrios, Tramaca and Tur-Bus, US$3, 2½ hours; to **Iquique**, by bus and minibus along coastal road, Barrios, Tramaca and Turisnorte, 4 hours, US$7, frequent. To **Chuquicamata** and **Calama**, Tur-Bus, 2 a day, 3 hours, US$5. No direct services to **Santiago**, go via Antofagasta or take Tramaca or Flota Barrios to Vallenar or La Serena and change. Bus company offices are on 21 de Mayo.

Routes north and east of Tocopilla

East of Tocopilla a good paved road climbs a narrow valley 72 kilometres to the Pan-American Highway. From here the road continues east across the Pan-American Highway to Chuquicamata: the first 62 kilometres east of the Pan-American Highway is in good condition, the last part is very poor.

The coastal road runs north from Tocopilla to Iquique, 244 kilometres, offering fantastic views of the rugged coastline and tiny fishing communities. The customs post at Chipana-Río Loa, Km 90, searches all southbound vehicles for duty-free goods; long delays. Basic accommodation is available at San Marcos, a fishing village, at Km 131. At Chanaballita, Km 184, there is a hotel, cabañas, camping, restaurant, shops. There are campsites at the former salt mining town of Guanillos, Km 126, Playa Peruana, Km 129 and Playa El Aguila, Km 160.

Calama

Calama lies in the oasis of the Río Loa. Initially a staging post on the silver route between Potosí and Cobija, it has grown in this century as a commercial and residential centre for nearby Chuquicamata. It is an expensive modern town. Although there is little to do, travellers en route to Bolivia may find it a useful point to stay for a day or two to get used to the altitude. It is the departure point for buses to San Pedro de Atacama and the weekly train to Bolivia.

Population: 106,970
Altitude: 2,265m
Phone code: 055
202 km NE of Antofagasta,
Colour map 1, grid C2

Calama can be reached from the north by Route 24, which is in poor condition, via Chuquicamata. Or, from the south, you can take the paved Route 25 leaving the Pan-American Highway 98 kilometres north of Antofagasta at Carmen Alto, which has petrol and food. This road passes many abandoned nitrate mines, or *oficinas*.

Sights

Two kilometres from the centre on Avenida B O'Higgins is the **Parque El Loa**, which contains a reconstruction of a typical colonial village built around a reduced-scale reproduction of Chiu Chiu church. ■ *1000-1800 daily*. Nearby in the park is the **Museo Arqueológico y Etnológico**, with an exhibition of pre-hispanic cultural history. ■ *Tuesday-Friday 1000-1330, 1430-1800, Saturday 1100-1830, Sunday 1530-1830. Getting there: colectivos 4, 5, 6 or 18 from the centre.*

Essentials

L2 *Lican Antai*, Ramírez 1937, T341621. With breakfast, good service and good restaurant, TV. Recommended. **L2** *Park*, Camino Aeropuerto 1392, T319900, F319901 (Santiago T233-8509). First class, pool, bar and restaurant. Recommended. **L3** *Hostería Calama*, Latorre 1521, T342817. Comfortable, good food and service. **L3** *Quitor*, Ramírez 2116, T341716. Good. **A1** *Alfa*, Sotomayor 2016, T342496. Comfortable. **A2** *Mirador*, Sotomayor 2064, T/F340329. With bath, **B** without, clean, helpful. Recommended. **A2** *Olimpo*, Santa Maria 1673, T342367. Good. **A3** *Casablanca*, Sotomayor 2160, T341938. Clean. **A3** *Res John Kenny*, Ecuador 1991, T341430. Modern, clean, friendly, parking.

C *Genesis*, Granaderos 2148, T342841, near Tramaca and Geminis bus terminals, clean. Recommended. **C** *Hostal Coco*, Sotomayor 2215, T310591. Clean, hospitable,

Sleeping
■ *on map page 190*
Price codes:
see inside front cover

with breakfast. **D** *El Loa*, Abaroa 1617, T341963. English spoken. **D** *Res Splendid*, Ramírez 1960, T341841, with bath, **D** without. Clean, hot water, good. **D** *Hostal Internacional*, Velázquez 1976, T342927. Overpriced. **D** *Res Casa de Huéspedes*, Sotomayor 2079. Poor beds, basic, clean, hot shower. **D** *San Sebastián*, Pinto 1902, T343810. With bath, good beds, meals available, family run.

E pp *Capri I*, Vivar 1639, T342870. Without bath, **D** with bath, basic. **E** pp *Capri 2*, Ramírez 1880. Basic, safe. **E** *Claris Loa*, Granaderos 1631, T311939. Clean, quiet. **E** *Los Andes*, Vivar 1920, T319079. Good beds, noisy. **E** pp *Palermo*, Sotomayor 1889, T341283. **E** pp *Hostal Valle de la Luna*, Sotomayor 2326, T342114, with breakfast.

Eating
● *on map*

Bavaria, Sotomayor 2095. Good expensive restaurant with cafetería downstairs, real coffee, open 0800, also at Latorre 1935. *Comedor Camarino*, Latorre 2033. *Lascar*, Ramirez 1917. Good value *almuerzo*. Recommended. *Mariscal JP*, Félix Hoyos 2127. Best seafood in town, not cheap. *Continental*, Vargas 2180. Good seafood and fish, cheaper but less charm. *Los Adobes de Balmaceda*, Balmaceda 1504. Parrillada, expensive. *Mexico*, Latorre 1986. Genuine Mexican cuisine, expensive, live music at weekends. *Nueva Victoria*, Vargas y Abaroa. Good inexpensive *almuerzos* and à la carte, popular with locals. Highly recommended. Several Chinese including *Nueva Chong Hua*, Albaroa 2006, good; *Canton*, Vargas 1925; *Jing Long*, Latorre 2005.

Calama centre

■ **Sleeping**	10 Hostería Calama	19 Universo
1 Alfa	11 Lican Antai	
2 Capri 1	12 Los Andes	● **Eating**
3 Capri 2	13 Mirador	1 Bavaria
4 Casablanca	14 Olimpo	2 Club Croata
5 Claris Loa	15 Quitor	3 Di Giorgio
6 El Loa	16 Residencial Casa de	4 Los Adobes de
7 Genesis	Huespedes	Balmaceda
8 Hostal Internacional	17 Residencial John Kenny	5 Mariscal JP
9 Hostal Valle de la Luna	18 Residencial Splendid	6 Tropicana

N

0 metres 100
0 yards 109

The slow train to Oruro

The line between Calama and Oruro in Bolivia is the only section of the old Antofagasta and Bolivia railway line still open to passenger trains. It is a long, slow journey, theoretically taking 36 hours (in reality often up to 48 hours), but it is well worthwhile for the scenery. The journey is very cold, both during the day and at night (-15°C). From Calama the line climbs to reach its highest point at Ascotán (3,960 metres); it then descends to 3,735 metres at Cebollar, skirting the Salar de Ascotán. Chilean customs are at Ollagüe, where there is a delay of five to six hours while an engine is sent from Uyuni. Immigration formalities are conducted on the train but passengers are required to disembark with their luggage, to be searched on the Bolivian side. There are money changers on the train but beware of forged notes. From the border the line runs to Uyuni, 174 kilometres northeast, crossing the Salar de Chiguana and running at an almost uniform height of 3,660 metres. Uyuni is the junction with the line south to the Argentine frontier at Villazón.

Tropicana, Sotomayor 2043. Good for fresh fruit juices. On the Plaza 23 de Marzo: *Club Croata*, excellent value 4-course *almuerzo*, good service; *Apumanque*, good 6-course *almuerzos*, opens 0900. Recommended; *D'Alfredo Pizzeria*, vast and uninviting but good pizzas and *almuerzos*; *Di Giorgio*; pizzas, good coffee, ice cream, opens 0900. Recommended.

Supermarkets *El Cid*, Vargas 1942; *El Cobre*, Vargas 2148. **Market** at Antofagasta between Latorre and Vivar. | **Shopping**

Local Car hire: *IQSA*, Abaroa 1484, T310281. *Localiza*, Mackenna 2279, T/F342143. *Hertz*, Latorre 1510, T341380; *Avis*, Gallo 1985A, T319797; *Maxso*, Abaroa 1930, T212194; *Budget*, Granaderos 2925, T341076 and at airport, T311325. A four-wheel drive jeep (necessary for the desert) costs US$87-118 a day. Rates are sometimes much lower at weekends. A hired car, shared between several people, is an economic alternative for visiting the Atacama region. | **Transport** *Car hire is not readily available in San Pedro de Atacama*
   Bicycle Spares *Cicles Miranda*, Sotomayor 2271, T342769.

Long distance Air: LanChile/Ladeco and Avant to Santiago via Antofagasta. Taxi to town US$6 (courtesy vans from hotels *Calama*, *Alfa* and *Lican Antai*).

Bus: No main terminal, buses leave from company offices: Tramaca, terminal at Granaderos 3048, T340404 (colectivo 14 from centre), office at Sotomayor 1961; Tur Bus, Ramirez y Balmaceda; Pullman Bus, Sotomayor 1808; Géminis, O'Higgins 078; Kenny Bus, Vivar 1954; Flota Barrios, Ramírez 2298 To **Santiago** 22-24 hours, US$35-40 (sálon cama US$70); to **Arica**, Tramaca overnight, US$16, 8 hours, or change in Antofagasta; to **Valparaíso/Viña del Mar**, US$35; to **Iquique**, 8 hours, US$15-20 semi-cama, overnight only. To **La Serena**, usually with delay in Antofagasta, 15 hours, US$30. To **Chuquicamata** (see below). To **San Pedro de Atacama** Tur Bus daily 1100, Frontera 6 a day, US$2.50, 1½ hours; to **Antofagasta**, 3 hours, several companies, for example Tramaca, hourly on the half-hour till 2130, US$6.
   To Argentina Tramaca services from Iquique and Antofagasta to **Salta** call at Calama, details above, book well in advance, US$50, 22 hours.

Train: To Uyuni and Oruro (Bolivia), weekly service, Wednesday 2300 (in theory), US$15 to Uyuni, US$20 to Oruro, journey time to Oruro up to 48 hours. Book seats in advance (passport essential) from railway station. Catch the train as early as possible: although seats are assigned, the designated carriages may not arrive; passengers try to occupy several seats to sleep on but will move if you politely show your ticket. Sleeping bag and/or blanket essential. Restaurant car and waiter service; food is also available at Ollagüe.

Remember that between October and March, Chilean time is 1 hour later than Bolivian

A freight train with 1 or 2 passenger cars attached leaves Calama for Ollagüe Saturday 2300, return departure unknown, check details beforehand, buy ticket a few hours before departure, US$5 one way, not crowded. Note that there is no connecting passenger train and riding on goods trains from Ollagüe into Bolivia is not allowed. No accommodation in Ollagüe.

Directory **Airline offices** *LanChile*, Latorre 1499, T341477/341494 and airport T311331. *Avant*, Cobija 2188, T343064/343066, F343070 and airport T342646. *Ladeco*, Ramírez 1858, T312626. **Banks** Rates are generally poor especially for TCs. *Corp Banca*, Sotomayor 2041. Visa, ATM. *Finandes*, Latorre 1763. Mastercard. **Casas de Cambio:** *Moon Valley Money Exchange*, Paseo Peatonal Local 12. Mon-Sat. Others on Sotomayor at Nos 1826, 1837, 1891, most open Sat. Try also shop at Ramírez 1434 and *La Media Luna* clothes store, Ramírez 1992 (poor rates). At weekends try Tramaca or Morales Moralitos bus offices or *farmacias* (poor rates). Poor rates for buying and selling Bolivian currency. **Communications** **Post Office:** Granaderos y V Mackenna. 0830-1300, 1530-1830, Sat 0900-1230, will not send parcels over 1 kg. **Telecommunications:** *CTC*, Sotomayor 1825. *Entel*, Sotomayor 2027. **Internet access:** *Centro Internet*, Vargas 2014, T/F310434. *Cybercafé*, Vargas 2014, piso 2, T318925, US$6/hour. **Consulates** *Bolivia*, Sr Reynaldo Urquizo Sosa, Bañados Espinoza 2232, Apdo Postal 85, T341976. Open (in theory only) 0900-1230 and 1530-1830, Mon-Fri, friendly, helpful. **Laundry** *París*, Vargas 2178. *Universal*, Antofagasta 1313 (cheapest). *Lavexpress*, Sotomayor 1887. Good, speedy. **Tour companies & travel agents** Several agencies run 1-day and longer tours to the Atacama region, including San Pedro; these are usually more expensive than tours from San Pedro and require a minimum number for the tour to go ahead. Reports of tour quality are mixed – poorly maintained vehicles and poor guides. Those with positive recommendations including: *Talikuna Explorer*, Gral Velázquez 1948, T342595. *Turismo El Sol*, Abaroa 1614, T340152. *Moon Valley*, Sotomayor 1814, T/F317456. Very helpful, excursions, cycle rental. *Turismo Tujina*, Ramirez 2222, T/F342790. Also *Azimut 360*, T/F333040, azimut@reuna.cl, www.azimut.cl. Tours to the Atacama desert, mountaineering expeditions to Licanábur and Llullaillaco. **Tourist offices** Latorre 1689, T345345/316400. Map of town, helpful. Open Mon-Fri 0900-1300, 1430-1900. *Automóvil Club de Chile*, Av Ecuador 1901, T/F342770.

Chuquicamata

Population: 13,000
Altitude: 2,800m
Phone code: 055
Colour map 1, grid C2

Sixteen kilometres north of Calama, Chuquicamata is a clean modern town serving the world's largest open-cast copper mine, employing 8,000 workers and operated by Codelco, the state copper corporation. Although copper has been mined here since pre-Inca times, it was the Guggenheim brothers who introduced modern mining and processing techniques after 1911 and made Chuquicamata into the most important single mine in Chile.

Everything about Chuquicamata is huge: the pit from which the ore is extracted is four kilometres long, two kilometres wide and 630 metres deep; the giant trucks, with wheels over three metres high, carry 255 ton loads and work 24 hours a day since the pit is floodlit at night. In other parts of the plant 60,000 tons of ore are processed a day. Although the ore extracted is low grade, refined copper of 99.98 percent purity is produced. Since 1986 output has been over 500,000 tonnes a year.

■ *Guided tours, by bus, in Spanish (also in English if enough people) leave from the office of Chuqui Ayuda (a local children's charity) near the entrance at the top end of the plaza, Monday-Friday 1000 (though less frequently in low season – tourist office in Calama has details), one hour, US$2.50; register at the office half an hour in advance; passport essential. No filming permitted. Although the tour gives you an idea of the scale of the mining operation, you are restricted to the bus and do not see any of the processes.*

Copper: Chilean red gold

Although copper was mined in Chile in pre-Inca times, it only became important after independence. For much of the 19th century Chile was the world's leading copper producer, until new technology helped the US overtake her in 1882. After 1900, US investment and technology led to increased Chilean copper production, exploiting low-grade deposits through the use of large-scale open cast mining (as at Chuquicamata) and using new methods for separating the ore.

Copper was soon at the heart of a close relationship between Chile and the US. During the First World War, US demand for copper for arms manufacturing led to a 400% growth in Chilean copper production; by 1918, US investors controlled 87% of Chilean copper. Among the American corporations were the Chile Exploration Company, American Smelting, Kennecott and Braden, but by the 1960s two companies, Kennecott and Anaconda, dominated.

During the 1950s the role of the US in the Chilean economy became a controversial issue in Chilean politics; US ownership of copper, which in 1970 accounted for 78.5 percent of Chilean commodity exports, was seen as a symbol of Washington's domination. The Christian Democrat government of Eduardo Frei (1964-70) met the calls for nationalization with what it called Chileanization: under this the state took a controlling 51 percent share of the large companies. Complete nationalization was promised by Popular Unity in its 1970 election manifesto, but nationalization was popular not only on the left; many conservatives

supported it as a way of reducing US influence. The nationalization bill of 1971 passed through the Chilean Congress with the support of all parties. The large mines were taken over completely and placed under the control of CODELCO-Chile (Corporación Nacional del Cobre de Chile), which became the largest copper mining and refining company in the world.

Although the Pinochet government of 1973-90 sold off most state-run industries to the private sector, CODELCO was not touched. However, since the 1980s new mining laws have encouraged private investment in new mines. This has led to the opening of large new private mines and an increase in Chilean copper output from 1.6 million to 2.2 million metric tonnes between 1990 and 1995. The biggest new mine is La Escondida, where production began in 1990 and an output of 800,000 tonnes was planned for 1996, making it the world's leading mine. At Collahuasi, projected to start production in 1998, output of 330,000 metric tonnes a year was expected. Although some of CODELCO's older mines are in decline, it too is opening new mines.

Since 1982, Chile has once again been the world's leading producer of copper. Despite the growth of new exports such as fruit and wine, copper is likely to remain of central importance to the Chilean economy, as it has been since the collapse of nitrates in the 1920s.

Cheap lunches available at the *Club de Empleados* and at *Arco Iris* both facing the bus terminal. **Eating**

From Calama: yellow *colectivos* (marked `Chuqui') from the corner of the Plaza 23 de **Transport** Marzo, US$0.75. Buses to **Arica** at 2200 (weekends at 2300), US$16, 9 hours; to **Antofagasta**, US$6; to **Iquique**, US$14; to **Santiago**, US$28, 24 hours.

North and east of Calama

Several small towns and villages in the valley of the Río Loa, north and east of Calama, can be visited. The road is paved to Chiu Chiu and north to Conchi. **Chiu Chiu** was one of the earliest centres of Spanish settlement in the area. The church of **San Francisco**, dating from 1611, has roof beams of cactus and walls over one metre thick. Nearby is a unique, perfectly circular, very deep lake, called Chiu Chiu or Icacoia. Ancient rock carvings are to be found a few kilometres north in the Río Loa valley.

Population: 300
Altitude: 2,500m
33 km E of Calama

At **Lasana**, eight kilometres north of Chiu Chiu, there are the ruins of a pre-Inca *pukará*, a national monument; drinks are on sale. At **Conchi**, 25 kilometres north of Lasana, the road crosses the Río Loa via a bridge, built for the family in 1890; there is a spectacular view over the river from the bridge, but it is a military zone, so no photographs are allowed. Access to the river is by side tracks, best at Santa Bárbara. There is interesting wildlife and flower meadows and trout fishing in season. You can obtain a permit from Gobernación in Calama.

Population: 800

From Conchi a road branches east following the valley of the Río San Pedro, which has been a route for herders and silver caravans for centuries, to Inacaliri, from where a very poor road (four-wheel drive essential) runs south to Linzor and the geysers of El Tatio (see below, page 202). While there are several direct routes east from Chiu Chiu towards the geysers of El Tatio, only one is in good condition: just north of Chiu Chiu turn right off the Ollagüe road and continue until you reach a fork some 22 kilometres east of Chiu Chiu. Take the right fork, ignoring the large sign pointing leftwards to El Tatio; this leads to a very bad track via Linzor. At Km 47 a track turns off north to Caspana. At about Km 65 the main road climbs steeply up the Cuesta de Chita. At about Km 80, branch left to Tatio; this branch meets the main Tatio-San Pedro road some five kilometres further north.

Caspana is beautifully set among hills with a tiny church dating from 1641 and a museum with interesting displays on Atacameño culture. Basic accommodation is available at the village stores. A poor road runs north and east of Caspana through valleys of pampas grass with llama herds to **Toconce**, which has extensive prehispanic terraces set among some interesting rock formations. If visiting Toconce, check in with the *carabineros* in the plaza.

Population: 400
Altitude 3,305m

North and east of Calama & San Pedro de Atacama

Twenty kilometres west of Toconce is **Ayquina**, in whose ancient church is enshrined the statue of the Virgin of Guadalupe. Her feast-day is 8 September, when pilgrims come from far and wide. There is day-long group dancing to Indian rhythms on flute and drum. Towards sunset the Virgin is carried up a steep trail to a small thatched shrine, where the image and the people are blessed before the dancing is renewed at the shrine and all the way back to the village. The poor people of the hills gather stones and make toy houses all along the route: miniatures of the homes they hope to have some day.

Six kilometres north of Ayquina are the luke-warm thermal waters of the **Baños de Turi** and the ruins of a 12th-century *pukará* which was the largest fortified town in the Atacama mountains. Southwest of Ayquina is **Cupo**, which has a *fiesta*, San José, on 19 March. Between this village and Turi is a large, ruined prehispanic settlement at **Paniri** with extensive field systems, irrigation canals (including aqueducts) and a necropolis. Some of the fields are still in use. The area around Cupo is one of the best for seeing the Atacama giant cactus (*Notocereus atacamensis*). Flamingoes can be seen on the mud-flats. The Vega de Turi is an important site for the llama and sheep herders, who believe it has curative properties. At several times in the year, especially September, herders from a wide area congregate with their flocks.

The route to Ollagüe From Chiu Chiu a road runs to Ollagüe, 240 kilometres north on the Bolivian frontier. The first section to Estación San Pedro is in poor condition, but from Estación San Pedro to Ascotán it is worse. There is a *carabinero* checkpoint at Ascotán, the highest point of the road at 3,900 metres. North of Ascotán the road improves as it crosses the Salares de Ascotán and Ollagüe. ask at Ascotán or Ollagüe before setting out about the conditions, especially in December and January or August. There are many llama flocks along this road and flamingoes on the *salares*. There is no petrol between Calama and Uyuni in Bolivia. If you are really short, try buying from the *carabineros* at Ollagüe or Ascotán, the military at Conchi or the mining camp at Buenaventura. The only real answer is to take enough. **NB** The desert to the eastern side of the road is extensively covered by minefields.

Ollagüe

Situated 198 kilometres north of Calama on the dry floor of the Salar de Ollagüe, Ollagüe is surrounded by a dozen volcanic peaks of over 5,000 metres.

Population: 200
Altitude: 3,690m
Colour map 1, grid B3

Five kilometres south of Ollagüe is the sulphur mining camp of Buenaventura, which is situated at an altitude of 5,800 metres, only 150 metres short of the summit of Ollagüe Volcano. Camping is possible, and there are amazing views over the volcanoes and salt flats.

A 77 kilometre spur railroad of metre gauge runs north from Ollagüe to the copper mines of Collahuasi, but these cannot be visited. A road runs west fro Ollagüe to the sulphur mines, now closed, of Aucanquilcha, formerly the highest mine in the world at 5,300 metres, where there are the ruins of an aerial tram system. From the mine you can scramble to the summit of Aucanquilcha, at 6,176 metres, where there are superb views. A high clearance vehicle is needed to drive to the mine. An interesting excursion can be made north from Ollagüe to the village of **Coska** with its traditional agriculture and herds of llamas and alpacas.

Climate At this altitude nights are cold, the days warm and sunny. Minimum temperature at Ollagüe is -20°C, and at the mine, -37°C. There are only 50 millimetres of rain a year, and water is very scarce.

Pullman bus from Calama, US$8, 5 hours, Wednesday, Sunday; returns next day. There is no fuel in Ollagüe. Ollagüe can be reached by taking the Calama-Oruro train (see page 191) but, if you stop off, you will have to hitch back as the daily freight trains are not allowed to carry passengers. Hitching is difficult but the police may help you to find a truck.

Transport

Climate and altitude around San Pedro

Travellers to San Pedro de Atacama and the surrounding area should be prepared for the harsh climate and high altitudes of the interior. Gloves, a hat and a warm coat are essential for excursions from San Pedro, especially for the early morning trip to El Tatio. High factor sun cream and (again) a hat are necessary for the burning daytime sun. You should take plenty of water on any excursion. These precautions are particularly important for any trip over the frontier into the sparsely populated and remote border region of Bolivia, where daily temperatures can range from plus 25°C to minus 25°C and where afternoon winds can make it feel even colder.

Frontier with Bolivia: Ollagüe

Immigration and customs Open 0800-2000.

Sleeping There is nowhere to stay in Ollagüe, but police and border officials will help find lodgings.

Into Bolivia A poor road leads across the frontier and runs to Uyuni, 170 kilometres east. Trucks take a more northerly route across the Savar de Uyuni. Motorists are warned against using this route into Bolivia. There is the danger of getting lost on the many tracks leading over the deserted salt lakes, no gasoline between Calama (Chile) and Uyuni, and little hope of help with a breakdown on the Bolivian side unless you don't mind waiting for perhaps a week. After rain the route is impassable and even experienced guides get lost. Maps give widely differing versions of the route. Where the road has been built up, *never* forsake it for the appealing soft salt beside it. The salt takes a person's weight but a vehicle breaks through the crust into unfathomable depths of plasticine mud below.

San Pedro de Atacama

Population: 2,824
Altitude: 2,436m
Phone code: 055
Colour map 1, grid C3

Situated 103 kilometres by paved road southeast of Calama, San Pedro is an oasis town in the valley of the Río San Pedro. A small town of single-storey adobe buildings, San Pedro has become an important destination for travellers and the centre for excursions in this part of the Atacama. Owing to the clear atmosphere and isolation, there are wonderful views of the night sky after the electricity supply is switched off.

NB There is no food, water or fuel along the Calama-San Pedro road.

At Paso Barros Arana (Km 58) there is an unpaved turning to the left which leads through interesting desert scenery to the small, mud-brick village of Río Grande. Look out for vicuñas and guanacos on the pass. The main road skirts the Cordillera de la Sal about 15 kilometres from San Pedro. There are spectacular views of the sunset over to the Western Cordilleras. The old unpaved road to San Pedro turns off the new road at Km 72 and crosses this range through the Valle de La Luna (see **Excursions** below), but should only be attempted by four-wheel drive vehicles. This road is partly paved with salt blocks.

Archaeology of the Atacama

From very early times, people settled along the northern coast of Chile, sustained by the food supply from the Pacific Ocean. Since about 7,600 BC, fisherfolk and foragers lived in relatively large groups in permanent settlements, such as the Quebrada de Conchas, just to the north of Antofagasta. They fished with fibre nets, sometimes venturing inland to hunt for mammals.

About 2,000 years later the successors of these people, the 'Chinchorros', developed one of the deepest characteristics of Andean cultures, veneration for their ancestors. The role of the dead in the world of the living was vital to the earliest Andean people. As a link between the spiritual and the material world, the ancestor of each local kin group would protect his clan. The expression of these beliefs came in the form of veneration of the ancestors' bodies; sacrifices were made to them, funeral rites were repeated, and precious grave offerings were renewed. In the arid climate of the Atacama, the people observed how bodies were naturally preserved. The skilled practice of mummification was thus developed, over a period of 3,000 years,

dedicated to preserving the dead as sacred objects and spiritual protectors.

Another major cultural practice of northern Chile was the use of hallucinogens. Grave remains found in the region, dating from about 1,000 AD, include leather bags containing organic powder, wooden tablets and snuffer tubes. The tablets and snuffers were often decorated with supernatural figures, such as bird-headed angels, winged humans, star animals and other characters familiar in altiplano cultures. Although the origins and function of taking hallucinogens is not known for certain (see page 485), it is thought that the practice may have been brought down to the coast by traders from the highlands. There were also 'medicine men' who travelled throughout the central and south central Andes dispensing the drugs and healing the sick. As with cures still practised in the Andes and Amazonia, it is possible that the drugs were taken as part of religious rituals, and often for a combination of spiritual and physical healing.

Huw Clough

History

The main centre of the Atacameño culture which flourished in this region before the arrival of the Incas around 1450, San Pedro was defended by a *pukará* (fortress) at Quitor, three kilometres north. The cultivable land around was distributed in 15 *ayllos* (socio-economic communities based on family networks) and irrigation channels were built. San Pedro was visited by both Diego de Almagro and Pedro de Valdivia and the town became a centre of Spanish colonial control; a mission was established in 1557. After independence the town became an important trading centre on the route between Cobija on the coast and Salta in Argentina, but the decline of Cobija and the rise of copper-mining led to San Pedro's replacement as an economic centre by Calama.

Sights

The **Iglesia de San Pedro**, dating from the 17th century, is supposedly the second oldest church in the country. It has been heavily restored and the tower was added in 1964. The roof is made of cactus; inside, the statues of Mary and Joseph have fluorescent light halos. Nearby, on the Plaza, is the **Casa Incaica**, the oldest building in San Pedro.

Museo Arqueológico This is the collection of Padre Gustave Paige, a Belgian missionary who lived in San Pedro between 1955 and 1980. It is now under the care of the Universidad Católica del Norte. One of the most important museums in northern Chile, it traces the development of pre-hispanic Atacameño society. It is well organized; the labels (in Spanish only) on displays are good and there is a comprehensive booklet in Spanish and English. Graham Greene observed "the striking feature of the museum is the mummies of Indian women with their hair and dresses intact dating from before the Conquest, and a collection of paleolithic tools which puts the British Museum in the shade". There is no heating: so wear warm clothing. ■ *US$2.50, Monday-Friday, 0800-1200, 1500-1900; Saturday, and Sunday, 1000-1200, 1500-1800; summer, Monday-Friday 0900-1200, 1400-1800, Saturday-Sunday 1000-1200, 1400-1800.*

Excursions

For Toconao, the Salar de Atacama and the Geysers of El Tatio, all of which can be visited on tours from San Pedro, see below

Valle de la Luna is 12 kilometres west, with fantastic landscapes caused by the erosion of salt mountains. The valley is crossed by the old San Pedro-Calama road. Although buses on the new road will stop to let you off where the old road branches off 13 kilometres northwest of San Pedro (signposted to Peine), it is far better to travel from San Pedro on the old road, either on foot (allow three hours there, three hours back; no lifts), by bicycle or by car. The Valle is best seen at sunset. Take water, hat, camera and torch. Also consider spending the night to see the sunrise (take warm clothes and plenty of water). Agencies in San Pedro offer tours, departing 1530, returning 2200, US$10 per person, but make sure agency departs in time for arrival in the Valle before sunset.

Three kilometres north of San Pedro along the river is the **Pukará de Quitor**, a pre-Inca fortress restored in 1981. The fortress, which covers 2.5 hectares on a hillside on the west bank of the river, was stormed by the Spanish under Pedro de Valdivia, 1,000 defenders being overcome by 30 horsemen who vaulted the walls. The path involves fording the river several times. A further four kilometres up the river there are ruins at Catarpe, which was the Inca administrative centre for this region. At **Tulor**, 12 kilometres southwest of San Pedro, there is an archaeological site where parts of a village (dated 500-800 BC) have been excavated. The road is impassable to cars, but it is worth a visit on foot and you can sleep in two reconstructed huts, or take a tour, US$5. Nearby are the ruins of a 17th century Spanish-style village, abandoned in the 18th century because of lack of water.

Essentials

San Pedro has electricity in the evening (until 2400), but take a torch (flashlight) for walking at night. *Residenciales* supply candles, but better to buy them in Calama beforehand. San Pedro is an expensive town and accommodation is particularly expensive in January and February when it may also be scarce. Drink bottled water as the local supply is not drinkable.

Sleeping

■ *on map*
Price codes: see inside front cover

L1 *Explora*, luxury full board and excursion programme, 3 nights, 4 nights and 8 nights, advance booking only (Av Américo Vespucio Sur 80, 5 piso, Santiago T2066060, F2284655, explora@entelchile.net). **A1** *Terrantai*, Tocopilla, T851140, F851032 (Casilla 10). Comfortable, good restaurant. **A2** *El Tatio*, Caracoles, T851092, F851052. Comfortable, small rooms, bargain off season, English spoken. **A2** *Hostería San Pedro*, Solcor, T851011. Pool (residents only), petrol station, cabins, hot water, constant electricity, restaurant (good *almuerzo*) and bar. No credit cards or TCs. **A2** *Kimal*, Atienza y Caracoles, T/F851030. Comfortable, excellent restaurant. **A2** *La Casa de Don Tomás*, Tocopilla, T/F851055. Good accommodation, good restaurant. Recommended. **A2** *Tulor*, Atienza, T851027, F851063. Good service, excellent restaurant. Recommended. **A3** *Res Corvatsch*, Antofagasta, T851101, F851052. With bath, **C** without, German, English spoken. Recommended. **A3** *Res Licancábur*, Toconao, T851007. With bath, **C** without, clean, nicely furnished.

Antofagasta, Calama & San Pedro

B *Hostal Takha-Takha*, Caracoles, T851038. With bath, **C** without, camping **E** pp. Laundry facilities. **B** *Katarpe*, Atienza, T851033. Comfortable, quiet, friendly. Recommended. **B** *Res Juanita*, on the plaza, T851039. With bath, **D** without, hot water, good value, restaurant. Recommended. **B** *Supay*, Toconao, T851076. Constant hot water and electricity, good breakfast, English spoken, good beds. Recommended. **B** *Tambillo*, Antofagasta, T/F851078. Nice place, good service. Recommended.

C *Res Rayco*, Antofagasta, T851008. Without bath, good value. **C** *La Quinta Adela*, Toconao, good but expensive without breakfast. **D** *Hostal Edén Atacameño*, Toconao, T851154, no singles, also camping **F** pp. **E** pp *Pukará*, Tocopilla. Cold water, basic, unfriendly, no singles. **D** *Res Chiloé*, Atienza, T851017. Without hot water, good meals, laundry facilities, good beds, good value. **D** *Res Don Rául*, Caracoles, T851138. Without bath, hot water, basic, small rooms. **D** *Res Florida*, Tocopilla, T851021. Without bath, basic, clean, hot water evenings only, laundry facilities, no singles. **D** *Sonchek*, Calama, T851112. Without bath, also dormitories, simple, clean, kitchen and laundry facilities, English, French spoken, very friendly. Highly recommended. **E** *Casa de Nora*, Tocopilla, T851114. Family accommodation, simple rooms, lovely patio. Recommended.

Camping *Camping Kunza*, Antofagasta y Atienza, T851183, US$4 pp.

Paacha, Caracoles. Excellent 4 course *almuerzo*, extensive menu, best in town, live music at weekends. *La Casona*, Caracoles. Excellent food, good service. *Adobe*, Caracoles. Good breakfast menu (open 0900), excellent food, pleasant atmosphere. *Estaka*, Caracoles. Very good cuisine, good service. Recommended. *Tulor*, Atienza. First class pizzeria, also à la carte menu, real coffee. *Sonchek*, Calama. Chilean and international cuisine with some vegetarian dishes, real coffee, good service. Warmly

Eating
● *on maps*
Price codes:
see inside front cover

Antofagasta, Calama & San Pedro

San Pedro de Atacama

■ Sleeping
1 Edén Atacameño
2 El Tatio
3 Hostería San Pedro
4 Katarpe
5 Kimal
6 La Casa de Don Tomás
7 Licancábur

8 Residencial Chiloé
9 Residencial Corvatsch
10 Residencial Don Rául
11 Residencial Florida
12 Residencial Juanita
13 Residencial Rayko
14 Sonchek
15 Supay

16 Takha-Takha
17 Tambillo
18 Terrantai
19 Tulor

● **Eating**
1 Casa Piedra
2 La Casona

3 La Estaka
4 Paacha

▲ **Other**
1 Cosmo Andino Expediciones
2 Labra Turismo

N
Not to scale

recommended. *Casa Piedra*, Caracoles. Good breakfast (open 0900), very good *almuerzo*, good sandwiches, cosy atmosphere, nice music. *Café Tierra Todo Natural*, Caracoles. Fruit juice, real coffee, yoghurt, good for breakfast. *Hosteria San Pedro*, good value *almuerzo*. *Sumaj Jallpa*, Caracoles. Fast food, cheap, popular with locals. *Tambo*, Toconao y Caracoles, bar with live music at weekends.

Sports **Climbing**: Licancábur (5,916m) on the frontier with Bolivia can only be climbed from the Bolivian side, see box on page 206. **Swimming Pool**: *Piscina Oasis*, at Pozo Tres, 3 km southeast, was drilled in the late 1950s as part of a mineral exploration project, open all year 0500-1730 daily. US$1.50 to swim, sometimes empty. Worth asking around for a lift before walking there. Camping US$4 and picnic facilities, very popular at weekends.

Transport **Local** **Bicycle hire**: *Pangea*, Tocopilla, T851111. Most reliable, has best mountain bikes, rental US$2 per hour, US$17 per day. Treks organized, very knowledgeable. Warmly recommended. Several other agencies offer cycle hire.

Car hire: some agencies in San Pedro may offer vehicle hire, but you should check vehicle condition and insurance very carefully as there are reports of accidents involving uninsured and badly serviced vehicles.

Buses To **Calama**, Tur Bus, once a day (continues to Antofagasta); Frontera 6 a day, US$2.50, 1½ hours. Frequencies vary with more departures in January/February and some weekends, fewer out of season. Book in advance to return from San Pedro Sun evening. Frontera also run to Toconao. Daily direct service to Antofagasta, 1100. Tramaca services from Iquique and Antofagasta to Salta (Argentina) stop in San Pedro (see under Antofagasta for details); book in Calama, Iquique or Antofagasta.

Directory **Banks** *Banco del Estado*, in Casona Municipal, ATM. *Cambio Atacama*, Toconao. Open daily 1030-1800, rates posted outside, good rates for US$ cash, poor rates for TCs. Best not to try changing TCs in San Pedro, take cash. If stuck try *Eztaka* restaurant or pay for an excursion using TCs.

Communications **Post Office**: on Padre Le Paige, opposite Museo Archeológico. **Telephone**: *CTC*, Caracoles. *Entel* on the Plaza, open Mon-Fri 0900-1300, 1800-2000. Fax for incoming calls 851052.

Tour companies & travel agents The main tours are to the Valle de la Luna (see above), the Salar de Atacama and the Geysers of El Tatio (see below). These run most days in season, subject to demand at other times. Other tours include Laguna Miscanti and an archaeological tour to Quintor, Tulor and Catarpe. There has been a boom in tour agencies in recent years but quality is very mixed: avoid cut-price operators and try to check out vehicles and guides before booking. Report any complaints to the Municipalidad or to Sernatur. There are about 10 agencies, but some are impermanent and/or open for only part of the year. Best is *Cosmo Andino Expediciones*, Caracoles, T/F851069, cosmoandino@entelchile.net. English, French, German, Dutch spoken, good vehicles, good drivers, experienced guides, excellent book exchange. Owner Martin Beeris is very knowledgeable about the region. Highly recommended. *Labra Turismo*, Caracoles, T851137/851165. English, German spoken, reliable, owner Mario Banchón an expert guide. Recommended. Others include: *Expediciones Corvatsch*, Tocopilla. Operated jointly by *Res Corvatsch* and *Res Florida*, good vehicles, casual service, offer discounts for package tours with accommodation. *Atacama Inca Tour*, Plaza, T851062. Recommended but not always open. *Pachamama Tours*, Toconao, T851067. Open for part of the year. For tours to Bolivia the specialists are *Turismo Colque*, Caracoles, T851109, who offer tours across the frontier into Bolivia including 1-day tour to Laguna Verde (US$90 per person) and 3-day tours to Laguna Colorado and the Salar de Uyuni (see below); TCs, Visa and Mastercard all accepted, reliable, hires sleeping bags, recommended, has agencies in Uyuni and La Paz. *Desert Adventures*, Caracoles S/N, T/F851067, desert-adventure@hotmail.com, offers excursions to all the major sites, modern fleet of vehicles, excellent guides. **Tourist offices** Sernatur kiosk in the plaza, rarely open.

Antofagasta, Calama & San Pedro

El Tatio

The highest geyser in the world, El Tatio was formed as a result of water percolating through the porous volcanic rock until it gets trapped above a layer of impermeable rock. Here it comes into contact with intensely hot rock and is heated. As there is little space for it to expand and boil, pressure builds up until, eventually, the water explodes to the surface, rushing out through cracks and fissures. On the way up, the very hot water dissolves the silica and other minerals in the surrounding rock. In the cold dry air at the surface the boiling water evaporates, leaving behind tiny crystals of silica and chloride.
    Naomi Peirce

The geysers of El Tatio

Situated 122 kilometres east of Calama at an altitude of 4,321 metres, the geysers of El Tatio are a popular attraction. From San Pedro the geysers are reached by a maintained road which runs northeast, past the **Baños de Puritama** (28 kilometres), then on a further 94 kilometres. The geysers are at their best 0630-0830, though the spectacle varies: locals say the performance is best when weather conditions are stable. A swimming pool has been built nearby. There is a workers' camp which is empty apart from one guard, who will let you sleep in a bed in one of the huts, **G** per person, take food and sleeping bag. From here you can hike to surrounding volcanoes if adapted to altitude. There is no public transport and hitching is impossible. If going in a hired car, make sure the engine is suitable for very high altitudes and is protected with antifreeze; four-wheel drive is advisable. If driving in the dark it is almost impossible to find your way: the sign for El Tatio is north of the turn off. **NB** People have been killed or seriously injured by falling into the geysers, or through the thin crust of the mud.

Tours Agencies in San Pedro operate tours to El Tatio, departing 0330, arriving at the geysers 0700, US$22, including breakfast. These offer opportunities to swim, in the hot thermal pool and to visit the Baños de Puritama on the return journey. Take warm clothing and swimming costume. Some agencies offer tours to El Tatio and Calama.

South of San Pedro de Atacama

From San Pedro to Toconao, 37 kilometres south, the road (well-surfaced) runs through groves of acacia and pepper trees. There are many tracks leading to the wells (pozos) which supply the intricate irrigation system. Most have thermal water but bathing is not appreciated by the local farmers. The groves of trees are havens for wildlife especially rheas (ñandu) and Atacama owls.

About four kilometres before Toconao, vehicle tracks head east across the sand to a hidden valley two kilometres from the road where there is a small settlement called **Zapar**. Here are some well preserved pre-hispanic ruins on the rocky cliffs above the cultivated valley. The sand is very soft and a four-wheel drive vehicle is essential.

Antofagasta, Calama & San Pedro

This village is on the eastern shore of the Salar de Atacama. All houses are built of bricks of white volcanic stone, which gives the village an appearance totally different from San Pedro. The 18th century church and bell tower are also built of volcanic stone. East of the village is an attractive gorge called the Quebrada de Jérez. Nearby is the quarry where the stone *sillar* is worked; it can be visited. The stones sound like bells when struck. Worth visiting also are the vineyards which produce a unique sweet wine, and the tree-filled gorges with their hidden fields and orchards. There are three basic *residenciales*; accommodation is also offered at the Restaurant Lascar, which has good simple food. Camping is possible along the Quebrada de Jérez.

Toconao
Population: 500
Altitude: 2,600m
Colour map 1, grid C3

Transport Frontera buses daily from San Pedro, 1100, 1800, return 0700, US$1.30.

South of Toconao is one of the main entrances to the Salar de Atacama, 300,000 hectares. Rich in minerals including borax, potassium and an estimated 40 percent of world lithium reserves, the Salar is home to the pink flamingo and other birds (though these are usually only visible at a distance). The air is so dry that you can often see right across the Salar. ■ *US$3*. Three areas of the Salar form part of the **Reserva Nacional de los Flamencos**, in seven sectors totalling 73,986 hectaresa, administered by Conaf in San Pedro.

Salar de Atacama
The third largest expanse of salt flats in the world

Tours Agencies in San Pedro offer excursions to Toconao and the Salar, returning via the Quebrada de Jérez, US$12 plus park entry, usual departure 1530.

South of San Pedro de Atacama

▲ Sections of the Reserva Nacional Los Flamencos

Antofagasta, Calama & San Pedro

Routes south of Toconao

From Toconao the road heads south through the scenic villages of **Camar**, where handicrafts from cactus may be bought, and **Socaire**, which has llama wool knitwear for sale. Twenty kilometres south of Socaire is the beautiful **Laguna Miscanti** (*Altitude*: 4,350 metres) which is part of the Reserva Nacional Los Flamencos. After Socaire the road goes on to the mine at Laco, with one poor stretch below the mine, before proceeding to the Paso de Sico, which has replaced the higher, more northerly Guaytiquina pass, at 4,295 metres, also spelt Huaytiquina, to Argentina.

Ten kilometres south of Toconao the old road branches east towards Guaytiquina. In a deep *quebrada* below Volcán Láscar is the small agricultural settlement of **Talabre**, with terracing and an ancient threshing floor. Above the *quebrada* is an isolated, stone-built cemetery. Large flocks of llamas graze where the stream crosses the road below the Láscar volcano at 5,154 metres. After a steep climb, you reach the **Laguna Lejía** at 4,190 metres, where flamingoes abound. You then pass through the high plains of **Guaytiquina** (4,275 metres), where only a few herdsmen are found. This crossing is not open for road traffic to Argentina.

South from Toconao by 67 kilometres, on a road that runs along the eastern edge of the Salar de Atacama, is the attractive village of **Peine**, which is the site of the offices of the lithium extraction company. There is also a thermal pool where you can swim. Woollen goods and knitwear are made here and there is a daily bus by Frontera from San Pedro. To the east of the village lies a group of beautifully coloured hills, whose colours are more vibrant at sunset, with good views over the Salar de Atacama. A path leads across these hills to Socaire, allow two days. It is worth asking if the company's access road can be used to visit the Salar de Atacama's spectacular salt formations. Other villages worth visiting include Tilomonte and Tilopozo, south and west of Peine.

From Peine a road (64 kilometres) crosses the Salar de Atacama; it joins a road which runs from San Pedro down the west side of the Salar and continues south to **Pan de Azúcar**, an abandoned railway station. Here it meets the paved road which leads from the Pan-American Highway, 50 kilometres south of Antofagasta via La Escondida, a modern copper mine with an output of copper higher than any other mine in the world, to Socompa on the Argentine border. Between Pan de Azúcar and Socompa (poor road) is Monturaqui, the source of the green onyx which is much used for carving in northern Chile.

Parque Nacional Llullaillaco Situated southeast of Antofagasta on the Argentine frontier, this recently created park covers 263,000 hectares and includes Cerro Llullaillaco at 6,739 metres, the second highest peak in Chile, as well as three other peaks over 5,000 metres: Cerro de la Pena at 5,260 metres, Guanaqueros, 5,131 metres, and Aguas Calientes, 5,070 metres. The park is inhabited by large numbers of guanacos and vicuñas. Access is via a poor road which turns off south from the La Escondida-Socompa road at Imilac, 10 kilometres east of La Escondida. Visits by arrangement only with Conaf in Antofagasta.

Frontier crossings from San Pedro

There are several routes into Bolivia and Argentina from San Pedro de Atacama.

There are three crossings; the best is the most northerly, the **Paso de Jama** at 4,200 metres, 165 kilometres southeast of San Pedro, which is reached by a paved road that runs via the Salar de Tara which forms a sector of the Reserva Nacional de los Flamencos.

Frontier with Argentina

The main alternative to this, **Paso de Sico** at 4,079 metres, lies further south, 207 kilometres southeast of San Pedro, and is reached by a poor road which runs via Toconao and Socaire (see above, page 204). This pass has replaced the higher **Paso de Guaytiquina** at 4,275 metres. The most southerly crossing is **Paso de Socompa**, 3,865 metres, which is reached by a poor road from Pan de Azúcar (see page 204).

Immigration There is a Chilean immigration and customs post at Paso Socompa, open 0800-2000. Chilean immigration and customs formalities for Paso de Jama and Paso de Sico are dealt with in San Pedro de Atacama, open 0900-1200, 1400-1600. Incoming vehicles are searched for fruit and dairy products.

Crossing by private vehicle Check road conditions with the *carabineros* and at immigration in San Pedro as these crossings are liable to be closed by heavy rain in summer and blocked by snow in winter.

Transport Bus: For services from Antofagasta, Calama and San Pedro to Jujuy and Salta, see above. **Hitching**: try the immigration post in San Pedro; Spanish is essential.

Into Argentina On the Argentine side of the frontier all these roads link up and continue to San Antonio de los Cobres (where Argentina customs and immigration formalities take place) and Salta. Transport using the Paso de Jama crossing usually

Antofagasta, Calama & San Pedro

The route to Argentina via the Paso de Jama

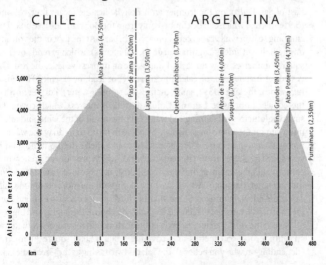

Climbing Licancábur

Licancábur, 5,916 metres, on the frontier between Chile and Bolivia, can only be climbed from the Bolivian side; the Chilean side is mined.

From Laguna Verde drive to the pre-hispanic pukará, about 15 kilometres further southwest. From here you need to start out at 0500 at the latest; follow the riverbed straight up and hold right to the ridge after about three hours climbing; there are red flags to show you the way.

After about five hours you will pass the grave of a tourist killed in 1989, a reminder that the mountain is dangerous. After about eight hours you reach a flat section; from here it is still 1½ hours to the summit. To descend, go straight down the riverbed, allowing at least four to five hours. Take plenty of water. Beware of falling rocks. Note that there is no rescue service.

Patrick Frehner and Andrea Nicodemus, Trogen, Switzerland.

---

follows a more northerly alternative via Susques, where there is accommodation, and Jujuy. The most southerly route via Paso de Socompa is perhaps the most spectacular, crossing saltflats and wide expanses of desert, but this route is virtually unused.

Frontier with Bolivia There are two crossings, the more northerly of which, via Ollagüe, is described above (see page 196). The more southerly crossing is at **Hito Cajones**, 45 kilometres east of San Pedro via a poor road which turns off the paved road towards Paso de Jama at La Cruz, eight kilometres southwest of the frontier. Laguna Verde (see below) is seven kilometres north of Hito Cajones. There is no public transport: do not be tempted to hitch to the frontier as you risk being stranded without water or shelter at sub-zero temperatures. The most practicable method of crossing this frontier is with a tour from San Pedro (see below).

Immigration Chilean immigration and customs are in San Pedro, open 0900-1200, 1400-1600. Incoming vehicles are searched for fruit, vegetables and dairy products.

Bolivian Consulate See under Calama.

Into Bolivia: The Salar de Uyuni

East of San Pedro, on the frontier with Bolivia, lies the Licancábur volcano (5,916 metres) which can be climbed only from the Bolivian side, see box. The climbing season is all year except January-February. At the foot of the volcano on the Bolivian side is **Laguna Verde** (4,400 metres), which extends over 17 square kilometres; its wind-lashed waters are an impressive jade, the result, it is said, of magnesium, or calcium carbonate, or lead, or arsenic. There is a *refugio* near the lake (US$2, small, mattresses, running water). Further north is the equally impressive **Laguna Colorada** (4,278 metres) which covers 60 square kilometres; its flaming red waters are the result of the wind and afternoon sun on the micro-organisms which live in it (up to midday the water is pretty normal in colour). The water is less than a metre deep but the mud is very soft. The shores are encrusted with borax, which provides an arctic white contrast with the waters of the lake. The pink algae in the lake provide food for the rare James flamingos, which live here along with the more common Chilean and Andean flamingos. Some 40 other bird species can also be seen. Further north still, north of Ollagüe, is the **Salar de Uyuni**, the largest and highest salt lake in the world, an increasingly popular attraction for visitors. Situated at an altitude of 3,650 metres and covering 9,000-12,000 square kilometres (depending on who you believe), the Salar is twice as big as the Great Salt Lake in the United States. The depth of the salt varies from two to 20 metres. Driving across it is one of the most fantastic experiences in South America, especially in June/July when the bright blue skies contrast with the blinding-white salt. After particularly wet rainy seasons the Salar is covered in water, which adds to the surreal experience.

The Salar de Uyuni, Laguna Colorada and Laguna Verde are usually visited by **Tours** tours from the Bolivian town of **Uyuni** (*Population*: 10,000; *Altitude*: 3,665 metres), where accommodation, money exchange and transport to La Paz, Oruro and Potosi are all available. However, Turismo Colque in San Pedro (see page 200) also offers this tour from San Pedro and will drop passengers off for Uyuni, although some report that to see the colour changes on Laguna Colorada the trip is best done from Uyuni.

NB If you intend to travel independently in this region do not underestimate the dangers of getting stuck without transport or accommodation at this altitude. Do not travel alone and seek full advice in advance.

Antofagasta, Calama & San Pedro

Iquique, Arica and the Far North

8

Though much of the far north of Chile is covered by the Atacama desert, this region has much to attract the visitor. The two main cities are Iquique and Arica, both situated on the coast. Iquique, which retains traces of the nitrate boom of the late 19th century to which it owes its existence, is the base for trips to the thermal springs of Mamiña and the mountain resort of Pica. Arica, just south of the Peruvian frontier, is an important route centre with regular bus services along the international highway to La Paz, Bolivia. Between Iquique and Arica the Atacama is dotted with abandoned nitrate mines and ancient geoglyphs.

Inland a chain of four national parks protects much of the Andean highland plateau. The northernmost of these, the Parque Nacional Lauca, offers some of the most stunning scenery in northern Chile including snow-capped volcanoes, lakes and lava fields and varied birdlife: it is easily reached from Arica along the international road to Bolivia. Further south are three other parks which are much less accessible: the Reserva Nacional Las Vicuñas, which covers large expanses of high grassland; the Monumento Nacional Salar de Surire, centred on a salt lake with a large flamingo population; and the Parque Nacional Volcán Isluga which includes four volcanoes including the active Isluga.

Background

History

As elsewhere in northern Chile, the early Spanish settler population was small in numbers. Settlement was concentrated largely in the oases of the *sierra*, where the climate was easier and where malaria, the scourge of the coast, was not found. From an early date Arica became one of the principle ports for the silver trade from Potosí, but the coast remained sparsely inhabited until the

The far north

The camels of South America

The llama, alpaca, guanaco and vicuña are all camelids, or South American camels, adapted for the mountainous terrain by having narrower feet than the desert forms. There are estimated to be some 7.7 million camelids, over half of them in Peru. All four species can be seen in Chile, though three of these are only found in the north. The relationships between camelids is very confused: fertile offspring arise from matings between all of them. There is a long-held view that both the llama and the alpaca are descended from wild guanaco.

Guanaco (lama guanicae), coffee coloured with a darker head and tail and weighing up to 55 kilograms, were once found throughout Chile except in rainforest areas. Both a grazer and browser, it lives in deserts, shrub lands, savannah and occasionally on forest fringes. In many areas hunted to extinction, an estimated 20,000 now survive in the far north, especially in the Parque Nacional Lauca, in coastal areas between Antofagasta and Lago Rapel and in the far south including the Parque Nacional Torres del Paine.

Vicuña (lama vicugna), weighing up to 20 kilograms, are like half-sized guanaco, though with a yellower coat and coffee coloured head and tail. Hunted almost to extinction, there were only around 400 in Chile in 1970. Protection has increased their numbers to around 12,000, mainly in the far north and at altitudes of 3,700-4,800 metres.

Alpaca (lama paco) are domesticated animals, weighing 20-30 kilograms, but appearing much larger because of their wool. Colours vary between black, coffee coloured, mahogany, grey and white. An estimated 20,000 can be found in drier parts of the northern altiplano.

Llama (lama glama) are also domesticated and are usually found with alpacas. Larger than alpacas and weighing up to 55 kilograms, their wool varies in colour but is shorter than that of alpacas. They are found only in the area of their domestication which occurred around Lake Titicaca some 4,000-5,000 years ago. Used as pack animals, males can carry loads of up to 40 kilograms. There are some 40,000 in the Tarapacá and Antofagasta regions of Chile.

19th century. At the time of independence the whole of this area became part of Peru as the provinces of Tarapacá and Arica, before coming under Chilean control as a result of the War of the Pacific. After the war Iquique and Tarapacá province shared in the nitrate boom of the late 19th century (see page 180).

Geography

The Atacama Desert extends over most of the Far North. The Cordillera de la Costa slowly loses height north of Iquique, terminating at the Morro at Arica: from Iquique northwards it drops directly to the sea and, as a result, there are few beaches along this coast. Inland the central depression, the *pampa*, 1,000-1,200 metres high, is arid and punctuated by salt flats south of Iquique. Between Iquique and Arica it is crossed from east to west by four gorges. East of the central depression lies the *sierra*, the western branch of the Andes, beyond which is a high plateau, the *altiplano* (3,500 metres-4,500 metres) from which rise volcanic peaks, the highest of which include Parinacota (6,350 metres), Pomerape (6,250 metres), Guayatiri (6,064 metres), Acotango (6,050 metres), Capurata (5,990 metres), Tacora (5,988 metres) and Tarapacá (5,825 metres).

Northwards from Pisagua several rivers flow west from the *sierra*; the more northerly of these, the Ríos Lluta and San José, provide water for Arica. In the *altiplano* there are a number of lakes, the largest of which, Lago Chungará, is one of the highest lakes in the world. The main river draining the *altiplano*, the Río Lauca, flows eastwards into Bolivia.

John North, The 'Nitrate King'

In the history of northern Chile few people have played a more controversial role than John North, known in both Chile and Britain as the 'Nitrate King'. Born in Leeds in 1842, North arrived in Chile at the age of 24 and worked as a railway engineer in Caldera and Iquique. In 1875 he began supplying water to Iquique by boat from Arica. During the War of the Pacific North and his partner, John Harvey, bought large numbers of shares in the Peruvian nitrate companies of the Atacama at low prices. When after the war, the Chilean government unexpectedly recognised ownership of the shares, North had acquired six nitrate mines and made a fortune. Some suggest that North and Harvey, a mining engineer employed by the Chilean government, had inside knowledge of the decision to recognise the shares.

North returned to London in 1882 and built a large empire of companies with interests in northern Chile. By 1889 he controlled 15 nitrate mines, four railway companies including the Nitrate Railways Company which monopolized rail transport around Iquique, the Bank of Tarapacá and London and the Nitrate Provisions Company, which supplied food to the nitrate oficinas. North's efforts to establish a monopoly over nitrate transport were opposed by President Balmaceda and, when the president came into conflict with the Chilean Congress in 1891, North provided £10,000 for the Congressional war effort which was to overthrow the President.

By this time North was a famous figure in London, spending ostentatiously on his business and society friends; his mansion at Avery Hill, Eltham, was the scene of great parties; he owned racehorses and sponsored other sports. In 1895 he stood for parliament as a Conservative, but was narrowly defeated. He died, of a heart attack, in May 1896 and his funeral was attended by huge crowds. By the time of his death nitrate stocks had gone into decline, but North had quietly sold most of his shares, shifting his wealth into coal mining in South Wales, gold mining in Australia, trams in Cairo, cement in Belgium and rubber plantations in the Congo.

Climate

The coastal strip and the *pampa* are rainless; on the coast temperatures are moderated by the Pacific Ocean, but in the *pampa* variations of temperature between day and night are extreme, varying between 30°C and 0°C. In the *sierra* temperatures are lower, averaging 20°C in summer and 9°C in winter. The *altiplano* is much colder, temperatures averaging 10°C in summer and -5°C in winter. Both the *sierra* and the *altiplano* are affected by storms of rain, snow and hail (*invierno boliviano*). Coastal regions receive *camanchaca* (sea mist).

Economy

Over 90 percent of the population of this area lives in the two coastal cities, Arica and Iquique. The sea provides the main source of wealth. Iquique is the principal fishing port in Chile, unloading 35 percent of the total national catch and the city has important fish processing industries. Mining is much less important than in other parts of northern Chile, but silver and gold are mined at Challacollo and copper at Sagasca, near Tarapacá. Fruit is grown in the Valle de Azapa, the oasis formed by the Río San José, and in the *sierra* around Pica. The Azapa valley also produces olives. Vegetables and alfalfa are grown in the oases of the *sierra*. Commerce is an important source of local employment: Arica benefits from its position as a port for Bolivian goods and its proximity to Peru, while Iquique is the site of a duty free zone.

Iquique

Situated 492 kilometres north of Antofagasta, Iquique is the the capital of Región I (Tarapacá) and one of the main ports of northern Chile. The name of the town is derived from the Aymara word ique-ique, meaning place of 'rest and tranquillity'. The city is situated on a rocky peninsula at the foot of the high Atacama pampa, sheltered by the headlands of Punta Gruesa and Cavancha.

Population: 145,139
Phone code: 057
Colour map 1, grid B2

Iquique is a major duty free centre. The main Free Zone, the Zofri, lies north of town along Amuñategui: it is a giant shopping centre selling a wide range of duty-free imported products including electronic goods, used cars, motorcycles and good quality camping equipment. ■ *Monday-Friday 0800-2000, Saturday 080-1400. Colectivo from the centre US$0.50.* Another duty-free zone, Mall Los Américas, has been opened south of the centre on Avenida Héroes de la Concepción. ■ *Limit on tax free purchases US$650 for foreigners, US$500 for Chileans. All vehicles travelling south from Iquique are searched for duty-free goods at Quillagua on the Pan-American Highway and at Chipana on Route 1, the coastal road.*

History

Although the site was used as a port in pre-hispanic times, it remained sparsely populated throughout the colonial period. Even in 1855, when the port had begun to export nitrates, the population was about 2,500. The nitrate trade transformed the city, bringing large numbers of foreign traders and creating a wealthy élite. Though partly destroyed by an earthquake in 1877, the city became the centre of this trade after its transfer from Peru to Chile at the end of the War of the Pacific.

Sights

In the centre of the old town is **Plaza Prat** with a clock tower and bell dating from 1877. On the northeast corner of the Plaza is the **Centro Español**, built in Moorish style by the local Spanish community in 1904; the ground floor is a restaurant, on the upper floors are paintings of scenes from Don Quixote and from Spanish history by the Spanish artist, Vicente Tordecillas. On the south side of the Plaza is the **Teatro Municipal**, built as an opera house in 1890; the façade features four women representing the seasons. Three blocks north of the Plaza is the old **Aduana** (customs house) built in 1871; in 1891 it was the scene of an important battle in the Civil War between supporters of President Balmaceda and congressional forces. Part of it is now the **Naval Museum**. Five blocks east along Calle Sotomayor is the Railway Station, now disused, built in 1883 and displaying several old locomotives. Along Calle Baquedano, which runs south from Plaza Prat, are the attractive former mansions of the 'nitrate barons'. Adorned with columns and balconies, these date from between 1880 and 1903 and were constructed from timber imported from California. The finest of these is the **Palacio Astoreca**, Baquedano y O'Higgins, built in 1903, subsequently the Intendencia and now a museum.

Sea lions and pelicans can be seen from the harbour. There are cruises around the harbour from the passenger pier, US$2.65, 45 minutes, minimum 10-15 people.

Museums **Museo Naval**, Sotomayor y Baquedano, focuses on the Battle of Iquique, 1879 (see box, page 268). ■ *US$0.50. Tuesday-Saturday 0930-1230, 1430-1800, Sunday and holidays 1000-1300.*

Museo Regional, Baquedano 951, contains an archaeological section tracing the development of pre-hispanic civilizations in the region; an important ethnographical collection of the Isluga culture of the altiplano (c400 AD) and of contemporary Aymara cultures. There is also a section devoted to the Nitrate Era which includes a model of a nitrate *oficina* and the collection of the nitrate entrepreneur, Santiago Humberstone. ■ *US$1. Monday-Friday 0800-1300, 1500-1900, Saturday 1030-1300, Sunday (in summer) 1030-1300.*

Palacio Astoreca, Baquedano y O'Higgins, fine late 19th century furniture and exhibitions of shells. ■ *US$1. Tuesday-Friday 1000-1400, 1500-1900, Saturday/Sunday 1000-1300.*

Excursions

Humberstone, a large nitrate town, now abandoned, at the junction of the Pan-American Highway and the road to Iquique. At its height in 1940 the town had a population of 3,700. Though closed since 1961, you can see the church, theatre, *pulpería* (company stores) and the swimming pool (built of metal plating from ships' hulls). ■ *Donation invited. Guided tours Saturday-Sunday. Leaflets available.* Nearby are the ruins of several other mining towns including Santa Laura, which has the only nitrate processing plant still intact. Transport to/from Iquique: take any bus to/from Arica or Antofagasta, or a colectivo for Pozo Almonte from Sgto Aldea y Barros Arana, US$2 (there is a phone for contacting taxi company for return journey). Humberstone and Santa Laura can be visited on tours arranged by local agencies (see below).

To the **Geoglifos de Pintados** (see page 223) take any bus south, US$2.50, and walk from the Pan-American Highway then hitch back or flag down a bus. Many other sites around Iquique, including the Gigante del Atacama (see page 223), are difficult to visit without a vehicle. Hire a car and drive south along the Pacific coast to see sealions, fishing villages and old salt mines, including the ghost town of Guanillos.

Essentials

Sleeping
■ *on map*
Price codes:
see inside front cover
Accommodation is
scarce in the weeks
before Christmas as
many Chileans visit
Iquique to shop
in the Zofri

L3 *Arturo Prat*, Plaza Prat, T411067, F423309. 4-star, pool, health suite. **L3** *Gavina*, Balmaceda 1497, T413030, F411111. **L3** *Hostería Cavancha*, Los Rieles 250, T434800, F431039. 4-star, south of city, on water's edge. Nearby is **L3** *Terrado*, Los Rieles 126, T437878.

A1 *Icaisa*, Orella 434, T412324, F428462. **A2** *Atenas*, Los Rieles 738, T431100, F424349. Good service and food. Recommended. **A2** *Barros Arana*, Barros Arana 1330, T412840, F426709. Clean, modern, good value. **A2** *Cano*, Ramirez 996, T416597, F422032. **A2** *Carani*, Latorre 426, T413646, F425124. **A2** *Majestic Playa Brava*, Playa Brava 3118, T443226, F431039. With breakfast, good. **A3** *Belén*, Tarapacá 1002, T/F413644. **A3** *Inti-Llanka*, Obispo Labbé 825, T/F413858. Helpful. **A3** *Playas*, Gral Hernán Fuenzalida 938, T/F429111. Small, friendly. **A3** *Riorsa*, Vivar 1542, T/F420153. **A3** *Tamarugal*, Tarapacá 369, T413910. Central, clean, good restaurant.

B *Hostal Casa Blanca*, Gorostiaga 200, with bath and breakfast. **B** *Durana*, San Martín 294, T/F428085. Helpful. **B** *Hostal Cuneo*, Baquedano 1175, T428654. Modern, clean, pleasant. **B** *Phoenix*, Aníbal Pinto 451, T/F411349. Overpriced, poor value. **B** *Res Catedral*, Labbé 235, T/F413360. **B** *Wilson*, Wilson 422, T/F415522.

C *Continental*, Lynch 679, T429145. Central, nice rooms, good value. **C** *Danino*, Serrano 897, T417301, F443079. **C** *Res Condell*, Thompson 684, T413984. With bath, clean, friendly. **C** *Res Nan-King*, Thompson 752, T423311. Clean, good value. **C** *Hostal Mamiña*, Tarapacá 933, T413218. With bath, good value. Warmly recommended.

Iquique centre

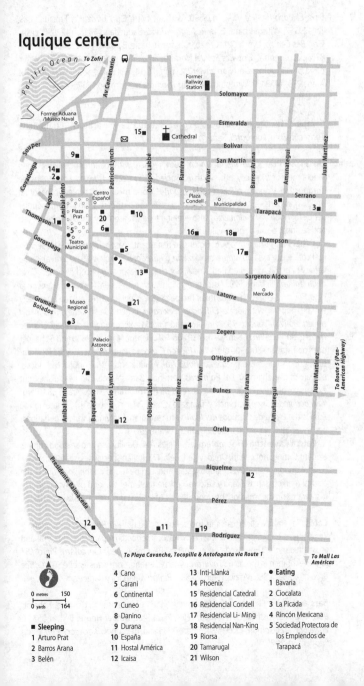

Iquique, Arica & the Far North

N

0 metres   150
0 yards   164

■ **Sleeping**
1 Arturo Prat
2 Barros Arana
3 Belén

4 Cano
5 Carani
6 Continental
7 Cuneo
8 Danino
9 Durana
10 España
11 Hostal América
12 Icaisa

13 Inti-Llanka
14 Phoenix
15 Residencial Catedral
16 Residencial Condell
17 Residencial Li- Ming
18 Residencial Nan-King
19 Riorsa
20 Tamarugal
21 Wilson

● **Eating**
1 Bavaria
2 Ciocalata
3 La Picada
4 Rincón Mexicana
5 Sociedad Protectora de
   los Emplendos de
   Tarapacá

D pp *España*, Tarapacá 465. Without bath, friendly, warm water, dirty. **D** pp *Hostal América*, Rodríguez 550, T/F427524. Near beach, clean, good value. **D** pp *Hostal San Francisco*, Latorre 990, T427524. Clean, hot water, noisy. **D** *Res Li Ming*, Barros Arana 705, T421912. Clean, good value, small rooms.

E pp *El Paso*, Bolívar 754, T425690. Without bath. **E** pp *Errázuriz*, Errázuriz 889, T/F429557. Without bath. **E** pp *Res Baquedano*, Baquedano 1315, T422990, clean. **E** pp *Res Centro*, Lynch 621. Cheap, run down, basic. **E** pp *Res Los Troncos*, Serrano 826, clean, central. **E** pp *Res Sol del Norte*, Juan Martínez 852, T421546. Cold water, basic, small rooms. **E** pp *San Javier I*, Lynch 97, T427641, and *San Javier II*, Barros Arana 210, T428408. Without bath. **E** pp *Thompson*, Thompson 837, T411734. Without bath.

Camping No site but wild camping possible on La Brava beach. **Equipment**: *Tunset*, in Zofri; *Lombardi*, Serrano 447.

Eating
● *on maps*
Price codes:
see inside front cover

On Plaza Prat *Club de la Unión*, roof terrace with panoramic views, open lunchtimes only, pricey but worth it. *Sociedad Protectora de los Empleados de Tarapacá*, reasonable prices. *Casino Español*, good meals well served in beautiful building, expensive, "a good place to celebrate your birthday". *Club Croata*, popular venue for good value *almuerzos*, also evening meals, reasonably priced. *Colonial*, fish and seafood, popular, good value.

Others *Bavaria*, Pinto 926. Expensive restaurant, reasonably priced café serving real coffee, snacks and *almuerzo*. *Pizzeria d'Alfredo*, Los Molles (Playa Brava). Large variety of pizzas, well-prepared pastas, not cheap, reasonably priced *almuerzo*. *Casa degli Italiani*, Serrano 520. Authentic Italian cuisine, excellent 4-course *menu de la casa*. Recommended. *La Tarantela*, Tarapacá 399. Popular bar/restaurant, open early till late, popular with locals. *El Rincón Mexicano*, Lynch 754. Tex-Mex, reasonably priced. *Bolivia*, Serrano 751. *Humitas* and *salteñas*. Recommended. Many Chinese *chifas* including *Win Li*, San Martin 439 and *Sol Oriental*, Martínez 2030 and 6 cheaper ones on Tarapacá 800/900 blocks. *La Picada Curicana*, Pinto y Zegers. Good local cuisine, good value *menu de la casa*. *Rapa Nui*, Amuñategui 715. Popular with locals, beware of overcharging. *Las Palmeras*, Serrano y Barros Arana. For meat dishes, not expensive, good value *almuerzo*. *Las Tejas de Barros Arana*, Barros Arana 684. Peruvian *parrillada*. *Snappy*, Lynch y Tarapacá. Cheap snacks, open early till late. In the Zofri is the *Plaza de Comidas del Mall*, with restaurants serving a variety of national and international cuisine including cheap *almuerzos*.

Caleta Cavancha *El Sombrero*, Los Rieles 704. Quality fish and seafood cuisine, elegant setting, not cheap. *Otelo*, Valenzuela 775. Italian specialities, seafood, pricey. Several good, inexpensive seafood restaurants can be found on the 2nd floor of the central market, Barros Arana y Latorre. Beware the expensive and poor value tourist restaurants on the wharf on the opposite side of Av Costanera from the bus terminal.

Cafés Several excellent cafés in the centre including: *Via Pontony*, Baquedano y Zegers. Also fruit juices and *empanadas*. Recommended. *Tropical*, on Plaza Prat and at Baquedano y Thompson. Juices, snacks. Recommended. *Cioccolata*, Pinto 487 (another branch in the Zofri). *Tavarúa*, Lynch y Serrano. *Contactos*, Labbé 501. *Coffee Break*, Tarapacá 380. *Vizzio*, Tarapacá 398. *Pinina*, Tarapacá y Ramirez.

Bars and pubs For late night food, drink, video entertainment, dancing: *Taberna Barracuda*, Gorostiaga 601; *Mascarrieles*, Plaza Prat; *Timber House*, Bolívar 553. In Playa Brava: *El Galpón*, 11 de Septiembre 1985 and, next door, *Black Jack Pub*, 11 de Septiembre 1975.

Cinema *Cine Tarapacá*, Serrano 202. Shows foreign films. Also in Mall las Américas. **Entertainment**
Casino, Balmaceda 2755. Open nightly, entry to salóns, US$22.50. Plays, ballet, dance
and concerts in the Teatro Municipal.

Bathing Beaches at Cavancha just south of town centre, good, and Huaiquique, rea- **Sports**
sonable, popular between November and March. Restaurants at Cavancha. Piscina
Godoy, fresh water swimming pool on Av Costanera at Aníbal Pinto and Riquelme,
open evening, US$1. **Surfing** Iquique offers some of the best surfing in Chile with
numerous reel breaks along the coast south of the city, not for beginners. **Fishing
equipment** *Ferretería Lonza*, Vivar 738. *Ferretería La Ocasión*, Sgto Aldea 890.
Fishing for broadbill swordfish, striped marlin, yellowfin tuna, oceanic bonito, March
till end of August. **Tennis** *Club de Tenis Huantajaya*, Av Costanera Sur 3607, T38194
for temporary membership.

See page 221 for the festival of the *Virgen del Carmen* in La Tirana, 70 kilometres east **Festivals**
of Iquique, **10-16 July**.

Most of the city's commerce is in the two Free Zone centres. **Bookshops** Andrés **Shopping**
Bello, Héroes de la Concepción 2855, excellent range.

Local Car hire: expensive: *Hertz*, Souper 650, T/F426316. *IQSA*, Labbé 1089, **Transport**
T/F412068, at airport T410925. *Alfa*, Colectivo O'Higgins, Local 1, T/F415999. *Budget*,
Portales 2070, T/F430353. *Procer*, Serrano 796, T/F413470, at airport T407019.
Jofamar, Libertad 1156, T/F411639. *Localiza*, Bolívar 615, T416332, F416095, at air-
port T407034. *GP Car Rental*, O'Higgins 169, T/F425295. *Dollar*, at airport, T283722.
Motorcycle mechanic: Sergio Cortez, *Givet*, Bolívar 684. Highly recommended. In
the Zofri there is a wide range of motorcycle tyres. **Bicycles**, Redolfi, Latorre 786. Sales,
parts, repairs. Try also the Zofri.

Long distance Air: Diego Aracena international airport, 35 kilometres south at
Chucumata. Taxi T413368. Airport bus to city centre, US$3. LanChile/Ladeco and
Avant fly daily to Arica, Antofagasta and Santiago.

Buses: terminal at north end of Patricio Lynch (not all buses leave from here); bus
company offices are near the market on Sgto Aldea and Barros Arana. All southbound
buses are stopped for a luggage check on leaving the duty free zone of Region I at
Quillagua on the Pan-American Highway and at Chipana on the coastal Route 1. To
Arica, buses and *colectivos*, frequent, US$8, 4½ hours; to **Antofagasta**, US$15, 8
hours. To **Calama**, 8 hours, US$13. To **Tocopilla** along the coastal road, buses and
minibuses, several companies, 4 hours, US$7; to **La Serena**, 17 hours, US$25; to **Santiago**, 24 hours, several companies, US$30 (US$50 for Barrios *salón cama*).
   International buses: Géminis (Obispo Labbé y Sotomayor) to **La Paz** (Bolivia) via
Oruro (US$30), Thursday and Saturday 2300, 22 hours, US$32. Also Litoral, Esmeralda
974, T423670. Tuesday, Saturday, Sunday 2300, US$32. To **Oruro** via Colchane several
companies including Delta, Tata Sabaya and Comet, all leave from Esmeralda y Juan
Martínez around 2100-2300, bargain for a good price. To **Salta** (Argentina) via Calama
and San Pedro; Tramaca twice a week, US$50.

Airline offices *Avant*, Pinto 55, T428800, F424094, airport T407007. *LanChile*, Vivar 675, **Directory**
T427600, airport T40736. *Iberia*, Vivar 630, T/F411878. *LAB*, Serrano 442, T/F418396, airport
T407015. *KLM*, Pinto 515, T423009. *Ladeco*, San Martín 428, T600-661-3000. **Banks** *Finandés*,
Tarapacá 441, Mastercard. *Corp Banca*, Uribe y Serrano, Visa. **Casas de Cambio:** *AFEX*, Serrano
396, changes TCs. *Money Exchange*, Lynch 548, Local 1-2. *Wall Street*, in the Zofri, sells Amex TCs
and changes them. Lots of ATMs in the Zofri. **Communications** Post Office: *Correo Central*,

Bolívar 485. **Telecommunications:** *CTC*, Labbé 399. *Entel*, Tarapacá 472. **NB** Correos, CTC, Chilexpress, Chilesat and Entel all have offices in the Plaza de Servicios in the Zofri. **Internet Access:** *Cybercafé*, Vivar y Latorre, piso 2, US$5/hour. **Consulates** *Bolivia*, Serrano, Pasaje Alessandri 429, p 2, Of 300, T421777. Mon-Fri 0930-1200. *Peru*, San Martín 385, T411466. **Hospitals** Dr Juan Noé, 18 de Septiembre, outpatient wing, no charge. **Language schools** *Academia de Idiomas del Norte*, Ramírez 1345, T411827, F429343, idiomas@chilesat.net. Swiss run, Spanish classes and accommodation for students. **Laundry** *Laverap*, San Martín 490; *Central Dry Clean*, Serrano 772. Both self-service laundries. **Tour companies & travel agents** *Iquitour*, Lynch 563, T/F412415, tour to Pintados, La Tirana, Humberstone, Pica, etc, no English spoken. *Viatours*, Baguedano 736, T/F417197, viatours@entelchile.net. *Situr*, Lynch 548, T/F428702. **Tourist offices** *Sernatur*, Serrano 145, Edif Econorte, 3 piso, oficina 303, T427586, F411523. Mon-Fri 0830-1630, very helpful. **Automóvil Club de Chile:** Serrano 154, T426772.

Routes around Iquique

Inland from Iquique there are several small towns which were the early centres of Spanish colonial settlement. Note that the rainy season in this area is mainly in January.

Pozo Almonte
Population: 5,400

Situated on the Pan-American Highway five kilometres south of the turning to Iquique, Pozo Almonte was the main service centre for the nitrate fields of the area. The **Museo Histórico Salitrero**, on the plaza, displays artefacts and photographs of the nitrate era. There is *Hotel Anakana*, Comercio 53, T751201, F751621 and *Hostería Fauda*, on the northern outskirts, T751396, F751025, with a restaurant. *Estancia Inn* is on Calle Comercial.

Mamiña

Population: 600
Altitude: 2,750m
Colour map 1, grid B2

A very popular thermal springs resort, Mamiña is reached by a road which runs east 74 kilometres from Pozo Almonte. Situated on a ridge, the village has pre-hispanic origins and is inhabited mainly by people of Aymara origin. The Aymara cultural centre, Kaspi-Kala, includes an artesania workshop and sales outlet. An Inca *pukará* (fortress) stands on a hilltop three kilometres east. Legend has it that one of its thermal pools cured an Inca princess. The church, built in 1632, is the only colonial Andean church in Chile with twin towers, each topped by a bell tower. In the nitrate period its agreeable climate and its thermal springs made it a resort for the wealthy: the Hotel Termas dates from this period. There is also a mud spring, the Baño Los Chinos (open 0930-1300) and good accommodation.

Sleeping
All the following are for full board in double rooms

A1 *La Coruña*, T09-5530051. Good Spanish cuisine, lovely views from hill-top site, horseriding. **A2** *Niña de Mis Ojos*, T420451. **A2** *Refugio del Salitre*, T751203, F420330. Swimming pool. **A3** *Llama Inn*, T09-5471246 (Iquique T/F419893). Room only, meals extra, swimming pool, good restaurant, good views, English spoken. Recommended. **A3** *Los Cardenales*, T5530934, F437755. 4-star, thermal baths, swimming pool with spring water, excellent cuisine in attractive restaurant, games room, lovely

Routes around Iquique

Distance in km

Mamiña

The site of abundant thermal springs as well as a unique mud spring, Mamiña has been a popular health resort since the nitrate era. The thermal springs are classified as being radioactive, are rich in sodium, potassium, sulphur, chlorides and silicates and are acknowledged to be valuable in treating ailments such as rheumatoid arthritis and sciatica as well as respiratory and digestive problems.

The Los Chinos thermal mud bath, which contains radioactive mud with natural deposits of vegetal mineral mud activated by the fermentation of certain algae, are seen as valuable in the treatment of many skin diseases such as psoriasis. The mud is allowed to dry on the skin after the bath and then washed off in one of the thermal springs.
    Simon Watson-Taylor

gardens, English, German spoken, delightful. Warmly recommended. **A3** *Res Cholele*, friendly. **A3** *Res Bacian*. **B** *Res Inti-Raimi*, with bath, also **E** pp dormitory accommodation, very pleasant, good restaurant, very good value. Warmly recommended. **A3** *Tamarugal*, T414663.

Bus From Iquique: *Minibuses Mollo*, Barros Arana 897, daily 0800, 1600, 2½ hours, US$6, from Mamiña 0800, 1800. *Turismo Mamiña*, Latorre 779, Monday-Saturday 0800-1600, also Sunday 1600, 2½ hours US$6, from Mamiña Tuesday-Saturday 0830, Monday-Saturday 1800.

Transport

Situated 10 kilometres east of the Pan-American Highway by a turning nine kilometres south of Pozo Almonte, La Tirana is famous for a religious festival to the Virgen del Carmen, held from 10 to 16 July. This attracts some 80,000 pilgrims. Over 100 groups dance night and day, starting on 12 July. All the dances take place in the main plaza in front of the church; no alcohol is served. Accommodation is impossible to find, other than in organized campsites (take tent) which have basic toilets and showers. There are two small museums: the Museo de la Virgen de La Tirana, which contains gifts to the virgin; and the Museo de La Tirana, which houses a collection of artefacts from the nitrate era.

La Tirana
Population: 550
Altitude: 995m

Thirty eight kilometres east of La Tirana, Matilla is an oasis settlement founded in 1760 by settlers from Pica. The village declined after 1912 when the waters of the Quebrada de Quisma were diverted to Iquique. The church (1887) is built of blocks of borax. Nearby is a **Museum** in the Lagar de Matilla, used in the 18th century for fermenting wine. ■ *Daily 0900-1700. Key from the kiosk in the plaza*. There is accommodation in the *Complejo Turístico El Parabien*, T431645, which has fully furnished *cabañas* and a pool. Near Matilla an unpaved and rough road runs southwest to meet the Pan-American Highway.

Matilla
Altitude: 1,160m

Pica

Four kilometres northeast of Matilla, Pica was the most important centre of early Spanish settlement in this region. In colonial times it produced a famous wine sold as far away as Potosí. Most of the older buildings including the church date from the nitrate period when it became a popular resort. The town is famous for its pleasant climate, its citrus groves and its two natural springs, the best of which is the Cocha Resbaladero. ■ *US$1. 0700-2000 all year. Changing rooms, snack bar, beautiful pool.*

Population: 4,000
Altitude: 1,325m
Colour map 1, grid B2

Iquique, Arica & the Far North

Sleeping C *Hostal Suizo*, Ibañez 210, T741551. With bath, modern, very comfortable. C *Hostería O'Higgins*, Balmaceda 6, T741322. With bath and breakfast, nicely furnished. C *Los Emilios*, Cochrane 213, T/F741126. With bath and breakfast, pool. C *San Andrés*, Balmaceda 197, T741319. With bath and breakfast, good restaurant, spacious, good value. E pp *Palermo*, Prat 500, T741129. Without bath, meals extra, spacious. Recommended. E pp *Res El Tambo*, Ibañez 68, T/F741041. Without bath, meals served, hospitable. Warmly recommended.

Cabañas *Res El Tambo* (see above) B, sleeps 4. *Miraflores*, in Ibañez, T741338, B, sleeps 3. *Mirador de Pica*, Resbaladero, T741061, A3, sleeps 6. *San José*, T741160, A3, sleeps 5.

Eating *Hotels San Andrés, El Tambo* and *Palermo*. *El Edén de Pica*, Riquelme 12. Best in town, speciality dishes, fine ice cream, lovely surroundings. *El Palomar*, Balmaceda 410. Good food, nice place, river trout. Recommended. Also disco at night. *La Palmera*, Balmaceda 115. Excellent *almuerzo*, popular with locals, inexpensive. *La Mía Pappa*, Balmaceda. Good selection of meat and fish, attractive location. *La Viña*, Ibañez 70. Good cheap *almuerzo*. Pica is famous for its *alfajores* filled with cream and honey, recommended.

Transport **Bus** From Iquique operated by 3 companies: *Santa Rosa*, Barros Arana 965, daily 0830 and 0930, 2 hours; from Pica 1700 and 1800, US$3; *San Andrés*, Sgto Aldea 790, daily 0930, return departure 1800, US$3; *Ramos Cholele*, Barros Arana 851, daily 0900, return departure 1900, US$3.

From Iquique to the Bolivian frontier

At Huara, 33 kilometres north of Pozo Almonte, a road turns off the Pan-American Highway and runs to Colchane, 173 kilometres northeast on the Bolivian frontier. 13 kilometres east of Huara, the road passes, on the right, the **Geoglifos de Cerro Unita**, the most outstanding of which is the **Gigante del Atacama**, a human figure 86 metres tall, reported to be the largest geoglyph in the world and best viewed from a distance.

At Km 23 a road branches off south to **Tarapacá** (*Altitude*: 1,350 metres), settled by the Spanish around 1560 and capital of the Peruvian province of Tarapacá until 1855, now largely abandoned. The major historic buildings, the Iglesia de San Lorenzo and the Palacio de Gobierno, are in ruins. From Km 25 the road is unpaved. At **Chusmisa** (*Altitude*: 3,650 metres), three kilometres off this road at Km 77 there are thermal springs: the water is bottled and sold throughout northern Chile. Basic accommodation is available in the forlorn and windy border town of **Colchane** (*Altitude*: 3,730 metres). Six kilometres northwest of Colchane is the southern entrance to the Parque Nacional Volcán Isluga (see below page 237).

Transport **Bus** Colchane can be reached by Kennybus from Iquique, 1 a week, returns after 2 hours. Bus services from Iquique to Oruro and La Paz also pass through Colchane.

Frontier with **Colchane** Open 0800-1300, 1500-1800 daily. On the Bolivian side an unpaved road
Bolivia leads to Oruro, 233 kilometres northeast.

From Iquique south towards Antofagasta

South of Pozo Almonte, the Pan-American Highway runs to Quillagua, 172 kilometres, where there is a customs post. All southbound vehicles including buses are searched. The road continues towards Antofagasta. At Km 24 the

Geoglyphs

Found as far south as the Río Loa and as far north as the Río Azapa near Arica, as well as along the Peruvian coast as far as Nazca, geoglyphs or geoglifos are one of the most visible traces left by ancient civilisations in the Atacama. Dating from an estimated 1000-1400 AD, these designs were made on the rocks using two different techniques: by scraping away the topsoil to reveal different coloured rock beneath or by arranging stones to form a kind of mosaic. They exhibit three main themes: geometrical patterns; images of animals, especially camelids, birds and snakes; humans, often holding or carrying instruments or weapons such as a bow and arrows. They are easily visible because they were intended to be seen, located on isolated hills in the desert, on the western slopes of the Cordillera de la Costa or on the slopes of quebradas (gorges).

Their significance is thought by some experts to be ritual, but others argue that they were often a kind of signpost pointing out routes between the coast and the sierra. The largest site is at Pintados, 96 kilometres south of Iquique, reached by turning off the Pan-American Highway towards Pica and then following a four kilometre track from which several panels can be seen, including representations of a large number of humans dressed in ponchos and feather head-dresses as well as geometrical designs and representations of animals and birds. Though there are more sites, the most important of the others are the following: at Tiliviche, 127 kilometres north of Iquique, some 600 metres south of the Pan-American Highway, where, on the southern side of the quebrada, a 300 metre panel can be seen representing a drove of llamas moving from the cordillera to the coast; at Cerro Rosita, 20 kilometres north of Huara near the Pan-American Highway, where the 'Sun of Huara' (an Aymara sun emblem) is visible on the eastern side of the hill; at Cerro Unitas, 15 kilometres east of Huara where geoglyphs are visible on the western and southern sides of an isolated hill. On the western slope is the Gigante del Atacama or Giant of the Atacama, probably the most famous of all the images: 86 metres high, this is a representation of an indigenous leader with a head-dress of feathers and a feline mask; to his left is a reptile, thought to link him to the earth god Pachamama, to his right is his staff of office.

(sidebar, vertical) Iquique, Arica & the Far North

road runs through the largest section of the **Reserva Nacional Pampa del Tamarugal** (the other two sections are around La Tirana and north of Huara) which is administered by Conaf. Covering a total of 100,650 hectares, the reserve includes plantations of tamaruga (Prosopis tamarugo), a tree species adapted to the dry climate and saline soils. The **Geoglifos de Pintados**, some 400 figures on the hillsides, representing humans, animals and birds as well as abstract designs, are situated some three kilometres west of the Pan-American Highway, turn off at Km 43.

From Iquique north towards Arica

The Pan-American Highway runs across the Atacama desert at an altitude of around 1,000 metres, with several steep hills which are best tackled in daylight. At night, sea mist, *camanchaca*, can reduce visibility.

Thirty three kilometres north of Pozo Almonte, Huara was once a town of 7,000 people, serving as a centre for the nearby nitrate towns but little evidence remains of that period apart from the railway station which is a national monument. Nearby are the huge and impressive geoglyphs of Cerro Unita, see above. Basic accommodation is available in the *Restaurant Frontera*.

Huara
Population: 400

Pisagua
Population: 200

At Zapiga, 47 kilometres north of Huara there is a cross roads: one branch leads west for 41 kilometres to **Pisagua**, formerly an important nitrate port, now a small fishing port. Several old wooden buildings here are national monuments including the Municipal Theatre (1892) and the Clock Tower (1887), but it is now largely abandoned. There are fish restaurants and it makes a pleasant stop for a meal. Pisagua was the site of a detention centre after the 1973 military coup: mass graves from that period were discovered near here in 1990. Accommodation is available in the friendly *Restaurant Acuario*, **F** per person. There is a campsite at the northern end of the beach.

Camiña
Population: 500
Altitude: 2,400m

A picturesque village in an oasis, Camina lies 67 kilometres east of Zapiga along a poor road (deep sand and dust).There is a basic *hostal* on the plaza, **E** per person. From here a terrible road runs to the Tranque de Caritaya, a dam 45 kilometres further northeast which supplies water for the coastal towns and which is set in splendid scenery with lots of wildlife and interesting botany (especially *llareta*).

At Km 57 north of Huara there is an interesting British cemetery dating from the 19th century: note the fine wrought-iron gates. Nearby from the highway there is a view of the **Geoglifos de Tiliviche** representing a group of llamas (signposted to left and easily accessible). Further north at Km 111, the **Geoglifos de Chiza** can be seen from the bridge which carries the Highway over the Quebrada de Chiza. At Km 172 a road runs east to **Codpa**, an agricultural community in a deep gorge with interesting scenery. From Codpa poor roads lead north and east through **Tignamar** and Belén to Putre.

Belén
Population: 150
Altitude: 3,240m

A tiny village founded by the Spanish in 1625, Belén was on the silver route between Potosí and the coast. It has two colonial churches: the older one, the Iglesia de Belén is one of the oldest (and smallest) churches in Chile; the other, the Iglesia de Carmen, dates from the 18th century. At Tignamar Viejo, an abandoned village 14 kilometres south, there is another colonial church.

Arica

Population: 174,064
Phone code: 058
Colour map 1, grid A1

Chile's most northerly city, Arica is 19 kilometres south of the Peruvian border. An oasis city, it lies at the foot of the Morro headland, fringed by sand dunes.

Arica is an important port and route centre; linked to the Bolivian capital La Paz by road, rail and an oil pipeline, it handles a large proportion of Bolivia's foreign trade. It is frequented for sea bathing by Bolivians as well as the locals. There are also fast road connections with the Peruvian city of Tacna, 54 kilometres north. Regrettably there are indications that Arica is also becoming a key link in the international drugs trade. There are large fishmeal plants and a car assembly factory.

History

During the colonial period Arica was important as the Pacific end of the silver route from Potosí. Independence as part of Peru and the re-routing of Bolivian trade through Cobija led to a decline from which the city recovered with the building of rail links with Tacna (1855) and La Paz (1913). The city came under Chilean control at the end of the War of the Pacific. The **Morro** in Arica was the site of an important Chilean victory over Peru on 7 June 1880.

Sights

The city is centred around the Plaza Colón, on which stands the cathedral of **San Marcos**, built in iron by Eiffel. Though small it is beautifully proportioned and attractively painted. It was brought to Arica from Ilo in Peru as an emergency measure after a tidal wave swept over Arica in 1868 and destroyed all its churches. Eiffel also designed the nearby **Aduana** (customs house) which is now the Casa de la Cultura. ■ *Monday-Saturday 1000-1300, 1700-2000.* Just north of the Aduana is the La Paz railway station; outside is an old steam locomotive (made in Germany in 1924) once used on this line. In the station is a memorial to John Roberts Jones, builder of the Arica portion of the railway. South of the Plaza Colón (about 10 minutes' walk) is the **Morro**, which offers fine views of the city.

Museums **Museo Arqueológico** of the University of Tarapacá, see under **Excursions** below. **Museo Histórico y de Armas**, on the summit of the Morro, contains weapons and uniforms from the War of the Pacific. ■ *US$1. December-February daily 0800-2200. March-November daily 0800-2030.*

Excursions

To the Azapa valley, east of Arica. At Km 13 is the **Museo Arqueológico San Miguel de Azapa**, part of the University of Tarapacá and worth a visit. It contains a fine collection of precolumbian weaving, pottery, woodcarving and basket work from the coast and the valleys as well as four mummified humans from the Chinchorro culture (8,000-10,000 BC), the most ancient mummies yet discovered. Comprehensive explanations are provided by booklets in English, French, German and Spanish, loaned free at the entrance. ■ *US$1.50, T224248. Daily 0900-2000 (2 January-28 February), 1000-1800 (1 March-31 December), closed 1 January, 1 May, 25 December. Getting there: Take a yellow colectivo from P. Lynch y Chacabuco, US$1.*

In the forecourt of the museum are several boulders with precolumbian petroglyphs. On the road between Arica and San Miguel several groups of geoglyphs of humans and llamas can be seen to the south of the road. On the opposite side of the valley at San Lorenzo are the ruins of a *pukará* (pre-Inca fortress) dating from the 12th century.

To the **Lluta valley**, north of Arica along Route 11, bus from MacKenna y Chacabuco: between Km 14 and Km 16, on the hillsides are the **Geoglifos de Lluta**, four groups of geoglyphs representing llamas and humans. The road continues through the Parque Nacional Lauca and on to Bolivia.

Iquique, Arica & the Far North

Essentials

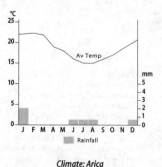
Climate: Arica

Sleeping **L3** *El Paso*, Gen Velásquez 1109, T/F231965. Bungalow style, excellent restaurant, lovely gardens, tennis court, pool. **A1** *Arica*, San Martín 599, 2 kilometres south on coast (frequent buses and colectivos), T254540, F231133. Lower rates off season, good value, excellent restaurant, tennis court, pool, lava beach (not safe for swimming). **A1** *Azapa*, Sánchez 660, Valle de Azapa, T244537, F244517. Attractive grounds,

Sleeping ■ *on map, page 226* *Price codes: see inside front cover*

also cheaper cabañas, good restaurant. **A1** *Star*, Playa Chinchorro, T/F211107. Fully furnished apartments. **A1** *El Jardín de Arica*, Valle de Azapa, T244537, F244517. Pool, tennis court, restaurant, attractive gardens. **A2** *Central*, 21 de Mayo 425, T252575, F251168. Attractive décor, usual luxury facilities, good service, nicely decorated. **A2** *Motel Saucache*, Sanchez 027, Valle de Azapa, T/F241458. Fully equipped *cabañas*, sleeps 2 or 4. **A2** *Savona*, Yungay 380, T231000, F231606. Comfortable, friendly, quiet. Highly recommended. **A2** *Sol de Arica*, Avalos 2041, T246050, F246113. Sauna, jacuzzi, pool. **A3** *Amadís*, Prat 588, T/F232994. Central, modern. **A3** *Americano*, Lagos 571, T/F252150, servturi@entelchile.net. Cable TV, sauna, gymnasium. **A3** *Concorde*, Velásquez 580, T252000, F230022. Busy popular restaurant, noisy, overpriced. **A3** *Diego de Almagro*, Sotomayor 490, T224444, F221248. Without breakfast, helpful, comfortable, parking. Recommended. Stores luggage. **A3** *King*, Colón 376, T232094, F251124. **A3** *Lynch*, Lynch 589, T231581/251959. **C** without bath, overpriced. **A3** *Plaza Colón*, San Marcos 261, T254424, F231244. Modern, comfortable. **A3** *San Marcos*, Sotomayor 387, T232970, F251815. Comfortable.

B *Aragón*, Maipú 344, T/F252088. With breakfast. **C** *Hostal 18*, 18 de Septiembre 524, T251727. With breakfast, good. **C** *Hostal Casa Mia Nona*, 21 de Mayo 660, T250597. Without breakfast. **C** *Jacora*, Sotomayor 540, T229234, F251240, pleasant patio, stores luggage. **C** *Res América*, Sotomayor 430, T254148, with bath, **E** pp without.

Arica centre

To Playa Chinchorro

To Shopping Center del Pacífico & Terminal for Buses to Tacna

To Main Bus Terminal, Airport, Pan-American Highway (North), for Peru, Parque Nacional Lauca & Bolivia

Pacific Ocean

Casino

Parque General Carlos Ibañez del Campo

Colectivos to Tacna

Muelle Turístico

Former Railway Station

Former Aduana

Plaza Colón

Cathedral

Plaza del Trabajador

Museo Histórico y de Armas

El Morro

To Hotel Arica, La Lisera, El Laucho, Playa Brava & Playa Corazones

Lastarria
Esmeralda
Juan Noé
Chacabuco
O'Higgins
18 de Septiembre
21 de Mayo
Sotomayor
San Marcos
Yungay
Ejército
El Morro
Maipú
Bolivian Consulate
Peruvian Consulate
Market
Thompson
Sangra

Maximo Lira
Pedro Montt
Arturo Prat
General Velásquez
Colón
Baquedano
Patricio Lynch
General Lagos
Blanco Encalada
San Martín
Gallo
Av Vicuña Mackenna
Angamos

To Poblado Artesanal, Pan-American Highway (South) & Azapa

N

0 metres 150
0 yards 164

■ **Sleeping**
1 Amadis
2 Aragón
3 Casa Mía Nonna
4 Central
5 Concorde
6 Diego de Almagro
7 El Paso
8 Hotel 18
9 Jacora
10 King
11 Lynch
12 Plaza Colón
13 Residencial América
14 Residencial Blanquita
15 Residencial Ecuador
16 Residencial Española
17 Residencial Jardín del Sol
18 Residencial Real
19 Residencial Velásquez
20 San Marcos
21 Savona
22 Stagnano

● **Eating**
1 Bavaria
2 Don Floro
3 El Rey del Marisco
4 Los Aleros del 21

Clean, hospitable. **C** *Res Ecuador*, Juan Noé 989, T251573. Noisy, breakfast extra, over-priced. **C** *Res Jardín del Sol*, Sotomayor 848, T232795. With bath, **D** without, with breakfast, comfortable, friendly, good value. Highly recommended.

D *Hostal Sammy*, Lagos 1066, T/F232469. With breakfast. **D** *Res Blanquita*, Maipú 472, T232064, F250062. Clean, pleasant. **D** *Res Caracas*, Sotomayor 867, T253688. Clean, with breakfast. **D** *Res Las Condes*, Mackenna 628, T/F254399, with breakfast. Helpful. Recommended. **D** *Res Real*, Sotomayor 578, T/F253359. Very friendly and helpful. Rec-ommended. **D** *Res Nilda*, Raul del Canto 947, T222743. Well furnished, kitchen and laundry facilities, near Playa Chinchorro. Recommended. **D** *Res Stagnano*, Gallo 294, T231254, F256687. With breakfast, very good value. Recommended.

E *Hostal Chez Charlie*, Paseo Thompson 236. Comfortable, without breakfast, good value. Recommended. **E** *Res Española*, Bolognesi 340, T231703. Without breakfast, central, basic, quiet. Recommended. **E** *Res Las Vegas*, Baquedano 120, T231355. Without bath, basic, friendly, dark rooms, hot water. **E** *Res Leiva*, Colón 347, T/F232008. Without bath, French spoken, cooking facilities, cycle hire. **E** *Res Los Portales*, Gallo 228, T/F226816, good value. **E** *Res Madrid*, Baquedano 685, T231479. Without bath or breakfast, poor beds, reductions for Hostelling International cards. **E** *Res El Sur*, Maipú 516, T252457. Clean but grim. **E** *Res Venecia*, Baquedano 739, T252877. Spotless, hot water, small rooms. Recommended. **E** pp *Res Las Condes*, MacKenna y Maipú, kitchen facilities, clean. **E** *Sra Gloria Martinez*, Pasaje 7, No 1026, Población Juan Noé, T241971. Friendly, helpful.

On Velásquez E *Res Chillán*, No 749, T251677. Noisy, poor beds. **E** *Res Ine'sa*, No 725, T231609. Comfortable, breakfast available, kitchen, laundry, good. **E** *Res Velásquez*, No 669, T231989. Basic, friendly, laundry facilities, cable TV. **E** pp *Res Pacífico*, No 611, T230567, with breakfast, cooking facilities. There are other cheap places along Velásquez 600 and 700 blocks, all **E-F**, some are reasonable, others to be avoided. In January-February the municipality supplies cheap basic accommodation, ask at the tourist office.

Camping Many sites at Villa Frontera, 15 kilometres north including *Gallinazos*, T232373. Full facilities, pool. *El Refugio de Azapa*, 3 ½ kilometres from Arica, T227545. At Playa Las Machas, 5 kilometres north, no water or facilities. Free camping (no facili-ties) at Playa Chinchorro. Camping at Playa Corazones, 8 kilometres south, (no water) is risky as there are reports of daylight mugging and robbery.

Acuario, Muelle Turístico. Good food in fishy environment, good value *menu de casa*. **Eating** *El Rey del Marisco*, Maipú y Colón. Excellent seafood, pricey. Recommended. ● *on map* *Maracuyá*, San Martín 0321. Seafood, splendid location on the coast, pricey. *Los Aleros del 21*, 21 de Mayo 736. Recommended for seafood and service. *Don Floro*, V MacKenna 847. Good seafood and steaks, good service. Highly recommended. *Snack Suceso Inn*, 18 de Septiembre 250. Good set meal and coffee. *La Jaula*, 21 de Mayo 293. Snacks, meals, not expensive. *Casanova*, Baquedano 397. Excellent but not cheap. *Yuri*, Maipú y Lynch. Good service, cheap lunches. Recommended. *Bavaria*, Colón 613. Good restaurant, pricey, coffee and cakes. *Govinda*, Bolognesi 430. Vege-tarian, good value lunches. *Scala*, 21 de Mayo 201. Excellent fruit juices, real coffee. *Carpaccio*, Velásquez 510. Restaurant and bar, live music from 2330 Wednes-day-Saturday. *El Tambo*, in Poblado Artesanal, Hualles 2025. For lunches, folk music and dancing on Friday/Saturday evenings. Several good Chinese restaurants includ-ing *Chin Huang Tao*, Lynch 317. Excellent, pricey but worth it; *Kau Chea*, 18 de Septiembre y Prat, good value; *Shaolin*, 18 de Septiembre 601. *La Bomba*, Colón 357, at fire station. Good value *almuerzo*, friendly service. *Capricho Latino*, 18 de

Septiembre 250. Good value *almuerzo*. *Cyclo*, Lynch 224. Seafood, pasta, reasonably priced. Recommended. *La Ciboulette*, Paseo Thompson 238. Good food, pleasant atmosphere, not expensive. Recommended. *Mi Viejo*, Maipú 436. Cheap meals and snacks. *El Arriero*, 21 de Mayo 385. *Parrillada*, also seafood and fish, expensive. Warmly recommended. *D'Aurelio*, Baquedano 369. Italian specialities, good pasta, seafood. *Las Tejas de Azapa*, Valle de Azapa Km 2, No 4301 *Parrillada*, seafood, pool, expensive. There are many cheap restaurants on Baquedano 600/700 blocks including *San Fernando*, No 601. Simple breakfast, good value *almuerzo*.

Cafés 3 good places all on 21 de Mayo and offering real coffee and outdoor seating: *Di Mango*, No 244. Juices, ice cream. *Caffelatte*, No 248. *Carlos Díaz León Snack Place*, No 388.

Bars **Pubs** *Puerto Navarrón*, Paseo Bolognesi. Open till 0400, live music at weekends. *Altillo Pub*, 21 de Mayo 260. *Barrabás*, 21 de Mayo 233. *France Tropicale Pub*, Baquedano 371. Open till dawn, live music weekends. French and English spoken.

Entertainment **Cinemas** *Colón,* 7 de Junio 190, T231165. *Cine Arte*, at the Biblioteca Publíca on Yungay.
    Music Peña folklorica of Andean music in the Poblado Artesanal, Friday and Saturday 2130.
    Discotheques *Avant Premier*, Santiago Flores 180 (taxi from centre US$5). *Soho*, Buenos Aires 209. For rock 'n' roll. *Sunset* and *Swing*, both $3\frac{1}{2}$ kilometres out of town in the Valle de Azapa. 2300-0430 weekends (taxi US$3).
    Theatre *Teatro Municipal de Arica*, Baquedano 234. Wide variety of theatrical and musical events, exhibitions. Recommended.

Sports **Bathing** Olympic pool in Parque Centenario, Tuesday-Sunday, US$2; take No 5A bus from 18 de Septiembre. The best beach for swimming is Playa Chinchorro, north of town (bus 24) but Playa Las Machas, further north, has strong currents. Buses 7 and 8 run to beaches south of town – the first two beaches, La Lisera and El Laucho, are both small and mainly for sunbathing. Playa Brava is popular for sunbathing but not swimming (dangerous currents). **Surfing** Good surfing at Playa Las Machas and Playa Chinchorro, north of the city, and at La Isleta and Playa Corazones, 9 kilometres south along coast road (take bus or colectivo). **Golf** 18-hole course in Valle de Azapa, open daily except Monday. **Tennis** *Club de Tenis Centenario*, Av España 2640. Open daily. **Paragliding** is practised on the mountains overlooking the city. Contact Escuela Profesional de Parapente Termica, Av La Tirana 3441, Depto C-37, T/F450675.

Shopping *Poblado Artesanal*, Plaza Las Gredas, Hualles 2825 (take bus 2, 3 or 7): expensive but especially good for musical instruments, open Tuesday-Sunday 0930-1300, 1500-1930; *Mercado Central*, Sotomayor y Sangra, recently renovated, fruit and vegetables, mornings only. *Feria Turística Dominical*, Sunday market, on Chacabuco between Velásquez and Mackenna, good prices for llama sweaters. Fruit, vegetable and old clothes market at Terminal del Agro at southeastern edge of town; take bus marked 'Agro' along 18 de Septiembre. Supermarkets at Baguedano y 18 de Septiembre, San Martín y 18 de Septiembre, Chacabuco y Lagos. **Cameras and film** *Profonor*, 18 de Septiembre y Lynch, recommended. Avoid Megaclor on 21 de Mayo for devloping film.

Transport **Local** **Bus**: buses run from Maipú, US$0.25. **Colectivos** run on fixed routes within city limit, US$0.30 per person (US$0.50 per person after 2000). **Car hire**: *Hertz*, Hotel El Paso, Gen Velázquez 1109, T231487. *Klasse*, Velásquez 760, Loc 25, T/F254498; *American*, Gen Lagos 559, T/F252234. *GP*, Copacabana 628, T252594, good reports. *Viva*, airport, T251121. For the Parque Nacional Lauca four-wheel drive and antifreeze are essential; if you wish to cross from the park into Bolivia you will need a permit from the hire company. Hertz provides the most reliable vehicles but check any rental vehicle for jack, lug wrench as well as the condition of both the fan belt (often dry and cracked) and the spare tyre. Crossing to Tacna (Peru) with a hire car can be difficult: Klasse can arrange the paperwork for this.

Motoring *Automóvil Club de Chile*: Chacabuco 460, T252878, F232780. **Car insurance**: at Dirección de Tránsito; may insist on car inspection. **Car service**: Shell, Panamericana Norte 3456; Esso, Portales 2462; Autocentro, Azola 2999, T241241. **Bicycles**: *Bicicletas Wilson*, 18 de Sept 583. Repairs, parts, sales, ATB specialists. **Motorcycle repairs**: Pablo Fernández Davils, El Salitre 3254, T212863, F212823.

Long distance **Air**: airport 18 kilometres north of city at Chacalluta, T222831. Taxi to town US$9, *colectivo* US$4-5 per person from Lynch y 21 de Mayo. Flights: to **La Paz**, LanChile/Ladeco and LAB; to **Santiago**, Ladeco, LanChile and Avant all via Iquique and Antofagasta. Book well in advance. To **Lima**, AeroPerú and others from Tacna (Peru), enquire at travel agencies in Arica.

Bus terminal (Rodoviario) northeast of centre at Av Portales y Santa María, T241390, reached by many buses and *colectivos* including No 8 and 18 (US$0.20, or US$0.45), taxi to centre US$2 (terminal tax US$0.25). All southbound luggage is carefully searched for fruit prior to boarding and is then searched again at Cuya on the Pan-American Highway. Bus company offices at bus terminal apart from the following: Flota Paco (La Paloma), Germán Riesco 2071 (bus U from centre); Humire, P Montt 662, T231891; Martínez, 21 de Mayo 575, T232265; Bus Lluta, Chacabuco y V Mackenna. Litoral, Chacabuco 454, T254702; Andes-Mar, Galerin Río San José, Av Santa María 2010, T 248200/232265.

To **Antofagasta**, US$18, 10 hours; to **Calama** and **Chuquicamata**, 8 hours, US$16, several companies, all between 2000 and 2200; to **Iquique**, frequent, US$8, 4½ hours, also *collectivos*, several companies, all with offices in the terminal; to **Santiago**, 28 hours, a number of companies, for example Carmelita, Ramos Cholele, Fénix and Flota Barrios US$40-45, also *salón cama* services, run by Fichtur, Flota Barrios, Fénix and others, US$75, Tramaca recommended (most serve meals though these vary in quality; generally better on more expensive services; student discounts available); to **La Serena**, 18 hours, US$30; to **Viña del Mar** and **Valparaíso**, US$40, also *salón cama* service, US$50.

International buses: to **La Paz, Bolivia**, Litoral, Monday, Wednesday, Saturday 0700, US$25 including lunch; Geminis, Monday, Wednesday, Friday 1000, US$20 without lunch; Chile Bus, Tuesday, Thursday, Saturday 1000, US$30 with lunch; Andes Mar, Monday, Thursday, Friday, Saturday 0800, Transalvador, Tuesday, Wednesday, Thursday, Friday, 0800, via border towns of Chungará (Chile) and Tambo Quemado (Bolivia, very cold at border – take blanket/sleeping bag, food, water and sense of humour), 8-10 hours. See page 231 for buses and *colectivos* to Tacna, Peru.

Motorists: it is illegal to take fruit and dairy products south of Arica: all vehicles are searched at Cuya, 105 kilometres south, and at Huara, 234 kilometres south. **Service stations** between the Peruvian border and Santiago can be found at: Arica, Huara, Iquique, Pozo Almonte, Oficina Victoria, Tocopilla, Oficina María Elena, Chuquicamata, Calama, Carmen Alto, Antofagasta, La Negra, Agua Verde (also fruit inspection post), Taltal, Chañaral, Caldera, Copiapó, Vallenar, La Serena, Termas de Soco, Los Vilos, and then every 30 kilometres to capital.

Hitchhiking: not easy to hitch south: try the Terminal del Agro off the Pan-American Highway (trucks leave Monday, Thursday and Saturday before 0700) and the Copec station opposite (reached by bus from Arica marked 'Agro' or *colectivo* No 8).

Iquique, Arica & the Far North

Directory **Airline offices** *LanChile*, 21 de May 345, T251641, F252600. *Ladeco*, 21 de Mayo 443, T255259, airport T211259. *Lloyd Aéreo Boliviano*, P Lynch 298, T251472, airport T/F216411. *Iberia*, Prat 391, 7 piso, oficina 7/8, T232079. *Avant*, 21 de Mayo 227, T/F232328, airport T216459.

Banks Street money changers on 21 de Mayo and its junction with Colón, mainly operate outside normal banking hours, accept TCs but at poor rates. *Corp Banca*, Bolognesi 317. Visa. ATM. *Finandes*, 21 de Mayo 560. Mastercard. **Casas de Cambio**: *Sol y Mar*, Colón 610, TCs not accepted. For TCs *Yanulaque*, 21 de Mayo 175, Mon-Fri 0900-1400, 1600-2000, Sat 0930-1330, and *Marta Daguer*, 18 de Septiembre 330, slow service, very high commission. Most large hotels also change cash. Rates for TCs are generally poor.

Communications Post Office: Prat 375. To send parcels abroad, contents must be shown to Aduana (first floor of post office), Monday-Friday 0800-1200. Packaging sold but take your own tape. **Telephones**: *Entel-Chile*, 21 de May 345. Open 0900-2200. *CTC*, Colón 430 and at 21 de Mayo 211. *VTR Telecommunications*, 21 de Mayo 477 and Colón 301. Telex, fax, telegrams. **Internet access**: *Biomar Technology*, Maipú 487.

Consulates *Bolivia*, 21 de Mayo 575, T231030. *Peru*, San Martín 220, T231020. *Germany*, 21 de Mayo 639, T231551.

Cultural centres Instituto Chileno – Británico de Cultura (library open Mon-Fri 0900-1200, 1600-2100) has newspapers, Baquedano 351, T231960, Casilla 653. *Instituto Chileno-Alemán de Cultura*, Camino Azapa 3727. *Instituto Cultural Chileno Norteamericano*, San Marcos 581.

Hospitals & medical services Dentist: *Juan Horta Becerra*, Latorre 565, oficina 202, T252497. Speaks English. *Rodrigo Belmar Castillo*, Latorre 565, oficina 306, T252047.

Laundry *Lavandería La Moderna*, 18 de Septiembre 457. US$4 per kg, open Sat till 2200.

Tour companies & travel agents *Globo Tour*, 21 de Mayo 260, T/F231085. Recommended for international flight bookings. *Latinorizons*, Thompson 236, T/F250007, latinor@entilchile.net. Specializes in tours to Lauca National Park. *Parmacota Expeditions*, Bolognesi 475, T/F251309. *AYCA Tour*, Covadonga 312, T/F240404. Archaeological and historical tours. *Ecotour Expediciones*, Bolognesi 460, T/F25000. *Turismo Payachatas*, Sotomayor y Bolognesi, T/F256981 (in Santiago: 11 de Septiembre 2214, oficina 71, T/F231-1292). *Transtours*, Bolognesi 421, T253927, F251675. *Turismo Daroch*, Bolognesi 360A, T/F254088. *Kijo Tour and Travel*, Bolognesi 357, T/F232245. Good for international travel. Most of these offer local tours and excursions to the altiplano at similar prices: city tour US$10; to Valle de Azapa US$12; to Parque Nacional Lauca one-day US$23, 2 days US$65 including accommodation; to Lauca and Isluga National Parks, 3 days US$200. Agencies pay up to 25% commission to hotels and residenciales which refer travellers; to get a lower price form a group of 5 or 6 travellers and negotiate direct with agencies. One-day tours to Lauca National Park are not really worthwhile but if limited to a one-day tour choose carefully. *Azimut 360*, Arzobispo Casanova 3, Providencia, Santiago, T 2-7358034, F 7772375, azimut@reuna.cl, www.azimut.cl. Tours to the Atacama Desert and mountaineering expeditions to Parinacota and Sajama.

Tourist offices *Sernatur*, Prat 375, piso 2. Open Mon-Fri 0830-1300, 1500-1830, T232101. Very helpful, English spoken, good map. *Automobile Club* Chacabuco 460, T252678. *Conaf*, Vicuña MacKenna 820, T/F250570, Monday-Thursday 0800-1300, 1400-1730, Friday 0800-1300, 1400-1630.

Frontier With Peru: Chacalluta

Immigration Open 0800-2400. A fairly uncomplicated crossing.

NB Between October and March Chilean time is 1 hour later than Peruvian, 2 hours later October to February or March, (varies annually).

Crossing by Drivers entering Chile are required to file a form, *Relaciones de Pasajeros* (4 copies; 8 if
private vehicle planning to return via this crossing), giving details of passengers, obtained from a sta-
tionery store in Tacna, or at the border in a kiosk near Customs. You must also present the original registration document for your car from its country of registration. The first checkpoints outside Arica on the road to Santiago also require the *Relaciones de Pasajeros* form. If you can't buy the form, details on a piece of paper will suffice or you can get them at service stations. The form is *not* required when travelling south of Antofagasta. Crossing to Tacna with a hire car is difficult: make sure you have the correct papers.

Facilities at the frontier but reported better rates in Tacna.

Colectivos: run from the bus terminal and bus company offices in Arica to **Tacna**, US$3 per person, 1½ hours, drivers take care of all the paperwork. 4 companies: Chile Lintur, Baquedano 796, T232048; Chasquitur, Chacabuco 320, T231376. San Marcos, Noé 321, T252528; Colectivo San Remo, Chacabuco 350, T251925; Bus from the terminal, US$2, also Taxibus, 2 hourly, US$4.

Tacna is 36 kilometres north of the frontier. The city was in Chilean hands from 1880 to 1929, when its citizens voted by plebiscite to return to Peru. There is a wide variety of hotels and restaurants as well as bus and air services to the rest of Peru, and a tourist office at Av Bolognesi 2088, T3778. The Peruvian side of the border is open 0900-2200.

From Arica to Bolivia

There are two routes from Arica to the Bolivian frontier

Via Chungará and Tambo Quemado Route 11 (paved to La Paz) turns off the Pan-American Highway 12 kilometres north of Arica and runs via Putre and Parinacota through the Parque Nacional Lauca (see page 232) to the frontier at Chungará. This is the route followed by most transport to Bolivia, including buses and trucks. Estimated driving time to La Paz six hours.

Chilean formalities are 7 kilometres west of the frontier open daily 0800-2000. Boliv- ian immigration and customs are at Tambo Quemado, just over the frontier (where there is a local barter market every other Friday). This is a relatively speedy crossing.

Bus there are 2 or 3 buses daily between Arica and La Paz; for details see under Arica.

Hitching the Chungará frontier post is a good place for hitching to La Paz.

Into Bolivia The road to Oruro and La Paz (Route 108) passes through the **Parque Nacional Sajama**. This park covers 60,000 hectares and contains the world's highest forest, consisting mainly of the rare Kenua tree (Polylepis tarapana) which survives at altitudes up to 5,200 metres. The scenery is wonderful and includes views of three volcanos: Parinacota (6,342 metres) and Pomerape (6,282 metres) both of which are on the frontier, and Sajama (6,530 metres) which is Bolivia's highest peak. Park administration is at Sajama village, 14 kilometres off Route 108 (*Population* 200; *Altitude* 4,200 metres) where there is also basic accommodation. There is also accommodation at Carahuara de Carangas, 111 kilometres northeast of Tambo Quemado. The main Oruro-La Paz highway is reached at Patacamaya, 104 kilometres south of La Paz, where there is basic accommodation and a Sunday market.

Via Visviri and Charalla This route is unpaved and should not be attempted in wet weather. It follows the La Paz-Arica railway line to **Visviri** (*Altitude* 4,069 metres), which is three kilometres from the Bolivian frontier and 12 kilometres from Peru (no crossing). There are markets on Wednesday and Saturday mornings and a Sunday morning market is held from 0900 north of the town at the frontier of the three countries. There is no fuel or accommodation. Visviri can also be reached by road from Putre.

Travelling in the Northern Altiplano

In all of the mountain areas of the north of Chile, it is important to note that weather and road conditions are very variable. The carabineros and military are very active trying to control the borders with Bolivia and Argentina, so they know about the conditions and are quite willing to tell, but only if asked. Some frontier areas are closed to visitors.

If you plan to stay in the mountains for any length of time, take small gifts for the locals, such as tea, sugar coffee, salad oil,

flour, or a few litres of fuel. Drivers should carry a tow-rope to assist other drivers. It is often possible to get people to bake bread etc for you, but you need to supply flour, yeast and salt if you are planning to do much cooking, then a good pressure cooker is indispensible (remember water boils at only 90°C at these altitudes). You may also have problems with kerosene stoves; petrol ones, though rather dangerous, are much more reliable.

Dr Lyndsey O'Callaghan.

Immigration Open 0800-2400. Chilean formalities are at Visviri, Bolivian formalities are conducted at Charaña, 10 kilometres east.

Transport **Bus** Martinez buses from Arica, Tuesday and Friday. *Colectivo* from Arica US$10. From Visviri take a jeep across the frontier to Charaña.

Into Bolivia In **Charaña** immigration is behind the railway station. Accommodation is available at *Alojamiento Aranda* (**G**). There are two routes, both poor, from Charaña towards La Paz, both of which meet at Viacha. Buses to La Paz, US$4, 6 hours, leave before 1000. Truck transport to La Paz leaves in the afternoon.

Parque Nacional Lauca

Colour map 1, grid A2 *Situated in the Andes and stretching from the entrance, 145 kilometres east of Arica to the frontier with Bolivia, this park is one of the most spectacular national parks in Chile. Declared a Biosphere Reserve by UNESCO, it is renowned for its birdlife.*

Access is easy as Route 11, the main Arica-La Paz road runs through the park. On the way from Arica at Km 90 there is a pre-Inca *pukará* (fortress) and a few kilometres further there is an Inca *tambo* (inn). From mid December to mid March during the rainy season and in August, when snowfall occurs, some roads in the park may be impassable; check in advance with Conaf or the Carabineros in Arica or Putre.

The park ranges in altitude from 3,200 metres to four peaks of over 6,000 metres, so beware of *soroche*, or altitude sickness unless you are coming from Bolivia. The park covers 137,883 hectares and includes a large lake, Lago Chungará, a system of small lakes, lagunas Cotacotani, and lava fields.

Population 1,200 **Putre** is a scenic Aymaran village, 15 kilometres west of the park entrance,
Altitude: 3,500m which provides an ideal base for exploring and acclimatization. Situated at the base of Volcán Taapacá (Spanish name Nevadas de Putre, 5,824 metres), it is surrounded by terracing dating from pre-Inca times which is now used for cultivating alfalfa and oregano. It has a church dating from 1670. The village is a good centre for hiking: an extensive network of trails lead to precordillerian villages. In the vicinity there are four archaeological sites with prehistoric cave paintings up to 6,000 years old. Five kilometres east by trail (11 kilometres by road) are the hot springs of Jurassi, with very hot water and a red mud bath.

Iquique, Arica & the Far North

Acclimatization for the Altiplano

Unless you are entering Chile from Bolivia, the high altitude of the altiplano encountered in the Parque Nacional Lauca presents specific health problems for the traveller to Chile. These should not be underestimated; anyone with circulation or respiratory problems would be advised to avoid the risks involved. Visitors to the park are advised to spend at least one night, preferably more, in Putre before moving on to higher altitudes. Drinking lots of water and/or mate de coca is also advised to compensate for the loss of body fluid caused by increased respiration and perspiration. You should, of course, take it easy, limiting exercise **before** *you get that familiar headache associated with* soroche *(altitude*

sickness), avoid smoking and take steps to get as much fresh air as possible, particularly if spending the night in a refugio. *In popular* refugios *there can be six to 10 people breathing the same air all night in a small room: to avoid the 3 am headache which often develops in such conditions leave a window open and keep the water bottle nearby. Sleeplessness is a common first night problem but is not a cause for concern.*

One-day trips to the park from Arica cannot really be recommended, either for health or for enjoyment: what should be a great trip amid incredible scenery can become an endurance exercise in a minibus full of passengers suffering from soroche.

At **Parinacota** (4,392 metres), 41 kilometres further east at the foot of the Payachatas volcano, there is an interesting 17th century church – rebuilt 1789 – with frescoes, silver religious objects and the skulls of past priests. Sr Sipriano keeps the key: ask for him at the kiosks and make sure you leave a donation. Most of the handicrafts sold in Parinacota are from Bolivia or Peru: a better place to buy locally made products is **Chucuyo**, 36 kilometres further east where local residents weave and knit from their own high quality alpaca wool.

From Parinacota an unpaved road runs to the Bolivian frontier at Visviri, 90 kilometres further north (see above). Cerro Guaneguane (5,300 metres), can be climbed from Parinacota; ask one of the villagers to accompany you as a guide (and pay them). Conaf maintains a nature trail which covers most plant and bird habitats, beginning at the Conaf pond in Parinacota and ending back in the village. Twenty kilometres southeast of Parinacota is **Lago Chungará**, one of the highest lakes in the world at 4,512 metres, a must for its views of the Parinacota, Pomerape, Sajama and Guallatire volcanoes. Overlooking the lake there is a Conaf *refugio* and campsite; vicuñas, llamas and alpacas can be seen grazing nearby. From here it is three kilometres to the Chilean passport control point and 10 kilometres to the Bolivian frontier at Tambo Quemado.

Park essentials

Putre A2 *Hostería Las Vicuñas*, T/F228564. Half board, bungalow-style, heating, restaurant, does not accept travellers' cheques, US$ cash or credit cards. **E** pp *Res La Paloma*. Newly renovated, indoor parking, no heating, good food, friendly. **E** pp *Res Rosamel*. Clean, pleasant, hot water, restaurant. **F** pp *Res Oasis*. Basic, no showers, good food, very friendly. **Camping** Sra Clementina Caceres, blue door on Calle Lynch, allows camping in her garden, lunches served. **Sleeping**

Iquique, Arica & the Far North

For all overnight stays in the park take a sleeping bag, food and candles Conaf refugios do not provide sheets or blankets

Inside the park **Lagunillas** (10 kilometres north of Parinacota on road to Visviri, turn left near lake) Sr Gumercindo Gutierrez provides accommodation, guide. **Chucuyo** *Res Copihue de Oro*, 1 room, 4 beds, no showers, restaurant. *Res Doña Mati*, 1 room, 5 beds, no shower, restaurant. *Restaurant Los Payachatas*. All 3 restaurants serve tasty alpaca dishes. **Parinacota** *Sra Francisca*, 3 beds, cooking facilities. *Uta Maillko* ('home of the condor' in Aymara), dormitory, home-cooked Aymara food. **D** pp *Conaf refugio*, many beds, cooking facilities, also camping US$12 per site, reserve in Putre. **B** *Casa Barbarita*, T300013, F222735. 2 bedrooms, cooking facilities, heating, naturalist library. **Lago Chungará** *Conaf Refugio*, 8 beds, wood stove, cooking facilities, camping, prices as in Parinacota, reserve in Putre.

Sports **Mountain climbing**: Arturo Gomez, who lives next to the Lipigas propane shop in Putre, is a climbing guide and local plant expert. Permits are required for climbing Parinacota, Pomerape, Taapacá and Guallatire volcanoes; these can be obtained from the Governor's office in Putre: the procedure is routine (passport required) but expect a delay of 1 or 2 days. To obtain permit in advance contact Departamento de Fronteras y Limites (DIFROL), Banderas 52, piso 5, Santiago, T6794200/6714110, listing the mountains you wish to climb. The best season for climbing is August-Novembver; avoid January-February.

Shopping Putre has markets where bottled water, fresh bread, vegetables, meat, cheese and canned foods can be obtained. The Cooperativo on the plaza is usually cheapest. Fuel is available from the Cali and Paloma supermarkets, but is cheaper at ECA, next to the Post Office. Buy all food for the park in Putre. Sra Daria Condori's shop on Calle O'Higgins sells locally made *artesanía* and naturally coloured alpaca wool. Organically grown vegetables are available from Freddy Blanco, opposite the Banco de Estado.

Parque Nacional Lauca

Conaf guardaparque station

Acclimatizing and birdwatching in Putre

Putre is an ideal place for getting used to the altitude of Lauca and birdwatching is an ideal way of doing it. The village is an ideal base for birdwatching: more than 70 species bave been registered near the village which is blessed with a variety of habitats. The area attracts both resident and migrant species while the open landscape provides an opportunity for really watching birds. Some species reach their southern limits near Putre, among them the canyon canastero, the black throated flower piercer, and the streaked tit-spinetail. There is even an occasional visitor from the northern hemisphere.

Barbara Knapton, Birding Alto Andino tour agency.

Transport

Bus *Flota Paco* buses (known as La Paloma) leave Arica for **Putre** daily at 0645, 4 hours, US$4, returning Sunday/Wednesday 1200, otherwise 1300; *Jurasi colectivo* leaves Arica daily at 0700, picks up at hotels, T222813, US$6.50. *Bolivia Litoral* bus from Arica to **La Paz** also runs along this route (charges full Arica-La Paz fare). *Martínez* buses run to **Parinacota** Tuesday and Friday.

Hitchhiking Hitching back to Arica is not difficult; you may be able to bargain with one of the tour buses. Trucks from Arica to La Paz rarely give lifts, but a good place to try is at the Poconchile control point, 37 kilometres from Arica. Most trucks for Bolivia pass Parinacota between 0700-1100.

Directory

Banks Bank in Putre changes TCs, and cash to pesos, but commission on TCs is very high. **Tours companies & travel agents** Tours: *Birding Altoandino*, Baquedano 299 (Correo Putre) T56-58300013, F56-58222735. Runs general tours and specialist birdwatching tours to remote areas of the park and to the Salar de Surire and Parque Nacional Isluga; English spoken, owner is an Alaskan biologist/naturalist. *Turismo Taki*, is located in Copaquilla, 45 kilometres west of Putre, 100 kilometres east of Arica: restaurant, camping site and excursions to nearby *pukarás*, Inca *tambo* and cemetery and the nearby Inca trail which connected the highlands with the coast, homemade bread, English and Italian spoken. One-day tours are offered by many travel agencies in Arica (addresses above), daily in season, according to demand at other times, US$23 with light breakfast and lunch. Longer tours are also available. You can leave the tour and continue on another day as long as you ensure that the company will collect you when you want (tour companies try to charge double for this). For 5 or more, the most economical proposition is to hire a vehicle in Arica but take at least 1 spare fuel can with a tightly fitting cap. While climbing from Arica stop several times to release excess pressure in fuel cans. For tyre repairs, ask for Andrés in Putre. If you wish to cross into Bolivia you will need written permission from the hire company.

Iquique, Arica & the Far North

The wildlife of Parque Nacional Lauca

Although the park lies very close to the lifeless Atacama desert, it receives more rain because of its altitude and the reward is a fairyland of volcanoes and highland lakes surrounded by brilliant green wetlands and vast expanses of puna grassland. The Río Lauca rises near Lago Chungará, then laces slowly through the park leaving marshy cushion bogs and occasional raceways and providing an arrayof habitats for the fauna of the altiplano.

The camelids are the stars of the park; thousands of domesticated llamas and alpacas, as well as the dainty, graceful, wild vicuña which now number over 18,000. The charming viscacha, seemingly a long tailed rabbit, but in fact belonging to the chinchilla family, can be seen perched sleepily on the rocks, backside toward the morning sun. Pumas, huemules (deer), foxes, skunks and armadillos are the more elusive mammals, some nocturnal, occupying the more remote reaches.

Lauca birdlife is spectacular with more than 120 species either resident or migrant. Lago Chungará is home to more than 8,000 giant coots, their bright orange legs,

never-ending nest building, and primordial cackling entertains all. In addition to coots, ducks and grebes, the wetlands provide a fine habitat for the puna plover, the rare diademed sandpiper plover, the puna ibis, Andean species of avocet, goose and gull, and an assortment of migratory shorebirds. Occasionally one can see three species of flamingoes at once, the Andean and the James (locally called parinas) and the more common Chilean flamingo. Trips through the drier grasslands can produce glimpses of the puna tinamou, always in groups of three, and the puna rhea, seen in October and November with 20 or 30 miniatures scooting along behind. Passerines occupy all the habitats in the park, some to 5,000 metres and above nearly to the snowline. There are Sierra finches, black siskins, tit-spinetails, earthcreepers, miners, canasteros, cinclodes, new names for most birders. After all this, don't forget to look up! Andean condors, mountain caracaras, aplomado falcons, black chested buzzard eagles and buteo hawks have all been seen in the skies above.

Barbara Knapton, Birding Alto Andino tour agency, Putre.

Reserva Nacional Las Vicuñas, Salar de Surire and Parque Nacional Volcán Isluga

Colour map 1, grid A2   These three parks, covering areas of the occidental range of the Andes south of Parque Nacional Lauca, are best visited from Arica or Putre as this permits acclimatization in Putre (Colchane and Enquelga, the alternatives, are too high). The route begins in the Parque Nacional Lauca at the dirt road (A235) which turns south off the Arica-La Paz highway one kilometre past Las Cuevas and ends at Huara on the Pan-American Highway, near Iquique. There is no public transport on this route and frequently no traffic of any sort passes for days on end between Las Cuevas and Isluga. The road is open all year round, but between January and March and in August it may be impassable because of deep mud and water while bridges may be washed out. Four-wheel drive is essential; take sleeping bags and stock up on fuel, drinking water and food for emergencies. Tours in this area, lasting two or four days, can be arranged in Putre.

Although many maps show roads descending from the *altiplano* from Surire to the Pan-American Highway and from Colchane to Camiña, do not be tempted to follow them. These roads are terrible in the dry season, dangerous and impassable in the rainy season; if stranded you could wait weeks for help to arrive. The only two safe routes between the *altiplano* and the Pan-American Highway are the international routes from Arica through Parque Nacional Lauca and from Huara to Colchane.

Reserva Nacional Las Vicuñas

Split off from Parque Nacional Lauca in order to permit mining, this reserve, reached by Route A235, stretches across 209,131 hectares, most of it rolling *altiplano* at an average altitude of 4,300 metres. The reserve is bisected by the Río Lauca along which riperian vegetation alternates with puna tola/grass-lands and many camelids can be seen; keep an eye open for condors, rheas and migrating peregrine falcons. Mina Chuquelimpie (not operating), one of the world's highest gold and silver mines, can be reached by a seven kilometre detour (clearly marked) off Route A235. Park administration is in **Guallatire**, a village 96 kilometres south of Las Cuevas at the foot of the smoking Guallatire volcano (6,060 metres); the village has a lovely *altiplano* church and a carabinero control post. At Km 139 the road reaches the Salar de Surire.

Sra Clara Blanca, an Aymaran weaver, offers overnight accommodation, food typical of the region, allows travellers to help with llamas and alpacas; house situated 1 kilometre east off A235 and reached by turning 10 kilometres after Chuquelimpie turnoff. **Guallatire** Conaf *refugio* has beds and cooking facilities, but is usually closed. Enquire at Conaf in Putre. *Restaurant Sanchez* (no sign), 1 block from carabinos, good lunch stews in an *altiplano* truckstop.

Sleeping & eating

Monumento Natural Salar de Surire

Situated at 4,300 metres and covering 17,500 hectares, the Salar de Surire is a drying salt lake with thermal springs and a year-round population of 12,000-15,000 flamingoes of three species (nesting season is January-March). It is open all year, but see advice above. Access is by Route A235. Administration is in **Surire**, 45 kilometres south of Guallatiri and 138 kilometres south of Putre. About half of the salar is mined for borax; sometimes Surire may be reached by getting a ride in a borax truck from Zapahuira, a road junction at Km 100 on the road from Arica to La Paz; trucks run sporadically depending on rainfall and the drop-off point is on the mine side of the Salar, 30 kilometres from the hot springs.

Conaf refugio, at Surire, 8 kilometres past the borax mine, 15 beds and cooking facili-ties, advance booking at Conaf in Arica essential. Campsite at Polloquere, 17 kilo-metres south of Surire in the southeastern corner of the salar, no facilities, no water, US$12 per site if Conaf check.

Sleeping

Parque Nacional Volcán Isluga

This park covers 174,744 hectares at altitudes above 2,100 metres. Although the lower parts of the park, at its southwestern end, lie in the hills of the precordillera, the heart of the park is situated between Laguna Aravilla with its flamingoes and the village of **Isluga**, where there is an 18th century Andean church and bell tower. Route A235 crosses the park, from the northern entrance, 40 kilometres south of Surire to the southern near Isluga. Northeast of Isluga under the smoking Volcán Isluga of 5,501 metres is the village of Encuelga, where Aymaran weavers can be seen working in the sand behind

This park includes some of the best volcanic scenery of northern Chile

Aymara and the birdlife of the Altiplano

The wealth and variety of the birdlife of the altiplano is reflected in the Aymaran language of the region's indigenous people. One measure of this influence can be seen in the names given to the lakes and mountains:

English	Aymara
flamingo	parina
lake	cota
Andean goose	guallata
place of the geese	guallatire
Rhea	suri
place of the rheas	surire

The Aymaran language also distinguishes between members of the same bird species according to gender or age and sometimes based upon their characteristic calls and songs. A condor chick, for example, is known as a condor chiuchi, based on the sounds it makes.

With grateful thanks to Sr Gumercindo Gutierrez, whose family has lived for centuries in Lagunillas, 10 kilometres north of Parinacota.

wooden wind breaks. There are three other peaks over 5,000 metres: Quimsachata (5,400 metres), Tatajachura (5,252 metres) and Latamara (5,207 metres). Wildlife varies according to altitude; there are large numbers of camelids and birds but fewer camelids and rheas than in Parque Nacional Lauca.

Park essentials Park administration is at Encuelga, but there are seldom guardaparques there. *Conaf refugio* in Encuelga, 6 beds and cooking facilities, reservation in Arica essential. There are also several basic residenciales in Colchane, which lies 6 kilometres south of the southern entrance (see above page 222).

Iquique, Arica & the Far North

The Central Valley

The Central Valley

Rancagua

Santiago

Curicó

Talca

Constitución

Pacific Ocean

Chillán

ARGENTINA

Concepción

Los Angeles

South of Santiago and extending as far south as the Río Biobío, with the snow-clad Andes to the east and the coastal range to the west, is the Central Valley, the agricultural heartland of the country. The major cities lie along the Pan-American Highway near the five main rivers which cross the Central Valley from east to west. From each of these cities roads lead west to resorts along the Pacific coast. To the south, near the mouth of the Río Biobío, are Concepción, the third largest city in Chile, and Talcahuano, the country's major naval port.

A region of small towns, farms and vineyards which is little visited by travellers, the Cental Valley offers insights into traditional Chilean society as well as a range of activities, including horseriding, watersports, (particularly in the Río Biobío), and visits to vineyards and thermal resorts. One of the latter, Termas de Chillán, also offers skiing. There are also four national parks of which two in the south are of particular interest: Laguna de Laja which is dominated by the active Antuco volcano, and Nahuelbuta, where the national tree, Araucaria araucana (the monkey puzzle) can be seen in large numbers.

Background

History

At the time of the first Spanish incursions, the Río Biobío and the lands south were inhabited by the Mapuche. Further north, in the Central Valley, the indigenous inhabitants, linguistically and culturally related to the Mapuche, had been conquered by the Incas in about 1470. On his second visit to Chile Pedro de Valdivia led an expedition southwards, founding Concepción in 1550 and a further seven cities south of the RíoBiobío. The Mapuche insurrection of 1598 and the Spanish defeat at Curalabo in 1599 led to a Spanish withdrawal north of the Río Biobío.

The Central Valley

The Mapuche uprising also led to the resettlement of many of the early Spanish settlers further north in the Central Valley where the land and inhabitants were divided up between the colonists. This was the origin of the hacienda which was to dominate social and economic life in the Central Valley for at least 200 years. The hacienda was a self-contained unit, producing almost everything needed and consuming its own produce. Until the 18th century there were no towns in the Central Valley, but from the 1740s the Spanish crown founded settlements in an attempt to increase its control. Towns were established at regular intervals along the main route south through the Central Valley: these included San Fernando (1742), Curicó (1743), Talca (1742), Cauquenes (1742) and Linares (1755).

After independence the Río Biobío continued to be the southern frontier of white settlement until in 1862 Colonel Cornelio Saavedra led an army south to build a line of ten forts, each four kilometres apart, between Angol and Collipulli. Following the occupation of the coast around Arauco in 1867 another line of forts was built across the Cordillera de Nahuelbuta. By 1881 the railway from Santiago had reached Angol, from where Chilean troops set out on the final campaign against the Mapuche.

Geography

This section covers three of the administrative regions of Chile, Regions VI (O'Higgins), VII (Maule) and VIII (Biobío). The Central Valley is a wide depression located between the Andes to the east and the Cordillera de la Costa to the west. The Andes gradually lose height as they continue southwards, although there are a number of high peaks east of Rancagua: Alto de los Arrieros, 5,000 metres, El Palomo, 4,986 metres, Tinguiririca, 4,280 metres. The Coastal Range is low at under 500 metres but south of the Río Biobío it forms a range of high peaks known as the Cordillera de Nahuelbuta. Five major rivers cross the Central Valley, cutting through the Coastal Range to reach the Pacific: from north to south these are the Ríos Rapel, Mataquito, Maule, Itata and Biobío. Of these the Biobío, one of the longest rivers in Chile, is the most important.

Climate

The northern parts of the Central Valley enjoy a type of Mediterranean climate with a prolonged dry season, but with more rain than Santiago. In general rainfall increases gradually from north to south both in amount and in duration, until around Concepción some rain falls in most months. The Central Valley itself receives less rain than the coastal range, but temperatures vary much more inland than in coastal areas.

Economy

The Central Valley is the agricultural heartland of Chile, transformed in the past 30 years by the growth of commercial export agriculture: wheat, maize, rice, sugar, beans, vegetables and fruit are grown throughout this area which also produces most of Chile's wine. Much of local industry is based on these products: rice mills, sugar mills, vegetable oil refineries and wineries are important sources of employment. While commercial forestry is based around the Río Biobío, it is important throughout the central valley. Fishing is of less importance, except around the Río Biobío: the coastline between Dichato and Arauco saw an important growth in large scale fishing and fish-processing in the 1980s and early 1990s.

The Central Valley

Rodeo – coming of age as a cow

During the summer months rodeo is one of the most popular sports in central and southern Chile. Teams (or colleras) of two riders on horseback compete throughout the season which culminates in the national championships held in Rancagua at the end of March. Eliminatory rounds are held in Osorno, Temuco, San Carlos, San Fernando, Vallenar and Los Andes, but most small towns in central southern Chile have their own media lunas (stadia) which may be used once a year only.

Rodeo owes its origins to the colonial period, when cattle roamed the open spaces and were rounded up to be identified and marked by their owners once a year in a rodeo. Based on the traditional view that heifers need to be broken in, the modern sport of rodeo is a test of the ability of two horses and their riders to work together.

The event takes place inside a stockade of thick upright timbers; although now circular, this is known as a media luna (crescent) after the design of the early rings: at two points the walls of the ring are covered by padded sections with a flag at either end of the section. Each collera competes by manoeuvring a heifer around the edge of the ring between the padded sections, stopping it at each padded section by pinning its hindquarters against the fence, before turning it in the opposite direction. This is done three times before the animal is released from the ring. Three judges give points (on a scale of one to seven) for skills of horsemanship and elegance.

It is one of the principles of rodeo that no heifer should be put through this performance more than once; for the heifer the event should come as a complete surprise. Since there are far more heifers than rodeos to break them in, many farms have their own rings, where heifers are broken in without an audience.

Rodeo is a good opportunity to see traditional Chilean rural customs: the huasos (cowboys) in wide-brimmed hats, brightly coloured ponchos and the carved wooden stirrups which were common in the 19th century, the fine horses and the cuecas (traditional dances) which sometimes follow the event.

The Biobío region is also a major industrial area. Concepción and the surrounding area are the second most important industrial area in Chile, partly as a result of the construction of the country's only steelworks at Huachipato in the 1950s and the development of major hydroelectric power plants along the Río Laja. Coal mining, however, which for many years was the mainstay of the coastal strip south of Concepción, went into decline in the 1980s and all the mines have now closed.

Moving on

Road and railway run south through the Central Valley; the railway has been electrified from Santiago to just south of Temuco. Along the road from Santiago to Temuco there are several modern motels. From Santiago to San Javier (south of Talca), the highway is dual carriageway, with two tolls of US$3 to pay. The highway between Santiago and Rancagua is dangerous for cyclists because of inattentive truck drivers.

The Rapel Valley

The Río Rapel is formed by the confluence of two much longer rivers, the Tinguiririca and the Cachapoal. The damming of the Río Rapel has created Lago Rapel, the largest artificial lake in Chile. In the valleys of the rivers Cachapoal, Claro and Zamorano the land is given over to fruit growing (including the estates of Viña Concha y Toro).

West of Rancagua are towns such as Doñihue, San Vicente de Tagua. Tagua and Peumo which have their roots in an indigenous past was replaced by the *huaso* (cowboy) and, more recently, by agroindustry. The main towns in the valley are Rancagua and San Fernando.

Rancagua

The capital of VI Región, Libertador General Bernardo O'Higgins, lies 82 kilometres south of Santiago, on the Río Cachapoal. Founded in 1743, it is a service and market centre for a rich agricultural area, easily visited from Santiago.

Population: 167,000
Phone code: 072
Colour map 3, grid B3

At the heart of the city is an attractive tree-lined plaza, the **Plaza de los Héroes** and several streets of single-storey colonial-style houses. In the centre of the plaza is an equestrian statue of O'Higgins. The **Merced** church, one block north, several times restored, dates from 1758. The main commercial area lies along Av Independencia which runs west from the plaza towards the bus and rail terminals.

The **Museo Histórico**, Estado y Ibieta, housed in a colonial mansion, contains collections of religious art and late 19th century furniture. ■ *US$1, Tuesday-Friday 0900-1230, 1430-1830, Saturday, Sunday 0900-1300.*

The Central Valley

Rancagua centre

■ **Sleeping**
1 Aguila Real   3 España   5 Rancagua
2 Camino del Rey   4 Portobello   6 Santiago

Not to scale

The battle of Rancagua

Rancagua was the scene of an important battle during the Wars of Independence. On 1-2 October 1814, Bernardo O'Higgins and his 1,700 Chilean patriots were surrounded in the centre of the town by 4,500 Royalist (pro-Spanish) troops. O'Higgins, who commanded his forces from the tower of the Merced church, managed to break out and escape. Following this defeat he was forced into exile in Argentina, while the Royalists re-established control over Chile. While in Argentina O'Higgins met up with San Martín who led the invasion force across the Andes which resulted in the final defeat of Spanish forces in Chile. Plaques in the centre of Rancagua mark the sites of the battle and a diagram in the Plaza de los Héroes shows the disposition of the troops. The battle resulted in the destruction of most of the buildings around the Plaza.

Excursions The thermal springs of **Cauquenes** are 28 kilometres east, reached by *colectivo* from Rancagua market. There is **A3** *Hotel Termas de Cauquenes*, T297226, which serves excellent food. It has a chapel and gardens. Five kilometres north of Cauquenes is the village of **Coya**, where the Chilean President has a summer residence.

Sleeping
■ *on map page 245*
Price codes:
see inside front cover

A2 *Camino del Rey*, Estado 275, T239765, F232314. 4-star, best. **A2** *Santiago*, Brasil 1036, T230855, F230822. Poorly maintained, friendly. **A3** *Aguila Real*, Brasil 1055, T222047, F237332. With breakfast. **B** *España*, San Martín 367, T230141. With bath, cheaper without, central, hot water, pleasant, clean. **B** *Rancagua*, San Martín 85, T232663, F241155. With bath, quiet, clean, secure parking. Recommended. **B** *Portobello*, Bueras 30, F238800. **E** pp *Res Ahumada*, Mujica 125, T225892, kitchen facilities, secure. Some 50 kilometres south (22 kilometres north of San Fernando) is *Hacienda Los Lingues*, see page 248.

Eating *Bravissimo*, Astorga 307, for ice cream. *Lasagna*, west end of Plaza, for bread and empanadas.

Festivals *National Rodeo Championships*, at the end of **March** in the Complejo Deportivo, north of the centre, US$10 per day (plenty of opportunities for purchasing cowboy items). *Festival del Poroto* (Bean Festival), **1-5 February**.

The Rapel Valley

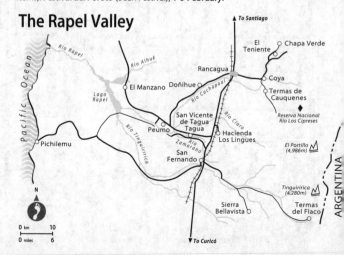

Motoring For car parts try *Aucamar*, Brasil 1177, T223594, and several others **Transport** around Brasil 1100-1200, better selection and prices in Santiago.

Bicycle spares Gustavo Sepúlveda, Bueras 481, T241413.

Train Main line services between Santiago and Concepción and Chillán stop here. Also regular services to/from Santiago on Metrotren, 1½ hours, 10-13 a day, US$2.

Bus Main terminal at Doctor Salinas y Calvo just north of the market but most buses for Santiago leave from terminal on O'Carrol. Tur Bus terminal at Calvo y O'Carrol. Many services from further south stop on the Pan-American Highway, 2 kilo-metres outside town. Frequent services to **Santiago**, US$3, 1¼ hours. To **Viña del Mar**, Tur Bus, US$6.

Banks *Afex*, Av Campos 363. For US$ cash. **Tourist offices** Germán Riesco 277, T230413, **Directory** F232297. Helpful, English spoken. Also municipal office in the Municipalidad on the Plaza de los Héroes. *Automóvil Club de Chile*, Ibieta 09, T239930, F239907.

Lago Rapel, southwest of Rancagua, is 40 kilometres in length and feeds the Rapel hydroelectric plant. Although much of the northern and southern shores of the lake are inaccessible by road, it is rapidly becoming a popular Chilean holiday destination. Most facilities are on the east shore around El Manzano, the main town. There are watersports at Bahía Skorpios.

Sleeping A1 *Punta Verde*, Bahía Skorpios, T591248. **C** *Hostería Playa Llallauquén*, T7515281 and many more. The eastern shore of the lake around El Manzano is lined with campsites (*Camping Punta Arenas*, 3 kilometres north of El Manzano, basic, cheap).

East of Rancagua

The **El Teniente** copper mine, one of the biggest in the country, lies 67 kilo-metres east. Owned by Codelco, it can only be visited by prior arrangement with the company. Nearby, on a private road above El Teniente, is the small **Chapa Verde** ski resort, owned by Codelco, but open to the public in season. It can only be reached by mine-transport bus (from Del Sol shopping centre on the northern outskirts of Rancagua, daily 0900, weekends in season every 15 minutes between 0800 and 0930). Equipment can be hired, no accommo-dation, lift tickets US$18 weekdays, US$25 weekends, obtainable only from resort office in Del Sol shopping centre.

Situated 50 kilometres southeast of Rancagua and 22 kilometres from the **Reserva** Termas de Cauquenes, the park covers 36,882 hectares of the valley of the Río **Nacional Río de** de los Cipreses at altitudes ranging from 900 metres to 4,900 metres. Park **los Cipreses** administration is at the entrance at the north end of the park, T297505. There is a campsite at Los Maitenes, 12 kilometres south of the entrance.

San Fernando

This town lies on the Río Tinguiririca 51 kilometres south of Rancagua. Founded *Population: 44,500* in 1742, it is capital of Colchagua Province and a service town for this fertile valley. *Altitude: 460m* From San Fernando a road runs east towards the Cordillera and divides: the *Phone code: 072* northern branch (75 kilometres) runs to the **Termas del Flaco** at 1,720 metres) *Colour map 3, grid B3* near the Argentine frontier. It has a poor campsite, *cabañas* and hotels, but it is open only in the summer when it attracts large numbers of visitors. The southern branch goes to the resort of **Sierra Bellavista**, a private *fundo* where many Santi-ago businessmen have holiday houses. Rodeos in October and November.

The Central Valley

Excursions **Los Lingues** is a private *hacienda* 20 kilometres northeast of San Fernando, 126 kilometres south of Santiago, where, it is said, the best horses in Chile are bred. Visits can be arranged to the 17th century house, a gift of the King of Spain. One-day tours including transport, rodeo and lunch are available. There is very expensive accommodation with an extra charge for breakfast or full board. The *hacienda* is a member of the French Hotels et Relais et Chateaux. Contact: Hacienda Los Lingues, Torre C de Tajamar, Of 205, Santiago, T235-2458/5446/7604, F235-7604, Tx 346060 LINGUES CK. To 6060 LINGUE.

Sleeping **On Av Rodríguez** **C** *Español*, No 959, T711098. **D** *Marcano*, No 968, T714759. **E** *Imperio*, No 770, T714595. With bath, clean. **D** *Pérez*, No 1028, T713328. Without bath.

Pichilemu West of San Fernando by 120 kilometres, of which 86 kilometres is paved,
Population: 6,827 Pichilemu is a coastal resort with a great many hotels and *residenciales*. It has several beaches, including the Punta Los Lobos beach, where international surfing competitions are held.

Sleeping **B** *Chile-España*, Ortúzar 255, T841270. **D** off season. Friendly, helpful, excellent restaurant, good value. **C** *Rex*, Ortúzar 34, T681003. Good breakfast, good value. **E** *Bahía*, Ortúzar 262. With breakfast, clean. **Camping** Campsites, US$15 per site, more expensive than *residenciales*.

Transport Andimar and Nilahue buses to **Santiago**, 4 hours, US$5.50.

The Mataquito Valley

The Río Mataquito, formed by the confluence of the Ríos Lontué and Teno, flows through the heart of the Chilean wine country reaching the Pacific near Iloca.

Curicó

Population: 103,919
Altitude: 200m
Phone code: 075
192 km to Santiago,
Colour map 3, grid C2

Curicó lies between the Ríos Lontué and Teno, 54 kilometres south of San Fernando. Founded in 1744, it is the only town of any size in the valley. In the **Plaza de Armas** there are lovely fountains with sculptures of nymphs, black-necked swans and a monument to the Mapuche warrior, Lautaro, carved from the trunk of an ancient beech tree. There is a steel bandstand, built in New Orleans in 1904, which is a national monument. On the western side of the plaza is the church of **La Merced**, which was badly damaged by an earthquake in 1986. Five blocks east is the church of **San Francisco**, a national monument, which contains the 17th century Virgen de Velilla, brought from Spain. At the junction of Carmen and Av San Martín is the imposing **Iglesia del Carmen**. To the east of the city is **Cerro Condell** offering fine views of the surrounding countryside and across to the distant Andes; it is an easy climb to the summit from where there are a number of walks.

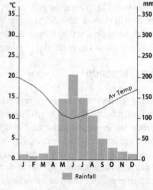

Climate: San Fernando

Torres wine bodega is five kilometres south of the city. To get there, take a bus for Molina from the local terminal or from outside the railway station and get off at Km 195 on the Pan-American Highway. ■ *T310455. 0900-1230, 1500-1730, no organized tour, Spanish only, worth a visit.*

Excursions

A2 *Comercio*, Yungay 730, T312443, F317001. With bath, also **B** without bath, clean. **A2** *Palmas Express*, Membrillar 728, T320066, F321425. **A2** *Turismo* (officially, Luis Cruz Martínez), Prat y Carmen, T310552, F310823. Modern, with breakfast, pleasant garden.

Sleeping
■ *on map*
Price codes:
see inside front cover

   Budget accommodation **C** *Res Ensueño*, Rodríguez 442, T312648. **D** *Res Alema*, Yungay 98, T/F314462. **D** *Renas Rahue*, Peña 410, T312194. Basic, meals, hot water, annex rooms have no ventilation. **D** *Res Central*, Prat 669. Good value. **D** *Res Colonial*, Rodríguez 461, T314103. Clean, patio, friendly. **D** *Res Montt*, M Montt 432, T312929. **D** *Savoy*, Prat 726. Basic. **E** *Prat*, Peña 427, T311069. Pleasant patio, friendly, clean, hot water, laundry facilities, large breakfast not included, parking.

El Fogón Chileno, Yungay 802. Good for meat and wines. *American Bar*, Yungay 647. Real coffee, small pizzas, good sandwiches, pleasant atmosphere, open early morning to late evening including weekends. Recommended. *Café-Bar Maxim*, Prat 617. Light meals, beer and wine. *Club de la Unión*, Plaza de Armas. Good. *Centro Italiano Club*

Eating
● *on map*

Curicó centre

■ **Sleeping**	9 Residencial Montt	4 El Fogón Chileno
1 Comercio	10 Residencial Rahue	5 Sant Angelo
2 Curicó Centro	11 Savoy	
3 Palmas Express	12 Turismo	Ⓢ **Banks**
4 Prat		1 Banco BCI
5 Residencial Alemana	● **Eating**	2 Banco BHIF
6 Residencial Central	1 American Bar	3 Banco de Chile
7 Residencial Colonial	2 Bavaria	4 Banco Santander
8 Residencial Ensueño	3 Club de la Unión	5 Banco Santiago

0 metres 50
0 yards 55

The Central Valley (vertical side text)

Social, Estado 531. Good, cheap meals. *Sant' Angelo*, Prat 430, excellent patisserie.

Festivals Mid March *Fiesta de la Vendimia* with displays on traditional wine making.

Transport **Motorcycle spares**, *Chaleco López Motos*, San Martín 171, T316191.

There is a toll (US$3) on the Pan-American Highway south of Curicó

Train Station is at the western end of Prat, 4 blocks west of Plaza de Armas, T310028. To/from Santiago, 4 a day, 2½ hours, US$6 *salón*, US$4 *turista*. To/from Chillán, 4 a day, 3 hours, US$7 *salón*, US$5 *turista*.

Bus Companies have their own terminals for interprovincial destinations. Local buses, including to coastal towns as well as some long distance services, from Terminal Plaza, Prat y Maipú. Pullman del Sur Terminal, Henríquez y Carmen; Tur bus Terminal southeast of centre on Manso de Velasco. Many southbound buses by-pass Curicó, but can be caught by waiting outside town. To **Santiago** Pullman del Sur, frequent, 2½ hours, US$5. To **Temuco**, LIT and Tur Bus, US$7. To **Llico**, Buses Díaz, US$3, 3 hours. To **Iloca**, US$2, regular in summer.

Directory **Banks** Major banks located around Plaza de Armas. *Casa de Cambio*, Merced 255, Local 106, no TCs.
see map for locations of banks **Communications** Post Office on Plaza de Armas. **Telephones:** *CTC*, Peña 650-A. **Internet access:** M y T Computación, Peña 430, T/F319865, mytcompu@entelchile.net. **Laundry** *Ecológico*, Yungay 411. *Lavacentro*, Yungay 437, expensive, good. **Tourist offices** In Goberación Provincial on Plaza de Armas. Mon-Fri 0900-1330, 1600-1800, helpful, has street map. *Automóvil Club de Chile*, Chacabuco 759, T311156. *Conaf*, Gobernación Provincial building, piso 1, Plaza de Armas.

Area de Proteccíon Radal Siete Tazas

The park is in two sectors, one at Radal, 65 kilometres east of Curicó, the other at Parque Inglés, nine kilometres further east. The most interesting sector is at Radal, where the Río Claro flows through a series of seven rock bowls (the *siete tazas*) each with a pool emptying into the next by means of a waterfall. The river then passes through a canyon, 15 metres deep but only one and a half metres wide, which ends abruptly in a cliff and a beautiful waterfall. There are several trails which are well marked. ■ *Entry US$2. The park is open October to March. Administration is in Parque Inglés.*

Sleeping **D** *Hostería La Flor de la Canela*, at Parque Inglés, T491613. Includes breakfast, good food. Highly recommended. **Camping** Campsite near entrance dirty, US$1 pp, shop. Also *Camping Las Catas*, 2 kilometres inside park, expensive, US$18/site, no shop.

Transport **Bus** Take a minibus to Molina, 26 kilometres south, from Terminal Plaza, frequent. From Molina buses run to the Parque Inglés daily in summer, 4 a day, 3 hours, US$2, last return 1700. Daily bus from Curicó in summer, 1330, 4½ hours, returns 0745 (Sunday 0700, returns 1900).

West of Curicó

Iloca From Curicó a road runs west to the mouth of the Río Mataquito and the popular resort of Iloca. Five kilometres north of Iloca is Puerto Duao, a fishing village with a good campsite.

Sleeping A3 *Iloca*, T887998, with breakfast, good views, run down. **B** *Hostería Iloca*, T671692. **Camping** *La Puntilla*, T314745, 2 kilometres north, also *cabañas*. *El Peñon*, 6 kilometres south. Reservations: Santiago, T6336099.

Transport Bus: from Terminal Plaza in Curicó, every hour in summer, less frequently off season, US$2.50, 2 hours.

Llico, north of Iloca, is a resort suitable for windsurfing: it can be reached **Llico** either by a coastal route or by an unpaved inland road which branches off at Hualañe, 74 kilometres east of Curicó.

Sleeping B *Hostería Atlántida 2000*, T400264, F312089, near beach. Small rooms, with breakfast. **D** *Hostería Llico*; **A3** *Res Miramar*, T400032. Good seafood restaurant, very small rooms but excellent. **D** *Pensión Chile*. Clean, friendly, rooms with bath have hot water, cheap meals.

Transport Bus: from Terminal Plaza in Curicó, by Bravo and Llomar companies, both daily 1230 and 1540, also Díaz, Monday-Saturday 1530, 3 hours.

A large lake surrounded by pine forest, Lago Vichuquén lies 114 kilometres **Lago Vichuquén** west of Curicó, just east of Llico. It is very popular with the wealthy and with watersports enthusiasts. Parts of the eastern shore of the lake are inaccessible by road, but there are full facilities on the western shore, particularly at Aquelarre.

Sleeping A1-A2 *Hostería Club de Yates*, T400018. Well-equipped, restful, good food. **A3** *Brujas del Lago*, T400020. **Camping** *Vichuquén*, on east shore, T400062. Full facilities. *El Sauce*, at north end of lake, F75400203. Good facilities.

Situated just north of Lago Vichuquén, 120 kilometres west of Curicó, this **Reserva** park, covering 604 hectares, is a natural sanctuary for over 80 species of birds, **Nacional** especially black-necked swans and other water fowl. Administration is four **Laguna Torca** kilometres east of Llico; campsite nearby. To get there, Take any bus from Curicó to Llico and get out near Administration. ■ *September-April*.

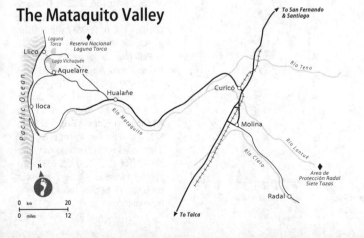

The Mataquito Valley

The Central Valley

The Maule Valley

The Río Maule, 240 kilometres long, flows from Laguna Maule in the Andes to the sea at Constitución. Its waters have been dammed east of Talca, providing power and creating Lago Colbún.

Talca

Population: 160,000
Phone code: 071
258 km to Santiago
Colour map 3, grid C2

Situated on the south bank of the Río Claro, a tributary of the Maule, Talca lies 56 kilometres south of Curicó. The most important city between Santiago and Concepción, it is a major manufacturing centre and the capital of VII Región, Maule. Founded in 1692, it was destroyed by earthquakes in 1742 and 1928.

Sights In the **Plaza de Armas** are statues looted by the Talca Regiment from Peru during the War of the Pacific. Just off the Plaza at 1 Norte y 2 Oriente is the **Museo O'Higginiano**, located in a colonial mansion which belonged to Juan Albano Pereira, tutor to the young Bernardo O'Higgins who lived here between the ages of four and 10. The house was later the headquarters of O'Higgins' Patriot Government in 1813-14, before his defeat at Rancagua. In 1818 O'Higgins signed the declaration of Chilean independence here: the room Sala Independencia is decorated and furnished in period style. The museum also houses a collection of regional art. ■ *US$1. Tuesday-Friday, 1030-1300, 1430-1845, Saturday/Sunday 1000-1300.* Eight kilometres southeast is **Villa Huilquilemu**, a 19th century hacienda, now part of the Universidad Católica del Maule, housing four museums, of religious art, handicrafts, agricultural machinery and wine. ■ *T242474. US$1. Tuesday-Friday 1500-1830, Saturday 1600-1830, Sunday 1100-1400. Getting there: reached by taking San Clemente bus.*

Sleeping
■ *on map*
Price codes:
see inside front cover

A2 *Inca del Oro*, Sur 1026, T239608, F239603. **A2** *Marcos Gamero*, 1 Oriente 1070, T223388, F224400. **A2** *Terrabella*, 1 Sur 641, T/F226555. **A3** *Plaza*, 1 Poniente 1141, T226150. Good commercial standard.

B *Hostal del Puente*, 1 Sur 407, T220930, F225448, lovely gardens, English spoken, parking. **B** *Res Maule*, 2 Sur 1381, T220995, without breakfast, overpriced. **C** *Amalfi*, 2 Sur 1265, T225703. Old-fashioned, central, good breakfast. **D** pp *Cordillera*, 2 Sur 1360, T221812, F233028, with bath, **C** without, good breakfast. **D** *Hostal Balcones del Maule*, 2 Norte 830, T230503. **D** *Oriente*, 10 Oriente 940. **E** pp *Hostal Alcázar*, 6 Oriente y 4 Norte, T233587, without bath, quiet, good value.

Pellarco, 18 kilometres northeast: **B** *Hosp Santa Margita*, T09-753-3753, F71-299799 (Casilla 1104, Talca), Swiss-run, meals served, open December-March only, reservation advised. **A3** *Cabañas Entre Ríos*, T223336, F220477 on the Pan-American Highway 8 kilometres north. (Santiago: San Antonio 486, of 132, T6333750, F6324791). Very good value, excellent breakfast, pool, very helpful owner. Highly recommended.

Climate: Talca
Rainfall

Casino de Bomberos, 2 Sur y 5 Oriente. Good value. *Bavaria*, 1 Sur 1370. Cheap lunches at *Casino Sociedad de Empleados*, 1 Norte 1025, and *Casino Club Deportivo*, 2 Sur 1313. Real coffee at *Mi Sandwich*, Plaza de Armas and at *Café Brasil*, nearby.

Eating
● *on map*

Regional folklore festival during first week of **January**.

Festivals

Cycle repairs: *Bicimotora Burgos*, 5 Oriente 1185.

Transport

Train Station at 2 Sur y 11 Oriente, T226254. To **Santiago**, 5 a day, US$5. To **Talca** and **Chillán**, 3 a day. To **Temuco**, 1 a day. To **Concepción**, Saturday and Sunday only. To **Constitución**, 4 a day, US$2, 2½ hours.

Bus Terminal at 12 Oriente y 2 Sur. To **Chillán**, frequent service, US$2; also frequent to **Constitución**, 2 hours, US$1.20. To **Puerto Montt**, US$14. To **Temuco**, US$12, 7 hours.

Banks *Banco Santander*, 1 Sur y 4 Oriente. *Edificio Caracol*, Oficina 15, 1 Sur 898. For US$ cash. **Communications** Post Office: 1 Oriente s/n. **Telephones:** *CTC*, 1 Sur 1156 and 1 Sur 835. **Laundry** *Lavaseco Flash*, 1 Norte 995; *Lavaseco Donini*, 6 Oriente 1120. **Tourist offices** 1 Poniente 1234, T233669. Open winter Mon-Fri 0830-1730; summer Mon-Fri 0830-1930. *Automóvil Club de Chile*, 1 Poniente 1267, T2232774.

Directory
see map for locations of banks

East of Talca

From Talca a road runs 175 kilometres southeast along **Lago Colbún** and up the valley of the Río Maule, passing through some of the finest mountain scenery in Chile to reach the Argentine frontier at Paso Pehuenche. At the western end of Lago Colbún is the town of Colbún. From here another road leads south and west to join the Pan-American Highway at Linares. There are thermal

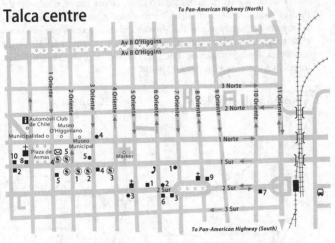

Talca centre

Sleeping
1 Amalfi
2 Casagrande
3 Cordillera
4 Inca del Oro
5 Marcos Gamero
6 Napoli
7 Oriente
8 Plaza
9 Residencial Maule
10 Terrabella

● Eating
1 Bavaria
2 Casino Club Deportivo
3 Casino de Bomberos
4 Casino Sociedad de Empleados
5 Centro Español

Ⓢ Banks
1 Banco BHIF
2 Banco de Chile
3 Banco Santander
4 Banco Santiago
5 Banco Sud Americano

0 metres 200
0 yards 218

The Central Valley

springs at Panimávida, five kilometres south of Colbún, and at Quinamávida, 12 kilometres south of Colbún.

Sleeping **A2** *El Colorado*, on north shore of Lago Colbún, T/F221750. **C** pp *Centro Portezuelo*, at Quinamávida, T09-7520510. Full board, large *estancia* offering forest trails, beaches, English spoken. Highly recommended. **Camping** There are several campsites east of Colbún on the south shore of Lago Colbún, including *Marina del Lago*, Km 11, T211743. *Marina del Condor*, Km 13, T211743. *El Mirador de Colbún*, Km 13, T213776. There are also 3 sites near Panimávida.

Transport **Bus**: To Lago Colbún, Los Cipreses bus, daily from Talca, T241949

Vilches Sixty three kilometres east of Talca, Vilches is the starting point for the climb to the volcanoes Quizapu, 3,050 metres, and Descabezado, 3,850 metres. For walks on Descabezado Grande and Cerro Azul, ice axe and crampons needed, contact recommended guide Carlos Verdugo Bravo, Probación Brilla El Sol, Pasaje El Nickel 257, Talca (Spanish only).

Sleeping **A2** *Hostería*, Vilches, T621463. With breakfast, use of kitchen, good food, *cabañas* **C** for 4 people, hospitable, pool, knowledgeable family (postal address: Casilla 876, Talca).

Transport 2 buses a day, US$1.50, 2-2½ hours, leave Talca 1300 and 1650, leave Vilches 0700 and 1730.

Reserva Nacional Altos del Lircay Situated just west of Vilches, this park covers 12,163 hectares and includes peaks up to 2,228 metres as well as several small lakes. Much of the park is covered with mixed forest including lenga, ñirre, coigüe, roble, raulí and copihue. Near the entrance are the administration and visitors' centre; nearby are the Piedras Tacitas, a stone construction supposedly built by the indigenous inhabitants of the region, and the Mirador Del Indio from where fine views over the Río Lircay. There are also two good hikes: to Laguna del Alto, eight hours via a lagoon in a volcanic crater; to El Enladrillado, a high basalt plateau from which there are great views, 12 hours. Entry US$1.

The Maule Valley

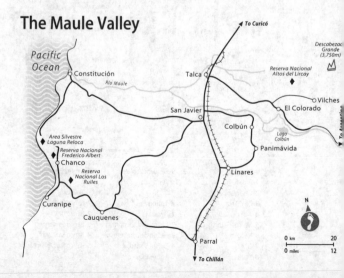

La Ruta del Vino

The Maule Valley is one of the largest wine-producing areas in Chile. Some 20 kilometres south of Talca, in the vicinity of the small town of San Javier, is the **Ruta del Vino San Javier-Villa Alergre**, covering 23 vineyards which can be visited. Although transport is essential for visiting most, those near San Javier can be visited without. A few have regular visiting hours which are given below; for the remainder advance notice is required. Further details can be obtained from the Municipalidad in San Javier.

1.	Alto de Pichivoque	73-322696
2.	Balduzzi	73-322138 (open Monday-Saturday 0900-1900)
3.	Carta Vieja	73-381612 (open Wednesday 1700-1800)
4.	Comávida	73-322696
5.	Concha y Toro	73-321767
6.	Cooperativa Lancomilla	73-322540
7.	Cremaschi	2-2311178
8.	El Aromo	71-242438
9.	El Durazno	09-7513368
10.	El Sauce	09-7513142
11.	Gabriel Court	73-322299
12.	Guzmán	73-328066
13.	J Bouchón	2-2469778 (open Wednesday 1500-1700)
14.	La Cabaña	73-322437
15.	Los Ciervos	73-321053
16.	Poxo de Oro	73-346004
17.	Saavedra	73-346006
18.	San Clemente	73-381474 (open daily 0900-2000)
19.	Santa Beatriz	73-321977
20.	Santa Berta	73-322478
21.	Santa Hilda	73-321367
22.	Segú Ollé	73-210078 (open Friday marnings)
23.	Tabontinaja	2-6238987

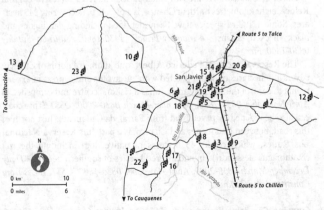

Frontier with **Argentina: Paso Pehuenche** Paso Pehuenche, 2,553 metres, is reached by unpaved road southeast from Lago Colbún, see above. On the Argentine side the road continues to Malargüe and San Rafael. The border is open December-March 0800-2100, April-November 0800-1900.

Constitución

Population: 28,748
Colour map 3, grid C2

Lying west of Talca at the mouth of the Río Maule, Constitución is reached by road (89 kilometres) from San Javier and a narrow gauge railway line which offers fine views over the Maule Valley. Founded in 1794, it is an industrial town situated in a major commercial logging area; there are naval shipyards and a giant cellulose factory; fishing is also important. Its main attraction is as a seaside resort, which is popular with Chileans in season. The beach, an easy walk from the town, is surrounded by very picturesque rocks. There are good views from Cerro Mutrún, at the mouth of the river, access from Calle O'Higgins.

Sleeping **A2** *Hostería Constitución*, Echeverria 460, T/F671450. Best. **A3** *Posada Colonial*, Blanco 390, T671213, F671335. **C** *Avendaño*, O'Higgins 681. Pleasant patio, restaurant, friendly, safe. **D** *Res Urrutia*, Freire 238, with breakfast, some rooms gloomy, laundry facilities. In Portales: **D** *Res Cristina*, No 368. Good. **D** *Res Santa Catalina*, No 320. There are many other *residenciales* in Freire 100-300 blocks, including *Res López*, No 153; *Res Familiar*, No 160; *Res Ramírez*, No 292, but book in advance from January to March.

Transport **Bus** To **Talca**, Empresa O'Higgins and Contimar, frequent, 2 hours, US$2. To **Cauquenes**, Empresa Amigo, 2½ hours, US$2.

Train To **Talca**, 2½ hours, US$2, 4 a day.

South of Constitución

A paved road runs from Constitución along the coast via Chanco and **Pelluhue** to **Curanipe**, 83 kilometres south, which has a beautiful black sand beach. Both Pelluhue and Curanipe are popular for surfing.

North of Chanco there are two small parks. The **Area Silvestre Laguna Reloca**, eight kilometres north of Chanco, is a private park covering 245 hectares. Some 130 bird species have been identified including flamingoes and black necked swans. ■ *Monday-Friday 1430-1800, Saturday-Sunday 0830-1800. Free.*

The **Reserva Nacional Federico Albert**, one kilometre north of Chanco, covers 145 hectares of dunes planted with eucalyptus and cypress in experiments to control the shifting sands. It has a visitors' centre and campsite. ■ *April-November 0830-1800, December-March 0830-2000, US$1.* This coast can also be reached by paved road from Parral via Cauquenes. Just north of this road, between Cauquenes and Chanco, is a park, the **Reserva Nacional Los Ruiles**, which covers 45 hectares of native flora including the *ruil* (Nothofagus alessandri), an endangered species of southern beech. ■ *Daily December-March 0830-2000, April-November 0830-1800, US$1. Buses from Constitución or Cauquenes.*

Sleeping **Curanipe** **C** *La Bahía*, Comercio 438, T556066. **C** *Pacífico*, Comercio 509, T556016. Pleasant, clean. Several others. Municipal campsite. **Pelluhue** (more expensive than Curanipe) **B** *Hostería Blanca Reyes*, Prat 615, T541022, F541061. Best. **C** *Hostal Casablanca*, Condell 1019, T541014. **D** *Res La Playa*, Prat 509. **D** *Pensión Rocas*, Condell 708, T541017, basic. Also lots of *cabañas*.

On the Pan-American Highway 88 kilometres south of Talca is Parral, cele- | **Parral**
brated as the birthplace of the Nobel Prize-winning poet Pablo Neruda (see also | *Population: 1,000*
under Santiago **Museums**, La Chascona, page 83, and Isla Negra, page 137). | *Altitude: 171m*
342 km S of Santiago

Sleeping B *Brescia*, Igualdad 195, T422675. Without bath, clean, good restaurant.
C *Res do Brasil*, Dieciocho 140, T462555. Clean, quiet, campsite.

The Itata Valley

The Río Itata and its longer tributary, the Río Ñuble, flow west reaching the Pacific some 60 kilometres north of Concepción.

Chillán

The capital of Ñuble province is 150 kilometres south of Talca and a service | *Population: 146,000*
centre for this agricultural area. Founded in 1580 and destroyed by the | *Altitude: 118m*
Mapuche, the city has been moved several times. Following an earthquake in | *Phone code: 042*
1833, the site was moved slightly to the northwest, though the older site, now | *Colour map 3, grid C2*
known as Chillán Viejo, is still occupied. Further earthquakes in 1939 and
1960 have ensured that few old buildings have survived. Chillán was the birthplace of Bernardo O'Higgins. Arturo Prat, Chile's naval hero, was born 50
kilometres away at Ninhue.

The city is centered around the Plaza O'Higgins. The modern cathedral, on the | **Sights**
plaza, is designed to resist earthquakes. The **San Francisco** church, three
blocks northeast of the Plaza, contains a **museum** of religious and historical
artefacts. ■ *Tuesday-Sunday 1500-1900, US$1.* Above the main entrance is a
mural by Luis Guzmán Molina, a local artist, which is an interpretation of the
life of San Francisco but placed in a Chilean context. The adjoining **convent**
(1835) was a big centre for missionary work among the Mapuche. Five streets
west of the Plaza is the neogothic **Iglesia Padres Carmelita**. Northwest of the
Plaza O'Higgins, on the Plaza Héroes de Iquique, is the **Escuela México**,
donated to the city after the 1939 earthquake. In its library are outstanding
murals by the great Mexican artists David Alvaro Siqueiros and Xavier
Guerrero which present allegories of Chilean and Mexican history. ■ *Daily
1000-1300, 1500-1830.* Three blocks further south is the **Museo Naval Arturo
Prat**, Collin y I Riquelme, which contains naval artefacts and models of Chilean vessels. ■ *Tuesday-Friday 0930-1200, 1500-1730.*

In **Chillán Viejo** (southwest of the centre) there is a monument and park on
the site of the birthplace of Bernardo O'Higgins; it has a 60 metre long mural
depicting his life (an impressive, but sadly faded, mosaic of various native
stones), and a **Centro Histórico y Cultural**, with a gallery of contemporary
paintings by regional artists. ■ *The park is open 0900-1300, 1500-1900.*
Half-way between the centre and Chillán Viejo on Av O'Higgins is the **Capilla
San Juan de Dios**, a small chapel dating from 1791.

Quinchamalí is a small village 27 kilometres southwest which is famous for | **Excursions**
the originality of its crafts in textiles, basketwork, black ceramics, guitars and | *See also box*
primitive paintings (see box). These are all on sale in Chillán market. The vil- | *on page 258*
lage holds a handicraft fair in the second week of February.

The Central Valley

Quinchamalí

Quinchamalí is one of the two most famous villages in Chile for producing black ceramic ware; the other, Pomaire, near Santiago, is much more influenced by tourism. Quinchamalí is a village of little houses hidden under large fruit trees; in these the women work with the clay while the men work on the land. Apart from items for domestic use, the women produce a wide range of other pieces including roosters, three legged pigs and women with children but the most popular is perhaps the guitarrera (a woman playing the guitar). The clay is mixed with sand to make it porous and to prevent it breaking when it is heated; the mixture is worked in two halves which are then joined and allowed to dry. The characteristic white patterns are made by incising with an old needle before the piece is wrapped in straw and heated over an open fire.

With grateful thanks to Luis Guzmán Molina.

Sleeping
■ *on map*
Price codes:
see inside front cover

A2 *Isabel Riquelme*, Arauco 600, T213663. **B** *Cordillera*, Arauco 619, on Plaza de Armas, T215211. 3-star, small, good. **B** *Floresta*, 18 de Septiembre 278, T222253. Quiet, old fashioned, friendly. **B** *Hostal De La Avenida*, O'Higgins y Bulnes, T230256. **A3** *Rucamanqui*, Herminda Martín 590 (off Plaza de Armas), T222704. Clean, spartan. **B** *Ruiz de Gamboa*, O'Higgins 493, T221013. **C** *San Bartoleme*, El Roble 585, T226721, with bath, parking, run down. **C** *Quinchamalí*, El Roble 634, T223381, F227365. Central, quiet, clean, hot water, heated lounge.

D *Claris*, 18 de Septiembre 357, T221983. Clean, friendly, run down. **D** *Hostal Cañada*, Libertad 269, T234515. Without breakfast or bath. **D** *Hostal 5 de Abril*, 5 de Abril y Constitución. Without bath. **D** *Libertador*, Libertad 85, T223155, without breakfast, parking, clean. **D** *Paso Nevado*, Libertad 219, T221827. Good. **D** *Chillán*, Libertad 85, basic. **D** *Res Su Casa*, Cocharcas 555, T223931. Clean, parking. Near the central terminal on Constitución are **D** *Res Vem-Sau*, No 96, T210958, and **D** *Res Chi-Can*, No 34. Both basic. **F** pp *Sonia Segui*, Itata 288, T214879, good beds, good breakfast, huge *almuerzo*, recommended, friendly, noisy.

Eating
● *on map*

Centro Español, Plaza de Armas. Separate bar with snacks, excellent. For real coffee: *Fuente Alemana*, Arauco 661, *Café de París*, Arauco 666, fine restaurant upstairs and *Café Europa*, Libertad 475. Recommended. *Club Comercial*, Arauco 745. Popular at lunchtime, good value *almuerzo*, popular bar at night. *O'Higgins*, O'Higgins y Libertad. Good value. *Jai Yang*, Libertad 250. Good Chinese. *La Cosa Nostra*, Libertad 398, Italian cuisine, German and Italian spoken, very good and reasonably priced. *La Copucha*, 18 de Septiembre y Constitución. Inexpensive meals and sandwiches. *La Masc'a*, 5 de Abril 544. Excellent cheap meals, *empanadas de queso*, drinks. Recommended. Good value cheap restaurants around the Mercado Municipal. In Chillán Viejo, *Los Adobes*, on Parque O'Higgins. Good food and service, reasonable prices. The Chillán area is well-known for its *pipeño* wine (very young) and its *longanizas* (sausages).

Shopping

Large *Mercado y Ferio Municipal* at Riquelme y Marpón which sells regional arts and crafts. Nearby is a large modern shopping centre, *Plaza El Roble*, at El Roble y Riquelme.

Festivals

Annual wine festival, *Fiesta de la Vendemia*, third week in March.

Transport

Train Station, Brasil opposite Libertad, 5 blocks west of Plaza de Armas, T222424. To **Santiago**, 3 trains a day, 5½ hours, *salón* US$7.

The Central Valley

Bus 2 long distance terminals: Tur Bus, Línea Azul, Tas Choapa and LIT all use central terminal at Brasil y Constitución. Other companies use the modern northern terminal at O'Higgins y Ecuador. Local bus terminal, Maipón y Sgto Aldea near the market. Buses to **Yumbel** and **Quinchamalí** (US$1, 30 minutes), leave from here. To **Santiago**, US$7-11, 5½ hours. To **Concepción**, Tur Bus and Línea Azul every 30 minutes, 1¼ hours, US$3. To **Curicó**, US$4. To **Tecumo**, US$5.

Motorcycle spares *Roland Spaarwater*, Ecuador 275, T/F232334.

Banks On the Plaza de Armas are *Banco BCI, Banco Santander* and *Banco de Chile* all with ATMs. **Directory** *Banco Sudamericano*, Arauco y El Roble. Poor rates. *Banco Santiago*, El Roble 580. *Corp Banca*. For Visa. Better rates than banks at *Casa de Cambio*, Constitución 550, or *Café de París* (ask for Enríque Schuler). **Communications Post Office:** In Goberación building on Plaza de Armas.

Chillán centre

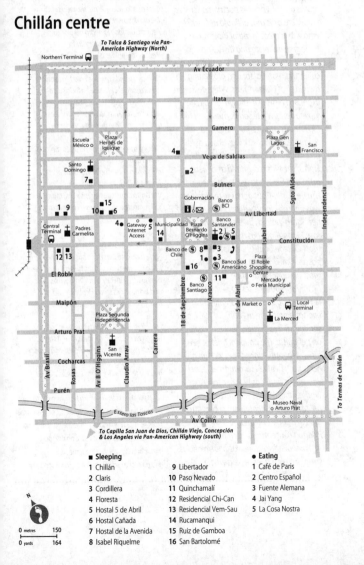

To Talca & Santiago via Pan-Americán Highway (North)

To Capilla San Juan de Dios, Chillán Viejo, Concepción & Los Angeles via Pan-American Highway (south)

To Termas de Chillán

The Central Valley

0 metres 150
0 yards 164

■ **Sleeping**
1 Chillán
2 Claris
3 Cordillera
4 Floresta
5 Hostal 5 de Abril
6 Hostal Cañada
7 Hostal de la Avenida
8 Isabel Riquelme
9 Libertador
10 Paso Nevado
11 Quinchamalí
12 Residencial Chi-Can
13 Residencial Vem-Sau
14 Rucamanqui
15 Ruiz de Gamboa
16 San Bartolomé

● **Eating**
1 Café de Paris
2 Centro Español
3 Fuente Alemana
4 Jai Yang
5 La Cosa Nostra

👉 *Violeta and the Parra family of Chillán*

Violeta and Nicanor Parra were two of the 11 children of Nicanor and Clarisa Parra. The family was brought up in Chillán. Their father, Nicanor, was a music teacher, while their mother, Clarisa, was a seamstress who played the guitar and sang. Most of the children were artistic in some way. Violeta sang with her sister Hilda in Santiago bars for several years. She also worked in the circus. Another child, Nicanor, became a professor of maths and physics. His poetry is discussed elsewhere, as is that of Pablo de Rokha, who was a great friend of Violeta.

Together Violeta and de Rokha travelled the length of Chile and abroad collecting material for and promoting their idea of Chilean-ness. While de Rokha expressed himself in the lyrical epic, Violeta sang, wrote songs, made tapestries, ceramics, paintings and sculpture. All her work was based on a philosophy of helping those in need. In France she was recognized as a great artist and her works were exhibited in the Louvre in 1964, but at home recognition was only grudgingly given. Neruda called her 'Santa Violeta'; the Peruvian novelist Jose Maria Arguedas described her as 'the most Chilean of all Chileans I could possibly know, but at the same time the most universal of all Chile'.

In the 1960s she set up her La Carpa de la Reina as a centre for popular art in the capital. It was here, in February 1967, that she committed suicide, her head resting on her guitar. The national grief at her funeral far outweighed the acclaim given her during her life. Her daughter Isabel was also a singer as was her son, Angel, whose radical views prompted the military government to arrest him after the 1973 coup and imprison him in the Pisagua concentration camp.

For Violeta, folklore was a form of class struggle. Her influence on a whole generation of Latin American folk singers was enormous and, without her, Salvador Allende would not have had the folkloric backing of Victor Jara, Inti-Illimani, Los Quilapayún and Angel and Isabel Parra themselves. After her death, her brother Nicanor, had published Décimas, a sort of autobiography in verse, full of simple humanity.

'Gracias a la vida'
Gracias a la vida que me ha dado tanto
Me dio dos luceros, que cuando los abro
Perfecto distingo lo negro del blanco
y en el cielo su fondo estrellado
y en las multitudes al hombre que yo amo

Gracias a la vida que me ha dado tanto.
Me ha dado el oído, que en todo su ancho
graba noche y día grillos y canarios;
martillos, turbinas, ladridos, chubascos,
y la voz tan tierna de mi bienamado ...

Gracias a la vida que me ha dado tanto.
Me ha dado la risa y me ha dado el llanto,
asi yo distingo dicha de quebranto,
los dos materiales que forman mi canto,
y el canto de ustedes que es el mismo canto
y el canto de todos que es mi propio canto.

'Thanks to Life'
I give thanks to life which has given me so much. It has given me two eyes, and when I open them I distinguish perfectly black from white, and in the sky its starry depths and in the crowds the man that I love.

I give thanks to life which has given me so much. It has given me hearing, which in all its breadth records night and day the crickets and canaries; hammers, turbines, barks and squalls, and the tender voice of my beloved...

I give thanks to life which has given me so much. It has given me laughter and it has given me tears, so that I can tell good fortune from despair, the two materials which make up my song, and your song which is the same song and everyone's song which is my own song.

The longest double chair in South America

There are 10 lifts in Chillán ski resort, including what the proud locals announce as the 'longest double chair in South America', but is better known as the oldest and slowest ride in the continent. Chillán is a snowboarders and off-piste skiers paradise as the extensive slopes include natural half-pipes, shutes and cornices. The skiing can be superb but be prepared for the slow lifts. Piste preparation is haphazard. Despite this Chillán has a lot of potential and soaking in the pools surrounded by trees after a hard day's skiing definitely makes up for all its shortcomings.

Josselyn van der Pol and Leandro Yáñez

Telephone: *Entel*, 18 de Septiembre 746. *CTC*, Arauco 625. **Internet Access:** *Gateway*, Libertad 360, T238855, gateway3@CTCrenuna.cl. **Tourist offices** 18 de Sept 455, at side of Gobernación, T223272, left-hand gallery. Street map of city, leaflets on skiing, Termas de Chillán, etc. *Automóvil Club de Chile*, O'Higgins 677, T212550. Two interesting publications on Chillán are: *Iconografía de Chillán, 1835-1939*, by Marco Aurelio Reyes (Universidad del Bío-Bío, 1989) which describes the history of Chillán up to the devastating 1939 earthquake with text, photographs and documents; and *Chillán me persigue*, by Luis Guzmán Molina, Sergio Hernández, Marco Aurelio Reyes and Norman Ahumada, which contains images of Chillán in drawings, poetry and prose (1995).

Termas de Chillán

Situated 82 kilometres east of Chillán by good road, paved for the first 50 kilometres, 1,850 metres up in the Cordillera at the foot of the double-cratered Chillán volcano are thermal baths and, above, the largest ski resort in southern Chile. There are two open-air thermal pools, officially for hotel guests only, and a health spa with jacuzzi, sauna, mud baths etc. The ski resort includes rental shops, restaurants, bars, ski school, first aid and nursery. Suitable for families and beginners and cheaper than centres nearer Santiago, Chillán has 10 ski lifts, 28 ski runs, the longest of which is 13 kilometres in length. It offers nordic, alpine randonnée and heli-skiing. The season runs from mid-December to the end of March. Weekly packages are available, but are not cheap. Lift pass is US$30 per day, US$20 for a half day. You can obtain information from Chillán Ski Centre, Barros Arana 261, or from Sociedad Hotelera de Montaña y Turismo Somontur, address below. Equipment can be hired also from the Chillán Ski Centre, for about US$25.

Sleeping At Las Trancas on the road to the Termas, 70 kilometres southeast of Chillán are **L1** *Gran Termas de Chillán*, T/F223576. 5-star, sports facilities, sauna, thermal pool and spa centre. **L3** *Pirigallo*, 3-star. Bookings for both via *Sociedad Hotelera de Montaña y Turismo Somontur*, Av Libertad 1042, Chillán, T223887, F223576, ventachi@termachillan.cl or Av Providencia 2237, Oficina P41, Santiago T233131, F2315963. **A2** *Los Pirineos*, T293839, and **A2** *Parador Jamón*, **Pan y Vino**, Casilla 618, Chillán, T222383, F220018. Arranges recommended horse riding expeditions. *Cabañas* also available in the village. **Camping** 2 kilometres from the slopes.

Transport Ski buses run from Libertador 1042 at 0800 and from Chillán Ski Centre, subject to demand, US$30 (including lift pass). Summer (January-mid March) bus service from **Anja**, 5 de Abril 594, Thursday, Saturday, Sunday only, 0730, US$5 return, book in advance. Taxi US$30 one way, 1½ hours. At busy periods hitching may be possible from Chillán Ski Centre.

The Central Valley

The Biobío Valley

The Río Biobío, which flows northwest from the Andes to reach the sea near Concepción, is 407 kilometres long, the second longest river in Chile. Its more important tributaries include the Ríos Laja, Duqueco and Renaico. Apart from Concepción and Talcahuano on the coast, the valley includes several other important cities, notably Los Angeles.

Climate The climate is very agreeable in summer, but from April to September the rains are heavy; the annual average rainfall, nearly all of which falls in those six months, is from 1,250 to 1,500 millimetres.

Concepción

Population: 210,000
Phone code: 041
516 km S of Santiago
Colour map 3, grid C1

The capital of Región VIII (Biobío), 15 kilometres up the Río Biobío, Concepción is the third biggest city in Chile. The conurbation of Concepción, Talcahuano, San Pedro and Chiguayante has a total population of 540,000. The most important city in southern Chile, it is one of the country's major industrial centres. To the south is an important forestry area. Talcahuano, Chile's most important naval base, is 15 kilometres north.

Founded in 1550, Concepción became a frontier stronghold in the war against the Mapuche after 1600. Destroyed by an earthquake in 1751, it was moved to its present site in 1764.

Sights In the centre is the attractive **Plaza de la Independencia**, where, in January 1818, Bernardo O'Higgins proclaimed the independence of Chile. Nearby are many of the official buildings including the modern Cathedral, the Municipalidad and the Palacio de la Justicia. Southeast of the Plaza is the **Parque Ecuador**, with the Galería de la Historia (see below). A few blocks north of the park is the Casa del Arte (see below). From the Parque Ecuador you can climb **Cerro Caracol**, to the south, from where there are panoramic views over the city and the river.

Museums Museo de Historia Natural de Concepción is 15 blocks north-east of the Plaza Independencia on Calle Maipú. ■ *Tuesday-Saturday 1000-1800, Sunday 1500-1730. US$1.*

The **Galería de la Historia**, Lincoyan y V Lamas, is an audiovisual depiction of the history of Concepción and the region; upstairs is a collection of Chilean painting. ■ *Free. Monday 1500-1830, Tuesday-Friday 1000-1330, 1500-1830, Saturday/Sunday 1000-1400, 1500-1930.*

The **Casa del Arte**, Roosevelt y Larena, contains the University art collection; the entrance hall is dominated by *La Presencia de América Latina*, by the Mexican Jorge González Camerena (1965), an impressive allegorical mural depicting Latin American history. Note especially the pyramid representing the continent's wealth, the figures of an armoured warrior and an Indian woman and the wounded cactus with parts missing, representing Mexico's

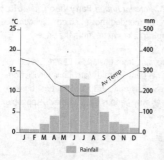

Climate: Concepción

Rainfall

Forestry – from monkey-puzzles to woodchips

The Río Biobío is the heartland of Chilean commercial forestry. Although the Cousiño family's Compañia Minera Lota experimented with new species and planted large areas for commercial foresty around Arauco in the 1880s, Chilean forestry owes its modern dynamism largely to a 1974 law which provided incentives for the development of the industry. Since 1974 over one million hectares of trees have been planted in the VII, VIII and IX Regions, mostly of Monterrey Pine (Pinus radiata), favoured for its fast growth and suitability for cellulose and construction timber. Normal growing periods are 10-15 years for trees destined for cellulose and 18-25 years for use as timber. Climatic conditions for forestry are particularly favourable in the area inland from Arauco, which has a high number of days of optimal temperatures and humidity for the growth of the Monterrey Pine, though this is now being replaced by faster growing species of eucalyptus.

Timber is a major industry in the Biobío region: there are four major cellulose plants in the Biobío valley, at La Laja, Concepción, Nacimiento and Mininco, as well as two more at Arauco on the coast. Timber trucks are a common feature on the roads of the region, and a common cause of traffic holdups.

Forestry development is not limited to the Biobío area: further south there are other signs of Chile's growing importance as a timber producer, for instance in the wood-chip mountains of Puerto Montt. While environmentalists voice concern at the disappearance of native species and particularly the threat to the ancient Araucada araucana, as well as the environmental damage produced by species such as the eucalyptus which extract most of the goodness from the soil, and plantations of pine which acidify the soil. Chile is rapidly becoming one of the great powers of world timber production.

---

defeat by the USA in 1845-1848. ■ *Free. Tuesday-Friday 1000-1800, Saturday 1000-1600, Sunday 1000-1300. Explanations are given free by University Art students.* There is another fine mural in the entrance hall of the railway station, *La Historia de Concepción* by Gregorio de la Fuente.

Museo y Parque Hualpen consists of a house built around 1885, which is now a national monument, and its gardens, donated to the city by Pedro del Río Zañartu. The museum contains beautiful pieces from all over the world, recommended. Further west in the park near the mouth of the Río Biobío, there are good opportunities for walking on the hills and several fine beaches including Playa Rocoto. ■ *Free. Tuesday-Sunday 0900-1230, 1400-1800. Getting there: take a city bus to Hualpencillo from Freire, ask the driver to let you out then walk 40 minutes, or hitch. You have to go along Av Las Golondrinas to the Enap oil refinery, turn left, then right (it is signed).*

Laguna San Pedro, on the far bank of the Río Biobío, has a beach and is where watersports are practised.

Museo Stom, southeast of Concepción, at Progreso 156, in Chiguayante, T362014, houses Mapuche artefacts.

Excursions

A1 *Alborada*, Barros Arana 457, Casilla 176, T/F242144. Good. **A1** *El Dorado*, Barros Arana 348, T229400, F231018. Comfortable, central, cafeteria, parking. **A2** *Concepción*, Serrano 512, T228851, F230948. Central, comfortable, heating, English spoken, recommended. **A3** *Alonso de Ercilla*, Colo Colo 334, T227984, with breakfast, recommended. **A3** *San Sebastián*, Rengo 463, T243412, F242710. With breakfast, parking. **B** *Ritz*, Barros Arana 721, T226696, F243249. Reasonable.

Sleeping
■ *on map, page 265*
Price codes:
see inside front cover

The Central Valley

B *Tabancura*, Barros Arana 790, p 8, T238348, F238350. Cean. Highly recommended.
B *Cecil*, Barros Arana 9, near railway station, T226603, with breakfast, clean, quiet.
Highly recommended.

C *Res Casablanca*, Cochrane 133, T226576. With bath, cheaper without, clean. **C** *Res Antuco*, Barros Arana 741, flats 31-33, T235485. Recommended. **C** *Res Central*, Rengo 673, T227309. With breakfast. **C** *Res Colo Colo*, Colo Colo 743, T234790. With breakfast. **C** *Res San Sebastián*, Barros Arana 741, flat 35, T242710, F243412. Recommended. Hostelling International reductions (both of these are entered via the Galería Martínez). **C** *Res Metro*, Barros Arana 464, T225305. Without bath, clean, poor showers. **C** *Res O'Higgins*, O'Higgins 457, T228303. With breakfast.

E pp *Pablo Araya*, Salas 643-C. **E** pp *Res Tiempo Libre*, Las Heras 646, T246525, clean, also short stay. **D** *Silvia Uslar*, Edmundo Larenas 202, T227449. Good breakfast, quiet, clean, comfortable. *El Naturista* restaurant lets out 2 rooms, **E** pp, clean, central. Good budget accommodation is hard to find.

Eating
• *on map*

El Rancho de Julia, Barros Arana 337. Argentine *parrillada*. *Piazza*, Barros Arana 323. Good pizzas. *Rincón de Pancho*, Cervantes 469 (closed Sunday). Excellent meat, also pasta and congrio, good service and ambience. *Novillo Loco*, Portales 539. Good, efficient service. *Le Château* Colo Colo 340. French, seafood and meat, expensive, closed Sunday. *Casino de Bomberos*, O'Higgins y Orompello, good value lunches.

Oriental *Yiet-Xiu*, Angol 515. Good, cheap. *Chungwa*, Barros Arana 270. **Big Joe Saloon**, O'Higgins 808, just off plaza. Popular at lunchtime, open Sunday evening, good breakfasts, vegetarian meals, snacks and pizzas. *Saaya 1*, Barros Arana 899. Excellent *panadería/pastelería/rotisería*. Highly recommended.

Vegetarian *El Naturista*, Barros Arana 244. Good fresh juices, soups and other dishes, closes 1800, English spoken. Highly recommended.

Cafés and bars Several *fuentes de soda* and cafés on Caupolicán near the Plaza de Armas including: *Fuente Alemana*, No 654. Recommended. *Café El Dom*, No 415, and *Café Haiti*, No 515, both open Sunday morning, good coffee. *Royal Pub*, O'Higgins 790. A posh snack bar. *Nuria*, Barros Arana 736. Very good breakfasts and lunches, good value. *QuickBiss*, O'Higgins between Tuscapel and Castellón. Salads, real coffee, good service, good lunches. *Café Colombia*, Aguirre Cerda. Good coffee, good atmosphere. *Treinta y Tantos*, Prat 356. Nice bar, good music, wide selection of *empanadas*, good breakfasts and lunches at the market. Recommended. *La Capilla*, Vicuña MacKenna 769, good ponches, popular, crowded.

Sports
Country Club: *Pedro de Valdivia*. Outdoor swimming pool, tennis. **Horseracing**: *Club Hípico*, north of the city on the road to Talcahuano. Race meetings Sunday and holidays.

Entertainment
Cinemas Multiscreen cinemas in the Plaza del Trebol shopping centre.
Discotheques *El Caríno Malo*, Barros Arana y Salas, bar, disco, live music, popular, not cheap.

Shopping
Main shopping area is north of Plaza de Armas. *Galería Internacional*, Caupolicán y Barros Arana is worth a visit (*El Naturista* vegetarian restaurant has a shop here at local 22). The market has excellent seafood, fruit and vegetables. *Las Brisas* supermarket, Freire y Lincoyán. There is a large modern shopping mall, the *Plaza del Trebol* north of the city off the road to Talcahuano (near the airport). Take any bus for Talcahuano.

Local Bicycle repairs: *Martínez*, Maipú y Lincoyán, very helpful. **Car hire**: *Hertz*, **Transport**
Prat 248, T230341; *Budget*, Arana 541, T225377. *Automóvil Club de Chile*, Caupolicán
294, T2250939. *Dollar*, at airport, T483661. *Full famas*, O'Higgins 1154, T248300,
F242385, airport T094403300.

Concepción

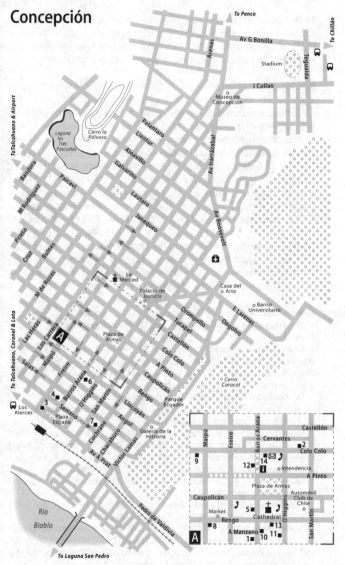

The Central Valley

N
Not to scale

■ **Sleeping**

1 Alborada	6 El Dorado	11 Residencial O'Higgins
2 Alonso de Ercilla	7 Residencial Casablanca	12 Ritz
3 Cecil	8 Residencial Central	13 San Sebastián
4 Concepción	9 Residencial Colo Colo	14 Tabancura
5 El Araucano	10 Residencial Metro	

Long distance Air: airport is north of the city, off the main road to Talcahuano. In summer, flights daily to and from Santiago (fewer in winter) and connections to Temuco, Puerto Montt and Punta Arenas. Airlines run bus services to the airport from their offices, leaving 1 hour before flight, US$2.50, also meet flights. Taxi US$8.

Train: station at Prat y Barros Arana, T226925. To **Santiago**, Rápido del Bío Bío overnight service, 9 hours, *económica* US$10; *salón* US$20, upper bunk US$30, lower bunk US$39; *departamento* US$80. Also local services to Laja and Yumbel. Booking offices at the station and at Galería Alessandri, Aníbal Pinto 478, local 3, T225286.

Bus: main long distance terminal, known as Terminal Collao, is 2 kilometres east, on Av Gen Bonilla, next to athletics stadium. (To the city centre take a Bus marked 'Hualpencillo' from outside the terminal and get off in Freire, US$0.40, taxi US$4.) Tur Bus, Línea Azul and Buses Bío Bío services leave from Terminal Camilo Henríquez 2 kilometres northeast of main terminal on J M García, reached by buses from Av Maipú in centre. To **Santiago**, 8½ hours, US$12. To **Valparaíso**, 9 hours, US$12 (most go via Santiago). To **Loncoche**, 7 hours, US$6.50. To **Puerto Montt** several companies, US$15, about 12 hours; to **Pucón** direct, 8 hours, US$8 in summer only, otherwise change at Temuco. To **Valdivia**, US$10; to **Los Angeles**, US$3. Best direct bus to **Chillán** is Línea Azul, 2 hours, US$2. For a longer and more scenic route, take the Costa Azul bus which follows the old railway line, through Tomé, Coelemu and Nipas on to Chillán (part dirt-track, takes 5½ hours). Services to **Coronel** (US$0.45), **Lota**, **Lebu**, **Cañete** and **Contulmo** are run by J Ewert (terminal next to railway station on Prat), by Los Alerces (terminal at Prat y Maipú) and by Jeldres, who leave from the main terminal. To **Talcahuano** frequent service from Plaza de Armas (bus marked 'Base Naval'), US$0.30, 1 hour, express US$0.50, 30 minutes.

Directory

Airline offices *Alta*, O'Higgins 734, Local 19, T252732. *LanChile*, Barros Arana 541, T25014/240025. *Ladeco*, Barros Arana y Lincoyán, T248824. *Aerolíneas Argentinas*, O'Higgins 650, Of 602.

Banks ATMs at banks. Most banks are on Av O'Higgins. Several *cambios* in Galería Internacional, entrances at Barros Arana 565 and Caupolicán 521, but check their rates first as these differ. *Cambios Fides*, local 58. Good rates for TCs. *Inter-Santiago*, local 31, T228914. *Afex*, local 57. No commission on TCs. Banks charge high commission on Tcs.

Communications Post Office: O'Higgins y Colo Colo. **Telephone**: *CTC*, Colo Colo 487, Angol 483. *Entel*, Barros Arana 541, Caupolicán 567, piso 2, Colo Colo 487. **Internet access**: Caupolicán 567, T245409, admin@cyberconce.cl, English spoken.

Cultural centres *Alliance Française*, Colo Colo y Lamas. Library, concerts, films, cultural events. *Chilean-British Cultural Institute*, San Martín 531 (British newspapers, library). *Chilean-North American Institute*, Caupolicán 301 y San Martín. Library.

Consulates *Argentina*, San Martin 472, Oficina 52, T230257, F230995.

Laundry Lincoyán 441. *Lavandería Radiante*, Salas 281. Open 0900-2030, very good. *American Cleaning*, Freire 817.

Tour companies & travel agents *South Expeditions*, O'Higgins 680, piso 2, oficina 218D, T/F232290, rafting and trekking expeditions, 1 and 2-day programmes.

Tourist offices Aníbal Pinto 460 on Plaza de la Independencia, T227976. Information on the more expensive hotels and *residenciales*. *Automóvil Club de Chile*, O'Higgins 630, Oficina 303, T245884. For information and car hire (T222070). *Codeff* (Comité Nacional pro Defensa de la Fauna y Flora) Caupolicán 346, Oficina east, p 4, T226649.

North of Concepción

A road runs north from Concepción along the coast through the suburbs of **Penco**, Km 12, and **Lirquén**, Km 15, a small, old, pretty town of wooden houses with a beach that can be reached by walking along the railway. There is plentiful cheap seafood for sale. **Tomé**, (*Population:* 38,000) 13 kilometres further north, is a small town set in a broad bay with long beaches. An interesting cemetery, Miguel Gulán Muñoz, is set on a cliff overlooking the ocean. **Dichato**, (*Population:* 3,000) nine kilometres further north along a hilly road offering fine views, is a beautiful fishing village and has the oceanographic centre of the University of Concepción. In summer it is a busy holiday resort. There is an interesting private museum, Museo del Mar, by Benjamín Ortega, free. You could also take a local bus to the tiny village of Cocholgüe.

Sleeping & eating Penco D *Hotel La Terraza*, T451422. **E** *Hosp Miramar*. Good, and *Casinoriente*. Good seafood restaurant. **Tomé D** *Roxy*, Sotomayor 1077, T650729. **E** *Linares*, Serrano 875, T651284. 7 kilometres before Tomé, on a hill, is *El Edén*, restaurant, bar and *cabañas*, **D**. **Dichato A3** *Chamaruk*, Daniel Vera 912, T683022. With bath, **C** without, clean, pleasant. **A2** *Manantial*, Aguirre Cerda 201, T683003. **B** *Kalifa*, Daniel Vera 813, T683027. With bath, restaurant. **C** *Chicki*, Ugalde 410, T683004. Wth bath, **D** without. **E** pp *Res Santa Inés*, República 540. Without bath; *albergue* in the school in summer.

Transport Línea Azul and Costa Azul buses from Concepción pass through all these villages, which can also be reached cheaply by *collectivo*.

The Biobío & Itata Valleys

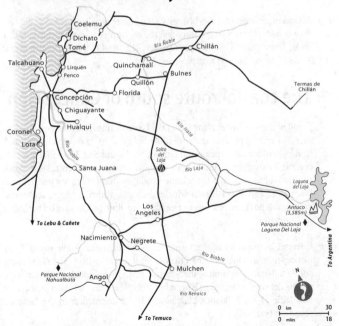

The Huáscar

At the outbreak of the War of the Pacific the Chilean navy blockaded Iquique, then an important Peruvian nitrate port. On 21 May 1879, the Peruvian Navy's huge ironclad, the Huáscar, and the smaller vessel, Independencia reached Iquique to lift the siege. Chile sent out two small wooden ships, the Covadonga and the Esmeralda, under Captain Arturo Prat to challenge them. Prat fought with ferocity.

When his damaged vessel, the Esmeralda, was rammed by the Huáscar, Prat called upon his men to follow him, boarded the enemy and continued fighting until he was killed. Chile later captured the Huáscar at the battle of Angamos near Mejillones, on 8 October 1879. Prat and his men are commemorated by a monument to the Héroes de Iquique in the Plaza Sotomayor in Valparaíso.

Talcahuano

Population: 244,000
Colour map 3, grid C1

Situated at the neck of a peninsula, Talcahuano has the best harbour in Chile. It is Chile's main naval station and an important commercial and fishing port. In the naval base you can visit the **Huáscar**, a relic of the War of the Pacific (see box). ■ *US$1.50. Tuesday-Sunday 0900-1130, 1400-1700. Photography is permitted, but passports must be handed in at the main gate.* On Península Tumbes is **Parque Tumbes**, owned by Codeff: paths lead along the coast, there are no services and no admission charge. Details are available from the Codeff office in Concepción.

Sleeping   **B** *De La Costa*, Colón 630, T545913. With breakfast. **B** *France*, Av. Pinto 44, T542130. With breakfast. **D** *Res San Pedro*, Rodríguez 22, T542145. With breakfast.

Eating   *Benotecas*, on seafront, a row of 4 restaurants sharing one window facing the harbour. Superb fish and seafood in each one, reasonable prices. Recommended. *El Alero de los Salvo*, Colón 3396. *La Aguada*, Colón 912. Shellfish dishes. *Domingo Lara*, Aníbal Pinto 450. Seafood specialities, excellent.

The coastal route south of Concepción

South of the Río Biobío is the **Costa del Carbón**, until recently the main former coal-mining producing area of Chile, linked with Concepción by road and bridge. Between Concepción and Lota are the Laguna San Pedro Chica, which is good for swimming, and Laguna Grande, a watersports centre, just across the Río Biobío. Nearer Lota are is the small Playa Negra with few peopleb and black sand and Playa Blanca with white sand, which is bigger and more crowded. It has bars, cafés and a free campsite. Both beaches are on the Bahía de Coronel.

Population: 80,000

Coronel in the heart of the former coal-mining area, 29 kilometres from Concepción, was the scene of a British naval defeat in 1914. The *Good Hope* and *Monmouth* were sunk by the *Scharnhorst* and a monument commemorating the defeat was erected in November 1989. The defeat was later avenged at the Battle of the Falklands/Malvinas with the destruction of the German squadron (see box).

The Central Valley

The Battles of Coronel and The Falklands, 1914

The British defeat at Coronel in November 1914 and their subsequent victory five weeks later in the Battle of the Falklands were part of a general struggle to control the sea and thus influence the outcome of the First World War in Europe. At the outbreak of war, the British navy set up a network of cruiser squadrons around the world to protect allied shipping and to drive German merchant shipping from the seas. At Coronel a small British force made up of three elderly cruisers and an armed merchant cruiser met a German squadron, which, under Vice-Admiral Graf von Spee, was en route to Germany via Cape Horn. The British were outgunned and lost two of their four vessels, Good Hope which blew up, and Monmouth which sank.

On 8 December when von Spee reached Port Stanley in the Falklands he sighted a larger British force in the harbour, including two battlecruisers, Invincible and Inflexible, sent by the British to deal with the German squadron. Von Spee attempted to flee. The ensuing battle was a series of duels which resulted in the sinking of four German vessels; the remaining one, Dresden, escaped and hid in Fiordo Leptepu, just north of Chaitén, until she was destroyed by the British in March 1915.

The Battle of the Falklands was the last sea battle decided purely by naval gunnery: henceforth submarines, torpedoes, mines and aircraft would also influence the outcome of naval warfare. Victory cleared the Pacific and South Atlantic of German shipping, an important part of the British strategy. Yet a questionmark remains over von Spee's decision not to attack the British vessels in harbour: faced with such a superior force his squadron was doomed, but it could have inflicted considerable damage on the port facilities and on the two battlecruisers which were relatively unmanoeuvrable in the confined space of Port Stanley harbour.

Steve Cobb

Lota

Forty two kilometres south of Concepción, Lota was, until recently, the site of the most important coal mine in Chile. Originally the property of the Cousiño family (see box on page 82), the mine closed in April 1997. The town is in two parts: Lota Alto, on the hill, is the original mining town, while Lota Bajo, below, is more recent. In the church on the main plaza you can see a virgin made of coal. Offshore is an island, Isla Santa María, which has basic accommodation and good beaches.

Population: 52,000
Colour map 4, grid A2

The **Parque de Lota**, covering 14 hectares on a promontory to the west of the town, was the life's work of Isadora Cousiño. Laid out by English landscape architects in the 19th century, it contains plants from all over the world, ornaments imported from Europe, romantic paths and shady nooks offering views over the sea, and peafowl and pheasants roaming freely. The mansion which was Isadora's home during her stays in Lota was destroyed in the 1960 earthquake. ■ US$2.50, no picnicking. 1000-1800 daily, till 2000 in summer. Near the entrance to the park is the **Museo Historíco de Lota**. ■ US$1. Daily 1000-2000 November -March, 1000-1800 April-October.

The **Coalmine**, the tunnels of which run almost entirely under the sea (the longest is 11 kilometres) can be visited; at the entrance is a small **Museo Minero**. ■ Guided tours led by former miners, daily 1000-1700, US$5, T870682.

C *Angel de Peredo*, Alessandri 169, T876824. *Res Roma*, Galvarino 233, T876257. Clean, friendly.

Sleeping

The Central Valley

Transport Buses to **Concepción**, 1½ hours, US$0.50. Many buses bypass the centre: catch them from the main road.

South of Lota the road runs past the seaside resort of **Laraquete** where there are miles of golden sands. At Carampangue, Km 24, it forks, running west to **Arauco** (*Population*: 12,000), the site of two cellulose factories. The other branch continues south, 52 kilometres, to Tres Pinos, where there is a turning for Lebu.

Sleeping Laraquete D *Laraquete*, on Gabriela Mistral (main street). Friendly, small rooms, poor bathrooms.. **D** *Hostal La Quinta*, T571993. Helpful, basic, good breakfast. Several *residenciales* close to beach; campsite near beach. **Arauco B** *Hostería Arauco*, Esmeralda 80, T551100. **D** *Plaza*, Chacabuco 347, T551265.

Lebu
Population: 20,000
Phone code: 041

A fishing port and coal washing centre, Lebu lies at the mouth of the Río Lebu 149 kilometres south of Concepción and is the capital of Arauco province. There are enormous beaches to both north and south, popular on summer weekends: three kilometres north at Playa Millaneco are caves with steep hills offering good walks and majestic views.

Sleeping A1 *Hostería Millaneco*, at Playa Millaneco, T511540, T511904. Offers *cabañas*, sleep 7, good restaurant. Recommended. **C** *Central*, Pérez 183, T/F511904. With bath, **E** pp without, clean, parking. Recommended. **D** pp *Gran* Pérez 309, T511939. With bath, **E** pp without, old fashioned, clean, *comedor*. **E** *Res Alcázar*, Alcázar 144. With breakfast, cold water, friendly.

Cañete

Population: 15,642
Phone code: 041
Colour map 4, grid A1

Twenty four kilometres south of Tres Pinos is **Cañete**, a small town on the site of Fort Tucapel where Pedro de Valdivia and 52 of his men were killed by Mapuche warriors in 1553. Three kilometres south on the road to Contulmo, is the **Museo Mapuche de Cañete** in a modern building supposedly inspired by the traditional Mapuche *ruca*; displays include Mapuche ceramics and textiles. Behind the museum is a reconstruction of a *ruca*. ■ *US$1.25. 0930-1230, 1400-1830, daily in summer, closed Monday in winter.*

Sleeping **B** *Hostería VIP's*, Av Bonilla, T/F611012. With breakfast. **C** *Alonso de Ercilla*, Villagrán 641, T611974. With bath, clean. **D** *Derby*, Mariñán y Condell, T611960. Without bath, clean, basic, restaurant. **D** *Nahuelbuta*, Villagrán 644, T611073. Clean, pleasant, parking. **E** *Comercio*, 7 de la Línea, T611218. Very pleasant, recommended. **E** *Gajardo*, 7 de la Línea 817 (1 block from plaza). Without bath, old fashioned, friendly, pleasant.

The coastal route south of Concepción

Caupolián

Caupolián was a Mapuche chief who led the resistance to the Spanish after the death of Lautaro in April 1557, launching an unsuccessful attack on the recently built fort of Concepción. The following year he was captured in a surprise raid on his camp, his wife revealing his identity to the Spanish by reproaching him for allowing himself to be taken alive and dashing her infant son to the ground. He was executed by being impaled, supposedly on the site of the modern Plaza Caupolián in Cañete.

Don Juanito, Riquelme 151. Very good, friendly. Recommended by the locals. Real coffee at **Café Nahuel**, off the plaza.

Eating

Bus Buses leave from 2 different terminals: J Ewert, Inter Sur and Thiele from Riquelme y 7° de la Línea; Jeldres, Erbuc and other companies from the Terminal Municipal, Serrano y Villagrán. To **Santiago**, Inter Sur, daily, 12 hours; to **Purén**, US$1.50; sit on right for views of Lago Lanalhue; to **Concepción**, 3 hours, US$3.50; to **Lebu** US$1.50; to **Angol** US$3.50; to **Tirúa**, Jeldres, frequent and J Ewert, 3 a day, 2 hours, US$2.

Transport

Lago Lleulleu and Tirúa

Lago Lleulleu is a peaceful lake covering 4,300 hectares. It lies 34 kilometres south of Cañete; to get there, turn off at Peleco, Km 11. The lake offers sandy beaches, many opportunities for camping and fine views of the coastal mountain range, but there are few facilities.

Tirúa, at the mouth of the Río Tirúa, is 78 kilometres south of Cañete. There are three *hospedajes* all **E**, including *Residencial Elimar*, T894902. The island of **Mocha**, visited by Juan Bautista Pastenes in 1544 and later by Sir Francis Drake, lies 32 kilometres offshore. Most of the island's 800 inhabitants live around the coast, the interior being of forests. The main settlement is La Hacienda where accommodation is available with families. Transport from Tirúa: ferry daily 0600, US$14; plane US$56 (ask the police to radio the plane which is based on Mocha). Buses run from Cañete to Tirúa.

Situated south of Cañete, Lago Lanalhue is surrounded by forested hills from which there has been extensive logging. Much less popular than the Lake District this area offers good opportunities for walking. A road runs south from Cañete along the north side of the lake to Contulmo at its southern end. Access to the lake shore is restricted as much of it is private property. Playa Blanca, 10 kilometres north of Contulmo, is a popular beach in summer (take any bus between Contulmo and Cañete). For further information on the area ask at the *Hostal Licahue* (see below).

Lago Lanalhue

Contulmo

This sleepy village at the foot of the Cordillera hosts a *Semana Musical* or music week in January. The wooden **Casa y Molino Grollmus**, three kilometres northwest along the southern side of the lake, are well worth a visit. The house, dating from 1918, has a fine collection of every colour of *copihue*, the national flower, in a splendid garden. The mill, built in 1928, contains the original wooden machinery. From here the track runs a further nine kilometres north to the *Posada Campesina Alemana*, an old German-style hotel in a fantastic spot at

Population: 2,000
Altitude: 31m
Colour map 4, grid A2

The Central Valley

The Central Valley

the water's edge. The **Monumento Natural Contulmo**, eight kilometres south of the village and administered by Conaf, covers 82 hectares of native forest.

Sleeping **Contulmo** **C** *Contulmo*, Millaray 116, T(messages)894903. With bath, **E** pp without, an attractive retreat, friendly and hospitable. Highly recommended. **E** pp *Central*, Millaray 131. Without bath, no sign, very hospitable. **On the lake A3** *Posada Campesina Alemana*. Open December-March, poor beds, own generator, fish come to hotel steps to be fed by guests, details from Millaray 135 in Contulmo. **B** *Hostal Licahue*, 4 kilometres north towards Cañete (T09-452-1781, Casilla 644, Correo Contulmo) T Santiago 2738417. With breakfast, also full board, attractively set overlooking lake, pool. Highly recommended. Also *cabañas*, **A1** , sleep 8, on far side of lake (connected by boat). *Hostería Lago Lanalhue*, reached from Tirúa road, on southern lakeside, T234981. **Camping at Playa Blanca** *Camping Elicura*. Clean, US$6. Recommended. *Camping Playa Blanca*. Clean. *Camping Huilquehue*, 15 kilometres south of Cañete on lakeside.

Transport **Bus** To **Concepción**, Thiele, US$4.50, 4 hours; to **Temuco**, Thiele and Erbuc, US$4; to **Cañete**, frequent, US$1.

Purén
Population: 7,572

Twenty kilometres further south, Purén is reached by crossing the Cordillera through dense forest (do this journey in daylight). Located in a major logging area, Purén was the site of a fortress built by Pedro de Valdivia in 1553 and destroyed soon after. It was a key stronghold of the Chilean army in the last campaign against the Mapuche (1869-1881) and there is a full-scale reconstruction of the wooden fort on the original site. There is **D** *Tur*, Dr Garriga 912, T793216 and *Central*, which is on the plaza. *Central* has excellent meals, but only lets rooms in the tourist season. **Lumaco**, 21 kilometres southeast, is the site of a major Mapuche festival, the *Fiesta de Piedra Santa* (see box on page 273).

Los Angeles

Population: 114,000
Altitude: 133m
Phone code: 043
Colour map 4, grid A2

Situated on the Pan-American Highway 110 kilometres south of Chillán, Los Angeles is the capital of Biobío province. Founded in 1739 as a fort, it was destroyed several times by the Mapuche. Located between the rivers Laja and Biobío at the heart of a wine, fruit and timber-producing district, it has become an important agroindustrial centre and is a pleasant, expanding city, with a large Plaza de Armas.

Colón is the main shopping street. There is a good daily market. There is swimming in the Río Duqueco, 10 minutes south by bus, US$0.80.

Sleeping
■ *on map*
Price codes:
see inside front cover

A3 *Mariscal Alcázar*, Lautaro 385 (Plaza de Armas), T/F311725. **B** *Gran Hotel Müso*, Valdivia 230 (Plaza de Armas), T313183, F312768, good restaurant open to non residents. **C** *Mazzola*, Lautaro 579, T321643. With breakfast. **C** *Res Santa María*, Plaza de Armas. Hot shower, TV, good beds. **C** *Winser*, Rengo 138. Overpriced but clean and friendly.

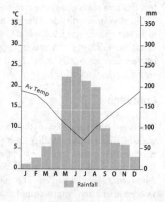

Climate: Los Angeles

Fiesta de la Piedra Santa

The ancient festival of the Holy Stone is celebrated every year on 20 January though Mapuche families start to arrive on the previous day. The women dress in their traditional costumes, with colourful belts and silver jewellery Each family carries a fowl which is sacrificed, covering the stone with blood, while they ask for favours or give thanks for favours received. A few drops of wine are also poured onto the stone before the rest is drunk. The stone is lit up by hundreds of candles and crosses made of straw or grass are placed over the blood, which sticks to them. Machis (shamans), surrounded by people from their communities, go up to the stone and, accompanied on their sacred instrument, the kultrung, they sing, dance and recite, while passing their knives over the diseased parts of the bodies of the sick. The festival continues through the night with singing, dancing, music and prayers.

Abridged and translated from Lengua y Costumbres Mapuches *by Orietta Appelt Martin, Imprenta Austral, Temuco, 1995.*

There are several residenciales (**C-D** range) around Colo Colo and Almagra. **E** Private house at Caupolicán 651, large breakfast, good value. Opposite is another, also No 651, basic, cheaper. **E** pp *Res Winser*, Colo Colo 335, T323782, small rooms.

16 kilometres north is **D** pp, also **F** pp *Hospedaje El Rincón*, Panamericana Sur Km 494, Cruce La Mona 2 kilometres east, T09-4415019, F043-317168, interbruna@ entelchile.net. Beautiful property beside a small river, restful. South American and European cuisine, including vegetarian (**B** pp full board), tours arranged, Spanish classes, horse riding, rafting, English, French and German spoken, kitchen facilities. Highly recommended ("one of the last corners in the garden of Eden"). *Antukelen*, Camino Los Angeles-Santa Bárbara-Ralco, 62. 7 kilometres southeast on the Alto Bío-Bío, reservations Siegfried Haberl, Casilla 1278, Los Angeles, T043-326097/09-4500210. Camping, US$15 per site, showers, German, English and French spoken, vegetarian food and other natural attractions; *cabañas*, natural therapy centre and excursions.

Los Angeles

■ Sleeping

1 Mariscal Alcázar	4 Residencial Santa Maria
2 Mazzola	5 Residencial Winser
3 Müso	6 Winser

0 metres 100
0 yards 109

The Central Valley

Eating   *El Arriero*, Colo Colo 235, T322899. Good *parrillas* and international dishes. *Di Leone*, Av Alemania 606. Good lasagne. *Julio's Pizzas*, Colón 542 and *Rancho de Julio*, Colón 720. Excellent *parrilla*. *Bavaria*, Colón 357. Good.

Transport   **Bus**   Long distance bus terminal on northeastern outskirts of town, local terminal at Villagrán y Rengo in centre. To **Santiago**, 9 hours, US$12, *Ejecutivo* US$23. To **Viña del Mar** and **Valparaíso**, 10 hours, US$14; to **Concepción**, US$2.50, 2½ hours; to Valdivia, US$7; to Chillán, US$2.50. To **Temuco**, US$5, hourly; to **Curacautín**, daily at 0600, 3 hours, US$4.

   Motorcycle spares   *Moto Stop*, Galvarino 487, T/F316987.

Directory   **Banks**   *Banco Santander*, Colón 500, Mastercard. *Corp Banca*, Colón 300, Visa. ATMs at banks and at supermarket at Av Alemaña 686. Banks are reluctant to change TCs or cash. Best rates at Agencia Interbruna, Caupolicán 350. **Communications**   Post Office: on Plaza de Armas. **Telephone:** *CTC*, on Colo Colo. *Entel*, Colo Colo 393. **Cultural centres**   *British Cultural Institute*, Vicuña 648. **Tourist offices**   On Caupolicán close to Post Office. *Conaf*, Ercilla 936. 0900-1300. *Automóvil Club de Chile*, Villagrán y Caupolicán, T322149.

Salto del Laja

Salto del Laja, 25 kilometres north of Los Angeles, is a spectacular waterfall where the Río Laja plunges 15 metres over the rocks.

Sleeping   **A3-B** *Hostería Salto del Laja*, Casilla 562, Los Angeles, T321706, F313996. With fine restaurant, 2 swimming pools and chalet-type rooms on an island overlooking the falls. Nearby are *Complejo Turístico Los Manantiales*, T/F314275. Also camping. Motels *El Pinar* and *Los Coyuches*.

Transport   **Bus**   Bus Bio-Bío from Los Angeles, US$1, 30 minutes – frequent; to Chillán, frequent, US$2.

Parque Nacional Laguna de Laja

Colour map 4, grid A3   Covering 11,600 hectares and situated 93 kilometres east of Los Angeles by a road which runs past the impressive rapids of the Río Laja, the park is dominated by the Antuco volcano (2,985 metres), which is still active, and the glacier-covered Sierra Velluda. The Laguna was created by the damming of the Río de Laja by a lava flow. It is surrounded by stark scenery of scrub and lava. Trees include a few surviving araucarias. There are 46 species of birds including condors and the rare Andean gull. The Visitors' Centre is one kilometre from park administration, which is four kilometres from the entrance.

The Central Valley

There is no clear path to the summit. From the Refugio Digeder at 1,400 metres **Climbing**
allow about six hours to ascend and start out early (0500) to allow time for the **Antuco**
descent which is exhausting. The volcano slopes are made of black scorias
blocks which are razor sharp; wear good strong boots and take water. From the
summit, where there are sulphur fumes, are fine views over the Sierra Velluda
and its glaciers and south to the smoking Villarrica volcano.

Take a bus from Los Angeles (ERS Bus, Villagrán 507) to Abanico then 4 kilometres to **Getting there**
park entrance. Alternatively take a bus to Antuco, US$1.35, 2 hours, weekdays 5 daily,
Sundays/festivals 2 daily, then hitch the remaining 24 kilometres to the park. Entry
US$1.50, (details from Conaf in Los Angeles)

Antuco **E** pp *Hostería El Mirador*, without bath. Most places are fully occupied by **Sleeping**
local workers. **Abanico** **E** pp *Hostería El Bosque*, restaurant, good campsite. **In the** *For the Parque Nacional*
park *Cabañas y Camping Lagunillas*, T314275 (or Caupolicán 332, oficina 2, Los *Laguna de Laja, take*
Angeles T3231066) 50 metres from the river, 2 kilometres from park entrance. Open *your own food as little is*
all year, restaurant, poor campsite US$2.50 per person. Camping not permitted on *available in Abanico or*
lake shore. 21 kilometres from the lake is the *Refugio Chacay* offering food, drink and *inside the park*
bed (**B** , T Los Angeles 222651, closed in summer). 2 other *refugíos*: *Digeder*, **E** , 11 kilometres from the park entrance and *Universidad de Concepción*, both on slopes of
Volcán Antuco, for both T Concepción 229054, office O'Higgins 740. Nearby is the
Club de Esquí de los Angeles with 2 ski-lifts, giving a combined run of 4 kilometres on
the Antuco volcano (season, May-August).

South of Los Angeles

The Pan-American (or Longitudinal) Highway (Ruta 5) bypasses **Mulchén**, a
small, old-fashioned town (32 kilometres; bus 45 minutes). It continues via
Collipulli, which has a campsite, Victoria, Púa and Lautaro to Temuco.

Angol

Situated at the confluence of the Ríos Rehue and Picolquén, Angol lies at the *Population: 39,000*
foot of the Cordillera de Nahuelbuta. Capital of the province of Malleco, it can *Altitude: 71m*
be reached from the Pan-American Highway by roads from Los Angeles and *Phone code: 045*
Collipulli. Though of limited interest to travellers, it is the main base for visit- *Colour map 4, grid A2*
ing the Parque Nacional Nahuelbuta, further west. Founded by Pedro de
Valdivia in 1552, Angol was seven times destroyed by the Mapucha Indians.
   The church and convent of **San Beneventura**, northwest of the attractive
Plaza de Armas, built in 1863, became the centre for missionary work among
the Mapuche. Worth visiting is **El Vergel**, five kilometres southeast, founded
in 1880 as an experimental fruit-growing nursery; it now includes an attractive
park with a wide range of trees and the **Museo Dillman Bullock** with displays
on archaeology and natural history. ■ *US$1. Daily 0830-1300, 1500-1800.*
Getting there: colectivo No 2.

B *Millaray*, Prat 420, T711570, with breakfast. **B** *Club Social*, Caupolicán 498, **Sleeping**
T711103. With breakfast. **C** *Olimpia*, Lautaro 194, T711517. **B** *Josanh-Paecha*,
Caupolicán 579, T711771. With breakfast, clean, good food. **D** pp *La Posada*, at El
Vergel, T712103. Full board, clean, friendly. **D** *Res Olimpia*, Caupolicán 625, T711162.
Good. **E** *Casa de Huéspedes*, Dieciocho 465. With breakfast, friendly. **E** *El Parrón*,
O'Higgins 345, T711370. **E** Vergara 651, chaotic but cheap.

The Central Valley

Camping On the road to Parque Nacional Nahuelbuta west of the city are *Las Quilas*, Km 21 *El Manzano*, Km 20.

Eating   *Carloncho*, Lautaro 447. Popular with locals. *Flores*, Caupolicán 330.

Transport   **Bus** Long distance terminal is at Chorrillos y Caupolicán. Local buses use the Terminal Rural, Ilabaca y Lautaro. To **Santiago** US$6.50, **Los Angeles**, US$1.20, or **Collipulli**. To **Temuco**, Trans Bío-Bío, frequent, US$2.50.

Car hire *Christopher Car*, Ilabaca 421, T/F715156.

Directory   **Banks** *Banco Bice*, Chorrillas 364. *Banco Santander*, Lautaro 399. **Tourist offices** O'Higgins s/n, across bridge from bus terminal, T711255. Excellent. *Conaf*, Prat 191, piso 2, T711870.

Parque Nacional Nahuelbuta

Colour map 4, grid A2   Situated in the coastal mountain range at an altitude of 800-1,550 metres, the park covers 6,832 hectares of forest and offers views over both the sea and the Andes. Good walks include: to Piedra el Aguila at 1,400 metres, four kilometres west of Visitors' Centre, where there is a *mirador* on top of a huge boulder; to Cormallín, five kilometres north of Visitors' Centre, from where you may continue to Cerro Anay, 1,402 metres, another *mirador*. ■ *Open all year (snow June-September).*

Wildlife   Although the forest includes many species of trees, the araucaria is most striking; with some over 2,000 years old, 50 metres high and two metres in diameter. There are also 16 species of orchids. Fauna include pudu deer, Chiloé foxes, pumas, black woodpeckers and parrots. There is a Visitors' Centre at Pehuenco, five kilometres from the entrance, open summer only 0800-1300, 1400-2000, offering small displays on fauna and flora.

Getting there   Bus to Vegas Blancas (27 kilometres west of Angol) 0700 and 1600 daily, return 0900 and 1600, 1½ hours, US$1.20, get off at *El Cruce*, from where it is a pleasant 7 kilometre walk to park entrance (entry US$4.50). Access is also possible by dirt road from Cañete, 40 kilometres west. Rough maps are available at the park entrance for US$0.25.

Sleeping   **Camping** Near Visitors' Centre, US$9 – there are many free campsites along the road from *El Cruce* to the entrance. Also at Cormallín, no facilities.

The Lake District

10

The Lake District

Extending from the Río Biobío south to the city of Puerto Montt, the Lake District is one of the most popular destinations for visitors to Chile. The main cities are Temuco, Osorno, Valdivia and Puerto Montt, but the most attractive scenery lies further east where a string of lakes, overlooked by volcanoes, stretch down the western side of the Andes. Much of this region has been turned into national parks. While the main lakes are readily accessible from the Pan-American Highway and offer a wide range of sporting and leisure activities, some of the smaller and less accessible lakes offer opportunities for those seeking a different type of escape.

The major lake resorts include Pucón on Lago Villarrica and Puerto Varas on Lago Llanquihue while the ports of Valdivia and Puerto Montt are also popular, the former for river-boat trips and the latter as a base for longer voyages south to Puerto Natales, Puerto Chacabuco and the Parque Nacional San Rafael and east across the lakes to the Argentine resort of Bariloche.

The Lake District

Background

History

After the Mapuche rebellion of 1598, Spanish settlement on the mainland south of the Río Biobío was limited to Valdivia. By the time of independence the only other Spanish settlement in this region was Osorno, refounded in 1796. The Chilean government did not attempt to extend its control into the Lake District until the 1840s. In 1845 all land south of the Río Rahue was declared the property of the state and destined for settlement and three years later Bernardo Philippi, a naturalist who had explored the lakes between Osorno and Lago Llanquihue between 1842 and 1845, was appointed colonization agent in Germany. In 1850 Vicente Pérez Rosales was sent to Valdivia to distribute lands to arriving European colonists.

The southern Lake District including the lands around Lago Llanquihue was settled, mainly by German immigrants, from the 1850s onwards. Further north Chilean troops began occupying lands south of the Biobío after 1862, but the destruction of Mapuche independence did not occur until the early 1880s when Chilean forces founded a series of forts in the area including Temuco (1881), Nueva Imperial (1882), Freire (1883) and Villarrica (1883). A treaty ending Mapuche independence was signed in Temuco in 1881.

White settlement in the area was further encouraged by the arrival of the railway, which reached Temuco in 1893, reducing the journey time from Santiago to 36 hours; the line was later extended to Osorno (1902) and Puerto Montt (1912). Railways encouraged the production of new crops to feed the cities further north; some of the elegant wooden mansions built with the new wealth can still be seen.

Geography

South of the Río Biobío the Andes and the passes over them are less high, and the snowline lower. The coastal range of mountains is also less high: the Cordillera de Nahuelbuta stops north of the Río Imperial and the coastal range then reappears intermittently, but at altitudes below 500 metres. The region between the cities of Temuco and Puerto Montt is one of the most picturesque lake regions in the world. There are some 12 great lakes of varying sizes, and dozens of smaller ones as well as imposing waterfalls and snowcapped volcanoes.

Main routes from the Pan-American Highway to the Lakes

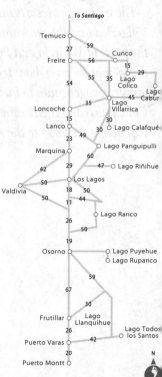

The Mapuche

The largest indigenous group in southern South America, the Mapuche now live mainly in communities south of the Biobío especially around Temuco. There are also reserves in the Argentine cordillera around Lago Nahuel Huapi. The name Mapuche is derived from the Mapuche for 'land' (mapu) and 'people' (che). They were known as Araucanians by the Spanish.

Never subdued by the Incas, the Mapuche successfully resisted Spanish attempts at conquest. At the time of the great Mapuche uprising of 1598 they numbered some 500,000, concentrated in the area between the Río Biobío and the Reloncaví estuary and mainly settled in the lands around the present day cities of Temuco, La Unión and Osorno. After 1598 200 years of intermittent war were punctuated by 18 peace treaties. So great was the Mapuche threat considered to be that Concepción became the base of the only standing army in Spanish America.

Although tools and equipment were privately owned, the Mapuche held land in common, abandoning it when it was exhausted by repeated use. This relatively nomadic lifestyle helps explain their ability to resist the Spanish. Learning from their enemies how to handle horses in battle they became formidable guerrilla fighters. They pioneered the use of horses by two men, one of whom handled the animal while the other was armed with bow and arrows. Horses also enabled them to extend their territory to the eastern side of the Andes. They also adopted aspects of Spanish life adding wheat, oats and apples (used for brewing chica de manzana) to their traditional crops.

The conquest of the Mapuche after 1862 was made possible by several developments, including the building of railways and the use of new weapons such as the breach-loading rifle. The settlement of border disputes between Chile and Argentina enabled Argentine troops to occupy the border crossings while the Chilean army subjugated the Mapuche. After 1881 the Mapuche were confined to reservations most of which were situated near large estates for which they provided a labour force. By the 1930s, living in more than 3,000 separate reservations, the surviving Mapuche had become steadily more impoverished and more dependent on the government. The agrarian reforms of the 1960s provided little real benefit to the Mapuche since it encouraged individual landholding; indeed some communal lands were sold off. It is estimated that the Mapuche now occupy only about 1½% of the lands they inhabited at the time of the Spanish conquest.

The Lake District

This landscape has been created by two main geological processes: glaciation and volcanic activity. Several of the lakes are glacial in origin: Lago Villarrica, for example, is the result of a glacial morraine forming a barrier across the valley of the Río Maichín. Others are volcanic, such as Lago Pirehueico, formed by lava flows from the Choshuenco volcano having dammed the Río Fuy. The main mountain peaks are also volcanic: the highest are Lanín (3,747 metres) and Tronador (3,460 metres), both on the Argentine border, followed by Llaima (3,050 metres), Lonquimay (2,865 metres), Villarrica (2,840 metres) and Tolhuaca (2,806 metres). The most active volcanoes include Llaima and Villarrica, which have errupted 22 and 10 times respectively this century.

Seven main river systems drain the Lake District, from north to south the ríos Imperial, Toltén, Valdivia, Bueno, Maullín, Petrohué and Puelo. Apart from the Imperial and the Puelo these gain much of their water from the lakes. The Río Bueno, 200 kilometres long, drains Lago Ranco and is joined by the ríos Pilmaiquén and Rahue, thus receiving also the waters of Lagos Puyehue and Rupanco: after the ríos Simpson and Baker, it carries the third largest water volume of any Chilean river. In most of the rivers there is excellent fishing.

The Lake District

♦ National parks
1 Monumento Natural Alerce Costero
2 Parque Nacional Alerce Andino
3 Parque Nacional Conguillio
4 Parque Nacional Huerquehue

5 Parque Nacional Malalcahuello Nalcas
6 Parque Nacional Puyehue
7 Parque Nacional Vicente Pérez Rosales
8 Parque Nacional Villarrica
9 Reserva Nacional Tolhuaca

The 1960 earthquake

Southern Chile is highly susceptible to earthquakes: severe quakes struck the area in 1575, 1737, 1786 and 1837, but the tremor which struck around midday on 22 May 1960 caused extensive damage throughout Southern Chile and was accompanied by the eruption of four volcanoes. The resulting tsunami (tidal wave) was felt as far away as New Zealand and Japan.

Around Valdivia the land dropped three metres, creating new lagunas along the Río Cruces to the north of the city. The tsunami destroyed all the fishing villages and ports between Puerto Saavedra in the north and Chiloé to the south. The earthquake also provoked several landslides. The greatest of these blocked the Río San Pedro near the point where it drains Lago Riñihue. The lake, which receives the waters of six other lakes, rose 35 metres in 24 hours. Over the next two months all available labour and machinery was used to dig channels to divert the water from the other lakes and to drain off the waters of Lago Riñihue, thus averting the devastation of the San Pedro valley.

Climate

The climate is cooler than further north; the summer is no longer dry, for rain falls all the year round, and more heavily further south. Rainfall decreases as you go inland: some 2,500 millimetres on the coast and 1,350 millimetres inland. Average daily temperatures in Valdivia are around 17°C in summer and 5°C in winter, with less variation between night and daytime than further inland. In the national parks to the east night temperatures even in summer can drop as low as −10°C. Beware if camping.

Out of season many facilities are closed, in season (from mid-December to mid-March), prices are higher and it is best to book well in advance, particularly for transport. Between mid-December and mid-January enormous horse-flies (*tábanos*) are a problem – do not wear dark clothes, especially black or navy blue.

Economy

Agriculture is the most important sector of the local economy. Cereals, potatoes, beans and sugar beet are grown throughout the region; cattle and sheep farming are more important further south than around Temuco. Despite the development of intensive fruit production since the early 1980s, much less fruit is grown than in the Central Valley. The farms are mostly medium sized, and no longer the huge haciendas found further north. The characteristic thatched or red tiled houses of the rural north disappear; they are replaced by the shingle-roofed frame houses typical of a frontier land rich in timber. Irrigation is unnecessary for agriculture. There is enough rainfall to maintain heavy forests, mostly of southern beech and native species, though increasingly of eucalyptus and other introduced varieties for the booming timber industry. Fishing is particularly important in the south of the region, where the growth of salmon farming is reflected in its presence on restaurant menus. Further north fishing is still largely small-scale, Puerto Saavedra and Quele being among the main fishing ports.

Industry has grown in importance in recent years, the main industries being connected to the region's produce, for example cereal mills, fish and meat processing plants, sugar beet plants, dairy processing and sawmills. Mining is of little significance, apart from small coal mines around Valdivia.

The Lake District

Crossing to Argentina

There are four main routes from the Lake District into Argentina:

1) From Pucón and Curarrehue to Junín de los Andes via Paso Tromen (see page 305).

2) From Panguipulli via Choshuenco and Lake Pirehueico to San Martín de los Andes via Paso Huahum (see page 311).

3) From Osorno and Entrelagos via the Parque Nacional Puyehue and Paso Puyehue to Bariloche (see page 325).

4) The Lakes Route, from Puerto Montt or Osorno via Ensenada, Petrohué and Lago Todos Los Santos to Bariloche (see page 339).

The Temuco Region

The northernmost city in the Lake District is Temuco, situated on the north bank of the Río Cautín, a tributary of the Río Imperial. North and east of Temuco are three national parks and several hot springs. West of the city in the valley of the Río Imperial are the market towns of Nueva Imperial and Carahue and, on the coast, the resort of Puerto Saavedra. This is an important agricultural region: wheat, barley, oats, timber and apples are the principal products of the area.

Temuco

Population: 225,000
Altitude: 107m
Phone code: 045
679 km S of Santiago
Colour map 4, grid A2

The capital of Región IX (Araucanía) is one of the fastest growing commercial centres in the south. Founded in 1881 following the final treaty with the Mapuche, the city lies near the heart of the biggest surviving Mapuche communities in the country.

The city is centred on the Plaza Aníbal Pinto, around which are the main public buildings including the cathedral and the municipalidad. On the plaza itself is a monument to La Araucanía featuring figures from local history. Nearby are fountains and a small Sala de Exposiciones, which stages exhibitions.

An important market town, Temuco offers the opportunity to see Mapuche women, in traditional costumes, at the produce market at Lautaroy Pinto, and *huasos* (cowboys), at the cattle auctions held on Thursday mornings in the stockyards on Calle Malvoa behind the railway station and at the Feria Agroaustral, just west of Temuco on the road to Nueva Imperial, on Friday from 1400 (take bus 4 from Calle Rodríguez). Traditional Mapuche spinning and weaving demonstrations are held at the *Casa de la Mujer Mapuche*, Prat 285, where textiles made by a co-operative of 135 Mapuche weavers are sold. ■ *Monday-Friday 0900-1300, 1500-1900.* North of the city is the **Monumento Natural Cerro Nielol** (entry US$1), offering fine views. There is an excellent visitors' centre run by Conaf and a fine collection of native plants in their natural environment, including the *copihue rojo*, the national flower. Cerro Nielol was the site of the signing of the final peace treaty between the Chilean army and the Mapuche (1881); it was signed under La Patagua, a tree which can still be seen.

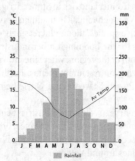

Climate: Temuco

Also highly recommended is the *Casa de Arte Mapuche*, Matta 25-A, T213085, Casilla 1682, for information on Mapuche arts and crafts speak to the director Rayen Kvyeh. There is also a bathing pool (US$1) and a restaurant (open 1200-2400).

Museo de la Araucanía, Alemania 84, houses a well arranged collection devoted to the history and traditions of the Mapuche nation; also a section on German settlement. ■ *US$1. Monday-Friday 0900-1700, Saturday 1100-1645, Sunday 1100-1400. Getting there: bus 1 from centre.* **Museums**

Parque Museo Ferroviario, Av Barros Arana three kilometres north of centre, contains 15 railway engines under restoration.

Chol Chol is a country town situated 30 kilometres northwest of Temuco by unpaved road through Mapuche country across rolling countryside with panoramic views. On a clear day it is possible to see five volcanoes. Nearer Chol Chol, a few traditional round *rucas* can be seen. For an overnight stay and information, contact Sra Lauriza Norváez, Calle Luzcano s/n, who prepares meals, and is very helpful. There are daily buses, laden with corn, vegetables, charcoal, animals as well as the locals, from Terminal Rural, Huincabus one hour, four times between 1100 and 1800, US$1. **Nueva Imperial** (*population* 12,000) is a market town 35 kilometres west by a paved road which follows the Río Imperial; cattle auctions are held here on Mondays and Tuesdays. From here the road continues to **Carahue** (*population* 7,869), where there is accommodation. This was the site of the Spanish colonial city of Imperial which was destroyed by the Mapuche. Further on is Puerto Saavedra, see page 288. **Excursions**

L3 *C'est Bayonne*, Vicuña MacKenna 361, T235510, F714915. With breakfast, small, modern, German and Italian spoken. **L3** *Terraverde*, Prat 0220, T239999, F239455. 5-star. **A2** *Nuevo Hotel de la Frontera*, Bulnes 726, T210718. With breakfast, excellent. Also *Hotel de la Frontera*, Bulnes 733, T/F212638. Same price. **A2** *Bayern*, Prat 146, T213915, F212291. Small rooms, clean, helpful. **A2** *Apart Hotel Don Eduardo*, Bello 755, T215554. Parking, suites with kitchen, recommended. **A3** *Luanco*, Aldunate 821, T213749, F214602. Apartments with kitchenette. **A3** *Tierra del Sur*, Bulnes 1196, T/F232439. Pool, sauna. **Sleeping**
■ *on map, page 286 Price codes: see inside front cover Do not confuse the streets Vicuña MacKenna and Gen MacKenna*

B *Chalet Alemán*, Varas 349, T212818. **B** *Continental*, Varas 708, T238973, F233830. Popular with business travellers, old fashioned building, old beds, excellent restaurant, the bar is popular with locals in the evening, cheaper rooms without bath. Recommended. **B** *Espelette*, Claro Solar 492, T234805. Helpful, quiet. **B** *Turismo*, Claro Solar 636, T210583. With bath, **C** without. Breakfast extra, restaurant, good value, good service, Hostelling International reductions. **C** *Oriente*, M Rodríguez 1146, T233232. Clean, recommended.

D *Alba Jaramillo*, Calbuco 583, near Av Alemania, T240042. With breakfast, clean. **D** *Hosp Aldunate*, Aldunate 187, T213548. Friendly, cooking facilities, also **E** dormitory accommodation. **D** *Casa Blanca*, Montt 1306 y Zenteno, T212740. Good breakfast, friendly. **D** *Hostal Argentina*, Aldunate 864. With breakfast, hot water, clean. **D** *Flor Acoca*, Lautaro 591. Hot water, breakfast, clean. **D** *Hosp Adriane Becker*, Estebáñez 881. Without bath, good breakfast, basic, friendly. **D** *Hosp Millaray*, Claro Solar 471. Simple, basic. **D** *Hostal Montt*, Manuel Montt 965, T211856. Parking, clean, friendly. **D** *Hospedaje La Araucaria*, Varas 552, T322820. **D** *Hospedaje 525*, T233982. Zenteno 525. Without breakfast, large rooms, clean, poor beds but good value. **D** *Rupangue*, Barros Arana 182. Hot shower, clean, helpful, good value. **D** *Sevilla*,

The Lake District

Aldunate 153. **D** *Las Heras 810*. Without breakfast, basic, clean. **D** *Blanco Encalada 1078*, T234447. Use of kitchen, friendly. Recommended. **D** *Bulnes 1006 y O'Higgins*. Good double rooms, hot water, above drugstore, ask for house key otherwise access limited to shop hours. **E** pp *Claro Solar 151*. With breakfast. Other private houses in same street. On Rodríguez, **E** pp *No 1311*. Friendly, clean, meals served. **E** pp *Res Temuco*, No 1341, T233721. Zenteno 486, T211269. Friendly, clean, hot water, recommended. **E** *San Martín 01760*, T246182. With breakfast, clean. **E** *Res Ensueño*, Rodríguez 442. Hot water, clean. Accommodation in private houses, category **D**, can be arranged by tourist office. Other *residenciales* and *pensiones* can be found in the market area.

Camping *Camping Metrenco*, on Pan-American Highway, Km 12.

Eating *Café Marriet*, Prat 451, Local 21. Excellent coffee. **On Bulnes:** *Dino's*, No 360. Good coffee. *Il Gelato*, No 420. Delicious ice cream. *Centro Español*, No 483. *Della Maggio*, No 536. Real coffee and light meals. *Cafetería Ripley*, Prat y Varas. Real coffee.

Temuco

To Long Distance Bus Terminal, Mall Temuco Shopping Centre, Santiago & the North

To Pacific Coast & the South via the Pan-American Highway

N

Not to Scale

■ **Sleeping**	6 Espelette	12 Nuevo Hotel de la
1 Argentina	7 de la Frontera	Frontera
2 Bayern	8 Hospedaje Aldunate	13 Sevilla
3 Casa Blanca &	9 Hospedaje Millaray	14 Terraverde
Hospedaje 525	10 Hospedaje La	15 Tierra del Sur
4 Chalet Alemán	Araucaria	16 Turismo
5 Continental	11 Luanco	

D'Angelo, San Martín 1199. Good food, pleasant, pricey. For cheap lunches try eastern end of Calle Lautaro or inside the municipal market (El Criollito has been recommended). *Pront Rapa*, Aldunate 421. For take-away lunches and snacks, recommended. *Ñam-Ñam*, Portales 802. Sandwiches etc, good. *La Cumbre del Cerro Nielol* (dancing), on top of Cerro Nielol. *Pizzeria Madonna*, M Montt 670, good atmosphere, good pizzas, reasonably priced. *HBH Bar*, M Montt 847, European style lager.

Cameras *Ruka*, Bulnes 394. Helpful, owner speaks German. **Shopping**
   Crafts Mapuche crafts and textiles are sold inside and around the municipal market at Aldunate y Portales.
   Supermarket Mall Temuco, a modern shopping centre north of city, bus 2, 7. *Frutería Las Vegas*, Matta 274. Dried fruit (useful for climbing/trekking).

Discotheque *Sol y Luna*, 10 kilometres south on road to Pucón, 2400-0600. **Entertainment**

Local Car hire: *Dollar*, at airport, T336512. *Christopher Car*, Varas 522, T/F215988. **Transport**
Hertz, Las Heras 999, T235385, US\$45 a day. *Budget*, Lynch 471, T214911. *Automóvil Club de Chile*, Varas 687, T248903 and at airport. *Puig*, Portales, 779. *Fatum*, Varas 983, T234199. *Euro*, MacKenna 426, T210311, helpful, good value.

Bicycle parts: *Oxford*, Andrés Bello 1040, T211869.

Motorcycle spares: *Terremoto*, Claro Solar 358, T312828, F312800.

Long distance Air: Manquehue Airport 6 kilometres southwest of city. LanChile and Ladeco to Santiago. LanChile and Ladeco to Osorno and Valdivia, Avant to Santiago, Puerto Montt and Punta Arenas. TAN flies to Neuquén, Argentina.

Train: station at Barros Arana y Lautaro Navarro, T233416. Ticket office at Bulnes 582, T233522, open Monday-Friday 0900-1300, 1430-1800, Sunday 0900-1300 as well as at station. To **Santiago**: overnight service, daily 2000, 12 hours. The dining car built in the early 1930s) and the sleeping car (1929) were both made in Germany. Sleeping car has hot showers. Fares: *económica* US\$13, *turista* US\$16, *salón* US\$22, *lower bunk* US\$50, *upper bunk* US\$38, *double compartment* US\$98, restaurant car expensive. No trains south of Temuco. Special bus services take train passengers to Valdivia, Osorno, Frutillar and Puerto Montt.

Bus: new long distance terminal north of city at Pérez Rosales y Caupolicán. Services to neighbouring towns leave from Terminal Rural, Pinto y Balmaceda or from bus company offices nearby: Erbuc, Miraflores y Bulnes; JAC, Balmaceda y Aldunate. To **Santiago** several companies, US\$18, 9-11 hours, most overnight. Cruz del Sur, 3 a day to **Castro**, 10 a day to **Puerto Montt** (US\$9, 5½ hours); to **Valdivia** US\$4; to **Osorno** US\$6; to **Concepción**, Bío Bío, US\$6, 4½ hours; to **Arica**, US\$55 or US\$70 *cama*; to **Antofagasta**, US\$45; to **Chillán**, 4 hours, US\$4.50-US\$7; to **Villarrica** and **Pucón** many between 0705 and 2045, 1½ hours, US\$3, and 2 hours, US\$3.50; to **Coñaripe**, 3 hours, and **Lican Ray**, 2 hours; to **Panguipulli**, Power and Pangui Sur, 3 hours, US\$3. Pangui Sur to **Loncoche**, **Los Lagos**, US\$4, **Mehuin** in summer only; to **Curacautín**, Erbuc, US\$2, 6 daily, 2¾ hours. To **Lonquimay**, Erbuc, 4 daily, 5½ hours, US\$3. Narbus to **Nueva Imperial, Carahue and Puerto Saavedra**, 6 a day; to **Laguna Captren**, Erbuc, Monday and Friday 1645, 4 hours, US\$3; to **Contulmo**, US\$4, 2 hours, **Cañete**, US\$4 and **Lebú**, Erbuc and Thiele.

The Lake District

Buses to Argentina: JAC to **Junín de los Andes** (US$25), **San Martín de los Andes** (US$25) and **Neuquén** (US$30), Wednesday and Friday 0400; also Igi Llaima and San Martín 3 a week each. Nar Bus from Terminal Rural to San Martín and Neuquén, Monday-Friday (San Martín buses go via Villarrica and Pucón when the Tromen Pass is open); Ruta Sur, Miraflores 1151, to **Zapala** (US$22) and Neuquén (US$28), via Paso Pino Hachado, Wednesday and Saturday 0400; La Unión del Sud, Miraflores 1285, same destinations Wednesday, Friday and Saturday. Fénix (address above) to **Buenos Aires** and **Mendoza**; to **Bariloche** via Osorno, Tas Choapa, US$23, daily.

Directory **Airline offices** *Avant*, Prat 515. Local 24, T270670, F270843, airport T339129. *LanChile*, Bulnes 667, T211339. *Ladeco*, Prat 565, Local 102, T214325. *Varig*, MacKenna 763, T213120. *TAN*, T210500. **Banks** ATMs at Banks on Plaza A Pinto: these include *Banco Santander, Banco Bice, Banco BCI, Banco Sud Americano, Banco de Chile*. Casas de Cambio: *Turcamb*, Claro Solar 733. *Christopher*, Prat 696, Oficina 419. Also at Bulnes 667, Local 202. *Inter-Santiago*, Bulnes 443, Local 2. *Comex*, Prat 471. All deal in dollars and Argentine pesos. **Communications** **Post Office:** Portales 839. **Telephones:** *CTC*, A Prat just off Claro Solar and plaza. Open Mon-Sat 0800-2400, Sun and holidays 1030-2400. *Entel*, Bulnes 303. Daily 0830-2200. **Consulates** *Netherlands*, España 494. Honorary Consul, Germán Nicklas, is friendly and helpful. **Laundry** Portales 1185, expensive. *Marva*, M Montt 415 and 1099. Mon-Sat 0900-2030. Aldunate 324. **Tourist offices** Bulnes 586, T211969. Open 0830-2030, all week in summer, 0900-1200, 1500-1700 Mon-Fri in winter. *Automóvil Club de Chile*: Varas 687, T213949. *Conaf*: Bilbao 931, T234420. **Tour companies and travel agents** *Turismo*, Claro Solar 988, T211278. *Turismo Nielol*, Claro Solar 633, T/F239497, offers towns to Parque Nacional Conquillo US$34, to Puerto Saavedra US$37, to Villarica volcano US$60.

Moving on

South of Temuco The Pan-American Highway (Route 5) runs south from Temuco through Loncoche and Lanco to Paillaco and Osorno. At Loncoche (Km 81; good place for hitching) the Philemon family workshop can be visited; the family specialize in fine carvings from native woods, of country and Mapuche scenes. At San José de la Mariquina, a road branches off Route 5 to Valdivia, 42 kilometres from the Highway (bus Lanco-Valdivia, Chile Nuevo, US$0.85, four a day, fewer at weekends).

West of Temuco

Puerto Saavedra

Population: 2,300

Eighty one kilometres west of Temuco, Puerto Saavedra lies behind a black volcanic standspit south of the mouth of the Río Imperial. Founded in 1897 at the mouth of the river, the town was destroyed in 1960 by a tsunami (tidal wave); few people were killed as they saw the water draining from the bay (the warning sign of a tsunami). There are now three distinct areas: Puerto Saavedra itself, inland, is the administrative centre; Maule, two kilometres south, is a fishing port with one poor *residencial*; Boca Budi, a further four kilometres south, is a resort with an enormous beach. From Puerto Saavedra a road leads north six kilometres to a free pedestrian ferry crossing over the Río Imperial to **Nehuentue** (*population* 700), on the north bank. From here launches may be chartered up the Río Moncul to **Trovolhue** (*population* 2,000), four hours.

Sleeping **Boca Budi**: **A3** *El Criollito*, T212583; *Lago Los Cisnes*, T251891; **E** *Sra Rita Sandoval Muñoz*, Las Dunas 01511. Lovely, knowledgeable. **Maule** **D** *Hosteleria Maule*, T634013. **Camping** *Rayen Lafquen*, in Boca Budi, El Cisne, in Maule.

Transport **Bus**: To Temuco (Terminal Rural), Nar Bus, three a day, 3¼ hours, US$2.50.

Orilie Antoine de Tounens

One of the more unusual European visitors to Southern Chile in the 19th century was Orilie Antoine de Tounens, a native of Périgueux in the Dordogne. His early reading of explorers' accounts of South America inspired Antoine to propose reuniting the 17 newly independent Spanish American states into a Monarchical Confederation with himself as king.

On arrival in South America in 1858 he decided instead to become King of the Mapuche. The widespread Mapuche belief that victory in their long struggle against the Chilean and Argentine governments would be brought about by the arrival of a new white chief meant that Antoine, an imposing figure with long black hair who wore a French coat and poncho and carried a curved sabre, was received better than might be expected. Antoine's proposals for the new coat of arms, flag and constitution of Araucania or Nueva Francia appealed to Quilapan, one of the Mapuche chiefs, and Antoine was duly crowned. The Chilean government was less impressed: when Antoine led a band of armed Mapuche to the Río Biobío to negotiate a peace settlement, the Santiago authorities had him arrested. Antoine's claims that he merely intended to build schools and encourage education were rewarded with a ten year prison sentence. French diplomats attempted to secure his release on the grounds of insanity. Eventually a compromise was arranged: the court ruled that although sane now, Antoine had been insane at the time of his offences so he was committed to an asylum in Santiago from which French diplomats were able to secure his release.

In France Antoine wrote his memoirs. His attempts to find benefactors to finance another visit to his kingdom were unsuccessful, but he returned secretly and penniless. With the Chilean government offering a reward for his head he was forced to flee. Back in France he sold bonds to finance another expedition, but the Chilean government objected to his activities and he was tried for selling fraudulent bonds. His final attempt to return was cut short when he was recognized disembarking at Bahía Blanca and deported by the Argentine government. Holding court in France, he sold specially minted coins, but was excommunicated by the Pope and the French government refused him the pension he claimed for services to his country of birth. Eventually his friends got him a job lighting street lamps. On his death in 1878 he left his crown to a cousin.

Lago Budi The only inland saltwater lake in Chile, Lago Budi lies south of Puerto Saavedra. Over 130 species of water bird, including black necked swans, visit it. On the east shore 40 kilometres by road south of Carahue is **Puerto Domínguez** (*population* 530), a picturesque little town famous for its fishing. On the west shore is Isla Huapi (also spelt Guapi), a peninsula with a Mapuche settlement (also known as Isla Huapi) of traditional thatched houses (*rucas*) and fine views of both the lake and the Pacific. Ideal for camping. Isla Huapi can be reached by ferry (*balsa*) either from about 10 kilometres south of Puerto Saavedra or from Puerto Domínguez (see below).

Sleeping Puerto Domínguez: **E** pp *Hostería Rucaleufú*, Alessandri 22. With good meals, clean, lake views. Highly recommended. **Camping** *Puaucho*, on Isla Huapi.

Transport Bus: to Puerto Domínguez from Temuco, 3 hours. **Ferry** The *Carlos Schalchli* ferry leaves Puerto Domínguez for Isla Huapi, Monday and Wednesday 0900 and 1700, returning 0930 and 1730, free, 30 minutes.

The Lake District

East of Temuco

Thirty kilometres east of Temuco a paved road branches off the Pan-American Highway and runs east to the Argentine frontier at Pino Hachado, passing through Curacautín and providing access to several national parks.

Curacautín
Population: 12,737
Altitude: 400m
Phone code: 045
Colour map 4, grid A2

A small town situated on the Río Cautín, Curacautín lies 84 kilometres by paved road, northeast of Temuco and 56 kilometres by paved road southeast of Victoria. Its main industry is forestry and there are several sawmills. It is a useful centre for visiting the nearby national parks and hot springs.

Sleeping & eating D *Plaza*, Yungay 157, T881256, main plaza. Restaurant good but pricey. E pp *Hostería Abarzúa*, T870011. Full board C pp, camping. E pp *Res Rojas*, Tarapacá 249. Without bath, good meals. Recommended. E pp *Turismo*, Tarapacá 140, T881116. Clean, good food, comfortable, best value. E pp Rodríguez 705 (corner of plaza). With breakfast, clean, kitchen facilities. *Camping Trahuilco*, 3 kilometres south. Expensive.
El Refugio is a popular eating place.

Transport Bus : terminal on the plaza. Buses to/from Temuco and Los Angeles.

Hot springs east of Curacautín

Termas de Manzanar, indoors, are 18 kilometres east of Curacautín and can be reached by bus from Temuco and Victoria. The hot springs cost US$5 and are open all year. The road passes the Salto del Indio (Km 14) a 60 metre high waterfall, before which there is a turn-off to Laguna Blanca (25 kilometres north, take fishing gear, ask Sernatur about trucks). Four kilometres beyond Manzanar is the Salto de la Princesa, a 50 metre waterfall.

Sleeping B *Termas de Manzanar*, T/F881200. Also simple rooms with bath. **D** *Hostería Abarzúa*, T870011. Simple, friendly. **D** pp *Hostería La Rotunda del Cautín*, T881256, F881569.

Termas de Río Blanco are situated 32 kilometres southeast of Curacautín at 1,046 metres on the slopes of the Sierra Nevada and near Lago Conguillio. To get there, take a bus to Parque Nacional Conguillio – see page 291 below – only at 1800.

The beautiful pine-surrounded **Termas de Tolhuaca** are 35 kilometres to the northeast of Curacautín by *ripio* road, or 57 kilometres by unpaved road from just north of Victoria; a high clearance four-wheel drive essential. The hot springs are open November-April daily, May-October weekends only.

Sleeping A2 *Termas de Tolhuaca*, T881164, F881211. With full board, includes use of baths and horse riding, very good. **E** pp *Res Roja*. Hot water, food, camping near the river, good.

Parque Nacional Tolhuaca

This park, two kilometres north of the Termas de Tolhuaca, covers 6,374 hectares of the valley of the Río Malleco at altitudes of 850 to 1,830 metres and includes the waterfalls of Malleco and Culiebra, and two lakes, Laguna Malleco and Laguna Verde. Superb scenery and good views of volcanoes from Cerro Amarillo. Park administration is near Laguna Malleco. ■ *December-April, with a campsite nearby.*

Getting there The park is reached either from Curacautín via the Termas de Tolhuaca (route open all year) or by dirt road from the Pan-American Highway 5 kilometres north of Victoria (four-wheel drive essential in winter and autumn). Bus from Victoria to San Gregorio (19 kilometres from park entrance) Monday, Wednesday, Friday 1715, return same days 0645.

The Lake District

Reserva Nacional Malalcahuello-Nalcas

Situated northeast of Curacautín, this 31,305 hectares park on the slopes of the **Lonquimay volcano** (2,865 metres) which is a popular ski resort (season May-November) is much less crowded than nearby Parque Nacional Conguillio. The volcano Lonquimay begun erupting on Christmas Day 1988; the new crater is called Navidad. To see it, access is made from Malalcahuello, 15 kilometres south and halfway between Curacautín and Lonquimay town. In Malalcahuello there is a steam-powered carpenter's shop.

Climbing Lonquimay From the ski lodge it is a one hour walk to the base of the mountain. Walk towards the ski lift and from there head to the spur to the left. Allow four hours for the ascent, one hour for the descent. Information from the Conaf lodge. Crampons and ice-axe are essential. The teacher at Malalcahuello school charges US$10 for transport to and from the volcano; Sra Naomi Saavedra at *Residencial Los Sauces* also arranges lifts.

Fishing The reserve is also a popular centre for fly-fishing: Sr Jorge Vio, at the ski lodge, provides information and acts as guide, US$40 per person per day, including transport but not equipment.

Sleeping **E** pp *El Encuentro*, Km 28 on Curacautín-Lonquimay road, T9-8849541, F881892, also dormitory accommodation and camping, cooking facilities, tours, English, German, French, Italian spoken. *Res Los Sauces*, **D** pp full board, or **E** pp with use of kitchen, hot water, good value. There is also a Conaf lodge. Accommodation is also available at the *Centro de Ski Lonquimay*, 10 kilometres from the bus stop, **B** pp with breakfast, full board also available, free camping, open all year, ski pass US$17.

Transport **Bus** Erbuc from Temuco, US$2 to Malalcahuello, 4 a day, 4 hours, 5½ to Lonquimay town, US$3. There is accommodation in Lonquimay, but no public transport to the volcano.

Parque Nacional Conguillio

Colour map 4, grid A3

Covering 60,833 hectares, the park, situated 80 kilometres east of Temuco, is one of the most popular in Chile, but is deserted outside January and February and weekends. In the centre is the **Llaima volcano** (3,050 metres), which is still active. There are two craters; the western crater was completely blown out in 1994 and it began erupting again in March 1996. There are two large lakes, Laguna Verde and Lago Conguillio, and two smaller ones, Laguna Arco Iris and Laguna Captrén. North of Lago Conguillio rises the snow covered extinct volcano Sierra Nevada, the highest peak of which reaches 2,554 metres.

Wildlife Much of the park is covered in forests of southern beech but the park is the best place in Chile to see araucaria forest which used to cover an extensive area in this part of the country (see box on page 293). Mature araucaria forest can be found around Lago Conguillio and on the slopes of Llaima. Other trees include cypresses, and *canelo* (winter's bark). Birdlife includes the condor, the black woodpecker and many waterfowl. Mammals include the marsupial *monito del monte*, pumas and pudú.

Climbing Llaima Crampons and ice-axe are essential except in summer (ask first). Climb south from *Guardería Captrén*, avoiding the crevassed area to the left of the ridge and keeping to the right of the red scree just below the ridge. From the ridge it is a straight climb to the summit. Beware of sulphur fumes at the summit. Allow five hours to ascend, two hours to descend. Information on the climb is available from Sr Torres at *Guardería Captrén*.

Walking There is a range of trails, from one kilometre to 22 kilometres in length. Details are available from park administration or Conaf in Temuco.

The Lake District

The route through the park from the south end is as follows: from the entrance, a 600 metre trail to Río Truful-Truful canyon and waterfall; eight kilometres to Laguna Verde; four kilometres to Laguna Arco Iris; four kilometres to Laguna Conguillio; six kilometres from Centro de Información Ambiental on Conguillio to Laguna Captrén; 10 kilometres to park limits and *guardería*.

Skiing Llaima ski resort, one of the prettiest in Chile, is reached by poor road from Cherquenco, 30 kilometres west (high clearance vehicle essential).

Park essentials Administration and information, open November-June, at Laguna Arco Iris, Laguna Captrén and at Truful-Truful. Out of season administration is at the western entrance. There is a Visitors' Centre at Lago Conguillio, open December-March. Conaf run a series of free slide lectures during daytime and evenings and short guided walks for adults and children during the summer, covering flora and fauna, Volcán Llaima and other subjects; details from the visitors' centre. Entry US$5.

Getting there There are 3 entrances: the northern entrance is reached by *ripio* road which continues through the park from Curacautín, 28 kilometres north; the southern entrance at Truful-Truful is reached by a *ripio* road from Melipeuco, 13 kilometres southwest; the western entrance, near the Llaima ski resort (see above) is reached by *ripio* road from Cherquenco. It is then a 2-3 day hike around Volcán Llaima to Lago Conguillio, dusty, but beautiful views of Laguna Quepe, then on to the Laguna Captrén *guardería*.

Sleeping In the park, **Laguna Captrén**: campsite US$20 per site including firewood but no other facilities. **Lago Conguillio**: campsite (US$20 per tent, hot water, showers, firewood), cheaper campsite (*camping de mochileros*, US$5 pp); *cabañas* **A3** summer only, sleep 6, gas stove, and café/shop but supplies are much cheaper in Temuco or Melipeuco. Book campsite with Conaf in the park; book *cabañas* with Jorge

Parque Nacional Conguillio

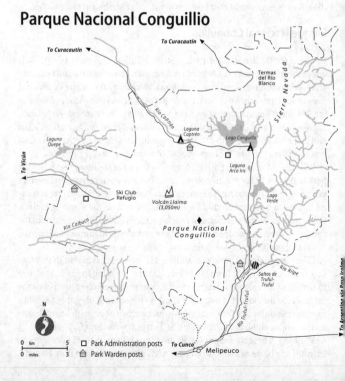

To Curacautín

To Curacautín

Termas
del Río
Blanco

Río Captrén

Laguna
Quepe

Laguna
Captrén

Lago Conguillio

S i e r r a   N e v a d a

To Vicún

Ski Club
Refugio

Volcán Llaima
(3,050m)

Laguna
Arco Iris

Lago
Verde

Río Calbuco

Parque Nacional
Conguillio

Saltos de
Truful-
Truful

Río Ripie

Río Truful-Truful

To Argentina vía Paso Icalma

N

| 0 km 5 | □ Park Administration posts |
| 0 miles 3 | ⌂ Park Warden posts |

To Cunco   Melipeuco

The Monkey Puzzle Tree

The Araucaria Araucana, known in Chile as the araucaria or pehuén and elsewhere called variously the Chilean pine, the umbrella tree and the parasol tree, this is the Chilean national tree. Very slow growing, it can grow up to 40 metres high; there are trees in several of the national parks which are believed to be over 300 years old. Though its natural habitat is on both sides of the Andes between 37° and 39° south, it is much more widespread in Chile than in Argentina. It was revered by the Mapuche who ate its cones and its sharp leathery leaves. Some isolated trees are still seen as sacred by the Mapuche who leave offerings to the tree's spirit. The characteristic cones can weigh up to one kilogram so take care sitting underneath!

Jane Norwich

Lefenda/Sra Silvia Weisser, Alvisur, Pedro de Valdivia 0631, Temuco, T/F214363, 213291. **In Melipeuco E** *Germania*, Aguirre 399, basic, good food. **E** *Pensión Hospedaje*, Aguirre 729, more spacious, recommended. **C** *Hosteria Hue-Telén*, Aguirre 15, Casilla 40, T693032 to leave message, good restaurant, free municipal campsite. Also *Camping Los Pioneros*, 1 kilometre out of town on road to the park, hot water. *Restaurant Los Troncos*, Aguirre 352, recommended.

Transport To the northern entrance: bus from Temuco Terminal Rural, Nar Bus, 5 daily, 0900-1830, 4 hours, US$1.30, ask driver to drop you at the road fork, 10 kilometres from park entrance, last back to Temuco at 1630. Bus from Curacautín to Laguna Captrén, Erbuc, Monday and Friday, 1730, summer only. To the western entrance: daily buses from Temuco to Cherquenco, from where there is no public transport to the park. Transport to the southern entrance can be arranged from Melipeuco (ask in grocery stores and *hospedajes*, US$25, one way). For touring, hire a four-wheel drive vehicle in Temuco. Several agencies in Temuco offer tours to the park, US$34, one day.

Frontier with Argentina

Paso Pino Hachado This pass of 1,884 metres can be reached either by unpaved road, 77 kilometres southeast from Lonquimay or by unpaved road 103 east from Melipeuco. On the Argentine side this road continues to Zapala.

Chilean immigration & customs In Liucura, 22 kilometres west of the frontier, open December-March 0800-2100, April-November 0800-1900. Very thorough searches and 2-3 hour delays reported.

Transport Buses from Temuco to Zapala and Neuquén use this crossing: see under Temuco.

Paso de Icalma This pass of 1,298 metres is reached by *ripio* road, 53 kilometres from Melipeuco. On the Argentine side this road continues to Zapala.

Chilean immigration Open December-March 0800-2100, April-November 0800-1900.

Lago Villarrica

Wooded Lago Villarrica, 21 kilometres long and about seven kilometres wide, is one of the most beautiful in the region, with snow-capped Villarrica volcano (2,840 metres) to the southeast.

Villarrica

Population: 36,000
Altitude: 227m
Phone code: 045
Colour map 4, grid B2

Pleasantly set at the extreme southwest corner of the lake, Villarrica can be reached by a 63 kilometre paved road southeast from Freire, 24 kilometres south of Temuco on the Pan-American Highway, or from Loncoche, 54 kilometres south of Freire, also paved. Less significant as a tourist resort than nearby Pucón, it is also cheaper. Founded in 1552, the town was besieged by the Mapuche in the uprising of 1599: after three years the surviving Spanish settlers, 11 men and 13 women, surrendered. The town was refounded in 1882.

There is a small museum, the **Museo Histórico** containing a collection of Mapuche artefacts, at Pedro de Valdivia y Zegers. ■ *Entry US$0.25, 0900-1930 Monday-Friday*. Next to it is the **Muestra Cultural Mapuche**, featuring a Mapuche *ruca* and stalls selling good quality handicrafts. The *costanera* offers good views of the volcano. For good views over the lake go south along Aviador Acevedo and then Poniente Ríos towards the *Hostería La Colina*.

Sleeping
■ *on map*
Price codes:
see inside front cover
Prices given are
high season
(January-February);
off-season 30-40%
lower

A1 *Hostería Kiel*, Koerner 153, T411631. **D** off season, lakeside, clean, friendly, good. **A1** *Hostería la Colina*, Ríos 1177, overlooking town, T411503, Casilla 382. With breakfast, large gardens, good service, good restaurant. Highly recommended. **A1** *Hotel y Cabañas El Parque*, 3 kilometres east on Pucón road, T411120, Casilla 65. Lakeside with beach, tennis courts, with breakfast, good restaurant with set meals. Highly recommended. **A2** *Hostería Bilbao*, Henríquez 43, T411452. Clean, small rooms, pretty patio, good restaurant. **A2** *Villarrica*, Koerner 255, T/F411641. **A2** *Yachting Club*, San Martín 802, T/F411191. **A3** *Bungalowlandia*, Prat 749, T/F411635. *Cabañas*, with comedor, good facilities. **A3** *Cabañas Traitraico*, San Martín 380, T411064, 100 metres from lake, sleep 6, TV, heating, kitchenette, parking. **A3** *El Ciervo*, Koerner 241, T411215. German spoken, beautiful location, pool. Recommended.

B *Kolping*, Riquelme 399, T/F411388. Good breakfast, recommended. **B** in summer, clean, good breakfast, lovely garden. Recommended.

C *Rayhuen*, Pedro Montt 668, T411571.

D *Fuentes*, Vicente Reyes 665, T411595, very basic, friendly, restaurant. **D** *Hosp Dalila Balboa*, San Martín 734, clean, cheap. **D** *La Torre Suiza*, Bilbao 969, T/F411213, zbinden@chilesat.net. Excellent breakfast, kitchen and laundry facilities, camping, cycle rental, book exchange, German, English spoken, repeatedly recommended. **D** *Villa Linda*, Valdivia 678, T411392, hot water, clean, basic, cheap, good restaurant. **D** *Yandaly*, Henríquez 401, T411452, good, English spoken.

D Several on Muñoz 400 and 500 blocks including *Res Victoria*, Muñoz 530, cooking facilities. Nearby, **D** *Vicente Reyes 854*, T414457. Good breakfast, limited bathroom facilities. **E** pp *Sra Nelly*, Aviador Acevedo 725, T412299, hot water all day, good value, camping, recommended. Rooms in private homes, all **E** pp: several in Bilbao including Eliana Castillo, No 537, clean, friendly; also in Koerner 300 block and O'Higgins 700 and 800 blocks. Urrutia 407, large breakfast, kitchen, clean; Matta 469, cooking facilities, clean.

Youth hostel E pp *Res San Francisco*, Julio Zegers 646. Shared rooms.

Camping Many sites east of town on Pucón road but these are expensive and it may be cheaper to stay in a hospedaje; those nearest to town are *El Edén*, T412772, 1 kilometre southeast of centre, US$4 pp. Recommended. *Los Castaños*, T412330, US$11 per site, and *du Lac*, T210466, F214495. Quiet, but buy supplies at *Los Castaños* which is cheaper.

Villarrica

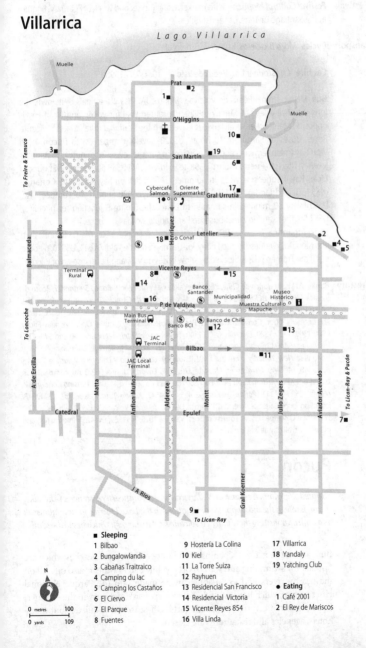

The Lake District

■ **Sleeping**		
1 Bilbao	9 Hostería La Colina	17 Villarrica
2 Bungalowlandia	10 Kiel	18 Yandaly
3 Cabañas Traitraico	11 La Torre Suiza	19 Yatching Club
4 Camping du lac	12 Rayhuen	
5 Camping los Castaños	13 Residencial San Francisco	● **Eating**
6 El Ciervo	14 Residencial Victoria	1 Café 2001
7 El Parque	15 Vicente Reyes 854	2 El Rey de Mariscos
8 Fuentes	16 Villa Linda	

N

0 metres	100
0 yards	109

Eating
● *on map, page 295*

Restaurant Alemán, Pedro de Valdivia 640, good. *El Rey de Mariscos*, Letelier 1030. Good seafood. *Rapa Nui*, Vicente Reyes 678. Good and cheap, closed Sunday. *The Travellers*, Letelier 753. Varied menu, Asian food, bar, English spoken. *Hotel Yandaly*, Henríquez 401. Good food. Recommended. *Café 2001*, Henríquez 379. Coffee and ice-cream, good. *El Tabor*, Epulef 1187, excellent but pricey. *El Viejo Bucanero*, Henríquez 552, good fixed price *almuerzo*, live music at weekends.

Festivals

Festival Cultural Mapuche, with market, usually in second week of February. Enquire at the Santiago or Temuco tourist office.

Transport

Cycles *Mora Bicicletas*, Körner 760, helpful.

Car hire *Christopher Car*, Pedro de Valdivia 1061, T/F413980.

Bus Main terminal Pedro de Valdiva y Muñoz; JAC has 2 terminals of its own, the long-distance one is at Muñoz y Bilbao, local terminal for Pucón and Lican-Ray is opposite. Many other local services leave from the Terminal Rural, Matta y Vicente Reyes. Buses to **Santiago**, 10 hours, US$20, several companies; to **Pucón**, both Vipu-Ray (main terminal) and JAC, services in summer every 30 minutes, 40 minutes journey, US$1; to **Puerto Montt**, US$8; to **Valdivia**, JAC, US$3.50, 5 a day, 2½ hours; to **Lican-Ray** frequent services in summer, JAC and Vipu-Ray, US$1; to **Coñaripe** (US$1.50) and **Liquiñe** at 1600 Monday-Saturday, 1000 Sunday; to **Temuco**, JAC, US$3 every 30 minutes in summer; to **Loncoche** (Route 5 junction for hitching), US$1.50. There are no direct buses to Panguipulli, go via Loncoche.

To **Argentina** Tuesday, Thursday and Saturday, Empresa San Martín (Muñoz 604) and Monday, Wednesday and Friday, Igi-Llaima, Pedro de Valdivia 611, US$20, 6 hours, but if the Tromen pass is blocked by snow buses go via Panguipulli instead of Pucón.

Directory

Banks ATMs: at *Banco de Chile*, Pedro de Valdiva y Pedro Montt, *Banco Santander*, Pedro de Valdiva 778, *Banco BCI*, Pedro de Valdivia y Alderete. *Casa de Cambio: Turcamb*, Henríquez 570. *Carlos Huerta*, Muñoz 417. Poor rates for TCs. *Cristopher*, Valdivia 1061. Good rates for TCs, rates are generally poor. **Communications** **Post Office:** Muñoz y Urrutia. Open Monday-Friday 0900-1300, 1430-1800. Saturday 0900-1300. **Telephones:** *Entel*, Henríquez 440 and 575. *CTC*, Henríquez 544, Chilesat, Henríquez 473. **Internet access** *Cybercafé Salmon*, Letelier y Henríquez. *New Yandaly*, Henríquez 401. **Laundry** *Lavandería y Lavaseco Villarrica*, Andrés Bello 348, T411449. *Lavacenter*, Alderete 770. *Todo Lavado*, Urrutia 669. **Tour companies & travel agents** *Turismo Repu-Pehuén*, Pedro de Valdivia 565, T/F412065. *Turismo Coñaripe*, P. Montt 525, T411111. *Politur*, Henriquez 475, T414547. *Karina Tour*, Letelier 825, T412048. Excursion prices: Parque Nacional Villarrica US$13, Villarrica Volcano US$55, Valdivia US$25, Termas de Coñaripe US$22. **Tourist offices** Valdivia 1070, T411162, F414261. Information and maps (open all day all week in summer).

Pucón

Population: 8,000
Altitude: 280m
Phone code: 045
Colour map 4, grid B2

Situated 26 kilometres east of Villarrica on the southeastern corner of the lake, Pucón is one of the most popular destinations in the Lake District, famous above all as a centre for visiting the Villarrica volcano (2,840 metres), which lies to the south.

Built across the neck of a peninsula, it has two black sand beaches which are popular for swimming and watersports. Whitewater rafting is also offered on the nearby rivers and excursions can be made into the Parque Nacional Huerquehue which lies east of the town. Expensive and busy in the summer, Pucón is also a centre for winter sports. Off-season it is quieter, but many hotels, agencies and restaurants are closed.

Sights

The main commercial centre lies between Avenida O'Higgins, the main avenue, and the *Gran Hotel Pucón*. From **La Peninsula**, west of town, there are fine views of the lake and volcano as well as pony rides and golf. Getting here involves crossing private land; ask for permission at the entrance. There is also a pleasant walk, along the **Costanera Otto Gudenschwager**, starting at the northern end of Calle Ansorena and following the lakeside north. Just south of O'Higgins, there is a large handicraft market where you can see spinning and weaving in progress.

Excursions

Excursions on the lake by launch are operated in summer from the landing stage at La Poza at the western end of O'Higgins, 1500, 1900, US$4, 2 hours. Walk two kilometres north along the beach to the mouth of the Río Pucón, with views of the volcanoes Villarrica, Quetrupillán and Lanín. There are boats to the mouth of the river from near the *Gran Hotel*, US$12, in summer only. To cross the Río Pucón: head east out of Pucón along the main road, then turn north on an unmade road leading to a new bridge; from here there are pleasant walks along the north shore of the lake to Quelhue and Trarilelfú, or northeast towards Caburga, see page 302, or up into the hills through farms and agricultural land, with views of three volcanoes and, higher up, of the lake.

Essentials

Prices given below are January-February. Off-season rates are 20-40 percent lower and it is often possible to negotiate.

L1-L2 *Del Lago*, Ansorena y Valdivia, T291000, F291200 (Santiago: San Sebastion 2839, Oficina 901, T245-6005, F245-6008), 5 star, pool, health suite, casino, cinema. **L1** *Antumalal*, 2 kilometres west, T441011, F441013. Very small, picturesque chalet-type, magnificent views of the lake, tennis court, lovely gardens, excellent, with meals, open year round, pool. **L1** *Gran Pucón*, Holzapfel 190, T441001. Restaurant, disco, sports centre, shared with **L3** *Condominio Gran Hotel* apartments. **L2** *Interlaken*, Colombia y Caupolicán, T441276, F441242. Chalets, recommended, water skiing, pool, travellers' cheques changed (open November-April), no restaurant. **L3** *Gudenschwager*, Pedro de Valdivia 12, T/F441156.

A1 *Araucarias*, Caupolicán 243, T441963, F441286. Clean, comfortable, indoor pool. **A1** *La Posada Plaza-Pucón*, Valdivia 191, T/F441088 (Santiago T/F5243325). With bath,

Sleeping
■ *on map, page 298*
Price codes:
see inside front cover
In summer, December to February, rooms may be hard to find. There are plenty of alternatives (usually cheaper) in Villarrica

The Lake District

cheaper without, full board available, also spacious cabins (**C** low season). **A1** *Munich*, Alderete 275, T/F442293. Modern, spacious, German and English spoken. **A2** *Oregon*, Fresia 260, T441977, F442433. Clean, good beds. **A2** *Hostería El Principito*, Urrutia 291, T441200. Good breakfast, clean, very friendly, recommended. **A2** *La Palmera*, Ansorena 221, T441083, F443127. **A3** *Kernayel*, 1 kilometre east at Camino International 1510, T/F442164, kernayel@cepri.cl. Apartments and *cabañas*, pool, comfortable.

B *Hosp Del Montanés*, O'Higgins 472, T441267. Good value, clean, TV, central, restaurant. **B** *Hostería Milla Rahue*, O'Higgins 460, T441610. Clean, good inexpensive restaurant.

C *La Tetera*, Urrutia 580, T/F441462, info@tetera.cl, www.tetera.cl. With bath and good breakfast, German and English spoken, book swap, Navimag reservations. Highly recommended. **C-D** *Hosp La Casita*, Palguín 555, T441712. Clean, laundry and

Pucón

To Camping Ainhoa

Lago Villarrica

Playa Grande

Costanera Otto Gudenschwager

Ramón Quezada

La Península

Costanera

Municipalidad

6 Holzapfel

4

3

P de Valdivia

20

7

1 ⑤

Alderete

25

26 **6** Off Limits

2

Gral Urrutia **5**

10

Sol y Nieve

15

⑤ 2

Av B O'Higgins

Trancura

22

14

Brasil

12

Psje Chile **11**

13 **9**

Uruguay

23

Paraguay

Perú

Perú

Camping La Poza

17

Camino a Villarrica

Ecuador

Caupolicán

Lincoyán

19

Palguín

Arauco

Colo Colo

Laundry

21 **8**

16

Fundación Lahuen

24 **7**

3

Eltit Supermarket

Apumanque

Servitour

Laundry

SCAI Club

Mercado Artesanal

Fresia

Ansorena

18

JAC

Politur

5 **2**

Condor

Laundry

Igi-Llaima

3

Camping Los Castaños

Laundry

Tur Bus

Las Araucarias

Sebastián Engler

La Poza

Costanera Sur

Colombia

To Villarrica

Legend

N		
0 metres 100		
0 yards 109		

■ Sleeping
1 Antumalal
2 Araucarias
3 Del Lago
4 Del Montanes
5 El Principito
6 Gran Pucón
7 Gudenschwager
8 Hospedaje Arauco
9 Hospedaje Eliana
10 Hospedaje El Refugio
11 Hospedaje Graciela
12 Hospedaje Irima
13 Hospedaje Lucia
14 Hospedaje Sonia
15 Hostal O'Higgins
16 Hostería iécole!
17 Interlaken
18 La Casita
19 La Palmera
20 La Posada
21 La Tetera
22 Lincoyán No 445
23 Lincoyán No 630
24 Milla Rahue
25 Munich
26 Oregon

● Eating
1 Café de la P
2 Club 77
3 El Mesón
4 Holzapfel Backerei
5 Mamas y Tapas
6 Puerto Pucón
7 Trabún

⑤ Banks
1 Banco BCI
2 Banco del Estado
3 Banco Santander

kitchen facilities, English and German spoken, large breakfast, garden, motorcycle parking, ski trips, Spanish classes, **D** off season. Recommended.

D *Hostal O'Higgins*, O'Higgins 136, T441153, F441334. Clean, cooking facilities. **D** pp *Hostería ¡école!*, Urrutia 592, T/F441675, trek@ecole.cl. With breakfast, no singles, also dormitory accommodation, **E** pp (sleeping bag essential), good vegetarian and fish restaurant, ecological shop, forest treks, rafting, biking, information, language classes, massage. **D** *Hosp Arauco*, Arauco 272, T442223, without bath, **C** with, without breakfast, noisy. **D** *Res Lincoyán*, Av Lincoyán, T441144. With bath, cheaper without, clean and comfortable.

In private houses, all **D** or **E** pp unless stated: *Familia Acuña*, Palguín 233 (ask at *peluquería* next door), without breakfast, hot water, kitchen and laundry facilities, dirty, good meeting place. **On Lincoyán:** Juan Torres, No 445, T441248. Poor bathrooms, noisy, cooking facilities. **B-C** *Hosp El Refugio*, No 348, T441347. With breakfast, good. **D** *Hosp Sonia*, No 485, T441269. Use of kitchen, very noisy and crowded, meals, friendly. No 630, friendly, clean. No 815, cooking facilities (information on climbing Villarrica). **D** *Hosp Irma*, No 545, T442226. Cooking facilities, clean. **D-E** pp *Hosp Lucía*, No 565, T441721. Friendly, quiet, garden, recommended, cooking facilities. Nearby is, **D-E** *Casa Eliana*, Pasaje Chile 225, T441851. Kitchen facilities. Highly recommended. **E** Adriana Molina, No 312. With breakfast, clean, helpful. **F** pp, No 630, T441043. Kitchen facilities, good value. *Hosp Graciela*, Pasaje Rolando Matus 521 (off Av Brasil). Good food. *Irma Villena*, Arauco 460. Clean, friendly. Recommended. **E** *Casa de Mayra*, Arauco 669, T441511. Kitchen facilities. **F** pp *Roberto y Alicia Abreque*, Perú 170. Basic, noisy, popular, kitchen and laundry facilities, information on excursions. **E** *Casa Richard*, Paraguay 140. Basic but friendly, cooking facilities. Recommended. Many other families have rooms – look for the signs or ask in bars/restaurants.

Camping Buy supplies in Villarrica (cheaper). Sites near Pucón include: *Ainoha*, 12 blocks north on lakeside. *La Poza*, Costanera Geis 769, T441435, **F** pp. *Los Boldos*, Pasaje Las Rosas, east of town. *Los Castaños*, O'Higgins 870, **F** pp. Other sites west along Lago Villarrica, including *Saint John*, Km 7, T441165, casilla 154, **F** pp. *Millaray*, Km 7, T212336, campsite. Also several sites *en route* to the volcano including *L'etoile*, Km 2, T442188, in attractive forest; *Mahuida*, Km 6. On the road to Tromen Pass, *Cabañas El Dorado*, US$18 for 2, good site, poorly maintained. Cheaper sites *en route* to Caburga. **Camping equipment** *Eltit Supermarket*, O'Higgins y Fresia. *Outdoors and Travel*, Lincoyán 361.

Eating
● *on map*
See also sleeping above

La Buonatesta, Fresia 243. Good pizzeria. *En Alta Mar*, Urrutia y Fresia, fish, seafood, very good but pricey. *El Fogón*, O'Higgins 480. Very good. *El Refugio*, Lincoyán 348. Some vegetarian dishes, expensive wine. *Puerto Pucón*, Fresia 251. Spanish, stylish, expensive. *Tijuna*, Fresia 303, Mexican, reasonably priced. **Cheap Restaurants:** *Trabún*, Palguin 348; *Coronado*, Urrutia 425; *Coppa Kavana*, Urrutia y Ansorena. **For real coffee:** *Café Brasil*, Fresia 477. *Café de la P*, O'Higgins y Lincoyán. *El Turista*, Fresia y Alderete. *Holzapfel Backerei*, Holzapfel 524. German café. Recommended. *La Tetera*, Urrutia 580. Wide selection of teas, good coffee, snacks, German spoken. Recommended. *Hostería école* (see under **Sleeping**). **Bars:** *Mamas y Tapas*, O'Higgins y Arauco. *Club 77*, O'Higgins 689; *Pub for you*, Ansorena 370. English-style pub. *Disco For You*, 2 kilometres east. Open all year (transport in summer from *Pub for You*).

Aerial sports Parapenting and paragliding, *Fabrice Pini*, Colo Colo 830, US$55 for half an hour. **Fishing** Pucón and Villarrica are celebrated as centres for fishing on Lago Villarrica and on the beautiful Lincura, Trancura and Toltén rivers. Local tourist office will supply details on licences and open seasons etc. *Off Limits*, Fresia 273, T441210, F441604, offlimitspucon@hotmail.com, fishing specialists, English spoken, offer

Sports

The Lake District

Pucón paradise

There are not many days during the season when you can enjoy skiing at Pucón in idyllic conditions, but on a sunny, windfree day with all the lifts working, this is one of the most mysterious and beautiful areas I *have skied in; smoke continuously billowing out of the crater; enormous lakes and a national park down below.*

Josselyn van den Pol and Leandro Yañez.

fly-fishing excursions US$100 per day, maximum 3 persons. Also fishing boat excursions, from US$190 for 2 persons. Some other tourist agencies also offer trips. **Hiking** to the Cañi Forest Sanctuary, overnight hikes are recommended, see below. **Horse riding** horse hire US$35 half day, US$55 full day, enquire at La Tetera. Also Centro de Turismo Ecuestre Huepil, T09-4534212, small groups, local excursions and three-day trips to Argentina. See also *Rancho de Callabos* at Termas de Palguín, page 304. **Skiing** on the slopes of the Villarrica volcano, see box and page 301. **Watersports** water-skiing, sailing, windsurfing at *Playa Grande*, the beach by *Gran Hotel* and La Poza beach end of O'Higgins (more expensive than Playa Grande, not recommended); Playa Grande: waterskiing US$10 for 15 minutes, Laser sailing US$11 per hour, sailboards US$10 per hour, rowing boats US$4 per hour. **Whitewater rafting** is very popular on the Río Trancura, east of Pucón; many agencies offer trips (see below), Trancura Baja (basic) US$15; Trancura Alta (advanced) US$25. 3-day excursions are also offered to the Río Bío Bío, (advanced), US$250 pp, with food, transport and equipment, October-March only.

Transport **Local** **Bicycle hire**: *Taller el Pollo*, Palguin 500 block; *Trancura*, O'Higgins 261, US$20 per day. Try also travel agencies, eg *Sol y Nieve*. **Car hire**: *Christopher Car*, O'Higgins 335, T/F449013. *Hertz*, Fresia 220, T441664, US$65 for cheapest car (including tax, insurance, and 200 kilometres free); same prices per day at Gran Hotel. *Pucón Rent A Car*, Camino Internacional 1395, T441922, kernayel@cepri.cl **Taxi**: Cooperative, T441009; individual member Oscar Jara Carrasco, T411992 (home in Villarrica).

Long distance **Bus:** No municipal terminal: each company has its own terminal: *JAC*, Uruguay y Palguin. *Tur Bus*, O'Higgins 1180, east of town. *Igi Llaima and Condor*, Colo Colo y O'Higgins. *LIT*, O'Higgins y Palguín. *Transportes Liucura*, O'Higgins 615.

JAC has most services to **Villarrica**, every 15 minutes, US$1. To **Valdivia**, US$5. To **Temuco** frequent, US$3, 2 hours, *rápido* US$3.50, 1 hour; for **Puerto Montt** go to Valdivia and change. To **Santiago**, 10 hours, US$18-25, many companies, Power cheapest (and least comfortable), overnight only; daytime go via Temuco; *cama* service by Tur-Bus and JAC, US$40. To **Paillaco** and **Lago Caburga** – see below. *Colectivos* to **Villarrica** from O'Higgins y Palguín. To **Argentina**: Buses from Temuco through to the Tromen Pass to Junín pass through Pucón, fares are the same as from Temuco.

Directory **Banks** ATMs: in *Banco Santander, Banco del Estado* and Eltit Supermarket, all on O'Higgins. *Banco BCI*, Fresia y Alderete, and in casino. Several *casas de cambio* on O'Higgins. Eltit supermarket also changes TCs but best to change TCs before arriving as rates poor. **Communications** Post Office: Fresia 183. **Telephone:** *CTC*, Gen Urrutia 472. *Entel*, Ansorena 299. **Laundry** Urrutia 520; Palguín 460; Fresia 224; Colo-Colo 475 and 478, several others. **Tour companies & travel agents** on O'Higgins: *Sol y Nieve* (esq Lincoyán, T/F441070, solnieve@entelchile.net). Excellent guides and equipment, repeatedly recommended. *Politur*, No 635, T/F441373, turismo@politur.com. *Servitour*, No 211, T441959. *Apumanque*, No 412, T441085. Poor equipment, good guides. *Turismo Florencia*, O'Higgins 480, T443026. *Hosteria école* (address above) *S.C.A.I. Club*, Palguín 465, T443449, F443436. All arrange trips to thermal baths, trekking to volcanoes, whitewater rafting, etc (prices: whitewater rafting and riding, see above; climbing Villarrica, US$50, 12 hrs, equipment provided; mountain bike hire from US$5 per hr to US$20 per day, ski hire and transport to slopes US$20 pp. Tours to Termas de Huife, US$20 including entry). Shop around: prices vary at times, quality of guides and equipment variable. For falls, lakes and *termas* it is cheaper, if in a group, to flag down a taxi and bargain. **Tourist offices** *Municipal Tourist Office*, O'Higgins y Palguín. Provides information and sells fishing licences (US$1 per month). The local hotel association runs an information office at Caupolicán y Brasil.

East of Lago Villarrica

Withing easy reach of Villarrica and Pucón are two more lakes, two national parks and several hot springs.

Parque Nacional Villarrica

This park, which covers 61,000 hectares, stretches from Pucón to the Argentine frontier near Puesco. There are three sectors: Villarrica Volcano, Quetrupillán Volcano and the Puesco sector which includes the slopes of the Lanín Volcano on the Argentine frontier. Each sector has its own entrance and ranger station.

Colour map 4, grid B2

The **Villarrica** volcano, 2,840 metres high and still active, lies eight kilometres south of Pucón. At the summit you can look down into the crater at the molten lava below: beware of the sulphur fumes – take a cloth mask moistened with lemon juice. On exceptionally clear days you can see six other volcanoes along the frontier between Chile and Argentina.

Entry US$8. Due to accidents, access to the Villarrica volcano sector is restricted only to groups with a guide and to individuals who can show proof of membership of a mountaineering club in their own country. Several agencies offer excursions, US$55-60 (plus park entry) including guide, transport to park entrance and hire of equipment (no reduction for those with their own equipment), good boots, crampons and ice picks essential. Also take sunglasses, sun block and plenty of water. At the park entrance equipment is checked. Entry is refused if the weather is poor. Travel agencies will not start out if the weather is bad and some travellers have experienced difficulties in obtaining a refund: establish in advance what terms apply in the event of cancellation and be prepared to wait a few days. Bargain for group rates. Conditions permitting, groups may carry ski and snowboard equipment for the descent. For information on guides, see above under **Tour companies & travel agents**. Also Alvaro Martínez, Cristóbal Colón 430; Juan Carlos, at Oliva's *pensión*, or his pool room on main street. Recommended. Many others, all with equipment; beware charlatans, ask at the tourist office. Crampons, ice axe, sunglasses can be rented for US$4 per day from the *Taller El Pollo* bicycle shop (address above) and from tour agencies.

Park essentials

There is a refuge without beds 4 kilometres inside the park, insecure and in desperate need of renovation. pampsite with drinking water, toilets, below refuge.

Sleeping

The Pucón resort, owned by the *Gran Hotel Pucón*, is situated on the eastern slopes of the volcano and reached by a badly maintained track, 35 minutes. A large modern base lodge offers equipment rental (US$15 per day, US$82 per week), ski instruction, first aid, restaurant and bar as well as wonderful views from the terrace. There are eight lifts, though rarely do more than two or three work. Lift tickets cost US$17-30 for a full day, depending on the season. The season is from July to November. Piste preparation is at best mediocre. Information on snow and ski lifts (and, perhaps, transport) from *Gran Hotel Pucón*. The snow is generally soft and good for beginners, though more advanced skiers can try the steeper areas.

Skiing

The Lake District

Lago Colico

One of the less accessible lakes, Lago Colico lies north of Lago Villarrica in a wild, remote setting. A road from Cunco runs east along the lake's northern shore leading to the northern tip of Lago Caburga, see below.

Sleeping **A2** *Trailanqui*, on riverbank 20 kilometres west of Lago Colico. Luxury, also suites, *cabañas* with kitchens, campsite (expensive), horseriding. Booking: Trailanqui, Portales 812A, Temuco, T/F045-214915. **Camping** 2 sites about half way along north shore: *Quichelmalleu*, Km 22 from Cunco, T573187. *Ensenada*, Km 26, T221441.

Lago Caburga

A very pretty lake in a wild setting 25 kilometres northeast of Pucón at an altitude of 700 metres, Lago Caburga (spelt locally Caburgua) is unusual for its beautiful white sand beach. Other beaches in the area are of black volcanic sand. The east and west shores of the lake are inaccessible to vehicles. The north shore can be reached by a road from Cunco via the north shore of Lago Colico. The village of Caburga, at the southern end is reached by a turning off the main road from Pucón to Argentina eight kilometres east of Pucón. Rowing boats may be hired US$2 per hour. Just off the road from Pucón, Km 15, are the **Ojos de Caburga**, beautiful pools fed from underground, which are particularly attractive after rainfall (entry US$0.50).

Lagos Villarrica, Caburga & Colico

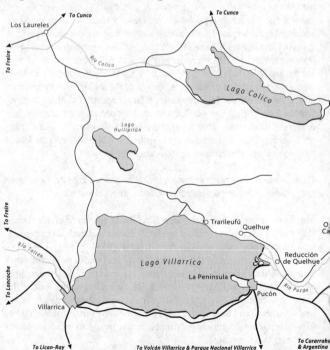

B *Hostería Los Robles*, 3 kilometres from Caburga village, T236989. Lovely views, good restaurant; campsite, expensive in season, but cheap out of season. The southern end of the lake is lined with campsites. No shops, so take own food. East of the lake is **D** pp *Landhaus San Sebastián*, F443057. With bath and breakfast, good meals, laundry facilities, good walking base.

Sleeping

JAC buses to Caburga, 4-6 daily; there are *colectivos* every 30 minutes from Brasil y Ansorena. Taxi day trips from Pucón, US$25 return. If walking or cycling, turn left 3 kilometres east of Pucón (sign to Puente Quelhue) and follow the track for 18 kilometres through beautiful scenery, recommended.

Transport

Parque Nacional Huerquehue

Located a short distance east of Lago Caburga, the park, covering 12,500 hectares at altitudes of 700-2,000 metres, includes steep hills, the highest of which is Cerro Araucano, and at least 20 lakes, some of them very small (the shapes of many of these are constantly changing). Tree species include araucaria and lenga. Entrance and administration are near **Lago Tinguilco**, the largest lake, on the western edge of the park. From the entrance there is a well signed track north up a steep hill to Lago Chico; there the track divides left to Lago Toro, right to Lago Verde. All three lakes are surrounded by trees and are very beautiful.

Colour map 4, grid B3

Park entrance is 7 kilometres (3 uphill, 3 down, 1 along Lago Tinguilco) from Paillaco, which is reached by a *ripio* road which turns off 3 kilometres before Caburga. Entry US$4. The park is open officially only January-March, but you can get in at other times. Adequate map available at entrance. Warden very helpful; people in the park rent horses and boats. Take your own food. Beware dogs along the paths to Lago Verde. There is a private car park, US$1, one and a half kilometres along the track.

Park essentials

Camping is not allowed in the park. At the park entrance there are 2 campsites, US$8. **D** pp *Refugio Tinquilco*, 3½ kilometres from park entrance, T7777673, F7351187, tinquilco@lake.mic.cl also **B** double with bath, meals served, cooking facilities, heating. At the southern end of Lago Tinquilco near the entrance, 2 German speaking families, the Braatz and Soldans, offer accommodation, **E** pp, no electricity, food and camping (US$6); they also rent rowing boats on the lake. Nidia Carrasco Godoy runs a *hospedaje* in the park, T09-4432725. **E** pp, with breakfast, hot water.

Sleeping

Playa Negra

Lago Caburga

Lago Toro

Lago Verde

Parque Nacional Huerquehue

Lago Tinguilco

Caburga

Termas de Quimey-Co

Termas de Huife

Termas Los Pozones

Río Liucura

N

Reserva Forestal Cañi

0 km 10
0 miles 6

To Termas de San Luis

The Lake District

Transport JAC bus from Pucón to Paillaco, 1½ hours, US$1, Monday-Friday 0700, 1230, 1700, Saturday/Sunday 1600, returns immediately. From Paillaco there is a connecting minibus service in summer to the park, US$1. Tour agencies arrange transport for groups, US$8 pp. Taxi US$34 return trip. Minibuses (no schedule) from Ansorena y Brasil.

Hot springs south of Huerquehue

South of the Huerquehue Park on a turning from the Pucón – Caburga road there are three sets of thermal baths.

Termas de Quimey-Co, about 29 kilometres from Pucón, are new, less ostentatious or expensive than Huife (see below), campsite, two cabins, hotel (*Termas de Quimey-Co*, T045-441903). **Termas de Huife** (*Hostería Termas de Huife*, T441222, PO Box 18, Pucón). Km 33, US$12 in season, US$9 off season, including use of one pool, modern, pleasant, picnicking not allowed (taxi from Pucón, US$23 return with taxi waiting, US$16 one way). **Termas los Pozones**, Km 35, are very popular with travellers, three large pools, little infrastructure, US$6 per day, US$8 at night.

Reserva Forestal Cañi

Situated south of Parque Nacional Huerquehue and covering 500 hectares, this is a private nature reserve owned by the Fundación Lahuén. It contains 17 small lakes and is covered by ancient native forests of coigue and lenga and includes some of the oldest araucaria trees in Chile. From its highest peak, *El Mirador*, (1,550 metres) there are panoramic views over neighbouring parts of Argentina and Chile, including four volcanoes: Lanín, Villarrica, Quetrupillán and Llaima.

Reserve essentials Tours with guide only, US$17 pp (take lunch), plus transport, also two-day tour with basic overnight accommodation, US$34 pp. Contact Fundación Lahuén, Urrutia 477, Pucón, T/F441660, lahuen@interaccess.cl or Hostería école (see Pucón page 299). As the reserve is above the snowline, tours are normally restricted to summer, though visits in winter are sometimes possible.

The route to Argentina

From Pucón a road runs southeast along the southern bank of the valley of the Río Tranquera to **Curarrehue** and the Argentine frontier. An unpaved road runs along the northern side of the valley to the **Termas de Menetue**, 21 kilometres east of Pucón, where there are two thermal pools, US$9 entry, and *cabañas*. At Km 18 on the Pucón-Curarrehue road there is a turning south 18 kilometres (*ripio*) to the **Termas de Palguín** (entry US$6). There are many hikeable waterfalls in the area; eg, six to seven kilometres from the turn-off for Termas de Palguín, Salto Palguín can be seen, but not reached; a further two kilometres Salto China (spectacular, entry US$1, restaurant, camping); one more kilometre to Salto del Puma (US$1) and Salto del León (US$2), both spectacular and 800 metres from the Termas. From Termas de Palguín a rough dirt road runs south to Coñaripe.

Sleeping The *Hotel Termas*, burnt down in 1988. Nearby is the **D** *Rancho de Caballos* (Casilla 142, Pucón), T441575. Restaurant with vegetarian dishes, laundry and kitchen facilities; also *cabañas* and camping, horse riding excursions US$50 per day, English, German spoken. **D** pp *Kila Leufu*, Km 20, full board, also offers tours, horse riding, mountain bike hire.

From Pucón take Bus Regional Villarrica from Palguín y O'Higgins at 1100 to the junction (10 kilometres from Termas); last bus from junction to the Termas at 1500, so you may have to hitch back. Taxi US$17. **Transport**

Near Palguín is the entrance to the **Quetrupillán** section of the Parque Nacional Villarrica. A high clearance vehicle is necessary; but horses are best. There is free camping and wonderful views over Villarrica Volcano and six other peaks. Palguin is also the starting point for a four to five day hike to Puesco, which offers great views over the Villarrica and Lanín volcanoes.

At Km 23 on the Curarrehue road a turning leads north to **Termas de San Luis**, from which it is 30 minutes' walk to Lago del León. For accommodation, there is the *Termas de San Luis,* T411388.

At Km 35 another turning leads north, 15 kilometres, to the **Termas de Pangui**, where there are three pools beautifully situated in the mountains, entry US$10; **C** *Hotel Termas*, T045-442039, F045-442040, good vegetarian meals, English spoken, tents that sleep three, and transport from Pucón. In Pucón Ansorena 547, Casilla 213, T442039, F442040.

From Curarrehue the road turns south to Puesco and deteriorates. It climbs via **Lago Quellelhue**, a tiny gem set between mountains at 1,196 metres to reach the frontier at the Mamuil Malal or Tromen Pass.

To the south of the pass rises the graceful cone of Lanín at 3,747 metres. Although extinct Lanín is geologically one of the youngest volcanoes in the Andes. It is climbed from the Argentine side. A four-hour hike from the Argentine customs leads to the *refugio* at 2,400 metres. The climb from here to the summit is not difficult but crampons and ice-axe are needed. **The Lanín volcano**
One of the world's most beautiful mountains

Paso Mamuil Malal or Tromen On the Argentine side the road runs south to Junín de los Andes, San Martín de los Andes and Bariloche. **Frontier with Argentina**

Chilean immigration & customs At Puesco, open December-March 0800-2100, April-November 0800-1900.

Sleeping Puesco A *Cabañas La Tranquera*, sleep 6, also dormitory **E** pp, restaurant, campsite. There is also a Conaf campsite at Puesco and another 5 kilometres from the frontier near Lago Tromen, free, no facilities.

Transport Daily bus from Pucón, 1800, 2 hours, US$2. To Pucón 0700.

The Lake District

The Seven Lakes

This group of lakes, situated south of Lago Villarrica, shares a common drainage system. Six of the lakes lie in Chile, with the seventh, Lago Lacár, in Argentina. Five of the lakes empty their waters into Lago Panguipulli from where in turn they flow into Lago Riñihue. The three western lakes, Calafquén, Panguipulli and Riñihue, were created by glacial morraine forming a barrier across steep river valleys. After the final peace settlement of 1882 the area around these lakes was reserved for Mapuche settlements. The southernmost lake, Lago Riñihue, is most easily reached from Valdivia and Los Lagos and is dealt with in a later section (see page 319).

Lago Calafquén

Colour map 4, grid B2   The most northerly of the seven lakes, Lago Calafquén, which covers 121 square kilometres, is a popular tourist destination, readily accessible by a paved road from Villarrica, along which there are fine views over Villarrica volcano. Wooded and dotted with small islands, the lake is reputedly one of the warmest and is good for swimming. Unpaved roads run round the lake.

Lican-Ray

Population: 1,700
Altitude: 207m
Phone code: 045
Colour map 4, grid B2
Situated 30 kilometres south of Villarrica on a peninsula on the north shore, Lican-Ray is the major resort on the lake. It is named after a legendary Mapuche woman, see box on page 308.

There are two fine beaches, one on each side of the rocky peninsula. Boats can be hired (US$2 an hour) and there are catamaran trips. Although very

The Seven Lakes

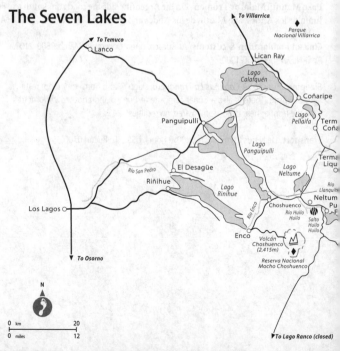

The Lake District

crowded in season, most facilities close by the end of March. Six kilometres to the east is the river of lava formed when the Villarrica volcano erupted in 1971.

On Playa Chica A3 *Becker*, Manquel 105, T431156. **C** *Hosp Los Nietos*, Manquel 125, T431078. Without breakfast. **On Playa Grande B** *Hostería Inaltulafquen*, Casilla 681, T431115, F410028. With breakfast and bath, English spoken, comfortable. **D** pp *Res Temuco*, G Mistral 515, T431130. Clean, without bath, with breakfast, good. **C** *Cabañas Cacique Vitacura*, Urrutia 825, sleep 2, also larger cabins, with kitchen (Santiago T2355302, F3639154, tradesic@intermedia.cl). **C** *Cabañas El Eden*, Huenuman 105. Sleep 6. *El Conquistador*, Cacique Millaqueo s/n. **Camping** Foresta, T211954, **B** for 6 persons, ½ kilometre east of town. *Prado Verde*, T431161, 1 kilometre east of town. 6 sites just west of town. Lots along north shore of Lago Calafquén towards Coñaripe. **Sleeping**

Café Ñaños, Urrutia 105. Very good, reasonable prices, helpful owner. *Restaurant-Bar Guido's*, Urrutia 405. Good value. **Eating**

Cycle hire US$3 per hour. **Horseriding** *Corral Club de Huasos*, US$6 per hour, summer only. **Boat** Boat trips US$3 voyages in catamaran; also voyages to islands US$11 per hour. **Sports**

Bus No central terminal; buses leave from offices around plaza. Buses from Villarrica (1 hour, US$1, JAC), frequent in summer; in January-February, there are direct buses from Santiago (Tur Bus, US$20, 10 hours) and Temuco (US$3, JAC). To Panguipulli, Monday-Saturday 0730. **Transport**

Tourist offices On plaza, open daily in summer, Monday-Friday off season. **Directory**

Coñaripe

ARGENTINA

Paso
irirriñe

ago
ueico

Parque
Nacional Lanín

Puerto
irehueico

Paso
Huahum

ago
scar

San Martín de
los Andes

To Junín de los Andes

To Junín de los Andes

Lying 21 kilometres southeast of Lican-Ray at the eastern end of Lago Calafquén, Coñaripe is another popular Chilean tourist spot. At first sight the village is dusty and nondescript, but its setting, with a black sand beach surrounded by mountains, is very beautiful. From here a road around the lake's southern shore leads to Lago Panguipulli (see below), 38 kilometres west, and offers superb views over Villarrica volcano.

Population: 1,253
Phone code: 045
Colour map 4, grid B2

The Lake District

D *Antulafquen*, homely. Entre Montañas, T317298. **E** pp *Hosp House*. With breakfast. Good meals. **Camping** Sites on both north and south sides of the lake, US$20 per site. Free camping on the beach. Also Isla Llanchahue, campsite on an island in Río Llanchahue, 5 kilometres east, T317360, F317200, **F** pp, also *cabañas*. **Sleeping**

The legend of Lican-Ray

At the height of the wars between the Spanish and the Mapuche a young Spanish soldier lost the rest of his unit and strayed into the forests near Lago Calafquén. Suddenly he saw a beautiful young Mapuche woman drying her hair in the sun and singing. As he did not want to frighten her he made himself visible at a distance and began to sing along. Singing, smiling and exchanging glances, they fell in love. She called him Allumanche, which means white man in Mapuche, and, pointing to herself, indicated that her name was Lican Rayan, meaning the flower of magic stone. They began to live together near the lake.

Her father, Curtilef, a powerful and fearsome chief, feared she might be dead. One day a boy came to him and said: "Lican Rayan is alive. I have seen her near the lake with a white man but she is not a prisoner: it is clear they are in love".

Lican Rayan saw the warriors coming to look for her. Knowing her father she feared what might happen, so she persuaded the soldier that they should

flee. They escaped by riding on logs to one of the islands. There they felt safe, but they could not light a fire against the cold because the smoke would give them away. The weather grew cooler, the north wind blew and it rained heavily. After several days, unable to bear the cold and thinking that the warriors would have given up the search, they lit a fire. The smoke was spotted by Curtilef's men, so they fled to another island further away but again they were discovered and had to escape. This happened so many times that, although they were never caught, they were never seen again.

In the town of Lican-Ray named after Curtilef's daughter, it is said that on spring afternoons it is sometimes possible to see a distant column of smoke from one of the islands, where Lican Rayan and the soldier are still enjoying their love of over 400 years.

Abridged and translated from Lengua Y Costumbres Mapuches by Orietta Appelt Martin, Imprenta Austral, Temuco, 1995.

Transport **Bus** To **Panguipulli**, several a day, US$1.50; to **Villarrica** US$1.50.

Southeast of Coñaripe From Coñaripe a road runs southeast over the steep Cuesta Los Añiques offering views of **Lago Pellaifa**, a tiny lake with rocky surroundings covered with vegetation and a small beach. The **Termas de Coñaripe** (Casilla 603, Lican-Ray, T411407), with four pools, accommodation, restaurant, cycles and horses for hire, are at Km 16, two kilometres from the lakeshore. Further south at Km 32 are the **Termas de Liquiñe** (hotel, Casilla 202, Villarrica, T/F063-317377, **A3** per person, full board, cabins, restaurant, hot pool, small native forest, tours offered; accommodation in private houses, **E** per person). Nearby there are several other thermal springs, though these have little infrastructure. There are tours to Liquiñe from Lican-Ray in summer, US$17, 0830-1830 with lunch. Eight kilometres north of Liquiñe is a road going southwest (20 kilometres) along the southeast shore of **Lago Neltume** to meet the Choshuenco-Puerto Fuy road (see below).

Frontier with Argentina: Paso Carirriñe Paso Carirriñe is reached by unpaved road from Termas de Liquiñe. It is open 15 October-31 August. On the Argentine side the road continues to San Martín de los Andes.

The Lake District

Lago Panguipulli and Panguipulli

Covering 116 square kilometres, Lago Panguipulli, the largest of the seven lakes, is reached by paved road from Lanco on the Pan-American Highway or *ripio* roads from Lago Calafquén. A road leads along the beautiful northern shore, which is wooded with sandy beaches and cliffs. Most of the south shore is inaccessible by road.

Situated on a hillside in the northwest corner of the lake in a beautiful setting, Panguipulli is the largest town in the area. The site of a Mapuche settlement, Panguipulli is Mapuche for 'hill of pumas'. The town grew as a railway terminal and a port for vessels carrying timber from the lakesides. The streets are planted with roses: it is claimed that there are over 14,000.

Population: 8,326
Altitude: 136m
Phone code: 063
Colour map 4, grid B2

On Plaza Prat is the **Iglesia San Sebastián**, built in Swiss-style with twin towers by the Swiss Padre Bernabé; its belltower contains three bells from Germany. From Plaza Prat the main commercial street, Martínez de Rozas, runs down to the lake. Catamaran trips are offered on the lake and excursions can be made to Lagos Calafquén, Neltume, Pirehueico and to the northern tip of **Lago Riñihue** at El Desagüe (see below, page 319). The road east to Coñaripe, on Lago Calafquén, offers superb views of the lake and of the Villarrica volcano.

B *Hostería Quetropillán*, Etchegaray 381, T311348. Comfortable. **B** *Cabañas El Mirador*, Carrera Pinto s/n, T311106. **B** *Hostal España*, O'Higgins 790, T311166, with breakfast. **C** *Cabañas Tío Carlos*, Etchegaray 377, T311215. **D** *Res Central*, J M Carrera y Valdivia. Clean, good breakfast. Recommended. **D** *Res La Bomba*, J M Carrera y R Freire. Quiet, friendly. **D** private house opposite *Quetropillán*. Clean, beautiful garden. **D** *Etchegaray 464*. For longer stays, clean, good breakfast. **D** *Sra Pozas*, Valdivia 251. Clean. **D** *Olga Berrocal*, JM Carrera 834. Small rooms. **D** *Hosp Familiar*, Los Ulmos 62, T311483. English, German spoken, kitchen facilities, helpful, good breakfast. **Youth**

Sleeping
■ *on map*
Price codes:
see inside front cover

Panguipulli

The Lake District

Hostel **E** *Albergue Juvenil*, Gabriela Mistral 1112, T311282, opposite bus terminal. **Camping** *El Bosque*, P Sigifredo 241, T311489. US$7.50 per site, clean, hot water. *Camping Lago Rinihue*, T461344, F461111, US$10/site. Also 3 sites at Chauquén, 6 kilometres southeast on the lakeside.

Eating *Didáctico El Gourmet*, restaurant of professional hotel school. Excellent food and wine, pricey but high quality, open in school terms only. *Café Central*, M de Rozas 750. Good cheap lunches, expensive evening meals. Cheap restaurants in O'Higgins 700 block.

Sports **Fishing** Excursions on Lago Panguipulli are recommended: good locations include Puntilla Los Cipreses, 30 minutes by boat; the mouth of the Río Huanehue, 11 kilometres east of Panguipulli; and the mouth of the Río Niltre, on the east side of the lake. Boat hire US$3. Fishing licences: from the Municipalidad (Monday-Friday), Librería Colón, O'Higgins 528 (daily) or from the *Club de Pesca*. **Watersports** Good rafting oportunities: on the Río Fuy, grade 4-5; Río San Pedro, varying grades, and on the Río Llanquihue near Choshuenco.

Festivals Last week of **January**, *Semana de Rosas*, with dancing and sports competitions.

Transport **Bus** Terminal at Gabriela Mistral y Portales. To **Santiago** daily, US$20. To **Valdivia**, frequent (Sunday only 4), several lines, 2 hours, US$3. To **Temuco** frequent, Power and Pangui Sur, US$2, 3 hours. To **Puerto Montt**, US$5. To **Calafquén**, 3 daily at 1200, 1545 and 1600. To **Choshuenco**, **Neltume** and **Puerto Fuy**, Buses La Fit 1000, 1500, 1630 (Monday-Saturday), 1800 (Sunday); Buses Huahum, Monday-Saturday 1130, 1530, also to Choshuenco and Neltume, Monday-Friday 1900. US$2, 2½ hours. To **Coñaripe** (with connections for Lican-Ray and Villarrica), 6 daily Monday-Friday, 1 Saturday, 1½ hours, US$2. No direct buse to Villarrica.

Directory **Banks** *Banco de Crédito e Inversiones*, Casa de Cambio, M de Rozas y Matta. Some shops accept US$ cash. Rates poor, TCs not accepted anywhere. **Tourist offices** In plaza, open December-February only.

Choshuenco

Population: 622
Colour map 4, grid B2

Forty five kilometres east of Panguipulli on the Río Llanquihue, Choshuenco lies at the eastern tip of the lake. To the south is the **Reserva Nacional Mocho Choshuenco** (7,536 hectares) which includes two volcanoes: Choshuenco (2,415 metres) and Mocha (2,422 metres). On the slopes of Choshuenco the Club Andino de Valdivia has ski slopes and three *refugios*. This can be reached by a turning from the road which goes south from Choshuenco to Enco at the east end of Lago Riñihue (see page 319). From Choshuenco a road leads east to Lago Pirehueico, via the impressive waterfalls of **Huilo Huilo**, where the river channels its way through volcanic rock before thundering down into a natural basin. The falls are three hours' walk from Choshuenco, or take the Puerto Fuy bus and get off at *Alojamiento Huilo Huilo*, Km 9 (one kilometre before Neltume) from where it is a five minute walk to the falls.

Sleeping **Choshuenco B** *Pulmahue*, T224402 ext 224, 3 star. **D** *Choshuenco*, T224402 ext 214, run down. Clean, good meals. Various *hosterías*, including **D** *Hostería Rayen Trai* (former yacht club), María Alvarado y O'Higgins. Good food, open all year. Recommended. *Rucu Pillán*, San Martín 85, T224402 ext 220. **Camping** On the beach. **Neltume D** *Restaurant Robles*, without bath, good beds. **E** *Pensión Neltume*, meals. **At Huilo Huilo E** pp *Alojamiento Huilo Huilo*. Basic but comfortable and well situated for walks, good food. Highly recommended.

Bus To Panguipulli 0645 and 0700.

Lago Pirehueico

Situated 21 kilometres southeast of Choshuenco at an altitude of 590 metres,   *Colour map 4, grid B2*
Lago Pirehueico is a 36 kilometre long, narrow and deep glacial lake, sur-
rounded by virgin *lingue* forest. It is totally unspoilt except for some logging
activity. There are, however, plans to build a huge tourist complex in Puerto
Pirehueico. There are no roads along the shores of the lake.

There are two ports on the lake: **Puerto Fuy** (*Population*: 300) at the northern end 21 kilometres southeast of Choshuenco, and **Puerto Pirehueico** at the
southern end; these are linked by a ferry service, see below. The two ports can
be reached by a road from Neltume which links Puerto Pirehueico and the
Argentine frontier crossing at Paso Huahum. The road south from Puerto Fuy
around the Choshuenco volcano and through rainforest to the Río Pillanleufú,
Puerto Llolles on Lago Maihue and Puerto Llifén on Lago Ranco, see below,
one of the most beautiful in Chile, is privately owned and closed to all traffic.

Puerto Pirehueico and Puerto Fuy **F** pp *Hosp Pirehueico*. **F** pp *Restaurant Puerto*   **Sleeping**
Fuy, cold water, good restaurant. Beds also available in private houses. **Camp-**
site Free camping on the beach in both Puerto Fuy and Puerto Pirehueico.

Bus Daily Puerto Fuy to Panguipulli, 3 daily, 3 hours, US$3. There is also a daily service   **Transport**
from Puerto Pirehueico via Paso Huahum to San Martín de los Andes in Argentina.
Ferry The *Mariela* sails from Puerto Fuy across the lake to Puerto Pirehueico, 2-3
hours, foot passengers US$1, cars US$21. This is a beautiful crossing (to take vehicles
reserve in advance at the *Hotel Quetropillán* in Panguipulli). **Schedule:** Novem-
ber/December and March/April from Pirehueico daily 1000, 1700, return 0700, 1400;
January/February from Pirehueico daily 1000, 1530, 2000, return 0700, 1300, 1800;
May-October from Pirehueico Monday-Saturday 1000, 1500, no Sunday service.

This pass of 659 metres is 11 kilometres southeast of Puerto Pirehueico. On the   **Frontier with**
Argentine side the road leads along the north side of Lago Lacar to San Martín   **Argentina: Paso**
de los Andes, 47 kilometres east, and Junín de los Andes. This crossing is usu-   **Huahum**
ally open all year.

Chilean Immigration Open summer 0800-2100, winter 0800-2000.

Valdivia

Surrounded by hills, Valdivia is one of the most attractive cities in Chile. It is set in   *Population: 110,000*
rich agricultural land receiving some 2,300 millimetres of rain a year and is the   *Phone code: 063*
capital of Valdivia province.   *839 km S of Santiago*
Colour map 4, grid B2

Situated about 15 kilometres inland, Valdivia lies at the confluence of two
rivers, the Calle Calle and Cruces which form the Río Valdivia. To the north of
the city is a large island, Isla Teja, where the Universidad Austral de Chile is
situated.

The German influence on Valdivia

From 1849 to 1875 Valdivia was a centre for German colonization of the Lake District and a comparatively small number of German and Swiss colonists settled in the city, exerting a strong influence on architecture and on the agricultural methods, education, social life and customs of the area. They established most of the industries which made Valdivia an important manufacturing centre until the 1950s. According to an 1884 survey all the breweries, leatherworks, brickworks, bakeries, machine shops and mills in Valdivia belonged to families with German surnames.

"By the end of World War I, Valdivia was one of the most flourishing centres of German colonization in the South of Chile. Oh these earthy German gentleman farmers who dream and sing of their new world utopia before crackling fires of hawthorn and cinnamon wood, and toast it with fiery shots of homemade booze!

Cowboys, loggers, contractors, shipbuilders, industrialists, merchants; in half a century they turned the unruly, inhospitable country to the south into an exclusive society, firm and resilient. A rough-hewn frontier world, yet one of poetic beauty where the winter rains blur the outlines of smoking pine cabins along the riverbanks, the lakeshores, and the tumbling sea." (Fernando Alegría, Allende: A Novel, Stanford University Press, 1993, page 9).

Little of the architectural heritage of this period survived the 1960 earthquake, but the city's German heritage can still be seen in some of its best cafés and restaurants and in the names of its streets.

History

Valdivia was one of the most important centres of Spanish colonial control over Chile. Founded in 1552 by Pedro de Valdivia, it was abandoned as a result of the Mapuche insurrection of 1599 and the area was briefly occupied by Dutch pirates. In 1645 it was refounded as a walled city, the only Spanish mainland settlement south of the Río Biobío. The coastal fortifications at the mouth of the river also date from the 17th century. From independence until the 1880s Valdivia was an outpost of Chilean rule, reached only by sea or by a coastal route through Mapuche territory.

Sights

The city is centred around the tree-lined **Plaza de la República**, three blocks east of which is the river and the **Muelle Fluvial**, the dock for boats down the river. A pleasant walk is along the **Costanera** (Avenida Prat) which runs from **Muelle Fluvial** north, under the bridge to Isla Teja and round the bend in the river as far as the bus terminal. On **Isla Teja**, on the western bank of the river, there is a **botanical garden** and **arboretum** with trees from all over the world. West of the botanical gardens is the **Parque Saval**, which has beautiful flowers in November. ■ *Entry US$0.50.*

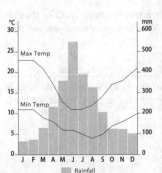

Climate: Valdivia

The Lake District

Museo Histórico y Antropológico is beautifully situated in the former man- **Museums**
sion of Carlos Andwandter, a leading German immigrant. Run by the University, it contains sections on archaeology and ethnography, German
colonization. Next door, in the former Andwandter brewery, is the **Museo de
Arte Moderno**. ■ *US$1.50. Tuesday-Sunday, 1000-1300, 1400-1800.*

Excursions

The district has lovely countryside of woods, beaches, lakes and rivers. The
various rivers are navigable and there are pleasant journeys by rented motor
boat on the Ríos Futa and Tornagaleanes around the Isla del Rey. Boat trips
can also be made around Isla Teja, offering views of birds and seals. For excursions to the coastal resorts of **Niebla** and **Corral** see below.

Santuario de la Naturaleza Río Cruces was flooded as result of the 1960
earthquake. There are lots of bird species are visible; tours by boat. *Isla del Río*,
daily 1415, six hours, US$15 each.

Valdivia

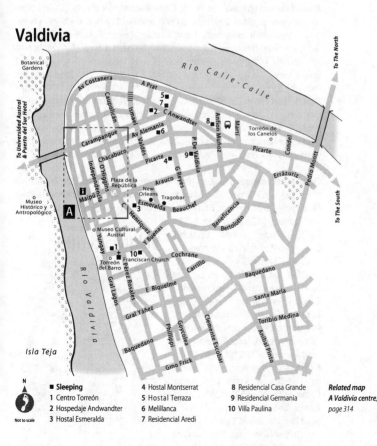

N
Not to scale

■ Sleeping	4 Hostal Montserrat	8 Residencial Casa Grande	*Related map*
1 Centro Torreón	5 Hostal Terraza	9 Residencial Germania	*A Valdivia centre,*
2 Hospedaje Andwandter	6 Melillanca	10 Villa Paulina	*page 314*
3 Hostal Esmeralda	7 Residencial Aredi		

The Lake District

Essentials

Sleeping
■ *on maps, pages 313 and 314*
Price codes: see inside front cover

L3 *Puerto del Sur*, Los Lingues 950, Isla Teja, T224500, F211046, 5 star, very good.

A2 *Pedro de Valdivia*, Carampangue 190, T/F212931. With breakfast, good. **A2** *Melillanca*, Alemania 675, T212509, F222740, with breakfast, modern. Recommended. **A2** *Naguilán*, Gen Lagos 1927, T212851/52/53, F219130. Clean, quiet, pool, good restaurant. **A2** *Villa del Río*, España 1025, T216292, F217851, restaurant expensive (try salmon in almond sauce), rents apartments with kitchen. **A3** *Palace*, Chacabuco y Henríquez, T213319, F219133. With breakfast, good, comfortable. **A3** *Villa Paulina*, Yerbas Buenas 389, T/F216372. Clean, pool. **A3** *Jardín del Rey*, Gen Lagos 1190, T218562, with breakfast.

B *Prat*, Prat 595, T222020. With good breakfast and bath, cable TV. **B** *Raitúe*, Gen Lagos 1382, T212503. **B** *Hostal Centro Torreón*, P Rosales 783, T212622. With breakfast, old German villa, nice atmosphere, cable TV, parking. **B** *Hostal Esmeralda*, Esmeralda 651, T215659, with bath, **C** without bath, also *cabañas*, parking.

Around the bus terminal On Picarte, **C** *Hostal Montserrat*, No 849, T215410. Without bath, with breakfast, poor beds. **D** *Res Germanía*, No 873, T212405. With breakfast, without bath, poor beds, clean, German spoken, Hostelling International reductions. **E** pp *Hostal del 900*, No 953. With breakfast. **E** *Hosp Elsa Martínez*, No 737, T212587. With breakfast, kitchen facilities, clean, friendly. Highly recommended. Several others. On A Muñoz, outside terminal: **E** pp No 345. With breakfast, clean, friendly. **E** pp No 353. Breakfast, hot water. Recommended. On Calle Anwandter **C** *Hostal Casa Grande*, No 880, T202035. With bath and breakfast, no singles, cable TV. Attractive old house, laundry facilities. Recommended. **E** pp *Hosp Aredi*, No 624, Casa 2, T290450. With breakfast, friendly, good value, *comedor*. **B** *Hostal La Terraza* No 624, Casa 4, T212664. With breakfast, very comfortable, lovely views, parking. **C** *Hosp Andwandter*, No 482, T218587, with bath and breakfast.

Cheaper accommodation **E** pp *Hosp Turístico*, Henríquez 745, T250086. Without bath, lovely villa in large gardens, friendly, large rooms, kitchen and laundry facilities, clean. Highly recommended. **E** pp *Hostal Arauco*, Arauco 869, with breakfast, kitchen and laundry facilities. **D** Arauco 935. Clean, friendly. **D** *Villa Beauchef*, Beauchef 844, with bath and breakfast. **E** pp, Gen Lagos 874, T215946. With breakfast, old German house, pleasant family atmosphere. Recommended. **C** *Hosp Universitaria*, Serrano 985, T218775. Breakfast, kitchen facilities, family atmosphere, clean, cheap meals. Recommended. **B** *Hosp Pérez Rosales*, Pérez Rosales 1037, T215607. With bath, **E** pp without, modern, small rooms, good beds, overpriced. **E** pp *Hostal Cochrane*, Cochrane 595. With breakfast. **E** pp Baquedano 664, with breakfast (but avoid laundry service). **E** pp Aníbal Pinto 1335, friendly and cheap. **E** pp Riquelme 15, T218909. With breakfast, friendly, clean, good value. **E** pp *Ana María Vera*, Beauchef 669, T218542. Clean, friendly,

Valdivia centre

hot water, good breakfast. **E** Picarte 2625, T216750, clean, German spoken, recommended. **D** *Hosp Internacional*, García Reyes 658, T212015. With breakfast, clean, helpful, English and German spoken, use of kitchen. Recommended. *Sra Paredes*, García Reyes 244. **D** with breakfast, hot water. Recommended. **G** pp *Albergue Juvenil*, García Reyes s/n, off Picarte. January/February only.

Campsite *Camping Centenario*, in Rowing Club on España, **E** per tent, overlooking river. *Isla Teja*, T213584, lovely views over river. White gas impossible to find, other than in pharmacies/chemists.

Cats Club, Esmerelda 657, good food, salad bar, pleasant ambience, not cheap. **Eating** *Delicias*, Henríquez 372. Recommended for meals and cakes, real coffee (open Sunday morning). *Derby*, Henríquez 314, large portions, good value. *Cervecería Kunstmann*, T292969, Camino Niebla s/n, German food, good beer. *New Orleans*, Esmerelda 652, large portions. *Selecta*, Picarte 1093. Pleasant, excellent fish and meat, not cheap. *Shanghai*, Andwandter y Muñoz. Pleasant Chinese, reasonably priced. For real coffee and sandwiches: *Dino*, Maipú y Rosales. *Palace*, Arauco y P Rosales. *Café Express*, Picarte 764. Real coffee. *Café Haussmann*, O'Higgins 394. Good tea and cakes. Several restaurants on the Costanera facing the boat dock have good food and good atmosphere: *La Ultíma Frontera*, Perez Rosales 787, (in Centro Cultural 787) real coffee, home made cakes etc. *Bar Olimpia*, Libertad 28. Always full, 24 hours, cheap, good meeting point. *Entrelagos*, Pérez Rosales 622. Ice cream and chocolates.

Bakery *La Baguette*, Libertad y Yungay. French-style cakes, brown bread. Repeatedly recommended.

Tragobar, Beauchef 620, great drinks, good music and ambience. *El Cantino*, **Bars** Andandter 385, Brazilian bar/restaurant. *La Bomba*, Caupolicán 337, old Valdivian bar, pleasant, empanadas. *Fuerte de Pedro*, Caupolicán 337, new restaurant/bar. *Bataclan*, Henriquez 326, live music.

Cinema In Chacabuco 300 block. Cine Club UACH, University campus, weekend **Entertainment** shows (not in summer).

Clubs Santa Elvira Golf Club (9 holes). Tennis, sailing, motor, and rowing clubs like **Sports** Phoenix on Teja Island. **Swimming** Indoor pool, Holzapfel y Las Tarrias, T220310, US$4, closed Monday.

Semana Valdiviana, in mid-February, culminates in Noche Valdiviana on the Satur- **Festivals** day with a procession of elaboratedly decorated boats which sail past the Muelle Fluvial. Accommodation is scarce at this time.

Film *Fotoquideon*, Picarte 417. For developing. *Fotoquick Agfa*, Picarte 430. *Kodak*, **Shopping** Picarte 382.

Supermarkets *Hiper-Unico*, Arauco 697. *Las Brisas*, Henriquez 522 (on plaza).

Bookshops *Librería/Centro Cultural 787*, Pérez Rosales 787, old mansion, hip bookstore, café, art exhibitions. *Librería Chiloé*, Caupolicán 410. *Librería Andrés Bello*, Independencia 635.

Car hire *Hertz*, Picarte 640, airport, T272273, T218316. *Turismo Méndez*, Gen Lagos **Transport** 1335, T213205. *Autovald*, Henríquez 610, T212786.

The Lake District

Spanish forts in the Río Valdivia

The Spanish fortifications at the mouth of the Río Valdivia were among the strongest in the empire. Although dating from just after the reoccupation of the city in 1645, they were greatly strengthened after 1760 owing to fears that Valdivia might be seized by the British. The main forts were rebuilt in brick and stone using the latest techniques of European military engineering. Large numbers of cannon were used to control access to the estuary. In all there were 17 forts: the main ones to see are at Niebla, Corral, Isla Mancera, Amargos and San Carlos. One other, San Luis de Alba de las Cruces, up the Río Cruces, can be visited by boat from Valdivia or by unpaved road from San José de la Mariquina.

These great fortifications were of little avail during the Wars of Independence: overnight on 2 February 1820 the Chilean naval squadron under Lord Cochrane seized San Carlos, Amargos and Corral and turned their guns on Niebla and Mancera which surrendered the following morning.

Air LanChile, Ladeco and Avant to/from Santiago every day via Temuco.

Bus Terminal at Muñoz y Prat, by the river. To **Santiago**: several companies, 13 hours, most services overnight, US$12-17 (Tur Bus good) *salón cama* US$45. Half-hourly to **Osorno**, 2 hours, several companies, US$5. To **Llifén**, 4 a day, US$2.50. To **Panguipulli**, US$3, Empresa Pirehueico, about every 30 minutes, US$3. Many daily to **Puerto Montt**, US$7, 3 hours. To **Castro**, US$10, 7 hours. To **Temuco**, US$3. To **Puerto Varas**, 2 hours, US$6. To **Frutillar**, US$4, 3 hours. To **Villarrica**, by JAC, 6 a day direct, 2½ hours, US$3.50, continuing to Pucón, US$4.50, 3 hours or take any bus to Loncoche and change. Frequent daily service to Riñihue via Paillaco and Los Lagos.

To Argentina: to **Bariloche** via Osorno, 10 hours, Bus Norte, US$20, and Tramaca. To **Zapala**, Igi-Llaima, Monday, Thursday, Saturday, 2300, change in Temuco at 0200, arrive Zapala 1200-1500, depending on border, US$34. To **Mendoza**, Fénix and Andesmar.

Directory **Airline offices** *Avant*, Chacabuco 408, T251431, F253467. *LanChile*, O'Higgins 386, T213042. *Ladeco*, Caupolicán 364, T213392. **Banks** *Banco del Estado*, Camilo Henríquez 562 (huge commission on TCs). Good rates for cash at *Banco Santander*, P Rosales 585, *Corp Banca*, Picarte 370, Visa. Will change cash and TCs. *Banco Santiago*, Arauco 149. Mastercard. *Turismo Cochrane*, Arauco 435. *Casa de Cambio* at Carampangue 325, T213305. *Turismo Austral*, Arauco y Henríquez, Galería Arauco. Accepts TCs. **Communications** Telephone Centres: *CTC*, Independencia 628, T252700. *Entel*, Pérez Rosales 601, T225334. Internet access: *Centro Internet Libertad*, Libertad 7, US$6/hour. **Laundry** *Au Chic*, Arauco 436. *Lavazul*, Chacabuco 300. Slow. Coin laundry: *Lavamatic*, Schmidt y Picarte (Mon-Sat 0930-2030). *Manantial*, Henríquez 809, T217609. **Tour companies & travel agencies** *Paraty Club*, Independencia 640, T215585. *Turismo Los Notros*, O'Higgins 189, T210533. *Turismo Conosur*, Maipu 129, T212757. **Tourist offices** Prat 555, by dock, T213596. Good map of region and local rivers, list of hotel prices and examples of local crafts with artisans' addresses. Helpful kiosk in bus terminal, mainly bus information. *Conaf*: Ismael Váldez 431, T218822. *Automóvil Club de Chile*: García Reyes 490, T250376. Also for car hire.

The Lake District

West of Valdivia

At the mouth of the Río Valdivia there are attractive villages which can be visited by road or by river boat. The two main centres are Niebla on the north bank and Corral opposite on the south bank. There is a frequent boat service between the two towns.

Niebla

Eighteen kilometres west of Valdivia, Niebla is a resort with seafood restaurants and accommodation. In mid-February there is a *Feria Costumbrista*, with lots of good food including *pullmay asado* and *paila marina*. To the west is the Fuerte de la Pura y Limpia Concepción de Monfort de Lemus, on a promontory. Built in 1671 and partially restored in 1992, it has an interesting museum on Chilean naval history. ■ *US$0.75. Sunday free, daily in summer 1000-1900, closed Monday in winter.* Tourist information and telephone office nearby. Six kilometres further round the coast is **Los Molinos**, a seaside resort set among steep wooded hills (campsite, lots of seaside restaurants including La Bahía which has good food, not cheap).

Colour map 4, grid B1

D *Hostería Riechers*, T/F282043. *Cabañas Fischer*, T282007, **C** per *cabaña*, camping. Worth bargaining out of season. **D** *Villa Santa Clara*, T282018 (Casilla 52, Valdivia), with breakfast, also *cabañas* **D** pp, cooking and laundry facilities. *Las Delicias*, T213566. With restaurant with 'a view that would be worth the money even if the food weren't good'. Also *cabañas* and camping. *Camping Rayen Quitral*.

Sleeping

Río Valdivia

The Lake District

Corral

Population 3,600
Colour map 4, grid B1

Situated 62 kilometres west of Valdivia by road, Corral is the main port serving the city and was, until the devastation of 1960, the site of the first steelworks in Chile. Visits can be made to the Castillo de San Sebastian, built in 1645; its three metre wide walls were defended by a battery of 21 guns. Inside is a museum. In summer re-enactments of eighteenth century battles in period costume are held, daily 1530 and 1730. Entry January-February US$4, March-December US$1. Further north along the coast are the remains of two other Spanish colonial forts: the Castillo San Luis de Alba, Km 3, and the Castillo de San Carlos, Km 4. The coastal walks west and south of Corral are splendid.

In midstream, between Niebla and Corral is **Isla Mancera** a small island, fortified by the Castillo de San Pedro de Alcántara, which has the most standing buildings. The island is a pleasant place to stopover on the boat trips, but it can get crowded when an excursion boat arrives.

Sleeping **E** *Res Mariel*, Tarapacá 36, T471290. Modern, clean, friendly, good value. *Hostería La Nave*. **E** *Hostería Los Alamos*, a delightful hideout for those seeking a quiet life. On Isla Moncera: **C** *Hostería Mancera*, T/F216296, open December-March, depending on weather, no singles, phone first: water not drinkable.

Transport **Boat** The tourist boats to Isla Mancera and Corral, offer a guided half-day tour (US$20 with meals – cheaper without) from the Muelle Fluvial, Valdivia (behind the tourist office on Av Prat 555), 1330 daily. **Bus** Buses to Niebla from Chacabuco y Yungay, Valdivia, roughly every 20 minutes between 0730 and 2100, 30 minutes, US$0.75 (continues to Los Molinos). There are occasional buses from Valdivia to Corral.

Resorts further north

San José de la
Mariquina
Population: 6,000

This small town, 42 kilometres north of Valdivia, lies on the Río Cruces. From here an unpaved road leads south along the river to the Castillo de San Luis de Alba (22 kilometres), a colonial fortification built in 1647 and largely rebuilt according to the original plans.

Mehuin

Twenty seven kilometres northwest of San José, Mehuin is a popular resort and fishing port with a long beach. Six kilometres further north is **Quele**, which has a good beach, but which is dangerous for bathing at high tide because of undercurrents (bathing is safer in the river near the ferry).

Sleeping **C** *El Nogal*, T/F451352, with bath and breakfast, good. **D** *Mehuin*, T219235, not very inviting. **D** *Playa*, T451376 **E** *Hosp Marbella*, clean, cheapest. **Quele**: there are two simple *residenciales*.

Transport **Bus**: from Valdivia, 2 hours, US$2.

Monumento Natural Alerce Costero

Covering 2,307 hectares, this newly designated park in the coastal mountain range, protects an area of alerce forest, though extensive of forest burnt down in 1975 can be seen in the distance. There is a Conaf *guardería* and *refugio*, from which a three kilometre trail leads to a 3,500 year-old alerce. Entry is free. Access is by a very poor road, 32 kilometres *ripio*, 20 kilometres unpaved, which runs northwest from La Unión, (see page 320).

Inland from Valdivia

A beautiful, unpaved road runs 61 kilometres east from Valdivia along the Río Calle Calle to Los Lagos, at the junction with the Pan-American Highway.

D *Roger*, Lynch 42, T261, disco on Saturday, recommended. *Turismo Tell*, 10 kilometres east. *Cabañas* and campsite, T09-653-2440, English, French and German spoken; two buses a day in summer.

Lago Riñihue

Thirty nine kilometres further east, Lago Riñihue is the southernmost of the   *Colour map 4, grid B2*
Seven Lakes. There is no road around the northern edge of the lake and the
road around the southern edge of the lake from Riñihue to Enco is closed
(except to jeeps in summer only), so Choshuenco at the southeast end of Lago
Panguipulli can only be reached by road from Panguipulli or Puerto Fuy.
Riñihue, a beautiful but very small and isolated village at the western end of
the lake, is worth a visit.

B *Hostería Huinca Quinay*, 3 kilometres east of Riñihue, T461347, F461406, *cabañas*,   **Sleeping**
restaurant. **E** *Restaurant del Lago* (no meals). Campsite by the lake. *El Desagüe*, 20
kilometres south of Panguipulli. **B** *Riñimapu*, T311388, comfortable, good value,
excellent food. *Vista Hermosa*, T/F311537.

Lago Ranco

One of the largest lakes, covering 41,000 hectares, and starred with islands, this   *Colour map 4, grid B2*
is also one of the most accessible as there is a road round its edge. This road is
terrible, with lots of mud and animals, including oxcarts, but it is worth taking
to see an older lifestyle, the beautiful lake, waterfalls and sunsets on the distant
volcanoes. It is better to travel anti-clockwise for the best views. To descend

Lagos Ranco & Maihue

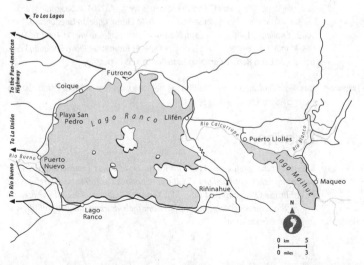

The Lake District

the worst hills; if you are walking, beware of the numerous guard dogs in the area. There is excellent fishing on the southern shore and several hotels organize fishing expeditions.

From the north the lake can be reached from the Pan-American Highway from Los Lagos or from a point 18 kilometres south of Los Lagos, 11 kilometres north of Paillaco. These two roads join and meet the road around the lake some five kilometres west of Futrono. From the south access is from **La Unión** (*Hotel Club Alemán*, Letelier 497, T322695) and **Río Bueno**, which are bypassed by the Pan-American Highway.

The main town on the northern shore is **Futrono** from where the road curves round the north of the lake to **Llifén**, Km 22, a picturesque place on the eastern shore. From Llifén, a visit can be paid to **Lago Maihue**, 33 kilometres further east, the south shore of which is covered by native forests. From Llifén the road continues via the Salto de Nilahue (Km 14) to **Riñinahue**, Km 23, at the southeast corner of the lake and **Lago Ranco**, Km 47, an ugly little town on the south shore, which has a museum with exhibits on Mapuche culture. On the western shore is **Puerto Nuevo**, where there are watersports and fishing on the Río Bueno. Further north, 10 kilometres west of Futrono is **Coique** with the best beach on the lake.

Sleeping **Futrono** B *Hostería Rincón Arabe*, T481262, F481330. *Puerto Futrono*, T481281. **E** *Hosp Futronhue*, Balmaceda 90, T481265, good breakfast. **F** pp in the Casa Parroquial. Note there is only one (dismal) pace in Futrono to eat in the evening. **Llifén** **A1** *Huequecura*, Casilla 4, T09-6535450. Includes meals and fishing services, good restaurant. **B** *Hostería Chollinco*, 3 kilometres out of town on the road towards Lago Maihue, T0638-202. Limited electricity, swimming pool. **C** *Hostería Lican*, T09-6535315, F Valdivia 218921. **Riñinahue** **A3** *Hostería Riñinahue*, Casilla 126, T491379, organizes fishing expeditions. *Hostería El Arenal del Nilahue*. **Lago Ranco** *Parque Thule*, T491293. **B** *Hostería Casona Italia*, T491225. **B** *Hostería Phoenix*, T491226. *Residenciales*, houses to let in summer. **Puerto Nuevo** **A1** *Hotel Puerto Nuevo*, very good.

Camping There are campsites all around Lago Ranco as well as several on Lago Maihue, though many open in summer only and prices are high. At **Futrono**: *Nalcahue*, 1 kilometre west, T481663, US$18 per site. *Bahía Las Rosas*, 1 kilometre east, US$18 per site, *Bahía Coique*, 9 kilometres west, T481264, autocamping, US$50 per site in summer, US$35 per site off season. At **Llifén**: *Callejón Huequecura*, 1 km south. *Chollinco*, 3 km east. At **Lago Maihue**: Puerto Llolles, at western end, no facilities. *Maqueo*, on eastern shore, US$18 per site. At **Riñinahue** *Playa Ranquil* US$10 per site. At **Lago Ranco**: *Camping Lago Ranco*, US$15 per site,

Transport **Bus** Cordillera Sur bus from Valdivia to Llifén, twice daily, once Sunday; from Osorno to Lago Ranco, Empresa Ruta 5, six daily.

Osorno

Population: 114,000
Phone code: 064
921 km S of Santiago
105 km N of Puerto Montt
Colour map 4, grid B2

Situated at the confluence of the Ríos Rahue and Damas, Osorno is a centre for visiting the lakes. Founded in 1553, it was abandoned in 1604 and was refounded by Ambrosio O'Higgins and Juan MacKenna O'Reilly in 1796. It later became one of the centres of German immigration; their descendants are still of great importance in the area.

The Lake District

Sights

On the large **Plaza de Armas** stands the modern, concrete and glass cathedral, with many arches, repeated in the tower, itself an open, latticed arch with a cross superimposed. West of the centre on a bend overlooking the river is the **Fuerte María Luisa**, named after the Spanish queen much painted by Goya, built in 1793, restored 1977, with only the river front walls and end turrets standing. East of the main plaza along Calle MacKenna are a number of late 19th century wooden mansions built by German immigrants, now preserved as national monuments. ■ *There are free tours of the city, Monday-Friday 1500 and 1700, January-February only. Book at municipal tourist office.*

Museums

Museo Histórico Municipal, Matta 809. Includes displays on natural history, Mapuche culture, refounding of the city and German colonization. ■ *Entrance in Casa de Cultura, US$1; Monday-Friday 1000-1230, 1430-1800, also Saturday 1000-1300, 1500-1800 and Sunday 1500-1800 in summer.* **Auto Museo Moncopulli**, 25 kilometres east of Osorno on Route 215, T204200; is the best motor museum in Chile. Exhibits include a Studebaker collection from 1852 to 1966. There is also a 1950s style cafeteria. ■ *Daily 1000-1900. Transport: Bus to Entre Lagos from the Mercado Municipal terminal.*

Excursions

Río Bueno (*population* 13,000), 30 kilometres north, is celebrated for its scenery and for fishing. There is a Spanish colonial fort dating from 1777, situated high above the river and offering fine views. Frequent buses from the Mercado Municipal terminal. At **Trumao**, a river port on the Río Bueno, 22 kilometres further west via La Unión, a launch may be taken to La Barra on the coast;

The Lake District

Osorno

■ Sleeping		● Eating
1 Colón 844	6 Hostal Rucaitué	12 Residencial Bilbao	1 Dino's
2 Del Prado	7 Interlagos	13 Residencial Bilbao II	2 La Paisana
3 Eduviges	8 Mendoza	14 Residencial Riga	3 Peter's Kneipe
4 Gran	9 Millantué	15 Residencial Schulz	4 Waldis
5 Hein	10 Pumalal	16 Waeger	
	11 Rayantu		

0 metres 100
0 yards 109

leaves Wednesday/Saturday only at 0900, five hours, returns Thursday/Sunday at 0900, US$9 return, no service in winter.

To the sea beaches at **Maicolpue**, 60 kilometres west (**D** *Hostería Müller*, on the beach, clean, good service, recommended campsite) and **Pucatrihue** (*Hostería Incalcar*, summer only) which are worth a visit in the summer (daily bus service) from the Mercado Municipal terminal.

Essentials

Sleeping
■ *on map, page 321*
Price codes:
see inside front cover

L3 *Rayantú*, Patricio Lynch 1462, T238114, F238116, 4-star. **L3** *Mendoza*, Mackenna 1040, T237111, F237113, 4-star. **L3** *Del Prado*, Cochrane 1162, T235020. Pool, garden, good meals, well-located, charming.

A1 *Waeger*, Cochrane 816, T233721, PO Box 802, F237080. 4-star, poor restaurant, comfortable. Recommended. **A2** *Gran*, O'Higgins 615, T233990, F239311. Cable TV, comfortable. **A3** *Eduviges*, Eduviges 856, T/F235023. Spacious, clean, quiet, attractive, gardens, also *cabañas*. Recommended. **A3** *Inter-Lagos*, Cochrane 515, T234695, F232581. With breakfast, garage, restaurant. **A3** *Pumalal*, Bulnes 630, T243520, F242477. With breakfast, modern, airy, clean. **A3** *Res Riga*, Amthauer 1058, T232945. Clean, pleasant. Highly recommended but heavily booked in season. **A3** *Res Schulz*, Freire 530, T237211. With bath, **B** without, overpriced, unwelcoming.

B *Hostal Rucaitué*, Freire 546, T239922, F310617. With breakfast, cable TV, comfortable. **B** *Millantué*, Errázuriz 1339, T242072, near bus terminal. With breakfast, parking. **B** *Res Hein*, Cochrane 843, T234116. With bath, **C** without, old-fashioned, spacious, family atmosphere. **B** *Res Bilbao*, Bilbao 1019, T236755, F321111. *Res Bilbao II*, MacKenna 1205, T242244. With breakfast, parking, restaurant.

Near terminal D Amunátegui 520. Good. **D** *Res Ortega*, Colón y Errázuriz. Parking, basic, clean, toilet facilities limited. **E** Anibal Pinto 1758, with breakfast, T238024. **D** *Germania*, Rodríguez 741. No hot water, cooking facilities. **E** pp *Res Sánchez*, Los Carrera 1595. Use of kitchen, noisy, basic, with breakfast. **E** pp *Hosp de la Fuente*, Los Carrera 1587. Basic, friendly. **E** pp Colón 844. With breakfast. **E** pp *Res San Diego*, Los Carrera 1551, with breakfast.

F pp *Res Carillo*, Angulo 454. Basic, clean. *La Paloma*, Errázuriz 1599, basic. *Richmond*, Lastarria 530, basic. *Silvane*, Errázuriz y Lastarria, T234429. Fairly basic. Private houses at Germán Hube, pasaje 1, casa 22, población Villa Dama, **E** pp, hot water, clean, use of kitchen. Recommended.

Camping Municipal site off Pan-American Highway near southern entrance to city, open January-February only, poor facilities, US$5 per site.

Eating
● *on map, page 321*

Peter's Kneipe, M Rodríguez 1039. Excellent German restaurant, not cheap. *Dino's*, Ramírez 898, on the plaza. Restaurant upstairs, bar/cafeteria downstairs, good. *Chung Hwa*, Matta 517, Chinese. *Shangri-La*, Ramon Freire 542, Local 16, Chilean and Nepalese cuisine, French, English spoken. Good food and service, pleasant atmosphere. Recommended. *La Paisana*, Freire 530. Arab specialities, not cheap. *Waldis*, on Plaza de Armas. Real coffee. *Travels* in bus terminal for cheap snacks. Bakery at Ramírez 977. Good wholemeal bread.

Sports

Skiing *Club Andino* O'Higgins 1073. For advice on possibilities.

Shopping

Ekono Supermarket, Colón y Errázuriz. For fishing tackle try *Climet*, Angulo 603 and *The Lodge*, Los Carrera 1291, local 5. *Alta Artesanía*, MacKenna 1069, excellent handicrafts, not cheap.

Car mechanic *Automotriz Salfa Sur SA*, Fco Bilbao 857; *Automotriz Amthauer*, **Transport**
Amthauer 1250.

Air LanChile/Ladeco daily flights to Santiago, via Temuco.

Bus Main terminal 4 blocks from Plaza de Armas at Errázuriz 1400. Left luggage open
0730-2030, bus from centre, US$0.30. To **Santiago**, frequent, US$16, *salón cama*
US$25, 16 hours. To **Valparaíso** and **Viña del Mar**, Tas Choapa, US$25. To **Arica**, Tas
Choapa, US$55. To **Concepción**, US$12. To **Temuco**, US$6. To **Panguipulli**, buses
Pirehueico, 4 a day. To **Pucón** and **Villarrica**, Tur Bus, frequent, US$6. To **Valdivia**, fre-
quent, 2 hours, several companies, US$5. To **Frutillar**, US$2.50, **Llanquihue**, **Puerto
Varas** and **Puerto Montt** (US$5) services by Varmontt every 30 minutes. To **Puerto
Octay**, US$1.50, Vía Octay company 6 daily between 0815-1930 (return 0800-1930)
Monday-Saturday, 5 on Sunday between 0800 and 2000 (4 return buses). To **Lago
Ranco**, (town) 6 a day, Empresa Ruta 5, 2 hours, US$2. To **Punta Arenas**, US$60-75,
Cruz del Sur, Turisbus, Eurobus and Bus Norte, all twice a week.

Local buses to **Entre Lagos**, **Puyehue** and **Aguas Calientes** leave from the
Mercado Municipal terminal, 1 block west of the main terminal. To Entre Lagos frequent services in summer, Expreso Lago Puyehue, T234919, and Buses Puyehue, 45
minutes, US$1, reduced service off-season; some buses by both companies also con-
tinue to Aguas Calientes (off-season according to demand) 2 hours, US$2; in summer
there are also services Maicolpué on the coast if demand is sufficient.

Airline offices *LanChile*, Matta 862, T236688, *Ladeco*, MacKenna 1098, T236102. **Banks** ATMs   **Directory**
at Banco BCI, MacKenna 801, Banco Santiago, MacKenna 787 (Visa). Casas de Cambio. *Cambio
Tur*, MacKenna 1010, T234846. *Turismo Frontera*, Ramírez 949, local 11 (Galería Catedral). If stuck
try *Travels* bar in bus terminal. **Communications Post Office:** O'Higgins 645. Also Telex.
Telephone: Ramírez at central plaza and Juan MacKenna y Cochrane. **Laundry** Prat 678 (allow at
least a day). **Tourist offices** *Sernatur*, provincial government office, on Plaza de Armas,
O'Higgins s/n, p 1, left, T234104. Municipal office in bus terminal and Kiosk on Plaza de Armas,
both open Dec-Feb. *Automóvil Club de Chile*: Bulnes 463, T232269. Information and car hire.

East of Osorno

From Osorno Route 215 runs east to the Argentine frontier at the Puyehue
Pass via the south shore of Lago Puyehue, Anticura and the Parque Nacional
Puyehue.

Lago Puyehue

Lying about 47 kilometres east of Osorno at an altitude of 207 metres and sur-   *Colour map 4, grid B2*
rounded by relatively flat countryside Lago Puyehue extends over 15,700 hect-
ares. The southern shore is much more developed than the northern shore
which is accessible only by unpaved road from the western end. At the western
end is **Entre Lagos** (*Population*: 3,358) and the **Termas de Puyehue** are at the
eastern end. ■ *Entry US$3.50 outdoor pools, US$15 indoor pools, 0900-2000.*

Entre Lagos **B** *Cabañas No Me Olvides*, with kitchen. **C** *Hosp Vista Hermosa*. With   **Sleeping &**
breakfast. **D** *Hostería Entre Lagos*, Ramírez 65, lake view, T371225. **D** *Villa Veneto*,   **eating**
Gral Lagos 602, T371203. **D** *Hosp Miraflores*, Ramírez 480, T371275, also *cabañas*.
D pp *Hosp Millarey*, Ramirez 333, T371251. With breakfast, excellent, clean, friendly.
Jardín del Turista, F371214. Very good restaurant, *cabañas*. *Pub del Campo*, F371220.
Highly recommended restaurant.

The Lake District

On the southern lakeshore *Chalet Suisse*, Km 55 (Casilla 910, Osorno, T Puyehue 647208, Osorno 234073). Restaurant with excellent food. *La Valenciana*, Km 53, T09-6433133. **B** *Posada Puntillo*, at Shell station, Km 62. **A1** *Motel Ñilque*, Santiago T2313417, or 09-647218, cabins, half-price May-October, fishing trips, watersports, car hire. **B** *Hostería Isla Fresia*, located on own island, T236951, Casilla 49, Entre Lagos. Transport provided.

At the Termas L2-A1 pp *Gran Hotel Termas de Puyehue*, T232157, F371272 (cheaper May to mid-December). 2 thermal swimming pools (one indoors, very clean), theatre, conference centre, well maintained, meals expensive, in beautiful scenery, heavily booked January-February (postal address Casilla 27-0, Puyehue, or T Santiago 2313417). Accommodation also in private house nearby, **E** pp full board.

Camping *Camping No Me Olvides*, Km 56. US$10. Also *cabañas*. *Playa Los Copihues*, Km 56.5 (hot showers, good), both on southern shore of Lake Puyehue. *Camping Playa Puyehue*, Km 75.

Transport **Bus** 2½ hours, schedule under Osorno; buses do not stop at the lakeside (unless you want to get off at *Gran Hotel Termas de Puyehue* and clamber down), but continues to Aguas Calientes.

Parque Nacional Puyehue

Colour map 4, grid B2 Located east of Lago Puyehue and stretching to the Argentine frontier, this park covers 107,000 hectares, much of it in the valley of the Río Golgol. On the eastern side are several lakes, including Lago Constancia and Lago Gris. There are two volcanic peaks: **Volcán Puyehue** (2,240 metres) in the north (access via a private road US$2.50) and **Volcán Casablanca**, (also called Antillanca, 1,900 metres).

At **Aguas Calientes**, four kilometres south of the Termas de Puyehue in a thickly forested valley, there is an open-air pool (dirty) with very hot thermal water beside the Río Chanleufú. ■ *0830-1900, US$1.50, children US$1, and a*

Lagos Puyehue & Rupanco

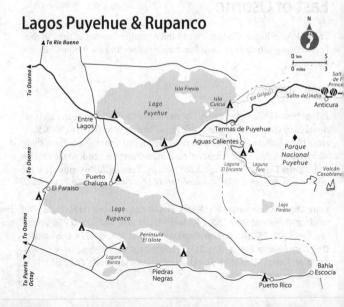

very hot indoor pool, open Monday-Friday (in season only) 0830-1230, 1400-1800, Saturday, Sunday and holidays (all year) 0830-2030, US$5, children US$3.

From Aguas Calientes the road continues 18 kilometres southeast past three small lakes and through forests to **Antillanca** on the slopes of Volcán Casablanca. In winter a one-way traffic system operates on the last eight kilometres: up 0800-1200 and 1400-1730, down 1200-1400 and after 1730. This is a particularly beautiful section, especially at sunrise, with views over Lago Puyehue to the north and Lagos Rupanco and Llanguihue to the south, as well as the snow-clad peaks of Calbuco, Osorno, Puntiagudo, Puyehue and Tronador forming a semi-circle. The tree-line on Casablanca is one of the few in the world made up of deciduous trees (*nothofagus* or southern beech). From Antillanca it is possible to climb Casablanca for even better views of the surrounding volcanoes and lakes, no path, seven hours return journey, information from Club Andino in Osorno. On the south side of the volcano there are caves (accessible by road, allow five hours from *Hotel Antillanca*). There are few mammals but waterfowl are common on the lake and condors can be seen near the volcanoes.

Skiing Attached to the *Hotel Antillanca* is one of the smallest ski resorts in Chile; there are three lifts, ski instruction and first aid available. Piste preparation is unreliable. Skiing is not difficult but quality depends on the weather: though rain is common it often does not turn to snow.

In the Anticura section of the park, northeast of Aguas Calientes, are three waterfalls, including spectacular 40 metres wide **Salto del Indio**. Legend has it that an Indian, enslaved by the Spanish, was able to escape by hiding behind the falls. Situated just off the road, the falls are on a marked path through dense forest which includes a 800 year old Coihue tree known as 'El Abuelo'.

Park administration is at Aguas Calientes; there is also a ranger station at Anticura. Leaflets on walks and attractions are available.

Sleeping A *Hotel Antillanca*, T235114. Includes free mountainbiking and parapenting, at foot of Volcán Casablanca, excellent restaurant/café, with pool, sauna, friendly club-like atmosphere. **Camping** *Chanleufu*, in Aguas Calientes. With hot water, US$25 per site, *cabañas* (**A3** in season, **C** off season) T236988. A small shop – better to take your own food, and an expensive café. *Los Derrumbes*, 1 kilometre from Aguas Calientes. No electricity, US$20 per site. Conaf *refugio* on Volcán Puyehue, but check with Conaf in Anticura whether it is open.

Transport See under Osorno for buses. No public transport from Aguas Calientes to Antillanca; try hitching – always difficult, but it is not a hard walk.

Frontier with Argentina: Paso Puyehue

This pass is reached by the paved Route 215 from Osorno via Entre Lagos and Lago Puyehue. On the Argentine side the road continues to Bariloche. *This route is liable to closure after snow*

Chilean immigration Open second Saturday in October-second Saturday in March 0800-2100, otherwise 0800-1900. The Chilean frontier post is at **Anticura**, 22 kilometres west of the border (*Hostería y Cabañas Anticura; Camping Catrue*). All luggage is passed through an X-ray machine.

Crossing by private vehicle For vehicles entering Chile, formalities are quick (about 15 minutes), but includes a search for fruit, vegetables and dairy produce.

The Lake District

To Anticura, bus at 1620 from Osorno, 3 hours. Several bus companies run daily services from Puerto Montt via Osorno to Bariloche along this route (see under Puerto Montt for details). Although less scenic than the ferry journey across Lake Todos Los Santos and Laguna Verde (see page 336) this crossing is cheaper, reliable and still a beautiful trip.

Lago Rupanco

Colour map 4, grid B2   Lying south of Lago Puyehue and considerably larger, this lake covers 23,000 hectares; much less accessible than most of the other larger lakes, it is less developed for tourism, although it is popular for fishing. Access from the northern shore is via two unpaved roads which branch off Route 215. **El Paraíso**, at the western tip of the lake, can be reached by an unpaved road which runs south from Entre Lagos. A 40 kilometre dirt road runs along the southern shore, via **Laguna Bonita**, a small lake surrounded by forest, and **Piedras Negras** to **Bahía Escocia** at the eastern end. From the south access is from two turnings off the road between Osorno and Las Cascadas.

Sleeping   **El Paraíso** *Hostería y Cabañas El Paraíso*, T236239. At **Piedras Negras** *Hostería El Islote* 7 kilometres east. **Bahía Escocia L3** *Puntiagudo Lodge*, T/F731515, also **A2**, with breakfast, very comfortable, good restaurant, fly fishing, horseriding, boat excursions, highly recommended. *Bahía Escocia Fly Fishing*, Casillon 1312, Osorno, T/F(064)-371515, offers excursions (advance booking required). There is no accommodation on the northern shore.

Camping *Puerto Chalupa*, on northern shore, T064-232680, F064-232741, US$28 per site. *Desague del Rupanco*, just south of El Paraíso, no facilities. Several on southern shore including at Puerto Rico.

Transport   **Bus** From Osorno to Piedras Negras from either *Minimarket El Capricho*, MacKenna y Colón, or Estaión Viejo (old railway station), leaves 1645, 1545 on Saturday, returns from Piedras Negras 0700.

Hacienda   Situated southeast of Lago Rupanco and covering 47,000 hectares, this haci-
Rupanco   enda, the largest milk-producer in Chile, invites day visitors and provides accommodation. Activities include horseriding, fishing, rafting, canoeing and sailing on Lago Rupanco. The main entrance is off the Osorno-Puerto Octay road. Accommodation **A3** in comfortable houses, full board, also camping, open all year. T/F064-203000.

Lago Llanquihue

The second largest lake in Chile and the third largest natural lake in South America   *Across this great blue sheet of water of 56,000 hectares can be seen three snowcapped volcanoes: the perfect cone of Osorno (2,680 metres), the shattered cone of Calbuco (2,015 metres), and the spike of Puntiagudo (2,480 metres), as well as, when the air is clear, the distant Tronador (3,460 metres).*

Colour map 4, grid C2   The largest towns, Puerto Varas, Llanquihue and Frutillar are all on the western shore, linked by the Pan-American Highway. Although there are roads around the rest of the lake the eastern shore is difficult to visit without transport: from Puerto Octay the eastern lakeside, with the Osorno volcano on your left, to Ensenada is very beautiful, but the road is narrow with lots of blind corners, necessitating speeds of 20-30 kph at best in places (see below). There is almost no public transport on this section and hitching is very difficult.

Puerto Octay

Fifty six kilometres southeast of Osorno, Puerto Octay is a small town at the north tip of the lake in a beautiful setting of rolling hills, hedgerows, German-style farmhouses and views over the Osorno volcano. Founded by German settlers in 1851, the town enjoyed a boom period in the late 19th century when it was the northern port for steamships on the lake: a few buildings survive from that period, notably the church and the enormous German-style former convent. Since the arrival of railways and the building of roads the town has declined. Three kilometres south along an unpaved road is the Peninsula of **Centinela** with accommodation, camping, a launch dock, bathing beaches, watersports. From the headland are fine views of the Osorno, Calbuco and Puntiagudo volcanoes as well as the Cordillera of the Andes; a very popular spot in good weather (taxi US$2.50 one way). The **Hotel Centinela**, idyllically situated, was built in 1913 as a summer mansion. Much less frequented by visitors than Frutillar or Puerto Varas, Puerto Octay offers an escape for those seeking peace and quiet.

Population: 2,000
Phone code: 064
Colour map 4, grid B2

Museums Museo el Colono, Independencia 591, has displays on German colonization. ■ *Tuesday-Sunday 0900-1300, 1500-1900, December-February only.* Another part of the museum, housing agricultural implements and machinery for making *chicha*, is just outside town on the road to Centinela.

Sleeping & eating

B *Haase*, Pedro Montt 344, T391193. With breakfast, attractive old building. **C** *Posada Gubernatis*, Santiago s/n, lakeside. Clean, comfortable. **E** pp *Hosp La Naranja*, Independencia 361. Without bath, with breakfast, restaurant, good views. **C** *Hosp Fogón de Anita*, 1 kilometre out of town, T391325. Good breakfast. **D** *Hosp Raquel Mardorf*, Germán Wulf 712. With enormous breakfast, clean, comfortable, owners

Lago Llanquique

The Lake District

German colonization in Llanquihue

The most important area of German agricultural colonization in Chile was around Lago Llanquihue. In 1845, when the Chilean government declared the area to be destined for colonization, it knew little about the area which was covered by dense virgin forest. Vicente Pérez Rosales, appointed to encourage settlement, travelled to Lago Llanquihue in 1851 and tried to sail around the lake in a dugout; it sank and, though Rosales swam to safety, his companion drowned.

To encourage settlement and help the new arrivals get started the government gave each adult male 75 cuadras of land plus an extra 12 cuadras for each son, a milking cow, 500 planks of timber, nails, a yoke of axen, a year's free medical assistance and medicines and Chilean citizenship on request.

The first groups of German colonists arrived in the area in 1852: one group settled around Maitén and Puerto Octay, another helped found Puerto Montt. The lives of these early settlers were hard and the risks great: in cutting a path between Puerto Montt and Lago Lanquihue, two young settlers strayed from the others and were never seen again. Yet within ten years they had cleared much of the forest round the lake and soon they were setting up small industries. In 1880, when the offer to colonists ended, unsettled land was auctioned in lots of 400-800 hectares. By then the lake was ringed by a belt of smallholdings and farms. The legacy of this settlement can be seen in the German-looking farmhouses around Puerto Octay and in many of the older buildings in Frutillar and Puerto Varas.

have *Restaurante La Cabaña* at No 713. Good. *Restaurante Baviera*, Germán Wulf 582. Cheap and good. **Camping** *El Molino*, beside lake. US$5 per person, clean, friendly, recommended. **Centinela** **C** pp *Hotel Centinela*, T391326. Run down but with superb views, also *cabañas*, restaurant with grand minstrels' gallery and bar, open all year. **E** pp *Hostería La Baja*, Casilla 116, T391269. Beautifully situated at the neck of the peninsula, with breakfast and bath. **Camping** Municipal site on lakeside, US$15 per site, T391326.

Transport Buses to **Osorno** 7 a day. To **Frutillar** (1 hour), Puerto Varas (2 hours) and Puerto Montt (3 hours) Thaebus, 8 a day. To **Las Cascadas** (see below) Monday-Friday 1700, return next day 0600. To Ensenada 0600, daily in season, less frequent out of season.

Directory **Tourist offices** Pedro Montt s/n, T276. Open Dec-Feb daily 0900-2100.

East of Puerto Octay

From Puerto Octay the road runs along the eastern shore of the lake to Ensenada. At Km 10 is **Playa Maitén**, 'highly recommended, nice beach, marvellous view to the Volcán Osorno, no tourists'. Twenty four kilometres further on is **Las Cascadas**, surrounded by picturesque agricultural land, old houses and German cemeteries: here there are attractive waterfalls in a gorge.

Sleeping *Centro de Recreación Las Cascadas*, T235377. **E** *Hostería Irma*, on lake, 2 kilometres past Las Cascadas, run by Tres Marías. Attractive former residence, good food, very pleasant. Several farms on the road around north and east side of the lake offer accommodation, look for signs. **Camping** *Centro de Recreación Las Cascadas* and Villa Las Cascadas picnic area (free); at Playa Maitén. Recommended.

Frutillar

Lying about half-way along the western side of the lake, Frutillar is in fact two towns: Alto Frutillar, just off the main highway, and Bajo Frutillar beautifully situated on the lakeside, four kilometres away.

Population: 5,000
Altitude: 70m
Phone code: 065
Colour map 4, grid C2

Sights

Bajo Frutillar is possibly the most attractive – and expensive – town on the lake: from its **costanera** there are superb views over the water with the forms of Calbuco and Osorno in the background. There is a large open-air chess board in the square outside the Club Alemán. At the northern end of the town is the **Reserva Forestal Edmundo Winckler**, run by the Universidad de Chile and extending over 33 hectares, with a guided trail through native woods. Named after one of the early German settlers, it includes a very good collection of native flora as well as plants introduced from Europe.

Colectivos run between the two towns, five minutes, US$0.50

Museo Colonial Alemán This museum includes a watermill, which does not turn, replicas of two German colonial houses with furnishings and utensils of the period and a blacksmith's shop with personal engravings for US$5. It also has a *campanario*, which is a circular barn with agricultural machinery and carriages inside, as well as gardens and a handicraft shop. It is well worth a visit. ■ *Daily 0930-1900 summer, Tuesday-Sunday 0930-1400, 1530-1800 winter, US$2.*

Museums

Essentials

North of Frutillar Bajo L3 *Salzburg*, T421589 or Santiago 2061419. Excellent restaurant, sauna, mountain bikes, arranges tours and fishing. *Hostal Cinco Robles*, Casilla 100, T421351. With breakfast, other meals on request, parking. **A** *3 Los Maitenes*, 3 kilometres north, T/F339130, hosterialosmaool@chilnet.cl.

Frutillar Bajo B *Casona del 32*, Caupolicán 28, T421369. Casilla 101. With breakfast, comfortable old house, central heating, English and German spoken. **On Philippi A2** *Klein Salzburg*, No 663, T421201. **C** *Hosp El Arroyo*, No 989, T421560. With breakfast. Highly

Sleeping
■ *on maps, pages 329 and 330*
Price codes:
see inside front cover
During the annual music festival accommodation should be booked well in advance; alternatively stay in Frutillar Alto or Puerto Varas

Frutillar Bajo

To Puerto Octay

To Reserva Forestal Edmundo Winkler

Caupolicán

S Junginger

18 de Septiembre

Carlos Richter

Museo Colonial Alemán

Prat

Balmacada

San Martín

Municipalidad o Public toilets o

O'Higgins

M Montt

A Varas

Las Piedras

Pérez Rosales

M Rodríguez

P Aguirre

21 de Mayo

Lago Llanquihue

To Llanquihue

N

0 metres 200
0 yards 218

■ **Sleeping**
1 Am See
2 Casona del 32
3 El Arroyo
4 Hospedaje Trayén
5 Hospedaje Vivaldi
6 Klein Salzburg
7 Los Maitenes
8 Salzburg
9 Winkler

● **Eating**
1 Bierstube
2 Casino de Bomberos
3 Club Alemán

The Lake District

recommended. **C-D** *Hosp Costa Azul*, No 1175, T421388. Mainly for families, good breakfasts. **C** *Winkler*, No 1155, T421388. Discount to Hostelling International members, cabins, friendly. Recommended. **D** pp *Hosp Vivaldi*, No 851, T421382. *Sra Edith Klesse*, quiet, comfortable, excellent breakfast and lodging, also family accommodation. Recommended. **D** *Las Rocas*, No 1235, T421397. With breakfast. **D** *Residenz/Café am See*, No 539. Good breakfast. **C** No 451, T421204, clean, good breakfast. **D** *Hosp Trayén*, No 963, T421346. Basic, clean. **D** *Pérez Rosales 590*. Excellent breakfast. **In Frutillar Alto D** *Faralito*, Winkler 245. Hot water, cooking facilities (owner can be contacted at shop at Winkler 167, T421440). **E** pp *Hosp Juana Paredes*, Anibal Pinto y Winkler, T421407, recommended, also *cabañas*, **B**, sleep 5, parking. Several along Carlos Richter (main street). Cheap accommodation in the school in Frutillar Alto, sleeping bag required.

Camping *Playa Maqui*, 7 kilometres north of Frutillar, T339139. Fancy, expensive. *Los Ciruelillos*, 2 kilometres south, T339123. Most services. Try also Sr Guido González, Casa 3, Población Vermont, T421385. **G** pp. Recommended.

Eating
• *on maps, pages 329 and 330*

Andes, Philippi 1057, good set menus and à la carte. *Club Alemán*, Av Philippi 747. Good but not cheap, hostile to backpackers. *Casino de Bomberos*, Philippi 1060. Upstairs bar/restaurant, best value, open all year, memorable painting caricaturing the firemen in action. *Bierstube*, Varas y Philippi. Open 1600-2400. Several German-style cafés and tea-rooms on Calle Philippi eg *Salón de Te Frutillar*, No 775. *Der Volkladen*, O'Higgins y Philippi. Natural products, chocolates and cakes, natural cosmetics.

Festivals In late **January to early February** there is a highly regarded classical music festival.

Transport **Car mechanic** *Toirkens*, Los Carrera 1260, highly recommended.

Bus to **Puerto Varas** (US$0.75) and **Puerto Montt** (US$1.25), frequent, Varmontt and Full Express. To **Osorno**, Varmontt 1¼ hours, US$3. To **Puerto Octay**, Thaebus, 6 a day. Most buses leave from opposite the Copec station in Alto Frutillar.

Directory **Communications** *Post Office*, San Martín y Pérez Rosales, Monday-Friday 0930-1230, 1430-1800, Saturday 0900-1230. **Tourist offices** On lakeside opposite *Club Alemán*, helpful. *Viajes Frutillar*, Richter y Alissandre in Alto Frutillar. Run tours. **Useful services** Toilet, showers and changing cabins for beach on O'Higgins. *Cema-Chile* shop, Philippi y O'Higgins.

Llanquihue

Population: 9,422
Phone code: 065

Twenty kilometres south of Frutillar, Llanquihue lies at the source of the Río Maullín which drains the lake. The site of a large dairy processing factory, it is the least touristy town on the lake and offers uncrowded beaches and a cheaper alternative to Puerto Varas and Frutillar. There is a German style beer festival at the end of January with German music.

Frutillar Alto

To Osorno
To Puerto Octay
JA Rios
Pinto
Montt
Pan American Highway
Av Alessandri
C Winkler
San Pedro
To Frutillar Bajo
Carlos Richter
N
18 de Septiembre
Tte Jiménez
Av 11 de Septiembre
0 metres 100
0 yards 109
To Puerto Varas & Puerto Montt

A3 *Siete Lagos*, Errázurriz 132, T242020. **B** *El Cisne*, M Montt s/n, T242726. *Cabañas.* **Sleeping**
Posada Alemana, Errázuriz 517, T242629. Several *hospedajes*. **Camping** North of
Llanquihue are *Baumbach*, Km 1, T242643, on lakeside, meals available. *Playa
Werner*, Km 2, T242114, on lakeside. *El Totoral*, Km 8, T339123, also *cabañas*.

Puerto Varas

*Situated on the southwestern corner of the lake, Puerto Varas is the commercial
and tourist centre of Lago Llanquihue and a residential centre for Puerto Montt
20 kilometres to the south. In the 19th century, it was the southern port for shipping on the lake; it is now an expensive resort, popular with Argentine tourists.*

Population: 16,000
Phone code: 065
Colour map 4, grid C2

Sights

Parque Philippi, on top of a hill, is a pleasant place to visit; walk up to *Hotel
Cabañas del Lago* on Klenner, cross the railway and the gate is on the right. The
views are a bit restricted by trees and the metal cross at the top is unattractive
(so is the electric clock which chimes the quarter-hours in town). The centre
lies at the foot of the hill, but the town stretches east along the lake to Puerto
Chico where there are hotels and restaurants. The Catholic church, in monumental Baroque style, built by German Jesuits in 1918, is a copy of the church
in Marieenkirche in the Black Forest; worth a visit. North and east of the **Gran
Hotel Puerto Varas** (1934) are a number of German style mansions dating
from the early 20th century: there are plans to turn one of these, the **Casa
Kuschel**, into a museum.

Excursions

Puerto Varas is a good base for trips around the lake. A paved road runs along
the south shore to Ensenada on the southwestern corner of the lake. Two of the
best beaches are Playa Hermosa, Km 7 and Playa Niklitschek, Km 8, where an
entry fee is charged. **La Poza**, at Km 16, is a little lake to the south of Lago
Llanquihue reached through narrow channels overhung with vegetation; **Isla
Loreley**, an island on La Poza is very beautiful (frequent boat trips, US$1.50); a
concealed channel leads from La Poza to yet another lake, the Laguna
Encantada. At Km 21 there is a watermill being converted into a museum. For
the continuation of this road to Ensenada and for transport between Puerto
Varas and Ensenada, see below.

Essentials

L3 *Los Alerces*, Pérez Rosales 1281, T233039. 4-star, with breakfast, new cabin complex, attractive.

Sleeping
■ *on map page 332*
Price codes:
see inside front cover
Accommodation is
expensive, it is cheaper
to stay in Puerto Montt

A1 *Colonos del Sur*, Del Salvador 24, T233369, F233394. Good views, good restaurant,
tea room. **A1** *Cabañas del Lago*, Klenner 195, T232291, F232707. On Phiippi hill overlooking lake, superb views. Also self-catering *cabañas* sleeping 5 (good value for
groups), cheaper rates in low season, heating, sauna. **A1** *Antonio Varas*, Del Salvador
322, T232375, F232352. Very comfortable. **A1** *Terrazas del Lago*, Pérez Rosales 1571,
T/F232622, (in Santiago, San Antonio 477, T/F6392829/6395240), good breakfast,
views over Osorno volcano, restaurant. **A2** *Bellavista*, Pérez Rosales 60, T232011,
F232013. Cheerful, recommended, restaurant, overlooking lake. **A3** *Cabañas
Ayentemo*, Pérez Rosales 1297. Clean, comfortable, friendly, T/F232270.

The Lake District

A3 *Licarayén*, San José 114, T232305, F232955. Overlooking lake, comfortable, 'enthusiastically recommended'. Book in season, **C** out of season, clean, friendly, 'the perfect place for bad weather or being ill'.

B *Del Bosque*, Santa Rosa 714, T232897, F236000. With breakfast, recommended. **B** *Hosp Loreley*, Maipo 911, T232226. Homely, quiet. Recommended. **B** *Merlín*, Walker Martínez 584, T/F233105. Good beds, excellent restaurant. Highly recommended. **B** *Motel Altué*, Pérez Rosales 1679, T232294. With breakfast. **B** *Cabañas Amancay*, Walker Martínez 564. With breakfast, German spoken. Recommended.

C *Agatha Haus*, Route 5 on southern outskirts, very relaxed, German spoken. **C** *Casa Familiar*, Maipo 1010, T232880. With breakfast, cable TV, very comfortable. **C** *El Greco*, Mirador 134, T233388. Modern, good. **C** *Hostal Chancerel*, Decher 400, T/F234221. Also offers tours. **C** *Hostal Erika*, Maipa 0290, T233760. Also *cabañas*. **C** *Rincón Aleman*, San Francisco 1004, T232087. **C** *Villa Germania*, Nuestra Sra del Carmen 873, T233162. Also *cabañas*.

D *Hosp Las Rosas*, Santa Rosa 560, with bath and good breakfast. **D** *María Schilling Rosas*, La Quebrada 752. Recommended. **D** pp *Hosp Las Carmelas*, Imperial y Rosario. Excellent, helpful, good meals, lends books including some in English. Highly recommended. **D** pp Andrés Bello 321. Nice atmosphere, good breakfast. **D** *Res Alemana*, San Bernardo 416, T232419. With breakfast, without bath, clean. **D** *Hosp Don Raúl*, Salvador 928, T234174. Laundry and cooking facilities, very friendly, clean, recommended. Camping **F** pp.

Puerto Varas

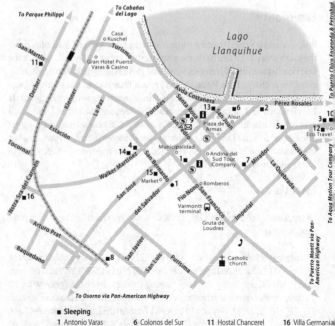

■ **Sleeping**

1 Antonio Varas	6 Colonos del Sur	11 Hostal Chancerel	16 Villa Germania
2 Bellavista	7 El Greco	12 Hostal Erika	
3 Cabañas Amancay	8 Hospedaje Don Raúl	13 Licarayén	● **Eating**
4 Cabañas Ayentemo	9 Hospedaje Ellenhaus	14 Merlín	1 Café Danés
5 Casa Azul	10 Hospedaje Loreley	15 Residencial Alemana	

The Lake District

Calle Imperial **D** *Hosp Imperial*, 653, T232451. Clean, including breakfast, central, recommended. Several other family *hospedajes* on same street. **D** *Hosp Ellenhaus*, Walker Martínez 239, T233577. Kitchen and laundry facilities, luggage stored, lounge, hospitable, highly recommended. **D** pp *Outsider*, San Bernardo 318, T/F232910, outsider@telsur.cl. With bath, real coffee, meals, also horseback trekking, rafting, sea kayaking, climbing. German and English spoken. **D** pp *Casa Azul*, Mirador 18, T232904, casaazul@telsur.cl. Without breakfast, kitchen facilities, good beds, book exchange, English, German spoken, recommended. **D** pp *Santa Rosa y Martínez*, good atmosphere, kitchen facilities, good meeting place.

E pp *Elsa Pinto*, Verbo Divino 427. Clean. **E** pp *Pío Nono 474*, T233172. With breakfast. **E** pp *Colores del Sur*, Santa Rosa 318, T338588. Dormitory accommodation without breakfast, good meeting place.

F pp *Maria Angélica Banda*, Del Salvador 1026. With breakfast, meals served.

Camping On south shore of Lago Llanquihue east of Puerto Varas: Km 7, *Playa Hermosa*, T Puerto Varas 338283, Puerto Montt 252223, fancy, US$23 per site, bargain off season. Recommended. Take own supplies. Km 8, *Playa Niklitschek*, T338352, full facilities. Km 10, *Los Troncas*, US$10 per site, no beach access. Km 20, *Playa Venado*.

Eating *Aníbal*, Del Salvador y Santa Rosa, Italian, cheap, tasty. *Café Danés*, Del Salvador 441. Good coffee and cakes. *Club Alemán*, San José 415, good value. *Coffee Break*, San José 319, real coffee. *Donde El Gordito*, downstairs in market. Immense portions, very popular. *Domino*, Del Salvador 450. Good, cheap. *El Amigo*, San Bernardo 240. Large portions, good value. At the Puerto Chico end of Pérez Rosales are *Costa Azul*, No 01071, recommended. *Espigas*, Martínez 417, local 3. Vegetarian. *Ibis*, No 1117. Warmly recommended. Expensive motel restaurants just beyond it aren't worth visiting, although service is friendly. *El Molino*, café next to an old water mill, on road to Ensenada 22 kilometres east.

Sports **Cycle hire** *Travel Art*, Imperial 0661, T232198. Check equipment carefully. *Thomas Held Expeditions*, Martínez 239, T/F311889. US$20 per day. **Fishing** The area around Puerto Varas is popular for fishing. Licence (obligatory), obtainable from the Municipalidad. Fishing expeditions are organized by *Quiroz Hnos*, Estación 230, T233771, 235693. **Horse riding** Fundo Molino Viejo, 2 kilometres north, T338033. Guided tours, minimum 2 persons. See also below under **Tour Companies and Travel Agents**.

Shopping **Supermarkets** *VYH Meistur*, Walker Martínez. Good selection, reasonably priced. **Bookshop** *El Libro del Capitán*, Martiínez 417, book swap, large selection in German and English.

The Lake District

Transport **Bus** Varmontt terminal, San Francisco 500 block. To **Santiago**, Varmontt, Igi Llaima, Cruz del Sur and others, US$24, semi cama US$36, cama US$48. To **Puerto Montt**, 30 minutes, Varmontt and Full Express every 15 minutes, US$0.50; same companies, same frequency to Frutillar (US$0.75, 30 minutes) and **Osorno** (US$3.50, 1¼ hours). To **Valdivia** US$6, 3 hours to Temuco, US$10. To **Bariloche**, services from Puerto Montt stop here. For Andina del Sud via Lago Todas Los Santos, see under Puerto Montt. To Cochamó via Ensenada, 3 a day, US$2. Minibuses to Ensenada and Petrohué leave from San Bernardo y Martínez.

Train There are no longer passenger services but tickets may be booked for the Temuco-Santiago train (but not for *clase economica*) from the station on Av Klenner, T232210, open 0900-1230, 1500-1830.

Directory **Banks** *Turismo Los Lagos*, Del Salvador 257 (Galería Real, local 11). Open daily 0830-1330, 1500-2100, Sun 0930-1330, accepts TCs, good rates. *Banco Osorno*, Del Salvador 399. Good rates. **Communications** Post Office: San José y San Pedro. Del Salvador y Santa Rosa. *Entel*, San José 413. **Internet Access** Av Gramado 560, 2 piso. **Laundry** *Lavanderia Delfin*, Martínez 323, expensive. **Tour companies & travel agents** *Alsur*, Del Salvador 100, T/F232300, alsur@telsur.cl. Rafting on Río Petrohue. Good camping equipment, tours. *Andina del Sud*, Del Salvador 243, T232511. Operate 'lakes' trip to Bariloche, Argentina via Lago Todos los Santos, Peulla, Cerro Tronador (see under Puerto Montt, **To Argentina**), plus other excursions, good. Also *Eco Travel*, Av Costanera s/n, T233222. *Aqua Motion* San Pedro 422, T/F232747, aquamotn@telsur.cl. *Tranco Expeditions*, Santa Rosa 190. Imperial 0699, T/F232747, for trekking, rafting and climbing, German and English spoken, good equipment. Outsider, San Bernardo 318, T232710, English and German spoken, offer one, three and ten-day trips on horseback (see below under Cochamó). Several others. Most tours operate in season only (1 Sep-15 Apr). **Tourist offices** San Francisco 441, T232402, F233315. Open 0900-2100 in summer, helpful, find cheap accommodation, also art gallery.

Ensenada

Phone code: 065
Colour map 4, grid C2 Despite its lack of a recognizable centre, Ensenada, 47 kilometres east of Puerto Varas, is beautifully situated at the southeast corner of Lago Llanquihue. A good half-day trip is to Laguna Verde, about 30 minutes from *Hotel Ensenada*, along a beautiful circular trail behind the lake (take first fork to the right behind the information board), and then down the road to a secluded campsite at Puerto Oscuro on Lago Llanquihue.

Sleeping **A2** *Ensenada*, Casilla 659, Puerto Montt, T/F212018. With bath, olde-worlde, good food (closed in winter), good view of lake and Osorno Volcano, runs tours, hires mountain bikes (guests only). Also *hostal* in the grounds, cooking facilities, much cheaper but not that cheap. **C** *Hosp Ensenada*, T338278. Very clean, excellent breakfast, **D** off-season. Recommended. **C** *Cabañas Villa Ensenada*, T338278 extension 344, sleeps 4. Bargain off season. About 2 kilometres from town is **C** *Pucará*, also with good restaurant (the steaks are recommended). **C** *Ruedas Viejas*, T338278 extension 312, for room, or **D** in *cabañas*. About 1 kilometre west from Ensenada, Hostelling International reductions, basic, damp, hot water, restaurant. **C** *Hosp Arena*, T338278. With breakfast. Recommended. **D** *Cabañas Brisas del Lago*, T212012. On beach sleep 6, good restaurant nearby, highly recommended, supermarket next door. **D** *Hosp Opazo*, with breakfast, friendly. **E** pp *Hosp* above Toqui grocery. Cheapest in town, basic, quiet, hot water, use of kitchen, beach in the back yard, recommended. **Camping** *Trauco*, 4 kilometres west, T212033. Large site with shops, fully equipped, US$4-9 pp. Also at Playa Larga, 1 kilometre east of *Hotel Ensenada*, US$10 and at Puerto Oscuro, 2 kilometres north, US$8.

Canta Rana, recommended for bread and *kuchen*. **Ruedas Viejas**, the cheapest. **Eating**
Donde Juanito, Km 44, excellent value set lunch, US$5. Most places closed off season,
a few pricey shops. Take your own provisions.

Minibuses run from Puerto Varas, frequent in summer. Buses from Puerto Montt via **Transport**
Puerto Varas to Cochamó also stop here. Hitching from Puerto Varas is difficult.

Tour companies & travel agents *Patagonia Adventures*, T212030, F212031. **Southern Chile** **Directory**
Expeditions, T213030. **Guide:** Ludwig Godsambassis, owner of *Ruedas Viejas*, who works for *Aqua*
Motion in season, works independently as a trekking guide out of season and is very
knowledgeable about flora and fauna.

Volcán Osorno

One of the lasting images of Lago Llanquihue is the near perfect cone of the *Colour map 4, grid C2*
Osorno Volcano of 2,652 metres, situated north of Ensenada on the eastern
edge of the lake. Although the peak lies on the edge of the Parque Nacional
Pérez Rosales, it is climbed from the western side which is outside the park.
Access is via two roads which branch off the Ensenada-Puerto Octay road
along the eastern edge of Lago Llanquihue: one at Puerto Klocker, 20 kilometres south of Puerto Octay, the other two kilometres north of Ensenada.

Climbing Weather permitting, *Aqua Motion* (address under Puerto Varas),
organize climbing expeditions with local guide, transport from Puerto Montt or
Puerto Varas, food and equipment, US$150 per person, payment in advance
(minimum group of two, maximum of six with three guides) all year, setting out
from the *refugio* at La Burbuja. *Aqua Motion* check weather conditions the day
before and offer 50 percent refund if climb is abandoned due to weather. From
La Burbuja it is six hours to the summit. Only experienced climbers should
attempt to climb right to the top, ice climbing equipment essential. Conaf checks
equipment and only allow experienced climbers to continue.

"Unlike many other volcanoes Osorno has some interesting ice climbing on
crevasse walls and between high seracs (although you avoid the technical stuff
if you go on a tour). Best for this are the southern and southeastern slopes.
There is a large ice cave on the north slope." Simon Harvey.

There are three *refugios*, two of them south of the summit and reached from the **Sleeping**
southern access road: **La Burbuja**, the former ski-club centre 14 kilometres north of
Ensenada (1,250 metres) and the **Refugio Teski Ski Club**, just below the snow line,
D pp, meals served. On the northern slopes, 20 kilometres east of Puerto Klocker is the
Refugio La Picada (950 metres), **D** pp.

The Lake District

Parque Nacional Vicente Pérez Rosales

Colour map 4, grid C2

Established in 1926, this is the oldest national park in Chile. It covers 251,000 hectares and stretches east from Lago Llanquihue to the Argentine frontier. It contains a large lake, Lago Todos Los Santos and three major volcanic peaks: Osorno, Puntiagudo and Tronador. Several other peaks are visible, notably Casablanca to the north and Calbuco to the south.

The most beautiful of all the lakes in southern Chile

Lago Todos los Santos is a long irregularly shaped sheet of water. There are no roads round it and only people with houses on the lake are allowed boats on it. The waters are emerald green; the shores are deeply wooded and several small islands rise from its surface. In the waters are reflected the slopes of Volcán Osorno. Beyond the hilly shores to the east are several graceful snow-capped mountains, with the mighty Tronador in the distance. To the north is the sharp point of Cerro Puntiagudo, and at the northeastern end Cerro Techado rises cliff-like out of the water. The lower mountain slopes are covered with Valdivian forest. The lake is fed by several rivers, including the Río Peulla to the east, the Ríos Techado and Negro to the north and the Río Blanco to the south. At its western end the lake is drained by the Río Petrohue. The ports of **Petrohué** at its western and **Peulla** at its eastern ends are connected by boat. Sheltered from the winds, the lake is warm and is a popular location for water sports and swimming. Trout and salmon fishing are excellent in several parts including Petrohué.

Parque Nacional Pérez Rosales & the lakes route to Argentina

Climbing Puntiagudo and Tronador

Tronador, 3,460 metres, offers many technical possibilities, with both easy and difficult stretches on the upper slopes. It is usually climbed from the Argentine side. There is no road on the Chilean side so a four to five day hike is required. Moreover glaciers on the western (Chilean) slopes make climbing difficult and pose safety problems. There is a basic hut on the Chilean side.

Puntiagudo, 2,490 metres, is the most distinctive peak in the Lake District as a result of its sharp volcanic plug summit which is much steeper than the lower slopes. Only ever climbed a few times, it poses considerable climbing problems because of the 75-90° upper slopes and the very poor loose rock, though it may be easier in winter when there is more snow and ice. The southern side is the most difficult. Access is from the northern side of Lago Todos Los Santos or from the southern side of Lago Rupanco.

The only scheduled vessel on the lake is the Andino del Sud service with connections to Bariloche (Argentina), but private launches can be hired for trips. **Isla Margarita**, the largest island on the lake, with a lagoon in the middle of it, can be visited (in summer only) from Petrohué.

Petrohué, 16 kilometres northwest of Ensenada, is a good base for walking tours around the foot of Osorno Volcano, or for lookouts over it, eg Cerro Picada. Near the Ensenada-Petrohué road, 6 kilometres west of Petrohué, is the **Salto de Petrohué** (entrance, US$1.50). The falls were formed by a relatively recent lava flow of hard volcanic rock. Near the falls is a snack bar; there are also two short trails, the *Sendero de los Enamorados* and the *Sendero Carileufú*.

Peulla, is a good starting point for hikes in the mountains. The *Cascadas Los Novios*, signposted above the *Hotel Peulla*, are a steep walk, but are stunning once you reach them. Good walk also to Laguna Margarita, four hours, take water.

On the south shore of Lago Todos Los Santos is the little village of **Cayutué**, reached by hiring a boat from Petrohué, US$30. From Cayutué (no camping on the beach but there are private sites) it is a three-hour walk to Laguna Cayutué, a jewel set between mountains and surrounded by forest. Good camping and swimming. From here it is a five hour hike south to Ralún on the Reloncaví Estuary (see below): the last half of this route is along a *ripio* road built for extracting timber. This is part of the old route used by missionaries in the colonial period to travel between Nahuel Huapi in Argentina and the island of Chiloé.

North of the lake are the **Termas de Callao**, reached by hiring a boat to the uninhabited El Rincón from Petrohué. Arrange for the boat to wait or collect you later. "It is 3½-4 hours walk through virgin forest beside the Río Sin

The Lake District

Nombre. The path twice crosses the river by rickety hanging bridges. The slopes immediately beside the river and path are steep, giving the impression that the forest is even more gigantic than it actually is. Just before the baths is a house: collect the keys and pay. The Termas are two large Alerce tubs in a cabin." (Simon Harvey). Nearby is a modern comfortable *refugio*.

The park is infested by *tavanos* in December and January: cover up as much as possible with light coloured clothes which may help a bit. In wet weather many treks in the park are impossible and the road to Puerto Montt can be blocked.

Park essentials Conaf office in Petrohué with a visitors' centre, small museum and 3D model of the park. There is a *guardaparque* office in Puella. No maps of treks are available in the park.

Sleeping **Petrohué A2** *Hostería Petrohué*, T/F258042. With bath, excellent views, log fires, cosy; owner, Franz Schirmer, a former climbing guide, can advise on activities around the lake. **L3** *Fundo El Salto*, near Salto de Petrohué. Very friendly, run by New Zealanders, mainly a fishing lodge, good home cooking, fishing trips arranged. Casilla 471, Puerto Varas. **E** pp *Familia Küschel* on other side of river (boat across). With breakfast, electricity only 3 hours in evening, dirty (rats), noisy, poor value, camping possible. Albergue in the school in summer. Conaf office can help find cheaper family accommodation. There is a shop with basic supplies and some of the houses sell fresh bread.
Peulla A1 *Hotel Peulla*, (reservations: Casilla 487, Puerto Montt), T253253, including dinner and breakfast, direct personal reservations, cheaper out of season. Beautiful setting by the lake and mountains, restaurant and bar, poor meals, cold in winter, often full of tour groups (tiny shop at back of hotel). **D** pp *Res Palomita*, 50 metres west of hotel. Half board, family-run, simple, comfortable but not spacious, separate shower, book ahead in season, lunches.

Petrohué Camping: at Petrohué on far side beside the lake, US$4 per site, no services (local fishermen will ferry you across, US$0.50). At Peulla, opposite Conaf office, US$1.50. Ask the commander of the military garrison at the beach nearest the hotel if you can camp on the beach; no facilities. Good campsite 1¾ hours walk east of Peulla. Small shop in Andino del Sud building in Petrohué but best to take your own food.

Transport **Minibuses** From Puerto Varas to Ensenada continue to Petrohué, frequent in summer.

Boats The Andino del Sud catamaran between Petrohué and Peulla costs US$30 day return or one way (book in advance); it leaves Petrohué at 1030, Peulla at 1500 (not Sunday, 2 hours – most seating indoors, no cars carried, cycles free), commentaries in Spanish and English. Take own refreshments as those sold on board are very expensive. This is the only public service across the lake and it connects with the Andina del Sud tour bus between Puerto Montt and Bariloche (see page 348). Local fishermen make the trip across the lake and for a group this can be cheaper than the public service, allow 3½ hours. If planning to go to Bariloche in stages, book through to Bariloche in Petrohué, not Peulla because onward connections from Peulla may be full and the accommodation is not so good there. **NB** It is impossible to do this journey independently out of season as then there are buses only as far as Ensenada, there is little traffic for hitching and none of the ferries takes vehicles.

The lakes route to Bariloche via Lago Todos Los Santos

This popular route from Puerto Montt to Bariloche, involving ferries across Lago Todos Los Santos, Lago Frías and Lago Nahuel Huapi is outstandingly beautiful whatever the season, though the mountains are often obscured by rain and heavy cloud.

The journey is as follows: by bus via Puerto Varas, Ensenada and the Petrohué falls (20 minutes stop) to Petrohué, where there is a connection with catamaran service (1¾ hours) across Lago Todos Los Santos to Peulla. Lunch stop in Peulla two hours (lunch not included in fare: *Hotel Peulla* is expensive, see above for alternatives). Chilean customs are in Peulla, followed by a two-hour bus ride through the Paso Pérez Rosales to Argentine customs in Puerto Frías, 20 minute boat trip across Lago Frías to Puerto Alegre and bus (15 minutes) from Puerto Alegre to Puerto Blest.

From Puerto Blest it is a beautiful one hour catamaran trip along Lago Nahuel Huapi to Puerto Panuelo, from where there is a one hour bus journey to Bariloche (bus drops passengers at hotels, camping sites or in town centre). From 1 May to 30 August this trip is done over two days with overnight stay in Peulla, add about US$89 to single fare for accommodation in *Hotel Peulla*. (Baggage is taken to *Hotel Peulla* automatically but for alternative accommodation see above.) This journey is operated only by Andino del Sud (for contact details, see page 348). Bus from company offices in Puerto Montt daily at 0800; the fare is US$110 one way. Note that the trip may be cancelled if the weather is poor; there are reports of difficulty in obtaining a refund. If you have time buy the boat sections in Puerto Montt or Puerto Varas and do the rest of the trip yourself (though this will probably involve walking sections since there is little transport for hitching).

Paso Pérez Rosales Chilean immigration is in Peulla, 30 kilometres west of the frontier, open summer 0800-2100, winter 0800-2000.

Frontier with Argentina

Into Argentina

Bariloche is a popular destination and centre for exploring the Argentine Lake District. Beautifully situated on the south shore of Lago Nahuel Huapi, the streets rise steeply along the edge of a glacial morraine. West of the city on the shores of the lake is the resort of Llao Llao, where the famous *Hotel Llao Llao*, looks out over chocolate box scenery. Nearby are two ski resorts and boat excursions can be made on the lake and to other parts of the Argentine Lake District. There is a wide range of accommodation as well as air and bus connections to Buenos Aires and other destinations in Argentina. For more complete details see the *Argentina Handbook* or the *South American Handbook*.

Population 77,750

The Reloncaví Estuary

The Reloncaví estuary situated east of Puerto Montt and south of the Parque Nacional Pérez Rosales, is the northernmost of Chile's glacial inlets. Recommended for its local colour, its sea lions, dolphins and its peace, it is relatively easily reached from Puerto Montt by a road which runs along the wooded lower Petrohué valley south from Ensenada and then follows the eastern shore of the estuary to join the Camino Austral.

The Lake District

Ralún

Colour map 4, grid C2   A small village situated at the northern end of the estuary, Ralún is 31 kilometres southeast from Ensenada by a poorly paved road. On the outskirts of the village there are thermal baths, US$2, reached by boat, US$2.50 across the Río Petrohué. Ralún is the departure point for a five hour walk north to Laguna Cayutué in the Parque Nacional Vicente Pérez Rosales, see above. There is a village shop and post office, with telex. A road branches off and follows the western side of the estuary south, 36 kilometres to Lago Chapo, giving access at the eastern end to Parque Nacional Alerce Andino (see page 383).

Sleeping   **A3** *Cabañas Ralún*, T/F(065)-278286, Santiago 6321675. **B** *Cabañas Villa Margarita*, Santiago T2361817. **E** pp *Restaurant El Refugio* rents rooms. **E** pp *Navarrito*, restaurant and lodging. **F** pp *Posada Campesino*, simple, clean, without breakfast, very friendly. **E** pp *El Encuentro*. The *Hotel Ralún*, T/F233457/278286, at south end of the village, which burnt down in 1992, has *cabañas*, **L2**, sleep 6.

Transport   Bus from Puerto Montt, 5 a day, Bohle, between 1000 and 1930, 4 on Saturday, return 0700-1830, US$2. Also Fierro services from Puerto Montt, see below.

Cochamó

Population: 1,000   Seventeen kilometres south of Ralún on the east shore of the estuary, Cochamó
Colour map 4, grid C2   is a pretty village situated in a striking setting, with the estuary and volcano behind. There is a fine wooden church, similar to those on Chiloé, dating from 1900.

Sleeping   **D** *Hosp Maura*, JJ Molina 12, beautifully situated, good food. **D** *Cochamó*, T216212. Basic but clean, friendly, often full with salmon farm workers, good meals, recommended, and a large number of *pensiones* (just ask), eg **E** pp *Mercado Particular Sabin*, Catedral 20, next to *Hotel*. **E** pp *Hosp Edicar*, without bath, spacious, recommended. **E** pp *Restaurant Copihue*. *Camping Los Castaños*, T216212 (Reservations Casilla 576, Puerto Montt).

Eating   *Reloncaví*, next to *Hotel*. *Donde Payi* opposite church.

Sports   **Horseriding (trekking with packhorses)** *Campo Aventura* (Casilla 5, Correo Cochamó) T/F232910, outsider@telsur.cl, offer accommodation at their base camp 4 kilometres south of Cochamó (**E** pp, kitchen, sauna, camping) and at their other base, a renovated mountain house in the valley of La Junta. Specialize in horseback and trekking expeditions along the Gaucho trail between the Reloncaví Estuary and the Argentine frontier, 2-10 days. They also offer a 2 week excursion on horseback to the ranch in Cholila, Argentina, where Butch Cassidy and the Sundance Kid lived from 1902 to 1905.

The **Gaucho Trail** east to Paso León on the Argentine frontier was used in the colonial period by indians and Jesuit priests and later by gauchos. The route runs along Río Cochamó to La Junta, then along the north side of Lago Vidal, passing waterfalls and the oldest surviving Alerce trees in Chile at El Arco, three to four days by horse, five to six days on foot, depending on conditions (best done December-March). From the border crossing at Paso León it is a three-hour walk to the main road to San Carlos de Bariloche.

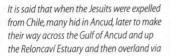

The legend of Cochamó

It is said that when the Jesuits were expelled from Chile, many hid in Ancud, later to make their way across the Gulf of Ancud and up the Reloncaví Estuary and then overland via
Cochamó to Bariloche. Along the way they buried the valuables they were carrying, including hoards of gold, silver and coin.

Puelo

Further south, on the south bank of the Río Puelo, Puelo is a most peaceful place (ferry crossing); accommodation is available at one of the restaurants (**F** per person) and with families – try Roberto and Olivia Telles, simple, clean, no bath/shower, meals on request, or Ema Hernández Maldona; two restaurants. From here the road continues 36 kilometres further southwest to Puelche on the Camino Austral.

Colour map 4, grid C2

Transport

Bus Fierro services from Puerto Montt, Monday-Saturday 1230 and 1600, Sunday 0900 and 1500 via Puerto Varas (departure 30 minutes later), Ensenada, Ralún and Cochamó. Departures from Cochamó Monday-Saturday 0745 and 1645, Sunday 1100 and 1500.

Boat In summer boats sail up the Estuary from Angelmó. Tours from Puerto Montt US$30. Off season the *Carmencita* sails once a week, leaving Puelo Sunday 1000 and Angelmó Wednesday 0900 (advisable to take warm clothes, food and seasickness pills if windy).

Puerto Montt

The capital of Región X (Los Lagos), Puerto Montt lies on the northern shore of the Seno de Reloncaví 1,016 kilometres south of Santiago. It was founded in 1853 on the site of a Mapuche community known as Melipulli, meaning four hills, as part of the German colonization of the area. Good views over the city and bay are offered from outside the Intendencia Regional on Av X Region.

Population: 110,139
Phone code: 065
Colour map 4, grid C2

It is an important centre for the salmon farming industry. Its port is used by fishing boats and coastal vessels, and is the departure point for vessels to Puerto Chacabuco, Laguna San Rafael and for the long haul south to Puerto Natales. A paved road runs 55 kilometres southwest to Pargua, where there is a ferry service to Chiloé.

Sights

The **Plaza de Armas** lies at the foot of steep hills, one block north of Av Diego Portales, which runs east-west parallel to the shore. Two blocks west of the square is the **Iglesia de los Jesuitas** on Calle Gallardo, dating from 1872, which has a fine blue-domed ceiling; behind it on a hill is the **campanario** (clock tower). The little fishing port of **Angelmó**, two kilometres west along Av Diego Portales, has become a tourist centre; it has many seafood restaurants, very popular with Chileans, and handicraft shops (reached by buses and *colectivos* Nos 2, 3 and 20 along Diego Portales, US$0.30 each).

The Lake District

The Poet and the Sea

"We sing to the sea"
At that time I was unaware,
Frankly, even of my own name,
I hadn't written my first poem,
Nor shed my first tear;
My heart was nothing more, nothing less
Than a forgotten kiosk in a square.
It so happened that one day my father
Was exiled to the South, to far off
Chiloé Island where the winter
Is like an abandoned city.
I left with him and without thinking we
arrived
In Puerto Montt one clear morning.
My family had always lived
In the Central Valley or in the mountains,
So that never, in our house, did we think
about
Or talk about the sea.
On this point I only knew what was
taught in public school...
We got down from the train among flags
And a solemn fiesta of bells
When my father took me by the arm
And turning his eyes to the white,

Free and eternal foam which navigates
In the distance towards some nameless
country,
Said to me as if uttering a prayer
In a voice which still rings in my ear:
"That, my boy, is the sea." ...
I began to run, headlong,
As if desperate towards the beach
And for an unforgettable moment I stood
In front of that great lord of battles ...
How long our greeting lasted
I cannot put into words.
I can only add that on that day
The need and the anguish was born in my
mind
To create in verse what in wave after
wave
God created ceaselessly in my vision...
It is, in truth, that since the world began,
The voice of the sea has been in my being.

Translated from "se canta al mar", Nicanor
Parra, Obra gruesa (Santiago: Editorial
Andrés Bello, 1983), pages 18-20.

Museums **Museo Regional Juan Pablo II**, Diego Portales 997 near bus terminal, documents local history. It has a fine collection of historic photos of the city; also memorabilia of the Pope's visit. ■ *Daily 1030-1800, US$1.*

Excursions

Puerto Montt is a popular centre for excursions to the Lake District: Puerto Varas, Frutillar, Puerto Octay and Ensenada are all in easy reach. The wooded **Isla Tenglo**, offshore from Puerto Montt and reached by launch from Angelmó (US$0.50), is a favourite place for picnics. There are magnificent view from the summit. The island is famous for its *curanto*, served by restaurants in summer. Boat trips round the island from Angelmó, 30 minutes, US$8. **Chinquihue** (the name means "place of skunks") west of Angelmó, has many seafood restaurants, with oysters as a speciality. East of Puerto Montt, **Chamiza**, up the Río Coihuin, has fine fishing. There is a bathing beach with black sand, which is polluted, at **Pelluco**, four kilometres east of Puerto Montt (accommodation including *cabañas*; several good seafood restaurants and discotheques – see below). **Isla Guar**, an island in the Seno del Reloncaví may be visited by boat from Angelmó harbour (1600, two hours); boat returns from the other end of the island at 0730. The north shore is rocky. If you are lucky you can stay at the church, but it may be best to camp.

West of Puerto Montt the Río Maullín, which drains Lago Llanquihue, has some attractive waterfalls and good fishing (salmon). At its mouth is the little fishing village of **Maullín**, founded in 1602 (B *Motel El Pangal*, five kilometres away, T244). Southeast of here, on the coast, is Carelmapu; three kilometres

The Lake District

away is an excellent beach, Playa Brava (*cabañas*). **Calbuco**, centre of the fishing industry (*Hotel Colonial*, T461546; several others; municipal campsite. *Restaurant San Rafael*, recommended) with good scenery, is on an island linked to the mainland by a causeway. It can be visited direct by boat or by road (the old coast road from Puerto Montt is very beautiful). South of Puerto Montt is the **Parque Nacional Alerce Andino** (see below under **Camino Austral**)

Essentials

A1 *Vicente Pérez Rosales*, Varas 447, T252571. With breakfast, some rooms noisy, excellent restaurant, seafood, fine views, tourist and climbing information. Recommended. **A1** *O'Grimm*, Gallardo 211, T252845, F258600. With breakfast, cosy restaurant with occasional live music, central. **L3** *Viento Sur*, Ejército 200, T258701, F258700. 4-star, excellent, good restaurant, sauna, gym, excellent views. **A2** *Burg*, Pedro Montt y Portales, T253941. Modern, central heating, centrally located, good, interesting traditional food in restaurant. **A2** *Colón*, Pedro Montt 65, T264290, F264293, good value. **A1** *Club Presidente*, Portales 664, T251666. 4-star, with breakfast, very comfortable, also suites. English spoken. Recommended. **A1** *Don Luis*, Urmeneta y Quillota, T259001, F259005. Heating, very good, good restaurant. **A3** *Montt*, Varas y Quillota, T253651. Also **C** without bath, clean, friendly, good value, good restaurant. **A3** *Raysan*, Benavente 480, T256151. Helpful. **A3** *Millahue*, Copiapó 64, T253829, F253817, and apartments at Benavente 959, T/F254592. With breakfast, modern, good restaurant.

A3 *Colina*, Talca 81, T253501. Restaurant, bar, car hire, noisy. Recommended. **B** *Le Mirage*, Rancagua 350, T255125, F256302. With breakfast, small rooms, clean. **B** *El Candil*, Varas 177, T253080. Run down. Also has **C** *Res Candil*, Illapel 87 nearby.

    C pp *Hostal Pacífico*, J J Mira 1088, T256229. With bath, **D** pp without, with breakfast, cable TV, parking, comfortable. Recommended. **C** *Res Embassy*, Valdivia 130, T253533. With bath, **E** pp without, clean, stores luggage. Recommended. **C** pp *Res Urmeneta*, Urmeneta 290, T253262. With bath, **D** pp without, clean, comfortable. Recommended. **C** pp *Res La Nave*, Ancud y Varas, T253740. With bath, **E** pp without, clean, inexpensive restaurant.

Budget accommodation Near the bus terminal: **C** *Hosp Polz*, J J Mira 1002,T252851. With breakfast, clean, warm, good beds. Recommended. **D** *Res El Turista*, Ancud 91, T254767. With bath, with breakfast, noisy. **D** *Res El Talquino*, Pérez

Sleeping
■ *on map, page 344*
Price codes:
see inside front cover
Accommodation is
expensive in season,
much cheaper off
season

Puerto Montt: Angelmó

To Route 5

To Chinquihue & Route 5

Ecuador
Chorrillos
Miraflores

Naval Headquarters

Skorpios

Gobernación Marítima
Handicraft stalls
Transmarchilay
Navimag
Handicraft stalls

Restaurant de las Antigüedades

Freight Port

Av Angelmó

Travellers'

Seafood Restaurants

To Bus Terminal & Centre

Canal Tenglo

Isla Tenglo

N

| 0 | metres | 200 |
| 0 | yards | 218 |

The Lake District

Rosales 114, T253331. Hot water, clean. **D** *Res Punta Arenas*, J J Mira 964. With breakfast, basic but clean. The following are all **E** pp: *Casa Gladis*, Ancud y Mira. Dormitory style, kitchen and laundry facilities, crowded. *Walglad*, Ancud 112. With breakfast, clean, run down. *Hosp Leticia*, Lota 132, T256316. With breakfast. Basic, safe, cooking facilities. Recommended. *Res Central*, Lota 111, T257516. Clean, use of kitchen, good beds. Recommended. **E** *Hosp Godoy*, Goecke 119, T266339. With breakfast, clean, cooking facilities, poor bathroom. Goecke 245, T258688, kitchen and laundry facilities. **E** Goecke 347, T288954, without breakfast, helpful. *Vista Hermosa*, Miramar 1486, T268001, without bath, quiet, helpful, fine views.

Near the Plaza de Armas: **D** *Res Calipso*, Urmeneta 127, T254554. Without bath, clean. Hostelling International discounts. **D** *Res La Alemana*, Egaña 82, T255092. With breakfast, German spoken, run down. The following are all **E** pp in Calle Huasco: **E** pp *Hosp Frente al Mar*, *no 6*, T260126, with breakfast, kitchen, also *cabañas*. *No 16*, T254709. With breakfast, basic. *No 126*, friendly. Recommended. *No 130*, cooking facilities, home made bread. Recommended. Antonio Varas 840, basic, including breakfast. Antonio Varas 770, T254720, with breakfast.

All E per person unless otherwise stated **Other budget accommodation**: **D** *Casa Haraldo Steffen*, Serrano 286, T253823. With breakfast, 15 minutes walk from centre, small clean rooms, run down, only 1

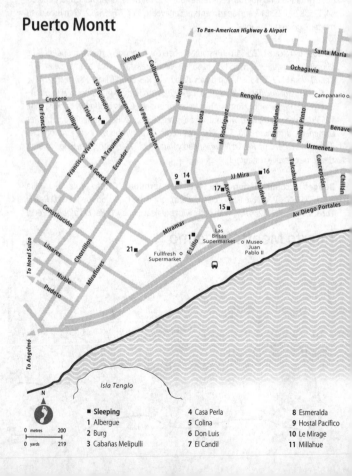

Puerto Montt

To Pan-American Highway & Airport

Santa María

Ochagavia

Campanario

Benave

Vergel

Calbuco

Allende

Rengifo

Los Guindos

Crucero

Manzanal

V Perez Rosales

Lota

M Rodriguez

Freire

Baquedano

Anibal Pinto

Dr Fonecks

Philippi

Trigal

A Traumann

Ecuador

Urmeneta

Francisco Vivar

A Goecke

JJ Mira

Talcahuano

Concepción

Chillán

Valdivia

Ancud

Constitución

Av Diego Portales

Miramar

Linares

Chorrillos

Miraflores

E Lillo

Las Brisas Supermarket

Museo Juan Pablo II

Nuble

Fullfresh Supermarket

Pudeto

To Hotel Suizo

To Angelmó

Isla Tenglo

N

| 0 metres | 200 |
| 0 yards | 219 |

■ **Sleeping**
1 Albergue
2 Burg
3 Cabañas Melipulli

4 Casa Perla
5 Colina
6 Don Luis
7 El Candil

8 Esmeralda
9 Hostal Pacífico
10 Le Mirage
11 Millahue

bathroom. **D** pp *Alda González*, Gallardo 552, T253334. With bath, **E** pp without, with breakfast, cooking facilities, English, German spoken, good value. *Esmeralda*, Libertad 395, T255649. **F** pp *El Tata*, Gallardo 621, floor space. Very basic, popular, packed in summer. **D** Aníbal Pinto 328, with breakfast, popular, laundry facilities, ten minutes walk from centre. Recommended. Balmaceda 300, with breakfast, clean, friendly. Balmaceda 283, clean, hospitable. Trigal 309, T259923, use of kitchen, clean, with breakfast. **D** pp *Casa Perla*, Trigal 312, T262104. With breakfast, French, English spoken, helpful, friendly, meals, Spanish classes offered off season, recommended. *Casa Patricia*, Trigal 361. Family run, clean, welcoming. *La Familia*, Bilbao 380, T256514. Hot water, very clean, comfortable. *Sra María Oyarzo*, Subida Miramar 1184, T259957. With breakfast, friendly, basic (no heating, hot water next door), clean, good beds. *Res Emita*, Miraflores 1281. With breakfast with homemade bread, clean, friendly, safe. *Vivar 1141*, T255039. With breakfast, hot water. *Baquedano 247*, T252862. Friendly, clean. *Hostal Independencia*, Independencia167, T277949, also Av Angelmo 2196, T257938, opposite Navimag terminal, Hostelling International reductions. **D** pp *Hosp Suizo*, Independencia 231, T/F252640. With breakfast, clean, German, Italian spoken, painting and Spanish classes. *Hostal Rocco*, Pudeto 233,T/F272897, Hostelrocco@hotmail.com Without bath, with breakfast, real coffee, English spoken. **On Allende** No 119, T258638. Clean, friendly. Recommended. *Hosp Montesinos*, No 121, T255353. With breakfast, clean. Recommended. *El Forastero*,

The Lake District

Colo Colo 1350, T263342. With good breakfast, very clean. *Albergue* in school opposite bus station, **F** pp sleeping bag on floor, cold showers, kitchen and laundry facilities, but no security, open 2 January-15 February only.

Cabañas: Lots of *cabañas*, both on the outskirts of the city, eg *El Toqui*, Huasco 213, T255824; *Melipulli*, Libertad 610, T253325, and outside especially in Pelluco, eg *Rucaray*, T252395; *El Rincón de Gabriel*, T251293.

Camping 'Wild' camping possible along the sea front. Several sites west of Puerto Montt: *El Ciervo*, 3 kilometres west, good. *Camping Municipal* at Chinquihue, 10 kilometres west (bus service). Open October-April, fully equipped with tables, seats, barbecue, toilets and showers, small shop, no kerosene. *Camping Anderson*, 11 kilometres west, American run, hot showers, private beach, home-grown fruit, vegetables and milk products. *Camping Los Alamos*, T25667, 13 kilometres west. Nice views, poor services, stray dogs, US$17 per site. *Camping Metri*, 30 kilometres southeast on Caminó Austral, T251235. Fierro bus, US$2 per tent.

Eating *Embassy*, Ancud 106. Very good, pricey. *Club de Yates*, Juan Soler s/n. Excellent,
Look out for local expensive seafood. *Centro Español*, O'Higgins 233. Expensive but very good. *Balzac*,
specialities such as Urmeneta y Quillota. Very good, pricey. *Club Alemán*, Varas 264. Old fashioned, good
curanto and picoroco al food and wine. *Café Real*, Rancagua 137. For *empanadas*, *pichangas*, *congrío frito*, and
vapor, a giant barnacle cheap lunches. *Costa de Reloncaví*, Portales 736. Good, moderate prices. *Café*
whose flesh looks and *Alemana*, Rancagua 117. Real coffee, good. *Rincón Sureño*, Talca 86. Poor meat
tastes like a crab dishes, good fish. *Dino*, Varas 550. Restaurant upstairs, snacks downstairs (try the lemon juice). *Don Pancho*, in old railway station. Good. *Café Amsel*, (in *Hotel Burg*) Pedro Montt y Portales. Superb fish but not cheap, real coffee. *Plato's*, Portales 1014, Galería Comercial España. Cheap, good. Also in the Galería is *El Rinconcito*, a good bar. Cheap food at bus terminal (all credit cards accepted). In **Angelmó**: many small seafood restaurants in the old fishing port, very popular, lunches only, ask for *té blanco* (white wine – they are not legally allowed to serve wine). *Pancho Pub*, Angelmó 2456 (above *Travellers*). Real coffee, vegetarian dishes, English spoken, recommended. *Asturias*, Angelmó 2448. Limited menu. Often recommended. *Restaurant de las Antiqüedades*, Av Angelmo, attractive and unusual décor, real coffee, interesting menu. **In Pelluco** *Pazos*, T252552. Best curanto in Puerto Montt. *Azurro*, T318989. Italian. Several other seafood restaurants. **In Chinquihué** *Kiel*, T255010. Excellent, not cheap. *La Casona*, T255044.

Bakery *La Estrella*, Antonio Varas 984. Self-service, good.

Entertainment *Casa del Arte Diego Rivera*, off Plaza de Armas. Temporary exhibitions, concerts, plays.

Discos Several in Pelluco including *Cocodrilo* and *Black Hole*; also *Star*, on Route 5 north.

Sports Aerial Sports: Felix Oyarzo Grimm, owner of the *Hotel O'Grimm* can advise on possibilities, especially parachuting. **Fishing**: Luis Wellman, at the *Hotel Don Luis* is very knowledgeable about fishing in the area. **Football**: stadium opposite Marina del Sur yacht club. **Gymnasium**: Augusto Trautmann 1320, T254957. **Sailing**: 2 Yacht Clubs in Chinquihué: *Marina del Sur* (MDS), T/F251958. Modern, bar and restaurant, sailing courses, notice board for crew (*tripulante*) notices, MDS Charters office (also Santiago T/F2318238) specializes in cruising the Patagonian channels. Charters US$2,200-8,500 per week depending on size of boat. *Club de Deportes Náuticas*, founded by British and Americans in 1940s, more oriented towards small boat sailing, windsurfing, watersports. **Rafting and Water Sports:** *Alsur*, Antonio Varas 445, T/F287628.

Large modern shopping mall, *Paseo del Mar*, Talca y Antonio Varas. Woollen goods **Shopping** and Mapuche-designed rugs can be bought at roadside stalls in Angelmó and on Diego Portales opposite the bus terminal. Prices are much the same as on Chiloé, but quality is often lower.

Camera repairs and film Torres Color, Rancagua III, for photo developing, efficient.

Supermarkets *Las Brisas* and *Fullfresh* opposite bus terminal. Open 0900-2200 daily.

Bookshops *Libros*, Diego Portales Portales 580. Small selection of English novels, also maps.

Local Car hire: *Hertz*, Antonio Varas 126, T259585, helpful, English spoken. *Automóvil* **Transport** *Club de Chile*, Ensenada 70, T254776, and at airport. Others are *Avis*, Urmeneta, 1037, T253307, and at airport. *Budget*, Gallardo 450, T254888 and at airport. *Dollar* (*Hotel Vicente Pérez Rosales*), Antonio Varas 447. *First*, Antonio Varas 447, T252036; *Formula Uno*, Santa María 620, T254125, highly recommended. *Autovald*, Diego Portales 1330, T256355, cheap rates. *Travicargo*, Urmeneta 856, T257137/256438. *Automotric Angelmó*, Talca 79, cheap and helpful. *Full Famas*, Diego Portales 506, T258060, F259840, and airport, T263750, friendly, helpful, good value, has vehicles that can be taken to Argentina.

Motorcycle repairs: Miguel Schmuch, Urmeneta 985, T/F258877.

Cycle repairs: 3 on Urmeneta, none very well stocked, including *Oxford*, Urmeneta 908, T272960.

Boat hire: Lucinda Cárdenas, Manuel Montt Pasaje 7, Casa 134, Angelmó, for trips around the harbour or to Tenglo island.

Long distance Air: El Tepual Airport, 13 kilometres northwest of town. ETM bus from bus terminal 1½ hours before departure, US$2. ETM also run a minibus service to/from hotels, US$4 pp, T294292. Taxi to Puerto Varas, US$20. To **Santiago** at least 2 daily flights by LanChile, Ladeco and Avant. To **Punta Arenas**, LanChile, Ladeco and Avant (cheaper) daily; in January, February and March you may be told that flights are booked up; however, cancellations may be available from the airport. Avant also flies to **Valdivia** and **Temuco**.

International flights To **Bariloche** and **Neuquén (Argentina)**, TAN, twice a week, 40 minutes. To **Balmaceda**, LanChile and Avant, daily. To **Chaitén**, Aeromet, Monday-Friday 1200, US$40; also Aerosur and Aero Vip. To **Port Stanley** (Falkland Islands/Islas Malvinas), from Santiago via Punta Arenas, LanChile, Saturday, US$280, return same day.

Bus: very crowded terminal on seafront at Diego Portales y Lota, has telephones, restaurants, *casa de cambio* left luggage (US$1.50 per item for 24 hours). To **Puerto Varas** (US$0.50), **Llanquihue**, **Frutillar** (US$1.25) and **Osorno** (US$5) minibuses every few minutes, Varmontt, Expreso Puerto Varas, Thaebus and Full Express. To **Ensenada** and **Petrohué** Buses JM at least 3 a day. To **Ralún**, **Cochamó** and **Puelo**, Fierro, 2 a day. To **Pucón**, US$12, 2 daily in summer only, 6 hours. To **Santiago**, express, US$18-25, *cama* US$45, several companies including Tur Bus, very good, 14 hours, Tas Choapa *Royal Class* US$33. To **Temuco** US$9, to **Valdivia**, US$7; **Concepción**, US$15. For services to **Chiloé**, see page 359. To **Punta Arenas**, Austral, Turibus and Ghisoni, between 1 and 3 times a week, US$53-70 depending on company, (bus goes through Argentina via Bariloche – take US$ cash to pay for meals etc in Argentina), 32-38 hours. Book well in advance in January-February and check if you need a multiple-entry Chilean visa; also book any return journey before setting out.

The Lake District

Buses to Argentina via Osorno and the Puyehue pass Daily services to **Bariloche** on this route via Osorno, US$20, 6-10 hours, are run by Cruz del Sur, Rio de la Plata, Tas Choapa and Bus Norte. Tas Choapa services also run to Mendoza, Buenos Aires, Montevideo and Rio de Janeiro. Out of season, services are reduced. Buy tickets for international buses from the bus terminal, not through an agency. If intending to return by this route, buy an open return ticket as higher fares are charged in Argentina. Book well in advance in January and February. Hitchhiking on this route is difficult and may take as long as 4 days. For the route to Argentina via Lago Todos Los Santos see below.

Motoring: when driving north out of Puerto Montt (or out of Puerto Varas, Frutillar, etc), look for signs to 'Ruta 5'.

Shipping offices in Puerto Montt: *Navimag* (Naviera Magallanes SA), Terminal Transbordadores, Angelmó 2187, T253318, F258540. *Skorpios*, Angelmó 1660 y Miraflores (Castilla 588), T252619, Tx370171 NATUK CL. *Transmarchilay Ltda*, Terminal Transbordadores, Angelmó 2187, T270416/270420, F270415.

Directory **Airline offices** *Avant*, Benavente 431, T278317, F278318, airport 278317. *Don Carlos*, Quillota 127, T253219. *LanChile*, San Martín 200, T253141/253315. *Ladeco*, Benevente 350, T253002. *TAN*, T250071.

Banks ATMs at banks including Banco Santiago, Urmeneta 541. Banco Santander, Antonio Varas 501. Also at Las Brisas supermarket and in the Terminal Transbordadores. For Visa *Corp Banca*, Pedro Montt y Urmeneta. Good rates. Commission charges for TCs vary widely. *Casas de Cambio*. Good rates at *Galería Cristal*, Varas 595, *El Libertador*, Urmeneta 529-A, local 3, and *Turismo Latinoamericano*, Urmeneta 531. *Travellers* travel agent in Angelmó (address below) has exchange facilities. *La Moneda de Oro* at the bus terminal exchanges Latin American currencies (Mon-Sat 0930-1230, 1530-1800). *Afex*, Portales 516. *Turismo Los Lagos*, Varas 595, local 13.

Communications Post Office: Rancagua 120. Open 0830-1830 (Mon-Fri), 0830-1200 (Sat). Telephone Office: Pedro Montt 114 and Chillán 98. Entel, Averas between Talca and Pedro Montt. Internet access: Antonio Varas 629.

Consulates *Argentina*, Cauquenes 94, piso 2, T253996, quick visa service. *Germany*, Antonio Varas y Gallardo, piso 3, Oficina 306. Tues/Wed 0930-1200. *Spain*, Rancagua 113, T252557. *Netherlands*, Chorillos 1582, T253003.

Laundry *Center* Antonio Varas 700. *Lavatodo*, O'Higgins 231; San Martín 232; *Unic*, Chillán 149. *Yessil't*, Edif Caracol, Urmeneta 300. *Nautilus*, Av Angelmó 1564, cheaper, good service. *Narly*, San Martín 187, Local 6, laundry prices generally high (US$7 for 3 kg).

Tour companies & travel agents *Andina del Sud*, very close to central tourist kiosk, Varas 437, T257797. Sells a daily tour at 0830 (not Sun) to Puerto Varas, Parque Nacional V Pérez Rosales, Petrohué, Lago Todos los Santos, Peulla and back (without meals US$27, with meals US$37), and to other local sights, as well as skiing trips to the Osorno volcano (see below for trip to Bariloche). *Eureka Turismo*, Varas 449, T250412, F255146, helpful, German, English spoken. *Travellers*, Av Angelmó 2456, Casilla 854, T262099, F258555, gochile@entelchile.net, close Navimag office. Open Mon-Fri 0900-1330,1500-1830, Sat 0900-1400 for booking for Navimag ferry *Puerto Edén* to Puerto Natales, Osorno volcano trips and other excursions, money exchange, flights, also sells imported camping equipment and runs computerized tourist information service, book swap ('best book swap south of Santiago'), map display, TV, real coffee, English-run, recommended. *Petrel Tours*, San Martín 167, oficina 403, T/F255558. Recommended. *Reloncaví*, Angelmó 2448, T288080, F288081. *Patagonia Verde*, Diego Portales 514. Mountaineering, fishing, trekking, horseriding. Many other agencies. Most offer 1-day excursions to Chiloé (US$20) and to Puerto Varas, Isla Loreley, Laguna Verde, and the Petrohué falls: these tours are much cheaper from bus company kiosks inside the bus terminal, eg Bohle, US$17 to Chiloé, US$11 to the lakes. Some companies eg *Reloncaví*, also offer 2-day excursions along the Camino Austral to Hornopirén, US$76 including food and accommodation.

Tourist offices *Sernatur* office in Gobernación Provincial building on Plaza de Armas, daily in summer 0900-1300, 1500-1900, Mon-Fri in winter 0830-1300, 1400-1800. Ask for information on Chiloé as this is often difficult to obtain on the island. *Sernatur* is in the Intendencia Regional, Av Décima Región 480 (p 3), Casilla 297, T254580/256999, F254580, Tx270008. Also kiosk on Plaza de

On board the Puerto Edén

"When the boat began loading there was a mild stampede, especially for us economy class (or dungeon class) passengers: we didn't want to end up in one of the top bunks, which require elaborate climbing equipment to reach and which give only three inches of headroom. There were two 24-occupant dungeon-class barracks, each equipped with two toilets and one shower, located at the very bottom of the ship, scattered alongside the engine room, the generator, the anchor-chain-dropping room and the rock-concert-amplifier-testing room. It was loud.

What did we do all day? Not much. The ship felt like an airport waiting room. People read, played cards, drank and slept. The scenery was indeed 'breathtakingly beautiful and rugged' but it was too windy and cold to stay outside for long, so we usually settled for glancing out of the ship's tiny windows. At Puerto Edén we were awakened by the release of the anchor which, in dungeon class, sounded as though it had been dropped through the ceiling. We weren't sure whether to wake up or abandon ship. Nearly 200 of us decided to go ashore. We each wore a bright orange life jacket so, naturally, we were easily identifiable to the locals who were eager to do business with us. After a few hours of stocking up on the requisite souvenirs, we went back and steeled ourselves for the rough sea crossing. The waves, relative to the boat's size, were not threatening, but they hit the boat directly on her port side and created an impressive nauseating effect. Some passengers took seasickness pills and wandered down to their rooms to pass out. Others drank wine or beer till this had the same effect.

Perhaps the highlight of the trip was a tug-o-war on the upper cargo deck against the crew. The passengers, who had spent too much time sitting around and too little time loading and unloading cargo ships, were trounced. Team gringo fared better, however, in the ensuing soccer match: adding to the excitement were the obstacles on the 'pitch': huge metal rivets every few metres and a 20 tonne freight elevator.

Doug Lansky Tucson Daily Star.

Armas run by the municipality, open till 1800 on Sat, town maps available, but little information on other places. *Telefónica del Sur* and *Sernatur* operate a phone information service (INTTUR), dial 142 (cost is the same as a local call). Dial 149 for chemist/pharmacy information, 148 for the weather, 143 for the news, etc. The service operates throughout the Tenth Region. *Sernatur* in Puerto Montt has a reciprocal arrangement on information with Bariloche, Argentina. **Conaf**: Ochogavia 458, but cannot supply details of conditions in National Parks. **Automóvil Club de Chile**: Esmeralda 70, T252968. **Parque Pumalin**, Buin 356, T251911/255145.

Sea routes south of Puerto Montt

Puerto Montt is the departure point for several popular voyages along the coast of southern Chile. All sailings are from Angelmó. Shipping offices in Puerto Montt are listed above. All shipping services should be checked carefully in advance as schedules change frequently.

To Puerto Natales

One of the highlights of many journeys to Chile is the 1,460 kilometre voyage on the ferry *Puerto Edén* between Puerto Montt and the southern port of Puerto Natales. The route south is as follows: from Puerto Montt across the Seno Reloncavi and the Golfo de Ancud between the mainland and the large island of Chiloé, then south through the Canal Moraleda and the Canal

See colour map at the end of the book for ferry routes

The Lake District

Errázuriz, which separate the mainland from the outlying islands before sailing west through the Canal Chacabuco to Bahía Anna Pink and across the open sea and the infamous Golfo de Peñas (Gulf of Sorrows) to reach a series of channels, Canal Messier, Angostura Inglesa, Fiordo del Indio and Canal Kirke which provide one of the narrowest routes for large shipping in the world.

The only regular stop on this route is at the fishing village of **Puerto Edén** on Isla Wellington, one hour south of the Angostura Inglesa. This is a fishing village with three shops, with scant provisions, one off-licence, one café, but no hotel or camping facility, nor running water. Population is 180, plus five *carabineros* and the few remaining Alacaluf Indians. It is, though, the drop-off point for exploring Isla Wellington, which is largely untouched, with stunning mountains. If stopping here, take all food; maps (not very accurate) are available in Santiago. The *Puerto Edén* charges US$50 between Isla Wellington and Puerto Natales.

The ferry, *Puerto Edén*, operated by Navimag sails this route once a week from 1 November to 30 April, departing from Puerto Montt on Mondays. The voyage takes four days and three nights; the fare ranges from US$220 each economy (including meals) to US$792 each in various classes of cabin (also including meals); 10 percent discount on international student cards in cabin class only, fares 10-20 percent lower in March-April. Payment by credit card or foreign currency is generally not accepted. Economy class accommodation is basic, in 24-berth dormitories and there is limited additional space for economy class passengers when the weather is bad. Apart from videos, entertainment on board is limited. Economy class and cabin passengers eat the same food but in separate areas (economy class are very cramped). The food is variable (some say it is good, others disagree). This is a ferry which also carries cargo (including cattle and sheep) rather than a cruise liner; it is cheaper to fly and quicker to go by bus via Argentina but the voyage is spectacular. Standards of service and comfort vary, depending on the number of passengers and weather conditions. Take seasickness tablets.

Booking   Economy class can only be booked, with payment, through Navimag offices in Puerto Montt and Puerto Natales. Economy tickets are frequently sold on the day of departure when conditions in the Navimag office can be chaotic. Cabin class can be booked in advance through *Travellers* in Puerto Montt (see **Tour companies**, above), through Navimag offices in Puerto Montt, Puerto Natales and Punta Arenas, or through Cruceros Austalis (Navimag parent company) in Santiago. All of these have their own ticket allocation: once this is used up, they have to contact other offices to request spare tickets. Book well in advance for cabin class departures between mid-December and mid-March especially for the voyage south. Puerto Natales to Puerto Montt is less heavily booked. Note that departures are frequently delayed – or even advanced – by weather conditions.

To Puerto Chacabuco

Both *Navimag* and *Transmarchilay* operate regular sailings between Puerto Montt and Puerto Chacabuco, 80 kilometres west of Coyhaique, 24 hours. Though beautiful, this voyage means that travellers miss out on the attractions of the Camino Austral. The Navimag ferry *M/N Evangelista* sails this route twice a week throughout the year except in January-February when it operates every four days. In January-February the vessel continues once a week from Puerto Chacabuco to visit Laguna San Rafael, 21-24 hour excursion. Fares Puerto Montt-Puerto Chacabuco range from US$125-250 for first class, depending on which cabin and number of occupants, to US$145 for tourist class and

US$40-70 for reclining seats (*butacas*). Return fares on the excursion to Laguna San Rafael from Puerto Montt are much higher, ranging from US$300 to US$1,000 first class return. It is slightly cheaper to sail from Puerto Montt to Laguna San Rafael and then disembark in Puerto Chacabuco. Vehicle charges between Puerto Montt and Puerto Chacabuco: cars US$150, motorcycles US$20, cycles US$35. The Transmarchilay ferry *El Colono* sails twice a week from Puerto Montt to Puerto Chacabuco, once every four days in January-February, also once a week in January-February from Puerto Chacabuco to Laguna San Rafael. Fares are similar to those on *Evangelistas*.

For fares from Puerto Chacabuco to Laguna San Rafael on these services see under Puerto Chacabuco.

These vessels have been described as "floating buses"; apart from those in cabins, passengers sleep in their seats and there is little space for luggage. There is a small canteen; long queues if the boat is full. Food is expensive so take your own.

To Laguna San Rafael

The m/n *Skorpios 1* and *2* of Constantino Kochifas C leave Puerto Montt on Saturday at 1100 for a luxury cruise with stops at Puerto Aguirre, Melinka, Laguna San Rafael, Quitralco, Castro (each ship has a slightly different itinerary) and returns to Puerto Montt on Friday at 0800. The fare varies according to season, type of cabin and number of occupants: a double ranges from US$465 (low) to US$660 (high) on *Skorpios 1* and from US$770 (low) to US$1,100 (high) on *Skorpios 2*, which is the more comfortable of the two. It has been reported that there is little room to sit indoors if it is raining on *Skorpios 1*, but generally service is excellent, the food superb and at the glacier, you chip your ice off the face for your whisky. (After the visit to San Rafael the ships visits Quitralco Fiord where there are thermal pools and boat trips on the fiord.)

Patagonia Connection SA, Fidel Oteíza 1921, Oficina 1006, Providencia, Santiago, T225-6489, F274-8111, operates *Patagonia Express*, a catamaran which runs from Puerto Chacabuco to Laguna San Rafael via Termas de Puyuhuapi, see page 389. Tours lasting 4 to 6 days start from Puerto Montt and include the catamaran service, the hotel at Termas de Puyuhuapi and the day excursion to Laguna San Rafael. High season 20 December-20 March, low season 11 September-19 December and 21 March-21 April. High season fares for a 4-day tour from US$940, all inclusive, highly recommended.

Other routes

The Navimag ferry *Alejandrina* sails to Chaitén (for the trip along the Camino **Chaitén** Austral) Tuesday, Thursday, Saturday in summer, reduced service off season, 10 hour crossing. Fares: passengers US$22, *literas* US$33, cars US$100, cycles US$11. The Transmarchilary ferry *Pincoya* also sails this route on Friday 2200. Fares similar to Navimag.

The m/n *Bohemia* makes six day/five night trips from Puerto Montt to Río **Río Negro** Negro, Isla Llancahué, Baños Cahuelmó and Fiordo Leptepu/Coman, US$545-720 per person depending on season (Antonio Varas 947, T254675, Puerto Montt).

Chiloé

11

Chiloé

The large island of Chiloé and the smaller islands east of it are one of the most distinctive areas of Chile. The islands' culture, strongly influenced by centuries of isolation during the colonial period and by the mixture of early Spanish settlers and Huilliche indians, reflects a history of heavy dependence on the sea. A land of small fishing villages and farms; Chiloé is famous for its wooden churches, some of them dating back to the late colonial period. In February and March most towns and villages celebrate their annual fiestas; traditional foods such as curanto *are served and there are sports events and dancing. With their mild climate, the result of the influence of the sea, and peaceful lifestyle, the islands are a popular destination for travellers and are ideal for a few days' stopover at any time of the year.*

Background

Officially known as Chiloé Grande, the island of Chiloé is 250 kilometres long, 50 kilometres wide and covers 9,613 square kilometres. The Cordillera de la Costa, the coastal mountain range, runs down the western side of the island, though at altitudes below 1,000 metres. South of Castro there is a gap in the range in which there are two lakes, Lago Huillinco and Lago Cucao. Thick forests cover most of the western and southern parts of the island which are sparsely populated. In summer the hillsides are a patchwork quilt of wheat fields and dark green plots of potatoes and the roads are lined with wild

Chiloé

The Jesuits in Chiloé

The Jesuits arrived in Chiloé in 1608 and the first Jesuit residence was established four years later. Although in Chiloé they established few of the missions for which they became famous in other parts of the continent, by the time they were expelled in 1767 there were 79 churches on the island. The key to their influence lay in their use of fiscales, indigenous people freed from the duty to work for the Spanish and trained to teach Christian doctrine and ensure that everyone observed prayers and other religious duties. One fiscal was appointed for every 50 inhabitants. On 17 September each year, two missionaries set sail from Castro in small boats, taking with them statues of saints and other essential supplies. They spent the next eight months sailing round the islands, visiting all the parishes in a set order. In each parish they spent three days, carrying out weddings and baptisms, hearing confessions and reviewing the work of the fiscales.

Most of the old churches for which Chiloé is famous date from after the expulsion of the Jesuits, but some writers claim that their influence can still be seen, for example in the enthusiasm for education in the island which has long boasted one of the lowest illiteracy rates in the world. Many villages, meanwhile still have fiscales who are, by tradition, responsible for keeping the church keys.

---

flowers. Most of the population of 116,000 live on the sheltered eastern side of Chiloé Grande. There are two main towns, Ancud and Castro, and many fishing villages. East of the island are several groups of smaller islands, where the way of life is even more peaceful; the largest of these islands, Quinchao, Lemuy and Mechuque are described below. Good centres for exploring Chiloé are Castro and the smaller town of Chonchi which lies just to the south.

History

The original inhabitants of Chiloé were the Chonos, who were pushed south by the Huilliche invading from the north. The first Spanish sighting was by Francisco de Ulloa in 1553; a Spanish expedition was despatched from the mainland five years later and in 1567 Martín Ruiz de Gamboa took possession of the islands on behalf of Spain. The small Spanish settler population divided the indigenous population and their lands between them. The rising of the Huilliche after 1598 which drove the Spanish out of the mainland south of the Río Biobío left the Spanish community on Chiloé, some 200 settlers in 1600, isolated. During the 17th century Chiloé was served by a single annual ship from Lima, though on occasions even this failed to arrive. In 1600 and 1642 the island was attacked by Dutch pirates. Following a violent earthquake in 1646 the Spanish population asked the Viceroy in Lima for permission to leave, but this was refused. Much of Chiloé's distinctive character derives from the following 200 years of separation from the mainstream of Spanish colonial development.

The islanders were the last supporters of the Spanish Crown in South America. When the Chilean partriot leaders rebelled the last of the Spanish Governors fled to the island and, in despair, offered it to Britain. George Canning, the British Foreign Secretary, turned the offer down. The island finally surrendered to the patriots in 1826.

Chiloé

Curanto

Particularly associated with Puerto Montt and Chiloé, curanto is a very filling fish, meat and seafood stew, which is delicious despite the rather odd combination of ingredients. Though of prehispanic origins, it has developed over generations by adding new ingredients. In its original pre-conquest form a selection of fish was wrapped in leaves and baked over hot stones in a hole.

Could this way of cooking have come from the Pacific islands where pit baking is still practised? With the arrival of the Spanish, the dish was modified to include pork, chicken and white wine. Nowadays it is usually cooked in a large pan and then it is often advertised as pullmay to distinguish it from the pit-baked form.
Jaime Baez

Climate

Chiloé has a maritime climate; temperatures are moderated by the sea.

The west coast, exposed to strong Pacific winds, is wet for most of the year. The sheltered east coast and the offshore islands are drier, though frequently cloudy and are seldom cold even in winter.

Art and architecture

The availability of wood and the lack of metals have left their mark on the architecture of Chiloé. Some of the earliest of the island's churches were built entirely of wood, using wooden pegs instead of nails. These early churches often displayed some German influence as a result of the missionary work of Bavarian Jesuits. Three notable features were the *explanada* or porch which ran the length of the front of the church, the not-quite semi-circular arches and the central position of the tower directly above the door. In the 19th century the original design was often modified. Few of the oldest churches have survived the ravages of fire, earthquakes and the weather, but there are still over 150 churches on the islands mostly built of wood.

The houses (*rucas*) of the indigenous population were thatched and throughout the 19th century thatch continued in widespread use. Two features of local architecture often thought to be traditional are in fact late 19th century in origin. The use of thin tiles (*tejuelas*) made from alerce wood was partly the result of the influence of the German settlers around Puerto Montt. These tiles, which are nailed to the frame and roof in several distinctive patterns, overlap to form an effective protection against the wet climate. *Palafitos* or wooden houses built on stilts over the water, were once popular in all the main ports, but are now mainly found in Castro.

The islands are also famous for their traditional handicrafts, notably woollens and basketware, which can be bought in all the main towns and on some of the smaller islands, as well as in Puerto Montt.

Modern Chiloé

Although the traditional mainstays of the economy, fishing and agriculture, are still important, salmon farming has become an important source of employment. Seaweed is harvested for export to Japan. Tourism provides a seasonal income for a growing number of people, especially in Castro. The relatively high birth rate and the shortage of employment in Chiloé have led to regular emigration. Chilotés have settled throughout Chile, were prominent as shepherds in late 19th century Patagonia and are an important source of labour for the Argentine oil industry.

Chiloé's distinctive history and its maritime traditions are reflected in the strength of its unique folklore, much of which is in the form of traditional tales.

Ferry Chiloé's main transport connections are with Puerto Montt to the north, although a ferry service also connects the port of Quellón in the south of the island with Chaitén and the Camino Austral. The straits of Chacao separate the north of the island from the mainland: frequent vehicle ferry services are operated by several companies across these straits between **Pargua**, on the mainland (55 kilometres southwest of Puerto Montt) and **Chacao**, on the island, 30 minute crossing, cars US$10 one way, foot passengers US$1. For details of ferry services between Quellón and Chaitén see page 373. **Transport**

Bus Frequent bus services, which connect with ferry sailings, operate between Ancud and Castro, the main towns on Chiloé, and Puerto Montt. Buses drive onto the ferries; passengers can get out of the bus. Fares and other details are given under destinations. There are also direct services to/from other cities, including Santiago, Osorno, Valdivia, Temuco and Los Angeles. Transport to the island is dominated by Cruz del Sur, who also own Trans Chiloé and Regional Sur and, in Castro, operate from their own terminal. Cruz del Sur also operate their own ferries, which give priority over cars to Cruz del Sur. The only independent bus operator to the island is Queilén Bus.

Pargua *Hotel La Ruta. Res El Porvenir.* **Chacao** E pp *Hosp Angelino.* E pp *Pensión Chiloé.* **Sleeping**

Ancud

Situated on the northern coast of Chiloé 34 kilometres west of the Straits of Chacao, Ancud lies at the mouth of a great bay, the Golfo de Quetalmahue. Less important than Castro, it is a good centre for visiting the villages of northern Chiloé.

Population: 23,148
Phone code: 065
Colour map 4, grid C1

Sights

Founded in 1767 to guard the shipping route around Cape Horn, the city was defended by two fortresses, the Fuerte San Antonio and, on the far side of the bay, Fuerte Ahui. The port is dominated by the **Fuerte San Antonio**, built in 1770, the site of the Spanish surrender of Chiloé to Chilean troops in 1826. Close to it are the ruins of the **Polvorín del Fuerte** (a couple of cannon and a few walls). One kilometre north of the fort is a secluded beach, **Arena Gruesa**. Two kilometres east is a **Mirador** offering good views of the island and across to the mainland. The small fishing harbour at Cochrane y Prat, is worth a visit, especially in the evening when the catch is landed.

Near the Plaza de Armas is the **Museo Regional**, with an interesting collection on the early history of Chiloé as well as replicas of a traditional Chiloté thatched wooden house and of the small sailing ship *Ancud* (see box on page 360). ■ *US$1. Summer daily 1100-1900, winter Tuesday-Friday 0900-1300, 1430-1830, Saturday 1000-1330, 1430-1800.* **Museums**

Chiloé

The voyage of the Ancud

The opening of regular steamship services through the Straits of Magellan in the early 1840s and the seizure of the Falkland Islands/Ilas Malvinas by the British in 1833 revived European interest in the route to the Pacific. Alarmed at reports of a French expedition to claim the Straits, President Bulnes ordered the dispatch of the Ancud. The vessel, which sailed from Ancud on 23 May 1843, was captained by John Williams of Bristol, who was accompanied by the naturalist Bernardo Philippi, eleven sailors, eight soldiers, two women, three dogs, two pigs and a pregnant goat. After a three month voyage the party landed at Puerto Hambre, one day before the arrival of a French warship. Captain Williams's voyage was later commemorated by the naming of the Chilean naval base on Isla Navarino Puerto Williams in his honour.

Excursions

Faro Corona is the lighthouse on Punta Corona, 34 kilometres west along the beach, which, though unsuitable for swimming, offers good views with interesting birdlife. Bus from Ancud 0645; return departure 1730. Take food and drink.

Pumillahue is 27 kilometres southwest, on the Pacific coast. About three kilometres from Pumillahue there is a penguin colony situated on an island: hire a fishing boat to see it, US$6 per person. There are buses from Ancud Monday-Saturday 0645, Monday-Friday 1200, Saturday 1400, Monday-Friday 1600.

Caulín is east of Ancud along the north coast where there are good beaches; fresh oysters at *Hotel Lyon*. The road goes along the beach and is only passable at low tide.

Essentials

Sleeping
■ on map
Price codes:
see inside front cover

A1 *Hostería Ancud*, San Antonio 30, T/F622340, 622350. Overlooking bay, attractive, very comfortable, friendly and helpful, restaurant. **A3** *Galeón Azul*, Libertad 751, T622567, F622543. **A3** *Lydia*, Pudeto y Chacabuco, T622990, F622879. With bath, **B** without bath. Poor beds, small rooms, overpriced. **A3** *Lacuy*, Pudeto 219 near Plaza de Armas, T/F623019. With breakfast, restaurant. Recommended. **A3** *Montserrat*, Baquedano 417, T/F622957. With breakfast, clean, good views, small rooms. **A3** *Cabañas Las Golondrinas*, end of Baquedano at Arena Gruesa, T622823. Superb views, with kitchenette, overpriced.

B *Hostería Ahui*, Costanera 906, T622415. With breakfast, modern, clean, good views, restaurant. **B** *Polo Sur*, Costanera 630, T622200. With bath, good seafood restaurant, not cheap, avoid rooms overlooking disco next door. **B** *Res Weschler*, Cochrane 480, T622318. With bath, **D** without. Clean, view of bay. **B** *Res Germania*, Pudeto 357, T/F622214. With bath, **C** without, parking, comfortable, clean. **C** *Madryn*, Bellavista 491, T622128. With bath, also meals, clean. **C** *Lluhay*, Cochrane 458, T/F622656, meals served, recommended.

D *Caleta Ancud*, Bellavista 449. Good breakfast, good restaurant. **D** *Hosp Alto Bellavista*, Bellavista 449, T622384. With sleeping bag on floor much cheaper. **D** *Hosp Capri*, Ramírez 325. Good breakfast. **D** *Hosp Alinar*, Ramírez 348. Clean, hospitable. **D** *Hosp Santander*, Sgto Aldea 69. With bath, **E** without, clean. Recommended. **D** *Res MaCarolina*, La Torre 558, T622458. With breakfast. **E** pp Errázuriz 442. With breakfast, cold water. **E** pp Elena Bergmann, Aníbal Pinto 382. Clean, friendly, use of kitchen, parking. **F** pp Aníbal Pinto 1340, with breakfast. Several others on same street. **E** pp Pudeto 331, T622535. Without bath, old fashioned. Recommended. **E** pp Lautaro 947,

T2980. Clean, friendly. **E** pp Sra Lucía, San Martín 705. **E** pp *San Bernardo*, Errázuriz 395, T622657. With bath and breakfast, clean. **E** pp *Hosp San José*, Pudeto 619. With breakfast, large rooms, great views, good beds. **E** pp *Hosp Blanca Vargas*, Blanco Encalada 579, T624343, with breakfast. **E** pp *Hosp Miranda*, Mocopulli y Errázuriz, with breakfast comfortable. In summer the school on Calle Chacabuco is used as an *albergue*.

Camping At Arena Gruesa beach, at north end of Baguedano are: *Arena Gruesa*, F623428. US$15 per site, and *Chiloé*, T622961, F2363647. US$15 per site. *Playa Gaviotas*, 5 kilometres north, T09-6538096, also has *cabañas*. US$20 per site. *Playa Larga Huicha*, 9 kilometres north. **E** per site, hot water, electricity.

Good lunches at *Hotel Polo Sur*. **On Pudeto**: *Carmen*, No 159. Chilean cooking, *pasteles*. *Coral*, No 346. Good, not cheap. *Jardín*, No 263. Good local food, not cheap. *Lydia*, No 254. Chilean and international. *Macaval*, Chacabuco 691. *El Trauco*, Blanco y Prat. Seafood excellent. Highly recommended. *La Pincoya*, on Prat next to harbour. Seafood. *El Cangrejo*, Dieciocho 155. Seafood highly recommended. *Hamburguería*, Av Prat. Much better than name suggests, good seafood. *Mar y Velas*, Serrano 2. Beautiful views, good food. *El Timon*, Yungay y Allende, small, cheap, good value.

Eating
● on map
Seafood restaurants in market area

Bus Long distance terminal on eastern outskirts at Av Prat y Marcos Vera, reached by bus 1 or Pudeto *colectivos*. Local buses leave from the Terminal Rural at Pedro Montt

Transport

Ancud

Sleeping
1 Ahui
2 Alto Bellavista
3 Cabañas Las Golondrinas
4 Galeón Azul
5 Germania
6 Hospedaje Miranda
7 Hostería Ancud
8 Lacuy
9 Lydia
10 Madryn
11 Montenegro
12 Montserrat
13 Polo Sur
14 Santander
15 Wechsler

● **Eating**
1 Carmen
2 Coral
3 El Cangrejo
4 La Pincoyá

Chiloé

☞ *El Trauco and La Fiura*

Visitors to Chiloé should beware of these two famous figures from local mythology. El Trauco is held to be responsible for unwanted pregnancies, especiailly among young girls. A small, ugly and smelly man who wears a small round hat made of bamboo and clothing of the same material, he usually carries a small stone hatchet, with which he is reputed to be able to fell any tree in three strokes. He spends much of his time haunting the forests, sitting on fallen tree trunks and weaving his clothes.

El Trauco specializes in seducing virgins. He uses his magic powers to give them erotic dreams while they are asleep; they wake and go to look for him in the forest and are seduced by his eyes. Despite his ugliness, he is irresistible and the girl throws herself on the ground. You should

be careful not to disturb the Trauco while he is thus occupied: those who do so are immediately deformed beyond recognition and sentenced to die within twelve months.

La Fiura, a small ugly woman, lives in the forests near Hualdes where she is reputed to bathe in the streams and waterfalls combing her hair with a crystal comb. Known as the indefatigable lover of bachelors, she attracts her victims by wearing colourful clothes. As the man approaches he is put to sleep by her foul breath. After La Fiura has satisfied her desire, the unfortunate man goes insane. Refusing her advances is no escape either: those who do so, whether animals or men, are so deformed that they become unrecognizable.

Brian Grady.

538. To **Santiago**, Cruz del Sur, salón cama, US$36, 24 hours. To **Castro**, frequent, 1½ hours, Cruz del Sur/Regional Sur US$2.50, Queilén Bus US$2. To **Chonchi** US$3. To **Quellón**, Cruz del Sur/Regional Sur, 11 daily, US$5. To **Puerto Montt**, 2 hours, frequent services by Cruz del Sur US$5, Regional Sur US$4.50, and Queilén Bus US$4. To **Quemchi** via the coast 2 hours, US$1.50. To **Achao** (from Terminal Rural) 2 a day, but it is quicker to take any bus south to Mocopulli and then take a *colectivo*, US$1.50.

Directory **Banks** ATM at Banco BCI. *Casa de Cambio* on Ramírez, 1 block up the hill from the Plaza de Armas. **Communications** **Post Office:** on corner of Plaza de Armas at Pudeto y Blanco Encalada. **Telephone:** Plaza de Armas. Open Mon-Sat 0700-2200. **Tour companies & travel agents** *Turismo Ancud*, Pudeto 219, Galería Yurie, T2235, Tx297700, ANCD CL. *Paralelo 42*, Prat 28, T2458, F2656. Recommended for tours to the Río Chepu area, including 2-day kayak trips, guide Carlos Oyarzun (also at *Res MaCarolina*). Recommended. **Tourist offices** *Sernatur*, Libertad 665, T622665, 622800. Open Mon-Fri 0900-1300, 1430-1800.

Longer excursions

Chepu, on the coast southwest of Ancud and reached along a poor *ripio* road, is famed for its river and sea fishing. It is a base for exploring the drowned forest and river environment of the Río Chepu and its tributaries, inhabited by a wide range of birds. It is also the entrance to the north part of the Parque Nacional Chiloé, see Cucao, page 370. At **Río Anguay** (also known as **Puerto Anguay**) there is a camping site and *refugio*. From here it is a one and a half hour walk to Playa Aulén which has superb forested dunes and an extinct volcano.

Activities Boat trips can be organized in Río Anguay to Laguna Coluco, one hour up the Río Butalcura (a tributary of the Río Chepu). Two day trips, navigating the ríos Grande, Carihueco and Butalcura, usually start further inland and finish at Río Anguay. These can be arranged in Ancud. This area offers great opportunities for horse-riding with long beaches for galloping. Try Sr Zuñipe or Sr Uroa (recommended), US$5 per hour (ask at the *refugio* in Río Anguay).

Access is from the Pan-American Highway, 26 kilometres south of Ancud by a 24 kilo- **Transport**
metres dirt road. Alternatively there is a two day coastal walk from Ancud: you can take the daily bus to Pumillahue (0645, return 1330) or hitch. The route is difficult to follow so take food for 3 days and wear light-coloured clothes in summer to protect against *tavanos*. There is no public transport.

Ancud to Castro

There are two alternative routes: direct along the Pan-American Highway, cross-ing rolling hills, forest and agricultural land, or via the east coast along unpaved roads passing through small farming and fishing communities and offering good views of rural life in Chiloé.

The two main towns along the coastal route, Quemchi and Dalcahue, can also be reached by roads branching off the Pan-American Highway.

Quemchi

Fifty six kilometres south of Ancud via the coastal road (68 kilometres south   *Population: 2,000*
via the Pan-American Highway), Quemchi is a quiet town with long beaches.   *Colour map 4, grid C1*
Miniature boats are made in the village. Four kilometres from Quemchi is Isla Aucar, once linked by bridge (now ruined) where there is a church and where black necked swans can be seen.

F pp *Hosp El Embrujo*, Pedro Montt 431, T651262. **F** pp *Hosp La Tranquera*, Yungay   **Sleeping**
40, T651250. Without bath, basic.

Dalcahue

Seventy four kilometres south of Ancud via the Pan-American Highway,   *Population: 3,000*
Dalcahue is more easily reached from Castro, 30 kilometres further south. It is   *Colour map 4, grid C1*
one of the main ports for boats to the offshore islands, including Quinchao and Mechuque (see below). The wooden church on the main square dates from the 19th century. The market is on Sunday, from 0700 to 1300. It has good quality goods, but bargaining ispractically impossible. There is a tourist kiosk in sea-son. **Tenaún**, 40 kilometres east, is an interesting fishing village with a church dating from 1837.

D-E *La Feria*, Rodríguez 17, T641293. Without bath, basic. **D-E** *Res Playa*, Rodríguez 9.   **Sleeping &**
Basic. **E** *Hosp Puteman*, Freire 305, T330. Clean, basic. **E** *Res San Martín*, San Martín 1,   **eating**
T641207. Basic, clean, also meals. **E** *Hosp Mary*, Tte Merino 10, T641260, also sells handicrafts.
    Restaurant La Dalca, Freire 502. Good food and service. Recommended.

Sea kayaking is offered by Altue Active Travel from its sea kayaking centre, 3 kilo-   **Sports**
metres south of Dalcahue. Details of Altue under Santiago.

Buses to Castro, hourly, 40 minutes, US$1. Also *colectivos* to Castro and to Achao,   **Transport**
US$1.50.

Chiloé

Quinchao

The island of Quinchao is a short ferry journey from Dalcahue. Its main settlement is **Achao**, 25 kilometres southeast of Dalcahue, a quiet, pretty fishing village and market town serving the smaller islands offshore. The town owes its origins to a Jesuit mission on the site; its wooden church, built in 1730 is the oldest surviving church in Chiloé. Saved by a change of wind from a fire which destroyed much of the town in 1784, it is a fine example of Chiloté Jesuit architecture. The original construction was without use of nails. There is a small museum, US$1. There is another fine church in the small village of Quincha, nine kilometres further south.

Sleeping & eating **D** pp *Hosp Achao*, Serrano 061, T661373. Without bath, good, clean. **D** pp *Hostería La Nave*, Prat y Aldea, T/F661219. With bath. **E** pp without bath, with breakfast, restaurant with fine views over bay. **D** *Plaza*, Plaza de Armas, T661283. With bath and breakfast, clean, good. **D-E** *Hosp Chilhue*, Zañartu 021. Without bath, with breakfast, clean. **E** pp *Hosp Sao Paulo*, Serrano 52. Basic, poor beds, hot water.

For eating, try *Arrayan*, Zañartu 19. *Restaurant Central*, Delicias. Simple, cheap, good. Good food at the *Hostería La Nave*.

Transport **Bus** Arriagada buses from Ancud, 5 daily. For bus services from Castro see page 367. **Ferry** From Dalcahue, frequent, free for pedestrians and cyclists.

Directory **Tourist offices** Serrano y Progreso (Dec-Mar only).

Mechuque and the Chauques Islands

The Chauques are a group of 16 islands, interconnected by sandbars which are crossable at low tide. The largest island Mechuque, east of Dalcahue, has one village and offers splendid walking country.

Sleeping Accommodation with the schoolteacher's son or with Sra Dina del Carmen Paillacar, **E**, good meals. Recommended.

Transport **Boat** From Tenaún, departing Wednesday 1730, returning Thursday, 2½ hours, US$2.50 one way.

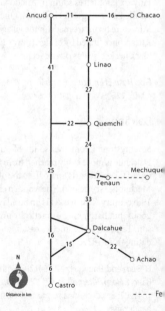

Ancud to Castro

Ancud —11— —16— Chacao
26
Linao 41
27
Quemchi —22—
24
Mechuque 25
—7— Tenaun
33
Dalcahue 16
15 22
Achao
N
6
Castro
Distance in km
---- Fe

Castro

The capital of Chiloé, Castro lies 88 kilometres south of Ancud on a fiord on the east coast. The centre is situated on a promontory, from which there is a steep drop to the port. Castro is the major tourist centre of the island; its central location and good communications make it a good base for excursions to Dalcahue and the offshore islands and to Chonchi and the Parque Nacional Chiloé.

Population: 20,000
Phone code: 065
Colour map 4, grid C1

Sights

On the Plaza de Armas is the large **Cathedral**, strikingly decorated in lilac and orange, with a splendid wood panelled interior, built by the Italian architect, Eduardo Provosoli and dating from 1906. South of the Plaza on the waterfront is the **Feria Artesanal**, where local woollen articles such as hats, sweaters, gloves can be found, but note that many of the articles sold are imported from elsewhere in South America. Nearby are several *palafito* restaurants, built on stilts above the water. More *palafitos* can be seen on the northern side of town and by the bridge over the Río Gamboa. There are good views of the city from **Mirador La Virgen** on Millantuy hill above the cemetery.

Museo Regional on Esmeralda, one block south of the Plaza de Armas, contains history, folklore, handicrafts and mythology of Chiloé and photos of the effects of the 1960 earthquake. ■ *Summer Monday-Saturday 0930-2000, Sunday 1030-1300; winter Monday-Saturday 0930-1300, 1500-1830, Sunday 1030-1300.*

Museums

Museo de Arte Moderno is in the Parque Municipal, about three kilometres northwest of the centre. It is reached by following Calle Galvarino Riveros up the hill west of town, from where there are fine views. ■ *T632787, F635454. 1000-2000.*

Excursions

There is a pleasant walk through woods and fields to **Puntilla Ten Ten** and the Peninsula opposite Castro. It is a two hour round trip; turn off the Pan-American Highway, two kilometres north of town. **Nercón**, four kilometres south, has a fine wooden church, which was restored in 1996.

Essentials

A1 *Hostería Castro*, Chacabuco 202, T632301, F635668. With breakfast, good restaurant, wonderful views. **A1** *Unicornio Azul*, Pedro Montt 228, T632359, F632808. Good views over bay, comfortable, restaurant, English spoken. **A2** *Gran Alerce*, O'Higgins 808, T632267. Heating, helpful, breakfast, also has *cabañas* and restaurant 4 kilometres south of Castro. **A3** *Motel Auquilda*, Km 2 north on the Pan-American Highway, T632458.

B *Cabañas Pleno Centro*, Los Carrera 346, T635092, sleeps 2, also larger, with kitchen. **B** *Casita Española*, Los Carrera 359, T635186. Heating, TV, parking. Recommended. **B** *Chilhue*, Blanco Encalada 278, T632956. With bath, good. **B** *Casa Kolping*, Chacabuco 217, T/F633273. **C** *Costa Azul*, Lillo 67, T632440. With bath, **D** without. Friendly. **C** *Casa Blanca*, Los Carrera 308, T/F632726. With breakfast, without bath, clean, modern, warm, also *cabañas*, sleeps 5.

Sleeping
■ *on map, page 366*
Price codes:
see inside front cover

Chiloé

South of Castro on the road to Chonchi A2 *Cabañas Centro Turístico Nercón*, Km 5, T632985, with bath, hot water, heating, restaurant, tennis court. **A3** *Cabañas Trayen*, Km 5, T633633. **B** off season, lovely views. **A3** *Posada Alemana*, Km 5, noisy. **B** *Cabañas Llicaldad*, Km 6, T635080 (or Esmeralda 269, Castro), also camping.

Cheaper accommodation on San Martín C *Hostal Quelqún*, No 581, T632396. With bath, **E** pp without, heating, helpful. **D** *Res Mirasol*, No 815. Basic, friendly, noisy. **E** pp *Hosp Chiloé*, No 739. Breakfast, clean. Recommended. **E** pp *Hosp Guillermo*, No 700. Clean, cheap. **E** *Pensión Victoria*, No 747. Small rooms, clean, pretty. **E** pp *Res Capullito*, No 709. Clean, friendly, quiet. **F** pp No 879. With big breakfast, central, clean. Highly recommended. **F** pp Lidia Low, No 890. With good breakfast, warm showers, use of kitchen.

Other budget accommodation D *Hilton*, Ramírez 385. Good value, friendly, restaurant. **D** *Hosp Sotomayor*, Sotomayor 452, T632464. With breakfast, quiet, small beds. **D** Los Carrera 658. No sign, with breakfast, clean, friendly. Recommended. **D** *Res El Gringo*, Lillo 51. Without bath, good views, overpriced. **E** pp Chacabuco 449. Good beds, clean, quiet, friendly, water only warm. **E** pp Eyzaguirre 469. Comfortable. Recommended. **E** pp Freire 758. Breakfast, clean, good value. **E** pp *Hosp* of Jessie Toro,

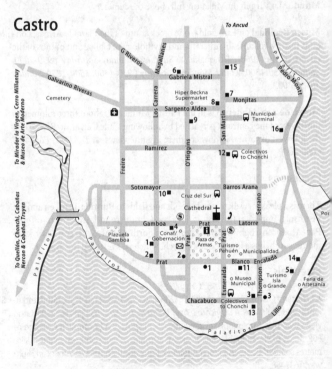

Castro

To Ancud

To Quellón, Chonchi, Cabañas Nercón & Cabañas Trayen

To Mirador la Virgen, Cerro Millantuy & Museo de Arte Moderno

Cemetery

Galvarino Riveras

G Riveras

Magallanes

Los Carrera

Gabriela Mistral

Hiper Beckna Supermarket

Sargento Aldea

San Martín

Monjitas

Municipal Terminal

Ramírez

O'Higgins

Freire

Colectivos to Chonchi

Sotomayor

Barros Arana

Cruz del Sur

Serrano

Cathedral

Gamboa

Plazuela Gamboa

Conaf/ Gobernación

Prat

Latorre

Plaza de Armas

Turismo Pehuén

Municipalidad

Prat

Blanco

Encalada

Museo Municipal

Turismo Isla Grande

Feria de Artesanía

Esmeralda

Chacabuco

Colectivos to Chonchi

Thompson

Lillo

Palafitos

Palafitos

Palafitos

Por

Pedro Montt

N

Not to scale

■ Sleeping		
1 Cabañas Pleno Centro	8 Hospedaje Guillermo	15 Residencial Mirasol
2 Casa Blanca	9 Hospedaje Llapui	16 Unicornio Azul
3 Casa Kolping	10 Hospedaje	
4 Casita Española	Sotomayor	● Eating
5 Costa Azul	11 Hostal Chilhue	1 Del Mirador
6 Gran Alerce	12 Hostal Quelcun	2 La Brújula del Cuerpo
7 Hospedaje Chiloé	13 Hostería Castro	3 Sacho
	14 Residencial El Gringo	

Chiloé

Las Delicias 287. With good breakfast, helpful, clean, spacious, good bathrooms, also *cabañas*. Recommended. **E** pp *Hosp El Mirador*, Barros Arana 127, T633795. Good breakfast, kitchen facilities, good views, very clean. **E** *Hosp Llapui*, O'Higgins 657. Run down, with breakfast. **E** pp *Hosp Tonque*, Pasaje Díaz 170, T632773. Without breakfast, clean, hot water. **E** pp Los Carrera 560, T632472. Clean, hot water. **E** pp María Zuñiga, Barros Arana 140, T635026. With breakfast, clean, comfortable, cooking facilities, friendly, secure. Recommended. **E** pp O'Higgins 415, Dpto 41. Quiet, very clean, hot water. **E** pp O'Higgins 765. Clean, friendly. **E** pp *Res La Casona*, Serrano 488, above TV shop. With breakfast. Recommended. **E** pp *Hosp Bellavista*, Barros Arana 151, clean, good views. **E** pp Los Carrera 785, T632989, with good breakfast. **E** Serrano 407. Breakfast, friendly, warm water. **F** pp *Hosp Polo Sur*, Barros Arana 169, T635212. Cooking facilities, wonderful views, noisy. Basic accommodation December-February in the Gimnasio Fisical, Freire 610, T632766. **F** with breakfast, clean.

Camping *Pudú*, 10 kilometres north on the Pan-American Highway, T/F632476. Also *cabañas*, hot showers, sites with light, water, children's games. Several sites along road south towards Chonchi including: *Montpellier*, Km 2; *Santa Elba*, Km 4; *El Chiloté*, Km 4.5, US$15 per site, also *cabañas*; *Llicaldad*, Km 6, T638188/635080, US$16 per site.

Palafito restaurants near the Feria Artesanía on the waterfont offer good food and good value, including Rapu Nui, *Brisas del Mar* and *La Amistad*. *Gipsy*, O'Higgins 548. Chinese. *Del Mirador*, on Plaza. Meat and seafood specialities. *Sacho*, Thompson 213. Good sea views. *Don Camilo*, Ramírez 566. Good food, not expensive. Recommended. *Stop Inn Café*, Prat y Chacabuco. Good coffee. *Chilo's*, San Martín 459. Good lunches. *El Curanto*, Lillo 67. Seafood including *curanto*. Recommended. In the market, try *milcaos*, fried potato cakes with meat stuffing. *La Brújula del Cuerpo*, Plaza de Armas. Good coffee, snacks.

Eating
● *on map*
Breakfast before 0900 is difficult

Hiper Beckna supermarket, Sargento Aldea y O'Higgins. See above for market. Cema-Chile outlet on Esmeralda, next to Museo Regional. **Bookshops** *El Tren Libros*, Thompson 229, and *Annay Libros*, Serrano 357, both sell books in Spanish on Chiloé, often cheaper than Santiago bookshops. Also *Libros Chiloé*, Blanco Encalada 204. Cassettes of typical Chiloté music are widely available.

Shopping

Bus There are 2 terminals. Cruz del Sur services depart from Cruz del Sur terminal (T632389) on San Martín behind the Cathedral. Other services leave from the Municipal Terminal, San Martín, 600 block (2 blocks further north). Frequent services to **Ancud** (1½ hours) and **Puerto Montt** (3½ hours) by Cruz del Sur, Trans Chiloé and Queilén Bus. Cruz del Sur also run to **Osorno**, **Valdivia**, **Temuco**, **Concepción** and **Santiago**. Bus Norte to **Ancud**, **Puerto Montt**, **Osorno** and **Santiago** daily; to **Punta Arenas**, Queilén Bus, Monday, 36 hours, US$60.

Transport

Chiloé

Frequent services to **Chonchi**, choose between buses (Cruz del Sur, Queilén Bus and others), minibuses and *colectivos* (from Ramirez y San Martín and Esmeralda y Chacabuco). Arroyo and Ocean Bus both run to **Cucao** for the **Parque Nacional Chiloé**, 1 a day off season, more services in summer, US$2. To **Dalcahue** frequent services by Gallardo and Arriagada, also *colectivos* from San Martín 815. To **Tenaún**, daily 1200. To Achao (US$2) on the island of Quinchao via **Dalcahue** and **Curaco de Vélez** (US$1.50), Arriagada, 4 daily, 3 on Sunday, last return from Achao 1730. To **Puqueldón** on the island of Lemuy, Gallardo, Monday-Saturday, 4 a day, US$2; to **Quellón**, Cruz del Sur/Trans Chiloé, frequent (US$2); to **Queilén**, Queilén Bus, 4 a day; to **Quemchi**, 1 a day, Queilén Bus, 1½ hours, US$2.50.

Directory **Banks** *Banco de Chile*, Plaza de Armas. ATM. Accepts TCs (at a poor rate). *BCI*, Plaza de Armas. Mastercard and Visa ATM. Better rates from Julio Barrientos, Chacabuco 286. Cash and TCs. **Communications** Phone Office: Latorre 289. *Entel* O'Higgins between Sotomayor and Gamboa. **Post Office:** on west side of Plaza de Armas. **Hospitals & medical services** Doctor: *Muñoz de Las Carreras*, near police station. Surgery 1700-2000 on weekdays. Recommended. **Laundry** *Lavandería Adolfo*, Blanco Encalada 96. Quick, reasonably priced. *Clean Centre*, Serrano 440. **Tourist offices** Kiosk run by local hotels and agencies, on Plaza de Armas opposite Cathedral. *Conaf* in Gamboa behind the Gobernación building. **Tour companies and travel agents** *Turismo Pehuén*, Blanco Encalada y Esmeralda, LanChile/Ladeco agents. Horseriding excursions. *Turismo Queilén*, Gamboa 502, T632776. Good tours to Chonchi and Chiloé National Park. Recommended. *LanChile* agency, Thompson 245. *Ladeco* agency on Serrano, opposite *Hostería Castro*. *Turismo Isla Grande*, Thompson 241, Transmarchilay and Navimag agency. Local guide Sergio Márquez, Felipe Moniel 565, T632617, very knowledgeable, has transport. **Tour prices:** to Parque Nacional Chiloé US$25, to Mechuque US$37.

Castro to Quellón

The Pan-American Highway continues south to Quellón, the southernmost port in Chiloé. There are paved side roads to Chonchi and unpaved ones to Cucao and Parque Nacional Chiloé. From Chonchi a road runs south to Queilén. This road, now being paved, winds across forested hills, and is probably the most attractive on the island especially in autumn.

Chonchi

Population: 4,000
Phone code: 065
Colour map 4, grid C1

A picturesque fishing village 23 kilometres south of Castro, Chonchi is a good base for exploring the island. Known as the *Ciudad de los Tres Pisos*, or 'the city built on three levels', it was, until the opening of the Panama Canal, a stopping point for sailing ships. In the years which followed the demand for cypress made it the cypress capital of Chile: big fortunes were made and the grand timber mansions in the town date from this period. In the 1950s the town boomed as a free port, but in the 1970s it lost that status to Punta Arenas. Its harbour is now the supply point for the salmon farms almost as far south as Coyhaique.

On the plaza is the church, built in neo-classical style in 1880 on the site of the first church which was erected in 1745.

From the plaza Calle Centenario, with several attractive but sadly neglected wooden mansions, drops steeply to the harbour. Fishing boats bring in the early morning catch which is carried straight into the nearby market. There is another 18th century church at Vilopulli, five kilometres north.

Museums **Museo de las Tradiciones Chonchina**, Centenario 116, houses artefacts donated by local families reflecting life in the early 20th century. ■ *Monday-Saturday 1000-1300, 1500-1900, Sunday 1500-1700.*

Sleeping **A3** *Posada Antiguo Chalet*, Gabriela Mistral, T671221. **B** in winter, charming, beautiful location, very good. **B** *Cabañas Amankay*, Centenario 421, T671367. Homely, kitchen facilities. Recommended. **D** *Esmeralda by the Sea*, on waterfront 100 metres south of the market,

Castro to Quellón

Distance in km

Castro
20
Cucao
34
Chonchi
Ichmac
3
Aldachildo
Puqueldón
9
5
16
Detif
46
75
Queilén
Quellón
···· Ferry

Chiloé

The legend of the potato

A chief on Chiloé, a place populated by seagulls, wanted to make love like the gods.

When pairs of gods embraced, the earth shook and tidal waves were set moving. That much was known, but no one had seen them.

Anxious to surprise them, the chief swam out to the forbidden isle. All he got to see was a giant lizard, with its mouth wide open and full of foam and an outsized tongue that gave off fire at the tip.

The gods buried the indiscreet chief in the ground and condemned him to be eaten by the others. As punishment for his curiosity, they covered his body with blind eyes.

Oreste Plath, Geografía Del Mito Y La Leyenda Chilena, *Santiago, 1973, quoted in Eduardo Galeano,* Genesis, *Methuen, 1986.*

T/F671328, gredycel@entelchile.net (Casilla 79). With breakfast, attractive, welcoming, English spoken, cheap meals served, good beds, boat trips offered, information. Highly recommended. **D** *Hosp Chonchi*, O'Higgins 379, T671288. Full board available, good value. Recommended. **D** *Hosp Mirador*, Alvarez 198. With breakfast, friendly, clean. Recommended. **D** *Huildin*, Centenario 102, T671388. Without bath, old fashioned, good beds, also *cabañas* **A3**, garden with superb views, parking. **E** *Res Turismo*, Andrade 299, T257. Without bath, with breakfast. **E** Baker at Andrade 184. Clean, friendly. **E** Aguirre Cerda 160. There are other *hospedajes* on Irarrazával, eg Nos 181, 189.

Camping *Los Manzanos*, Aguirre Cerda y Juan Guillermo, T671263. US$12 per site.

La Parada, Centenario 133. Very friendly, good selection of wines, erratic opening hours. Recommended. *El Alerce*, Aguirre Cerda 106. Excellent value. *El Trébol*, Irarrazával 187. Good views over harbour. *La Quila*, Andrade 183. Popular with locals. **Eating**

Handicrafts from *Opdech* (Oficina Promotora del Desarrollo Chilote), on the waterfront, and from the *parroquia*, next to the church (open October-March only). **Shopping**

Bus Buses and taxis to Castro, frequent, US$0.75, from main plaza. To Puerto Montt US$7. Services to Quellón and Queilén from Castro and Puerto Montt and from Castro to Cucao also call here. **Transport**

Boat To Chaitén, via the outer islands, 8 hours (including one hour stopover on one of the islands), US$15 low season (October-December; March-May), US$20 high season (January-February), bicycles US$10; departures 0800, Tuesday, Wednesday, Friday high season, weather permitting; tickets from *Hospedaje Esmeralda by the Sea*.

Banks Nicolás Alvarez, Centenario 429. Cash only. **Tourist offices** Kiosk on the main plaza in summer. **Directory**

Lemuy

This island, covering 97 square kilometres, lies offshore opposite Chonchi and offers many good walks along quiet unpaved roads through undulating pastures and woodland. From the ferry crossing a road runs east across the island to **Puqueldón**, the main settlement. At Km 3 there is a fine 19th century wooden church at Ichuac. There are other also old churches at Aldachildo, nine kilometres east of Puqueldón, and at Detif, 16 kilometres south of Puqueldón in the extreme south of the island.

Population: 4,200
Colour map 4, grid C1

When Cucao had everything

'Long ago', Don Antonio began, 'Cucao had everything - cows, horses, sheep, goats, everything - and the rest of Chiloé had nothing. One day a sheep was born with three horns, and its fame spread. A stranger came to see the sheep and stayed the night. In the morning the people woke to find all their animals gone. They followed the tracks and came to a river. There was an old man sitting on the bank.

"Have you seen the thief who stole our animals?" they asked.

"That was no thief," the man said. "That was the King of the Land."

'And ever since the people of Cucao have nothing and the rest of the island is rich.'

Bruce Chatwin, What Am I Doing Here? Picador; 1989.

Sleeping **E** pp *Restaurant Lemuy* and *Café Amancay*. Both in Puqueldón, both clean, without bath, good. **Camping** *Los Isleños*, 1½ kilometres from Puqueldón, T09-6548498.

Transport **Bus** 4 a day except Sunday from Castro. **Ferry** Service from Puerto Huicha, 4 kilometres south of Chonchi, approximately every 30 minutes, foot passengers free.

Queilén

Colour map 4, grid C1 Forty six kilometres by a very beautiful road southeast from Chonchi, Queilén is a pretty fishing village with long beaches and wooden pier. There is the basic *Pensión Chiloé*, without bath, **F** per person and the friendly *Restaurant Melinka*.

Transport Buses to Castro, Queilén Bus, 6 a day, 4 on Saturday, 3 on Sunday, 2 hours, US$2.50.

Cucao

One of only two settlements on the west coast of Chiloé, Cucao lies 40 kilometres west of Chonchi. The road is paved as far as Huillinco, Km 12, a charming village on Lago Huillinco with an **E** per person *residencial* with good food, or stay at the Post Office. Cucao lies at the southern edge of the southern section of the Parque Nacional Chiloé. There is an immense 20-kilometre beach with thundering Pacific surf and dangerous undercurrents.

Sleeping & **E** pp *Hosp Paraíso*, T633040. Friendly. **E** pp *Posada Cucao*, T633040. With breakfast, **eating** hot water, meals, friendly. **E** pp with full board or *demi-pension* at *Provisiones Pacífico* (friendly, good, clean, no hot water). Meals and good homemade bread. Recommended. **E** pp *Casa Blanca*, T633040. With breakfast. **F** pp *Parador Darwin*, with breakfast, good food with vegetarian options, real coffee. Highly recommended. **Camping** Several campsites including *Parador Darwin*. Check prices carefully first. *Lago Mar*, 2 kilometres east, T635552. US$12 per site. *Las Luminarias* sells excellent *empanadas de machas* (*machas* are local shell fish).

Transport Two buses a day from Castro via Chonchi in season, last departure 1600, reduced service off-season; hitching is very difficult.

Chiloé

Parque Nacional Chiloé

I've been to Cole Cole three times and for me it's paradise. I've always walked there; it's a long hike and it takes all day, but it's really rewarding. Take plenty of water as it can get very hot in summer and drinkable water is hard to come by until you reach the Río Cole Cole. The walk from Cole Cole to Río Anay takes about two hours; the trail can be difficult in some places if you have a large pack, so I would recommend it as a day trip from Cole Cole. Near the beginning of the trail there is an absolutely fabulous stand of mature Arrayanes; they are stunning to look at in the afternoon with shafts of sunlight highlighting the cinammon coloured bark. Once you reach Río Anay you can wade or swim across the river to reach a beautiful secluded fine beach from where you have a fantastic view of dolphins playing in the huge breakers.
Sean Partridge, Montevideo.

Parque Nacional Chiloé

The park, which is in three sections, covers extensive areas of the wild and uninhabited western side of the island. Much of it is covered by temperate rainforest. The largest sector is the southernmost and is reached from Cucao. The northern sector is reached from Chepu (see page 362). The third section is a small island, Metalqui, off the coast of the northern sector. The southern sector, 35,207 hectares, is entered via a bridge one kilometre north of Cucao, where there is an administration centre with limited information and a guest bungalow for use by visiting scientists; applications to Conaf via your embassy. In 1998 the bridge connecting Cucao and the park collapsed. While it is being replaced boats offer ferry service, US$0.50, no change given. ■ *Park entry US$2.50. No access by car. Maps of the park are available. Refugios are inaccurately located.*

A path runs three kilometres north from the administration centre to Laguna Huelde and then north a further 12 kilometres to Cole Cole, where there is a dirty *refugio* and free camping. From the path there are great views and the journey is best done on horseback, which takes nine hours round trip. Take lots of water and your own food. The next *refugio* is at Anay, nine kilometres further north. There are several other walks but signposts are limited. Many houses in Cucao rent horses at US$2.50 per hour, US$22 per day. If you hire a guide you pay for his horse too. Horseflies are bad in summer so wear light coloured clothing.

Wildlife Much of the park is covered by evergreen forest. The park marks the southern limit of the Chilean Alerce. Fauna include the Chiloé fox and pudú deer. There are over 110 species of birds including cormorants, gulls, penguins and flightless ducks.

Sleeping No accommodation in the park, but several places in Cucao. There are several campsites near the administration centre as well as others between Laguna Huelde and Cole Cole. *Refugios* at Cole Cole and Anay are described above.

Transport For transport to northern sector see under Chepu, page 362; for southern sector see under Cucao.

Quellón

Population: 7,500
Phone code: 065
Colour map 5, grid A2

The southernmost port in Chiloé, 92 kilometres south of Castro, Quellón is the departure point for ferries to Chaitén. Most of the town's commercial activity lies along the attractive waterfront on Costanera Pedro Montt.

There are pleasant beaches nearby at Quellón Viejo four kilometres west (old wooden church), Punta de Lapa, seven kilometres west, and Yaldad, nine kilometres west. The launch *Puerto Bonito* sails three times daily in summer from the pier, to tour the bay passing Punta de Lapa, Isla Laitec and Quellón Viejo, US$12.50. A trip can also be made to Chaiguao, 11 kilometres east, where there is a small Sunday morning market; horses can be hired US$2.50 per hour; kayaks with a guide, US$2.50 per hour.

Museo de Nuestros Pasados, Ladrilleros 225, includes reconstructions of traditional Chiloté house and mill. **Museo Municipal** is on Gómez García.

Essentials

Sleeping
■ *on map*
Price codes:
see inside front cover

B *Melimoyu*, Pedro Montt 375, T681250. Clean, good beds, parking. **C** pp *El Chico Leo*, Pedro Montt 325. Without bath. **D** *Playa*, Pedro Montt 427, T68127. With breakfast, without bath. Clean. **E** pp *G Laris*, Pedro Montt 45, with breakfast. **E** pp *Hosp La Paz*, La Paz 370, T681207. With breakfast, hot water. **E** pp *La Pincoya*, La Paz 064, T681285. **E** pp *Res Esteban*, Aguirre Cerda 351. **E** pp *Res Estrella del Mar*, Gómez García 248. Without bath, basic, poor value. **F** pp *Club Deportes Turino*, Ladrilleros y La Paz 024. Floor space and camping, cold water, kitchen facilities, basic. Open December-February only. *Albergue*, Ladrilleros, near Carrera Pinto. **F** pp *Las Brisas*, Pedro Montt 555, T681413. Without bath, basic. **G** pp locals, **F** pp foreigners, dormitory accommodation. **At Punta de Lapa Camping** Five sites in Punta de Lapa. Also sites without services at Chaiguao and Yaldad. *Leo Man*, chalets and *cabañas*, and *Cabañas y Camping Las Brisas*.

Quellón

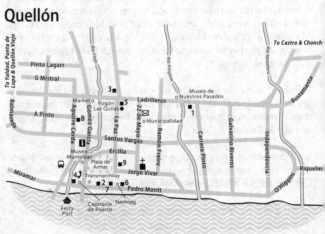

N
Not to scale

■ **Sleeping**
1 Albergue
2 El Chico Leo
3 La Pincoya

4 Las Brisas
5 Los Suizos
6 Melimoyu

7 Playa
8 Residencial Esteban
9 Turino Club Deportes

Rucantú on Pedro Montt. Good food, good value. *El Coral*, 22 de Mayo. Good, reason- **Eating** ably priced, superb views. *Los Suizos*, Ladrilleras 399, Swiss cuisine, good. *Fogón Las Quilas*, La Paz 053, T206. Famous for lobster. Recommended.

Bus To Castro, 2 hours, frequent, Cruz del Sur, US$3; also services to Ancud and **Transport** Puerto Montt.

Ferry To **Chaitén**: in summer (January-early March) the Navimag ferry *Alejandrina* sails to Chaitén, on the mainland, Monday, Wednesday, Friday and Sunday; 5 hour crossing, off-season reduced service. Fares: passengers US$19, reclining seats (*literas*) US$28, cars US$88, cycles US$11. The ship continues ftom Chaitén to Puerto Montt. The Transmarchilay ferry *Pincoya* sails to Chaitén Wednesday 1500. Fares similar to Navimag. To **Puerto Chacabuco**: the Transmarchilay ferry *Pincoya* also sails to Puerto Chacabuco Saturday 1900 all year round, 24 hour voyage.

Banks *Banco del Estado* on Ladrilleros. US$12 commission on TCs, credit cards not possible, **Directory** no commission on US$ cash. **Laundries** *Lavandería Ruck-Zuck*, Ladrilleras 392. **Shipping offices** *Transmarchilay*, Pedro Montt 457, T681331. *Navimag*, Pedro Montt 383. **Tourist offices** Kiosk on Plaza de Armas. Open mid-Dec to mid-Mar. Ask about *hospedajes* not listed in their information leaflet.

Chiloé

The Camino Austral

12

The Camino Austral

Before the opening of the Camino Austral the long stretch of the country south of Puerto Montt was inaccessible to most travellers. Stretching well over 1,000 kilometres and sparsely populated, this is an area of deep fjords, snow capped mountains, rushing rivers and dense temperate rainforest. The only town of any size, Coyhaique, lies far south of Puerto Montt in the valley of the Río Simpson. South of Coyhaique are Lago General Carrera, the largest lake in Chile, and the Río Baker, one of the longest rivers in the country. Further south still is a great icecap, the Campo de Hielo Sur, which feeds the magnificent glacier at Laguna San Rafael, which can be visited by ship or by air. Coyhaique enjoys good air connections with Puerto Montt and Santiago while Puerto Chacabuco, just west of Coyhaique, can be reached by ferry from Puerto Montt. Most of this region, however, can only be visited by travelling along the Camino Austral. There is no direct overland route to the far south of Chile as the Camino Austral ends just north of the Campo de Hielo Sur .

Background

History

The original inhabitants were Tehuelches (Tzónecas, or Patagones), who lived on the pampa hunting guanacos, ñandúes (rheas) and huemules (a large indigenous deer, now almost extinct), and Alacalufes (Kaweshour, or Canoeros), who were coast dwellers living off the sea. See **Archaeology and Prehistory**, page 487 and **The original Patagonians** box, page . There is archaeological evidence, notably cave paintings, in the vicinity of Lago General Carrera, for example at Cueva de la Guanaca, near Lago Lapparent, and Cueva de las Manos, on the Argentine side of the frontier near Chile Chico. The arrival of the Spaniards, who called the region Trapananda, led to little more than exploration of the coast by navigators and missionaries.

This was the last territory to be occupied by the Chilean state after independence from Spain. In the late 19th century expeditions up the rivers led by George Charles Musters (1869) and Enríque Simpson Baeza (1870-72) were followed by a failed attempt to found a settlement at the mouth of the Río Palena in 1884. Fearing that Argentina might seize the territory, the Chilean government appointed Hans Steffen to explore the area. His seven expeditions (1892-1902) were followed by an agreement with Argentina to submit the question of the frontier to arbitration by the British crown.

Chile's first attempt to occupy the area was by granting concessions to three large cattle companies. Although the companies undertook to export their produce through Chile and to encourage settlement, it was much easier to use routes through Argentina and they had little interest in colonization. Until the 1920s there were few settlers and few towns; early pioneers settled along the coast and supplied themselves from Chiloé. The first estimate, in 1907, gave the population as 197. By 1920 this had risen to 1,660 and by 1930, 8,886 inhabitants were in the region. Although the first town, Balmaceda was founded in 1917, followed by Puerto Aisén in 1924, the first road, between Puerto Aisén and Coyhaique, was not built until 1936. It was not until the 1960s when new roads were built and airstrips were opened in small towns that the integration of this region with the rest of the country began to take place.

The Camino Austral: Puerto Montt to Puerto Cisnes

Pudu

To see a pudu (Pudu pudu) in the wild is truly a gift. These miniature deer, approximately 40 centimetres tall and weighing only 10 kilograms, are ideally adapted to the dense undergrowth of the temperate rainforests of Chile and Argentina. Reddish-brown in colour (the males grow two short spiked antlers) the pudu is the smallest member of the deer family in the world. They scoot along on trail systems which weave around in the undergrowth leaving behind miniscule two centimetre long cloven tracks. They are reported to live solitary lives, perhaps due to the dense habitat in which they live. Native to southern Argentina and Chile, the pudu is listed in Chile as vulnerable to extinction, largely due to habitat loss, but also because their unique appearance has led to poaching for zoos: between 1983 and 1985 more than 600 glimpse of one these animals is while travelling along the Camino Austral.

Robert Terwilliger.

Geography

South of Puerto Montt the sea has broken through and drowned the central valley between the Andes and the coastal mountain range. The higher parts of the latter form a maze of islands, stretching for over 1,000 kilometres and separated from the coast by tortuous fjord-like channels.

The Camino Austral: Mañihuales to Puerto Yungay

The Andes are much lower than further north and eroded by glacial action: towards the coast they rise in peaks such as San Valentín (4,058 metres), the highest mountain south of Talca; inland they form a high steppe around 1,000 metres. The other mountain peaks in this area include Fitzroy (3,340 metres), Lautaro (3,380 metres), Maca (2,960 metres), Hudson (2,600), Jeinimeni (2,600 metres) and Alesna (2,480 metres). To the south of Coyhaique are two areas of highland covered by ice and glaciers, known as *campos de hielo* (ice fields). The Campo de Hielo Norte, over 100 kilometres from north to south and some 50 kilometres from west to west, includes the glaciers San Rafael, San Quintin and Steffen. The Campo de Hielo Sur covers a larger area, stretching south from the mouth of the Río Baker towards Puerto Natales.

Five main rivers flow westwards: from north to south these are the Futaleufú or Yelcho, the Palena, the Cisnes, the Simpson or Aisén and the Baker. The latter, 370 kilometres long, is the third longest river in Chile. Only the Cisnes and the Simpson are entirely

The Camino Austral

Climbing volcanoes along the Camino Austral

The many volcanoes along the Camino Austral offer climbing opportunities of varying degrees of difficulty, though in this part of the country most climbs usually take only one or two days and there are no problems with soroche. Corcovado (2,600 metres), a beautiful mountain with a sharp summit situated 40 kilometres south of Chaitén and visible from parts of Chiloé, is particularly difficult. Most are much easier; such as Volcán Yates, further north near Puelche.

in Chile, the other three being largely fed from Argentina. The three largest lakes in this region, Lago General Carrera (the largest in Chile), Lago Cochrane and Lago O'Higgins are also shared with Argentina. This is one of the most sparsely populated areas of Chile, with fewer than 100,000 inhabitants, most of whom live in Coyhaique or in nearby Puerto Aisén.

Climate

January and February are probably the best months for a trip to this region

There is no real dry season. On the offshore islands and along the coast annual rainfall is over 2,000 millimetres. Westerly winds are strong especially in summer. Temperatures vary little between day and night. Inland on the steppelands the climate is drier and colder.

Economy

Agriculture is limited by the climate and poverty of the soil. Potatoes and cereals are among the major crops, while sheep farming is more important than cattle. Chile Chico and the shores of Lago Gen Carrera enjoy a warm microclimate which allows the production of fruit. Fishing remains important as a source of employment in the inland channels. Forestry plays a growing role in the economy: wood is used for construction and in towns such as Coyhaique is in such demand in winter for fuel that it costs as much as petrol. It is also increasingly exported, often as woodchips. Zinc, lead and copper are mined, but of these only zinc is produced in major quantities. Manufacturing is mainly restricted to processing local agricultural produce.

The Camino Austral

Travelling along the Camino Austral is one of the greatest journeys Chile has to offer: described on Chilean maps as a camino ripio (paved with stones), it stretches over 1,000 kilometres. Much of it passes through virgin rainforest, from Puerto Montt to its ultimate destination, the small community of Villa O'Higgins. Beyond this, the icefields of the Campo de Hielo Sur prevent further construction.

Southern Chile, altitude & climate

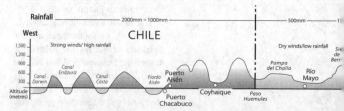

The Camino Austral by bike

I would highly recommend cycling the Camino Austral, but give yourself plenty of time to be able to enjoy it. Going by bus is way too fast and hitching can be frustrating: you can easily wait a day and a half for a ride and in the high season hitching can be competitive, with up to 20 people trying to get a ride out of the same place. In emergencies or if you are pushed for time, it is fairly easy to catch a bus, although you may need to wait a day to make a connection. Buses charge extra for the bikes. Stock up on provisions in major towns. Bread is generally available in small towns or houses en route. Free camping is fairly easy to find and water is easily available from small streams or by asking at nearby houses.

If you have to stop riding for a section, Puerto Cisnes to Coyhaique is a long stretch of tree 'cemeteries' as a result of massive burning by the original colonists of the area. The road conditions of the Camino vary, but the uphill stretches (cuestas) are manageable. An especially rainy section is through the Parque Nacional Queulat. If it looks like rain, try to head for the camping areas which have covered spaces for fires and picnic tables. There may be a charge for camping. The circuit around Lago General Carrera via Puerto Ibáñez and Chile Chico can be done by bus or bicycle but involves a ferry journey across the lake; the scenery is spectacular but there are some very challenging passes on the southern shore of the lake. If possible travel from Cochrane towards Chile Chico to take advantage of the spectacular views of the Andes. Hitching this section is close to impossible: hitching south of Cochrane would be a lost cause.

Carrie Wittner, San José, California.

Before the opening of what was originally rather grandly called the Carretera Austral General Augusto Pinochet, the Chilean mainland between Puerto Montt and Punta Arenas had been poorly connected to the remainder of the country, relying on overland transport through Argentina, limited airline services and irregular coastal shipping. Communications between communities in this area were also poor: roads ran east-west linking up with the Argentine road system.

Although the road has helped transform the lives of many of the inhabitants of the small towns and villages of this part of Chile and is rapidly becoming a tourist destination, the motivation behind its construction was mainly geopolitical: ever since independence Chilean military and political leaders have stressed the importance of occupying the southern regions of the Pacific coast and preventing any incursion by Argentina. Building the Camino Austral was just as much a means of occupying and securing territory as colonization of this area had been in the early years of the 20th century.

Begun in 1976, the central section of the Camino Austral, from Coyhaique to Chaitén, was opened in 1983. Five years later the northern section, linking Chaitén with Puerto Montt, and the southern section, between Coyhaique and Cochrane, were officially completed. Since then work has continued taking the road south of Cochrane towards Villa O'Higgins.

The road can be divided into three sections: Puerto Montt-Chaitén (242 kilometres) with two or three ferry crossings; Chaitén-Coyhaique (435 kilometres); and Coyhaique-Puerto Yungay (421 kilometres). There is also a branch which runs along the

The Camino Austral

☞ *Buses along the Camino Austral*

Most of the buses which ply the Camino Austral are minibuses operated by small companies and often they are driven by their owners. Services are less reliable than elsewhere in Chile and timetables change frequently as operators go out of business and new ones start up. Perhaps one of the major reasons for this is the cost of operating vehicles over the gravel and stone surfaces of the Camino Austral: buses need regreasing after every return *trip between Chaitén and Coyhaique; spare parts are expensive and have to be flown in from Puerto Montt; in summer tyres may have to be changed every month. Fuel is also more expensive than in other parts of Chile. Anxious to maintain rural services, the government offers subsidies on some routes especially in winter and some operators shift to those routes in winter when the Camino Austral is less busy.*

southern shore of Lago General Carrera to Chile Chico; one part of this was the most expensive to build as a route had to be cleared along the sheer rock face of the lake. The Puerto Montt-Chaitén section can only be travelled in summer when the ferries are operating, but an alternative route, through Chiloé to Chaitén, exists.

Most of the villages along the Camino are of very recent origin and consist of a few wooden houses, some of which offer accommodation and other services to travellers. Although tourist infrastructure is growing rapidly, motorists should carry adequate fuel and spares, especially if intending to detour from the main route, and should protect their windscreens and headlamps. Some sections of the road can be difficult after heavy rainfall. Unleaded fuel is available as far south as Cochrane. Cyclists should note the danger of stones thrown up by passing vehicles. See box on page 381 for further information on cycling the Camino Austral. Hitching is increasingly popular in season, but be prepared for long delays and allow at least three days from Chaitén to Coyhaique.

Puerto Montt to Chaitén

This section of the Camino Austral, 242 kilometres long, passes two national parks and the private Parque Pumalin. The route includes two ferry crossings. Before setting out, it is imperative to check when the ferries are running and, if driving, make a reservation: do this at the Transmarchilay office in Puerto Montt, rather than in Santiago. The alternative to this section is by ferry from Puerto Montt or Quellón to Chaitén.

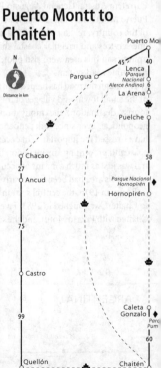

Puerto Montt to Chaitén

N
Distance in km

Puerto Mo
45 40
Lenca
(Parque Nacional Alerce Andino) 6
Pargua
La Arena

Puelche

Chacao
27
Ancud

58

Parque Nacional Hornopirén
Hornopirén

75

Castro

99

Caleta Gonzalo
Parc Pum

60

Quellón

Chaitén

The Camino Austral

The road heads west out of Puerto Montt, through Pelluco and after an initial rough stretch follows the shore of the beautiful Seno Reloncaví passing the southern entrance of the Parque Nacional Alerce Andino, Km 40.

Parque Nacional Alerce Andino

Situated between the Seno Reloncaví to the south and west and Lago Chapo to the northeast, this park covers 39,255 hectares of steep forested valleys rising to 1,500 metres, some 50 small lakes and many waterfalls. The park contains one of the best surviving areas of alerce trees, some over 1,000 years old, with the oldest estimated at 4,200 years. Wildlife includes pudú, pumas, vizcachas, condors and black woodpeckers. Lago Chapo (5,500 hectares) feeds a hydro-electric power station at Canutillar, east of the park. There are four ranger posts: at Río Chaicas, Lago Chapo, Laguna Sargazo and at the north entrance. There are basic *refugios* at Río Pangal, Laguna Sargazo and Laguna Fría and camping sites at Río Chaicas and the north entrance. There is very little information at the ranger posts; a map is available from Conaf in Puerto Montt.

Colour map 4, grid C2

There are 2 entrances: 2.5 kilometres from Correntoso (35 kilometres west of Puerto Montt) at the northern end of the park and 7 kilometres west of Lenca (40 kilometres south of Puerto Montt) at the southern end.

Access

Parque Nacional Alerce Andino

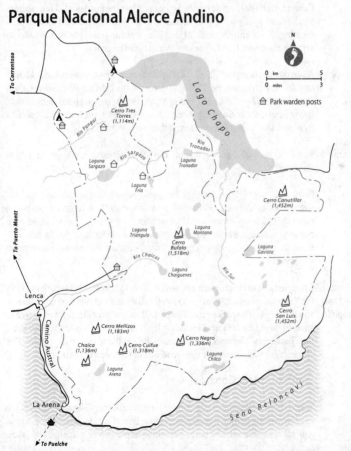

The Camino Austral

Transport To the northern entrance: take Fierro or Río Pato bus to Correntoso (or Lago Chapo bus which passes through Correntoso), several daily except Sunday, then walk. To the southern entrance: take any Fierro bus to Chaicas, La Arena, Contau and Hornopirén, US$1.50, getting off at Lenca sawmill, then walk (signposted).

La Arena

Colour map 4, grid C2 Forty six kilometres south of Puerto Montt (allow one hour), La Arena is the site of the first ferry, across the Reloncaví Estuary to Puelche.

Transport **Ferry** 30 minutes, 10 crossings daily December-March, reduced service off season. Arrive at least 30 minutes early to guarantee a place; buses have priority, cars US$5.

Hornopirén

Population 1,100 Also called Río Negro, Hornopirén lies 58 kilometres south of Puelche at the
Colour map 4, grid C2 northern end of a fjord and at the foot of the Hornopirén volcano. Although a branch of the Camino Austral runs round the edge of the fjord to Pichanco, 35 kilometres further south, Hornopirén is the departure point for the second ferry, to Caleta Gonzalo. There is excellent fishing in the area and Hornopirén is a base for excursions to the Hornopirén volcano (1,572 metres) and to Lago Cabrera which lies further north. At the mouth of the fjord is **Isla Llancahué**, a small island with a hotel and thermal springs, which is reached by boat on a crossing which affords views of dolphins and fur seals (phone the hotel to arrange transport, US$25 one way shared between group).

Sleeping **A3** *Termas de Llancahué*, T09-65-38345, full board, good food, thermal pool. **A3** *Holiday Country*, O'Higgins 666, T263062, restaurant, also *cabañas*. *Hornopirén*, Carrera Pinto 388, T255243 (Casilla 650, Puerto Montt) highly recommended, also *cabañas*. Lots of other *cabañas*. **Camping** Good site next to the *Hostería Setca*, US$14 per site. Four more sites south of Hornopirén on the road to Pichanco.

Transport **Bus** Fierro daily 0800 and 1500 from Puerto Montt. There are no buses south from Hornopirén.

Ferry In January-February only the Transmarchilay ferry *Mailen* sails daily from Río Negro to Caleta Gonzalo, 1500; return departures daily 0900. Fares: vehicles over 4 metres US$88, under 4 metres US$75, foot passengers US$11, cycles US$9. Advance booking required: there can be a two-day wait. *Chaitur* (address under Chaitén) organize transport between the ferry port in Caleta Gonzalo and Chaitén to connect with ferry services.

Parque Lying just east of Hornopirén and covering 48,232 hectares, this park includes
Nacional the Yates volcano (2,187 metres) as well as the basins of two rivers, the Blanco
Hornopirén and the Negro. The park protects some 9,000 hectares of alerce forest as well as areas of mixed native forest including lenga and coigue. From the entrance a path leads eight kilometres east up along the Río Blanco to a basic *refugio*. The entrance is 16 kilometres by *ripio* road east of Hornopirén, entry free.

South of Caleta Gonzalo

Situated on the southern edge of the Fiordo Reñihue, Caleta Gonzalo is the base for visiting Parque Pumalín, see below. From Caleta Gonzalo the Camino Austral runs through the park, climbing steeply before reaching two lakes,

Lago Río Negro and Lago Río Blanco. The coast is reached at Santa Bárbara, 48 kilometres south, where there is a black sand beach, good campsite and swimming. **NB** Do not camp close to the water.

Created by the US billionaire Douglas Tomkins, this private reserve extends over 267,000 hectares and is in two sectors, one just south of the Parque Nacional Hornopirén and the other stretching south and east of Caleta Gonzalo to the Argentine frontier. Its purchase aroused controversy especially in the Chilean armed forces, who perceived it as a threat to national sovereignty. Covering large areas of the western Andes, most of the park is covered by temperate rainforest. Seen by many as one of the most important conservation projects in the world, the park is intended to protect the lifestyles of its inhabitants as well as the physical environment.

Parque Pumalin

In Caleta Gonzalo there is a restaurant, *cabañas* and campsite as well as visitors' centre and demonstrations of agricultural techniques in the region. There are also three marked trails into the park: to a waterfall, *Cascadas Escondidas*; to an area of very old alerce trees; and to Laguna Tronador.

Chaitén

The capital of Palena province, Chaitén is important as a port for ferries to Puerto Montt and Quellón and is a growing centre for adventure tourism and fishing excursions. Visits are also possible to a sea lion colony offshore on Isla Puduguapi. There are good views over the Corcovado Bay from Avénida Corcovado.

Population: 3,258
Phone code: 065
Colour map 4, grid C2

Essentials

A2 *Mi Casa*, Av Norte, T/F731285, on a hill offering fine views – recommended. Comfortable, sauna, gymnasium, restaurant, good value set meal. **A3** *Brisas del Mar*, Corcovado 278, T731284, F731294. *Cabañas*, sleep 4. **B** *Schilling*, Corcovado 230, T731295. With breakfast, heating, restaurant. **C** *Los Colonos*, Juan Todesco 77. With bath, shabby, without breakfast.

Sleeping
■ on map, page 386
Price codes:
see inside front cover
The ferry from Quellón is met by people offering accommodation

D *El Triángulo*, Juan Todesco y Corcovado, T731312. Without bath or breakfast. **D** *Hostería Llanos*, Corcovado 378, T731332. Without bath, with breakfast, good beds, unwelcoming. **D** *Res Astoria*, Corcovado 442, T731263. Without bath or breakfast, clean. **D** *Sebastián*, Riveros 163, T731225, without bath, with breakfast. **E** pp *Hosp Watson*, Ercilla 580. Use of kitchen, clean, friendly. **E** pp *Casa Rita*, Rivero y Prat. (**F** pp for floor space, **G** pp for camping), use of kitchen, clean, open all year, heating. Recommended. **E** pp Martín Ruiz, Camino Austral 1 kilometre north. With breakfast, friendly, nice views. **E** pp *Hosp Recoba*, Libertad 432, T731390. With breakfast, clean, friendly, good meals. **E** pp *Hosp Hogareño*, Pedro de Valdivia 129, T731413, with breakfast, meals. **Camping** *Los Arrayanes*. 4 kilometres north, with hot showers and close to sea, good.

El Canasto del Agua, Prat 65, *El Quijote* O'Higgins 42. Bar, snacks. *Flamengo*, Corcovado 218. Popular with travellers. *Mahurori*, Independencia 141.

Eating
● on map, page 386

Fishing There is excellent fishing nearby, especially to the south in the ríos Yelcho and Futaleufú and in lagos Espolón and Yelcho. Fishing licences are sold at the Municipalidad.

Sports

The Camino Austral

Transport
Fuel is available

Air Flights to Puerto Montt by Aerosur, AeroVip and Aeromet (daily 1200, 35 minutes, US$40). AeroVip also fly to Castro. Bookings can be made through *Chaitur*.

Bus Terminal at O'Higgins 67. Minibuses are operated along the Camino Austral to **Coyhaique** by several companies; in summer up to 6 a week, in winter 2 a week with overnight stop in La Junta or Puyuguapi. Departures usually 0800-0900. The agent for all these services is *Chaitur* (details below). To La Junta US$11, 4 hours; to Puyuguapi, US$13, 5 hours; to Coyhaique, US$24, 11 hours. Minibuses usually travel full so are unable to pick up passengers en route. Hitching the whole route takes several days, but you must be prepared for a day's wait if you find yourself out of luck. To **Futaleufú**, Monday-Saturday 1530, Sunday 1700, 5 hours.

Boat Service to Chonchi (Chiloé) via the smaller islands off the coast, 8 hours (including one hour stopover on an island), departures 0800, Wednesday, Saturday, low season (October-December, March-May), Tuesday, Thursday, Saturday high season (January-February) US$15 low season, US$20 high season, bicycles US$10. Tickets from *Chaitur*.

Ferry Port about 1 kilometre north of town. To **Quellón**: In summer (January-early March) the Navimag ferry *Alejandrina* sails to Quellón, on Chiloé, Monday, Wednesday, Friday and Sunday, 5 hour crossing, off-season reduced service. The Transmarchilay ferry *Pincoya* sails to Quellón Saturday 1000. Fares under Quellón. To **Puerto Montt** The Navimag ferry *Alejandrina* sails to Puerto Montt Monday, Thursday, Saturday in summer, reduced service off-season, 10 hour crossing. The Transmarchilay ferry *Pincoya* also sails this route Wednesday 2100. Fares under Puerto Montt.

Chaitén

Directory

Banks Exchange: *Banco del Estado*, O'Higgins y Libertad, charges US$10 for changing travellers' cheques. **Shipping offices** *Transmarchilay*, Corcovado 266, T731273. *Navimag*, Carrera Pinto 108, T731570. **Tour companies & travel agents** *Chaitur*, O'Higgins 67, in bus terminal, T731429, F731266, nchaitur@hotmail.com. Excursions, trekking, horseriding, fishing, trips to Pumalin park, English spoken, friendly and helpful. Recommended.

N

0 metres   150
0 yards   164

■ **Sleeping**
1 Brisas del Mar
2 El Triangulo
3 Hospedaje Corcovado
4 Hospedaje Don Carlos
5 Hospedaje Elizabéth
6 Hostería Llanos
7 Hostería Sebastián
8 Los Alerces
9 Los Colonos
10 Mi Casa
11 Residencial Astoria
12 Schilling

● **Eating**
1 Canasta del Agua
2 El Quijote
3 Flamengo

Chaitén to Coyhaique

This section of the Camino Austral, 422 kilometres long, runs through small villages and passes through the Parque Nacional Queulat. Roads branch off east to the Argentine frontier and west to Puerto Cisnes.

Amarillo

At Amarillo, 25 kilometres south of Chaitén there is a turning to the **Termas de** *Colour map 5, grid A3*
Amarillo, five kilometres west, which consist of two wooden sheds with a very hot pool inside, US$3, and an outdoor swimming pool. From here it is possible to hike along **the old trail to Futaleufú**, four to seven days, not for the inexperienced, be prepared for wet feet all the way. The trail follows the Río Michinmawida, passing the volcano of the same name, to Lago Espolón, see below. A ferry with a sporadic schedule crosses the lake taking cargo only to Futaleufú. There is superb salmon fishing in the rivers, and the local people are very friendly.

B *Termas de Amarillo*, at the Termas, T731326. Also camping and *cabañas*. **In the vil-** **Sleeping**
lage: **B** *Hostería Galpones del Volcán*, T/F731605. **E** *Res Marcela*, T264442. Also
cabañas, camping. **E** *Hosp Las Rosas*.

Chaitén to Coyhaique

Distance in km

Puerto Cárdenas

Situated 46 kilometres south of *Colour map 5, grid A3*
Chaitén, Puerto Cárdenas lies on the northern tip of **Lago Yelcho**, a beautiful glacial lake on the Río Futaleufú surrounded by hills and frequented by anglers. The *Isla Monita Lodge* offers packages for anglers and non-anglers on a private island in the lake, as well as fishing in many nearby locations; contact *Turismo Grant*, PO Box 52311, Santiago, T6395524, F6337133. Further south at Km 60, a path leads to **Ventisquero Yelcho**, a two hour walk.

Two *residenciales* including **C** *Res Yelcho*. **Sleeping**
Clean, full board available. *Cabañas Yelcho en La Patagonia*, 7 kilometres south on lakeshore, also camping, cafetería.

The Camino Austral

The route to Futaleufú and Argentina

Southeast of Chaitén the Argentine frontier is reached in two places, Futaleufú and Palena along a road which branches off at **Villa Santa Lucía** (Km 81), where there are 30 houses, a military camp, one small shop and bread available from a private house. The road to the border is single track, gravel, passable in a regular car, but best with a good, strong vehicle; the scenery is beautiful. At **Puerto Ramírez**, Km 30, at the southern end of **Lago Yelcho** the road divides: the north branch runs along the valley of the Río Futaleufú to **Futaleufú** while the southern one continues to Palena. **Lago Espolón**, west of Futaleufú, reached by a turning 41 kilometres northeast of Puerto Ramirez, is a beautiful lake in an area enjoying a warm microclimate: 30°C in the day in summer, 5°C at night. The lake is warm enough for a quick dip but beware of the currents. There are *cabañas*, **E** per person, US$3.75 for a motor home, and a campsite. Aníbal, who owns the campsite, sells meat, bread, beer and soft drinks and will barbecue lamb. The Río Futaleufú and Lago Espolón provide excellent fishing, ask for the Valebote family's motorboat.

Sleeping **Villa Santa Lucía** Several places on main street: at No 7 (Sra Rosalía Cuevas de Ruiz, basic, meals available), No 13 (breakfast extra) and No 16 (not bad), all **F** pp, none has hot water. **Puerto Piedra** *Pensión Alexis*. Campsite nearby. **Puerto Ramírez** *Hostería Río Malito*. Rooms, camping, fishing.
    Futaleufú *Hostería Río Grande*, O'Higgins y Balmaceda, T258633 anexo 320. **D** *Hosp Adolfo*, O'Higgins s/n, T258633 anexo 256. **D** *Hosp El Campesino*, Prat 107, T258633. **E** pp *Res Yamara*, O'Higgins s/n, without bath. Recommended. **E** *Res Carahue*, O'Higgins 322, T258633. Very basic, kitchen facilities. **D** *Continental*, Balmaceda 597, T258633, anexo 222. Basic, hot water, clean. Recommended. Cheap restaurant. Several others. **At Palena** *La Frontera*, T741240. *Res La Chilenita*, T258633.

Transport **Air** Airport 1 kilometre east of Futaleufú. Aerosur flights from Chaitén to Futaleufú, Tuesday and Friday, US$62, January-February only. **Bus** To Chaitén daily, 5 hours. To Puerto Montt via Argentina, Monday, Friday 0800, 13 hours, US$35, Transportes Cuchichi (T731280).

Directory **Banks** *Banco de Chile* in Futaleufú, changes US dollars and Argentine pesos. **Tour companies & travel agents** At Futaleufú: Futaleufú Expediciones, O'Higgins 397, T/F258634. Organize rafting, canyoning, trekking and horseriding expeditions.

Frontier with Argentina

Futaleufú **Chilean immigration** At the frontier, at the bridge over the Río Grande, 8 kilometres east of Futaleufú. This is no straight forward crossing

Entering Chile Continue from Futaleufú towards Puerto Ramírez, but outside Ramírez, take the right turn to Chaitén (left goes to Palena).

Exchange If entering Chile change money in Futaleufú (poor rates); nowhere to change at the border. If entering Argentina pay the bus fare to Esquel in dollars and then change in Esquel.

Transport From Futaleufú a bus runs to the border, Monday and Friday 0900, 1800, US$3, 30 minutes, from Balmaceda 419. From the Argentine side there are connecting services to Trevelin and Esquel.

Chilean immigration At Palena, 8 kilometres west of frontier.   **Palena**

Expreso Yelcho bus from Chaitén Tuesday, Thursday, 0830, US$12, 5½ hours.   **Transport**

Both crossings lead to **Trevelin**, which is 45 kilometres east of Futaleufú, 95   **Into Argentina**
kilometres east of Palena. Trevelin is an offshoot of the Welsh Chubut colony   *Population: 4,000*
on the Atlantic side of Argentine Patagonia. It has accommodation, restau-
rants, tea rooms and a tourist office.

At **Esquel** 23 kilometres northeast of Trevelin, there is a much wider range of   *Population: 23,000*
services as well as transport connections for Bariloche and other destinations.
Esquel is a base for visiting the Argentine Parque Nacional Los Alerces and for
journeys on La Trochita, or the Old Patagonian Express.

La Junta

From Villa Santa Lucía the Camino Austral follows the Río Frío and then the   *Population: 736*
Río Palena to La Junta, a drab, expensive village at the confluence of Río   *Colour map 5, grid A3*
Rosselot and Río Palena, 151 kilometres south of Chaitén. **Lago Rosselot**, surrounded by forest and situated in the **Reserva Nacional Lago Rosselot**
(12,725 hectares), nine kilometres west of La Junta, can be reached by a road
which heads west, 74 kilometres, to Lago Verde and the Argentine frontier.

C *Hostería Valdera*, Varas s/n, T314105. With breakfast and bath, very good value.   **Sleeping**
C *Hostal Espacio Tiempo*, T314141. Restaurant, fishing expeditions. **D** *Café Res*
Patagonia, Lynch 331, T314115. Good meals, small rooms, limited bathrooms. **E** pp
Res Copihue, Varas 611, T314184. Without bath, good meals, changes money at very
poor rates. At Lago Risopatrón there is a Conaf campsite.

Fuel is available. Buses to Coyhaique, twice a week in winter, more in summer,   **Transport**
US$13, 7 hours. To Chaitén, US$11, 4 hours, Tuesday/Thursday 0730. Also
Chaitén-Coyhaique buses.

Puyuguapi

From La Junta the Camino Austral runs south along the western side of Lago   *Population: 500*
Risopatrón, to Puyuguapi (also spelt Puyuhuapi), 45 kilometres further south.   *Phone code: 068*
Located in a beautiful spot at the northern end of the Puyuguapi Fjord, the vil-   *Colour map 5, grid A3*
lage was founded by four Sudeten German families in 1935. Puyuguapi is
famous for its carpet factory, founded in 1945, by one of these settlers: the factory, situated at the western end of the village, can be visited.

   From Puyuguapi the road follows the eastern edge of the fjord along one of
the most beautiful sections of the Camino Austral. There are views of the
Termas de Puyuhuapi, a resort on the western edge of the fjord 18 kilometres
southwest of Puyuguapi and accessible only by boat: there are several springs
with 40°C water filling three pools near the beach. Baths cost US$15 per per-
son, children under 12 US$10, take food and drink. This resort can be visited
with four and six day tours run by *Patagonia Connections SA* (see page 100. See
also page 399 for details of its services to Laguna San Rafael).

L3-A1 *Hotel Termas de Puyuhuapi* (price depends on season and type of room).   **Sleeping**
Including use of baths and boat transfer to hotel, full board US$40 extra, good restau-
rant. Recommended. For reservations: *Patagonia Connection SA*, Fidel Oteíza 1921,
Oficina 1006, Providencia, Santiago (Metro Pedro do Valdivia), T2236489, F2748111 or

The Camino Austral

directly at the *Hotel Termas de Puyuhuapi*, T325103, 325129, F325117. (See also under **Sea routes south of Puerto Montt**.) Boat schedule from jetty, 2 hours walk from town, 0930, 1000, 1200, 1230, 1830, 1900, US$3 each way, 10 minutes crossing. **B** *Res Alemana*, Otto Uebel 450, T325118. A large wooden house on the main road, owned by Sra Ursula Flack Kroschewski, comfortable. Highly recommended. **B** *Hostería Ludwig*, on the road south, T325131. Excellent, German spoken. Highly recommended. **E** pp *Hosp El Pino*, Hamburgo s/n, T325117. Homemade bread, friendly. **E** pp *pensión* of Sra Leontina Fuentes, Llantureo y Circunvalación. Clean, hot water, good breakfast for US$1. **E** pp *Hostería Elizabeth*, Llautured y Henríquez. With breakfast, clean, good meals. **A3** *Cabañas Fiordo Queulat* (T Coyhaique 233302). Recommended. There is a dirty campsite by the fjord behind the general store which is behind the service station.

Eating   *Café Rossbach* with limited menu. Not cheap, excellent salmon. There are 2 bars.

Transport   **Bus** Transport out of Puyuguapi is very scarce. Artetur (O'Higgins 039, T325101) to Coyhaique and La Junta twice a week, to Chaitén once a week (Tuesday), Transaustral twice a week to Coyhaique.

Parque Nacional Queulat

Colour map 5, grid A3   Covering 154,093 hectares of attractive forest around Puyuguapi, the park is, according to legend, the place where the rich Cuidad de los Césares once was. The Camino Austral passes through the park. In the north of the park is **Lago Risopatrón**; 24 kilometres south of Puyuguapi is the beautiful **Ventisquero Colgante** (hanging glacier). ■ *US$3*. From here the Camino Austral climbs out of the Queulat valley through a series of hairpin bends offering fine views of the forest and several glaciers. Near the pass (500 metres) is the Salto Pedro García waterfall. Five kilometres further, near the southern entrance to the park, a path leads off to the Salto del Cóndor waterfall. Boat trips can be made on Lago Risopatrón. Administration is in the Conaf office in La Junta. There is an information centre near the Ventisquero Colgante.

Sleeping   **A3** *Cabañas El Pangue*, at north end of Lago Risopatrón, T/F325128, meals served, boat hire. *Cabañas Lago Queulat*, on Seno Queulat. Campsite nearby, US$3.50. *Hospedaje* 5 kilometres north of the Ventisquero Colgante. Conaf campsites 12 kilometres north of Puyuguapi on shores of Lago Risopatrón, and near the Ventisquero Colgante, cold water, basic. Reservations T(67)212125.

Puerto Cisnes

Population: 1,784   Puerto Cisnes is an attractive settlement at the mouth of the Río Cisnes, *Colour map 5, grid A3*   reached by a road, 33 kilometres long, which branches west off the Camino Austral about 59 kilometres south of Puyuguapi. Fuel is available.

The Río Cisnes, 160 kilometres in length, is recommended for rafting or canoeing, with grand scenery and modest rapids except for the horrendous drop at Piedra del Gato; there is a 150 metre cliff at Torre Bright Bank. Good camping in the forest.

Sleeping   **B** *Manzur*, Dunn 75, T346453. *Cabañas*. **C** *Hostal Michay*, Mistral 112, T346462. **C** *Res El Gaucho*, Holmberg 140, T346483. With breakfast, dinner available, welcoming, hot water. *Pensión* at Carlos Condell y Dr Steffen. **D** pp. With breakfast, hot shower, friendly.

Transport   To **Coyhaique**, Colectivos Río Cisnes, daily 0630, US$13, Colectivos Basoli 2 a week, US$13, also Múnoz 2 a week, US$13.

The price of settlement

Two legacies of the Chilean government's attempts to encourage settlement in this area are the large expanses of burnt tree stumps to be seen especially around the Río Palena and Mañihuales and the shifting of the port facilities from Puerto Aisén to Puerto Chacabuco. A law of 1937 offered settlers ownership of land provided it was cleared of forest: smoke from the forest fires which followed could be seen from the Atlantic coast. So much soil was washed into the rivers that the Río Aisén silted up preventing vessels reaching Puerto Aisén.

Rio Cisnes to Coyhaique

Eighty nine kilometres south of Puyuguapi is Villa Amengual (*Population*: 152) with a **D** *Hospedaje Christian*. At Km 92 a road branches west 104 kilometres to the Argentine border via La Tapera. Chilean immigration is 12 kilometres west of the frontier and is open daylight hours only. On the Argentine side the road continues to meet up with Route 40, the north-south road at the foot of the Andes.

The **Reserva Nacional Lago Las Torres** is 98 kilometres south of Puyuguapi and covers 16,516 hectares. It includes the wonderful Lago Las Torres, which offers good fishing and a small Conaf campsite. Further south at Km 125 a road branches east to El Toqui where zinc, gold and silver are mined. From here the Camino Austral is paved.

Villa Mañihuales(*Population*: 2,000) at Km 148 is near the **Reserva Forestal Mañihuales** (1,206 hectares) where there is a huemul reserve. The forests were largely destroyed by forest fires in the 1940s, but the views are good. ■ *Entry US$1.*

A *Cabañas El Mirador;* **E** pp *Res Bienvenido*. Clean, friendly, and restaurant. **E** pp *Villa Mañihuales*. Friendly, breakfast. **Sleeping**

Bus to **Coyhaique**, Trans Mañihuales, one a day except Sunday. **Transport**

13 kilometres south of Villa Mañihuales a branch road (*ripio*) forks east towards Coyhaique via Villa Ortega, Km 28, where the *Restaurant Farolito* takes guests, **D**. Recommended. The main road continues (paved) for a further 49 kilometres to join the Coyhaique-Puerto Aisén highway (Route 240).

Coyhaique

Located 420 kilometres south of Chaitén, Coyhaique lies in the broad green valley of the Río Simpson surrounded by mountains. Founded in 1929, it is the administrative and commercial centre of Región XI. It provides a good base for hiking, skiing and fishing excursions in the area.

Population: 36,367
Phone code: 067
Colour map 5, grid B3

Sights

The town is centred around an unusual pentagonal plaza, on which stand the Cathedral, the Intendencia and a handicraft market. Two blocks northeast of the plaza at Baquedano y Ignacio Serrano there is a monument to El Ovejero (the shepherd). Outside the city on the west bank of the Río Simpson is the

The Camino Austral

The Huemul

The Andean huemul (Hippocamelus bisulcus) is a mountain deer native to the Andes of southern Chile and Argentina. Sharing the Chilean national crest with the Andena condor, the huemul (pronounced 'way-mool') is a medium sized stocky cervid adapted to survival in rugged mountain terrain. Males grow antlers with two main tines each side (with occasionally a third or fourth) and have distinctive black face masks. Huemul tend to occur in small groups of two to five, usually a breeding pair accompanied by offspring. The rutting season is at its height in February and March; females give birth to a single fawn in November or December.

Although it used to range from just south of Santiago to the Straits of Magellan, human pressures including livestock grazing and habitat loss have pushed the huemul to the brink of extinction. Current numbers are unknown but are estimated at 1,000-1,500. A small and dwindling group of 60 animals survive in the Nevados de Chillán in central Chile, their northernmost presence.

The remaining known populations are scattered throughout the southern regions of Argentina and Chile.

The huemul is the focal point of both national and international conservation efforts, carried out primarily by CONAF and the Comite pro la Defensa de la Fauna y Flora de Chile (CODEFF). The current focus is on halting and reversing the decline in numbers in central Chile and on determining more precisely numbers and distribution further south.

The huemul is a shy animal which tends to avoid human contact: with luck you may view a small group along the Camino Austral, but your best chance of seeing them is in one of two reserves managed by CONAF: the Reserva Nacional Río Claro which lies on the southeastern corner of the larger Reserva Nacional Río Simpson just outside Coyhaique and the Reserva Nacional Tamango, near Cochrane. To visit either of these you will need to be accompanied by a warden: enquire first in Coyhaique or Cochrane to make sure someone is available.

Robert Terwilliger.

Piedra del Indio, a rock outcrop which looks like a face in profile, which is best viewed from the Puente Simpson.

Museums **Museo Regional de la Patagonia Central** in the Casa de Cultura, Baquedano 310, has sections on history, mineralogy, zoology and archaeology as well as photos of the building of the Camino Austral. ■ *US$1. Monday-Friday 0900-2000 (summer), Saturday/Sunday 1000-2000 (winter).*

Excursions

Reserva Nacional Coyhaique — Five kilometres northwest off the Camino Austral is this reserve, which covers 2,150 hectares of forest (mainly introduced species). Park administration is at the entrance. There is a basic campsite at Laguna Verde and another at Casa Bruja, four kilometres and two kilometres respectively from the entrance, US$4, and a *refugio* three kilometres from the entrance. ■ *US$1.*

Reserva Nacional Río Simpson — Situated around the valley of the Río Simpson west of Coyhaique and crossed by the road to Puerto Aisén, the park covers 40,827 hectares, most of it steep forested valleys and curiously shaped rounded hills rising to 1,878 metres. One of these, near the western edge of the park is known as *El Cake Inglés*. There are beautiful waterfalls and good views of the river and very good fly fishing. Wildlife includes pudú, pumas and huemul as well as a variety of birds ranging from condors to several species of ducks. Administration is 32 kilometres west of

The Camino Austral

Coyhaique, just off the road; campsite near the turning to Santuario San Sebastián, US$5.

Transport Take any bus between Coyhaique and Puerto Aisen.

Southwest to **Lagos Atravesado** (20 kilometres) and **Elizalde** which offer good fishing, yachting and camping. Southeast to **Lagos Frío**, **Castor** and **Pollux**, all of which offer good fishing. The **Monumento Natural Dos Lagunas**, 25 kilometres east on the Coyhaique Alto road, is a small park which includes Lagos El Toro and Escondido, worth a visit. ■ *US$1. Camping US$12 per site.*

Essentials

The tourist office has a full list of all types of accommodation, but look out for notices in windows since any place with less than 6 beds does not have to register with the authorities.

L3 *Hostería Coyhaique*, Magallanes 131, T231137. In large gardens.

A2 *Los Ñires*, Baquedano 315, T232261, F233372. With breakfast, comfortable, parking. **A3** *Austral*, Colón 203, T232522. Hot water, clean, English spoken, tours arranged, friendly. Recommended. **A3** *Libanés*, Simpson 367, T234242. **A3** *Luis Loyola*, Prat 455, T234200. **A3** *San Sebastian*, Baquedano 496, T233427. Small.

Sleeping
■ *on map*
Price codes:
see inside front cover

Coyhaique

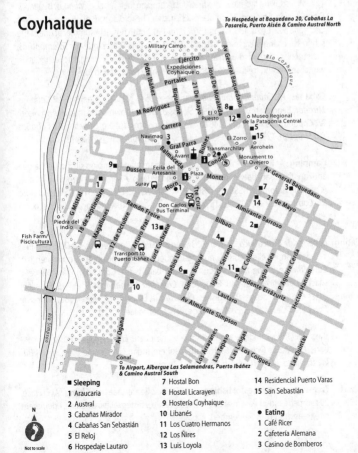

To Hospedaje at Baquedano 20, Cabañas La Pasarela, Puerto Aisén & Camino Austral North

To Airport, Albergue Las Salamandras, Puerto Ibáñez & Camino Austral South

The Camino Austral

■ Sleeping	7 Hostal Bon	14 Residencial Puerto Varas
1 Araucaria	8 Hostal Licarayen	15 San Sebastián
2 Austral	9 Hostería Coyhaique	
3 Cabañas Mirador	10 Libanés	● Eating
4 Cabañas San Sebastián	11 Los Cuatro Hermanos	1 Café Ricer
5 El Reloj	12 Los Ñires	2 Cafetería Alemana
6 Hospedaje Lautaro	13 Luis Loyola	3 Casino de Bomberos

N
Not to scale

B *El Reloj*, Baquedano 444, T231108. With restaurant, comfortable. **B** *Hostería Araucarias*, Vielmo 71, T232707. **B** *Hostal Bon*, Serrano 91, T231189. With breakfast, friendly, clean, also *cabañas* **D** pp, good meals served. Highly recommended.

C *Hostal Licarayen*, Carrera 33A, T233377 (Santiago T7431294). With bath and breakfast, no singles. Recommended. **C** *Res Puerto Varas*, Serrano 168, T/F235931. With bath, also **D** without, restaurant and bar, tatty.

The following are **E** pp unless otherwise stated: *Hosp* at Baquedano 20, Patricio y Gedra Guzmán, T232520. Room in family home, use of kitchen, breakfast with home-made bread, tent sites with bathroom and laundry facilities, by the river. **E** pp *Hosp Pierrot*, Baquedano 130, T221315. Highly recommended, internet access. English spoken, hospitable. Recommended. Manuel Torres, Barroso 957. Hot water, use of kitchen, good. Several cheap places on Av Simpson, for example *Casa El Fondo*, No 417. Clean, friendly. **E** pp No 571, breakfast extra. **F** pp at No 649. **C** *Hostal San Cayetano*, No 829, T/F231555. With bath, also **D** without, cooking facilities, good. **E** pp *Casa Irene*, 12 de Octubre 503, with breakfast, kitchen and laundry facilities. *Los Cuatro Hermanos* Colón 495, T232647. Without breakfast (more with), hot water, clean. **E** pp Baquedano 274. Small rooms, very good. **D** *Res Mónica*, Lillo 664, T234302. **C** *Hosp Lautaro*, Lautaro 532, T231852. Clean, comfortable, kitchen facilities, large rooms. **D** pp Lautaro 269, T235202, with parking, English spoken, internet access, kitchen facilities. Recommended. **E** pp *Hosp Ogana*, Av Ogana Pasaje 8, 185, T232353, cooking facilities, with breakfast, camping, helpful, also *cabañas*, **B**, sleep 3. **E** pp *Pensión América*, 21 de Mayo 233. Other cheap places, **E** pp: Baquedano 444; Cochrane 532, Colón 133, Colón 166, Colón 190. Youth hostel in summer at one of the schools (it changes each year), **F** pp with sleeping bag. **D** *Albergue Las Salamandras*, 2 kilometres south of town in attractive forest, T/F211865. Camping, kitchen facilities, winter sports and trekking, (June-October). Highly recommended.

Cabañas AL *Cabañas San Sebastián*, Freire 554, T231762. Sleeps 5. **L3** *Cabañas Mirador*, Baquedano 848, T233191. Sleeps 8. West of town on road to Puerto Aisén: **A2** *Cabañas La Pasarela*, T234520. Km 1.5. Good atmosphere, *comedor*. **A2** *Cabañas Río Simpson*, T232183. Km 3, cabins for 5, fully equipped, horse hire, fishing.

Sernatur in Coyhaique has a full list of all sites in XI Región **Camping** At Baquedano 20, see above. There are many camping sites in Coyhaique and on the road between Coyhaique and Puerto Aisén, for example at Km 1, (*Camping Alborada*, US$8.50, T238868, hot shower), 24, 25, 35, 37, 41, 42 (*Camping Río Correntoso*, T232005. US$15 per site, showers, fishing, Automobile Club discount) and 43.

Eating *Loberías de Chacabuco*, Barroso 553. Good seafood, slow service. *La Olla*, Gen Prat 176. Spanish, excellent cuisine, not cheap, good value lunches, highly recommended. *Café Oriente*, 21 de Mayo y Condell. Good bakery, tea. *Café Kalu*, Prat 402. Beer, snacks. *Café Ricer*, Horn 48. Good food. *Cafetería Alemana*, Condell 119. Excellent cakes and coffee, vegetarian dishes. *El Mastique*, Bilbao 141, cheap, good. *Casino de Bomberos*, Gen Parra 365. Wide range, very good value.

● on map, page 393 Most places, except the Casino de Bomberos, are closed on Sunday evenings

Bars *Piel Roja*, Condell y Moraleda, nice atmosphere. *El Puesto*, live music at weekends. *Pub*, 12 de Octubre 361. Nice atmosphere and music. Around the corner is *Bar West*, Bilbao y 12 de Octubre. Western style.

Sports Excellent opportunities for **fishing** in the Coyhaique area, see box. **Skiing** At El Fraile, 29 kilometres southeast near Lago Frío: there are 5 pistes, 2 lifts, cafetería, equipment hire (season June to September).

Coyhaique: the angler's paradise

Coyhaique is the greatest centre for fishing in Chile; each summer the international fishing fraternity converge on the town for the season which runs from 15 November to 15 April. The weather is changeable, with hot sunshine (20-30°C) interspersed with showers; evenings are cool and the wind can lower temperatures particularly when fishing in river gorges. A warm jersey and lightweight waterproofs are advisable as well as total sun block protection.

Rivers range from the typically English slow chalk stream to the fast flowing Andean snowmelt torrents, requiring a variety of angling techniques. On the outskirts of Coyhaique, the spectacular Río Simpson teems with both Rainbow and Brown trout. The Simpson offers over 60 kilometres of world class angling. It is renowned for its exciting evening hatches (sedge and mayfly) which take place throughout the season. Anglers will find that, pound for pound, these are some of the best fighting fish to be found anywhere. Catches in excess of five pounds are frequent and Rainbow trout weighing over

12 pounds have been landed.

Located near the Argentine border a scenic one hour drive from Coyhaique, the Río Nirehuao is a fly-fisher's dream. Throughout the season the Brown trout feed voraciously on grasshoppers and dragonfly. The easy wading and moderate casting distances make this river an all-time favourite.

South of Coyhaique the Río Baker, rising from South America's second biggest lake, Lago General Carrera, offers anglers a unique fishing experience in its turquoise blue water. The Baker is huge and intimidating, as are its fish: rainbows up to 12 pounds lurk in its deep blue depths and anglers regularly take fish in the four to seven pound range. The Río Cochrane, a tributary of the Baker, also holds large Rainbows and if it were possible for a river to be clearer than 'gin-clear' this would be it. The Cochrane is mainly a 'sight-fishing' experience which requires skill, patience and an experienced guide.

Major JA Valdés-Scott.

Shopping Feria de Artesanía on the plaza. Cema-Chile on plaza, between Montt and Barroso. Brautigam, Horn 47. Fishing gear, camping. Supermarket Wyhmeister, Lautaro y Cochrane and Multimas, Prat y Lautaro, both open till 2300. Central, Magallanes y Bilbao. Open daily till 2230. Food, especially fruit and vegetables, is more expensive than in Santiago.

Transport Local Bicycle rental: Figón, Simpson y Colón, T234616, check condition first, also sells spares. Repairs Bilbao 500 block, poor supply of spares but good service. Also Tomás Enríque, Madrid Urrea, Pje Foitzick y Libertad, T252132. Bicycle spares from several shops on Simpson. Car hire: Automóvil Club de Chile, Bolívar 194, T231649. Rents jeeps and other vehicles. AGS, Av Ogana 1298, T235354, F231511. Los Carrera, Carrera 330, T/F231010. Budget, Parra 215. Traeger-Hertz, Baquedano 457, T231648. Automundo AVR, Bilbao 509. Cars may be taken across Argentine border and may be returned to a different office. Four-wheel drive recommended for Camino Austral. Buy fuel in Coyhaique, several stations. Taxis: Fares 50 percent extra after 2100. Colectivos congregate at Prat y Bilbao, standard fare US$0.50.

Long distance Air: There are two airports. Tte Vidal, about 5 kilometres south-west of town (including a steep climb up and down to the Río Simpson bridge). Taxi US$5. This airport handles smaller aircraft. Don Carlos to Chile Chico (Monday, Wednesday, Friday, US$36), Cochrane (Monday and Wednesday, 45 minutes, US$65), Tortel (Monday, US$91), and Villa O'Higgins (Wednesday US$100), recommended only for those who like flying, with strong stomachs, or in a hurry. (Don Carlos also flies to Cochrane from Balmaceda.) Balmaceda, 56 kilometres southeast

The Camino Austral

of Coyhaique via paved road, 5 kilometres from the Argentine frontier at Paso Huemules. Balmaceda is used by LanChile, Ladeco and Avant for flights from Santiago via Puerto Montt for Coyhaique. There are also flights by Don Carlos to Chile Chico, Tuesday, Thursday, Saturday, US$41. Airlines run connecting bus services to/from Coyhaique (leave Coyhaique 2 hours before flight), US$2. Minibuses also operate, collecting/delivering to hotels, US$4.50, several companies including Travell, T230010, Transfer, Lautaro 828, T233030. Taxi from airport to Coyhaique, 1 hour, US$6. **Car hire at airport** Río Baker, T272163.

Bus: Terminal at Lautaro y Magallanes but few buses use this: most leave from bus company offices: Turibus, Baquedano 1171, T231333. Don Carlos, Subteniente Cruz 63, T232981. Suray, Prat 265, T238387. Pudu, 21 de Mayo 1231, T231008. Artetur, Muñoz and Basoli all from Gen Parra 337, T232167. Full listing of bus services from tourist information.

To/from **Puerto Montt**, via Bariloche, all year, Turibus, Tuesday and Friday 1700, US$35, with connections to Osorno, Valdivia, Temuco, Santiago and Castro, often heavily booked. To **Punto Arenas** via Coyhaique Alto and Comodoro Rivadavia, Bus Sur, Tuesday 1600, US$55. To **Comodoro Rivadavia**, Turibus, Monday, Friday, also Giobbi, Tuesday, Saturday, from terminal, US$30, 12 hours. To **Puerto Aisén** minibuses run every 45 minutes, 1 hour journey, Suray and Don Carlos, US$2, with connections for Puerto Chacabuco. There are daily buses to **Mañihuales**, Trans Mañihuales (daily 1700).

To **Puerto Ibáñez** on Lago Gen Carrera, *colectivos* (connect with *El Pilchero* ferry to Chile Chico) from your hotel 0530-0600, 3 hours, book the day before, US$7; several operators including Colectivos Sr Parra, T251073, or try contacting drivers along Prat between Errázuriz and Lautaro, to Bajada Ibáñez, (the turning for Puerto Ibanez off the Camino Austral) Aerobus from bus terminal, Monday, Wednesday, Friday 1000, return next day, US$5.45, and Pudú, Tuesday and Saturday 0815.

Buses on the **Camino Austral** vary according to demand: north to **Chaitén**, several companies including B and V, Tuesday, Saturday, and Artetur, Wednesday, Sunday, approximately 12 hours, US$24; in winter these stop overnight in La Junta. To **La Junta**, Morales, T232216, Tuesday, Saturday, US$13. To **Puerto Cisnes**, Muñoz, Wednesday, Saturday, US$11, also Colectivos Río Cisnes (Horn 51) daily 1430, US$13. South to **Cochrane** Pudú, Wednesday, Saturday; Don Carlos, Tuesday, Saturday; Acuario 13, Friday, Monday; and Los Ñadis, Sunday, charging US$23, 10-12 hours.

Routes to Argentina: options are given below and under Balmaceda, Chile Chico and Cochrane. Many border posts close at weekends. If looking for transport to Argentina it is worth going to the local Radio Santa María, Bilbao y Ignacio Serrano, and leaving a message to be broadcast.

Directory **Airline offices** *Avant*, Gen Parra 302, T211073, F237571. *Emperador*, Bilbao 222. *LanChile*, Gen Parra 215, T231188. **Banks** *Banco Santander*, Condell y 21 de Mayo. Mastercard ATM, no exchange. For dollars, TCs and Argentine pesos. *Turismo Prado*, 21 de Mayo 417, T/F231271. TCs accepted. *Lavaseco* Gen Parra 55. **Communications** Post Office: Cochrane 202. Open Mon-Fri 0900-1230, 1430-1800, Sat 0830-1200. **Internet access:** Bilbao 144. *CTC*, Bilbao y 12 de Octubre. **Telephone Office:** at Barroso 626. Open till 2200, opens on Sun about 0900. **Language schools** *Baquedano International Language School*, Baquedano 20, at *Hosp* of Sr Guzmán (see Sleeping above), T232520, F231511, pguzmanm@entelchile.net. US$300 per week course including lodging and all meals, 4 hrs a day person-to-person tuition, other activities organized at discount rates. **Laundry** *QL*, Bilbao 160. **Shipping** *Transmarchilay*, 21 de Mayo 447, T231971, F232700, Tx377003 MARCHI CK. *Navimag*, Ibáñez 347, T233306, F233386. *Greenline*, T238947, services to Termas de Chiconal and Laguna San Rafael, charters. *Sotramin* (services on Lago General Carrera), Moraleda y Portales, T233515. **Tour companies & travel agents** *Aerohein*, Baquedano 500, T/F232772, aerohein@entelchile.net offer air tours to Laguna San Rafael. *Cabot*, Dussen 357, T/F230101, Cabot@entelchile.net. Offer horseriding excursions to Cerro Castillo, (US$70, 2 days) and other tours. *El Puesto Expeditions*, Moraleda 299, T/F233785, elpuesto@entelchile.net, hiking, fishing, climbing. *Patagonia Travel Service*, Condell 149, T237795, offer fishing tours on Lago Riesco and near Puerto Chacabuco. *Turismo Prado*, address in Banks above and *Expediciones Coyhaique*, Portales 195, T/F232300, both offer tours of local lakes and other sights, arrange Laguna San Rafael trips, etc. *Prado* does historical tours, while *Expediciones* does fishing trips and excursions down the Río Baker. *Turaustralis*, Moraleda 589, T/F239696, hsaldivia@hotmail.com. Fishing, horseriding, bird watching, trips to the lakes. *Turismo Aysén*, Barroso 626, T238036, F235294. Fishing, horseriding tours. *Turismo Queulat*, 21 de Mayo 1231, T/F231441. Trips to Queulat glacier, adventure and nature tourism, fishing, etc. *Aventura*, Gen Parra 222, T234748. Offers rafting. *Alex Prior*, T234732. For fly fishing. Tours only operate in season. **Tourist offices** *Sernatur*, Bulnes 35, T231752, F233949, sernatur-coyhai@entelchile.net. Municipal kiosk on the plaza. *Conaf*: office, Ogana 1060. Maps (photocopies of 1:50,000 IGM maps) from Dirección de Vialidad on the plaza.

Frontier crossings to Argentina

This crossing is reached by a *ripio* road which runs east of Coyhaique.   **Coyhaique Alto**
On the Argentine side the road leads through Río Mayo and Sarmiento to Comodoro Rivadavia on the Atlantic seaboard.

At Coyhaique Alto, 43 kilometres west of Coyhaique, 6 kilometres west of the frontier,   **Chilean** open May-August 0800-2100, September-April 0700-2300.   **immigration**

For buses between Coyhaique and Comodoro Rivadavia see above.   **Transport**

Around Coyhaique

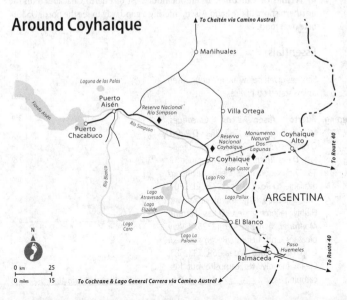

Paso Huemules This crossing is reached by a paved road, Route 245, which runs southeast, 61 kilometres from Coyhaique, via Balmaceda airport, which is five kilometres west of the frontier. There is no accommodation at the frontier or at the airport and no public transport from the frontier to the airport. See above for transport from the airport to Coyhaique. On the Argentine side a *ripio* road runs via Lago Blanco (fuel) to join Route 40, 105 kilometres west of Paso Huemules.

Chilean immigration Open May-July 0800-2100, September-April 0700-2100.

Puerto Aisén

Population: 13,050
Phone code: 067
Colour map 5, grid B3

Situated 65 kilometres west of Coyhaique and 426 kilometres south of Chaitén, Puerto Aisén lies at the confluence of the rivers Aisén and Palos. The climate here is much wetter than in Coyhaique: it is said to rain 370 days a year. Dating from the 1920s, the town grew as the major port of the region though it has now been replaced by Puerto Chacabuco, 15 kilometres further down the river. There are few vestiges of the port left, just some boats high and dry on the river bank when the tide is out and the foundations of buildings by the river, now overgrown with fuchsias and buttercups. To see any maritime activity you have to walk a little way out of town to Puerto Aguas Muertas where the fishing boats come in.

The town is linked to the south bank of the Río Aisén by the Puente Presidente Ibáñez, the longest suspension bridge in Chile. From the far bank a paved road leads to **Puerto Chacabuco**; a regular bus service runs between the two. The harbour is a short way from the town.

Excursions

There is a good walk north to **Laguna Los Palos**, 10 kilometres north of Puerto Aisén. Lago Riesco, 30 kilometres south of Puerto Aisén, can be reached by unpaved road following the Río Blanco. In season the *Apulcheu* sails regularly to **Termas de Chiconal**, about one hour west of Puerto Chacabuco on the northern shore of the Seno Aisén, offering a good way to see the fjord, US$30, take own food.

Essentials

Services given below are in Puerto Aisén unless stated otherwise.

Sleeping
■ *on map*
Price codes:
see inside front cover
Accommodation can be hard to find, most is taken up by fishing companies in both ports

Puerto Aisén A3 *Los Caicahues*, Michimalonco 660, T332888. **D** *Plaza*, O'Higgins 237, T332784. Without breakfast. **D** *Res Aisén*, Serrano Montaner 37, T332725. Good food, clean, full board available. **D** *Roxy*, Aldea 972, T332704. Friendly, clean, large rooms, restaurant. Highly recommended. **D** *Res Serrano Montaner*, Montaner 471, T332574. Very pleasant and helpful. Recommended. **E** pp *Yaney Ruca*, Aldea 369, T332583. Clean, friendly. No campsite but free camping easy.

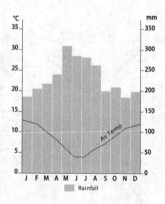

Climate: Puerto Aisén

Puerto Chacabuco A2 *Parque Turístico Loberías de Aisén*, Carrera 50, T351115, F351188. Accommodation overpriced, best food in the area, climb up steps direct from port for drink or meal overlooking boats and mountains before boarding ferry. **D** *Moraleda*, O'Higgins 82, T351155. No other places to buy food or other services.

Gastronomía Carrera, Cochrane 465. Large, very good, popular. *Café Rucaray*, south side of Plaza de Armas.

Eating
● *on map*

Local festival of folklore, second week in **November**.

Festivals

Bus To **Puerto Chacabuco**, **Don Carlos** and **Suray**, every 30 minutes-1 hour, US$1, frequent *colectivos*, US$0.50. To **Coyhaique**, Don Carlos minibuses, 8 a day, Suray minibuses every 45 minutes-1 hour, both charge US$2, 1 hour journey.

Transport

Ferry to Puerto Montt Both the Transmarchilay ferry *El Colono* and the Navimag ferry *Evangelistas* sail to Puerto Montt via the Canal Moraleda twice a week, 24 hours, all year service (fares under Puerto Montt). **To Quellón** The Transmarchilay ferry *Pincoya* sails to Quellón on Chiloé via Melinka and Puerto Aguirre, Monday 1800, 24 hours, all year service. **To Laguna San Rafael** In January and February both *El Colono* and *Evangelistas* make an excursion from Puerto Chacabuco to Laguna San Rafael. Departures on Saturday, return Sunday, 21-24 hour voyage. Fares including food: *El Colono* suite US$640 per person; *butaca* US$210-295; *Evangelistas* suite US$750 per person, *literas* US$370, semi-*cama* US$200. For fares from Puerto Montt to Laguna San Rafael see under Puerto Montt.

    Patagonia Connection SA, Fidel Oteíza 1921, Oficina 1006, Providencia, Santiago, T2256489, F2748111, operates *Patagonia Express*, a catamaran which runs from Puerto Chacabuco to Laguna San Rafael via Termas de Puyuhuapi, see page 351 for further details. **Shipping Offices**: *Agemar*, Tte Merino 909, T332716, Puerto Aisén; *Navimag*, Terminal de Transbordadores, Puerto Chacabuco, T351111, F351192; *Transmarchilay*, Av O'Higgins s/n, T351144, Puerto Chacabuco. It is best to make reservations in these companies' offices in Puerto Montt, Coyhaique or Santiago (or, for Transmarchilay, in Chaitén or Ancud). For other trips to Laguna San Rafael, see below;

Puerto Aisén

out of season, they are very difficult to arrange, but try Edda Espinosa, Sgto Aldea 943. Boat information is posted at Café Rucaray.

Directory   **Banks**   *Banco de Crédito*, Prat. For Visa. *Banco de Chile*, Plaza de Armas. Only changes cash, not TCs. **Communications**   Post Office: on south side of bridge. **Telephone Office:** on south side of Plaza de Armas, next to *Café Rucaray*. **Tourist offices**   In Municipalidad, Prat y Sgto Aldea, 1 Dec to end-Feb only, helpful.

Lago General Carrera

Colour map 5, grid B3   *Straddling the frontier with Argentina at an altitude of 350 metres, Lago General Carrera (Lago Buenos Aires in Argentina) covers 184,000 hectares, 98,900 hectares of which are in Chile. The largest lake in Chile (and the second largest in South America), it is now reckoned to be the deepest lake in the continent; depth soundings in 1997 established its maximum depth as 590 metres.*

One of the main Chilean rivers flowing into the lake is the Río lbañez, which is fed by the glaciers of the Hudson volcano. At its western end, near Puerto Bertrand, the lake empties into the Río Baker, which carries a greater volume of water than any other river in Chile.

The lake itself is a beautiful azure blue; the Chilean end is surrounded by predominantly Alpine terrain and the Argentine end by dry pampa. To the north there are fine views of Cerro Castillo. The major eruption of Volcán Hudson in 1991, polluted parts of the lake and many rivers, but the waters are now clear. The effects can still be seen in some places where there is a metre-thick layer of ash on the ground.

Climate   Sheltered from the prevailing west winds by the Campo de Hielo Norte, the region prides itself in having the best climate in southern Chile with some 300 days of sunshine; much fruit is grown as a result especially around Chile Chico. Rainfall is very low for this area.

The main towns, Puerto Ibáñez on the north shore and Chile Chico on the south, are connected by a ferry, the *Pilchero*, but there are also two, much longer, overland routes between Coyhaique and Chile Chico: through Argentina or along the Camino Austral which runs west around the lake.

Puerto Ibáñez

Population: 800   The principal port on the Chilean section of the lake, Puerto Ibáñez is reached
Colour map 5, grid B3   by taking a branch road, 31 kilometres long, from Bajada Ibañez 97 kilometres south of Coyhaique. There are some fine waterfalls, the Salto Río Ibañez, six kilometres north.

Sleeping   **E** pp *Res Ibáñez*, Bertrán Dixon, T423227. Clean, warm, hot water. Unnamed hospedaje at Bertrán Dixon 31. **E** *Vientos del Sur*, Bertrán Dixon 282. **D** *Hostería Doña Amalia*, Bajada Río Ibañez. Fuel (sold in 5 litre containers) available at Luis A Bolados 461 (house with 5 laburnum trees outside). **Camping**   Municipal campsite, T423234, US$7 per site, open December-March.

Transport   **Minibus**   To Coyhaique, 2½ hours, US$7. There is a road to Perito Moreno, Argentina, but no public transport.

Ferry   The car ferry, *El Pilchero*, sails from Puerto Ibáñez to Chile Chico, daily (except Thursday, Sunday) 0900, return departures Monday-Wednesday, Friday, 1730,

Sunday 1500. Fares for cars US$33, for passengers US$3.50, 2¾ hours crossing, bicycles US$2.50. Number of passengers limited to 70; reservations possible. This is a very cold crossing even in summer: take warm clothing. Buses and jeeps meet the ferry in Puerto Ibáñez for Coyhaique.

Around the lake on the Camino Austral

The southernmost section of the Camino Austral currently ends at Puerto Yungay, 442 kilometres south of Coyhaique, but the final 92 kilometre stretch beyond this to Villa O'Higgins is nearing completion. The section around the north and western sides of Lago General Carrera is reckoned by many people to be the most spectacular. A branch road along the southern shore of Lago General Carrera connects with the small town of Chile Chico near the Argentine frontier.

Branching off Route 245, the paved highway between Coyhaique and Balmaceda, 41 kilometres southeast of Coyhaique, the Camino Austral runs southwest through the **Reserva Nacional Cerro Castillo**. Extending over 179,550 hectares, this park is named after the fabulous **Cerro Castillo** (2,675 metres) which resembles a fairytale castle with rock pinnacles jutting from a covering of snow. The park also includes Cerro Bandera (2,040 metres) just west of Balmaceda and several other peaks in the northern wall of the valley of the Río Ibáñez. There is a *guardería* at the northeastern end of the park near Laguna Chinguay and a Conaf campsite nearby, US$5 per site, T067-237070. At Km 83 the road crosses the Portezuelo Ibáñez (1,120 metres) and drops through the Cuesta del Diablo, a series of bends which offer fine views over the Río Ibáñez.

Lago General Carrera

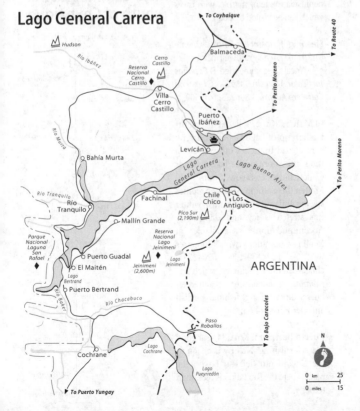

The Camino Austral

Villa Cerro Castillo, Km 98, eight kilometres beyond Bajada Ibañez (the turning for Puerto Ibañez) is a village in a narrow gorge, where there are two *residenciales* (one at Aguirre Cerda 35, **D**, with good meals) and a grocery store. Nearby is the **Monumento Nacional Manos de Cerro Castillo**, where traces of ancient rock paintings, estimated at 10,000 years old, have been found.

The road climbs out of the valley, passing the aptly named Laguna Verde and the Portezuelo Cofré. It descends to the boggy Manso valley, with a good campsite at the bridge over the river, watch out for mosquitoes. This area was seriously affected by the ash from Volcán Hudson.

Bahía Murta
Population: 600

Five kilometres off the Camino Austral at Km 203 is this village, situated on the northern tip of the central 'arm' of Lago General Carrera. Bahía Murta dates from the 1930s when it lived from exporting timber to Argentina via Chile Chico. From here the road follows the lake's western shore; the colour of the water is an unbelievable blue-green, reflecting the mountains which surround it and the clouds above.

Sleeping E pp *Res Patagonia*, Pasaje España 64, T419601, very basic, without bath.
E pp *Res Lago Gen Carrera*, Av 5 de Abril y Colombia, T419601. Excellent meals, also has cabin with own store. Free camping by the lake, good views of Cerro Castillo.

Río Tranquilo
Population: 400

This village at Km 228 is where the buses stop for lunch: fuel is available at the ECA store from a large drum (no sign). Nearby is the **Catedral de Mármol**, a peninsula made of marble, with caves which can be visited by boat.

Sleeping B *Hostal Los Pinos*, 2 Oriente 41, T411637, family run, well maintained, good meals. Recommended. **D** *Cabañas Jacricalor*, 1 Sur s/n, T419500. **C** *Hostería Carretera Austral*, 1 Sur 223, T419500.

El Maitén, Km 279, lies at the southwestern tip of Lago General Carrera: here a road branches off west along the south shore of the lake towards Chile Chico, see below. South of El Maitén the Camino Austral becomes steeper and more bendy and in winter this stretch is icy and dangerous. Accommodation is available at Mallín Colorado, two kilometres west, T2741807, F2042785, chile@patgonia-pacific.cl, which has *cabañas*, adventure activities, horseriding, rafting, fishing, English and German spoken,

Puerto Bertrand, Km 284, is a good place for fishing. Nearby is a sign to the Nacimiento del Río Baker: the place where the Río Baker is reckoned to begin.

The Camino Austral south of Coyhaique

Coyhaique
35
El Blanco
6
15 — Balmaceda
56
8 31 — Puerto Ibáñez
Villa Cerro Castillo
93
5 — Bahía Murta
25
Río Tranquilo
50
El Maitén — 122 — Chile Chico
11
Puerto Bertrand
59
Cochrane
100
Puerto Yungay
▼ To Villa O'Higgins

N

Distance in km

The Camino Austral

Sleeping A3 *Hostería Campo Baker*, T411477, *cabañas*, sleeps four. *Casa de Huéspedes*. Dormitory accommodation. One small shop. For excursions contact Jonathan Leidich, T411330, for rafting, horseriding and other activities, highly recommended.

Beyond Puerto Bertrand the road climbs up to high moorland, passing the confluence of the Ríos Neff and Baker, before winding south along the east bank of the Río Baker to Cochrane. The scenery is splendid all the way; in the main the road is rough but not treacherous. Watch out for cattle on the road and take blind corners slowly.

South of Lago General Carrera

The southern shore of the lake is reached by a road (opened 1994) which branches off the Camino Austral at El Maitén.

At **Puerto Guadal** 10 kilometres east of El Maitén, there are shops, a post office and petrol.   *Population: 500*

Sleeping & eating D *Hostería Huemules*, Las Magnolias 382, T411202. With breakfast, good views. **E** pp *Res Maitén*, Las Magnolias. There is also *Patagonia Lodge* on the shores of Lago General Carrera, T2-7358034, F7772375, azimut@reua.cl. *Restaurant La Frontera*, Los Lirios y Los Pinos.

Transport Bus: Pudú bus to Cochrane Wednesday, Saturday. Sr Sergio Haro Ramos runs a minibus service, connecting with Pudú buses from Cochrane, Thursday, Sunday, US$10.

Further east along the shore, just past the village of **Mallín Grande**, Km 40, the road runs through the **Paso de las Llaves**, a 30 kilometre stretch carved out of the rock-face overlooking the lake. This was the most expensive section of the Camino Austral. The road climbs and drops, offering wonderful views over the lake and over the ice-fields to the west. At Km 74 a turning runs to **Fachinal**, where there is no accommodation though people will let you stay for free if you have a sleeping bag. A further eight kilometres east there is an open cast mine which produces gold and other precious metals.

The Camino Austral

The War of Chile Chico (1917)

Chile Chico dates from 1909 when Chilean settlers crossed from Argentina and occupied the land. In the previous year the Chilean government had granted 80,000 hectares of land between Lago General Carrera and Lago Cochrane to cattle ranchers from the Sociedad Explotadora Río Baker. In the showdown which followed the ranchers were driven out by the settlers, but it was not until 1931 that the Chilean government finally recognized the town's existence.

Chile Chico

Population: 2,200
Phone code: 067
Colour map 5, grid B3

A quiet, friendly but dusty town situated on the lake shore 122 kilometres east of El Maitén, Chile Chico lies near the Argentine border. At the centre of a fruit growing region, it has an annual festival at the end of January. There is a small museum; outside is a boat which carried cargo on the lake before the opening of the new road along the southern shore of the lake. There are fine views from the Cerro de las Banderas at the western end of town.

The country to the south and west of Chile Chico, with weird rock formations and dry brush-scrub, provides good walking for the mountaineer. The northern and higher peak of Cerro Pico del Sur (2,168 metres) can be climbed by the agile from Los Cipres (beware dogs in farmyard). You will need a long summer's day and the 1:50,000 map. Follow the horse trail until it peters out, then navigate by compass or sense of direction until the volcano-like summit appears. After breaching the cliff ramparts, there is some scrambling and a 10 foot pitch to the summit, with indescribable views of the Lake and the Andes. (Brian Spearing).

Sleeping **A3** *Austral*, O'Higgins 501, T411461, welcoming, very clean. Recommended. **B** *Hostería de la Patagonia*, Camino Internacional s/n, T411337, F411414. Full board, clean, excellent food, English, French and Italian spoken, trekking, horse-riding and white-water rafting organized (Casilla 91, Chile Chico, XI Region). Recommended. **C** *Res Aguas Azules*, Rodriguez 252, T411320. **C** *Ventura*, Carrera 29, T411311. Modern. **D** *Casa Quinta No me Olvides/Manor House Don't Forget Me*, Camino Internacional s/n, without bath. Clean, cooking facilities, warm, camping. Recommended. Tours arranged to Lago Jeinimeni and Cueva de las Manos. **D** *Hosp Don Luis*, Balmaceda 175, T411384. Clean, meals available. **E** pp *Plaza*, O'Higgins y Balmaceda. Basic, clean. Recommended. **Camping** Free campsite at Bahía Jarra, 15 kilometres northwest.

Eating Apart from *Hostería de la Patagonia* and *Residenciales*: *Cafetería Loly y Elizabeth* on Plaza serves coffee and delicious icecream and cakes, expensive. *Café Holiday*, Calle Gonzalez, good coffee, friendly. Supermarket on B O'Higgins.

Transport **Air** Don Carlos to Coyhaique Monday, Wednesday, Friday, US$36; Don Carlos to Balmaceda, Tuesday, Thursday, Saturday, US$41.

Minibus These run along the south side of the lake to **Cochrane**, Transportes Ales, T411739, Tuesday, Friday, US$20. To **Puerto Guadal**, Sr Sergio Haro Ramos, T411251, Wednesday, Saturday, minibus service, US$10, which connects in Puerto Guadal with Pudú service for Cochrane. See page 400 for ferry service to Puerto Ibañez and connecting minibus services to Coyhaique.

Directory **Banks** Best to change money in Coyhaique or Argentina: dollars and Argentine pesos can be changed in small amounts at shops and cafés including *Café Loly y Elizabeth*, but at poor rates. **Tourist offices** On O'Higgins. Ask here or at the Municipalidad for help in arranging tours.

The Camino Austral

Reserva Nacional Lago Jeinimeni

Situated south of Chile Chico, this park covers 160,000 hectares and includes two lakes, Lago Jeinemeni and Lago Verde which lie surrounded by forests in the narrow valley of the Río Jeinimeni. There are impressive cliffs, waterfalls and small glaciers. Wildlife includes huemul deer, pumas and condors. Activities include fishing for salmon and rainbow trout, trekking and rowing. A good map is essential. Access is via an unpaved road which branches south off the road to Los Antiguos and crosses five rivers, four of which have to be forded. At Km 42 there is a small lake, Laguna de los Flamencos, where large numbers of flamingoes can be seen. The park entrance is at Km 53; just beyond is a ranger station; two kilometres further, at the eastern end of Lago Jeinemeni, there is a campsite and fishing area. ■ *Entry US$1.50, Camping US$3.* Take all supplies. A good map is essential. The park is open all year but access may be impossible between April and October due to high river levels. ■ *Getting there: lifts may be possible from Chile Chico: try Juan Núñez, Hernán Trizzando 110, for a lift on a timber truck, or ask in the Conaf office.*

Frontier with Argentina

A road runs east from Chile Chico to the Argentine frontier 3 kilometres east. From the frontier it is 5 kilometres further to Los Antiguos. Open September-April 0700-2300, May-August 0800-2100.

Chile Chico: Chilean immigration

Minibuses from Chile Chico to Los Antiguos are run by 2 companies, Arcotrans, T411358, and Transportes Padilla, T411224, US$3, (payable in US$ or Argentine pesos only) 45 minutes including formalities (once a day each company at weekends).

Transport

Los Antiguos is also a fruit growing town. There is an annual cherry festival in mid-January. Salmon fishing is also possible. There is accommodation. From here buses run weekdays to Comodoro Rivadavia via Perito Moreno, US$20, seven hours.

Into Argentina
Population: 1,500
Altitude: 326m

Perito Moreno, 67 kilometres east of the frontier has a few hotels, a campsite, a restaurant and money exchange services. There is one flight a week Perito Moreno-Río Gallegos. 118 kilometres south is the famous **Cueva de las Manos** where the walls of a series of galleries are covered with painted human hands and animals, 10,000 years old.

Population: 3,000
Altitude: 400m

South of Lago General Carrera

Cochrane

Sitting in a hollow on the northern banks of the Río Cochrane, **Cochrane** is 343 kilometres south of Coyhaique. There is a small museum. ■ *Monday-Friday 0830-1300, 1430-1800.* It is a simple place, sunny in summer, good for walking and fishing.

Population: 3,000
Colour map 5, grid C3

Excursions can be made to **Lago Cochrane**, which straddles the frontier with Argentina (the Argentine section is called Lago Puerredón). The lake, which extends over 17,500 hectares, offers excellent fishing. The views from the reserve are superb, over the town, the nearby lakes and to the Campo de Hielo Norte to the west. On the northern shores of the lake is the **Reserva Nacional Tamango**, which covers 6,925 hectares of lenga forest and is home to one of the largest colonies of the rare huemal as well as guanaco, foxes and lots of birds including woodpeckers and hummingbirds. ■ *Entry US$3. 0830-2100 December-March, 0830-1830 April-November. Guided visits to see the huemal, Tuesday, Thursday, Saturday, US$60 for a group of 6 people. Tourist facilities are rudimentary. Campsites at Los Correntadas, US$10 per site, also* cabañas, *and Los Coigües, US$13 per site, also* cabañas. *Details and booking through Conaf office on the main plaza (T422164).*

Sleeping **A3** *Ultimo Paraíso*, Lago Brown 455, T522361. **B** *Hostería Wellmann*, Las Golondrinas 36, T522171. Hot water, comfortable, warm, good meals. Recommended. **B** *Res Rubio*, Tte Merino 871, T522173. Very good, breakfast included, lunch and dinner extra. **D** *Res Sur Austral*, Prat 334, T522150. With breakfast, hot water, also good. **D** *Residencia Cero a Cero*, Lago Brown 464, T522158. With breakfast, welcoming. In summer it is best to book rooms in advance. **D** *Res El Fogón*, San Valentín 135, T522240. **E** pp *Hosp Cochrane*, Dr Steffens 451, T522377, good meals, camping. Recommended. **E** pp *Hosp Paola*, Lago Brown 150, T522215, also camping. **D** pp *Café Rogery*, Tte Merino 502, cabañas, sleep 5, kitchen facilities.

Eating *El Farolito*, Tte Merino 546. *Café Rogery*, Tte Merino 502.

Sports **Horseriding** Horses can be hired for excursions in the surrounding countryside. Try Don Pedro Munoz, T522244, F522245.

Transport **Air** Don Carlos to Coyhaique, Monday, US$65.

Bus Company agencies: *Pudú* Tte Merino 499, T/F522122. *Don Carlos*, Prat 344, T/F522150. *Los Ñadis*, Los Helechos 490, T/F522196. *Acaurio 13*, Río Baker 349, T/F522143. Pudu and Don Carlos run 2 buses a week to **Coyhaique**, **Los Ñadis** and **Acaurio** 1 a week, US$23. To **Vagabundo**, Los Ñadis and Acaurio 13, 4 a week, US$9. Petrol is available, if it hasn't run out, at the Empresa Comercial Agrícola (ECA) and at the Copec station.

Directory **Tour companies & travel agents** *Samuel Smiol*, T522487. Offers tours to the icefields and mountains, English spoken. Excursions can also be arranged through Guillermo Paso, Transportes Los Ñadis.

To Argentina 17 kilometres north of Cochrane, a road through Villa Chacabuco and Paso Roballos (78 kilometres), enters Argentina (and continues to Bajo Caracoles); no public transport, road passable in summer but often flooded in spring.

South of Cochrane

The Camino Austral has been built a further 122 kilometres south of Cochrane to Puerto Yungay. In 1999 most of the final stretch to Villa O'Higgins had also been completed. At Km 45 there is a free *refugio*. From *Vagabundo*, Km 98, where there is a *refugio* with four beds, boats sail down the Río Baker to Tortel. This is a beautiful trip through thick forest with views of snow-capped mountains and waterfalls. **Tortel**, a village built on a hill at the mouth of the river, has no streets, only wooden walkways ('no hay ni una bicicleta'). It trades in wood with Punta Arenas and fishes for shellfish. From here you can hire a boat to the **Ventisquero Jorge Montt** five hours southwest or to the **Ventisquero Steffens**, north on the edge of the Parque Nacional San Rafael.

Ask for Doña Berta Muñoz, **D** pp full board. "Expect fresh mutton meals and if you are **Sleeping**
squeamish about seeing animals killed don't look out of the window when they
butcher the two lambs a day on the front porch." Carrie Wittner. **E** pp Sergio Barrio,
also **D** pp full board, good food. Free accommodation is also available at the Centro
Abierto, ask at the Municipalidad.

Air Don Carlos to Coyhaique, Monday and Wednesday from Cochrane (US$65), **Transport**
Tortel, Monday (US$91), and Villa O'Higgins, Wednesday (US$100).

Bus Minibuses from Cochrane.

Boat From Vagabundo to Tortel, Tuesday, Sunday 1500, 3 hours, US$2. From Tortel
to Vagabundo, Tuesday, Sunday 0900, 5 hours (upstream). **Charters** Charter boats
can be arranged through Viviana Muñoz or Hernán Ovando at the Municipalidad,
T/F211876. Prices: to Ventisquero Jorge Montt, US$220 return, 11 hours, 8-15 passen-
gers. To Ventisquero Steffens, US$110 return, 8 hours, 8-15 passengers. To Puerto
Yungay, US$110 return, 8 hours, 6-10 passengers.

Villa O'Higgins lies near the Argentine frontier at the northeastern end of an   *Population: 350*
'arm' of Lago O'Higgins which straddles the frontier (Lago San Martín in   *Colour map 5, grid C3*
Argentina). On the lake are large numbers of icebergs which have split off the
glaciers of the Campo de Hielo Sur which lies to the west. Accommodation is
available at the *Hospedaje Patagonia*, **E** per person without bath. Boat trips are
offered by Adolfo Güinao Velásquez. Horses can be hired. Tourist information from the Municipalidad, T211849.

Until the Camino Austral is finished, Villa O'Higgins can only be reached by air. Don   **Transport**
Carlos air taxi fly from Balmacedo US$80, from Cochrane US$50.

Parque Nacional Laguna San Rafael

*Laguna San Rafael is one of the highlights for many travellers to Chile. Situated
west of Lago General Carrera and some 200 kilometres south of Puerto Aisén, the
Ventisquero San Rafael is one of many which flow off the giant Campo de Hielo
Norte. About 45 kilometres in length the glacier flows into the Laguna San Rafael
which empties into the sea northwards via the Río Tempano. Towering 30 metres
above water level, the glacier calves small icebergs which are carried across the
laguna and out through the Río Tempano. Around the shores of the laguna is
thick vegetation and above are snowy mountain peaks.*

Laguna San Rafael and the Campo de Hielo Norte are part of the Parque
Nacional Laguna San Rafael, which extends over 1.74 million hectares. In the
national park are puma, pudú (miniature deer), foxes, dolphins, occasional
sealions and sea otters, and many species of bird. Walking trails are limited
(about 10 kilometres in all) but a lookout platform has been constructed, with
fine views of the glacier.

Park essentials

Park entry fee is US$6. At the glacier there is a small ranger station which gives infor-
mation; a pier and two paths have been built. One path leads to the glacier. The rangers are willing to row you out to the glacier in calm weather, a three hour trip.

The Camino Austral

Laguna San Rafael

The trip in the rowboat is an awesome venture. At first it is fairly warm and easy to row. Gradually it gets colder when the wind sweeps over the icy glacier (be sure to take warm clothes – a thick sweater, and waterproof jacket are recommended – Ed). It gets harder to row as small icebergs hinder the boat. Frequently somebody has to jump onto an iceflow and push the boat through. The glacier itself has a deep blue colour, shimmering and reflecting the light; *the same goes for the icebergs, which are an unreal, translucent blue. The glacier is very noisy; there are frequent cracking and banging sounds, resembling a mixture of gun shots and thunder. When a hunk of ice breaks loose, a huge swell is created and the icebergs start rocking in the water. Then great care and effort has to be taken to avoid the boat being crushed by the shifting icebergs; this is a very real danger.*

Robert af Sandeberg (Lidingö, Sweden)

Transport   The only ways there are by plane or by boat: **Air** Air Taxis from Coyhaique by Aerohein and Don Carlos (addresses under Coyhaique), US$200 each if party of 5; some pilots in Puerto Aisén will fly to the glacier for about US$95 each, but many are unwilling to land on the rough airstrip. **Sea** The official cruises are: *Skorpios I* and *II* (see under Puerto Montt); Navimag's *Evangelistas* and Transmarchilay's *Colono* (see under Pto Chacabuco); *Patagonia Express*, a catamaran which sails from Puerto Montt to Laguna San Rafael via Termas de Puyuhuapi, in tours lasting 4-6 days (see page 389); *Iceberg Express*, a catamaran which offers 12-hour luxury cruises from Puerto Chacabuco; in Santiago, Av Providencia 2331, oficina 602, T3350580, F3350581. *Pamar*, Pacheco Altamirano 3100, T256220, Puerto Montt, September-March only; Compañía Naviera Puerto Montt has 2 vessels: the *Quellón*, with 6-day, 6-night tours to the Laguna from Puerto Montt via various ports and channels (US$900); Puerto Montt, Diego Portales 882, T/F252547; Puerto Chacabuco T351106. *Odisea* and *Visun*, motorized sailing boats, December to March, in Santiago, Alameda B O'Higgins 108, local 120, T6330883, in Puerto Aisén, Sgto Aldea 679, T332908, 6-day trips from Puerto Chacabuco to Laguna San Rafael. Various private yachts can be chartered in Puerto Montt for 6-12 passengers to Laguna San Rafael. Local fishing boats from Puerto Chacabuco/Puerto Aisén take about 18-20 hours each way, charging the same as the tourist boats. Ask for Jorge Prado at the port (he takes a minimum of 7, more expensive than others); Andino Royas, Cochrane 129; Justiniano Aravena, Dr Steffen 703; Rodrigo Azúcar, Agemar office, T332716; or Sr Ocuña, ask at the port. These unauthorized boats may not have adequate facilities and may not be licensed for the trip.

The Camino Austral

The Far South

13

410

The Far South

A land of fjords, glaciers, lakes and mountains, Chilean southern Patagonia is a very popular destination for visitors. The great attraction is the Parque Nacional Torres del Paine; justly famous for its glaciers, its glacial lakes and three distinctive columns (the 'towers' after which the park is named) which point vertically like fingers from the Paine massif. Torres del Paine should not be missed, but this region has other attractions including the glaciers which descend from Monte Balmaceda at the southern end of the Parque Nacional Bernardo O'Higgins. The base for visiting both parks is Puerto Natales, which is often reached on the ferry Puerto Eden from Puerto Montt. Most other visits to this area begin in Punta Arenas, the most southerly city in Chile, and one of the most attractive. A short distance from Puerto Natales, on the Argentine side of the frontier, is more spectacular scenery, notably the famous Perito Moreno Glacier and the mountainous area around Fitz Roy. These, and the small town of Calafate, the base for visiting this region, are also covered in this chapter.

Background

History

Although southern Patagonia was inhabited from the end of the ice ages, the first Europeans did not visit until the 16th century. In 1519 Hernando de Magallanes, a Portuguese sailor serving the Spanish crown, sailed through the Straits that bear his name. The strategic importance of the Straits, connecting Europe with the Pacific, was quickly recognized: soon Spanish naval and merchant ships were using the route, as were mariners from other countries including Francis Drake on his world voyage (1578). However the route

The far south

The original Patagonians

Southern Patagonia was originally inhabited by four indigenous groups, all of whom followed nomadic lifestyles. The Tehuelches, who lived along the eastern side of the Andes as far north as modern-day Bariloche, were hunters of guanaco and rheas. In the 18th century they began to domesticate the wild horses of the region and sailed down the Patagonian rivers to reach the Atlantic coast. They were very large: it is said that the name Patagonia originates from the Spanish qué patagón (what a large foot) on discovering Tehuelche footprints in the sand. The Onas, also hunter-gatherers, lived further south on Tierra del Fuego which they reached at the end of the final ice age when the island was still connected to the mainland. The Yaganes (or Yahgan), who lived largely by fishing further south around the Beagle Channel, traded with the Onas and sailed as far south as Cape Horn. The final group, the Alacalufes lived on the islands along the west coast between the Magellan Straits and the Golfo de Penas further north. They survived in these inhospitable conditions by fishing and hunting seals. A small community survives at Puerto Edén on Isla Wellington.

The fate of all these groups was very similar. The granting by the Chilean government of large land concessions in the late 19th century ended the nomadic life-style of the Tehuelches and the Onas. The Yaganes and the Alacalufes were killed by diseases and alcohol introduced by whalers and sealers. The fate of the Onas was particularly tragic. Many were hunted down and slaughtered by gunmen employed by goldminers and ranchers: the gunmen were paid for each pair of ears they presented. José Fagnano, a Salesian missionary, attempted to save them by taking them to the missions which he founded on Dawson Island in 1888 and near Río Grande in Argentina five years later. Few survived diseases and the change of lifestyle.

became less important after 1616 when the Dutch sailors Jacob le Marie and Cornelius van Schouten discovered a quicker route round Cape Horn.

Although at independence Chile claimed the far southern territories along the Pacific coast, little was done to carry out this claim until 1843 when, concerned at British activities in the area and at rumours of French plans to start a colony, President Bulnes ordered the preparation of a secret mission. The expedition, on board the vessel *Ancud*, established Fuerte Bulnes on a rocky point; the fort was abandoned in 1848 in favour of the new settlement of Punta Arenas.

Geography

This chapter covers the Chilean part of southern Patagonia as well as adjoining areas of Argentina around El Calafate and the Parque Nacional Los Glaciares. Chilean southern Patagonia stretches south from the icefields of the *Campo de Hielo Sur* to the *Estrecho de Magallanes* (Straits of Magellan) which separate South America from Tierra del Fuego. The coastline is heavily indented by fiords; offshore are numerous islands, few of which are inhabited. The remnants of the Andes stretch along the coast, seldom rising above 1,500 metres. Mountains above this altitude include the Cordillera del Paine (several peaks over 2,600 metres) and Cerro Balmaceda (2,035 metres). Most of the western coast is covered with thick rainforest, but further east is grassland.

Together with the Chilean part of Tierra del Fuego and Isla Navarino, this part of Chile is adminstered as Región XII (Magallanes). The whole region (and the adjoining areas of Argentina) are sparsely populated. Although Región XII covers 17.5 percent of Chilean territory, its population is around 171,000, under one percent of the Chilean total. This population is overwhelmingly urban: 160,000 live in towns, most of them in Punta Arenas, the main settlement.

The Far South

Climate

Strong, cold, piercing winds blow, particularly during the spring, when they may exceed 100 kilometres an hour. These bring heavy rain to coastal areas, over 4,000 millimetres a year on the offshore islands. Further east the winds are much drier; annual rainfall at Punta Dungeness at the east end of the Straits of Magellan is only 250 millimetres. Along the coast temperatures are moderated by the sea: summer temperatures are more variable, though seldom rising above 15°C. In winter snow covers the country, except those parts near the sea, making many roads more or less impassable, except on horseback. The winds parch the ground and prevent the growth of crops, except in sheltered spots and greenhouses. When travelling in this region, protection against the ultra-violet rays of the sun is essential.

Economy

Sheep farming is still important to the local economy; much of the meat is exported to Islamic countries, whereas locally produced beef is mainly sold domestically. Potatoes are an important crop, but owing to the climate most other vegetables are grown under cover. Although fishing is perhaps the oldest economic activity in the region, it has been transformed by the growth of salmon farming. Forestry has become more important but also controversial as a result of the use of native forests for woodchips for export to Japan, Taiwan and Brazil. Although oil production has declined as reserves have become depleted, large quantities of natural gas are now produced. About 33 percent of Chilean coal comes from large open cast coal mines on the Brunswick Peninsula, northwest of Punta Arenas; most of it is shipped to the thermal power stations of northern Chile. Tourism is growing rapidly, making an increasingly important contribution to the local economy.

Punta Arenas

Population: 110,000
Phone code: 061
Colour map 7, grid B1

The most southerly city in Chile, and capital of Región XII, Punta Arenas lies 2,140 kilometres south of Santiago. It is situated on the eastern shore of the Brunswick Peninsula facing the Straits of Magellan at almost equal distance from the Pacific and Atlantic oceans. The city is a centre for the local sheep farming and fishing industries and exports wool, skins, and frozen meat. It is also the home of La Polar, the most southerly brewery in the world. Although it has expanded rapidly, particularly in recent years, it remains tranquil and pleasant.

Good roads connect the city with Puerto Natales, 247 kilometres north, and with Río Gallegos in Argentina. Punta Arenas has certain free-port facilities; the Zona Franca is 3½ kilometres north of the centre, on the righthand side of the road to the airport.

History After its foundation in 1848, Punta Arenas became a penal colony modelled on Australia. In 1867 it was opened to foreign settlers and given free port status. From the 1880s it prospered as a refuelling and provisioning centre for steam ships and whaling vessels. It also became a centre for the new sheep *estancias* since it afforded the best harbour facilities. The city's importance was reduced overnight by the opening of the Panama Canal in 1914.

Sheep

Although Bernardo Philippi, Governor of Punta Arenas, imported a few sheep from Chiloé in 1852, sheep farming did not become big business until the 1880s. In 1877 Governor Diego Almeyda brought 300 sheep from the Falkland Islands/Islas Malvinas; they were sold to a British merchant who left them on Isla Isabel in the Magellan Straits. Other merchants established sheep on other islands, where they could not stray and could be easily protected from Tehuelche hunters.

Sheep-farming was not without risks: up to 50 percent of the sheep died on the voyage from the Falklands/Malvinas, while fencing and other equipment were *expensive. However the high price of wool made it worth while especially once the settlement of frontier disputes with Argentina in 1881 enabled the Chilean government to distribute land around Punta Arenas and on Tierra del Fuego. In 1884 alone 570,000 hectares were handed out in 90 lots in the Punta Arenas area. The main beneficiaries were a few local families, whose names are recalled in the street names of Punta Arenas. Their newly acquired lands were converted into sheep estancias, the equipment and many of the shepherds and other workers being brought from the Falklands/Malvinas, New Zealand and Britain.*

Sights

Around the **Plaza Muñoz Gamero** are a number of former mansions of the great sheep ranching families of the late 19th century. See the **Palacio Sara Braun**, which dates from 1895 and which now houses the *Hotel José Nogueira*, see below. In the centre of the plaza is a statue of Magellan with a mermaid and two Fuegian Indians at his feet. According to local wisdom those who rub the big toe of one of the Indians will return to Punta Arenas. Just north of the plaza on Calle Magallanes are the **Palacio Braun Menéndez** (see below) and the **Teatro Cervantes**, which is now a cinema: the interiors of both are worth a visit. Further north, at Av Bulnes 929, is the **Cemetery**, with a **statue of Indicito**, the little Indian (now also an object of reverence, bedecked with flowers, the left knee well-rubbed, northwest side of the cemetery), cypress avenues, and many memorials to pioneer families and victims of shipping disasters. ■ *0800-1800 daily.*

C Pedro Montt runs E-W, while C Jorge Montt runs N-S

West of the Plaza Muñoz Gamero on Calle Fagnano is the **Mirador Cerro de La Cruz** offering a view over the city. Nearby on Waldo Seguel are two reminders of the British influence: the **British School** and **St James Church** next door. The **Parque María Behety**, south of town along 21 de Mayo, features a scale model of Fuerte Bulnes and a campsite, popular for Sunday picnics.

Museo Regional Salesiano Mayorino Borgatello covers the history of indigenous peoples, sections on local animal and bird life, and other interesting aspects of life in Patagonia and Tierra del Fuego, excellent. ■ *In the Colegio Salesiano, Av Bulnes 374, entrance next to church, Tuesday-Saturday 1000-1200 and 1500-1800, Sunday 1500-1800, hours change frequently, entry US$2.50.*

Museums

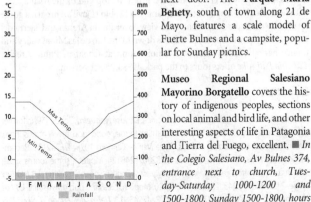

°C / mm

35 · 800
30 · 700
25 · 600
20 · 500
15 · 400
10 · 300
5 · 200
0 · 100
-5 · 0

J F M A M J J A S O N D

Max Temp
Min Temp
Rainfall

Climate: Punta Arenas

The Far South

☛ *Dar-es-Salaam and Aberdeen?*

Today the wooden huts in Punta Arenas have given way to a mishmash of sandstone, concrete and brick. In characteristic New World fashion the town's grid layout pays no attention to topography, and streets continue straight up the hill behind the main square, giving way to steps where the gradient becomes too steep. On the stylish Avenida España, houses of the well-to-do sit smugly behind privet hedges: mock Luytens 'Bayko' styles cheek by jowl with Spanish haciendas, mid-European chalets, modernist Bauhaus blocks and Californian picture-house ranches. In the square itself more solemn Edwardian styles prevail, their dignity preserved in lemon-tinged stonework as yet unsullied by pigeon droppings. The feeling somehow combines the exotic promise of Dar-es-Salaam with the dourness of Aberdeen.

John Pilkington, An Englishman In Patagonia, Century, 1991.

Museo de Historia Regional Braun Menéndez is located in the former mansion of Mauricio Braun, built in 1905. Recommended. Part is set out as room-by-room regional history, the rest of the house is furnished. Guided tours are in Spanish only. ■ *Magallanes 949, off Plaza de Armas, T244216, closed Monday. Open (summer) Tuesday-Friday 1100-1600, Saturday/Sunday 1100-1400 and (winter) 1100-1300, entry US$2.*

The **Instituto de la Patagonia**, Av Bulnes Km 4 north (opposite the University), T244216, houses the **Museo del Recuerdo**, an open-air museum with artefacts used by the early settlers, pioneer homes, and botanical gardens. ■ *Outdoor exhibits open Monday-Friday 0800-1800, indoor pavillions: 0830-1115, 1500-1800.*

Museo Naval y Maritimo, Pedro Montt 981. ■ *Tuesday-Sunday 0930-1230, 1500-1800.*

Excursions

Reserva Forestal Magallanes, seven kilometres west of town and known locally as the Parque Japonés, extends over 13,500 hectares and rises to 600 metres. Follow Independencia up the hill; three kilometres from the edge of town take the right turning for Río de las Minas. The entrance to the reserve is two kilometres beyond, there you will find a self-guided nature trail, one kilometre long, free leaflet. The road continues through the woods for 14 kilometres, passing by several picnic sites. From the top end of the road a short path leads to a lookout over the Garganta del Diablo (Devil's Throat), a gorge formed by the Río de las Minas, with views over Punta Arenas and Tierra del Fuego. From here a slippery path leads down to the Río de las Minas valley and thence back to Punta Arenas. Administration at Conaf in Punta Arenas. *Turismo Pali Aike offers tours to the park, US$3.75 per person.*

Essentials

Sleeping
■ *on map, page 418*
Price codes: see inside front cover Hotel prices are substantially lower during winter months (April-September)

Most hotels include breakfast in the room price. **L2** *José Nogueira*, Bories 959, in former Palacio Sara Braun, T248840, F248832. Beautiful loggia, good food, lovely atmosphere. Recommended. **L3** *Cabo de Hornos*, Plaza Muñoz Gamero 1025, T/F242134. Recommended. **L3** *Finis Terrae*, Colón 766, T228200, F248124. Modern, some rooms small, safe in room, rooftop café/bar with lovely views, English spoken, parking. **L3** *Isla Rey Jorge*, 21 de Mayo 1243, T222681, F248220. Modern, pleasant, pub downstairs. **L3** *Los Navegantes*, Menéndez 647, T244677, F247545. **L3** *Tierra del Fuego*, Colón 716, T/F226200. Good breakfast, parking. Recommended. *Café 1900* downstairs.

La Anónima

The centre of Punta Arenas bears witness to the influence of the people who benfitted most from the Chilean government's distribution of lands in the area after 1881: José Menéndez, whose Estancia San Gregorio covered 90,000 hectares; his neighbours Sara and Maunco Braun at the Pecket Harbour Estancia; their associate Juan Blanchard; and José Noguiera, who married Sara Braun. After Noguiera's death in 1893, his holdings were merged into Braul & Blanchard, which became the largest commercial landowner in Chile; their factory at Puerto Bories, north of Puerto Natales, processed and exported meat from all over southern Argentina and Chile

Further opportunities came the way of Menéndez and Braun & Blanchard after 1899. Following the meeting between the Argentine and Chilean Presidents in Punta Arenas, the Argentine government allowed Chilean entrepreneurs to invest in Argentine Tierra del Fuego. José Menéndez founded two estancias in the Río Grande area, which were named after himself and after his wife, Maria Behety,

while Braun & Blanchard established the Estancia Sara, near San Sebastián.

Although the two companies were linked by the marraige of Maurico Braun to José Menéndez's daughter Josefina, rivalry between them was intense until both were hit by an economic crisis in 1907. In the following year they merged their holdings into the Sociedad Anónima Importadora y Exportado de la Patagonia, usually known simply as La Anónima, and in 1910 they moved their headquarters to Buenos Aires. In the following years the company extended its influence over southern Argentina; apart from its extensive landholdings, it established a chain of general stores in 45 cities and towns, built slaughter houses, meat-processing plants and port facilities, and operated shipping services, newspapers and radio stations. Its continued existence can be seen in Argentina in the form of the supermarket chain known simply as La Anónima.

A2 *Hostería Yaganes*, Camino Antiguo Norte Km 7.5, T211600, F211948. *Cabañas* on the shores of the Straits of Magellan, nice setting. **A1-A2** *Apart Hotel Colonizadores*, Colón 1106, T243578, F244499. Clean, fully furnished apartments (2 bedrooms **A1**, 1 bedroom **A2**) discounts for long stay. **A3** *Colonizadores*, 21 de Mayo 1690, T244144, F226587. **A3** *Hostal Carpa Manzano*, Lautaro Navarro 336, T/F248864. Recommended. **A3** *Cóndor del Plata*, Colón 556, T247987, F241149. Excellent breakfast. **A2** *Mercurio*, Fagnano 595, T/F242300. TV and phone, good restaurant and service. Recommended. **A3** *Plaza*, Nogueira 1116, piso 2, T241300, F248613. (**B** without bath), pleasant, good breakfast.

B *Hostal del Sur*, Mejicana 151, T227249, F222282, large rooms, excellent breakfast. Highly recommended. **B** *Monte Carlo*, Colón 605, T/F243438, also **D** pp without bath, traditional, charming, good food. **B** *Hostal Patagonia*, Croacia 970, T249970, without bath. **B** *Savoy*, Menéndez 1073, T241951, F247979. Pleasant rooms but some lack windows, good place to eat. **B** *Ritz*, Pedro Montt 1102, T224422. Old, clean and cosy. Recommended (Bruce Chatwin stayed here: see his name in the guest book). **B** *Hotel El Pionero*, Chiloé 1210, T248851, F248263. With bath. **C** *Res Central*, No 1 España 247, T222315, No 2 Sanhueza 185, T222845. With bath (**D** without). Comfortable. **B** *Hostal de la Avenida*, Colón 534, T247532. Good breakfast, friendly, safe. Recommended. **B** *Hostal Del Estrecho*, Menéndez 1048, T/F241011. With breakfast and bath.

C *Albatros,* Colón 1195, T223131. Without bath, good. **C** *Hosp Lodging*, Sanhueza 933, T221035. With bath, **E** pp without, clean, heating, modern. **C** *Res Sonia Kuscevic*, Pasaje Darwin 175 (Angamos altura 550), T248543. Popular, Hostelling International discounts, with bath, breakfast, hot water, heating, parking.

D *Casa Dinka,* Caupolicán 169, T226056. With breakfast, use of kitchen, noisy. **D** *Hostal Calafate*, Lautaro Navarro 850, T248415, F228205, with large breakfast. **D** pp *Res Roca*, Magallones 888, T243903. Without bath, clean. **D** pp *Res Rubio*, España 640,

T226458. With bath, helpful. Accommodation available in many private houses, usually **E** pp, ask at tourist office. **D** *Sra Carlina Ramírez*, Paraguaya 150, T247687. Motorcycle parking, meals, safe, quiet. Recommended.

E pp *The Pink House*, Caupolicán 99, T222436. With breakfast, clean. **D** *Hostal O'Higgins*, O'Higgins 1205, T225205, F243438. With breakfast, very clean. **D** *Hostal Paradiso*, Angamos 1073, T224212. With bath, breakfast, parking, use of kitchen. Recommended. **E** *Hosp Nena*, Boliviana 366, T242411. Friendly, with large breakfast. **E** pp, España y Boliviana, T247422. Without bath, clean, friendly, use of kitchen. **E** Sanhueza 750. Homely. Recommended. **E** pp *Hosp Independencia*, Independencia 374, T227572, with breakfast, kitchen facilities, camping. **E** pp *Alojamiento Golondrina*, Lautaro Navarro 182, T229708, kitchen facilities, meals served, English spoken. Recommended.

Punta Arenas

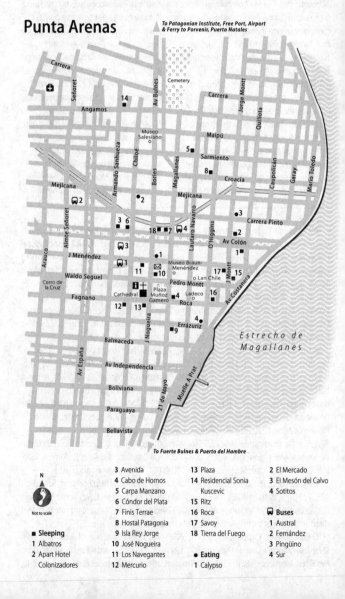

N	3 Avenida	13 Plaza	2 El Mercado
	4 Cabo de Hornos	14 Residencial Sonia	3 El Mesón del Calvo
	5 Carpa Manzano	Kuscevic	4 Sotitos
	6 Cóndor del Plata	15 Ritz	
Not to scale	7 Finis Terrae	16 Roca	**Buses**
	8 Hostal Patagonia	17 Savoy	1 Austral
■ **Sleeping**	9 Isla Rey Jorge	18 Tierra del Fuego	2 Fernández
1 Albatros	10 José Nogueira		3 Pingüino
2 Apart Hotel	11 Los Navegantes	● **Eating**	4 Sur
Colonizadores	12 Mercurio	1 Calypso	

F pp *Alojamiento Prat*, Sgto Aldea 0520. Clean. Recommended. **F** pp *Backpackers Lodging*, O'Higgins 646, T220567, without breakfast, helpful. Dormitory accommodation may also be available at the Salvation Army hostel, Bellavista 577. Kitchen, hot showers, clean. Dormitory accommodation, **F** pp, also at the Colegio Pierre Fauré, Bellavista 697, in January/February.

Camping There are no campsites in or near the city.

Main hotels Good value set lunches and dinners at *Cabo de Hornos*, excellent restaurants at *Los Navegantes* and *José Nogueira* which has a lovely dining room.

El Mercado, Mejicana 617, open 24 hours, reasonably priced set lunch, expensive à la carte. *Centro Español*, Plaza Muñoz Gamero 771, above Teatro Cervantes. Large helpings, limited selection, reasonably priced. *El Mesón del Calvo*, Jorge Montt 687. Excellent, seafood, lamb, small portions, pricey. Recommended. *Sotitos*, O'Higgins 1138. Good service and cuisine, excellent. Recommended. *Lucerna*, Bories 624. Excellent meat, reasonably priced, good. *Calypso*, Bories 817. Open Sunday evening, busy at night, smoky, cheap. *Bianco's Pizza*, Bulnes 01306. Excellent pizzas. Recommended. *El Quijote*, Lautaro Navarro 1087. Good sandwiches and fish dishes. Highly recommended. *Asturias*, Lautaro Navarro 967. Good food and atmosphere. *La Casa de Juan*, O'Higgins 1021. Spanish food. *El Estribo*, Carrera Pinto 762. Good grill, also fish. *Yaganes*, Camino Antiguo Norte Km 7.5. Beautiful setting, weekend buffet. *Golden Dragon*, Colón 529. Chinese, expensive. *La Terraza*, 21 de Mayo 1288. Sandwiches, *empanadas* and beer, cheap and good. *La Taberna del Club de la Unión*, Plaza Muñoz Gamero y Seguel. For drinks. For economic set lunches several along Chiloé: *Restaurant de Turismo Punta Arenas*, No 1280. Good, friendly. Recommended. *Los Años 60 The Mitchel*, No 1231. Also serves beer and 26 varieties of sandwiches, open 24 hours. *Parrilla Apocalipsis*, Chiloé esq Balmaceda. *Carioca*, Menéndez 600 y Chiloé. *Parrilla*, cheap lunches, snacks and beer, very friendly. *Lomit's*, Menéndez 722. Cheap snacks and drinks, open when the others are closed. *Kiosco Roca* (no sign), Roca 875. Early morning coffee. Cheap fish meals available at stalls in the *Cocinerías*, Lautaro Navarro south of the port entrance. Excellent *empanadas*, bread and pastries at *Pancal*, 21 de Mayo 1280. Also at *La Espiga*, Errázuriz 632. Excellent pastries at *Casa del Pastel*, Carrera Pinto y O'Higgins.

Lobster has become more expensive because of a law allowing only lobster pots. *Centolla* (king crab) is caught illegally by some fishermen using dolphin, porpoise and penguin as live bait. There are seasonal bans on *centolla* fishing to protect dwindling stocks, do not purchase *centolla* out of season. At times *centolla* fishing is banned because the crabs can be infected with a disease which is fatal to humans. If this ban refers to the *marea roja* (red tide), it does not affect crabs, only bivalve shellfish. Mussels should not be picked along the shore owing to pollution and the *marea roja*.

Eating
● *on map*
Many eating places close on Sunday

Bars & nightclubs *The Queen's Club*, 21 de Mayo 1455. *Sexywoman*, Av España. *Tentación*, Av Colón. Recommended.

Discotheques *Jack*, Carrera Pinto y Bories. *Yordi*, Pedro Montt 937. *Borssalino*, Bories 587. **On the southern outskirts**: *Torreones*, Km 5.5, T261985. *Salsoteca*, Km 5. **To the north**: *Drive-In Los Brujos*, Km 7.5, T212600.

Entertainment

Golf 9-hole golf course 5 kilometres south of town on road to Fuerte Bulnes. **Skiing** Cerro Mirador, only 9 kilometres west from Punta Arenas in the Reserva Nacional Magallanes, is one of the few places where you can ski with a sea view. Transtur buses 0900 and 1400 from in front of *Hotel Cabo de Hornos*, US$3 return, taxi US$7. Daily lift-ticket, US$7; equipment rental, US$6 per adult. Mid-way lodge with food, drink and equipment. Season June to September, weather permitting. Contact the Club Andino, T241479, about crosscountry skiing facilities. Also skiing at Tres Morros.

Sports

The Far South

Shopping For leather goods and sheepskin try the Zona Franca; quality of other goods is low and prices little better than elsewhere; Monday-Saturday 1030-1230, 1500-2000 (bus E or A from Plaza Muñoz Gamero; many *colectivos*; taxi US$3). Handicrafts at *Pingüi*, Bories 404, (also stocks books on Tierra del Fuego, Patagonia and Antarctica). *Artesanía Ramas*, Independencia 799, *Chile Típico*, Carrera Pinto 1015, *Indoamérica*, Colón y Magallanes and outdoor stalls at the bottom of Independencia, by the port entrance.

Cameras Wide range of cameras but limited range of film, from Zona Franca. *Foto Sánchez,* Bories 768, for Fuji film and *Fotocentro*, Bories 789, for Agfa: all have same day print-processing service.

Chocolate Hand made chocolate from *Chocolatería Tres Arroyos*, Bories 448, T241522. *Chocolatería Regional Norweisser*, José Miguel Carrera 663. Both good.

Supermarkets *Listo*, 21 de Mayo 1133. *Cofrima*, Lautaro Navarro 1293 y Balmaceda. *Cofrima 2*, España 01375. *Marisol*, Zenteno 0164.

Transport
All transport is heavily booked from Christmas through to March: advance booking strongly advised

Local Car hire: **NB** You need a hire company's authorization to take a car into Argentina. *American Rent a Car*, Menéndez 631, T/F240852, try bargaining, friendly. *Hertz*, O'Higgins 987, T248742, F244729, English spoken. *Australmag*, Colón 900, T242174, F226916. *Autómovil Club*, O'Higgins 931, T243675, F243097, and at airport. *Budget*, O'Higgins 964, T241696. *Internacional*, Sarmiento 790-B, T228323, F226334. Recommended. *Willemsen*, Lautaro Navarro 1038, T247787, F241083. Highly recommended. *Lubac*, Magallanes 970, T/F242023/247060. *Todoauto*, España 0480, T212492, F212627.

Car repair: *Automotores del Sur*, O'Higgins 850, T224153.

Taxis: ordinary taxis have yellow roofs. *Colectivos* (all black) run on fixed routes, US$0.50 for anywhere on route. Reliable service from *Radio Taxi Austral*, T247710/244409.

Cycle parts: *José Aguila Quezada*, Arauco 2675, T265399. **Motorcycle parts**: *Violic*, Sanhueza 285, T241606, also in the Zona Franca.

Long distance Air: Carlos Ibáñez de Campo Airport, 20 kilometres north of town (served by Punta Arenas-Puerto Natales buses). Bus service by Buses Transfer (address below) scheduled to meet flights, US$2.50. LanChile, DAP and Ladeco have their own bus services from town, US$2.50; taxi US$12. The airport restaurant is good. To **Santiago**, LanChile, Ladeco and Avant daily US$220, via Puerto Montt (sit on right for views). When no tickets are available, go to the airport and get on the standby waiting list. To **Porvenir**, Aerovías DAP daily at 0815 and 1730, return 0830 and 1750 (US$20), plus other irregular flights, with Twin-Otter and Cessna aircraft. (Heavily booked with long waiting list so make sure you have your return reservation confirmed.) Military (FACh) flights approx twice a month to Puerto Montt US$30, information and tickets from airforce base at the airport, Spanish essential, T213559; need to book well in advance. It is very difficult to get space during the summer as all armed forces personel and their families have priority over civilians. For flights to Puerto Williams see page 468.

International services To Argentina: to Ushuaia, Aerovías DAP twice a week. To Río Grande, Kaiken 5 a week. Reserve well in advance from mid-December to February. To Falkland Islands/Islas Malvinas, LanChile, Saturdays, US$230 (flies via Río Gallegos, Argentina, once a month).

Bus timetables are printed daily in La Prensa Austral

Bus company offices: *Pingüino* and *Fernández*, Sanhueza 745, T242313, F225984. *Tecni Austral*, Lautaro Navarro 975, T223205. *Pacheco*, Colón 900, T242174. *Bus Sur*, Colón y Magallanes, T244464. *Austral Bus*, Menéndez 565, T247139, T/F241708.

The Far South

Gesell, Menéndez 556, T222896. *Los Carlos*, Plaza Muñoz Gamero 1039, T241321. *Turbus*, Errázuriz 932, T/F225315. *Buses Transfer*, J Menéndez 631, T220766.

Bus services: buses leave from company offices. To **Puerto Natales**, 3½ hours, Fernández, Austral Bus, and Buses Sur, several every day, last departure 2000, US$7, book in advance. *In-Tur* (see **Tour companies**, below) runs a twice daily circuit Punta Arenas-Puerto Natales-Torres del Paine in minibuses with snack, English-speaking guide and including National Park entry. Service runs mid-October to mid-April. Tur Bus, Ghisoni and Austral have services through Argentina to **Osorno, Puerto Montt** and **Castro**. Fares: to Puerto Montt or Osorno US$60-75 (cheaper off season) 36 hours; to Castro US$ 67-83 (uncomfortable, not recommended); Tur Bus continues to **Santiago**, US$95 (cheaper in winter), 46 hours.

To **Río Gallegos**, Argentina, Pingüino daily 1200, return 1300; Ghisoni, daily except Friday, 1000; Magallanes Tour, Tuesday 1000. Fares US$20-22, officially 5 hours, but can take up to 8 (taxi to Río Gallegos US$130). Services to Buenos Aires, Pinguino, via Río Gallegos, US$120. To **Río Grande**, Hector Pacheco, Monday, Wednesday, Friday 0730 via Punta Delgada, return Tuesday, Thursday and Saturday, 0730, 10 hours, US$27, heavily booked. To **Ushuaia** via Punta Delgada, 14 hours, book any return at same time. Tecni Austral, Tuesday, Thursday, Saturday 0800, US$48; Tolkeyen, Monday, Wednesday, Friday 0800, US$50. Alternatively, Tecni Austral runs daily from Río Grande to Ushuaia at 0730 and 1800, 4 hours, US$20.

Ferry: for services to Porvenir, Tierra del Fuego, see page 455.

Shipping Services For *Navimag* services Puerto Montt – Puerto Natales, see under Puerto Montt, page 349 (confirmation of reservations is advised). Visits to the beautiful fjords and glaciers of Tierra del Fuego are highly recommended. Comapa runs a once a fortnight 22-hour, 320-kilometres round trip to the fjord d'Agostino, 30 kilometres long, where many glaciers come down to the sea. The luxury cruiser, *Terra Australis*, sails from Punta Arenas on Saturday via Ushuaia and Puerto Williams; details from Comapa. Advance booking (advisable) from Cruceros Australis SA, Miraflores 178, piso 12, Santiago, T6963211, F331871. Government supply ships are recommended for the young and hardy, but take sleeping bag and extra food, and travel pills. For transport on navy supply ships to Puerto Williams, enquire at Tercera Zona Naval, Lautaro Navarro 1150, or ask the captain direct, but be prepared to be frustrated by irregular sailings and inaccurate information. All tickets on ships must be booked in advance January-February.

Most cruise ships leave from Ushuaia. Other than asking in agencies for possible empty berths on the few cruise ships which call here, the only possibility is with the Chilean navy. The navy itself does not encourage passengers, so you must approach the captain of the vessel in the port. Spanish is essential. The two naval vessels, the *Galvarino* and the *Lautaro*, charge US$80 pp per day. There is no accurate schedule. Accommodation includes 4 meals a day (2 with meat), laundry facilities. Take twice as much film as you think you'll need. During the voyage across the Drake Passage albatrosses, petrels, cormorants, penguins, elephant seals, fur seals, whales and dolphins can be sighted.

To Antarctica

From Punta Arenas there are 3 routes to Calafate and Río Gallegos: 1) northeast via Route 255 and Punta Delgada to the frontier at Kimiri Aike and then along Argentine Route 3 to Río Gallegos. 2) north along Route 9, turning 9 kilometres before Puerto Natales for Dorotea (good road) and then northeast via La Esperanza (fuel, basic accommodation). 3) Via Puerto Natales and Cerro Castillo on the road to Torres del Paine joining the road to La Esperanza at Paso Cancha.

Overland to Argentina

The Far South

Directory **Airline offices** *Avant*, Roca 924, T228312, F220735, airport 219507. *LanChile*, Lautaro Navarro 999, T241232, F222366. *Ladeco*, Lautaro Navarro 1155, T/F241100/223340. *Aerovías DAP*, O'Higgins 891, T223340, F221693. Open 0900-1230, 1430-1930.

Banks open Mon-Fri **Banks** *Banco BCI*, 21 de Mayo 1199. *Banco Santiago*, on Plaza Muñoz Gamero, Visa. *Banco*
0830-1400 *Santander*, Magallanes 997. *Corp Banca*, Magallanes 944. Most have ATMs. *Casas de cambio* open Mon-Fri 0900-1230, 1500-1900, Sat 0900-1230. Outside business hours try *Buses Sur*, Colón y Magallanes, kiosk at *Calypso Café*, Bories 817 and the major hotels (lower rates). *Corp Banca*, Magallanes y Menéndez. Argentine pesos can be bought at *casas de cambio*. Good rates at *Cambio Gasic*, Roca 915, Oficina 8, T242396. German spoken. *La Hermandad*, Lautaro Navarro 1099, T243991. Excellent rates, US$ cash for Amex TCs and credit cards. *Sur Cambios*, Lautaro Navarro 1001, T225656. Accepts TCs. *Kiosco Redondito*, Mejicana 613, in the shopping centre, T247369.

Communications Post Office: Bories 911 y Menéndez. Mon-Fri 0830-1930, Sat 0900-1400. **Telecommunications:** for international and national calls and faxes (shop around as prices vary). *CTC*, Plaza Muñoz Gamero. Daily 0800-2200. *CTC*, Roca 886, local 23. Daily 0900-2030. *Entel*, Lautaro Navarro 957. Mon-Fri 0830-2200, Sat-Sun 0900-2200. *Telex-Chile/Chile-Sat*, Bories 911 and Errázuriz 856. Daily 0830-2200, also offers telex and telegram service. *VTR*, Bories 801. Closed Sat afternoon and Sun. For international calls and faxes at any hour *Hotel Cabo de Hornos*, credit cards accepted, open to non-residents. **Internet access:** *Austrointernet Services*, Bories 687, piso 2, T/F229279/227971, US$6 per hour. *Canadian Language Institute*, O'Higgins y Carrera Pinto, US$5 per hour.

Consulates *Argentina*, 21 de Mayo 1878, T261912. Open 1000-1400, visas take 24 hrs, US$25. *Brazil*, Arauco 769, T241093. *Belgium*, Roca 817, Oficina 61, T241472. *Denmark*, Colón 819, Depto 301, T221488. *Finland*, Independencia 660, T247385. *Germany*, Pasaje Korner 1046, T241082, Casilla 229. *Italy*, 21 de Mayo 1569, T242497. *Netherlands*, Sarmiento 780, T248100. *Norway*, Independencia 830, T242171. *Spain*, Menéndez 910, T243566. *Sweden*, Errazúriz 891, T224107. *United Kingdom*, Roca 924, T247020.

Hospitals & medical services Dentists: *Dr Hugo Vera Cárcamo*, España 1518, T227510. Recommended. *Rosemary Robertson Stipicic*, 21 de Mayo 1380, T22931. Speaks English. Hospitals: *Hospital Regional Lautaro Navarro*, Angamos 180, T244040. Public hospital, for emergency room ask for *La Posta*. *Clínica Magallanes*, Bulnes 01448, T211527. Private clinic, medical staff is the same as in the hospital but fancier surroundings and more expensive.

Laundry *Lavasol*, the only self-service, O'Higgins 969, T243067. Mon-Sat 0900-2030, Sun (summer only) 1000-1800, US$6 per machine, wash and dry, good but busy. *Lavaseco Josseau*, Carrera Pinto 766, T228413.

Shipping offices *Navimag*, Independencia 830, T244400, F242003. *Comapa* (Compañía Marítima de Punta Arenas), Independencia 830, T244400, F247514.

Tour companies & travel agents *Turismo Lazo*, Angamos 1366, T/F223771. Wide range of tours. Highly recommended. *Turismo Aventour*, Nogueira 1255, T241197, F243354. English spoken, specializes in fishing trips, organize tours to Tierra del Fuego. *Turismo Comapa*, Independencia 840, T241437, F247514. Tours to Torres del Paine, Tierra del Fuego, also trips to the Falklands/Malvinas, charter boats to Cape Horn and Isla Magdalena. *Turismo Runner*, Lautaro Navarro 1065, T247050, F241042. Adventure tours. *Arka Patagonia*, Ignacio Carrera Pinto 946, T248167, F241504. All types of tours, rafting, fishing, etc. *Turismo Pehoé*, Menéndez 918, T244506, F248052. Organizes tours and hotels, enquire here about catamaran services. *Turismo Aonikenk*, Magallanes 619, T228332. Recommended. *Turismo Pali Aike*, Lautaro Navarro 1129, T223301. *El Conquistador*, Menéndez 556, T222896. Recommended. *Turismo Viento Sur*, Fagnano 565, T/F225167. For camping equipment, fishing excursions, English spoken, good tours. Recommended. *Turismo Patagonia*, Bories 655 local 2, T248474, F247182. Specializes in fishing trips. Most organize tours to Torres del Paine, Fuerte Bulnes and *pingüineras* on Otway sound: shop around as prices vary. Sr Mateo Quesada, Chiloé 1375, T222662, offers local tours in his car, up to 4 passengers. *In-Tur* is an association of companies which aims to promote tourism in Chilean Patagonia. The members are *Arka Patagonia*, *Turismo Aventour*, *Turismo Pehoé*, *Turismo Runner*, *Aerovías DAP* and *Hostería Las Torres* (in the Parque Nacional Torres del Paine). The head office is at Errázuriz 840, p 2, Punta Arenas, T/F229049, which can be contacted for information. See **Bus**, above, for In-Tur's SIB bus to Torres del Paine.

Tourist offices *Sernatur*, Waldo Seguel 689, Casilla 106-D, T241330. At the corner with Plaza Muñoz Gamero, 0830-1745, closed Sat and Sun. Helpful, English spoken. Kiosk on Colón between Bories and Magallanes Mon-Fri 0900-1300, 1500-1900, Sat 0900-1200, 1430-1730, Sun (in the summer only) 1000-1230. Turistel Guide available from kiosk belonging to *Café Garogha* at Bories 831. *Conaf*, Menéndez 1147, piso 2, T223841. Open Mon-Fri.

Longer excursions

Situated 56 kilometres south of Punta Arenas, Fuerte Bulnes is a replica of the **Fuerte Bulnes**
wooden fort erected in 1843 by the crew of the Chilean vessel *Ancud*. Nearby is
Puerto Hambre. Tours by several agencies, US$12. At the intersection of the
roads to Puerto del Hambre and Fuerte Bulnes, 51 kilometres south of Punta
Arenas, is a small marker with a plaque of the Centro Geográfico de Chile, ie
the midway point between Arica and the South Pole.

Fifty three kilometres south, covering 18,814 hectares, this reserve has older **Reserva Forestal**
forest than the Magallanes Reserve and sphagnum bogs. There is a three hour **Laguna Parrillar**
walk to the tree-line along poorly marked paths. There are fine views from the
Mirador. There is no public transport, radio taxi US$60.

Seventy kilometres north of Punta Arenas, Seno Otway is the site of a colony of **Seno Otway**
Magellanic penguins which can be visited (November-March only). Rheas
and skunks can also be seen. Tours by several agencies, US$12, entry US$4;
taxi US$35 return.

A small island 25 kilometres northeast, Isla Magdalena is the location of the **Isla Magdalena**
Monumento Natural Los Pingüinos, a colony of 150,000 penguins. Deserted
apart from the breeding season (November-January), the island is administered by Conaf. Magdalena is one of a group of three islands, the others are
Marta and Isabel, visited by Drake, whose men killed 3,000 penguins for food.
It can be visited by boat with Comapa, address above: Tuesday, Thursday, Saturday, 0800 (December-February), two hours each way, with two hours on the
island, return 1400, coffee and biscuits served, US$30, subject to cancellation
if windy; full refund given. Recommended.

The Far South

Port Famine (Puerto Hambre)

In 1582 Felipe II of Spain, alarmed by Drake's passage through the Straits of Magellan, decided to establish a Spanish presence on the Straits. A fleet of 15 ships and 4,000 men, commanded by Pedro Sarmiento de Gamboa, was despatched in 1584. The ships were scattered by storms, only three arriving with 300 men on board. With his small force Sarmiento founded two cities: Nombre de Jesús on Punta Dungeness at the eastern entrance to the Straits and Rey Felipe near Puerto Hambre.

Disaster struck when their only remaining vessel broke its anchorage in a storm; the ship, with Sarmiento on board was blown into the Atlantic. After vain attempts to re-enter the Straits, Sarmiento set sail for Río de Janeiro where he organized two rescue missions: the first ended in shipwreck, the second in mutiny. Captured by English corsairs, Sarmiento was taken to England where he was imprisoned. Released by Elizabeth I, he tried to return to Spain via France, where he was gaoled again. Until his death in 1608, Sarmiento besieged Felipe II with letters urging him to rescue the men stranded in the Straits.

When the English corsair Thomas Cavendish sailed through the Straits in 1587 he found only one survivor at Rey Felipe, the remainder having hanged themselves, or starved owing to the lack of supplies and the inhospitable climate. Cavendish named the place Port Famine.

North from Punta Arenas

From Punta Arenas a road runs to Puerto Natales, 247 kilometres north; the southbound lane is paved; the northbound lane is *ripio* but is being paved. Arond Villa Tehuelches, 100 kilometres north of Punta Arenas, a sign invites you to see '*Panchito*', a tame condor, US$0.25. Fuel is available in Villa Tehuelches.

Sleeping Along this road are several hotels, including **C** *Hostería Río Verde*, Km 90, east off the highway on Seno Skyring, T311122, F241008. Private bath, heating. **B** *Hostal Río Penitente*, Km 138, T331694. In an old *estancia*. Recommended. **C** *Hotel Rubens*, Km 183, T226916. Popular for fishing. *Hostería Llanuras de Diana*, Km 215 (30 kilometres south of Puerto Natales), T248742, F244729 (Punta Arenas), T411540 (Puerto Natales). Hidden from road, beautifully situated. Highly recommended.

Puerto Natales

Population: 15,000
Phone code: 061
Colour map 6, grid B3

Situated 247 kilometres north of Punta Arenas, Puerto Natales lies on the eastern shore of the Seno Ultima Esperanza (Last Hope Sound) amid spectacular scenery and is the jumping-off place for the magnificent Balmaceda and Torres del Paine national parks. There are fine views over the Seno Ultima Esperanza to the Peninsula Antonio Varas.

Founded in 1911 it grew as an industrial centre: at Puerto Bories, six kilometres north, there was the biggest meatpacking factory in Patagonia; though much of the old plant was destroyed by fire, the administration buildings and housing can be visited. Until recent years the town's prosperity was based upon employment in the coal mines of Río Turbio, nearby in Argentina.

Museo de Agostini in the Colegio Salesiano at Padre Rossa 1456, has one room on Tierra del Fuego fauna. ■ *Free*. **Museo Histórico Municipal**, Bulnes 285. ■ *Tuesday-Sunday 1500-1800*.

The Far South

Local Wildlife

A good place to photograph rheas (ñandúes) and guanacos is a few kilometres north of the checkpoint at Kon Aiken, the turnoff for Otway. Antarctic cormorants can be seen sitting on offshore rocks from the road to Fuerte Bulnes. The local skunk (chingüe) is apparently very docile and rarely sprays. Also look out for foxes and the Great Horned Owl.

Arthur Shapiro (Dept of Zoology, University of California, Davis).

Excursions

A recommended walk is up to **Cerro Dorotea** which dominates the town, with superb views of the whole Seno Ultima Esperanza. It can also be reached by any Río Turbio bus.

For excursions to the Torres del Paine and the Monte Balmaceda national parks, see below

Monumento Natural Cueva Milodón (50 metres wide, 200 metres deep, 30 metres high), 25 kilometres north, contains a plastic model of the prehistoric ground-sloth whose bones were found there in 1895. Evidence has also been found here of occupation by early Patagonian humans some 11,000 years ago. Nearby there is a visitor's centre with good displays on the mylodon and on local geology, summaries in English. There is free camping once the US$4 entrance fee has been paid. Buses J and B regular service US$7.50; taxi US$18 return or check if you can get a ride with a tour; both Adventur and Fernández tour buses to Torres del Paine stop at the cave.

Estancia Rosario, T410836, on the Peninsula Antonio Varas on the western side of the Seno Ultima Esperanza, offers lunches, horseriding, US$22 per person for three hours, and other activities, transport across the sound included.

Essentials

In season cheaper accommodation fills up quickly after the arrival of the *Puerto Edén* from Puerto Montt

Sleeping
■ *on map, page 426*
Price codes:
see inside front cover
Most prices include breakfast

L3 *Eberhard*, Pedro Montt 58, T411208, F411209. Excellent views, restaurant.
L3 *Costa Australis*, Pedro Montt 262, T412000, F411881. Modern, good views, popular cafeteria. Recommended.

L3 *Martín Guisinde*, Bories 278, T412770, F412820. Pub, restaurant, modern. Recommended. **A1** *Palace*, Ladrilleros 209, T411134. Good food, overpriced. **A2** *Juan Ladrilleros*, Pedro Montt 161, T411652, F412109. Modern, with bath, good restaurant, clean. Recommended. **A2** *Glaciares*, Eberhard 104, T412189, F411452. New, snack bar. **A2** *Hostal Sir Francis Drake*, Phillipi 383, T/F411553. Good views, snack bar. Recommended. **A3** *Hostal Lady Florence Dixie*, Bulnes 659, T411158, F411943. Modern, friendly. Recommended. **A3** *Lukoviek*, Ramirez 324, T411120, F412580, with breakfast, restaurant, helpful. **A3** *Lago Sarmiento*, Bulnes 90, T411542. Good views, restaurant. **A3** *Saltos del Paine*, Bulnes 156, T413608. Excellent.

B *Blanquita*, Carrera Pinto 409. Quiet. Recommended. **B** *Hostal Melissa*, Blanco Encalada 258, T411944. With bath. **B** *Natalino*, Eberhard 371, T411968. Clean and very friendly (tours to Milodón Cave arranged), **C** without bath, parking. **B** *Hostal Reymar*, Baquedano 414, T/F411434, with breakfast, good restaurant. **B** *Amerindia Concept*, Bories y Costanera, also **E** pp dormitory accommodation, lovely views, rock climbing courses and tours, good meeting place, slide shows, pizzeria. Recommended.

C *Hostal Los Antiguos*, Ladrilleros 195 y Bulnes, T/F411488. Without bath, pleasant. **C** *Res Carahue*, Bulnes 370, T411339. With breakfast, laundry facilities, pleasant. **C** *Bulnes*, Calle Bulnes 407, T411307. With breakfast, good, stores luggage. **C** *Hostal Puerto Natales*, Eberhard 250, T411098. With bath.

The Far South

D *Res Centro*, Magallanes 258A, T411996. With bath. **D** *Res Sutherland*, Barros Arana 155. With bath, welcoming, clean, kitchen facilities. **D** *Res Asturias*, Prat 426, T412105, with breakfast, kitchen facilities, cosy.

E pp *Hosp Niko's*, Ramirez 669, T412810, with breakfast, good meals, English spoken, also dormitory accommodation, **F** pp, recommended. **E** pp *Hosp La Chila*, Carrera Pinto 442. Use of kitchen, welcoming, luggage store, bakes bread. Recommended. **E** pp *Hosp María José*, Magallanes 646. Cooking facilities, helpful. **E** pp *Hosp Gamma/Milodón*, El Roble 650, T411420. Cooking and laundry facilities, evening meals, tours. **E** pp *Los Inmigrantes*, Carrera Pinto 480. Good breakfast, clean, kitchen facilities, equipment rental, luggage store. Recommended. **E** pp *Res El Mundial*, Bories 315, T412476. Use of kitchen, good value meals, luggage stored. Recommended. **E** pp *Tierra del Fuego*, Bulnes 29. Clean, will store luggage, good. **E** pp *Casa de familia Bustamante*, Bulnes 317, T411061. Clean, good breakfast, helpful, luggage store. Recommended. **E** pp *Hosp Elsa Millán*, Elcano 588. Good breakfast, homemade bread, dormitory-style, popular, hot water, warm, friendly, cooking facilities. Recommended. **E** pp *Res Dickson*, Bulnes 307, T411218. Good breakfast, clean, helpful, cooking and laundry facilities. Recommended. **E** pp *Pensión Ritz*, Carrera Pinto 439. Full pension available, friendly. **E** pp *Res Temuco*, Ramírez 310, T411120. Friendly, reasonable, good food, clean. **E** pp *Hosp Laury*, Bulnes 222. With breakfast, cooking and laundry facilities, clean, warm, friendly. **E** pp *Almirante Nieto*, Bories 206. Use of kitchen, dormitory accommodation, sleeping bag necessary, good meeting place, friendly. **D** pp *Casa Cecilia*, Tomás Rogers 60, T/F411797/413875, redcecilia@entelchile.net. With bath, also **E** pp without bath, with breakfast, clean, cooking facilities, English, French and German spoken, kitchen facilities, heating, camping

Puerto Natales

■ Sleeping	10 Juan Ladrilleros	20 Residencial Carahue
1 Amerindia Concept	11 Lady Florence Dixie	21 Residencial Niko's
2 Blanquita	12 Lago Sarmiento	22 Residencial Temuco
3 Bulnes	13 Laury	23 Sir Francis Drake
4 Casa Cecilia	14 Lukoviek	
5 Costa Australis	15 Martín Guisinde	● Eating
6 Dickson	16 Melissa	1 Centro Español
7 Eberhard	17 Natalino	2 La Ultima Esperanza
8 Famatina	18 Palace	
9 Glaciares	19 Puerto Natales	

equipment rental, information on Torres del Paine, tours organized, credit cards accepted, internet access, airline tickets sold. Warmly recommended **E** pp *Patagonia Adventure*, Tomás Rogers 179, T411028. Dormitory style, and private rooms, friendly, clean, use of kitchen, breakfast, English spoken, camping equipment for hire, book exchange. Recommended. **E** pp Sra Bruna Mardones, Pasaje Don Bosco 41 (off Philippi). Friendly, meals on request. **E** pp *Casa de familia Alicia*, M Rodríguez 283. With breakfast, clean, spacious, luggage stored, helpful. Recommended. **E** pp *Don Bosco*, Padre Rossa 1430. Good meals, pancakes for breakfast, use of kitchen, helpful. Recommended. Motorcycle parking, luggage store. **E** *Res Nataly*, O'Higgins 657. Dormitornies. **E-F** pp *Casa Teresa*, Esmeralda 463. Good value, warm, cheap meals, quiet, friendly. Recommended. Tours to Torres del Paine arranged. **F** pp *Res Lago Pingo*, Bulnes 808, T411026. Basic, with breakfast, laundry, use of kitchen, luggage stored, English spoken; similar at O'Higgins 70, 431 and Perito 443.

North of Puerto Natales are: **A2** *Cabañas Kotenk Aike*, 2 kilometres north of town, T412581, F225935, sleep 4, very comfortable. **L3-A2** *Cisne de Cuello Negro*, a former guest house for meat buyers at the disused meat packing plant, 5 kilometres from town at Km 275 near Puerto Bories, T411498 (Av Colón 782, Punta Arenas, T244506, F248052). Friendly, clean, reasonable, excellent cooking. Recommended. **C** *Hotel 3 Pasos*, 40 kilometres north, T228113. Simple, beautiful. In Villa Cerro Castillo, 63 kilometres north. **B** *Hostería El Pionero*, T/F411646/691932 anexo 722. With bath, country house ambience, good service, horses available for hire for Torres del Paine.

Hotels in the countryside open only in summer months: dates vary For accommodation in the Torres del Paine area, see below

Don Alvarito, Blanco Encalada 915. Hospitable. El Marítimo, Pedro Montt 214. Seafood and salmon, good views, popular, slow service. *Mari Loli*, Baquedano 615. Excellent food, good value. *La Ultima Esperanza*, Eberhard 354. Recommended for salmon, seafood, enormous portions, not cheap but worth the experience. *Andrés*, Ladrilleros 381. Excellent, good fish dishes, good service. *Tierra del Fuego*, Bulnes 29. Cheap, good, slow service. *Café Midás*, Tomas Rogers 169, has book swap. *Melissa*, Blanco Encalada. Good coffee and sandwiches. *Centro Español*, Magallanes 247. Reasonable. *La Frontera*, Bulnes 819. Set meals, good value. Cheap meals at *Club Deportivo Natales*, Eberhard 332. *Cristal*, Bulnes 439. Good sandwiches and salmon, good value. *La Repizza*, Blanco Encalada 294. Good value. *La Esquina*, Magallanes y Eberhard. Good bar.

Eating
● *on map*

Discos *El Cielo*, Esmeralda y Ramírez. *Milodón*, Blanco Encalada.

Entertainment

Camping equipment *Patagonia Adventures*, Tomás Rogers 179. *Casa Cecilia*, Tomás Rogers 54. German, French and English spoken, imported gear, also for sale.

Sports

The Far South

Recommended. Check all equipment and prices carefully. Average charges, per day: tent US$6, sleeping bag US$3-5, mat US$1.50, raincoat US$0.60, also cooking gear, US$1-2. (**NB** Deposits required: tent US$200, sleeping bag US$100.) Note that it is often difficult to hire walking boots. Camping gas is widely available in hardware stores, eg at Baquedano y O'Higgins and at Baquedano y Esmeralda. **Fishing** Tackle for hire at *Andes Patagónicos*, Blanco Encalada 226, T411594, US$3.50 per day for rod, reel and spinners; if you prefer fishing with floats, hooks, split shot, etc, take your own. Other companies up to 5 times as expensive.

Shopping **Handicrafts** *Ñandu*, Eberhard 586. Popular. Also at Baquedano y Chorillos.

Shoe repairs *París*, Miraflores between Blanco Encalada and Baquedano.

Supermarket *El Favorito*, Bulnes 1008. 24-hour supermarket Bulnes 300 block, markets good, food prices variable so shop around. Cheaper in Punta Arenas.

Transport **Local Bicycle hire**: *Casa Cecilia*, (see under **Sleeping**). **Bicycle repairs**: *El Rey de la Bicicleta*, Ramírez 540, good, helpful. **Car hire**: *Andes Patagónicos*, Blanco Encalada 226, T411728, US$85 per day including insurance and 350 kilometres free. *Avis*, Bulnes 632, T411775. *Todoauto*, Bulnes 20, T412837. US$110 per day for high clearance vehicle, others US$80 per day, or US$85 with driver. Hire agents can arrange permission to drive into Argentina, but this is expensive and takes 24 hours to arrange. **Mechanic**: Carlos González, Ladrilleros entre Bories y Eberhard. Recommended.

Long distance Bus: to **Punta Arenas**, several daily, 3½ hours, US$7. Bus Fernández, Eberhard 555, T411111, Bus Sur, Baquedano 534, T411325 and Bus Transfer, Baquedano 414, T421616. Book in advance. To **Coyhaique** via Calafate, Urbina Tours, 4 days, US$120 (November-March). Out of season the only service to rest of Chile is with Austral Bus, Tuesday to Puerto Montt, US$150, book days in advance.

    To Argentina: to Río Gallegos direct, Bus Sur, US$22, Tuesday and Thursday 1830 and El Pingüino, Wednesday and Saturday 1100, US$13; hourly to **Río Turbio**, Lagoper, (Baquedano y Valdivia), Turisur, Bus Sur, Cootra, US$3, 2 hours (depending on Customs – change bus at border). To **Calafate**, take 0630 Cootra bus to Río Turbio and change, US$20, otherwise travel agencies run several times a week depending on demand, 7 hours, US$20, shop around, reserve 1 day ahead.

Ferry The *Navimag* ferry Puerto Edén sails every Friday in summer to Puerto Montt, less frequently off season (see page 349).

Directory **Airline offices** *LanChile/Ladeco*, Tomás Roger 78. **Banks** *Banco Santiago*, Bulnes y Blanco
Poor rates for TCs, which Encalada. Mastercard and Visa, ATM. **Casas de cambio** *Enio America*, Blanco Encalada 266 where
cannot be changed into Argentine pesos can be changed. *Cambio Stop*, Baquedano 380. Good for cash (also arranges
US$ cash tours). Another 2 at Bulnes 683 and 1087 (good rates; also Argentine pesos). Others on Prat. Shop around as some offer very poor rates. **Communications** Post Office: Eberhard 417. Open Mon-Fri 0830-1230, 1430-1745, Sat 0900-1230. **Telephones**: *CTC*, Blanco Encalada 23 y Bulnes. Phones and fax. *Entel*, Baguidano y Bulnes. **Internet access**: *El Rincón de Tata*, Prat 236 also at *Casa Cecilia*, *Amerindia*, *Concept*, *Hosp María José* (see under **Sleeping**). **Laundry** *Servilaundry*, Bulnes 513. *Lavandería Catch*, Bories 218, friendly service. *Tienda Milodón*, Bulnes. Cheap. *Liberty*, Bulnes 513, or try Sra María Carcamo (at *Hosp Casa Teresa* at 1000-1200, 1800-2200). Good service, more expensive. **Shipping** Navimag: Pedro Montt 262 Loc B, Terminal Marítimo, T/F411421. **Tour companies & travel agents** *Michay*, Baquedano 388, T411149/411957 (Pedro Fueyo recommended). *Knudsen Tours*, Blanco Encalada 284, T411531. Recommended. *Onas* and *Andescape*, Eberhard y Blanco Encalada, T412707 (Casilla 78). *Servitur*, Pratt 353, T411028. *Turismo Zaahj*, Prat 236. T412260, F411355. Recommended. *Turismo Cabo de Hornos*, Pedro Montt 380. *Turismo Tzonka*, Carrera Pinto 626, T411214. *Turismo Luis Díaz*, Blanco

Encalada 189, T411654, for tours to Perito Moreno glacier (Argentina). Reports of the reliability of agencies, especially for their trips to Torres del Paine National Park, are very mixed. It is better to book tours direct with operators in Puerto Natales than through agents in Punta Arenas. Several agencies offer tours to the Perito Moreno glacier in Argentina, 1 day, US$70 without food or park entry fee, 14 hour trip, 2 hours at the glacier. (Take US$ cash or Argentine pesos as Chilean pesos not accepted.) **Tourist offices** Kiosk on waterfront, Av Pedro Montt y Phillipi; maps for US$1 from Eberhard 547. *Conaf*, O'Higgins 584.

Parque Nacional Bernardo O'Higgins

Often referred to as the **Parque Nacional Monte Balmaceda**, this park covers *Colour map 6, grid B2* large expanses of the icefields of the Campo de Hielo Sur and the fjords and offshore islands further west, including Isla Wellington. The park is uninhabited; the small community of Puerto Edén on Isla Wellington is outside the park limits, see page 350. Though the park is inaccessible except by air and sea, the southernmost section of the park, around Monte Balmaceda (2,035 metres) lies at the northern end of the Seno Ultima Esperanza and can be reached by boat from Puerto Natales. Two boats *Nuestra Senora de las Nieves*, *21 de Mayo* and *Alberto de Agostini* sail daily from Puerto Natales in summer and on Sunday only in winter (minimum 10 passengers), when weather conditions may be better with less cloud and rain, US$55 (or US$50 cash). After a three hour journey up the Sound, the boat passes the Balmaceda Glacier which drops from the eastern slopes of Monte Balmaceda (2,035 metres). The glacier is retreating; in 1986 its foot was at sea level. The boat docks one hour further north at Puerto Toro, from where it is a one kilometre walk to the base of the Serrano Glacier on the north slope of Monte Balmaceda. On the trip dolphins, sea lions (in season), black-necked swans, flightless steamer ducks and cormorants can be seen.

Bookings direct through Turismo 21 de Mayo, Ladrilleros 171, T/F411478 or from Eberhard 554, T411978 or through travel agencies, expensive lunch extra, take own food, drinks available on board. Take warm clothes, hat and gloves. This trip can also be combined with a visit to Torres del Paine. You have to pay full return fare on the boat and you need a permit from Conaf. There is a route from Puerto Toro along the Río Serrano to the Torres del Paine administration centre, 35 kilometres, guided tours along this are available, four hours. It is also possible to travel from Puerto Toro along the Río Serrano by boat to the Paine administration centre, four hours, US$60, details from *Casa Cecilia* in Puerto Natales.

Parque Nacional Torres Del Paine

Situated 145 kilometres northwest of Puerto Natales and covering 181,414 hect- *Colour map 6, grid B2* *ares, this national park, a Unesco Biosphere Reserve, is a must for its wildlife and spectacular scenery. The scenery is superb, with constantly changing views of fantastic peaks, ice-fields, vividly coloured lakes of turquoise, ultramarine and grey, and quiet green valleys. In the centre of the park is a granite massif from which rise the Torres (Towers) and Cuernos (Horns) of Paine, oddly shaped peaks of over 2,600 metres. The valleys are filled by beautiful lakes at altitudes of 50 metres to 200 metres above sea level.*

There are 15 peaks above 2,000 metres, of which the highest is Cerro Paine Grande (3,050 metres). On the western edge of the Park is the enormous *Campo de Hielo Sur* icecap; four main glaciers (*ventisqueros*), Grey, Dickson,

Zapata and Tyndall, branch off this and drop to the lakes formed by their meltwater. Two other glaciers, *Francés* and *Los Perros*, descend on the western side of the central *massif*.

The park enjoys a micro-climate especially favourable to wildlife and plants: there are 105 species of birds including 18 species of waterfowl and 11 birds of prey. Particularly noteworthy are condors, black-necked swans, rheas, kelp geese, ibis, flamingos and austral parrots. The park is one of the best places on the continent for viewing large numbers of guanacos and rheas. Apart from guanacos 24 other species of mammals can be seen including hares, foxes, *huemules* (a species of deer), pumas and skunks. Over 200 species of plants have been identified. The park is open all year round, although snow may prevent access in the winter: warmest time is December-March, although it can be wet and windy. The spring months of October-November are recommended for the wild flowers. In winter there can be good, stable conditions and well-equipped hikers can do some good walking.

Torres del Paine has become increasingly popular with foreigners and Chileans alike: in 1996 it received 51,000 visitors, most during the summer months of January and February, which, if possible, should be avoided. Despite the best efforts to manage this large influx of visitors rationally, their impact is starting to show. Litter has become a problem especially around the *refugios* and camping areas. Please take all your rubbish out of the park and remember that toilet paper is also garbage.

Allow a week to 10 days to see the park properly

The park is administered by Conaf: the administration centre is in the south of the park at the northern end of Lago del Toro (open 0830-2000 in summer, 0830-1230, 1400-1830 off season). The Centre provides a good slide show at 2000 on Saturday and Sunday and there are also excellent exhibitions on the flora and fauna of the park (Spanish only), but no maps or written information to take away. For information in Spanish on weather conditions phone the administration centre (T691931). There are six ranger stations (*guarderías*) staffed by rangers (*guardaparques*) who give help and advice and will also store luggage (except at Laguna Amarga where they have no room). Rangers keep a check on the whereabouts of all visitors: you are required to register and show your passport when entering the park. You are also requested to register at a ranger station before setting off on any hike. There are entrances at Laguna Amarga, Lago Sarmiento and Laguna Azul. Entry for foreigners: US$15 (proceeds are shared between all Chilean national parks), climbing fees US$800.

Warning It is vital not to underestimate the unpredictability of the weather (which can change in a few minutes), nor the arduousness of some of the stretches on the long hikes. Rain and snowfall are heavier the further west you go, and bad weather sweeps off the *Campo de Hielo Sur* without warning. It is essential to be properly equipped against cold, wind and rain. The only means of rescue are on horseback or by boat; the nearest helicopter is in Punta Arenas and high winds usually prevent its operation in the park.

Hikes

There are about 250 kilometres of well marked trails. Visitors must keep to the trails: cross-country trekking is not permitted. **NB** The times indicated should be treated with caution: allow for personal fitness and weather conditions.

El Circuito The most popular hike is a circuit round the Torres and Cuernos del Paine: usually it is done anticlockwise starting from the Laguna Amarga *guardería*. From Laguna Amarga the route is north along the western side of the Río Paine

An impression of Torres del Paine

Torres del Paine is one of the most impressive mountain areas on Earth. There are few comparable sites with almost 1,000 metre vertical shafts of basalt with conical caps atop steep forested talus slopes. These are the remains of frozen magma in ancient volcanic throats, everything else having been eroded; the highest is 3,243 metres and may be seen from near sea-level. As well as these spectacular mountains the surrounding forest, with lakes, glaciers and open country is truly magnificent. Although outposts of civilization exist near the edges of the park it is quite easy to escape its influences in a few hours trekking.

Wildlife abounds; guanacos and condors are common, and other mammals and birds quite abundant. I recall a very peculiar scratching sound on the corrugated iron roof of a hut one morning, and emerged to find a large condor was roosting on the ridge but having difficulty

securing a good grip with its claws. The region is sufficiently far south for the worst of the biting invertebrates to be only a minor problem.

Vegetation is typical South Andean. Although few trees reach great size, several valleys are thickly forested and little light penetrates. The grassland is distinct from the monotony of the pampa and dispersed sclerophyl forest. A complex series of lakes and streams leads into fjords extending sinuous distances from the sea. These are another attraction; many are glacial fed (and thus very cold); fortunately some strategic footbridges exist.

Much of the park was once a cattle ranch. This explains some of the older refugios which were huts where gauchos lived during round-up. Most cattle have now gone leaving the few hotels as the only commerce.

RK Headland, Scott Polar Research Institute, Cambridge.

to Lago Paine, before turning west to follow the Río Paine to the southern end of Lago Dickson. From here the path runs along the wooded valley of the Río de los Perros before climbing steeply to Paso John Gardner (1,241 metres, the highest point on the route), then dropping to follow the Grey Glacier southeast to Lago Grey, continuing to Lago Pehoé and the administration centre. There are superb views, particularly from the top of Paso John Gardner.

Although some people complete the route in less time, it normally takes five to six days. In theory, lone walkers are not allowed on this route; camping gear must be carried. The circuit is often closed in winter because of snow. The longest lap is 30 kilometres, between Refugio Laguna Amarga and Refugio Dickson (10 hours in good weather), but the most difficult section is the very steep slippery slope between Paso John Gardner and *Campamento Paso*. Although most people go anti-clockwise round the circuit, some advise doing it clockwise so that you climb to Paso John Gardner with the wind behind. The major rivers are crossed by footbridges, but these are occasionally washed away.

The W This route combines several of the hikes described separately below. From *Refugio Laguna Amarga* the first stage runs west via *Hostería Las Torres* and up the valley of the Río Ascensio via *Refugio Chileno* to the base of the Torres del Paine (see below). From here return to the *Hostería Las Torres* and then walk along the northern shore of Lago Nordenskjold via *Refugio Los Cuernos* to *Campamento Italiano*. From here climb the Valley of the Río del Francés (see below) before continuing to *Refugio Pehoé*. From here you can complete the third part of the 'W' by walking west along the northern shore of Lago Grey to *Refugio Grey* and Glaciar Grey before returning to *Refugio Pehoé*. A popular alternative to *El Ciruito*, this route can be completed without camping equipment as there is adequate accommodation in *refugios*. Allow four to five days.

The Far South

Valley of the Río del Francés From *Refugio Pehoé* this route leads north across undulating country along the western edge of Lago Skottberg to *Campamento Italiano* and then follows the valley of the Río del Francés which climbs between (to the west) Cerro Paine Grande and the Ventisquero del Francés and (to the east) the Cuernos del Paine to *Campamento Británico*. Allow two and a half hours from Refugio Pehoé to *Campamento Italiano*, two and a half hours further to *Campamento Británico*. The views from the *mirador* above *Campamento Británico* are superb.

Parque Nacional Torres del Paine

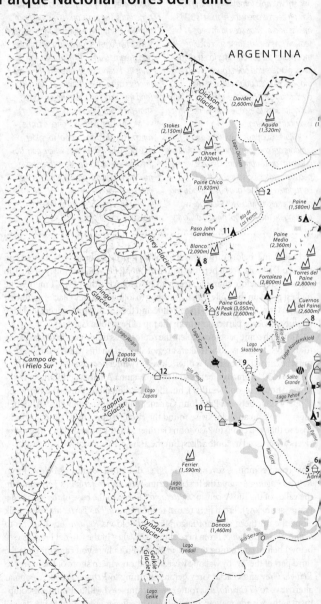

To Lago Pingo

From *Guardería Grey* (18 kilometres west by road from the administration centre) follow the Río Pingo, via *Refugio Pingo* and *Refugio Zapata* (four hours), with views south over Ventisquero Zapata (plenty of wildlife, icebergs in the lake) to reach the lake (five hours from *Guardería Grey*). Ventisquero Pingo can be seen three kilometres away over the lake. Two short signposted walks from Guardería Grey have also been suggested: one is a steep climb up the hill behind the ranger post to **Mirador Ferrier** from where there are fine

■ **Sleeping**
1 Explora
2 Hostería Estancia Lazo
3 Hostería Lago Grey
4 Hostería Las Torres
5 Hostería Pehoé
6 Posada Río Serrano

⌂ **Refugios**
1 Chileno
2 Dickson (Andescape)
3 Grey (Andescape)
4 Lago Paine
5 Lago Toro (Conaf)
6 Laguna Amarga
7 Laguna Verde
8 Los Cuernos
9 Pehoé (Andescape)
10 Pingo
11 Pudeto
12 Zapata

▲ **Camping**
1 Campamento Británico
2 Campamento Caírón
3 Campamento Chileno
4 Campamento Italiano
5 Campamento Japonés
6 Campamento Las Guardas
7 Campamento Las Torres
8 Campamento Paso
9 Laguna Azul
10 Las Torres
11 Los Perros
12 Río Serrano
13 Serón
14 Lago Pehoé

⌂ Ranger Stations (*guarderías*)

The Far South

Look under your feet

Few of the 50,000 people a year who visit Torres del Paine look closely at what they are treading on; a blanket of orchids, orange and yellow slipper plants (Calceolaria), Lathyrus (mauve sweet pea like flowers) and mauve Oxalis. In spring the hill slopes are a blaze of embothrium, with its brilliant red flowers, pernettya with its copious ruby-like fruits and calafate (Berberis buxifolia) a low shrub with bright yellow single flowers and delicate red/mauve berries. In damper shady areas are clumps of tiny three centimetre high Gunnera magellanica as well as the copihue (Lapageria rosea), the Chilean national flower.

Jane Norwich

views; the other is via a suspension bridge across the Río Pingo to the peninsula at the southern end of Lago Grey, from where there are good views of the icebergs on the lakes.

To the base of the Torres del Paine From *Refugio Laguna Amarga* the route follows the road west to *Hostería Las Torres* before climbing along the western side of the Río Ascensio via *Refugio Chileno* and *Campamento Chileno* to *Campamento Las Torres*, close to the base of the Torres and near a small lake. Allow one and a half hours to *Hostería Las Torres*, then two hours to *Refugio Chileno*, two hours further to *Campamento Torres* where there is a lake: the path is well-marked, but the last 30 minutes is up the morraine; to see the towers lit by sunrise (spectacular but you must have good weather), it's well worth humping camping gear up to *Campamento Torres* and spending the night. One hour beyond *Campamento Torres* is *Campamento Japonés*, a good camping site.

To Laguna Verde From the administration centre follow the road north two kilometres, before taking the path east over the Sierra del Toro and then along the southern side of Laguna Verde to the *Guardería Laguna Verde*. Allow four hours. This is one of the easiest walks in the park and may be a good first hike.

To Laguna Azul and Lago Paine This route runs north from Laguna Amarga to the western tip of Laguna Azul, from where it continues across the sheltered Río Paine valley past Laguna Cebolla to the *Refugio Lago Paine* at the western end of the lake. Allow 8½ hours.

Equipment A strong, streamlined, waterproof tent is essential if doing *El Circuito*. Also essential are protective clothing against wind and rain, strong waterproof footwear, compass, good sleeping bag, sleeping mat, camping stove and cooking equipment. In summer take shorts and sunscreen also. You are strongly advised to take all necessary equipment from Puerto Natales and not rely on availability at the Andescape *refugios*. Take your own food: the small shops at the Andescape *refugios* (see below) and at the *Posada Río Serrano* are expensive and have a limited selection. Note that rats and mice have become a major problem around camping sites and the free *refugios*. Do not leave food in your pack (which will be chewed through): the safest solution is to hang food in a bag on wire. Maps (US$3), are obtainable at Conaf offices in Punta Arenas or Puerto Natales. Most maps are unreliable but the one produced by Cartographia Digital, US$5, has been recommended as more accurate.

Park essentials

Hotels **L1** *Explora*, at Salto Chico on edge of Lago Pehoé, T411247. Ugly building but luxurious and comfortable, offering spectacular views, pool, gym, tours and transfer from Punta Arenas. (reservations: Av Américo Vespucci 80, piso 7, Santiago, T2066060/2288081, F2085479). **L3** *Hostería Pehoé*, T411390 (closed April-October). 5 kilometres south of Pehoé ranger station, 11 kilometres north of park administration, on an island with spectacular view across the Lake to Cerro Paine Grande and Cuernos del Paine, "a stunning location which is wasted", run down, overpriced (reservations. *Turismo Pehoé* in Punta Arenas or Antonio Bellet 77, office 605, T2350252, F2360917, Santiago). **L3** *Hostería Las Torres*, head office Lautaro Navarro 1125, Punta Arenas, T226054, F222641. **A2** off season, good restaurant, English spoken, horse-riding, transport from Laguna Amarga ranger station. Recommended. **L3** *Hostería Lago Grey*, T/F227528, or Punta Arenas T/F241042/248167. Good food, small rooms, on edge of Lago Grey. **A1** *Hostería Estancia Lazo*, on the eastern edge of the park, transport essential, (poor access road). Beautifully situated on Laguna Verde with spectacular views and good fishing, very friendly, comfortable, excellent food. Very highly recommended but an inconvenient base for visiting the park. (Reservations: *Operatur Patagónia*, Colón 822, T240513, F241153, Punta Arenas.) **A1** *Posada Río Serrano*, **B** off season. An old *estancia*, run down and overpriced, some rooms with bath, some with shared facilities, breakfast extra, near park administration, with expensive but good restaurant and a shop (reservations advisable: run by *Turismo Río Serrano*, Prat 258, Puerto Natales, T410684).

Refugios **F** *Refugio Lago Toro*. Near administration centre, run by Conaf, hot showers, cooking facilities, good meeting place, sleeping bag and mattress essential, no camping, open summer only – in the winter months another more basic (free) *refugio* is open near administration centre. The following are run by Andescape (for address in Puerto Natales see page 428; also office in Santiago): *Refugio Lago Pehoé*, on the northeast arm of Lago Pehoé. *Refugio Grey*, on the eastern shore of Lago Grey. *Refugio Lago Dickson*, *Refugio Los Chilenas*, in the valley of the Río Ascensio. *Refugio Los Cuernas*, on the northern shore of Lago Nordenskjold. All **D**, modern, closed in winter until 10 September, clean, with dormitory accommodation (sheets not provided), hot showers (US$2 for non-residents), cooking and laundry facilities, meals served, kiosk with basic food and other supplies, rental of camping equipment, campsite (US$3 pp), advance booking advisable. **D** *Refugio Las Torres*, owned by *Hostería Las Torres*, meals served, kitchen facilities.

Accommodation and meals in the Andescape *refugios* should be booked in advance in Puerto Natales (reservations can also be made, if space allows, by asking staff in one *refugio* to radio another).

In addition there are 6 free *refugios*: Zapata, Pingo, Laguna Verde, Laguna Amarga, Lago Paine and Pudeto. Most have cooking areas (wood stove or fireplace) but Laguna Verde and Pingo do not. These are in very poor condition.

Camping In addition to sites at the Andescape *refugios* there are the following sites: *Camping Serón* and *Camping Las Torres* (at *Hostería Las Torres*) both run by Estancia Cerro Paine. US$4, hot showers. *Camping Los Perros*, run by Andescape. US$4, shop and hot showers. *Camping Lago Pehoé* and *Camping Serrano*, both run by Turismo Río Serrano (address above). US$20 per site at former (maximum 6 persons, hot showers) and US$15 per site at latter (maximum 6 persons, cold showers, more basic). *Camping Laguna Azul*, hot showers, **D** per site. Free camping is permitted in 7 other locations in the park: these sites are known as *campamentos*. The wind tends to increase in the evening so it is a good idea to pitch tents early (by1600). Fires may only

Sleeping
■ *on map, page 432*

be lit at organized *camping* sites, not at *campamentos*. The *guardaparques* expect people to have a stove if camping. (**NB** These restrictions should be observed as forest fires are a serious hazard.) *Guardaparques* also require campers to have a trowel to bury their waste. Beware mice, which eat through tents. Equipment hire in Puerto Natales (see above).

Boat trips   From *Hostería Lago Grey* at the southern end of Lago Grey to the Grey Glacier, minimum 8 passengers, US$30 including refreshments, 2-3 hours, a stunning trip, recommended but often cancelled due to high winds. From *Refugio Lago Pehoé* to *Refugio Pudeto*, US$15 one way daily, from Pudeto 1030, 1600, from Pehoé 1200, 1530, 1 hour, in high season it is essential to reserve in advance at the *refugios* at either end or at *Turismo Tzonka* in Puerto Natales. Off-season, radio for the boat from *Refugio Pehoé*.

Transport   **Car hire**   Hiring a pick-up from ***Budget*** in Punta Arenas is an economical proposition for a group (up to 9 people): US$415 for 4 days. If driving there yourself, the road from Pto Natales is being improved: inside the park, the roads are narrow, bendy with blind corners; it takes about $3\frac{1}{2}$ hours from Puerto Natales to the administration, 3 to Laguna Amarga. Petrol available at Río Serrano, but fill up in case.

Horse hire   Baquedano Zamora, Blanco Encalada 226, Puerto Natales, T/F412911 (or contact via the Hostería El Pionero, Cerro Castillo, T691932 anexo 722).

Bus   Gomez, Servitur and JB Buses (addresses above) run daily bus services to the park from Puerto Natales leaving between 0630 and 0800, return departures 1500 from administration centre, 1600 from Laguna Amarga, 2½ hours journey to Laguna Amarga, 3 hours to the administration centre, US$10 one way, US$14 open return (return tickets are not interchangeable between all different companies), from early November to mid-April. In high season book in advance. See also under Punta Arenas
    For the daily In-Tur minibus service from Punta Arenas (in high season the buses fill quickly so it is best to board at the Administration): all buses wait at *Refugio Pudeto* until the 1430 boat from *Refugio Lago Pehoé* arrives. Travel between 2 points within the park (eg Pudeto-Laguna Amarga) US$3. At other times services by travel agencies are dependent on demand: arrange return date with driver and try to arrange your return date to coincide with other groups to keep costs down. Luis Díaz has been recommended, about $12 pp, minimum 3 persons. In season there are minibus connections from Laguna Amarga to the Hostería Los Torres and from the administration centre to Hostería Lago Grey.
    To go from Torres del Paine to Calafate (Argentina) either return to Puerto Natales and go to Río Turbio for bus to La Esperanza, or take a bus or hitch from the park to Villa Cerro Castillo border point (106 kilometres south of the administration), cross to Paso Cancha de Carreras and try to link with the Río Turbio-La Esperanza-Río Gallegos bus schedule, or hitch. (See Sleeping **North of Puerto Natales**, above.)

Tours   Several agencies in Puerto Natales including *Servitur, Knudsen, Zaahj, Scott Tours* and *Luis Díaz* offer 1-day tours by minibus, US$37.50 plus park entry; these give a good impression of the lower parts of the park, though you spend most of the day in the vehicle and many travellers would argue that you need to stay overnight to appreciate the park fully. José Torres of *Sastrería Arbiter* in C Bulnes 731 (T411637) recommended as guide. *Enap* weekend tours in summer cost US$45 including accommodation and meals. *Buses Fernández* offer 2-day tours, US$132 and 3-day tours (which includes trip to the Balmaceda Glacier) US$177. Before booking a tour check carefully on details and get them in writing: increasingly mixed reports of tours. Many companies who claim to visit the Grey Glacier only visit Lago Grey (you see the Glacier in the distance). After mid-March there is little public transport and trucks are irregular.

Onas Turismo (address under Puerto Natales **Tour companies**) runs trips from the Park down the Río Serrano in dinghies to the Serrano glacier and from there, on the *21 de Mayo* or *Alberto de Agostini* tour boats to Puerto Natales, US$90 each all inclusive. Book in advance.

Puerto Natales to Calafate (Argentina)

The small Argentine town of Calafate, the base for visits to the Parque Nacional Los Glaciares, is a short distance from Puerto Natales and can easily be visited.

Frontier with Argentina

From Puerto Natales the Argentine frontier can be crossed at three points, all of which meet Route 40 which runs to Calafate. These crossings are all open, subject to weather conditions, 24 hours a day from September to May, 0700-2300 June to August.

This crossing, 16 kilometres east of Puerto Natales, is reached by turning off Route 9 (the Punta Arenas road) at Km 14. On the Argentine side the road (*ripio*) runs east to meet Route 40. This crossing is open all year. **Paso Casas Viejas**

This crossing is reached by branching off Route 9 nine kilometres east of Puerto Natales and continuing north a further 11 kilometres. On the Argentine side this road (*ripio*) continues north to Route 40 via Río Turbio. **Villa Dorotea**

The most northerly of the three crossings, Cerro Castillo is reached by turning off the road north to Torres del Paine at Km 65. Chilean customs and immigration formalities are at Cerro Castillo; Argentine formalities are at Cancha Carrera, two kilometres further east. Accommodation is available at Cerro Castillo at the *Hostería El Pionero* (details under Puerto Natales) and at two *hospedajes*. On the Argentine side of the frontier the road meets Route 40. **Cerro Castillo**

Río Turbio

Only 30 kilometres northeast of Puerto Natales, Río Turbio is the site of Argentina's largest coalfield. Little visited by travellers, it is a good centre for trekking and horse riding. There is a **tourist office** in the Municipalidad. *Population: 8,000* *Phone code 02902*
  Visits can be made to one of the mines, **Mina Uno**, to the south of the town, and to the present mining and industrial area, on the eastern outskirts where there is a museum, the **Museo del Carbón**. ■ *Monday-Friday 0700-1200.* About four kilometres south of town is **Valdelén**, a ski resort, situated just inside the frontier on the slopes of Sierra La Dorotea.

A3 *Hostería Capipe*, at Dufour 9 kilometres west, T491240; **A3** *Gato Negro*, T4921226, also dormitory accommodation **E** pp; **E** pp *Hostería La Frontera*, an *albergue* at Valdelén; *Hostería Municipal* at Mina Uno. **Sleeping & eating** *Hotels almost always full*
  Restaurant El Ringo, near bus terminal, will shelter you from the wind.

Skiing Valdelén, with 6 *pistes*, is ideal for beginners. There is also scope for cross-country skiing nearby. Season runs from early June to late September, the *pistes* enjoying electric lighting to extend the short winter afternoons. **Sports**

The Far South

Transport **Air** Airport 15 kilometres southeast near 28 de Noviembre; taxi US$10 pp. LADE flights to Río Gallegos. **Bus** To Puerto Natales, 2 companies, US$4, regular. To Calafate, Quebek and Cootra, 6 hours, US$27.

The route to Calafate

There are two alternative routes. On clear days both offer fantastic views of Torres del Paine. The longest but easiest route runs east from the Cerro Castillo crossing, following the Río Coyle to **La Esperanza**, Km 123, where it meets the main Calafate-Río Gallegos road, 161 kilometres southeast of Calafate. The shorter route is via a very poor *ripio* road (marked Route 40) which turns off at Km 30 and runs northeast 70 kilometres to meet the Calafate-Río Gallegos road at El Cerrito, 91 kilometres southeast of Calafate. In winter both the Cerro Castillo crossing and this shorter route are closed. For public transport on this route see under Puerto Natales.

Sleeping **Fuentes del Coyle** 31 kilometres east of Cerro Castillo, there is a small bar which rents out rooms and a hotel, **D** pp, cold, dirty. **La Esperanza D** pp, *Restaurant La Esperanza*, bunk beds, with bath; also *cabañas* at the YPF service station.

El Calafate

Population: 4,000
Altitude: 225m
Phone code: 02902
312 km NW of Río Gallegos

This little town is situated on the southern shore of Lago Argentino, one of the largest lakes in the country. Founded in 1927, it is a modern town which has grown rapidly as a tourist centre for the Parque Nacional los Glaciares, which is 50 kilometres further west.

Sights

From the Centro Civico, visit Capilla Santa Teresita in Plaza San Martín. Walk to the top of the hill for the views of the silhouette of the southern end of the Andes, Bahía Redonda and Isla Solitaria on Lago Argentino. Just west of the town centre is Bahía Redonda, a shallow part of the lake; in winter when it freezes, ice skating and skiing are possible. At the eastern edge of Bahía Redonda is **Laguna Nimes**, a bird reserve where there are flamingoes, black necked swans and ducks, recommended. There is scope for good hill walking to the south of the town, while Cerro Elefante, west of Calafate on the road to the Moreno glacier is good for rock climbing.

Excursions

For excursions to the Moreno glacier, Upsala Glacier and Fitz Roy, see below. Travel by road to the most interesting spots is limited and may require expensive taxis. Tours can be arranged at travel agencies, or with taxi drivers at the airport who await arrivals.

Punta Gualicho, on the shores of Lago Argentino 15 kilometres east of town, has badly deteriorated painted caves. Several agencies run two-hour tours, US$16. The caves are on private property and may soon be closed to the public. Twelve kilometres east of Calafate on the edge of the lake there are fascinating geological formations caused by erosion.

El Galpón, 21 kilometres west, is an *estancia* offering evening visits from 1730 onwards which feature walks through a bird sanctuary where 43 species of birds have been identified, displays of sheep shearing and a barbecue as well

The Calafate

Whoever eats the fruits of the Calafate, *yellow/orange flowers dotted along its*
Berberis buxifolia, will return to *arching branches in spring. The deep*
Patagonia or so the story goes: whether *purple grape-like edible berries are also*
they do or not, they are likely to have *found singly or in pairs. Also known as the*
purple stained lips and fingers! This spiny, *Magellan barberry, its wood is used for*
shiny leaved, hardy shrub grows to two *making red dye.*
metres in height and has single bright *Jane Norwich*

as horseriding (visits at other times on request), transport arranged, English spoken; in Calafate T/F491793; Buenos Aires, Paseo Colón 221, 7th floor, T4343-3185, F4334-2669.

At **Lago Roca**, 40 kilometres south, there is trout and salmon fishing, climbing, walking, and branding of cattle in summer. There is good camping in wooded area and a restaurant.

Essentials

Calafate is very popular in January-February, when booking all transport in advance is recommended and accommodation can be difficult to find. Credit cards are not popular, apart from at hotels, and high commissions are charged.

L2 *Los Alamos*, Moyano y Bustillo, T491144, F491186, best, comfortable, very good food and service, extensive gardens, single-hole golf course. Recommended. **L3** *Frai Toluca*, Calle 6 No 1016, T/F491773/491593 (Buenos Aires T/F4523-3232), good views, comfortable, restaurant; **L3** *Hostería Kau-Yatun*, 25 de Mayo (10 blocks from town centre), T491059, F491260, many facilities, old *estancia* house, comfortable, restaurant and barbecues, horse-riding tours with guides; **L3** *El Mirador del Lago*, Libertador 2047, T/F491213, good accommodation, acceptable restaurant (wines not recommended), better not to take half-board.

A1 *Kalken*, V Feilberg 119, T491073, F491036, with breakfast, spacious. **A2** *Michelangelo*, Espora y Gob Moyano, T491045, F491058, with breakfast, modern, reasonable, good restaurant, accepts TCs (poor rates). **A2** *El Quijote*, Gob Gregores 1191, T491017, F491103. Recommended. **A3** *ACA Hostería El Calafate*, 1° de Mayo, T491004, F491027, modern, good view, open all year. **A3** *Hostería Schilling*, Paradelo 141, T491453, with breakfast, nice rooms, poor beds. **A2-3** *La Loma*, Roca 849, T491016 (Buenos Aires: Callao 433, 8a 'P', T/F4371-9123), with breakfast, modern (poor beds). Highly recommended, multilingual, restaurant, tearoom, spacious rooms, attractive gardens, also cheaper rooms, **D** pp, without bath.

B *Amado*, Libertador 1072, T491134, without breakfast, restaurant, good. **B** *Upsala*, Espora 139, T491166, F491075, with breakfast, good beds. Recommended. **B** *Cabañas Del Sol*, Libertador 1956, T491439 (**D** in low season), good meals, highly recommended. **B** *Hosp del Norte*, Los Gauchos 813, T491117, open all year, kitchen facilities, comfortable, owner organizes tours. Highly recommended. **B** *Paso Verlika*, Libertador 1108, T491009, F491279, with breakfast. **B** *Kapenke*, 9 de Julio 112, T491093, with breakfast, good beds. Recommended. **B** *Las Cabañitas*, V Feilberg 218, T491118, cabins, hot water, kitchen and laundry facilities, helpful. Recommended. **B** *Los Lagos*, 25 de Mayo 220, T491170, very comfortable, good value. Recommended. **B** *Hosp Cerro Cristal*, Gob Gregores 989, T491088, helpful. Recommended. **C** pp *Cabañas Nevis*, about 1 kilometre from town towards glacier, Libertador 1696, T491180, for 4 or 8, lake view, full board good value.

Sleeping
■ *on map, page 440*
Price codes:
see inside front cover
Many hotels are open
only from October to
April-May

The Far South

Budget accommodation D pp *Albergue & Hostal del Glaciar*, Los Pioneros, 200 metres off Avenida Libertador, T/F491243 (reservations in Buenos Aires T03448-69416 off season only), alberguedelglaciar@cotecal.com.ar. Discount for Hostelling International members, 1 September-Easter, Visa and Mastercard accepted, good kitchen facilities and lounge, English, German and Italian spoken, also rooms with bath (**B**) and sleeping bag space (**E** pp), restaurant, internet access, repeatedly recommended, tour agency *Patagonia Backpackers*, runs tours to Moreno glacier (US$32, repeatedly recommended) and elsewhere, free shuttle service from bus terminal, *poste restante*, Navimag agents. **E** pp *Lago Azul*, Perito Moreno 83, T491419, only 2 double rooms. Highly recommended. **E** pp *Hosp Jorgito*, Gob Moyano 943, T491323, without bath, basic, cooking facilities, heating, breakfast extra, often full, also camping. Recommended. **E** pp *Hosp Los Dos Pinos*, 9 de Julio 358, T491271, dormitory accommodation, cooking and laundry facilities, also cabins **C**, and camping **F** pp, arranges tours to glacier, popular. **E** pp *Hosp Buenos Aires*, Buenos Aires 296, 200 metres from terminal, T491147, kitchen facilities, helpful, good hot showers, luggage store. **E** pp *Hosp Alejandra*, Espora 60, T491328, without bath, good value, recommended; and airport, Navimag agents, book in advance in summer. **E** pp *Albergue Lago Argentino*, Campaña del Desierto 1050, T491423, near bus terminal, dormitory accommodation, limited bathrooms, kitchen facilities, English spoken, helpful. Some private houses offer accommodation: these include Enrique Barragán, Barrio Bahía Redonda, Casa 10, T491325, **E**, recommended. **F** pp *Apartamentos Lago Viedma*, Paralelo 158, T491159, F491158, hostel, 4 bunks to a room, cooking facilities. **F** pp *La Cueva de Jorge Lemos*, Gob Moyano 839, behind YPF station, bunk beds, bathroom, showers, kitchen facilities, popular and cheap. If in difficulty, ask at tourist office from which caravans, tents (sleep 4) and 4-berth *cabañas* may be hired, showers extra.

El Calafate

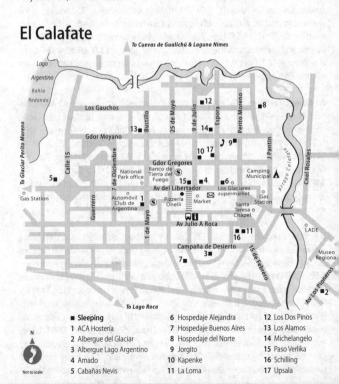

■ Sleeping	6 Hospedaje Alejandra	12 Los Dos Pinos
1 ACA Hostería	7 Hospedaje Buenos Aires	13 Los Alamos
2 Albergue del Glaciar	8 Hospedaje del Norte	14 Michelangelo
3 Albergue Lago Argentino	9 Jorgito	15 Paso Verlika
4 Amado	10 Kapenke	16 Schilling
5 Cabañas Nevis	11 La Loma	17 Upsala

N

Not to scale

In the Parque Nacional los Glaciares 40 kilometres west of Calafate on the road to the Moreno glacier: **L3** *Los Notros*, T/F491437, half-board, spacious, rooms with glacier views, recommended (in Buenos Aires: Talcahuano 1457, 7th floor, T825-4243, F815-7645). In the far south of the park on the shores of Brazo Sur: **A3** pp *Estancia Nibepo Aike*, T/F40966-20180, horse riding, expeditions, fishing, boat tours to glacier. Recommended. On the southern shore of Lago Viedma: **L3** pp *Estancia Helsingfors*, T/F40966-20719 (San Martín 516, Río Gallegos, or Buenos Aires T/F824-6623/3634), with breakfast, all other meals available, many treks, boat trips on Lago Viedma and flights over glaciers available, also riding, sheep-shearing. Recommended. **E** pp *La Leona*, T491418, 106 kilometres north of Calafate near east end of Lago Viedma, without bath, camping.

For accommodation in El Chaltén in the northern part of the park see below

Camping Municipal campsite behind YPF service station, T491344/491440, reservations off season 491829, US$4 pp, hot water, security, parillada, open 1 October-30 April. Three campsites in the park *en route* to the glacier: *Río Mitre*, near the park entrance, 52 kilometres from Calafate, 26 kilometres east of the glacier, US$3 pp; *Bahia Escondida*, 7 kilometres east of the glacier, toilets and hot showers, free but no water. Site at Arroyo Correntoso, 10 kilometres east of the glacier, no facilities but nice location and lots of firewood. Take food to all three. Another campsite is *Camping Río Bote*, 35 kilometres, on road to Río Gallegos.

Eating Excellent restaurant at *Hotel Los Alamos*. *Pizzeria Onelli*, Libertador 1197, reasonable, stays open out of season. *Pizzería Casablanca*, Libertador y 25 de Mayo, good breakfasts. *Michelangelo*, Espora y Gob Moyano, very expensive but magnificent steaks, trout, pastas. Recommended. *Paso Verlika*, Libertador 1108, small, 2 courses with wine US$16, credit cards 10% extra, good value. *Mi Viejo*, Libertador 1111, *parrilla*. *El Rancho*, 9 de Julio y Gob Moyano, large, cheap and good pizzas, popular, free video shows of the glacier. Highly recommended. *La Loma* (address above), friendly, home food. Good value fixed price menu at Albergue del Glaciar (see under **Sleeping**). Tea rooms: *Maktub*, Libertador 905, excellent pastries, pricey. *Bar Don Diego de la Noche*, Libertador 1603, lamb and seafood, live music, good atmosphere. *La Guanaconauta*, bar on Libertador.

Festivals People flock to the rural show on **15 February** (*Lago Argentino Day*) and camp out with much revelry; dances and *asados*. There are also barbecues and rodeo etc on *Día de la Tradición*, **10 November**.

Shopping **Supermarkets** *Los Glaciares*, Libertador y Perito Moreno, accepts Visa. *Alas*, 9 de Julio & Libertador. *Chuar ferretaria* selling white gas for camping (this is the only place for white gas).

Transport **Air** Lago Argentino airport, 1 kilometre east of town, with an all-weather runway (though flights may be suspended in severe weather). New airport under construction. Kaiken to Río Gallegos and Ushia. LADE to Río Turbio, Perito Moreno, Río Gallegos and Comodoro Rivadavia. Fares on LADE can be lower than on buses.

Bus Terminal on Roca, 1 block from Libertador. Bus schedule changes annually. To **Río Gallegos**, Interlagos Turismo daily at 0800 (summer) or 0915 Tuesday, Thursday, Saturday (winter); also Quebek (3 a day) and El Pinguiño daily at 0600 and 1630 (Wednesday, Friday, Saturday, in winter) 4½ hours, US$20-25, all via Río Gallegos airport. To **Río Turbio**, Cootra daily, 7 hours, US$27, Quebek, 2 a day, US$24, 4 hours. For Buenos Aires and northern destinations go to Río Gallegos and change (most departures in the evening). Taxi to Río Gallegos, 4 hours, US$200 irrespective of number of passengers, up to 5 people. To **Bariloche**, along Route 40, operated by Almafuerte

The Far South

Travel, 3 days with overnight stops in Puerto Moreno and Esquel, US$230, daily January/February, 3 times a week October-December, March, no service April-September, bookings through Chaltén Travel.

Direct services to Chile: COOTRA to **Puerto Natales** via Río Turbio, several times a week, 0700, US$23, 6 hours (recommended to book in advance). Bus Sur and Zahaj 0800, US$25. Travel agencies including *Albergue del Glaciar* run regular services in summer, on demand in winter, up to US$30, 5 hours. These connect at Cerro Castillo with buses from Puerto Natales to Torres del Paine (**NB** Argentine pesos cannot be exchanged in Torres del Paine).

Directory **Airline office** *Kaiken*, 25 de Mayo 43, T492072, F491854. **Banks** Take cash as there are no *Casas de Cambio*, and high commission is charged on TCs. There are ATMs but neither of these accept Visa or Mastercard. *Banco de Tierra del Fuego*, on 25 de Mayo, *Banco de la Provincia de Santa Cruz*, Libertador, 3% commission on TCs, 20%! commission on Visa and Mastercard advances. Travel agencies such as Interlagos change notes; *YPF garage* and *Chocolate El Calafate* and some other shops give good rates for cash; *Albergue del Glaciar*, 5% commission on TCs; *El Pingüíno* bus company, 6% commission; the *Scorpio* snack bar on Libertador is reported to give best rates; try also *Dos Glaciares supemarket*. Many businesses add 10% for credit card transactions. Note that US dollar notes are widely accepted. **Communications** Post Office: on Libertador; postal rates much lower from Puerto Natales (Chile) and delivery times much quicker. **Telephones:** run by Cooperativa Telefónica de Calafate, office on Espora, 0700-22400. Fax US$6.50 per page, cheaper from Puerto Natales, internet access. All services expensive, collect call impossible. **Laundry** *El Lavadero*, Libertador 1474, US$8 a load; also at *Hotel Cerro Cristal* (address above). **Tour companies & travel agents** Many agencies, most of them along Libertador, including *Interlagos*, No 1175, T491179, F491241. *Los Glaciares*, No 920, T491158, F491159, recommended, good value. *Hielo y Aventura*, No 935, T491053. *Upland Goose*, Roca 1004, Local 2, T491446, recommended. *El Pingüíno*, in terminal, T491273; Several hotels also organize tours by minibus including *Hosp del Norte* and *Albergue del Glaciar*. Most agencies charge the same rates for excursions: to the Moreno Glacier US$30 for a trip leaving 0830, returning 1800, without lunch, 3 hours at glacier; to Lago Roca, at 0830 return 1700, US$35; to Cerro Fitz Roy, at 0600 return 1900, US$50, Gualicho caves, 2 hours, US$16 (see **Excursions** above). Several agencies offer walking excursions on the Perito Moreno glacier, usually finishing with champagne or whisky with ice chipped from the glacier; these include *Hielo y Aventura*, 1½ hours, US$65 January-February and Holy Week, US$50 other times between 15 October and 15 March, plus US$15 for transport to the glacier, book ahead. Mountain bikes can be hired from Mariano Minich at Bike Way. **Tourist offices** Tourist office in bus terminal. Hotel prices detailed on large chart at tourist office; has a list of taxis but undertakes no arrangements. Helpful staff. October-April 0700-2200 daily. For information on the Parque Nacional los Glaciares, park office at Libertador 1302, T491005, Monday-Friday 0800-1500.

Parque Nacional Los Glaciares

This park, the second largest in Argentina, extends alang the Chilean frontier for over 170 kilometres and covers more than 660,000 hectares. Some 40 percent of the park is covered by the hielos continentales, giant ice fields which straddle the frontier.

Of the 47 major glaciers which flow from the ice fields, 13 run east descending into the park to feed two great lakes: Lago Argentino and, further north, Lago Viedma, both of which are heavily silted by glacial deposits. The Río La Leona, flowing south from Lago Viedma, links the two lakes. There are also about 190 smaller glaciers not connected to the ice fields.

East of the ice fields are areas of southern beech (nothofagus) forest, especially *lenga*, *ñire* and *guindo* (evergreen beech). Further east are areas of Patagonian steppe, with shrub vegetation including the *calafate*. Among over

100 bird species are the condor, the patagonian woodpecker, the austral parakeet, the green-backed firecrown as well as black-necked swans, Andean ruddy ducks and torrent ducks. Guanacos, grey foxes, skunks and rheas can be seen on the steppe while the endangered *huemul* inhabits the forest.

Climate

The climate is variable, depending on altitude and season. Temperatures in summer reach 20-25°C and even 30°C on occasions so wear sun block in summer. Rainfall ranges from 2,000 millimetres in the far west to 400 millimetres in the east, falling mainly between March and late May. The best time to visit is between October and March. Many facilities are closed off-season. Lighting fires is prohibited throughout the park.

Two sectors of the park are popular with travellers: the southern area around Lago Argentino and the northern area around Mount Fitz Roy. Access to the central sector, north of Lago Argentino and south of Lago Viedma, is difficult and there are few tourist facilities though *estancias* such as *Helsingfors* and *La Cristina* offer accommodation and excursions. The *Helsingfors* offers boat trips to the Viedma Glacier.

Lago Argentino

The source of the Río Santa Cruz, one of the most important rivers in Patagonia, Lago Argentino covers some 1,400 square kilometres. At its western end there are two networks of fiords (*brazos*), fed by glaciers (*ventis queros*). The major attraction in the park is the Moreno glacier; excursions also run to a group of four other glaciers further north, including the Upsala glacier. Ventisquero Moreno

This glacier, 80 kilometres west of Calafate, was until recently one of the few in the world still advancing. Some 250 kilometres long, it reaches the water at a narrow point in one of the fiords, Brazo Rico, opposite Peninsula Magallanes: five kilometres across and 60 metres high, it used to advance across Brazo Rico, blocking the fiord roughly every three years; as the water pressure built up behind it, the ice would break, reopening the channel and sending giant icebergs (*témpanos*) rushing down the appropriately named Canal de los Témpanos. This last occurred in February 1988. *Spectacular especially at sunset, the glacier is constantly moving and never silent*

The ice, with its vivid blue hues, is riven by crevasses; the noise as it cracks and strains can be heard at some distance. As pieces break off and collapse into the water, there is a dull roar. The glacier can be viewed from wooden catwalks (there is a fine of up to US$500 for leaving the catwalks) and by boat.

Tours From Calafate there are buses by Interlagos, US$30. Many agencies also run minibus tours, US$30 return (plus US$5 park entry) leaving 0800 returning 1800, giving 3 hours at glacier, book through any agency in Calafate, return ticket valid if you come back next day (student discount available). *Albergue del Glaciar* trips go out by a different route passing the *Estancia Anita* and have been repeatedly recommended. Walking tours on the glacier are offered by several agencies in Calafate, see above. Taxis, US$80 for 4 passengers round trip. Out of season, trips to the glacier are difficult to arrange, but you can gather a party and hire a taxi (*Remise Taxis* T491745/491044); take warm clothes, and food and drink. Ask rangers where you can camp out of season; there are no facilities except a decrepit toilet block.

The advance and retreat of the Moreno Glacier

The Moreno Glacier is frequently said to be in retreat as a result of global warming. Though the glacier no longer blocks Brazo Rico on a three yearly cycle as it last did in 1988, such statements must be treated with caution.

Glaciers are usually described by glaciologists as advancing, retreating or stable. This can cause confusion since even a retreating glacier will continue moving slowly forward; its frontage or snout retreats because it melts or breaks up at a faster rate than its forward movement. Though the Moreno glacier no longer behaves as it did until 1988, it is considered by glaciologists to be stable: its rates of forward movement and break-up are in a rough equilibrium.

One of the most puzzling things about glaciers is the way they change their behaviour. As far as is known, the Moreno glacier did not block Braza Rico until 1917;

*according to early scientific studies its snout was 750 metres away from the Magallanes Peninsula in 1900, a distance that had dropped to 350 metres by 1908. In 1917 the small dam formed by the ice broke after a few weeks; the next time the glacier blocked the fiord was in 1934-5. Between this date and 1988 the glacier moved forward more vigorously; in 1939 when it reached the Magallanes Peninsula again, the waters in Brazo Rico rose nine metres and flooded coastal areas, leading to attempts by the Argentine navy to bomb it from the air. These failed but the waters eventually broke through. After 1939 the glacier reached the Peninsula about every three years until 1988. Its changed behaviour since then **may** be related to global warming, but perhaps we also need to know why the glacier started advancing so vigorously in the first place.*

Boats Trips on the lake are organized by *Hielo y Aventura*, T491053, with large boats for up to 60 passengers: 'Safari Náutico', US$20 pp, 1 hour offering the best views of the glacier; or 'Minitrekking', US$67, day trip including 2½ hours' walk on the glacier. Recommended, but not for the fainthearted, take your own lunch.

The Upsala Glacier

The fiords at the northwestern end of Lago Argentino are fed by four other glaciers. The **Upsala** glacier is considered the largest in South America, 60 kilometres long and, with a frontage four kilometres wide and 60 metres high. **Spegazzini**, further south, has a frontage one and a half kilometres wide and 130 metres high. In between are **Agassiz** and **Onelli**, both of which feed **Lago Onelli**, a quiet and very beautiful lake, full of icebergs of every size and sculpted shape, surrounded by beech forests on one side and ice-covered mountains on the other.

Tours Tour boats from Punta Bandera, 50 kilometres west of Calafate, visit the Upsala glacier, Lago Onelli and glacier (restaurant) and the Spegazzini glacier, (check before going that access to the face of the Upsala glacier is possible), daily service in season on the catamaran *Serac*, US$90, or the motor boat *Nunatak* (slightly cheaper). The price includes bus fares and park entry fees – pay in dollars and take food. Bus departs 0730 from Calafate for Punta Bandera. One hour is allowed for a meal at the restaurant near Lago Onelli. Return bus to Calafate at 1930; a tiring day, it is often cold and wet, but memorable. Out of season it is extremely difficult to get to the glacier. Many travel agencies make reservations.

Fitz Roy and El Chaltén

In the far north of the park, 230 kilometres north of Calafate at the western end of Lago Viedma is **Cerro Fitz Roy** (3,405 metres), part of a granite massif which also includes the peaks of Cerro Torre (3,128 metres), Poincenot (3,076 metres), Egger (2,673 metres), Guillaumet (2,503 metres), Saint-Exupery (2,600 metres), Aguja Bífida (2,394 metres) and Cordón Adela (2,938 metres). Clearly visible from a distance, Fitz Roy towers above the nearby peaks, its

Parque Nacional Los Glaciares

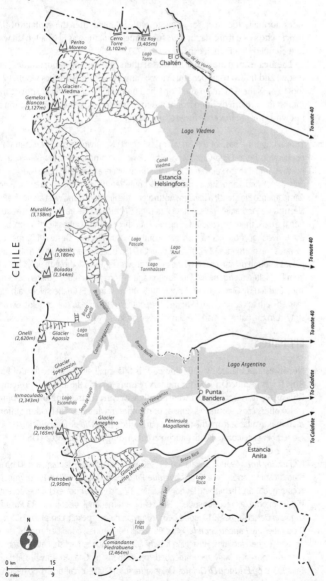

Peaks in the Fitz Roy Range

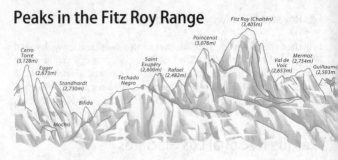

sides normally too steep for snow to settle. Named after the captain of the *Beagle* who saw it from afar in 1833 (its Tehuelche name was El Chaltén), it was first climbed by a French expedition in 1952.

The area around the base of the massif offers fine walking opportunities (see below) and there are stupendous views: "anyone within 500 miles would be a fool to miss them" (Julian and Cordelia Thomas). Occasionally at sunrise the mountains are briefly lit up bright red for a few seconds: this phenomenon is known as the *amanecer de fuego* ('sunrise of fire').

Hiking Trails around the base of the Fitzroy massif are: 1) Northwest from El Chaltén via a good campsite at Lago Capri, wonderful views, to Campamento Río Blanco, and, nearby Campamento Poincenot, 2-3 hours, from where a path leads up to Lago de los Tres (blue) and Lago Sucia (green), 2-3 hours return from the camps. 2). From Campamento Río Blanco a trail runs north along the Río Blanco and west along the Río Eléctrico via Piedra del Fraile (4 hours) to Lago Eléctrico. At Piedra del Fraile, just outside the park, there are *cabañas* (**E** pp with hot showers) and campsite, US$5 pp, plus expensive shop; from here a path leads south up Cerro Eléctrico Oeste (1,882 metres) towards the north face of Fitz Roy, 2 hours, tough but spectacular views. This route passes through private property: the owner allows you to walk through only. 3) West from El Chaltén along the Río Fitz Roy to Laguna Torre, beautifully situated at Cerro Torre and fed by Glaciar Torre, 3 hours. 4) Southwest from El Chaltén along a badly marked path to Laguna Toro (6 hours), the southern entrance to the ice fields. Do not stray from the paths. A map is essential, even on short walks.

El Chaltén

Phone code 02962 Northwest of Calafate by 230 kilometres is this small village at the foot of Fitz Roy. It was founded in 1985 for military reasons to settle the area and pre-empt Chilean territorial claims. Growing rapidly as a centre for trekking and climbing, it also offers cross-country skiing opportunities in winter. Local trekking information is available from the national park office. The *Día de la Tradición* on 10 November is celebrated with gaucho events, riding and a barbecue (US$5).

Sleeping **A3** *Fitz Roy Inn*, T493062 or Calafate 491368, with breakfast, restaurant, also **D** pp in shared cabins; opposite is **D** pp *Albergue Patagonia*, T461564/493019, dormitory accommodation, kitchen and laundry facilities, TV and video, book exchange, accepts TCs, comfortable, recommended, Hostelling International discounts. **A3** *Posada Lago del Desierto*, T493010, good beds, *comedor*, Italian spoken, camping US$5 pp. **D** pp *Albergue Rancho Grande*, T493005, small dormitories, good bathrooms, laundry and kitchen facilities, Hostelling International discounts, English, Italian, French, German spoken, highly recommended, reservations in Chaltén Travel, Calafate, T491833. **B** pp *Estancia La Quinta*, 3 kilometres from Chaltén, half-board, no heating, prepares lunch for trekkers. Recommended. **L3** *La Aldea*, T493040, 5-bed apartments. **D** pp *Casa de Piedra*, T493015, in shared cabins, also **A1** 4-bed cabins. **D** pp *Cabaña de Miguel*, shared cabins. **D** pp *Cabañas Cerro Torre*, T49306l, built for the Herzog film "El Grito de la Piedra", cabins sleep 4/6, kitchenette. **E** pp *Albergue Los Nires*, T493009, small dormitories, also camping, US$5 pp. **E** pp *Despensa 2 de Abril*, one room, cheapest. **Camping** *Camping Madsen* (free). *Ruca Mahuida*, T493018, very helpful, US$6 pp, showers, stores gear, recommended; 2 free campsites. A stove is essential for camping as firewood is scarce and lighting fires is prohibited in campsites in the National Park. Take plenty of warm clothes and a good sleeping bag. It is possible to rent equipment in El Chaltén, ask at park entrance. Equipment and cycles for hire at artesania shop on road to Camping Madsen, past Albergue Patagonia. All campsites in National Park free, no toilets, please bury your waste. Hot showers available at Albergue Patagonia and Confitería La Senyera, US$2.

La Senyera del Torre, excellent bread. Recommended. *Josh Aike*, excellent *confitería*, homemade food, beautiful building. Recommended. *The Wall Pub*, breakfasts and meals, interesting, shows videos of ascents of Fitz Roy and Cerro Torre.

Eating

The Fitz Roy area

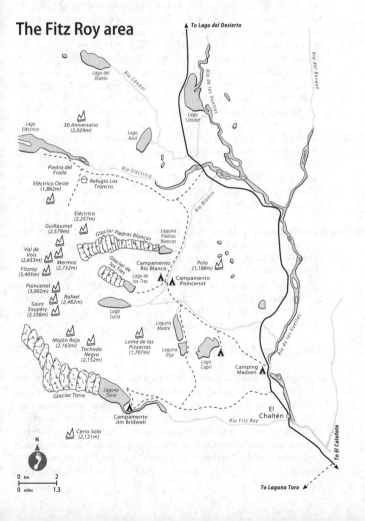

The Far South

Beware: flying ice

"One or two of the tourists who ignore the prohibition signs and walk down to the rocks overlooking the channel in front of the glacier always get washed away every season. They all think it won't happen to them, but it does; 60 metres of ice break off and hits the water just in front of them. But it isn't the water that kills them, its the chunks of flying ice."

Carlos Dupáez, Superintendent, Parque Nacional Los Glaciares, interviewed in the Buenos Aires Herald, 1 November 1997.

Shopping There are several small shops selling food, gas and batteries (*Dispensa 2 de Abril* is said to be cheapest) but buy supplies in Calafate (cheaper and more choice). Sra Isolina bakes the best bread. Fuel is available.

Sports **Climbing:** Base camp for climbing Fitz Roy is Campamento Río Blanco (see above). Most of the peaks in the Fitz Roy massif are for very experienced climbers as is the *Campo de Hielo Continental* (Ice Fields) which mark the frontier with Chile (no access from Chile). Ask Sr Guerra about hiring animals to carry equipment. Fitz Roy Expediciones, in Chaltén, T493017/F491364, owned by experienced guide Alberto del Castillo, organizes adventure excursions including on the *Campo de Hielo Continental*, 8 hours, US$75 including equipment, highly recommended, English and Italian spoken. For the ice fields guides are essential; necessary gear is double boots, crampons, pickaxe, ropes, winter clothing; the type of terrain is ice and rock and you need to be in good condition. The best time is mid-February to end-March; November-December is very windy; January is fair; winter is extremely cold. Permits for climbing are available at the national park information office.

Trekking The park information centre provides photocopied maps of treks but the best is one published by Zagier and Urruty, US$10 (Casilla 94, Sucursal 19, 1419 Buenos Aires, 4572-5766) and is available in shops in Calafate and Chaltén. For trekking by horseback with guides: Rodolfo Guerra, T493020; *El Relincho*, T493007; *Albergue Los Ñires*, T493009; Prices: Laguna Capri US$20; Laguna Torre, US$25, Río Blanco US$30, Piedra del Fraile US$30, Laguna Toro US$30.

Transport **Local Mechanic** Ask for Julio Bahamonde or Hugo Masias. **Bus** Daily services in summer from Calafate, 4 hours, US$25 one way, are run by Chaltén Travel 0800 return departure 1800, Caltur, 0700, return departure 1700, and Los Glaciares, 0800, return departure 1800. Best to book return before departure during high season. Day trips from Calafate involve too much travelling and too little time to see the area. Some agencies offer excursions, eg return travel by regular bus and 1 night accommodation US$79. Off season, travel is difficult: little transport for hitching. Agencies charge US$200 one way for up to 8 people, US$300 return.

The Lago del Desierto

Thirty seven kilometres north of El Chaltén and surrounded by forests, this lake is reached by an unpaved road which leads along the Río de las Vueltas via Laguna Condor, where flamingos can be seen. A path runs along the east side of the lake to its northern tip, from where a trail leads west along the valley of the Río Diablo to Laguna Diablo. There is a campsite at the southern end of the lake and *refugios* at its northern end and at Laguna Diablo. Excursions from El Chaltén by *Chaltén Travel* daily in summer; daily boat trips on the lake on *Mariana* 1030, 1330, 1630, 2 hours, US$30 (details and booking, *Hotel El Quijote*, Calafate).

Tierra del Fuego

14

Tierra del Fuego

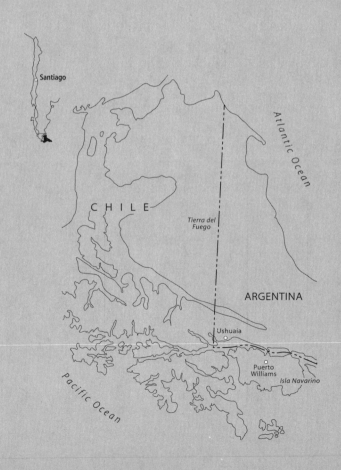

The largest island at the extreme south of South America, Tierra del Fuego is divided between Argentina and Chile; both are covered in this section, which also includes the Chilean island of Isla Navarino, to the south of Tierra del Fuego. Although northern Tierra del Fuego is flat windswept steppe, the south is a land of mountains, forests and lakes, usually visited from the Argentine city of Ushuaia, which is also a base for boat trips along the Beagle Channel. In winter there is also skiing. On the southern shore of the Beagle Channel is Puerto Williams, the one settlement on Isla Navarino.

Background

History

Human habitation of Tierra del Fuego dates back some 10,000 years; four indigenous groups, all now extinct, inhabited the island until the early 20th century. The most numerous, the Onas (also known as the Selk'nam), lived in the north as hunter-gatherers, living mainly on guanaco and several species of rodents. The southeastern corner of the island was inhabited by the Haus or Hausch, also hunter-gatherers, of whom very little is known. The same cannot be said for the Yaganes or Yámanas, who lived along the Beagle Channel and on the islands further south. A seafaring people who lived mainly on seafood, fish and seabirds, they were physically smaller than the Onas, but with a strongly developed upper body for rowing long distances. The fourth group, the Alacaluf, lived in the west of Tierra del Fuego as well as on the islands along the Chilean coast, surviving in these inhospitable conditions by fishing and hunting seals.

The first Europeans to visit the island were members of an expedition led by the Portuguese Fernão Magalhães, who, in 1520, sailed through the channel that bears his name. As a result of the extreme dangers of such a voyage and the failure of Sarmiento de Gamboa's attempt to found settlements along the

Tierra del Fuego

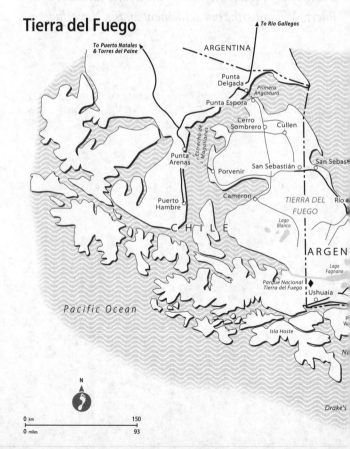

Straits in 1584, the indigenous population were left undisturbed until after South American independence.

Though Fitz Roy and Darwin visited in 1832, European settlement only occurred much later in the 19th century. In 1851 the South American Missionary Society, an Anglican society with missions on the Falkland Islands/Islas Malvinas, sent seven missionaries to Picton Island to establish a mission, but they were driven off by the Yaganes and the first successful mission was only established 18 years later, at Ushuaia.

The work of the missionaries was, however, disturbed by two developments: the discovery of gold and the growth of sheep farming. As in southern Patagonia, the settlement of the frontier disputes between Argentina and Chile was followed by a desire by both governments to populate the area by allocating large expanses of land for sheep farming. The main beneficiaries of this policy on Tierra del Fuego were the Menéndez and Braun families, already established in Punta Arenas.

Geography

Tierra del Fuego is separated from the South American mainland by the Magellan Strait to the north; to the east is the Atlantic Ocean; the Beagle Channel to the south separates it from the southern islands; a complex network of straits including the Whiteside, Gabriel, Magdalena and Cockburn channels divide it from the islands situated to the west.

South Atlantic Ocean

Harberton
Isla de los Estados
Isla Picton
Canal Beagle
Isla Nueva
a Lennox
ape Horn

The north of Tierra del Fuego is steppe but further south the island is crossed from east to west by the continuation of the Andes; in the Argentine sector these rise to around 1,500 metres, but in the Chilean part in the far southwest there are peaks of well over 2,000 metres. The main rivers drain into the Beagle Channel and into Lago Fagnano, the largest lake on the island, which straddles the frontier between Chile and Argentina and which drains west to the sea via the Río Azopardo. There are a number of other lakes including Lagos Yehuin and Chapelmuth, just north of Lago Fagnano in Argentine territory, and Lagos Blanco, Chico and Lynch in Chilean territory.

The northern and southern parts of the island have contrasting vegetation: the steppe is covered with grassland, while further south sub-Antarctic forests grow on hills up to about 600 metres. Poorly drained low-lying areas in the south are covered with Sphagnum moss. Native fauna include guanacos and red foxes; musk rats, beaver and rabbits have been

Gold fever

The Tierra del Fuego Gold Rush is closely linked to the name of Julio Popper, who settled in San Sebastián in 1887 where he founded the El Paramó mine. Popper died young in 1893, by which time his company had extracted 600 kilos of gold from El Paramó and from along the Beagle Channel. After his death, gold mining became a much larger scale business until, in 1909, the gold suddenly ran out. Despite its short life the gold rush had lasting consequences: among the prospectors from North America and Europe who arrived hoping to get rich, the largest group were Croats from Dalmatia, then part of the Austrian Empire; many of their descendants still live in the area.

introduced. In summer, wild geese and ducks can be seen and some 150 other bird species have been identified; the Bahia San Sebastián is an important area for migratory birds. Trout and salmon inhabit nearly all the lakes and rivers.

Climate

The island's climate is cold sub-Antarctic, though extremes of temperature are moderated by the sea and there are significant differences between the north and south of the island. In Ushuaia southwesterly winds prevail, ranging in force from 15 kilometres per hour to 100 kilometres per hour. September to March are the windy months, while winter is normally calmer. In winter, average daily temperatures hover around zero but in summer range from 13°C during the day to 5°C at night. Further north in Río Grande, where strong westerly winds blow up to 200 kilometres per hour almost all year round, average temperatures range from -3°C to 2°C in winter and from 5°C to 15°C in summer. Rainfall is higher in Ushuaia than further north, with slight seasonal variations; in Río Grande most rain falls in summer and autumn.

Government and economy

Chilean Tierra del Fuego forms part of Región XII (Magallanes), the capital of which is Punta Arenas. The Argentine section of the island is part of the Province of Tierra del Fuego, Antartida y Las Islas del Atlántico Sur, the capital of which is Ushuaia. The population of the Argentine sector is around 70,000, most of whom live in the two towns of Río Grande and Ushuaia. Chilean Tierra del Fuego has a population of some 7,000, the majority of whom live in Porvenir.

For many years the main economic activity of the northern part of the island was sheep farming, but Argentine government tax incentives to companies in the 1970s led to the establishment of new industries in Río Grande and Ushuaia and a rapid growth in the population of both cities; the subsequent withdrawal of incentives has produced increasing unemployment and emigration. The island is the site of the smallest and most southerly oil refinery in the world in Argentine San Sebastián. Tourism is increasingly important in Ushuaia.

Transport to Tierra del Fuego

Note that flights to and from the island are heavily booked in summer, especially in January, and that bus and ferry services are subject to cancellation due to weather conditions.

Tierra del Fuego

Shipwrecked in the Magellan Straits

The Estrecho de Magallanes, 534 kilometres long, was and still is a treacherous passage and over the centuries has claimed a long succession of victims. The hostile conditions which can prevail are perhaps best summed up in the words of Sir John Narborough: *"horrible like the ruins of a world destroyed by terrific earthquakes."*

From the Atlantic end the first navigational problem facing sailors is simply the difficulty of entering the Straits in the face of the fierce westerly gales which prevail, numerous sailing vessels having been forced back out to sea to wallow for weeks on end. Once in the straits the dangers are far from over: many ships have fallen victim to the notorious Williwaws, winds with the ferocity of tornados which spring up from nowhere, or the vicious Pamperos, which blow off the land with enough force to capsize a vessel.

Though in 1520 Magellan succeeded in passing through the straits which bear his name, few others managed to do so in the years which followed: of 17 ships which attempted the passage in the early 16th century, only one, the Victoria, succeeded in reaching the Pacific and returning to Europe. Twelve were lost near the eastern entrance and four returned in failure. The great attraction which drove these early navigators was the lure of a short route between Europe and the spices of the East. Once it was clear that there was no short route, it was still a useful way for Europeans to reach the rich Pacific ports of Peru and Chile without disembarking and crossing Mexico or Panama on foot or by mule.

Although by the 19th century the replacement of sail by steam and the development of advanced navigation techniques lessened the dangers, losses continued: in 1869, for instance, the Santiago, an iron paddle steamer built in Glasgow and owned by the Pacific Mail line, went down off Isla Desolación at the western end with a cargo of gold and silver; there are no records of any salvage operation having taken place. While the opening of the Panama Canal in 1914 provided an alternative route between the Atlantic and Pacific Oceans, increases in ships' size mean that the Straits are still a busy shipping route, though today the cargo is more commonly oil than gold and silver. Casualties still occur with, of course, the added risk of environmental disaster from oil spillage.

Nigel Pickford

There are two ferry crossings to Tierra del Fuego.

Ferries to Tierra del Fuego

Punta Arenas to Porvenir The *Melinka* sails from Tres Puentes (five kilometres north of Punta Arenas, bus A or E from Avenida Magallanes, US$1; taxi US$3) at 0900 daily except Monday in season, less frequently off season, 2½ hour crossing (can be rough and cold), US$6 per person, US$5 per bike, US$30 per vehicle. Return from Porvenir 1500 (1700 Sunday, no service Monday). Timetable dependent on tides and subject to change: check in advance. Reservations essential especially in summer (at least 24 hours in advance for cars), obtainable from *Agencia Broom*, Bulnes 05075, T218100, F212126. The ferry company accepts no responsibility for damage to vehicles on the crossing.

Punta Delgada to Punta Espora This crossing is via the *Primera Angostura* (First Narrows), 170 kilometres northeast of Punta Arenas. There are several crossings a day; schedules vary with the tides. Pedestrians and cycles free, US$14 per car one way. The ferry takes about four trucks and 20 cars; before 1000 most space is taken by trucks. There is no bus service to or from this crossing. If hitching, this route is preferable as there is more traffic.

Sleeping **In Punta Delgada** **E** per person *Hotel El Faro*. **C** *Hostería Tehuelche*, T061694433, at Kamiri Aike 17 kilometres from port. With restaurant.

Transport on Tierra del Fuego Throughout Tierra del Fuego the main roads are narrow and gravelled. The exceptions are San Sebastián (Argentina)-Ushuaia, which is paved, and the road for about 50 kilometres east of Porvenir, which is being widened. Fuel is available in Porvenir, Cerro Sombrero and Cullen (Chile), and Río Grande, Ushuaia and San Sebastián (Argentina).

Chilean Tierra del Fuego

Porvenir

Population: 4,500
Phone code: 061
Colour map 7, grid B1

Founded in 1894 as a port serving the sheep *estancias* of the island, **Porvenir** is the only town in Chilean Tierra del Fuego. There is a small museum, the **Museo Fernando Cordero Rusque**, Samuel Valdivieso 402, with archaeological and photographic displays on the Onas, as well as sections on natural history and gold mining.

Sleeping **Porvenir** **A2** *Los Flamencos*, Tte Merino, T580049. Best. **C** *Central*, Phillippi 298, T580077. Hot water. **C** *Hostal Patagonia*, Schythe 230, T580227. **C** *España*, Croacia 698, T380160. Good restaurant with fixed price lunch. *Res Los Cisnes*, Soto Salas 702, T580227. **C** *Rosas*, Phillippi, T580088. With bath, hot water, heating, restaurant and bar. Recommended. **E** pp *Res Colón*, Damián Ríobó 198, T580108. Also full board. **E** pp *Miramar* Santos Mardones 366 (**D** with full board). Clean, friendly, heaters in rooms, hot water, good.

For accommodation at San Sebastián see below **Elsewhere in Chilean Tierra del Fuego** At Cerro Sombrero, 46 kilometres south of Primera Angostura: **E** pp *Hostería Tunkelen*. Recommended. **F** *Pensión del Señor Alarcón*. Good, friendly. *Posada Las Flores*, Km 127 on the road to San Sebastián, reservations via *Hostal de la Patagonia* in Punta Arenas. *Refugio Lago Blanco*, on Lago Blanco, Punta Arenas T241197.

Eating *Club Croata*, Senoret y Phillippi, pricey. *Restaurante Puerto Montt*, Croacia 1169, for seafood. Recommended. Many lobster fishing camps where fishermen will prepare lobster on the spot.

Transport **Air** From Punta Arenas – weather and bookings permitting, Aerovías DAP, Oficina Foretic, T80089, Porvenir, fly daily except Sunday at 0815 and 1730 to Porvenir, return at 1000 and 1930, US$20. Heavily booked so make sure you have your return reservation confirmed. **Bus** Two a week between Porvenir and Río Grande (Argentina), Tuesday and Saturday 1400, 5 hours, Transportes Gessell, Duble Almeyda 257, T580488 (in Punta Arenas: José Menéndez 556, T222896). US$20 heavily booked; Río Grande-Porvenir, Wednesday and Sunday 0800. **Ferry** Terminal at Bahía Chilota, 5 kilometres west, see above for details. From bus terminal to ferry, taxi US$6, bus US$1.50. **Hitchhiking** Police may help with lifts on trucks from Porvenir to Río Grande; elsewhere is difficult as there is so little traffic.

Cameron, the only other settlement of any size on the Chilean part of the island, lies 149 kilometres southeast of Porvenir on the opposite shore of Bahía Inútil. From here a road runs southeast to Estancia Vicuña. East of Vicuña is Lago Blanco, surrounded by trees, good fishing; in the centre of the lake is Isla Victoria, with accommodation (see above). Beyond Vicuña a horse trail leads across the Darwin Range to Yendegaia. From there you will have to retrace your steps as it seems impossible to get permission to cross the unmanned border to Ushuaia or to get a Chilean exit stamp.

Bus To Cameron from Porvenir from Calle Manuel Señor, Monday and Friday 1700, US$10.

Transport

Exchange At *Estrella del Sur* shop, Santos Mardones.

Directory

The only legal frontier crossing between the Chilean and Argentine parts of Tierra del Fuego is 142 kilometres east of Porvenir. There are two settlements called San Sebastián, one on each side of the frontier, but they are 14 kilometres apart; taxis are not allowed to cross. Going into Argentina make sure you get an entry stamp for as long as you require. Entering Chile, no fruit, vegetables, dairy produce or meat permitted.

Frontier with Argentina: San Sebastián
Argentine time is 1 hr ahead of Chilean time, Mar-Oct

B *Hostería de la Frontera*, with bath, also basic accommodation in the annex, **E** pp, sleeping bag essential, dirty, no electricity.

Sleeping

Argentine Tierra del Fuego

Río Grande

Situated 87 kilometres south of San Sebastián, Río Grande lies on the southern edge of the Bahía San Sebastián, an important area in summer for migratory birds. The largest settlement in Tierra del Fuego, it is a sprawling modern town in windy, dust-laden, sheep-grazing and oil-bearing plains. The *frigorífico* (frozen meat) plant and sheep shearing shed are among the largest in South America. There is a small museum, the **Museo de Ciencias Naturales y História**, at El Cano 225. ■ *Tuesday-Friday 0900-1700. Saturday-Sunday 1500-2000.*

Population: 35,000
Phone code: 02964
Colour map 7, grid B2

The Salesian Mission of **La Candelaria** is 11 kilometres north along Route 3, has a historical museum housing a collection of Indian artefacts and also a natural history section. ■ *Monday-Saturday 1000-1230, 1500-1900, Sunday 1500-1900, US$1.50. Afternoon teas, US$3.* Nearby is the first parish church of Río Grande.

At **Estancia María Behety**, 18 kilometres southwest, horses can be hired. **Refugio Dicky** is a private bird sanctuary covering 1,900 hectares on Bahía San Sebastián.

Excursions

A2 *Atlántida*, Belgrano 582, T/F431914, without breakfast, restaurant, parking. **A2** *Posada de las Sauces*, El Cano 839, T/F430868/432895, with breakfast, good beds, comfortable, good restaurant, bar. Recommended. **A3** *Los Yaganes ACA*, Belgrano 319, T430823, F433897, comfortable, good expensive restaurant. **A3** *Federico Ibarra*, Rosales y Fagnano, T432485, with breakfast, good beds, large rooms, excellent restaurant. **A3** *Isla del Mar*, Güemes 963, T/F422883, next to bus terminal, with breakfast.

Sleeping
■ *on map, page 458*
Price codes: see inside front cover
Accommodation can be difficult to find if arriving at night

Budget accommodation **B** *Res Rawson*, Estrada 750, T425503, F430352, cable TV, clean, poor beds; **B** *Villa*, San Martín 277, T422312, without breakfast, warm ; **B** *Hosp Noal*, Rafael Obligado 557, lots of bread and coffee for breakfast, cosy. Recommended. **C** *Hostería Antares*, Echeverría 49, T421853; **C** *Avenida*, Belgrano 1001, T422561. No campsite. The gymnasium has free hot showers for men, as has the ACA garage on the seafront.

The Salesian Missions

Founded in 1893 by José Fagnano, La Candelaria was one of three missions set up by the Salesians to try to protect the Onas of Tierra del Fuego from the gold prospectors and estancieros (sheep farmers). The first was established in Punta Arenas in 1886; the second, on Isla Dawson, *two years later. The latter quickly attracted over 1,000 Onas, shipped there by the estancieros. It was finally closed in 1920, by which time the anthropologist Martín Gusinde counted only 276 surviving Onas, most of them on an estancia owned by the Bridges family, see box on page 461.*

Eating *Don Rico*, Belgrano y Pento Moreno, in ultra-modern building, closed Monday; *La Nueva Colonial*, Rosales 640, pizzeria, friendly; *Club de Pesca*, El Cano; *Rotisería CAI*, on Moreno, cheap, fixed price, popular with locals.

Shopping Food is cheaper than in Ushuaia. *La Nueva Piedmontesa*, Belgrano y Laserre, 24-hour food store; *Tia* supermarket, San Martín y Piedrabuena. Good selection.

Festivals *Trout Festival*, third Sunday in February; *Snow Festival*, third Sunday in July; *Woodsman Festival*, first week of December.

Transport **Local Car hire**: *Rent-a-Car*, Belgrano y Ameghino, T422657. *Avis*, El Cano 799, T/F422571 and airport; *Localiza*, at airport, T430482. **Mechanic** and VW dealer: *Viaval SRL*, Pento Moreno 927.

Long distance Air: Airport 4 kilometres west of town. Bus US$0.50. Taxi US$5. To **Buenos Aires**: *Aerolíneas Argentinas*, daily, 3½ hours direct and Lapa daily (except

Río Grande: centre

■ **Sleeping**
1 Antares
2 Atlántida
3 Avenida
4 Federico Ibarra
5 Hosp Noal
6 Isla del Mar
7 Los Yaganes
8 Posada de las Sauces
9 Residencial Rawson
10 Villa

N
Not to scale

Saturday). To **Ushuaia**: *Aerolíneas Argentinas* and *Kaiken*, daily. LADE also to **Río Gallegos**, continuing to **Comodoro Rivadavia** via Calafate. Kaiken flies to **Calafate** daily except Sunday and to **Punta Arenas**.

Buses: All buses leave from terminal, El Cano y Güemes. To **Porvenir**, Chile, 5 hours, Gesell, Wednesday, Sunday, 0800, US$20; to **Punta Arenas**, Chile, via Punta Delgada, 10 hours, Pacheco, Tuesday, Thursday, Saturday 0730, US$30, Los Carlos, Monday, Friday, 0700, US$30; to **Ushuaia**, Tecni Austral, 4 hours, daily 0730 and 1800, US$21 and Los Carlos, Tuesday, Saturday 1700; sit on right for better views, US$20.

Hitchhiking: Very difficult to hitch to Porvenir or north into Argentina (try the truck stop opposite the bus terminal or the police post 7 kilometres out of town). Hitching to Ushuaia is relatively easy in summer.

Directory

Airline offices: *Aerolineas Argentinas*, San Martín 607, T422711. *Lapa*, 9 de Julio 747, T432620. *LADE*, Laserre 425, T422968. *Kaiken*, Perito Moreno 937, T430665. *TAN*, Moyano 516, T422885. **Banks**: *Banco de la Nación Argentina*, San Martín 200. *Banco del Sud*, Rosales 241, cash advance on Visa. *Superkiosko*, Piedrabuena y Rosales, cash only. **Communications**: Post Office: Piedrabuena y Ameghino. **Laundry**: *El Lavadero*, P Moreno y 9 de Julio. **Tour companies & travel agents**: *Yaganes*, San Martín 641, friendly and helpful. **Tourist offices**: Tourist information at the Municipalidad, on Elano, Mon-Fri.

Ushuaia

The most southerly town in Argentina, and one of the most expensive, Ushuaia is 234 kilometres southwest of Río Grande by a new road via Paso Garibaldi. Founded in 1884 it is the provincial capital. Situated on the northern shore of the Beagle Channel, its streets climb steeply towards snow-covered Cerro Martial to the north. There are fine views over the green waters of the Beagle Channel and the snow-clad peaks. The mainstays of the local economy are fishing and tourism.

Population: 30,000
Phone code: 02901
Colour map 7, grid C2

The **Presidio** or old prison, Yaganes y Gobernador Paz, at the back of the Naval Base, houses the **Museo Marítimo**, with models and artefacts from seafaring days, the **Museo Antártico** and, in the cells, the **Museo Penitenciario**, which details the history of the prison. ■ *Daily 1000-1200, 1600-2300, US$5, students US$3.* **Museo Territorial**, Maipú y Rivadavia, T21863, ■ *Monday-Friday 0900-1300, 1630-1930, US$3.* Small but interesting display of early photos and artefacts of the local Indian tribes; relics from the missionaries and first settlers, as well as natural history section. Known as the 'museum at the end of the world' (you can get a stamp in your passport). Highly recommended. The building also contains a bookshop and post office, open afternoons when the main one is closed.

Museums

Cerro Martial offers fine views down the Beagle Channel and to the north, about seven kilometres behind the town; to reach the chairlift (*Aerosilla*, US$5) follow Magallanes out of town, allow one and a half hours. Pasarela and Kaupen run minibus services, several departures daily in summer, US$5 return. There is skiing on the glacier in winter.

Excursions

Harberton, T422742, 85 kilometres east of Ushuaia, is the oldest *estancia* on the island. Run by descendants of its founder, the British missionary Thomas Bridges, it offers guided walks through protected forest and refreshments are sold in the *Manacatush confitería*. Camping is possible. Access is from a dirt road which branches off Route 3, 40 kilometres east of Ushuaia and runs past

See also box on page 462

Tierra del Fuego

> ### Fauna of the Beagle Channel
>
> *Many bird-species can be viewed from the shore or on a boat-trip along the Channel. These include the Black-browed Albatross , the Antarctic Giant Petrel, the Southern Fulmar, the Great Glebe, the Kelp Goose (the male of which is an unmistakable white), Imperial and Rock Cormorants, Steamer ducks, Kelp gulls,*
>
> *the South American tern, the Black Oystercatcher, the Snowy Sheatbill and the Antarctic Skua. The shores of the Beagle Channel are also breeding grounds for several sea mammals, including the Southern Sea Lion and the Southern Fur Seal.*
>
> *Santiago de la Vega*

Lago Victoria, then 25 kilometres through forest before the open country around Harberton. Some parts of the road are bad; tiring driving, five hours there and back. Tours are offered by agencies in Ushuaia. By land these cost US$30 plus US$6 entrance; take your own food if not wishing to buy meals at the Estancia. For excursions to Harberton by boat see below.

Other excursions include: to the **Parque Nacional Tierra del Fuego** (see below); to the **Río Olivio** falls; to **Lagos Fagnano** and **Escondido**.

Sea trips
Note that the Beagle Channel can be rough

Excursions can be booked through most agencies. The main trips are: to the sea lion colony at Isla de los Lobos, two hours on the *Ana B*, US$35, four hours on the *Tres Marías*, US$40; to Lapataia Bay and Isla de los Lobos, five hours on

Ushuaia

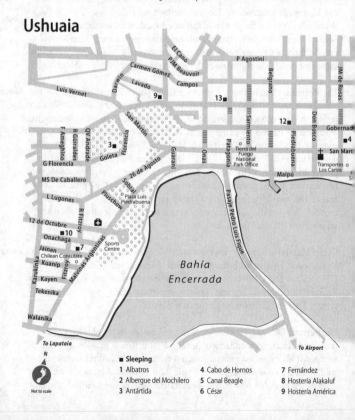

■ Sleeping

1 Albatros	4 Cabo de Hornos	7 Fernández
2 Albergue del Mochilero	5 Canal Beagle	8 Hostería Alakaluf
3 Antártida	6 César	9 Hostería América

Thomas and Lucas Bridges

An orphan from Bristol, Bridges was so named because he was found as a child under a bridge with the letter T on his clothing. Bridges arrived in Tierra del Fuego in 1871 with his wife, young daughter and his adoptive father, Rev Despard, an early Christian missionary; he remained when Despard left after a massacre of Christians by the Indians. Until his death in 1898, Bridges lived near the shores of the Beagle Channel, first at Ushuaia and then Harberton, devoting his

life to his work with the Yámanas (Yaganes) and compiling a dictionary of their language. Of his six children the most famous was Lucas (1874-1949), who, after spending his early life among the Yámanas and Onas and learning their languages, became an outspoken defender of their rights and an opponent of the early sheepfarmers. His memoirs, The Uttermost Part of the Earth *(1947), trace the tragic fate of the native population with whom he grew up.*

the *Ezequiel MB*, US$35; to Isla de los Lobos and Estancia Harberton, six hours on the *Luciano Beta*, US$75, Tuesday, Thursday, Saturday; to Isla de los Lobos and the Isla Martillo Penguin colony, four hours on the *Luciano Beta*, US$60. Some tour agencies imply that their excursions to Harberton go to the *estancia* though in fact they only go to the bay; others go by inflatable launch from main boat to shore. Check thoroughly in advance. Food and drink on all boats is expensive, best to take your own.

10 Maitén
11 Malvinas
12 Mustapic
13 Torres al Sur
14 Ushuaia

NB Prices double on 12 December and accommodation may occasionally be hard to find December-March – the tourist office will help with rooms in private homes and with campsites. Accommodation, food and drink are all expensive. There is no Youth Hostel in Ushuaia. Hostel for sporting groups only at Haruwen Sports Complex.

On the road to the Martial Glaciar overlooking the city are: **L2** *Las Hayas*, Km 3, T430710, F430719. Colourful large rooms, pool, and **L1** *del Glacier*, Km 3.5, T430640, F430636. Modern, casino, pool rooms, shuttle to/from *Hotel Albatros*. Also outside the city **L3** *Tolkeyen*, at Estancia Río Pipo 5 kilometres from town, T422637. With recommended restaurant Tolkeyen (see below). **L3** *Ushuaia*, Laserre 933, 1 kilometre north of town, T430671, F424217. With breakfast, restaurant, sauna.

A1 *Albatros*, Lasserre y Maipú, T430003, F430666. Modern, includes breakfast, good views. **A1** *Las Lengas*, Florencia 1722, T423366, F424599. Superb setting, heating, good dining room. **A2** *Cabo de Hornos*, San Martín y Rosas, T422187, F422313. Comfortable,

Sleeping
■ *on map*
Price codes: see inside front cover

Tierra del Fuego

Estancia Harberton

In a land of extremes and superlatives, Harberton still stands out as special. The oldest estancia on Tierra del Fuego and the oldest house on the island, it was built in 1886 on a narrow peninsula overlooking the Beagle Channel. Its founder, the missionary Thomas Bridges, was given the land by President Roca for his work among the local Indians and for his help in rescuing the victims of the numerous shipwrecks in the channel. Harberton is named after the Devonshire village where his wife Mary was born. The farmhouse was prefabricated by her carpenter father and then assembled on a spot chosen by the Yamana Indians as the most sheltered. The English connection is still evident in the neat garden of lawns, shrubs and trees between the jetty and the farmhouse. Behind the buildings is a large vegetable garden, a real rarity on the island. Visitors will notice that there is much more wildlife around the estancia than in the Tierra del Fuego National Park, probably owing to the remoteness of Harberton.

Still operating as a working farm, mainly with cattle and sheep, Harberton is run by Thomas Goodall, great-grandson of the founder. Visitors receive a conducted tour of the farm buildings and immediate surroundings: though there are guides, Thomas in his dungarees and horn-rimmed glasses, and his wife, Natalie, are usually also on hand.

Natalie is an internationally recognized expert on whales and dolphins, which accounts for the whale jawbone arch over the garden entrance. There is also a 'house of bones' where dolphin, whale and seal carcasses are cleaned and labelled for research, and entire skeletons displayed. Harberton is well worth the visit, particularly by sea as the voyage up the Beagle Channel is equally memorable.

Philip Horton

good value, restaurant not open to non-residents. **A2** *Canal Beagle*, Maipú y 25 de Mayo, T421117. Restaurant. **A2** *César*, San Martín 753, T421460, F432721. Comfortable, including breakfast. Recommended. **A2** *Malvinas*, Deloqui 615, T422626, F424482. Without breakfast, helpful, central heating. Recommended. **A3** *Fernández*, Onachaga y Fitzroy, T421192. With breakfast, good beds, overpriced. **A3** *Posada Fin del Mundo*, Valdez 281, T422530. Family atmosphere. Recommended.

B *Capri*, San Martín 720, T421833. Without breakfast. **B** *Hostería Alakaluf*, San Martín 146, T436705. Without breakfast, quiet. Recommended. **B** *Hostería América*, Gobernador Paz 1665, T423358, F431362. Without breakfast, modern. **B** *Maitén*, 12 de Octubre 140, T422745, F422733. Good value, 1 kilometre from centre, no singles, 10% discount for ISIC and youth card holders. **B** *Mustapic*, Piedrabuena 238, T/F423557. Multi-lingual owner, breakfast.

Budget accommodation D pp *Albergue de Mochilero*, 25 de Mayo 237. Small dormitories with kitchen facilities. **D** pp *Alojamiento Internacional*, Deloqui 395, 1st Floor, T423483/423622. With bath, kitchen facilities, good meeting place. Recommended. **D** pp *Hosp Torres al Sur*, Gobernador Paz 1437, T30745, toresur@hostels.org.ar. Dormitories, heating, good atmosphere, kitchen facilities. Highly recommended. **E** pp *Casa Azul*, Las Primulas 283, Barrio Ecológico, T434769. Floor space. **E** pp *Casa del Turista*, Belgrano 236, T421884. Large kitchen, helpful.

List of private accommodation available from the tourist office. Many people offer rooms in private houses at the airport **Accommodation in private homes A3** *Julio Linares*, Deloqui 1522, T423594, **B** without bath. **A3** *Miguel Zapruscky*, Deloqui 271, T421316. **B** without bath, parking, kitchen, English spoken. Recommended. **B** *Zulema Saltzmann*, Roca 392 y Campos. Clean and friendly. *Sr Ueno*, 12 de Octubre 432, T24661. Full board US$10 per person. Recommended. *La Fiaka*, Deloqui 641, T22669, **C** pp. Clean, warm, cooking facilities. Recommended. **B** *Hosp María Cristina Navarrete*, 25 de Mayo 440, T423068. Without bath or breakfast, cooking facilities. **B** *Familia Cárdenas*, 25 de Mayo 345, T21954.

Without bath or breakfast, quiet. **E** pp *Silvia Casalaga*, Gobernador Paz 1380, T423202. Dormitories, comfortable, heating, breakfast extra, no sign. Recommended. **D** pp *Hosp Turístico*, Magallanes 196. Good views. **E** pp *Posada de los Angeles*, Gobernador Paz 1410. Basement, good kitchen. **D** pp *Adrienne Grinberg*, Bouchard y Rivadavia, T423148. With breakfast, warm, English, French spoken.

Lago Escondido B *Hostería Petrel*, 54 kilometres north of Ushuaia, on the road to Río Grande (bus departs 0900, returns 1500, US$17 return, minimum 4 people), T424390. Trout fishing possible, boat rides, friendly staff.

    Lago Fagnano B *Hostería El Kaiken*, T492208, 100 kilometres north of Ushuaia on a promontory. Also **C** cheaper rooms and bungalows, good site.

Camping *Club Andino Ushuaia*, on the outskirts at Alem 2873, T/F422335. With kitchen, shop, US$5 per person. West of Ushuaia are: *Camping Río Pippo*, US$4 per person, reached by bus no 2. *Ushuaia Camping Municipal* (Km 8), US$15 per tent, toilets, cold showers. East of town on Route 3 are: *Camping del Solar del Bosque* (Km 14), US$5 per person, hot showers. *Camping Río Tristen*, in the Haruwen Winter Sports complex (Km 36), T/F424058. US$5 per tent, electricity, bar, restaurant. Inside the Parque Nacional Tierra del Fuego (entry fee US$5) is *Camping Lago Roca*, 18 kilometres west of Ushuaia, at Lapataia, by forested shore of Lago Roca. With good facilities, dirty, showers (US$3), noisy, reached by bus January-February, small shop, cafeteria. There are also 3 free sites with no facilities: *Ensenada Camping*, 14 kilometres from Ushuaia. *Camping Las Bandurrias* and *Camping Laguna Verde*, both 21 kilometres from Ushuaia. Hot showers, free, at YPF on main road.

Facilities at Kaiken and Petrel are open all year round. These inns are recommended for peace and quiet

Barcleit 1912, Fadul 148. Cordon bleu cooking at reasonable prices. *Kaupé*, Roca 470. English spoken, excellent food and wine. Expensive. Recommended. Best place to eat lamb is at *Tolkeyen*, 5 kilometres from town. *Mi Viejo*, Campos 758. *Tenedor libre*, good value. *Los Amigos*, San Martín 130. Quick service, some cheap dishes. *Volver*, Maipú 37. Sea view, good food and service, not cheap. *Quick*, San Martín 130. Clean, good service. Recommended. 10% discount for ISIC card holders. *Split*, Piedrabuena 238. *Pizzería*, offers same discount, cheap. *Café de la Esquina*, San Martín y 25 de Mayo. Recommended. *Turco*, San Martín 1460. Cheapest in town, friendly. *Der Garten*, *confitería*, San Martín 638, in Galería shopping arcade. Excellent homemade chocolate sold at a shop at San Martín 785. *Helados Massera*, San Martín 270-72. Good. The coffee bar at the airport is very expensive. Ask around for *centolla* (king crab) and *cholga* (giant mussels). *Barcito Ideal*, San Martín 393. Good, cheap, very popular with travellers. *Moustacchio*, San Martín 298. Good fish, good *tenedor libre*. *Bidu Bar*, San Martín 898. Good music, lunches, good meeting place.

Eating

A popular spot at night is the disco *Siglo* at 9 de Julio y Maipú. Other discos are *Barny's*, Antártida Argentina just off San Martín and *Garage*, San Martín 20; El Ñaupe, Gobernador Paz y Fadul. Bar with live music.

Entertainment

12 October: *Founding of Ushuaia*.

Festivals

Good boots at *Stella Maris*, San Martín 443.

Shopping

    Bookshop At San Martín y 9 de Julio (Lapataia Arcade). Film is cheaper in Chile.

Sports Centre on Malvinas Argentinas on west side of town (close to seafront). Ice skating rink at Ushuaia gymnasium in winter. Beachcombing can produce whale bones. **Fishing** Trout, season 1 November-31 March, licences US$20 per week, US$10 per day. Contact Asociación de Caza y Pesca at Maipú y 9 de Julio, which has a small museum. Fishing excursions to Lago Fagnano are organized by *Yishka*,

Sports

Tierra del Fuego

Gobernador Godoy 115, T431535, F431230. **Skiing, hiking, climbing** Contact Club Andino, Fadul 5. **Skiing** A downhill ski run (beginner standard) on Cerro Martial. There is another ski run, Wallner, 3 kilometres from Ushuaia, open June-August, has lights for night-skiing and is run by Club Andino. The area is excellent for cross country skiing; *Caminante* organizes excursions 'off road'. Twenty kilometres northeast of Ushuaia is Valle Tierra Mayor, a large flat valley with high standard facilities for cross country skiing, snow shoeing and snowmobiling; rentals and a cafeteria; bus in the morning and 1400 from *Antartur*, San Martín 638. The Haruwen Winter Sports complex is 36 kilometres east on Route 3.

Supermarkets *Surty Sur* (with clean toilets, San Martín y Onas), good stock, Visa accepted, climbing and trekking clothes at European prices and *Sucoop*, Paz 1600.

Transport **Local** **Car hire**: Tagle, San Martín y Belgrano, T422744. Good, also **Río Grande**, Elcano 799, T422571, and **Localiza**, in *Hotel Albatros* and at airport. Recommended. T430663.

Long distance **Air**: New airport 4 kilometres from town, taxi US$5 (no bus). Services are more frequent in high season; in winter weather often impedes flights. In the summer tourist season it is sometimes difficult to get a flight out, it may be worth trying Río Grande. Aerolíneas Argentinas and LAPA to Buenos Aires 5 hours. To **Río Grande**, Kaiken, US$36, LADE, US$14. To **Río Gallegos**, LADE twice a week, US$39, also Kaiken, LAPA and Aerolíneas Argentina and Austral, US$50-63. LADE to **Comodoro Rivadavia** via Río Grande, Río Gallegos, Calafate (US$55), Gobernador Gregores and Perito Moreno on Wednesday (to Calafate only in summer). To **Punta Arenas**, DAP twice a week, US$91, LanChile, US$95.

At the airport ask around for a pilot willing to take you on a 30 minute flight around Ushuaia, US$38 per person (best to go in evening when wind has dropped). Alternatively ask about flights at the tourist office in town. Aerial excursions over the Beagle Channel with local flying club, hangar at airport, 3-5 seater planes, 30 minutes.

Train: A Decauville gauge train for tourists runs along the shore of the Beagle Channel between the Fin del Mundo station west of Ushuaia and the boundary of the Parque Nacional Tierra del Fuego, 4½ kilometres, 3 departures daily, US$26 (tourist), US$30 (first class), plus US$5 park entrance and US$3 for bus to the station. Run by Ferrocarril Austral Fueguino with new locomotives and carriages, it uses track first laid by prisoners to carry wood to Ushuaia; tickets from Tranex kiosk in the port, T430709. Sit on left outbound.

Bus: To **Río Grande** 4 hours, Los Carlos, 0300, US$20, and Tecni Austral daily 0730, 1800, US$21. To **Punta Arenas** via Punta Delgada, Tecni Austral, Monday, Wednesday, Friday, 0730, 14 hours, US$48; Tolkeyen, Tuesday, Thursday, Saturday 0630, 14 hours, US$50. Bus company offices: Los Carlos, *Ticatur Turismo*, San Martín 880, T422337; Tecni Austral, 25 de May 50, T423396/423304. *Tolkeyen*, Maipu 237, T/F437073.

Hitching: Trucks leave Ushuaia for the refinery at San Sebastián Monday-Friday, but hitching is very difficult (easier via Bahía Azul and Punta Delgada where there is more traffic). A good place to hitch is from police control on Route 3.

Shipping: To **Puerto Williams** (Chile) No regular sailings. Yachts based at the Club Náutico carry charter passengers in summer, returning the same day; enquire at the Club, most possibilities in December because boats visit Antarctica in January. Luxury cruises around Cape Horn via Puerto Williams are operated by the Chilean company, *Tierra Aaustral*, 7/8 days, US$1,260.

To **Antarctica** Most tourist vessels to Antarctica call at Ushuaia and, space permitting, take on passengers. Enquire at *Rumbo Sur* or other agencies. All agencies charge similar price, US$2,200 per person for 8/9 day trip, though prices may be lower for late availability, which are posted in window of *Rumbo Sur*.

Airline offices *LADE*, Av San Martín 552, T421123, airport T421700. *Aerolíneas Argentinas*, Roca 116, T421218, airport 421265. *LAPA*, 25 de Mayo 64, T432112, F430532. *Kaiken*, San Martín 884, T432963, or at airport, T422620, 423049.

Directory

Banks Banks open 1000-1500 (in summer). Credit cards useful as difficult to change TCs and very high commission (up to 10%), *Banco del Sud*, Maipú 600. *Banco de la Nación Argentina*, Rivadavia y San Martín, only bank which accepts Chilean pesos. Cash advance on Mastercard at *Banco de Tierra del Fuego*, San Martín 1044, accepts Amex TCs. *Casa de Cambio* include *Gredi Sol*, 25 de Mayo 50. Tourist agencies and the *Hotel Albatros* also give poor rates. *Listus* record shop, San Martín 973, sweet shop next door, or *Caminante* travel agency for better rates for cash.

Communications Post Office: San Martín y Godoy. Mon-Fri 0900-1300 and 1700-2000, Sat 0830-1200. **Telephones:** San Martín 1541. **Internet access:** *Don Guido Cybercafé*, Godoy 45. US$10 per hr, also offers mailbox facilities for email, 0800-2400.

Embassies & consulates *Chile*, Malvinas Argentinas y Jainen, Casilla 21, T421279. *Finland*, Gobernador Paz y Deloqui. *Germany*, Rosas 516. *Italy*, Yaganes 75.

Laundry Rosas 139, between San Martín and Deloqui. Open weekdays 0900-2100, US$8.

Tour companies & travel agents All agencies charge the same fees for excursions: Parque Nacional Tierra del Fuego, 4 hrs, US$19; Lago Escondido, 5 hrs, US$25; Lagos Escondido and Fagnano, 8 hrs, US$30. With 3 or 4 people it is often a little more expensive to hire a *remise* taxi. The 2 largest agencies are: *Rumbo Sur*, San Martín 342, T430699. Runs a range of tours on water and on land and offers a 2-day package to Calafate, US$150 including transport and hotel, good value. Also organizes bus to ski slope, very helpful; and *Tolkeyen*, 12 de Octubre 150, T422237. Recommended. Others include *Antartur*, Maipú 237, T423240. *All Patagonia*, Fadul 26, T430725, F430707. Amex agent. *Caminante*, Don Bosco 319, T432723, F431040. Organizes walking tours, horse riding, equipment rental, English and German spoken. Highly recommended. *Kilak*, Kuanip 67, T422234. For horse-riding tours. Recommended guide: Domingo Galussio, Intervú 15, Casa 211, (9410) Ushuaia, bilingual, not cheap (US$120). Recommended.

Tourist offices San Martín 660, T424550, "best in Argentina", literature in English, German and Dutch, helpful, English spoken. Large chart of hotels and prices and information on travel and staying at Estancia Harberton. Has noticeboard for messages. Open Mon-Fri 0830-2030, Sat and Sun 0900-2000. *National Park Office*, San Martín 1395, has small map but not much information. The *ACA* office on Maipú also has maps and information.

Parque Nacional Tierra del Fuego

Covering 63,000 hectares of mountains, lakes, rivers and deep valleys, the park stretches west to the Chilean frontier and north to Lago Fagnano, though large areas are closed to tourists to protect the environment. The lower parts are forested; tree species include lenga, ñire and coihue. Birdlife includes several species of geese, such as kelp geese, as well as ducks, Magellanic woodpeckers and austral parakeets. Introduced species, like rabbits, beavers and muskrats, have done serious environmental damage. Near the Chilean frontier, beaver dams can be seen and with much luck and patience the beavers themselves. Stand still and down-wind of them: their sense of smell and hearing are good, but not their eyesight.

There are several beautiful walks: the most popular ones are an interpreted trail along Lapataia Bay, good for birdwatching; a five kilometre walk along

Lago Roca to the Chilean frontier at Hito XXIV; and a two and a half kilometre climb to Cerro Pampa Alta which offers fine views. Good climbing on Cerro Cóndor, recommended. There are no recognized crossing points to Chile. In winter the temperature drops to as low as -12°C, in summer it goes up to 25°C. Even in the summer the climate can often be cold, damp and unpredictable. The *Club Andino* in Ushuaia has a booklet explaining routes in the park (in Spanish) and a poor map.

Park essentials The park entrance is 12 kilometres west of Ushuaia. Park administration is at **Lapataia Bay**. Entry US$5. In summer buses and mini-buses, US$5, to the park are run by several companies: *Pasarela*, Fadul 5, T421735, leaving from Maipú y Fadul; *Kaupen*, T434015, leaving from Maipú y 25 de Mayo, and *Eben-Ezer*, T431133, leaving from San Martín y 25 de Mayo; Timetables vary with demand, tourist office has details. *Caminante* also runs a 1 day excursion to the Park, including trek, canoeing, *asado* lunch, US$70 inclusive (small groups, book early). Ask at the tourist office about cycling tours in the park, US$65 full day, also 'Eco Treks' available and cultural events. It is possible to hitch as far as Lapataia.

Sleeping See above for **Camping** possibilities.

Parque Nacional Tierra del Fuego

Isla Navarino (Chile)

Situated on the southern shore of the Beagle Channel, Isla Navarino is totally unspoilt and beautiful, with a chain of rugged snowy peaks, magnificent woods and many animals; apart from large numbers of beaver which were introduced to the island and have done a lot of damage, guanacos and condors can be seen inland.

Puerto Williams

Population: 1,500
Phone code: 061
Colour map 7, grid C2

The only settlement on the island is Puerto Williams, a Chilean naval base. Situated about 50 kilometres east of Ushuaia (Argentina) at 54° 55' 41" south, 67° 37' 58" west, Puerto Williams is the most southerly place in the world with a permanent population. It is small, friendly and remote (it suffered a serious fire in 1994).

Tierra del Fuego

Isla de los Estados

"This long (75 kilometre) and guarded island lies east of Tierra del Fuego. Except for the caretakers of the lighthouse and an occasional scientist, few people ever set foot on this cloud-shrouded reserve of Fuegian flora and fauna that no longer exist on the main island. During the 18th and 19th centuries, large numbers of ships were wrecked or lost in the treacherous waters surrounding this island. Much gold, silver and relics await salvage." Robert T Cook.
Further information and tours from Rumbo Sur, San Martín 342, Ushuaia.

Museums **Museo Martín Gusinde**, known as the **Museo del Fin del Mundo** ('End of the World Museum') is full of information about vanished Indian tribes, local wildlife, and voyages including Charles Darwin and Fitzroy of the *Beagle*, a 'must'. ■ *1000-1300, 1500-1800 (Monday-Thursday); 1500-1800 (Saturday-Sunday), Friday closed (subject to change). Entrance US$1.*

Excursions Sights include beaver dams, waterfalls, the Villa Ukika, two kilometres east of town, the place where the last descendants of the Yaganes people live, and the local *media luna* where rodeos are held. One kilometre west of the town is the yacht club; the wharf is a sunken 1930s Chilean warship. Outside the Naval headquarters you can see the bow section of the *Yelcho*, the tug chartered by Shackleton to rescue men stranded on Elephant Island. For superb views, climb Cerro Bandera which is reached by a path that runs from the dam seven kilometres west of the town (three to four hours round trip, steep, take warm clothes). No equipment rental on island; buy food in Punta Arenas.

Sleeping **A3** *Hostería Walla*, on the edge of Lauta bay, T4223571. Two kilometres out of town (splendid walks), very hospitable. **D** *Jeanette Talavera*, T4621150, sim@entelchile.net. Small dormitories, kitchen and laundry facilities. **D** per person *Pensión Temuco*, Piloto Pardo 224. Also half board, comfortable, hospitable, good food, hot showers. Recommended. You can also stay at private houses. You can camp near the *Hostería*: collect drinking water from the kitchen. There are several small grocery stores. Beware drinking water from the rivers without purification. **E** per person. *Hostería Camblor*, T4621033, meals served. **E** per person *Res Onashaga* (run by Señor Ortiz – everyone knows him). Cold, run down, good meals, helpful, full board available.

Transport **Air** From Punta Arenas by air, Aerovías DAP, daily 1400, return departure 1530, US$150 return. Book well in advance; 20 seater Cessna aircraft and long waiting lists (be persistent). Luggage allowance 10 kg (US$2 per kg extra). Sit on the right leaving Punta Arenas: the flight is beautiful, with superb views of Tierra del Fuego, the Cordillera Darwin, the Beagle Channel, and the islands stretching south to Cape Horn. Free transport from DAP office in Punta Arenas to the airport. Also army flights available (they are cheaper), but the ticket has to be bought through DAP. Aeropetrel will charter a plane, if a sufficiently numerous party is raised, to Cape Horn (US$2,600 for 8-10 people).

Ferry From Ushuaia (Argentina), the *Tres Marías*, once a week in summer, 3-4 hour crossing, US$65 per person, take own lunch; irregular service in winter, and frequent schedule changes.

Boats from Punta Arenas: *Ñandú* or *Ultragas* leaves on a fixed schedule every 10 days, about midnight, reclining chairs, no food, US$50 one way, including meals, 24-36 hours. Enquire at the office, Independencia 865, next to service station. The *Navarino* leaves Punta Arenas in third week of every month, 12 passengers, US$150

Shackleton, 'Yelcho' and the rescue from Elephant Island

Shackleton's 1914-16 expedition to cross the Antarctic is one of the epics of polar exploration. Shackleton's vessel, Endurance, which left England in August 1914 with 28 men aboard, became trapped in pack-ice in January 1915. After drifting northwards with the ice for eight months, the ship was crushed by the floes and sank. With three boats, supplies and the dogs, the group set up camp on an ice floe which continued to drift north for eight months. In April 1916, after surviving on a diet largely of seals and penguins, the party took to the boats as the ice broke up. After seven days at sea they reached Elephant Island. From there Shackleton and five other men sailed 1,300 kilometres in one of the boats on a 17 day voyage to South Georgia, where there were whaling stations. On reaching the south shore of South Georgia, Shackleton and two men crossed the island (the first such crossing and achieved without skis or snowshoes) to find help. Shackleton, from whom nothing had been heard by the outside world (Endurance had no radio) since leaving the island 18 months before, was not at first recognized.

Though the British government was sending a rescue vessel to Elephant Island, the delays involved led Shackleton to seek help locally. After ice had prevented two rescue attempts, the first from South Georgia and the second from the Falkland Islands/Islas Malvinas, Shackleton went to Punta Arenas, where the British community raised £1,500 to buy Emma, a small schooner with a wooden hull (best for the pack-ice) which was towed towards Elephant Island by the tug Yelcho; but, after continuing alone, Emma was threatened by ice and the attempt was abandoned. Shackleton pursuaded the Chilean authorities to permit a fourth attempt using Yelcho after meteorological conditions had changed. Leaving Punta Arenas on 25 August 1916, the vessel encountered thick fog, but, unusually for the time of year, little ice, and it quickly reached Elephant Island where the men, who had endured an Antarctic winter under upturned boats, were down to four days of supplies.

Though the expedition failed to cross Antarctica, Shackleton's achievement was outstanding: despite the loss of Endurance, the party had survived two Antarctic winters in extreme conditions without loss of life. Shackleton himself returned to the region in 1921 to lead another expedition, but in January 1922, though aged only 47, he suffered a fatal heart attack while in South Georgia.

one way; contact the owner, Carlos Aguilera, 21 de Mayo 1460, Punta Arenas, T228066, F248848 or via *Turismo Pehoé*. The *Beaulieu*, a cargo boat carrying a few passengers, sails from Punta Arenas once a month, US$300 return, 6 days. Navy and port authorities in Puerto Williams may deny any knowledge, but everyone else knows when a boat is due.

Boat trips: ask at the yacht club on the off chance of hitching a ride on a private yacht to Cape Horn. Luxury cruises around Cape Horn are run by *Tierra Austral* for US$800, 6 days. Captain Ben Garrett offers recommended adventure sailing in his schooner *Victory*, from special trips to Ushuaia to cruises in the canals, Cape Horn, glaciers, Puerto Montt, Antarctica in December and January. Write to Victory Cruises, Puerto Williams (slow mail service); Fax No 1, Cable 3, Puerto Williams; phone (call collect) asking for Punta Arenas (Annex No 1 Puerto Williams) and leave message with the Puerto Williams operator.

Directory **Airline offices** *Aerovías DAP*, *LanChile*, *Ladeco* in the centre of town. **Communications** Post Office: closes 1900. **Telephone**: *CTC*. Mon-Sat 0930-2230, Sun 1000-1300, 1600-2200. **Telex**. **Tourist offices** Near the museum (closed in winter). Ask for details on hiking. Maps available.

Chilean Pacific Islands

15

Chilean Pacific Islands

Far out in the Pacific are two Chilean island possessions, the Juan Fernández Islands, famed for Alexander Selkirk's enforced stay (the inspiration for Robinson Crusoe) and the Polynesian island of Rapa Nui, better known as Easter Island. While neither of these is on the itinerary of most visitors to Chile, both can be reached relatively easily by air from Santiago.

Juan Fernández Islands

History

Population: 500
Phone code: 032
Colour map 3, grid B2

The islands are named after Joao Fernández, a Portuguese in the service of Spain, who was the first European to visit in 1574. Although they were frequented by pirates and corsairs over the following 150 years, it was not until after 1750 that the Spanish took steps to defend them, founding San Juan Bautista and building seven fortresses. During the Wars of Independence the islands were used as a penal colony, the Spanish deporting here Chilean independence leaders captured after the Battle of Rancagua. In 1915 two British destroyers, HMS *Kent* and *Glasgow* cornered the German cruiser, *Dresden*, in Bahía Cumberland. The German vessel, which was scuttled, still lies on the bottom; a monument on shore commemorates the event and, nearby, unexploded shells are embedded in the cliffs. Some of the German crew are buried in the cemetery.

Geography

Situated 667 kilometres west of Valparaíso, this group of small volcanic islands is a national park administered by Conaf. There are three islands: Isla Robinson Crusoe (4,794 hectares) which was the home (1704-9) of Alexander Selkirk (the original of Defoe's *Robinson Crusoe*); Isla Alejandro Selkirk (4,952 hectares) the largest, and Isla Santa Clara (221 hectares), the smallest. Selkirk's cave on the beach of Robinson Crusoe is shown to visitors. The only settlement is San Juan Bautista, a fishing village of simple wooden frame houses, located on Bahía Cumberland on the north coast of Isla Robinson Crusoe: it has a church, schools, post office, and radio station. The islands are famous for *langosta de Juan Fernández* (a pincerless lobster) which is sent to the mainland. In summer, a boat goes once a month between Robinson Crusoe and Alejandro Selkirk if the *langosta* catch warrants it, so you can visit either for a few hours or a whole month.

Best time for a visit:
October-March

The islands enjoy a mild climate and the vegetation is rich and varied: the Juan Fernández palm, previously used widely for handicrafts, is now a protected species, but the *sandalo* (sandalwood tree), once the most common tree

Isla Robinson Crusoe

Chilean Pacific Islands

Yachting

Each February, a yachting regatta visits the islands; setting out from Algarrobo, yachts sail to Isla Robinson Crusoe, thence to Talcahuano and Valparaíso. At this time Bahía Cumberland is full of colourful and impressive craft, and prices in restaurants and shops double for the duration.

Thomas G Lammers, Department of Botany, University of Miami.

on the islands, is now extinct owing to its overuse for perfumes. Fauna includes wild goats, hummingbirds and seals. The islands were declared a UN World Biosphere Reserve in 1977. **Take insect repellent**.

Sights

The remains of the **Fuerte Santa Bárbara**, the largest of the Spanish fortresses, overlook San Juan Bautista. Nearby are the **Cuevas de los Patriotas**, home to the deported Chilean independence leaders. South of the village is the **Mirador de Selkirk**, the hill where Selkirk lit his signal fires. A plaque was set in the rock at the look-out point by British naval officers from HMS *Topaze* in 1868; nearby is a more recent plaque placed by his descendants. Selkirk, a Scot, was put ashore from HMS *Cinque Ports* and was taken off four years and four months later by a privateer, the *Duke*. The Mirador is the only easy pass between the north and south sides of the island. Further south is the anvil-shaped **El Yunque**, 915 metres, the highest peak on the island, where Hugo Weber, a survivor from the *Dresden*, lived as a hermit for 12 years: some remains of his dwelling can be seen. The only sandy beach on Robinson Crusoe is **Playa Arenal**, in the extreme southwest corner, two hours by boat from San Juan Bautista.

Essentials

San Juan Bautista C pp *Alejandro Selkirk*. Clean, good food, full board **A** pp. Recommended (Santiago T5313772). **A1** *Hostería Robinson Crusoe*, T751069. Full board. **L3** *Daniel Defoe*, at Aldea Daniel Defoe, F751075 (Santiago T5313772). **A2** *Hostería Villa Green*, T751049, F751044. Good. **B** *Charpentier*, F751020 (Santiago T2245691).

Sleeping
Lodging with villagers is difficult

Air Air taxi daily in summer (subject to demand) from Santiago (Los Cerrillos airport, US$395 round trip), by three companies: Transportes Aéreas Isla Robinson Crusoe, Monumento 2570, Maipú, Santiago, T531-4343, F531-3772; Lassa, Av Larraín 7941, La Reina, Santiago, T273-4354, F273-4309; Servicio Aéreo Ejecutivo, Apoquindo 8750, Torra 3, Local 4, T/F2293419. Luggage allowance 10 kilograms. Planes land on an airstrip in the west of the island; passengers are taken by boat to San Juan Bautista (1½ hours, US$10 one way).

Transport

Sea The boat service, about every 3 weeks from Valparaíso on the *Río Baker* and *Charles Darwin*, is for cargo and passengers, modest accommodation, 36-hour passage; *Agentur*, Huérfanos 757, oficina 601, T337118, Santiago. *Pesquera Chris*, Cueto 622, Santiago, T681-1543, or Cochrane 445 (near Plaza Sotomayor), Valparaíso, T216800, 2-week trips to the island (5 days cruising, a week on the island), from US$200 return. No fishing or cargo boats will take passengers.

Banks No exchange facilities. Only pesos and US$ cash accepted. No credit cards, no TCs.

Directory

Easter Island

Geography

Population 3,000
Phone code: 032

Isla de Pascua or Rapa Nui lies in the Pacific Ocean just south of the Tropic of Capricorn and 3,790 kilometres west of Chile; its nearest neighbour is Pitcairn Island. The island is triangular in shape, with an extinct volcano at each corner. The original inhabitants called the island Te Pito o te Henua, the navel of the world. The population was stable at 4,000 until the 1850s, when Peruvian slavers, smallpox and emigration to Tahiti (encouraged by plantation owners) reduced the numbers. Of the current population about 500 are from the mainland. There is one village on the island, Hanga Roa, where most of the population live. About half the island, of low round hills with groves of eucalyptus, is used for horses and cattle, and nearly one-half constitutes a national park (entry US$10, payable at Orongo). The islanders have preserved their indigenous songs and dances, and are extremely hospitable. Tourism has grown rapidly since the air service began in 1967. Paid work is now more common, but much carving is still done. The islanders have profited greatly from the visits of North Americans: a Canadian medical expedition left a mobile hospital on the island in 1966, and when a US missile-tracking station was abandoned in 1971, vehicles, mobile housing and an electricity generator were left behind.

Climate

Average monthly temperatures vary between 15-17°C in August and 24°C in February, the hottest month. Average annual rainfall is 1,100 millimetres. There is some rain throughout the year, but the rainy season is March-October, with the wettest weather in May. The tourist season is from September to April.

Rapa Nui - Easter Island

0 km 3
0 miles 2

Volcanos (extinct)

The formation of Easter Island

In geological terms Easter Island is not very old; potassium argon dating shows that its oldest part is under 2.5 million years old. It is located above a toectonic 'hot spot', an active upwelling of liquid rock emerging from beneath the crust of the earth and solidifying. Enough molten rock has poured out to form a mountain nearly 3,000 metres high, the altitude of the Easter Island volcano if measured from the sea bed. There are, however, no records of volcanic activity since human occupation of the island began. The three high peaks are all volcanic in origin and consist mainly of basalt. In the cliffs of Rano Kau different layers of basalt can be identified, indicating the existence of distinct lava flows. Caves have been formed where the lava has solidified on the outside but continued to flow downhill on the inside. On Terevaka, where the roofs of some of these caves have collapsed, long caverns up to 10 metres high can be seen.

The volcanic nature of the island contributed to the carving of the moai. Extremely hard basalt from Terevaka was used to make some of the hard tools for carving. Sharp edged implements were fashioned using obsidian, volcanic glass formed by lava cooling very rapidly. The moai themselves were carved from tuff, a porous rock much softer than basalt but also volcanic in origin, which can be found at Rano Raruka, a secondary cone on the side of Terevaka.

Unlike most Polynesian islands, Easter Island has no coral reef as winter temperatures are too cold for coral to survive. As a result the coastline has been eroded in parts to form steep cliffs, around Poike, Rano Kao and on the northern side of Terevaka.

Easter Island has no high central plateau and consequently there is little gully erosion which would normally lead to the development of streams and rivers. Moreover much of the island's rainfall drains away underground into the huge caverns formed by the collapse of basalt caves. As a result, although annual rainfall is usually above 1,000 millimetres, there is always a severe shortage of water and in many years several months of drought.

History

It is now generally accepted that the islanders are of Polynesian origin. Thor Heyerdahl's theories, as expressed in *Aku-Aku, The Art of Easter Island* (New York: Doubleday, 1975), are less widely accepted than they used to be, and South American influence is now largely discounted, see below.

European contact with the island began with the visit of the Dutch admiral, Jacob Roggeven, on Easter Sunday 1722, who was followed by the British navigator James Cook in 1774 and the French sailor Le Perouse in 1786. Between 1859 and 1862 over 1,000 islanders were transported as slaves to work in the Peruvian guano trade. The island was annexed by Chile in 1888. Until 1952 most of Easter Island was leased to a private company which bred sheep on its grasslands: a wall was built around the Hanga Roa area and the islanders were forbidden to cross.

Sights

The unique features of the island are the 600 (or so) *moai*, huge stone figures up to nine metres in height and broad in proportion. One of them, on Anakena beach, was restored to its probable original state with a plaque commemorating Thor Heyerdahl's visit in 1955. Other *moai* have since been re-erected. There is an anthropological museum in Hanga Roa, explanations in Spanish only. Most of the objects are reproductions because the originals were

Chilean Pacific Islands

Chilean Pacific Islands

The cultural development of Easter Island

Far from being the passive recipient of external influences, Easter Island shows the extent of unique development possible for a people left wholly in isolation. It is believed to have been colonized from Polynesia about 800 AD: its older altars (ahu) are similar to those of French Polynesia, and its older statues (moai) similar to those of the Marquesas Islands. The very precise stone fitting of some of the ahu, and the tall gaunt moai with elongated faces and ears for which Easter Island is best known were later developments whose local evolution can be traced through a comparison of the remains. Indigenous Polynesian society, for all its romantic idylls, was competitive, and it seems that the five clans which originally had their own lands demonstrated their strength by erecting these complex monuments. The moai were sculpted at the Rano Raraku quarry and transported on wooden rollers over more or less flat paths to their final locations; their red topknots were sculpted at and brought from the inland quarry of Puna Pau; and the rounded pebbles laid out checkerboard fashion at the ahu all came from the same beach at Vinapu. The sculptors and engineers were paid out of the surplus food produced by the sponsoring family: Rano Raraku's

unfinished moai mark the end of the families' ability to pay. Over several centuries from about 1400 AD this stonework slowed down and stopped, owing to the deforestation of the island caused by roller production, and damage to the soils through deforestation and heavy cropping. The birdman cult represented at Orongo is a later development after the islanders had lost their clan territoriality and were concentrated at Hanga Roa, but still needed a non-territorial way to simulate inter-clan rivalry." David Bulbeck, Adelaide.

The central feature of the birdman cult was an annual ceremony in which the heads of the lineages, or their representatives, raced to the islets to obtain the first egg of the sooty tern (known as the Manutara), a migratory seabird which nests on Motu Nui, Motu Iti and Motu Kao. The winning chief was named Bird Man, Tangata Manu, for the following year. It appears that, in the cult, the egg of the tern represented fertility although it is less clear what the status of the Tangata Manu actually was. The petroglyphs at Orongo depict the half-man, half-bird Tangata Manu, the creator god Make Make and the symbol of fertility, Komari.

removed from the island, but there are good descriptions of island life. ■ *Entry US$2. Tuesday-Friday 0930-1230, 1400-1730, Saturday/Sunday 0930-1230.*

A tour of the main part of the island can be done on foot, but this would need at least two days, either camping at Anakena or returning to Hanga Roa and setting out again the next day. Most correspondents, however, agree that this is far too quick. You could hire a vehicle to see more. From Hanga Roa, take the road going southeast past the airport; at the oil tanks turn right to Vinapu, where there are two *ahu* and a wall whose stones are joined with Inca-like precision. Head back northeast along the south coast, past Vaihu (an *ahu* with eight broken *moai*; small harbour); Akahanga (*ahu* with toppled *moai*); Hanga Tetenga (one toppled *moai*, bones can be seen inside the *ahu*), Ahu Tongariki (once the largest platform, damaged by a tidal wave in 1960, restored with Japanese aid). Turn left to Rano Raraku (20 kilometres), the volcano where the *moai* were carved. Many statues can be seen. In the crater is a small lake surrounded by reeds; swimming is possible beyond the reeds. There are good views.

The road heads north past 'the trench of the long-ears' and an excursion can be made to Poike to see the open-mouthed statue that is particularly popular with local carvers. Ask farmer for permission to cross his land. On Poike the earth is red; at the northeast end is the cave where the virgin was kept before marriage to the victor of ceremonies during the birdman cult; ask someone for directions. The road along the north coast passes Ahu Te Pito Kura, a round stone called the navel of the world and one of the largest *moai* ever brought to a platform. The road continues to Ovahe where there is a very attractive beach with pink sand and some rather recently carved faces and a cave.

From Ovahe, you can return direct to Hanga Roa or continue to Anakena, site of King Hotu Matua's village and Thor Heyerdahl's landing place. From Anakena, where there is a white sand beach and palm trees, a coastal path of variable quality runs west, passing interesting remains and beautiful cliff scenery. At Hanga o Teo, there appears to be a large village complex, with several round houses, and further on there is a burial place, built like a long ramp with several ditches containing bones. From Hanga o Teo the path goes west then south, inland from the coast, to meet the road north of Hanga Roa.

A six hour walk from Hanga Roa on the west coast passes Ahu Tahai (a *moai* with eyes and topknot in place, cave house, just outside town). Two caves are reached, one inland appears to be a ceremonial centre, the other (nearer the sea) has two 'windows' (take a strong flashlight and be careful near the 'windows'). Further north is Ahu Tepeu (broken *moai*, ruined houses). Beyond here you can join the path mentioned above, or turn right to Te Pahu cave and the seven *moai* at Akivi. Either return to Hanga Roa, or go to Puna Pau crater (two hours), where the topknots were carved

South of Hanga Roa is Rano Kau, an important site where the curious Orongo ruins can be seen. The route south out of Hanga Roa passes the two caves of Ana Kai Tangata, one of which has paintings. If on foot you can take a path from the Orongo road, just past the Conaf sign, which is a much shorter route to Rano Kau crater. A lake with many reed islands is 200 metres below. On the seaward side is Orongo (entrance US$11), where the birdman cult flourished, with many ruined buildings and petroglyphs. Out to sea are the 'bird islets', Motu Nui, Motu Iti and Motu Kao. It is very windy at the summit; good views at sunset, or under a full moon. It is easy to follow the road back to Hanga Roa in the dark.

In Hanga Roa is Ahu Tautira, next to a swimming area, with cold water, marked out with concrete walls and a breakwater. Music at the 0900 Sunday mass has been described as 'enchanting'. There is a cultural centre next to the football field, with an exhibition hall and souvenir stall.

Recommended reading There is a very thorough illustrated book by J Douglas Porteous, *The Modernization of Easter Island* (1981), available from Department of Geography, University of Victoria, BC, Canada, US$6. See also Thor Heyerdahl's work, details above; *Easter Island, Earth Island*, by Paul Bahn and John Flenley (Thames and Hudson, 1992) for a comprehensive appraisal of the island's archaeology. *Islas Oceánicas Chilenas*, edited by Juan Carlos Castillo (Ediciones Universidad Católica de Chile, 1987), contains much information on the natural history and geography of Juan Fernández and Easter Islands.

Anyone continuing into Polynesia or Melanesia from Easter Island will find David Stanley's *South Pacific Handbook* (Moon Publications Inc, PO Box 3040, Chico, CA 95927, USA, F1-916-345-6751) a useful guidebook.

Essentials

Time zone: Easter Island is always 2 hours behind the Chilean mainland, summer and winter time.

Street names In practice street names are rarely used. Directions are given by referring to local landmarks such as the church.

Cost of living Food, wine and beer are expensive, often twice the price of the mainland, because of freight charges, but local fish, vegetables, fruit and bread are cheap. Average prices: coffee/tea US$1, meals about US$10 or more, bread US$2 per kilogram, beer/cola US$2 in most bars and restaurants. Bring all you can from the mainland, but not fruit.

Tap water in Hanga Roa is safe to drink.

Sleeping
■ *on map*
Price codes:
see inside front cover
Unless it is a particularly
busy season there is no
need to book in
advance; mainland
agencies make
exorbitant booking
charges

Hanga Roa The accommodation list at the airport information desk only covers the more expensive places. Flights are met by large numbers of hotel and *residencial* representatives but it is cheaper to look for yourself. There are even reports of touts approaching passengers at Santiago airport prior to their flight to the island. Accommodation ranges from US$10-200. Note that room rates, especially in *residenciales* can be much cheaper out of season and if you do not take full board.

L3 *Hanga Roa*, Av Pont. Full board, T100299 (Santiago 6339130, F6395334). **L3** *Iorana*, Ana Magara promontory, 5 minutes from airport, T100312 (Santiago 633-2650). Friendly, excellent food, convenient for visiting Ana Kai Tangata caves.

A1 *Orongo Easter Island*, Policarpo Toro, half board (excellent restaurant), good service, nice garden. T100294, or Santiago 2116747. **A1** *Otai*, Te Pito Te Henua, T100250. Great location 2 minutes from sea, lovely gardens, no meals except breakfast. Recommended. **A1** *Victoria*, Av Pont, T100272. Friendly, helpful owner arranges tours. **A1** *Topara*, Atamu Kekena, T100223. 5 minutes from Hanga Roa, run down, very helpful, excellent restaurant. **A2** *Chez Joseph*, T100281. **A3** *Poike*, Petero Atamu, T100283. Homely, hot water.

Residenciales A1 *Res Pedro Atán*, T100329. Full board, Policarpo Toro. **A1** *Res Apina Nui*, Hetereki, T100292. (**B** low season, but bargain), good food, helpful, English spoken. **A2** *Res Kai Poo*, Av Pont, T100340. Small, clean, friendly with hot water. **A2** *Res Hanga Roa Reka*, T100433. Full board, good, friendly, camping. *Res El Tauke*, Te Pito Te Henua s/n, T100253. Same rates as *Hanga Roa Reka*, excellent, airport transfers, tours arranged. *Res Taheta One One*, T100257. Same rates, motorbike rental. **B** *Res Tahai*, Policarpo Toro, T100395. With breakfast, **A2** full board, nice garden. Recommended. **C** Anita and Martín Pate's guesthouse, T100593, opposite hospital in Hanga Roa, with breakfast, clean, good food. **D** per person *Chez Cecilia*, near Tahai Moai, T100499. Half board, speaks English and French, excellent food, camping. **D** María Goretti. With breakfast, camping. **C** pp *Res Viaka Pua*, Hanga Roa, T100377. Full board, comfortable, friendly. Recommended. **A3** Emilio and Milagrosa Paoa. With full board, tours.

Camping Free in eucalyptus groves near the Ranger's house at Rano Raraku (with water tank), and at Anakena, no water, make sure your tent is ant-proof. Officially, camping is not allowed anywhere else, but this is not apparently strictly enforced. Many people also offer campsites in their gardens, US$5-10 per person, check availability of water first; some families also provide food. Several habitable caves around the coast: for example between Anakena beach and Ovahe. If you must leave anything behind in a cave, leave only what may be of use to other campers, candles, oil, etc, certainly not rubbish. Camping equipment for hire at shop near the supermarket.

Most *residenciales* offer full board. Coffee is always instant. Beware of extras such as US$3 charge for hot water. It is worth booking a table in advance for evening meals. *Mama Sabina*, Av Policarpo Toro. Clean, welcoming. *Cowboy*, nearby, good food, not too expensive. *Ave Rei Pua*, limited menu, good tuna and lobster. *Tavake*, Av Policarpo Toro. *Pizzería*, opposite post office. Moderately priced. *Le Pecheur*, French run, unfriendly, expensive. *Kona Koa*, not cheap but good. *Ki Tai* for pizzas, snacks. *Pea*, Av Apina, pricey but pleasant with fine sea views.

Eating
● on map
Vegetarians will have no problems on the island

Discotheques There are two in Hanga Roa: *Maitaki* (open daily), east side of town, with pool table, and *Piriti*, near airport (open Thursday-Saturday). Action begins after 0100. Drinks are expensive: a bottle of pisco costs US$9, canned beer US$2.

Entertainment

Hiking Allow at least a day to walk the length of the island, one way, taking in all the sites. It is 5 easy hours from Hanga Roa to Rano Raraku (camp at ranger station); 5 hours to Anakena (camp at ranger station, but ask first). You can hitch back to Hanga Roa, especially at weekends though there are few cars at other times. Anyone wishing

Sports

Chilean Pacific Islands

Hanga Roa

Not to scale

■ Sleeping	6 Topara	3 Ki Tai
1 Chez Joseph	7 Victoria	4 Kona Koa
2 Hanga Roa		5 Le Pecheur
3 Iorana	● Eating	6 Mama Sabina
4 Orongo Easter Island	1 Ave Rei Pua	7 Pea
5 Otai	2 Cowboy	

Tapati or Semana Rapa Nui

Held each year in late January/early February, Tapati begins slowly but keeps on getting better as the fortnight goes on. It is organized as a huge competition between groups, many of them families, each of which elects a beauty queen. Families score points by participating in a wide variety of competitions including gastronomy, necklace-making, sculpting moai, body painting, dancing, singing, horse-racing, swimming, modified decathlon. In the most spectacular event,

men, dressed only in the traditional thong and with their bodies painted, compete to slide down the side of a volcano, sitting on a kind of sledge made from the trunks of two banana plants. Only for the tough guys!

Lots of tourists, especially from the Chilean mainland, visit at this time. It is best to stay in Hanga Roa, since it is easy to hitch to activities elsewhere.

Gert Van Lancker and Sandra Van Heyste, Vilvoorde, Belgium.

to spend time exploring the island would be well-advised to speak to Conaf first (T223236); they also give good advice on special interests (biology, archaeology, handicrafts, etc). **Horseback** The best way to see the island, provided you are fit, is on horseback: horses, US$20-25 a day. Tourist office provide a list of people hiring horses. A guide is useful. Try Emilio Arakie Tepane, who also leads horseback tours of the island (Spanish only) T100504.

Festivals *Tapati*, or *Semana Rapa Nui*, **end-January/beginning-February**. It lasts 2 weeks, see box on page 480. Only essential activities continue outside the festival.

Shopping On Av Policarpo Toro, the main street, there are lots of small shops and market stalls, which when it rains, and a couple of supermarkets; the cheapest is *Kai Nene* or *Tumukai*. Some local produce can be found free, but ask first. This includes wild guava fruit, fish, 'hierba luisa' tea, and wild chicken.

Cameras Film is readily available but is usually only Kodak 36 print rolls. No film developing on the island.

Handicrafts Wood carvings, stone moais, best bought from the craftsmen themselves, such as Antonio Tepano Tucki, Juan Acka, Hipolito Tucki and his son (who are knowledgeable about the old culture). The municipal market, left of church, will give you a good view of what is available – no compunction to buy. The airport shop is expensive. Good pieces cost between US$30 and 150. There are several souvenir shops on Av Policarpo Toro including *Hotu Matuu's Favorite Shoppe* where prices have been described as 'top dollar and she will not bargain', but she does have the best T-shirts. Handicrafts are sold at Tahai, Vaihu, Rano Raraku and Anakena. Bargaining is only possible if you pay cash.

Transport **Local** There are several taxis and in summer a bus goes from Hanga Roa to Anakena on Sunday at 0900, returning in the evening (unreliable). **Vehicle rental**: a high-clearance vehicle is better-suited to the roads than a normal vehicle. If you are hiring a car, do the sites from south to north since travel agencies tend to start their tours in the north. Jeep hire is available from main hotels but hire companies tend to have better vehicles. *Hertz*, Av Policarpo Toro, T100334. *Insular*, Policarpo Toro, T100480. Many other vehicle hire agencies on the same street. Jeep hire US$50-70 per day, US$10 per hour. There is no insurance available, drive at your own risk (be careful at night, many vehicles drive without lights). US$5-10 will buy enough fuel for a one-day trip around the island. **Motorbike rental**: about US$30 a day plus fuel

(Suzuki or Honda 250 recommended because of rough roads). **Bicycles**: some in poor condition, are available for rent for US$15 on main street or from *residenciales*.

Transport to Easter Island Air: Airport just south of Hanga Roa. The runway has been extended to provide emergency landing for US space shuttles. LanChile fly 4 days a week in high season (Saturday, Sunday, Tuesday, Thursday), 2 days a week low season (Sunday, Thursday) 5-5½ hours. Return to Santiago is Monday, Wednesday, Friday and Saturday (Monday, Friday out of season). Most flights continue to Papeete, Tahiti. LanChile office on Av Policarpo Toro, T100279; do not fly to Easter Island unless you have a confirmed flight out (planes are more crowded to Tahiti than back to Santiago) and reconfirm your booking on arrival on the Island. For details of LanChile air passes which include Easter Island and which must be purchased outside Chile, see **Essentials**, page 45. The fare in 1999 was US$812 return. Special deals may be available on flights originating outside Chile. Students studying in Chile eligible for 30 percent discount. Don't take pesos to Tahiti, they are worthless in French Polynesia.

   Airport tax: Flying from Santiago to Easter Island incurs the domestic tax of US$8. The airport tax for international flights from Easter Island to Tahiti is US$5.

Sea: There are no passenger services to Easter Island. Freight is brought by sea 3 times a year.

Banks US dollars are widely accepted though usually at a poor rate. Buy Chilean pesos on the mainland as local rates are poor. Bank next to tourist office, open 0900-1200 daily, charges US$18 commission on changing TCs, but you can change as many TCs for this fee as you like (and they can be in different names). Cash can be exchanged in shops, hotels, etc, at about 3% less than Santiago. Poor rates on Amex TCs at Sunoco service station but no commission. Amex TCs also changed by Kia-Koe Land Operator, *Hanga Roa Hotel*. Prices are often quoted in dollars, but bills can be paid in pesos. Amex credit cards are widely accepted, but cannot be used to obtain cash (but enquire at Sunoco service station). **Communications** Post Office: 0900-1700. **Telephones:** phone calls from the Chilean mainland are subsidized, at US$0.50 per minute, minimum 3 minutes. Calls to Europe cost US$10 for 3 mins, cheap rate Saturday 1400-1930. **Hospitals & medical services** There is a 20-bed hospital as well as 3 resident doctors, a trained nurse and 1 dentist on the island. **Tour companies & travel agents** *Mahinatur Ltda*, Av Hotu Matua, T100200, vehicle reservations in advance. Their guide, Christian Walter, is recommended. *Kia-Koe*, Av Policarpo Toro, T100282, *Schmidt Osterinsel Reisen*, office in *Hanga Roa Hotel*, T223600, F223532. English, French and German spoken, offers tours around the island and to caves, both US$15. Maps are sold on Av Policarpo Toro for US$15-18, or at the ranger station at Orongo for US$10. Many agencies, *residenciales* and locals arrange excursions around the island, eg *Aku-Aku Tours*, Krenia Tucki of *Res Kai Poo*, Fernando and Marcelo León (Pai Tepano Rano, recommended), Some go in jeeps, others will accompany tourists in hired vehicles (eg US$110 for 3), prices up to US$50 each per day. The English of tour guides is often poor. **Tourist office** *Sernatur Juumaheke*, T100255, Mon-Fri 0830-1300, 1400-1730.

Directory

Background

16

484

Background

History

Archaeology and prehistory

Some 50,000 years ago the very first peoples crossed the temporary land bridge spanning Asia and America at the Bering Straits, and began a long migration southwards. They were hunters and foragers, following in the path of huge herds of now extinct animals, such as mammoth, giant ground sloth, and descendants of the camel and horse. The first signs that these people had reached South America dated from around 14,000 BC, if not earlier.

Origins

Background

As sources of game in forested valleys dried up, some groups settled along the coasts, particularly drawn by the abundance of marine life provided by the cold Humboldt current in the Pacific. Some of the earliest evidence of humans in Chile have been found in the north, on the coast and in the parched Atacama desert. The coastal people lived on shellfish gathered by the shore, and on fish and sea lions speared from inflated seal-skin rafts.

One such group, the Las Conchas people, migrated from the inland valleys to the coast near Antofagasta around 7,500 BC. They were one of the first peoples in South America to take hallucinogenic drugs. Many graves excavated in this region contained mortars, which may have been used to grind up seeds also found nearby. These seeds contained an alkaloid similar to that found in the ayahuasca plant, which is also used for its hallucinogenic effects by modern peoples elsewhere on the subcontinent. Grave artefacts included bags, trays, and tubes that were used for inhaling the drug in the form of snuff, a method employed in curing and adivination practices in the Andean region and coastal Brazil today. Some of the trays and tubes found were decorated with images of supernatural beings and anthropomorphic figures, such as bird-headed angels, styles that are also common in the Andean regions of present-day Peru and Bolivia.

Gradually the nomadic lifestyle gave way to more settled occupation of fixed sites, with agricultural subsistence taking over from hunting. Remains of slingshot stones and what seem to be *bolas* (weights attached to cords used to bring down prey by entangling their legs) have been found alongside bones of mastodons in Monte Verde, near Puerto Montt. Other remains found nearby included agricultural tools and medicinal plants, hearths and house foundations, all indications that the site was inhabited for some time by one community and not just a hunters' temporary camp. Crop seeds were also found, including those of potatoes, evidence of very early contact with cultures from as far afield as the Central Andes. Some of these remains were found in a remarkable condition, owing to being buried in a peat bog; mastodon bones even had traces of meat on them. Lower levels at Monte Verde have been controversially dated from 34,000 years ago, but it is widely agreed that the site was settled as early as 10,000 years ago.

The beginnings of agriculture

By about 2500 BC agriculture was practised throughout much of Chile, as it was across the rest of the continent. Maize, beans, and squash have been found in northern Chile, from as early as 5000 BC, when they would have been cultivated to supplement food supplies from hunting and gathering. The extremely dry climate here is a great preservative, allowing archaeologists to build up a detailed picture of early life. The people lived in solidly built adobe houses, arranged in complexes around inner courtyards and corridors, such as can be seen in the village of Tulor in the San Pedro de Atacama oasis.

The link with Tiahuanaco These northern people had contacts with neighbouring highland communities (in present-day Bolivia, Argentina, and Peru), shown by the presence of plants and other goods found only in the adjacent regions. The important altiplano culture of Tiahuanaco in present-day Bolivia is thought to have had particularly close links with northern Chile, helping to stimulate the growth of settlements such as at San Pedro de Atacama. Trade with Tiahuanaco, through llama caravans bringing highland goods and produce, boosted the wealth and cultural development of the desert peoples. Some very fine textiles in particular, were found in this area, showing distinct design similarities with Tiahuanaco. The textiles were hand-spun and coloured with vegetable and cochineal dyes. Clothing and jewellery adornments containing feathers suggested contact even with tropical regions, although they may have obtained these through their altiplano intermediaries. Local ceramics were mostly plain and highly polished, but some items decorated with elaborate dragon-like figures had probably been traded with Tiahuanaco.

By about 500-900 AD the association between San Pedro de Atacama and Tiahuanaco had become even stronger. In return for trading their agricultural produce and other goods, it is thought that the Tiahuanaco people sought the copper, semi-precious stones, and use of grazing lands in northern Chile. Some graves from this period contained bodies with more elaborate clothing, jewellery, imported ceramics and other valuables, suggesting the existence of a wealthy élite, which was also common in central Andean cultures.

Following the demise of Tiahuanaco in about 1100 AD, a number of cultures arose in the adjacent area bordering southern Bolivia, northern Chile and Argentina, practising derivative agriculture, with terraces and irrigation, and producing ceramics in similar styles. In the Quebrada de Humahuaca in present-day Argentina several small defensive towns were built, with fortified walls and stone houses. Grave remains have revealed that metallurgy was well developed here; some bodies were adorned with pectorals, bracelets, masks, and bells made of copper, silver and gold. Bone tools were also found, and obsidian projectile points. Shells from the Pacific and ceramics from present-day Bolivian cultures, such as the Huruquilla, showed the existence of widespread trade links.

Mummification was practised from as early as 2500 BC by coastal peoples, and was also common further north in present-day Peru. The Chinchorro people buried their dead stretched out straight, in contrast to the foetal position used by other Chilean and Peruvian cultures. Internal organs and the brain were removed and the body stuffed with a variety of materials to preserve it. Sticks were attached to the limbs to keep them straight. A mask was placed over the face and a wig of real human hair attached to the head. The body was then coated in a layer of clay and wrapped in animal skins or mats. According to the person's status, they were often buried with their personal possessions, such as clothing, jewellery, musical instruments, and copper items.

By the beginning of the present era most people in Chile, as throughout South America, were leading settled lives in structured communities, farming, and to a greater or lesser degree producing ceramics, textiles, and worked metal objects, mostly in copper and silver. All the evidence shows that the metalwork was for personal use, not for tools or weapons, until the Inca era. People in southern Chile turned to agriculture at a much later date. In Araucania, a region around Temuco long noted for its foraging cultures, horticulture was not practised until around 500 AD. These people also had unusual burial practices; placing the body in an urn inside a funerary canoe, perhaps reflecting the local dependence on fishing for their livelihood. Elaborate artefacts found in some graves, with stone and copper jewellery as well as ceramic offerings, suggest a stratified society of both rich and poor.

At the peak of its growth in the 16th century, the Inca empire stretched deep into Chile, as far south as the Aconagua valley. The advancing armies of Inca Topa Yupanqui suppressed resistance in the valleys of the central region, and replaced local structures with their own military administration. They were finally stopped by hostile forest tribes at the Río Maule. This was the southernmost limit of the Inca Empire, some 2,400 miles south of the equator, and the deepest that any imperial movement had penetrated into the southern hemisphere.

Inca expansion

One major group, which survived the Inca incursion and resisted conquest by the Europeans right up until the 19th century AD was the Mapuche. They were concentrated in the central valley south and east of the Cordillera de Nahuelbuta. The Mapuche were primarily farmers, but also hunted and fished, both inland and along the coasts and lake shores. Their large cemeteries contained a variety of graves, some in canoes or stone chambers, and some in simple earthen graves, suggesting a social hierarchy. Grave goods were plentiful, with elaborate ceramics, wooden and stone artefacts, and jewellery made of copper and semi-precious stones.

Southernmost Patagonia and Tierra del Fuego, straddling present-day Chile and Argentina, are covered with dense forested hillsides and flat pampas grasslands. The climate here is harsh, with extremely cold winters and heavy rainfall all year round. Despite the apparently inhospitable conditions these regions were home to a sizeable population of hunting, fishing and gathering peoples from very early times continuously up to the 19th century AD. Bones of horses and extinct giant sloths have been found near to stone arrow heads, in sites such as Fells's Cave and Palli Aike Cave on the Magellan Straits, dating from approximately 8000 BC, as evidence of the earliest hunters.

The far south

Four distinct cultures developed here: the Haush, Ona, Yahgan, and Alacaluf. The oldest of these was the **Haush**, nomadic hunters of the guanaco mainly confined to the farthest southeastern tip of Tierra del Fuego, in present-day Argentina. The Haush hunted with bows and arrows, using guanaco skins for clothing and sometimes for covering their stick-framed houses. They also gathered shellfish and caught fish by the shore, using spears and harpoons.

The **Ona** people also hunted guanaco, ranging on foot across most of the Isla Grande of Tierra del Fuego in family groups. They were strong runners and tall people, some of them six foot tall; in fact, all these hunters and gatherers are thought to have been the tallest of the first South American peoples. They wore guanaco skin robes, fur side out, and also guanaco fur moccasins, known as *jamni*. They made open-topped shelters out of guanaco skins, which were weatherproofed with a coating of mud and saliva, and sometimes painted red. The Ona did not use harpoons or spears and only collected shellfish from beaches at low tide.

The **Yahgans** were nomadic coastal hunters, travelling in canoes up and down the coasts of the Beagle Channel and around the islands southwards to Cape Horn. They caught otters, fish, and seals, using spears and harpoons, and used slings and snares to catch birds. The Yahgans' houses were simple, made of sticks and grass, and they wore little clothing, perhaps a small seal skin and skin moccasins in winter.

Like the Yahgans, the **Alacalufes** were also nomadic coastal peoples, roaming from Puerto Edén in the Chilean channels, to Yendegaia, in the Beagle Channel. There was some contact with the Yahgan, with whom they would sometimes exchange goods and intermarry. The Alacalufes had similar lifestyles to the Yahgans, but developed various additions, such as raising a sail on their canoes, and using a bow and arrow in addition to the sling when hunting birds or guanaco.

Background

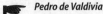

Pedro de Valdivia

Although Pedro de Valdivia joined the Spanish army as a young man in 1521, serving in Flanders and Italy, little else is known of his early life. In 1535 he was sent to Venezuela, where he joined an expedition sent to Peru to reinforce Francisco Pizarro. In 1537 he became aide de camp to Pizarro and sided with him in the war between the latter and Diego de Almagro, receiving an award of land and Indians in return. Shortly after he sold his property to finance an expedition southwards to Chile; setting off in 1540 accompanied by 12 white men, one white woman (Inés de Suárez), 1,000 Indians and a few black slaves. Travelling across the arid Atacama Desert, he reached the Copiapó Valley and then moved south to the Mapocho Valley, where he founded

Santiago. Receiving further supplies and reinforcements from Peru, he travelled north again, founding La Serena. After a brief expedition to Peru in 1547 where he helped in the defeat of Gonzalo Pizarro by troops sent from Spain, he returned to Chile in 1549, founding the cities of Concepción, Valdivia and Villarrica, before being killed in battle with the Mapuche at Fort Tucapel.

Although Valdivia's military career was as bloody and brutal as those of most of the conquistadores, he is seen by many historians as driven more by the spirit of adventure and the excitement of exploring unknown lands than by the desire to acquire gold and silver which motivated many including the Pizarro brothers with whom he was so closely associated.

Colonial history

Throughout the colonial period Chile, lacking important resources of precious minerals, inhabited by the warlike Mapuche and never less than four months' journey from Europe, was of relatively little importance to Spain except as a frontier zone. The first Spanish expeditions to Chile were led by Diego de Almagro and Pedro de Valdivia both of whom followed the Inca road from Peru to Salta and then west across the Andes. Almagro's expedition of 1535-1537, which included 100 Spaniards and some thousands of Indians, many of whom perished, reached the heartland, but, bitterly disappointed at not finding gold, returned to Peru almost immediately. Valdivia's expedition carried out what initially appeared to be a swift and successful conquest, founding Santiago in February 1541 and a series of other settlements in the following years. In the 1550s these Spanish settlements were shaken by a Mapuche rebellion which resulted in the death of Valdivia.

War against the Mapuche was to occupy the Spanish governors who succeeded Valdivia. Known by the Spanish as Araucanians, the Mapuche were fearsome opponents; they soon mastered the use of horses and were effective guerrilla fighters. In 1598 they began a general offensive which destroyed all of the Spanish settlements south of the Río Biobío, revealing the weakness of a colony whose Spanish population was under 8,000. Pushed back into the northern part of the Central Valley, the Spanish were forced to build a string of forts along the Río Biobío, guarded by a frontier army of 2,000 men, the only force of its type in Spanish America, financed by a special subsidy from the vice-regal capital of Lima. However, Chile was not important enough to warrant a full scale Spanish assault on the Mapuche and for the rest of the colonial period the Spanish presence south of the river would be limited to the island of Chiloé and to the coastal city of Valdivia.

Situated between the Biobío frontier to the south and the deserts to the north, colonial Chile developed as a compact society; most of its population inhabited the Central Valley and most trade was through Valparaíso. In this small isolated society

Town planning in the 16th century

Perhaps the most obvious influence of Spanish colonial settlement for the traveller is the characteristic street plan of towns and cities. Colonial cities were founded by means of an official ceremony which included the tracing of the central square and the holding of a mass. A series of Royal Ordinances issued in Madrid in 1573 laid down the rules of town planning. The four corners of the main plaza were to face the four points of the compass 'because thus the streets diverging from the plaza will not be directly exposed to the four principal winds, which would cause much inconvenience.' The plaza and the main streets were to have arcades which were seen as 'a great convenience for those who resort thither for trade.' Away from the plaza the streets were to be traced out by means of measuring by cord and ruler in the now-familiar grid-pattern. Once this was done building lots were to be distributed, those near the plaza being allocated by 'lottery to those of the settlers who are entitled to build around the main plaza'.

The Ordinances specified the principles underlying the distribution of the major public buildings: 'In inland towns the church is not to be in the centre of the plaza but at a distance from it in a situation where it can stand by itself, separate from other buildings so that it can be seen from all sides. It can thus be made more beautiful and it will inspire more respect. It should be built on high ground so that in order to reach its entrance people will have to ascend a flight of steps. Nearby the cabildo and the customs house are to be erected in order to increase its impressiveness but without obstructing it in any way. The hospital of the poor who are ill with non-contagious diseases shall be built facing the north and so planned that it will enjoy a southern exposure.'

The Ordinances also advised settlers on how to deal with hostility from the indigenous population: 'If the natives should wish to oppose the establishment of a settlement they are to be given to understand that the settlers desire to build a town there not in order to deprive them of their property but for the purpose of being on friendly terms with them; of teaching them to live in a civilized way; of teaching them to know God and His Law ... While the new town is being built the settlers ... shall try to avoid communication and intercourse with the Indians. Nor are the Indians to enter the circuit of the settlement until the latter is complete and in condition for defence and the houses built, so that when the Indians see them they will be filled with wonder and will realize that the Spaniards are settling there permanently and not temporarily.'

Royal Ordinances Governing the Laying Out of New Towns by Zelia Nuttall, Hispanic American Historical Review, *May 1922, pages 249-254.*

Background

racial intermixing was common; by the end of the 17th century there were few Indians, most having died, intermixed or escaped south of the Biobío. Most of the population was *mestizo* (mixed race), though the society was dominated by a small white élite.

During the colonial period the *hacienda*, or landed estate, was the most important feature of rural society in the Central Valley. In the 17th century Chilean agriculture expanded to meet demands for wheat, tallow, salted beef and cattle hides from Peru while hides were also sent to Potosí and mules to the great fair in Salta. These exports and the need to feed the frontier army led to the development of large scale agriculture. As the *haciendas* grew, small farmers and tenants were gradually forced to become *inquilinos*, a class of peasants tied to the land. The *inquilino* is regarded as the ancestor of the *huaso*, the Chilean cowboy, a figure seen as resourceful, astute, cunning and typically Chilean.

Although *haciendas* grew in response to food shortages, they were very self-contained; *haciendas* had their own supplies of food and clothing, their own vineyards, forges and workshops. Ownership of a *hacienda* was one of the clearest marks of upper class status although many were the property of religious orders. The *hacienda* remained at the centre of rural life in the Central Valley and social relations between landowners and *inquilinos* changed little until the Agrarian Reforms of the 1960s. Although no colonial *haciendas* remain, a few dating from the 19th century can be visited, notably Villa Huilquilemu, near Talca.

Chile was governed as part of the Viceroyalty of Peru, with its capital in Lima; until the 18th century all trade with Spain had to pass via Lima and trade with other countries was forbidden. This led to uncontrolled smuggling and by 1715 there were 40 French vessels trading illegally along the coast. In 1740 direct trade with Spain was permitted and in 1750 Chile was permitted to mint her own currency.

The War of Independence

Independence came to Spanish America as a result of Napoleon's invasion of Spain in 1808. As Spanish guerrilla forces fought to drive the French out, the colonial élites debated where their loyalties lay: to Napoleon's brother Joseph, now officially King? Or to the overthrown king, Ferdinand VII, now in a French prison? Or to the Spanish resistance parliament in Cadiz?

In 1810 a group of leading Santiago citizens appointed a Junta to govern until Ferdinand returned to the throne. Though they protested loyalty to Ferdinand, their move was seen as a challenge by the Viceregal government in Lima, which sent an army to Concepción. War broke out between the Chilean Patriots and these Royalist troops supporting Lima. The defeat of the Patriot army at Rancagua in October 1814 (see page 246) led to a restoration of colonial rule, but the turning point came in 1817 with the invasion of Chile from Mendoza by San Martín's Army of the Andes, a force of 4,000 men which defeated the Royalists at Chacabuco on 12 February 1817. A Royalist counter-attack was defeated at Maipó, just south of Santiago on 5 May 1818, putting an end to Royalist power in the Central Valley. The victory of the small Patriot navy led by Lord Cochrane (see box, page 125) at Valdivia in January 1820 helped clear the Pacific coast of Royalist vessels and paved the way for San Martín to launch his seaborne invasion of Peru.

The 19th century

In most of former Spanish America independence was followed by a period of political turmoil, marked by civil wars and dictatorship, which in some cases lasted until the 1860s. In Chile the overthrow of O'Higgins was followed by a brief period of instability but in 1830 conservative forces led by Diego Portales restored order and introduced the Constitution of 1833, which created a strong government under a powerful president. Portales, a Valparaíso merchant who never became president explained his actions thus: "If one day I took up a stick and gave tranquillity to the country it was only so that the bastards and whores of Santiago would let me get on with my work in peace". Chile became famous throughout Latin America as the great example of political stability: the army was reduced to 3,000 men and kept out of politics; after 1831 four successive presidents served the two successive five-year terms permitted under the constitution. However, this stability had its other side: civil liberties were frequently suspended, elections rigged, opponents exiled and power lay in the hands of a small landowning élite. Neither was the stability perfect: there were short civil wars in 1851, 1859 and 1891.

Bernardo O'Higgins

Born in 1778 in Chillán, O'Higgins was the illegitimate son of Ambrose O'Higgins, an Irishman who rose in the Spanish colonial service to become Governor of Chile and Viceroy of Peru and his Chilean mistress, Isabel Riquelme. At the age of 17 Bernardo was sent to study in London where he met Francisco de Miranda and other South American exiles who were plotting to overthrow Spanish colonial rule. Returning to Chile in 1802 after Ambrose's death, he inherited his father's estate and adopted his surname. After the collapse of Spanish rule, O'Higgins was elected to the first National Congress in 1811. When war broke out between the Chilean Patriots and Royalist forces, O'Higgins recruited his own troops, distinguishing himself in a number of battles and being wounded at El Roble in October 1813. In 1814 he was appointed Commander-in-Chief of the Patriot armies, but defeat at the Battle of Rancagua in October 1814 forced him to retreat with 2,000 men across the Andes to Mendoza. Here he met José de San Martín who was preparing an army to cross the Andes and free Chile from Spanish control as a first step to invading the Spanish stronghold of Peru. Returning to Chile with San Martín, O'Higgins led a risky and unauthorized cavalry charge at the Battle of Chacabuco on 12 February 1817 which assured victory. Four days later the Patriot leaders appointed O'Higgins Supreme Director.

Facing a renewed threat from a Royalist army moving north from Talcahuano, O'Higgins proclaimed Chilean independence in February 1818, but the following month his troops were defeated near Talca and he was badly wounded. A few weeks later, O'Higgins, still

recovering, galloped onto the battlefield at Maipó, at the head of reinforcements and embraced San Martín crying "Glory to the Saviour of Chile". San Martín replied "Chile will never forget the name of the illustrious invalid who, today, presented himself on the battlefield." This episode, known as 'The Embrace of Maipó', is one of the most famous in Chilean history.

As the head of the first Chilean government, O'Higgins remained personally popular, although many of the actions of his government were not. He abolished aristocratic titles and personally sketched the plans for a wide boulevard which was to run along a sheep-track on the outskirts of Santiago and which is now the Avenida Bernardo O'Higgins. Although the Creole élite disliked measures such as the prohibition of burial inside churches and the approval of a Protestant cemetery, opposition to his government was also partly the result of family rivalries. O'Higgins' constitution of 1822, which allowed for him to remain in office for another 10 years, provoked further opposition. After Gen Ramón Freire launched a rebellion in Concepción, O'Higgins was forced to resign on 23 January 1823. Six months later a British warship took him to Peru where he accompanied Simon Bolívar on the final campaign against Spanish forces. His final years were lived out on his estate in the Cañete valley, south of Lima. His support for a military insurrection in Chile in 1826 led to the Chilean government stripping him of all his honours but these were restored to him in 1842 shortly before his death in October of that year. He was buried in Lima and in 1869 his remains were returned to Chile.

Background

After 1879 Chilean territory was enlarged both northwards and southwards. Victory in the War of the Pacific gave her control over the nitrate-rich expanses of the Atacama desert. Although colonization schemes were begun in the Lake District in the 1850s, it was not until victory over Peru in the War of the Pacific was assured that the much enlarged army was sent to put an end to Mapuche independence and thus secure continuous Chilean control over the Pacific coastline south of Arica.

From the 1860s conflict between President and Congress became a constant feature of political life. Although the War of the Pacific brought the Chilean

The War of the Pacific, 1879-1883

One of the few major international wars in Latin America since independence, this conflict had its roots in a border dispute between Chile and Bolivia, the frontier between the two in the Atacama desert being ill-defined at the time of independence. There had already been one conflict: in 1836-1839, when Chile defeated Peru and Bolivia. Relations were complicated by the discovery of nitrates in the Atacama in the 1860s: in the Bolivian province of Antofagasta nitrates were exploited by Anglo-Chilean companies.

In 1878 the Bolivian government, short of revenue, attempted to tax the Chilean-owned Antofagasta Railroad and Nitrate Company. When the company refused to pay, the Bolivians seized its assets. The Chilean government claimed that the Bolivian action broke an 1874 agreement between the two states. When Peru announced that it would honour a secret alliance with Bolivia by supporting her, the Chilean president, Aníbal Pinto, declared war on both states.

None of the three states was prepared for war; they lacked skilled officers and adequate weapons. Control of the sea was vital and the few ironclad ships were far superior to wooden vessels. The Chileans blockaded the Peruvian nitrate port of Iquique with two wooden ships, the Esmeralda and the Covadonga. Peru sent her two best ironclads, the Huáscar and the Independencia, to Iquique. In the Battle of Iquique, 21 May 1879, the Esmeralda was sunk, but in the course of the battle the Independencia ran aground and was captured, thus altering the balance of forces between the two navies. Later in October 1879 off Angamos near Antofagasta, the two Chilean ironclads, Blanco Encalada and Cochrane, cornered the Huáscar and captured her (the Huáscar can be visited in the harbour of Talcahuano).

Rather than attack the Peruvian heartland, the Chileans invaded the southern Peruvian province of Tarapacá and then landed troops north of Tacna, seizing the town in May 1880 before capturing Arica, further south. In January 1881 fresh Chilean armies seized control of Lima. Despite these defeats, Peru did not sue for peace, although Bolivia had already signed a ceasefire, giving up her coastal province. Under the 1883 peace settlement Peru gave up Tapapacá to Chile. Although the provinces of Tacna and Arica were to be occupied by Chile for 10 years, it was not until 1929 that an agreement was reached under which Tacna was returned to Peru, while Chile kept Arica.

Apart from souring relations between Chile and her two northern neighbours to this day, the war gave Chile a monopoly over the world's supply of nitrates and enabled her to dominated the southern Pacific coast. Some idea of the war's importance in official Chilean history can be gained by the number of streets and squares named after the heroes of the war, especially Arturo Prat and Aníbal Pinto, and after the vessels Esmeralda and Blanco Encalada.

Peruvian province of Tacna, occupied by Chile 1883-1929, restored to Peru 1929

Provinces of Arica & Tarapacá, Peruvian until 1883, now part of Chile

Bolivian province of Antofagasta, before 1879, southern portion of which was claimed by Chile

— · · · — Present-day frontiers

- - - - - Peru-Bolivia frontier before 1879

— · — · — Original frontier between Chile & Bolivia

government a new source of income, the tax levied on nitrate exports, it also increased the rivalry for control of this income. When, in 1890 Congress rejected the budget, President Balmaceda announced he would use the 1890 budget for 1891. Congressional leaders denounced this as illegal and fled to Iquique, where they recruited an army which defeated Balmaceda's forces and seized the capital. Balmaceda took refuge in the Argentine embassy where he committed suicide. His defeat was important: between 1891 and 1924 Chilean presidents were weak figures and real power lay in Congress, dominated by the élite.

The 20th century

In the years before the First World War the income from nitrates helped build a large railway network, roads and ports and the best education system on the continent. However, the collapse of the nitrate industry during the First World War led to worker and student unrest which brought down the constitutional system in 1924 when the military intervened. A new constitution restored the strong presidency which had apparently served Chile so well in the nineteenth century, but the Great Depression brought further economic stress which resulted in a series of short-lived governments including a military-led 100-day Socialist Republic in 1932.

As economic conditions recovered in the 1930s, Chile became once again a model of political stability. Between 1932 and 1970 Chile developed a complex multiparty system: two left-wing parties, the Socialists and Communists, representing the urban workers and miners; the Conservative and Liberal parties, dating from the 19th century, representing the landowners; and the Radicals, a centre party representing the middle classes. The Radicals became the key to power, winning the presidency in 1938, 1942 and 1946. However, one major group remained excluded from political life: the peasants whose votes, controlled by their landlords, gave the Liberals and Conservatives their representation in Congress and enabled the landlords to block rural reform.

The 1958 election, in which the Socialist **Salvador Allende** narrowly failed to defeat the Conservative Jorge Alessandri, shook the right-wing parties and, in the aftermath of the Cuban Revolution, the US government. In 1964 the US and the Chilean right-wing threw their weight behind **Eduardo Frei**, a Christian Democrat who promised reforms in a 'revolution in freedom'. Frei's achievements in office were impressive: state ownership of 51 percent of the copper industry; minimum wage and unionization rights for agricultural workers; the 1967 agrarian reform which began replacing the *haciendas* with family farms. These measures raised hopes which could not be satisfied, especially in the countryside where workers now enjoyed rights to push for faster land reform. Hostility from the landowners was reflected in Congress where the National party, formed in 1966 by the merger of the Conservatives and Liberals, denounced the government. The president's Christian Democrat Party was divided between supporters and opponents of reform.

The 1970 election was narrowly won by Salvador Allende, heading a left-wing alliance called Unidad Popular. Allende's government launched an ambitious programme of reforms: banking, insurance, communications, textiles and other industries were taken over in the first year and the nationalization of copper was completed. After that the government ran into major problems: the nationalizations had depleted Chile's currency reserves; hostility by domestic business groups and the US led to capital flight and a US led boycott on international credit; an alliance between the Christian Democrats and National Party in Congress impeached several ministers; a series of anti-government strikes by truck drivers and professional groups brought the country to a halt in October 1972 and again in August 1973; annual inflation rose to over 300 percent in 1973.

Salvador Allende Gossens

Born in 1908 into an upper middle class Valparaíso family, Salvador Allende's childhood ambition was to be a doctor, like his grandfather Ramón Allende Padín, a respected Radical politician who became Serene Grand Master of the Chilean Freemasons. While studying medicine he discovered firsthand the appalling living conditions of the poor and the links between poverty and disease. Even before he qualified as a doctor he became active in politics and was briefly imprisoned during the Ibáñez dictatorship. He was a founder member of the Chilean Socialist party in 1933; at about the same time he became an active freemason.

Elected to Congress for Valparaíso at the age of 29, he served as Minister of Health in Aguirre Cerda's Popular Front government of 1939-1942. Elected to the Senate in 1945, he became Senate president in 1965. Allende was a candidate in four presidential elections. In 1952 he gained only 5.45 percent of the votes, but in 1958 as candidate of the Front for Popular Action, an alliance between the Socialists and Communists, he lost narrowly to the

right-wing candidate, Jorge Alessandri. Easily defeated in 1964 by the Christian Democrat, Eduardo Frei, he finally won the presidency in 1970: in a three-cornered race he gained 36 percent of the vote. Lacking a majority in Congress, heading a broad but divided coalition of eight parties and facing the hostility of much of the Chilean population and of Washington, Allende had increasingly little room for manoeuvre.

When news of the military revolt came through in the early hours of 11 September 1973, Allende went to the Moneda Palace and spoke twice on the radio before communications were cut. Though offered a flight out of the country in return for his resignation Allende refused and the Palace was bombed by three Hawker Hunter jets. Most accounts now accept that Allende committed suicide. He was buried in an unmarked grave in Viña del Mar. In September 1990 following the return to civilian rule his body was exhumed and transported to Santiago for a state funeral, thousands of people lining the route from the coast.

The coup of 11 September 1973, led by **General Augusto Pinochet,** was widely expected, the armed forces having received open encouragement from Allende's opponents in Congress, including the Christian Democrats and the opposition on the streets. The brutality shocked people who were accustomed to Chile's peaceful traditions. Left-wing activists and people mistakenly identified as leftists were arrested; thousands were executed; torture was widespread; at least 7,000 people were held in the national football stadium; by 1978 there were 30,000 Chilean exiles in Western Europe alone. With political parties and labour unions banned, the government adopted free market economic policies under the influence of Milton Friedman and the 'Chicago Boys'.

Under a new constitution, adopted in 1980, Chile became a 'protected democracy' based on the exclusion of political parties and the 'guardianship' of the armed forces who would put forward a single candidate for an eight-year presidential term in 1981. To no one's surprise the candidate was Pinochet, but his bid for a further eight-year term in a plebiscite in 1988 was unsuccessful.

As a result, presidential and congressional elections were held in 1989. A Christian Democrat, **Patricio Aylwin Azócar,** the candidate of the Coalition of Parties for Democracy (CPD, or Concertación), was elected President and took office in March 1990 in a peaceful transfer of power. General Pinochet remained as Army Commander although other armed forces chiefs were replaced. The new Congress set about revising many of the military's laws on civil liberties and the economy. In 1991 the National Commission for Truth and Reconciliation published a report with details of those who were killed under the military régime, but opposition by the armed forces prevented mass human rights trials.

General Augusto Pinochet Ugarte

Born in Valparaíso in 1915, the son of a customs officer who traced his ancestry to Breton immigrants, Pinochet entered the Escuela Militar (Military Academy) at the age of 17, graduating near the bottom of his class in 1936. His subsequent career included a posting to the Ecuadorean national military academy from 1956 to 1959. In 1964 he became deputy director of the Escuela Militar; among his publications were a history of the War of the Pacific and a textbook on geopolitics.

By 1969 he had risen to the rank of Brigadier General and the following year he became commander of the Santiago garrison, one of the most sensitive and influential postings in the Chilean army. When the Army Commander in Chief, General Carlos Prats González, became Minister of the Interior in the Allende government in 1972, Pinochet took over as acting Commander-in-Chief. He took over this post again in August 1973 on the resignation of Prats. Although Pinochet was a relatively unknown figure and was apparently a late convert to the coup plot against Allende, his position as head of the Army made him an automatic choice to become President of the military junta which took over.

In 1974 he became President of Chile, having increased his hold on power by his control over the regime's secret police, the DINA which was headed by a close colleague, Gral Manuel Contreras. Following his election in 1980 as the only candidate in the first elections held under the new constitution, he began a fresh eight-year term (1981-1989) during which he became the longest ever serving Chilean president. In 1986 he narrowly escaped an assassination attempt, escaping the bomb attack with minor bruises. Following his defeat in the 1988 referendum, he did not stand as a candidate in the December 1989 elections and handed over the presidency in March 1990.

Despite his advancing years and heart surgery in 1992 Pinochet insisted on remaining Commander-in-Chief of the Army until March 1998 as specified in the 1980 Constitution. He made it clear that he would oppose any moves to bring members of the armed forces to trial for human rights abuses committed during the dictatorship. In December 1990 questions in Congress and in the press about financial scandals involving army officers and his own son-in-law, led him to order all troops to report to barracks. In May 1993 he surrounded the Ministry of Defence with soldiers and ordered generals to wear battle dress to work for a day and in September 1996 he suggested that the armed forces should be prepared to carry out another coup if ever that became necessary.

With his stern features enhanced by dark glasses Pinochet became the stereotype of the 1970s South American dictator. Often seen as a bluff no-nonsense character, he is also noted for his astuteness, his suspicious mind, his ruthlessness and his hatred of democracy and political parties. Furious after his defeat in the 1988 referendum, Pinochet observed that another plebiscite long ago had elected Barrabas. Although Pinochet himself said in 1981 'not a leaf stirs in Chile without me moving it', it would be wrong to see his dominance as merely the result of repression and fear. To many Chileans who had hated Allende and feared his policies, Pinochet became a popular figure; the human rights abuses and destruction of democracy seen as a price worth paying.

Presidential elections in December 1993 resulted in victory for the Christian Democrat, Eduardo Frei, son of a previous president and candidate of the Concertación coalition, but in congressional elections held at the same time the Concertación failed to achieve the two-thirds majority in Congress required to reform the constitution, replace the heads of the armed forces and end the system of designated senators whose votes enabled the right-wing parties and the military to block reform. As a result Frei's presidency became an exercise in balancing the demands of the parties of the Concertación against the entrenched power of the military and the right-wing parties. In August 1995 Frei presented bills to Congress to make the necessary constitutional reforms. He also proposed that investigations continue into the disappearance of some 500 political prisoners under the military government. In spite of public support, the government was blocked on both issues. Although the Concertación won a comfortable victory in congressional elections in December 1997, they still failed to achieve the majority necessary to break the deadlock and the position of the military was strengthened in March 1998 when General Pinochet retired as army commander-in-chief and, as entitled under the constitution, as a former president who had held office for six years, took up his seat in the Senate.

General Pinochet's detention in London in October 1998 on a Spanish extradition warrant put the Frei government under great pressure: Pinochet's supporters demanded action while some of the government's supporters, especially in the Socialist party, were privately delighted. These debates were linked to the continuing demands from families of those who had disappeared for news of the whereabouts of the victims' corpses, and prosecutions of those responsible. As the December 1999 presidential elections approached the Socialist Ricardo Lagos, former Minister of Public Works and presidential candidate of the Concertación, remained the favourite to succeed Frei as president.

Land and environment

Geography

Chile is smaller than all other South American republics except Ecuador, Paraguay, Uruguay and the Guianas. Its territory is a ribbon of land lying between the Andes and the Pacific, 4,329 kilometres long and, on average, no more than 180 kilometres wide. Its range of climates and scenery, matched by few, if any other countries, poses great problems for surface communication and administration. Because of hostile environments the far north and extreme south are sparsely populated.

In the north Chile has a short 150 kilometres east-west frontier with Peru. In the far north its eastern frontier is with Bolivia – 750 kilometres long – but from San Pedro de Atacama south to Patagonia and Tierra del Fuego it shares over 3,500 kilometres of frontier with Argentina. In the main this frontier follows the crest of the Andes, but this is by no means the case throughout and there have been frequent frontier disputes with Argentina since independence. Chile has a short Atlantic coastline at the eastern end of the Straits of Magellan. Its sovereignty over the islands south of Tierra del Fuego gives it control over Isla Navarino, the site Puerto Williams, the most southerly permanent settlement in the world (apart from scientific bases in Antarctica). Various island archipelagos in the Pacific, including Easter Island/Rapa Nui and the Juan Fernández group, are under Chilean jurisdiction.

The Atacama Desert

Why is northern Chile so dry? We might perhaps expect otherwise anticipating that it would receive heavy rainfall off the Pacific. The answer to this question lies in the interaction of three processes which have combined to make the Atacama one of the driest environments on earth.

Situated between 10° and 30° south of the Equator, the Atacama falls within a zone of subtropical air pressure where warm, stable air is descending. As this air warms, its capacity to retain moisture increases, causing the lower atmosphere to remain dry. This low humidity and the lack of surface water for evaporation cause the clear desert skies which in turn lead to the very hot days and very cold desert nights. The Atacama is also affected by the rain shadow created by the Andes, which block the southeasterly trade winds. The third factor is the impact of the cold Humboldt Current: as this pushes north along the Pacific coast it is followed by the prevailing southeasterly winds but these are gradually pushed westwards and out over the Pacific by the rotation of the earth. This draws very cold water up from the Peru/Chile ocean trench towards the surface of the sea. Air crossing this cold water is cooled and its ability to hold water is reduced.

Where cool winds from the ocean blow onto the warm land surface fog is formed. Along the northern coast a heavy winter mist known as camanchaca *is common. In places this provides sufficient moisture for a limited vegetation cover to develop close to the coast.*

Naomi Peirce

Structure

Although there are surface remnants of older rock formations, notably in the coastal ranges between 30°S and 60°S, most have disappeared with the dramatic creation of the Andes which started around 80,000 years ago in the late Cretaceous Period and continues to this day. The South American Plate, moving westwards, meets the Nazca and Antarctic Plates which are moving eastwards and sinking below the continent. These two plates run more or less parallel between 26°S and 33°S and the friction between them creates a geologically unstable zone, marked by frequent earthquakes and volcanic activity. The area of Concepción has been particularly susceptible to both land and undersea quakes and the city was destroyed twice in the 18th century by tidal waves before being moved to its present site. The Quaternary Period was marked by the advance and retreat of the Antarctic Ice Sheet which at its maximum extent covered all of the Chilean Andes and the entire coastline south of Puerto Montt.

All of the Chilean Pacific islands were formed by underwater volcanoes associated with fracture zones between the Nazca and Antarctic Plates, Easter Island gaining its characteristic triangular shape from the joining together of three lava flows.

The Northern Desert

Northern Chile has a similar form to Peru immediately to the north; the coastal range rises to 1,000-1,500 metres; inland are basins known as *bolsones*, east of which lie the Andes. The Atacama Desert is, by most measures, the driest area on earth and some meteorological stations near the coast have never reported precipitation.

Water is therefore at a premium for those who inhabit the region between the Peruvian border and Copiapó. Water is piped in from the east and in the Andean foothills streams flow into alluvial fans on the eastern side of the inland basins which can act as reservoirs and may be tapped by drilling wells. One river, the Río Loa, flows circuitously from the Andes to Calama and then through the coastal range to the coast, but for most of its length is deeply entrenched and unsuitable for agriculture and there is no port at its mouth. East of Calama and high in the Andes are the geysers of El Tatio, more evidence of volcanic activity, which are fed by the summer rains which fall in this part of the Andes.

Background

 Glacial landscapes

Southern Chile provides some of the best examples of glacial landscapes on earth. One common sign of the region's glacial past are the U-shaped valleys, created as glaciers smashed their way through river valleys gouging out sides to leave a flat valley floor and steep sides. Good examples can be seen throughout the south, but perhaps one of the best is the Río Simpson between Coyhaique and Puerto Aisén. Sharp mountain ridges can often be seen high above these valleys: these have been caused by the eroding action of the ice on two or more sides. In some places the resulting debris or morraine formed a dam, blocking the

valley and creating a lake. This can be seen in several places in the Lake District where glacial morraines formed dammed narrow valleys to form Lagos Calafquén, Panguipulli and Riñihue.

The drowned coastline south of Puerto Montt also owes its origin to glaciation. The ice which once covered the southern Andes was so heavy that it depressed the relatively narrow tip of South America; subsequently once the ice melted and the sea level rose water broke through, leaving the western Andes as islands and creating the Chilean fjords, glaciated valleys carved out by the ice and now drowned.

Naomi Peirce

In the past, notably as the ice sheets retreated, there were many lakes in the depressions between the Coastal Range and the Andes. These dried out leaving one of the greatest concentrations of salts in the world, rich in mineral deposits especially nitrates, aided by the extreme aridity and the lack of sand at high altitudes and giving rise to extensive mining activity since the late 19th century.

Central Chile South of Copiapó the transition begins between the deserts of northern Chile and zone of heavy rainfall in the south. At first the desert turns to scrub and some seasonal surface water appears. Eventually rivers fed by winter rains follow deep trenches to reach the sea, allowing valley bottoms inland to be irrigated for agriculture.

Further south, near Santiago, the Central Valley between the Coastal Range and the Andes reappears, though most of the rivers flow westwards across it to reach the Pacific. With its heavier rainfall, forests, national parks and hot springs, this is one of the most attractive areas of the country.

South of Temuco lies the scenic Lake District, one of the most popular Chilean tourist destinations, with its many lakes formed by glaciation and volcanic activity, its attractive mountain scenery, its rich volcanic soils and fertile agricultural land.

Southern Chile South of Valdivia the Coastal Range becomes more broken until near Puerto Montt it becomes a line of islands as part of a 'drowned coastline' which extends all the way south to Cape Horn. The effects of glaciation can be seen in the U-shaped valleys and the long deep fjords stretching inland. There are few roads and many smaller settlements can only be reached by sea or air. This is a land of dense forests with luxuriant undergrowth which is virtually impenetrable and difficult to clear owing to the high water content. Further south towards Chilean Patagonia, coniferous forests are limited in expanse because glaciers have stripped the upper slopes of soil. Some of the remaining glaciers reach sea level, notably the San Rafael, which breaks off the giant icefields of the *Campo de Hielo Norte*.

The Andes The whole of Chile is dominated by this massive mountain range which reaches its highest elevations in Chile and the Argentine frontier regions. In the north, near the Peruvian border the ranges which make up the Andes are 500 kilometres wide, but the western ranges which mark the Chilean frontier, are the highest. Sajama, the highest peak in Bolivia, lies only 20 kilometres east of the border, along which are strung volcanoes such as Parinacota (6,330 metres) and Pomerape (6,240 metres). Further south, to the southeast of San Pedro de Atacama, lies the highest section of the Andes, which includes the peaks of Llullaillaco (6,739 metres) and Ojos del Salado (altitude from 6,864 metres to 6,879 metres to 6,908 metres depending on your source). Still further south, to the northeast of Santiago and just inside Argentina, lies Aconcagua (6,960 metres).

South of Santiago, the Andes begin to lose altitude. In the Lake District, the mountain passes are low enough in several places for crossing into Argentina. South of Puerto Montt, the Andes become more and more inhospitable, and lower temperatures bring the permanent snowline down from 1,500 metres at Volcán Osorno near Puerto Montt to 700 metres on Tierra del Fuego. Towards the southern end of the Andes are Mount Fitzroy (3,406 metres) just over the border in Argentina and the remarkable peaks of the Paine massif.

Climate

It is only to be expected that a country which stretches over 4,000 kilometres from north to south will provide a wide variety of climatic conditions. While temperatures vary less than might be expected, annual rainfall varies from zero in northern Chile to over 4,000 millimetres on the offshore islands south of Puerto Montt. Rainfall is heavier in the winter months (May-August) throughout the country, except for the northern altiplano.

Variations in the Chilean climate are, however, increased by two other factors: altitude and the cold waters of the Humboldt Current. The Andes, with their peaks of over 6,000 metres, are rarely more than 160 kilometres from the coastline. On average temperatures drop by 1°C for every 150 metres you climb. Moreover as it reaches the higher land warm air off the ocean is forced to rise, causing it to cool and condense as rain or snow over the mountains.

The Humboldt Current has perhaps even more impact. The current flows in a northeasterly direction from Antarctic waters until it meets the southern coast of Chile, from where it follows the coastline northwards. Cold polar air accompanies the current on its journey, eventually colliding with warmer air moving in from the southwest. The lighter warm air is forced to rise over the dense cold air, bringing rainfall all year round to the area south of the Río Biobío and rain in winter further north in the Central Valley.

The oceans also have a moderating effect on temperatures. Temperatures are generally moderate and decrease from north to south less than might be expected. As a result of the Humboldt Current temperatures in northern Chile are much lower than they are for places at corresponding latitudes such as Mexico. In the far south the oceans have the opposite effect and temperatures rarely fall below -6°C despite the high latitude. Detailed temperature and rainfall patterns are given in the text.

Flora

The diversity of Chilean flora reflects the geographic length and climatic variety of the country, in general terms ranging from the desert environment of the north via matorral scrub and sclerophyllous vegetation to the temperate rainforests of the south. Although the Andes constitute a great natural barrier, there are connections between the flora of Chile and that of the eastern side of the mountain range, most notably in the far north with the Bolivian altiplano and in the south with the temperate forests of Argentina.

Plant pirates

Botanists are plant lovers and still seeking new plant species in the varied ecosystems of Chile. Ever since the first Europeans reached Chile plants have been brought back to the 'old world'. One of the most notable plant hunters were Joseph Banks who visited Chile on Captain Cook's vessel *Endeavour* and documented 125 new plants including the ruby-fruited *Gaultheria mucronata*. Plant hunters were often sent at the request of botanical gardens or commercial nurseries. One of the most famous nurseries was Veitch & Sons who sent William Lobb to Chile in 1840: Lobb returned with seeds of the monkey puzzle tree (Araucaria araucana) as well as seedlings which were a huge commercial success. The most famous plant hunter was, of course, Charles Darwin who described many plants and the landscape in great detail. His description of the Ocoa are in the Parque Nacional la Campana still holds good today and the palms he considered ugly can still be seen. Of course botanical travel occurred in both directions: emigrants from Europe took many plants to Chile, notably Spanish broom (Genista hispanica) and vines for viniculture.

Jane Norwich

The Far North The extensive arid central plain of northern Chile, with its salt-flats and nitrate fields form one of the driest areas on earth: in parts of this desert it has never rained. Vegetation is limited to cacti, among them the *cardon* (Echinopsis atacamensis), and, in the Pampa de Tamarugal around Iquique, the *tamarugo* (Proposis tamarugo), a tree specially adapted to arid climates. On the western slopes of the Andes, along the eastern edge of the desert, ravines carry water which has permitted the establishment of small settlements and the planting of crops. The only native tree of this area, *queñoa* (Polylepis tomentella), heavily overexploited in the past, grows in sheltered areas, mainly near streams, at altitudes between 2,000 and 3,500 metres. Among cacti are the *candelabros* (genus Browningia) and, at higher altitudes (between 3,000 and 4,000 metres) the *ayrampus* (genus Opuntia).

The northern altiplano, with its poor soils, wide temperature ranges between day and night, high solar radiation and shortages of water, supports only sparse vegetation. Many plants found in this area, such as the *llareta* (genus Laretia) and the *tola* (genus Baccharis) have deep root systems and small leaves. Near streams there are areas of spongy, wet salty grass, known as *bofedales*.

To the west of the central plain the Pacific coastal area is almost complete desert, although in places the influence of the cold off-shore Humboldt Current is offset by the *camanchaca*, an early morning coastal fog which comes off the sea and persists at low altitudes, permitting the growth of vegetation, notably in the Parque Nacional Pan de Azúcar north of Chañaral, and around Poposo, south of Antofagasta, where about 170 flowering plants, including shrubs, bomeliacea and cacti can be found.

The Norte Chico Lying between the northern deserts and the matorral of central Chile, the Norte Chico is a transition zone: here annual rainfall averages from 30 to 100 millimetres increasing southwards. In the main dry areas native flora such as *pingo-pingo* (Ephedra andina), *jarilla* (Larrea nitida) and *brea* (Tessaria absinthioides) can be found. On the rare occasions when there is spring rainfall the desert comes to life in a phenomenon known as the 'flowering of the desert'. The central plain is crossed by rivers, in the valleys of which irrigation permits the cultivation of fruit such as chirimoya, papaya and grapes.

On the coast near Ovalle sea mists support a forest of evergreen species including the *olivillo* (Aextoxicon punctatum), *canelo* or winter's bark (Drimys winteri) amd *arrayán* (Luma chequen or Myrtus chequen) in the Parque Nacional Fray Jorge.

Fuschia magellanica

Although there are many varieties of fuchsia in Central and South America, the variety most commonly found in Chile is Fuschia magellanica. *First identified along the Magellan Straits during the voyage of HMS Beagle, this prolifically flowering shrub can be found as far north as Santiago, often growing in free-draining soil at the roadside or forest edge. Its scarlet calyx and violet petals last all summer long and into the autumn and its dark green leaves are found in whorls of three.*

Jane Norwich

Central Chile

The central valley, with its dry and warm summers and mild winters, is home to the *mattoral*, a deciduous scrubland ecologically comparable to the chaparral in California and consisting of slow-growing drought-resistant species with deep roots and small spiny sclerophyllous leaves. The original plant cover has been modified by human impact, particularly in the form of livestock agriculture, charcoal-burning and irrigation. In many areas, from the Río Limari in the north to the Río Laja in the south, the result is *espinal* (Acacia cavan), usually considered to be a degraded form of the original matorral and characterized by open savanna scattered with *algarrobo* trees (Prosopis chilensis). Along ravines and on western facing slopes there are areas of evergreen sclerophyllus trees including the *peumo* (Cryptocarpa alba), *litre* (Lithrea caustica) and *boldo* (Peumos boldos) and, along the banks of the great rivers, the *maiten* (Maytenus boaria or Maytenus chilensis) and a local species of willow can be found.

Towards the coast more hygrophilous species grow on hills receiving coastal fogs: among these are *avellano*, *lingue* (Persea lingue), *belloto* or northern acorn (Beilschmiedia miersii) and *canelo* as well as bromeliads and epiphytic lichens and mosses. Species of southern beech (Nothofagus) and the formerly endemic Chilean or ocoa palm (Jubea chilensis), grow under protection in the Parque Nacional La Campana between Santiago and Valparaíso.

Subantarctic temperate forests

Until this century subantarctic temperate forests extended south from the Río Bíobio to Cape Horn. As a result of the fragmentation of the great landmass of Gondwana some 120 million years ago, some of the species in these forests (Araucaria araucana, Nothofagus and Podocarpus salingus) share affinities with flora found in Australia and New Zealand as well as with fossils uncovered in Antarctica. Similar affinities of some insect groups have also been established. However the isolation of these subantarctic forests, with the nearest neighbouring forests 1,300 kilometres away in northwestern Argentina, has led to the evolution of many unique endemic species. Volcanic activity has also had an important influence on the development of plantlife in these forests.

Nowadays these forests are mainly of broad-leafed evergreen species; in contrast to temperate forests in the northern hemisphere there are few species of conifers. The dominant genus is the Nothofagus or southern beech, of which eight species are found in Chile. In the Maule area *roble* (Nothofagus obliqua) and *hualo* (Nothofagus glauca) can be found, while further south there is a gradual transitional change via the Valdivian rainforest, see below, to the southern deciduous Nothofagus forests. The latter, which can also be found at higher altitudes along the Andes, include the Patagonian and Magellanic forests. From the Valdivian forest south to the Magellanic forests all species of Nothofagus attract fungis from the genus Cyttaria and, especially in the south, the *misodendron* or South American mistletoe.

In between, from 41° south (around the Río Biobío) to 46° south, the Valdivian rainforest predominates. This is a complex and diverse environment, which includes ferns, bromeliads, lichens including old man's beard, and mosses, as well as a variety of climbing plants including the *copihue* or Chilean bell flower (Lapageria rosea) the

Background

Background

🐾 Southern beaches

Eight species of Nothofagus are native to South America. Some deciduous, some evergreen, they are found throughout the length of the country south of Santiago. The evergreen Nothofagus betuloides was used for canoes by the Yaghan Indians who called it sushci. The Nothofagus nervosa has leaves like a hornbeam and is a quick growing tree with good Autumn colour. Nothofagus dombeyi known as coihue or coigüe has shiny dark green evergreen leaves and is larger than Nothofagus betuloides; it can be seen at its stately best, growing to over 30 metres in height, at higher altitudes in the lake District. Nothofagus obliqua, which has toothed smooth leaves, is commonly known as roble. Nothofagus pumilo, well known for its vibrant red Autumn colour, is found at higher elevations, and has the common name of lenga.

Jane Norwich

national flower of Chile. Colourful flowering plants which can be easily identified include the firebush or *ciruelillo* (Embothrium coccineum), several species of alstromeria and berberis and, near streams, the fuschia. Near the Andes, for example in the Parque Nacional Puyehue, the forests are dominated by two species of Nothofagus, the evergreen *coihue* or *coigüe* (Nothofagus dombeyi) and the deciduous *lenga* (Nothfagus pumilio) as well as by the Podocarpus (Podocarpus salingus) and, near water, myrtle trees like the *arrayán*. The under-storey is dominated by tall *chusquea* bamboos.

In the northern parts of the Valdivian forest at altitudes mainly between 900 metres and 1,400 metres, there are forests of monkey puzzle trees (Araucaria araucana), Chile's national tree: the most important of these forests are in the Parque Nacional Nahuelbuta in the coastal cordillera and in the Parque Nacional Huerquehue in the Andean foothills.

Other species include the giant larch (Fitzroya cupressoides) known as the *alerce* or *lahuén*, which has some of the oldest individual specimens on earth (3,600 years). Athough this conifer grew extensively as far south as the 43° 30' south, being widespread both on Chiloé and in the Andes, excessive logging, initially in the colonial period, for shipbuilding, has destroyed most of the original larch forest. Some of the best examples of *alerce*, which is now a protected species, can be seen in the Parque Nacional Andino Alerce and the Parque Pumalin.

The Patagonian and Magellanic forests are less diverse than their Valdivian counterpart, mainly due to lower temperatures. The Magellanic forest, considered the southernmost forest type in the world, includes the evergreen Nothofagus betuloides, the deciduous *lenga* (Nothofagus pumilio) and Nothofagus antarctica, and the *canelo*. Firebush and berberis can also be found, as well as several species of orchids and beautiful species of Calceolaria or slipper plants. Shrubland in the south is mainly characterized by mounded shrubs, usually found in rocky areas. Common species include *mata barrosa* (Mullinum spinosum) a yellow-flowered shrub and *mata guanaco* (Anartrophyllum desideratum), a red-flowered shrub of the legume family. On most of the myriad small islands along the coast south of Chiloé tree growth is limited and much of the land is covered by moorland with bare rock and bogs.

The Pacific Islands In both the Juan Fernández Islands and Easter Island there are endemic species unique to the islands. In the forests of the Juan Fernández Archipelago at altitudes above 1,400 metres diverse but important species of ferns can be found as well as tree species such as *luma*, *mayu-monte*, giant naranjillo and the *yonta* or Juan Fernández palm, which, along with the ocoa palm, is one of only two palms native to Chile. The native forests of Easter Island were destroyed, first by volcanic activity and later by human impact, leaving an arid environment, covered partially with pasture. Although native species such as the *toromiro* can be found, introduced species such as the eucalyptus are more common.

Pablo Neruda on the forest

Under the volcanoes, beside the snow-capped mountains, among the huge lakes, the fragrant, the silent, the tangled Chilean forest... My feet sink down into the dead leaves, a fragile twig crackles, the giant rauli trees rise in all their bristling height, a bird from the cold jungle passes over, flaps its wings, and stops in the sunless branches. And then, from its hideaway, it sings like an oboe... The wild scent of the laurel, the dark scent of the boldo herb, enter my nostrils and flood my whole being... The cypress of the Guaitecas blocks my way... This is a vertical world: a nation of birds, a plenitude of leaves... I stumble over a rock, dig up the uncovered hollow, an enormous spider covered with red hair stares up at me, motionless, as huge as a crab... A golden carabus beetle blows it mephitic breath at me, as its brilliant rainbow disappears like lightning... Going on, I pass through a forest of ferns much taller than I am: from their cold green eyes 60 tears splash down on my face and, behind me, their fans go on quivering for a long time... A decaying tree trunk: what a treasure!... Black and blue mushrooms have given it ears, red parasite plants have covered it with rubies, other lazy plants have let it borrow their beards, and a snake springs out of the rotted body like a sudden breath, as if the spirit of the dead trunk were slipping away from it... Farther along, each tree stands away from its fellows... They soar up over the carpet of the secretive forest, and the foliage of each has its own style, linear, bristling, ramulose, lanceolate, as if cut by shears moving in infinite ways... A gorge; below, the crystal water slides over granite and jasper... A butterfly goes past, bright as a lemon, dancing between the water and the sunlight... Close by, innumerable calceolarias nod their little yellow heads in greeting... High up, red copihues dangle like drops from the magic forest's arteries... The red copihue is the blood flower, the white copihue is the snow flower... A fox cuts through the silence like a flash, sending a shiver through the leaves, but silence is the law of the plant kingdom... The barely audible cry of some bewildered animal far off... The piercing interruption of a hidden bird... The vegetable world keeps up its low rustle until a storm churns up all the music of the earth.

Anyone who hasn't been in the Chilean forest doesn't know this planet.

From Pablo Neruda, Memoirs, Penguin (1977) page 5-6.

Art and architecture

Arts and crafts

Chile's traditional crafts are in the main specific to particular places and all have a long history. Present-day handicrafts represent either the transformation of utilitarian objects into works of art, or the continued manufacture of pieces which retain symbolic value. A number of factors threaten these traditions: the loss of types of wood and plant fibres through the destruction of forests; the mechanization of farm labour, reducing the use of the horse; other agricultural changes which have, among other things, led to reductions in sheep farming and wheat growing; migration from the countryside to the city. On the other hand, city dwellers and tourists have created a demand for traditional crafts so their future is to some degree assured.

The Mapuche Although silverware is one of the traditional crafts of the Mapuche, its production is in decline owing to the cost of the metal. Traditional women's jewellery includes earrings, headbands, necklaces, brooches and *tupus* (pins for fastening the *manta*, or shawl). Each item has a Mapuche name (eg *chawai* for earrings). Nowadays, the most common item to be found for sale is earrings, but smaller and in simpler shapes than those worn by Mapuche women. It is a matter of debate whether Mapuche silversmiths had perfected their skills before the arrival of the Spaniards, but the circulation of silver coins in the 18th century gave great impetus to this form of metalwork. The Universidad Católica in Temuco is in charge of a project to ensure the continuance of the art.

The Mapuche are also weavers of sheep's wool, making ponchos, *mantas*, sashes (*fajas*), reversible rugs (*lamas*) with geometric designs, and bedspreads (*pontros*). The colours come from natural dyes. The main producing areas are around Lago Lanalhue, Chol Chol, Nueva Imperial and others (see pages 271 and 285).

Mapuche basketry is made for domestic, agricultural and fishing uses in Lago Lanalhue and the Cautín region. They also make musical instruments: the *trutruca*, a horn one and a half to four metres long, *pifilca* (or *pifüllka*), a wooden whistle, the *kultrún* drum, *cascahuilla*, a string of bells, and *trompe*, similar to a Jew's harp. Another craft from this region is the carving of horn or antler (*asta*) in Temuco, to make animals, birds, cups, spoons, etc.

Chiloé The island is famous for its woollen goods, hand-knitted and coloured with natural dyes. Clothing (such as sweaters, knitted caps, *mantas*, socks), rugs, blankets and patch dolls are sold locally and in Puerto Montt. The main knitting centres are Quinchao, Chonchi and Quellón. Other crafts of Chiloé are model boat building, and basketware from Quinchao and Quellón, not only baskets, but also mats and figurines such as birds and fish.

Items can be found in any part of the country where there are *huasos*: San Fernando, Chillán, Curicó, Colchagua, Doñihue and also in Santiago. Saddles of leather, wood and iron, wooden stirrups, leather reins, spurs, and hats of straw or other materials are the types of equipment you will see. The clothing comprises ponchos (long, simple in colour and design, used to keep out the rain and wind), *mantas* (shorter, divided into four with a great variety of colour), *chamantos* (luxurious *mantas*, double-sided, decorated with fine patterns of vines, leaves, flowers, small birds, etc) and sashes/*fajas* (either single or tri-coloured, made to combine with *mantas* or *chamantos*).

Cowboy equipment & clothing

Both men and women weave sheep or camelid wool in Isluga, see page 237. Each sex, however, makes different items. Men and women also weave in the villages in the vicinity of the Salar de Atacama, such as Tulor, page 198, not only items of clothing, bags, etc, but also wall-hangings. In the Elqui Valley, page 157, is Chapilca, which specializes in vegetable-dyed woollen *mantas*, rugs, covers, etc. Another centre for weaving is Quinamávida, page 254, where natural colours in browns and ochres are used for blankets, rugs and *mantas*.

Other textile-producing areas

The two most famous places for ceramics are Quinchamalí near Chillán, page 257, where the traditional black ware is incised with patterns in white and Pomaire, west of Santiago, page 105), which is renowned for its terracotta household items which are used in most Chilean homes. Less well known is the pottery of the Atacama zone, the clay figures of Lihueimo (Región VI), the household items, clay figurines and model buildings of Pilén de Cauquenes-Maule (Región VII) and the scented pottery of the nuns of the Comunidad de Santa Clara (Convento de Monjas Claras in Santiago and Los Angeles). These highly decorated pieces have been made since colonial times, when they achieved great fame.

Ceramics

Apart from the areas already mentioned, one of the great centres of basket-making is Chimbarongo, just south of San Fernando in the Central Valley. Here weaving is done in almost every household, usually by the men. One of the main materials used is willow, which is collected in June when it is still green and and then soaked in water for four months, at the end of which the bark peels off. The lengths of willow are split into four and finished with a knife. Baskets, chairs and lamps are the most common objects made. Willow is not the only fibre used. Many items are made from different types of straw, including the little boxes made of wheat; though the latter are produced throughout the country the most famous are from La Manga, Melipilla. Note also the yawl made for fishing, typical of Chiloé. Other important centres of basket-making are Ninhue-Hualte in Ñuble (Región VIII), Hualqui, 24 kilometres south of Concepción, and San Juan de la Costa, from the coast of Osorno, Región X.

Basketry

The people of the Atacama region edge trays and make little churches out of cactus wood; they also use cactus for drums and bamboo for flutes of various sizes. Different types of wood are used in the construction of guitars, *guitarrones*, harps and *rabeles* (fiddles), mainly in the Metropolitan Region. Villarrica, page 294, is a major producer of wooden items: plates, kitchen utensils, but especially decorative objects like animals and birds, jointed snakes and *picarones* (small figures which, when picked up, reveal their genitals). Another craft in wood is the ship in a bottle, made in Coronel, see page 268. In Loncoche, south of Temuco, a workshop specializes in fine carvings, in native woods, of country and Mapuche scenes.

Wood

This village, near the Termas de Panimávida, some 25 kilometres northeast of Linares (Región VII), specializes in beautiful, delicate items made from dyed horsehair: bangles and brooches in the shape of butterflies, little hats, flowers, etc.

Rari

Background

Lapis lazuli Mined in the Cordillera de Ovalle, this blue stone only found otherwise in Afghanistan is set in silver to make earrings, necklaces and bracelets. Many shops in Santiago sell the gemstone and objects that incorporate it, see **Shopping**, page 95.

Sources for this section are: *Artesanía tradicional de Chile*, Serie El Patrimonio Cultural Chileno, Ministerio de Educación, 1978; 'Visión estética de la cerámica de Quinchamalí', by Luis Guzmán Molina, *Atenea*, No 458 (Universidad de Concepción, 1988), pages 47-60; *Mapudungun, lengua y costumbres Mapuches*, by Orietta Appelt Martín (Temuco: Magin, 1995); *Arts and Crafts of South America*, by Lucy Davies and Mo Fini (Bath: Tumi, 1994). **Tumi**, the Latin American Craft Centre, specializes in Mexican and Andean products and produces cultural and educational videos for schools: at 23/2A Chalk Farm Road, London NW1 8AG (F0171-4854152), 8/9 New Bond Street Place, Bath BA1 1BH (T01225-462367, F01225-444870), 1/2 Little Clarendon Street, Oxford OX1 2HJ (T/F01865-512307), 82 Park Street, Bristol BS1 5LA (T/F0117-9290391). Tumi (Music) Ltd specializes in different rhythms of Latin America.

Fine art and sculpture

The colonial period There was little home-grown art during the colonial period in Chile, in cultural terms a peripheral territory of the vast Viceroyalty of Peru, but trade with other regions was extensive and Santiago in particular has good collections of non-Chilean colonial art. Perhaps inevitably, during the Spanish colonial era the Catholic church dominated the production of paintings and sculptures. The many new religious foundations needed images of Christ and the saints to reassure the Christian settlers and also to instruct the new converts, and without a strong local school Chile had to meet this demand from elsewhere. The importation of works from Spain was very costly because for taxation purposes all trade with the southern part of the Viceroyalty was required to pass first through Lima, so most patrons relied instead on the major colonial artistic centres of Cusco, Potosí and Quito to supply their requirements.

The churches and monasteries of Santiago give a vivid sense of the thriving art market in colonial Spanish America: sculptures shipped down the coast from Lima and from Quito via Guayaquil, canvases carried across the Andes on mule trains from Cusco and Potosí, and occasionally an itinerant Spanish-trained artist passed through in search of lucrative commissions. Extensive cycles of the lives of Christ, the Virgin and selected saints were popular: a cycle of 40 or 50 large canvases representing the exploits of, say, St Francis provided instant cover for large expanses of bare plaster, a good clear narrative and an exemplary life to follow. Such cycles would have been easy to commission because most Chilean examples are based either on engravings or on other painted cycles and they would also have been easy to hang in the correct sequence, not least because each canvas usually includes a cartouche with a helpful textual summary.

So, for example, San Francisco in Santiago has a cycle of 53 paintings of the life of St Francis painted in Cusco in the later 17th century. These are based on a similar cycle in the Franciscan monastery in Cusco by the Indian artist Basilio de Santa Cruz Pumacallao which is in turn derived from a series of European engravings. One of the Santiago paintings, the Funeral of St Francis of 1684, is signed by Juan Zapaca Inca, also, as his name suggests, an Indian and follower of Santa Cruz, and the whole series was probably produced under Zapaca's guidance. Wherever possible the artist has introduced bright-coloured tapestries and rich fabrics embellished with lace and gold embroidery, a mark of the continuing importance of textiles in Andean culture. This is a typical pattern for colonial art: a set of European engravings forms the basis for a large painted cycle which in turn becomes the source for further copies and derivatives. The narrative content and general composition remain constant while the setting, attendant figures, costume and decorative detail are often translated into an Andean idiom.

Background

There are, of course, many different categories of colonial art. The big painted cycles were produced more for the educated inhabitants of the monastic establishments than for a lay audience, and were intended for edification rather than devotion. Popular devotion tends to create increasingly decorated and hieratic images. A good example is that of the so-called Cristo de Mayo. Early in the 17th century Pedro de Figueroa, a friar of the Augustinian monastery in Santiago, carved a figure of the crucified Christ which still hangs in the church of San Agustín. This passionate, unusually defiant image was credited with miraculous powers after it survived a serious earthquake in Santiago in May 1647 (hence the popular name *de Mayo*). The only damage was that the crown of thorns slipped from Christ's head and lodged around his neck. A cult quickly grew up around the image, creating a demand for painted copies which are identifiable by the upward gaze, the distinctive necklace of thorns, and the evenly distributed lash marks across the body. The Carmelite convent of San José has a locally produced 18th century example of the Cristo de Mayo which includes attendant saints and garlands of bright flowers, the latter like pious offerings. The Jesuits, always adept at exploiting popular religious fervour, established an interesting local school of sculpture on the island of Chiloé where up until the late 19th century native craftsmen continued to produce boldly expressive Christian images.

Chile was one of the first countries in America to achieve independence from Spain and in the 19th century its distance from the old colonial centre of Viceregal power worked to its advantage in the field of art. The Lima-born artist José Gil de Castro who died in 1841, known as El Mulato Gil, accompanied Bernardo O'Higgins on the campaign for Chilean independence from 1814, working both as an engineer and map-maker and as a portrait painter. His portrait of O'Higgins of 1820 in the Museo Histórico Nacional in Santiago represents him as a towering giant of a man, immovable as the rocky mountains behind him, while in a painting in the Municipalidad of La Serena of 1818 San Martín is shown standing beside a writing desk, his hand inside his jacket in a distinctively Napoleonic pose, thoughtful and determined. The 19th century also brought European traveller-artists to Chile who helped to confirm the Chilean landscape, peoples and customs as legitimate subjects for paintings, including the German Johann Moritz Rugendas who lived in Chile from 1833 to 1845, and the Englishman Charles Wood (in Chile from 1819 to 1852). Examples of both artists' work can be seen in the Museo Nacional de Bellas Artes. The Frenchman Raymond Monvoisin also spent several years in Chile, from 1843 to 1857. His perceptive portraits of members of the government and the literary élite are interesting for the way in which they link the Chilean tradition of Gil de Castro with European sources, and after his return to France he produced the first major painting dedicated to an event from colonial history, the Mapuche hero Caupolicán taken prisoner by the Spaniards (1859, Museo O'Higginiano, Talca). Caupolicán was celebrated in Chile 10 years later in a bronze statue by Nicanor Plaza (1844-1914) erected on the Cerro Santa Lucía in Santiago, and although it originated as an entry for a competition organized by the US government for a statue to commemorate the Last of the Mohicans, it represents the incorporation of the Indian into national mythology.

The Chilean Academy of Painting was founded in 1849 and although its first presidents were mediocre European artists they too helped to make Chilean subject matter respectable, while the Academy acted as a focus for aspiring young artists. Antonio Smith (1832-1877) rebelled against the rigidity of the academic system, working as a political cartoonist as well as a painter, but his dramatic landscapes grow out of the gradual awakening of interest in Chilean scenery. He transforms the picturesque view into a heroic vision of mountains and valleys, full of air and space and potential. Cosme San Martín (1850-1906), Pedro León Carmona (1853-1899), Pedro Lira (1845-1912), Alfredo Valenzuela Puelma (1856-1909) and English-born

After independence

Background

Thomas Somerscales (1842-1927) extended the range of possible national subjects in the fields of landscape, portraiture, history and genre. The late 19th century saw a number of important commissions for nationalistic public statuary including the peasant soldier 'El Roto Chileno' in Santiago's Plaza Yungay by Nicanor Plaza's pupil Virginio Arias (1855-1941), and several monumental works by Rebecca Matte (1875-1929).

The 20th century From the later 19th century until well into the 20th century, Chilean painting was dominated by refracted versions of Impressionism. Artists such as Juan Francisco González (1853-1933) and Alfredo Helsby (1862-1933) introduced a looser technique and more luminous palette to create landscapes full of strong contrasts of sunlight and shadows, a tradition continued by, for example, Pablo Burchard (1873-1964), Agustín Abarca (1882-1953), Arturo Gordon (1883-1944) and Camilo Mori (1896-1973).

The Chilean avant-garde has been dominated by artists who have lived and worked for long periods abroad, many as political exiles. After studying with Le Corbusier in Switzerland and encountering the Surrealists in Paris, Roberto Matta (born 1911) moved to New York in 1939 and began painting uniquely unsettling space-age monsters and machines which circulate in a multi-dimensional chaos. Nemesio Antúnez (1918-1993) developed more earth-bound abstractions of reality: volcanic landscapes viewed through flames and falling rocks, or milling crowds, faceless and powerless. The younger generation includes Eugenio Dittborn (born 1943) who sends 'Airmail Paintings' around the world in an exploration of ideas of transition and dislocation and, because many contain photographs of victims of political violence, of anonymity and loss. Alfredo Jaar (born 1956) creates installations using maps and photographs to document the destructive exploitation of the world's resources, both human and natural. In recent years many exiles have returned home and Santiago is now a cultural centre of growing importance, with women particularly well-represented (for example Carmen Valbuena, born 1955, and Bernarda Zegers, born 1951). Chile is the home of an interesting ongoing project called 'Cuerpos Pintados', Painted Bodies, whereby artists from Chile and other Latin American countries are invited to Santiago to paint nude models in the colours and designs of their choice. Watch out for exhibitions of the stunning photographs which are the project's permanent outcome.

Culture

People

There is less racial diversity in Chile than in most Latin American countries. Over 90 percent of the population of 14.2 million is *mestizo*. There has been much less immigration than in Argentina and Brazil. The German, French, Italian and Swiss immigrants came mostly after 1846 as small farmers in the forest zone south of the Biobío. Between 1880 and 1900 gold-seeking Serbs and Croats settled in the far south, and the British took up sheep farming and commerce in the same region. The influence throughout Chile of the immigrants is out of proportion to their numbers: their signature on the land is seen, for instance, in the German appearance of Valdivia, Puerto Montt, Puerto Varas, Frutillar and Osorno.

There is disagreement over the number of indigenous people in Chile. The **Mapuche** nation (also called Araucanians), 95 percent of whom live around Temuco between the Biobío and Toltén rivers, is put at one million by Survival International, but much less by other, including official, statistics. For further details see under Temuco. There are also 15,000-20,000 **Aymara** in the northern Chilean Andes and 1200 **Rapa Nui** on Easter Island. A political party, the Party for Land and Identity, unites many Indian groupings, and legislation is proposed to restore indigenous people's rights.

The population is far from evenly distributed: Middle Chile, from Copiapó to Concepción and consisting 18 percent of the country's area, contains 77 percent of the total population. The Metropolitan Region of Santiago contains, on its own, about 39 percent of the whole population. Population density in 1995 ranged from 377 per square kilometre in the Metropolitan Region to 0.8 per square kilometre in Región XI (Aisén). *See also table on page 527*

The rate of population growth per annum is similar to those of Argentina and Uruguay, but lower than most of the rest of Latin America. The cities have higher birth and death rates than the rural areas but infant mortality is higher in the rural areas.

Since the 1960s heavy migration from rural areas has led to rapid urbanization. By 1995, 85.8 percent of the population lived in urban areas; the most urbanized regions were the Metropolitan Region (96.5 percent urban) and Región V (90.2 percent urban). Housing in the cities has not kept pace with this increased population; many Chileans live in slum areas called *callampas* (mushrooms) especially on the outskirts of Santiago.

Religion

According to the 1992 census the population is 76.7 percent Catholic and 13.2 percent Protestant. Membership of Evangelical Protestant churches has grown rapidly in recent years, from six percent in the 1970 census, especially in the Santiago and in Región XI where 22 percent of the population were members of Protestant Churches in 1992. The largest of these churches is the Pentecostal Methodist Church.

Education

Chilean literacy rates are higher than those of most other South American states; according to the 1992 census over 95 percent of the population above the age of 15 is literate. Census returns also indicated that among the over-25 age population eight percent had completed higher education, 42 percent had completed secondary education, and 44 percent had only completed primary education. Higher education provision doubled in the 1980s through the creation of private universities.

Literature

Background

From colonial times to independence

The long struggle of the Spaniards to conquer the lands south of their Peruvian stronghold inspired one of the great epics of early Spanish American literature, *La Araucana* by **Alonso de Ercilla y Zúñiga** (1533-1594). Published in three parts (1569, 1578 and 1589), the poem tells of the victories and defeats of Spaniards, such as Pedro de Valdivia, and the Araucanian Indians during Spain's efforts to push the empire's boundaries southwards. Like a subsequent work, *Arauco domado* (1596), by the criollo Pedro de Oña (1570-1643), the point of view is that of the conquering invader, not a celebration of Chilean, or American identity, although Ercilla does show that the people who resisted the Spaniards were noble and courageous. After Ercilla, literature written in what was to become Chile concentrated on chronicling either the physical or the spiritual conquest of the local inhabitants, which at times incorporated descriptions of the environment and the customs of the region, the first recognition of an identity different from imperial Spain.

Writing in the 18th and early 19th centuries tended to mirror the colonial desire to consolidate the territory which was in Spanish, rather than Mapuche hands. Post-independence, the move was towards the establishment of the new republic. To this end, the Venezuelan **Andrés Bello** (1781-1865) was invited to Santiago from London in 1829 to oversee the education of the new élite. Already famous for his literary journals and strong views on Romantic poetry, Bello made major contributions to Chilean scholarship and law. His main work was *Gramática de la lengua castellana destinada al uso de los americanos* (1847). As Jean Franco says, "He was one of the first of many writers to see that a general literary Spanish could act as an important cohesive factor, a spiritual tie of the Hispanic peoples" (page 30; see bibliographical note page 518).

A cultural haven

Chile's relative political stability in the 19th century helped Santiago to become a cultural centre which attracted many foreign intellectuals such as the Argentine Diego Sarmiento and the Nicaraguan Rubén Darío. At this time, Chilean writers were establishing a national literary framework to replace the texts of the colonial era. This involved the spreading of 'buenas costumbres', a republican education for the middle classes and the founding of a national identity. Realist fiction captured the public interest. **José Victorino Lastarria** (1817-1888) wrote *costumbrista* stories, portraying national scenes and characters. **Alberto Blest Gana** (1829-1904) enjoyed two periods of success as a novelist, heavily influenced by Balzac. His most popular novel was *Martín Rivas* (1862), the love story of a young man who wins a wife of a higher class. For some, Blest Gana's presentation of Santiago and its class structure is a worthy imitator of the French *comédie humaine*; for others his realism fails either to unite his themes to his sketches of Chilean life, or to rise above a pedestrian style.

20th century prose writing

Well into the 20th century, realism was the dominant mode of fiction, but in several guises. **Baldomero Lillo** (1867-1923) wrote socialist realist stories about the coal

Ariel Dorfman

As expressed in the subtitle of his fascinating recent memoir, Heading South, Looking North (1998), the literary and political career of Ariel Dorfman has taken the form of a 'bilingual journey', between the United States and South America, between English and Spanish. Born in Buenos Aires in 1942, his father's political activism saw the family – Russian Jewish immigrants to Argentina – expelled from Argentina in the mid-1940s, where they took up residence in New York, until McCarthyism sent the Dorfmans once more south in 1954, this time to Chile. Here the monolingual, English speaking, adolescent gradually made the Spanish language and Chilean politics and culture his main focus of activity until the military coup of 1973 sent him once again into exile, where he became one of the most articulate, bilingual voices against the military régime.

With the return to civilian government in 1990, he divides his time between Santiago and a professional post at Duke University, writing and broadcasting in both Spanish and English. Dorfman's work, as a poet, novelist, short story writer, essayist, playwright and more recently scriptwriter, is concerned, in his words, with, 'on the one hand, the glorious potential and need of human beings to tell stories and, on the other, the brutal fact that in today's world, most of the lives that should be telling those stories are generally ignored, ravaged and silenced.'

He is perhaps best known for his early critique of US cultural imperialism, How to Read Donald Duck (1971) and his Death and the Maiden (1990), later filmed by Roman Polanski, which deals with torture and resistance.

His prolific output includes the novels Moros en la costa, 1973, (Hard Rain), La última canción de Manuel Sendero, 1982 (The Last Song of Manuel Sendero), Mascara, 1988, Viudas, 1981, (Widows), Konfidenz, 1995 and The Nanny and the Iceberg, 1999; the plays Death and the Maiden, Reader (1995), Widows (1997) and 2 further plays co-written with is son Rodrigo, Mascara and Who's Who (1997); several volumes of essays and many poems (some collected in English as Last Waltz in Santiago and other poems of Exile and Disappearance, (1988). He often adapts his own work to different genres: Widows started as a poem, became a novel and later a play. Much of the work focuses on torture, disappearance, censorship and the exile condition, but also demonstrates staunch rebellion and resistance and optimism for our future.

Most of Dorfman's work is currently in print in English. His memoir Heading North, Looking South is essential reading. The plays, Death and the Maiden, Reader and Widows have been collected in the volume The Resistance Trilogy (1998). His latest novel is The Nanny and the Iceberg (1999).

Background

miners of Lebu: Sub terra (1904) and Sub sole (1907). Lillo and other regionalist writers shifted the emphasis away from the city to the countryside and the miserable conditions endured by many Chileans. Other novelists concentrated on the crisis of aristocratic values and the gulf between the wealthy and the deprived: eg **Luis Orrego Luco** (1866-1948), and **Joaquín Edwards Bello** (born 1887).

Another strand was criollismo, championed especially by short story writers like **Mariano Latorre** (1886-1955), whose main interest was the Chilean landscape which he described almost to the point of overwhelming his characters. A different emphasis was given to regionalism and criollismo by **Augusto d'Halmar** (Augusto Goeminne Thomson, 1882-1950), whose stories in La lámpara en el molino (1914) were given exotic settings and were labelled imaginismo. D'Halmar's followers, the Grupo Letras (1920s and 1930s), became openly antagonistic towards the disciples of Latorre, eg **Luis Durand** whose books of the 1920s and 1940s described in detail campesino life. Another branch of realism was the exploration of character through psychology in the books of **Eduardo Barrios** (1884-1963), eg El niño que enloqueció de amor (1915), El hermano asno (1922) and Los hombres del hombre (1950).

The decline of criollismo The anti-fascist views of a group of writers known as the Generation of 1938 (eg Nicomedes Guzmán, 1914-65, Juan Godoy, Carlos Droguett, born 1915, and others) added a politically committed dimension with support for the working class which coincided with the rise to power of the Frente Popular. At the same time, *Mandrágora*, a journal principally dedicated to poetry, introduced many European literary ideas, notably those of the surrealists. Its influence, combined with a global decline in Marxist writing after the Second World War and the defeat of the Frente Popular, contributed to a new generation in the 1950s whose main drive was the rejection of all the *ismos* that had preceded it. The novelists, short story writers and dramatists were characterized by existential individualism and political and social scepticism. Many writers started publishing in the 1950s, among them **Volodia Teitelboim** (born 1916), a communist exiled to the USSR after 1973, whose novels *Hijo del salitre* (1952) and *La semilla en la arena* (1957) were portrayals of the struggles of the Chilean masses (in 1979 he published *La guerra interna* a mixture of real and imaginary characters in post-coup Chile). Others of the Generation of 1950 were Enrique Lafourcade (born 1927), Claudio Giaconi (born 1927) and José María Vergara (born 1929).

Manuel Rojas (1896-1972) was brought up in Argentina, but his family moved to Chile in 1923. His first short stories, such as *Hombres del sur* (1926), *Travesía* (1934) and the novel *Lanchas en la bahía* (1932) were undoubtedly *criollista* in outlook, but he devoted a greater importance to human concerns than his *criollista* contemporaries. By 1951, Rojas' style had changed dramatically, without deserting realism. *Hijo de ladrón* (1951) was perhaps the most influential 20th-century Chilean novel up to that time. It describes the adventures of Aniceto Hevía, the son of a Buenos Aires jewel thief, who crosses the Andes to Valparaíso, ending up, after continually moving on, as a beachcomber. Nothing in his life is planned, or motivated by anything other than the basic necessities. Happiness and intimacy are only brief moments in an unharmonious, disordered life. Aniceto's adventures are continued in *Mejor que el vino* (1958), *Sombras contra el muro* (1963) and *La obscura vida radiante* (1971). To describe the essential isolation of man from the inside, Rojas relaxes the temporal structure of the novel, bringing in memory, interior monologue and techniques to multiply the levels of reality (to use Fernando Alegría's phrase).

The demise of *criollismo* put by some at 1959 coincided with the influence of the US Beat Generation and the culture epitomized by James Dean, followed in the 1960s by the protest movements in favour of peace, blacks' and women's rights. The Cuban Revolution inspired Latin American intellectuals of the left and the novel-writing 'boom' gained momentum. At the same time, the national political process which led ultimately to Salvador Allende's victory in 1970 was bolstered by writers, folk singers and painters who questioned everything to do with the Chilean bourgeoisie.

To the 1973 coup & beyond **José Donoso** (1924-1996) began publishing stories in 1955 (*Veraneo y otros cuentos*), followed two years later by his first novel, *Coronación*. The book describes the chaos caused by the arrival of a new maid into an aristocratic Santiago household and introduces many of Donoso's recurring themes: the closed worlds of old age and childhood, madness, multiple levels of reality, the inauthenticity of the upper classes and the subversion of patriarchal society. The stories in *Charleston* (1960), *El lugar sin límites* (1966), about a transvestite and his daughter who live in a brothel near Talca, and *Este domingo* (1966) mark the progression from *Coronación* to *El obsceno pájaro de la noche* (1970), a labyrinthine novel (Donoso's own term) narrated by a schizophrenic, throwing together reality, dreams and fantasy, darkness and light. Donoso achieved the same status as Gabriel García Márquez, Julio Cortázar and Mario Vargas Llosa with this, his most experimental novel. Between 1967 and 1981 he lived in Spain; in the 1970s he published several novels, including *Casa de campo* (1978), which relates the disintegration of a family estate when the children try to take it over. Back in Chile, he published, among others, *El jardín de al* *lado* (1981), which chronicles the decline of a middle-aged couple in exile in Spain, *Cuatro para Delfina* (1982), *La desesperanza* (1986) about the return of a left-wing singer from Paris to the daily horrors of Pinochet's regime, and was working on *El mocho* (about coal miners) at his death.

Another writer who describes the bad faith of the aristocracy is **Jorge Edwards** (born 1931). His books include *El patio* (1952), *Los convidados de piedra* (1978), *El museo de cera* (1980), *La mujer imaginaria* (1985) and *Fantasmas de carne y hueso* (1993). His book *Persona non grata* (1973) describes his experiences as a diplomat, including his expulsion from Cuba. **Fernando Alegría** (born 1918) spans all the movements since 1938. His work includes essays, highly respected literary criticism, poetry and novels. He was closely associated with Salvador Allende and was his cultural attaché in Washington in 1970-73. *Recabarren* was published in 1938, after which followed many books, among them *Lautaro, joven libertador del Arauco* (1943), *Caballo de copas* (1957), *Mañana los guerreros* (1964), *El paso de los gansos* (1975), about a young photographer's experiences in the 1973 coup, *Coral de guerra* (1979), also about brutality under military dictatorship, *Una especie de memoria* (1983), Alegría's own memoir of 1938 to 1973, and *Allende: A Novel* (1992). Having been so close to Allende, Alegría could not write a biography, he had to fictionalize it, he said. But the rise and fall of Allende becomes a realization that history and fiction are intimately related, particularly in that Chilean epoch.

The death of Salvador Allende in 1973 and with it the collapse of the left's struggle to gain power by democratic means was a traumatic event for Chilean writers. Those who had built their careers in the 1960s and early 1970s were for the most part exiled, forcibly or voluntarily, and thus were condemned to face the left's own responsibility in Allende's failure. René Jara (see bibliographical note, page 518) says that before 1970 writers had not managed to achieve mass communication for their ideas and 1970-73 was too short a time to correct that. Once Pinochet was in power, the task became how to find a language capable of expressing the usurping of democracy without simplifying reality. Those in exile still felt part of Chile, a country temporarily wiped from the map, where their thought was prohibited. Jara is here quoting **Ariel Dorfman**, in an afterword to the English edition of his most famous work *Death and the Maiden* (*La muerte y la doncella*), Dorfman says *"What we feel when we watch and whisper and ache with these faraway people from faraway Chile could well be that strange trembling state of humanity we call recognition, a bridge across our divided globe."* (London, 1990, page 61; new edition, Nick Hern, 1996).

There are many other contemporary male novelists who deserve mention, but this survey will confine itself to **Antonio Skármeta** (born 1940), another exile, in Germany, until 1980, who writes short stories, novels and directs in the theatre and cinema. His short-story collections include *El entusiasmo* (1967), *Desnudo en el tejado* (1969), *Tiro libre* (1973) and his novels *Soñé que la nieve ardía* (1975), *No pasó nada* (1980), *Ardiente paciencia* (1985) and *Match-ball* (1989). *Ardiente paciencia*, retitled *El cartero de Neruda* after its successful filming as *Il postino*, is a good example of Skármeta's concern for the enthusiasms and emotions of ordinary people, skilfully weaving the love life of a postman and a bar owner's daughter into the much bigger picture of the death of Pablo Neruda and the fall of Allende.

La casa de los espíritus (1982) by **Isabel Allende** (born 1942) was a phenomenally successful novel worldwide. Allende, a relative of Salvador Allende, was born in Peru and went into exile in Venezuela after the 1973 coup. *The House of the Spirits*, with its tale of the dynasty of Esteban Trueba, which ends with a thinly disguised description of 1973, was followed in 1984 by *De amor y de sombra*, set during the Pinochet régime. The main motivation behind these novels is the necessity to preserve historical reality (see the brief prologue to *Of Love and Shadows*, "Here, write it, or it will be erased by the wind"). The same thing applies in *Paula* (1994), Allende's letter to her daughter in a

Women novelists

Background

coma: a possible salvation from the devastation of not being able to contact Paula is through the 'meticulous exercise of writing'. She has also written *Eva Luna* (1987) and *Los cuentos de Eva Luna* (1990), about a fictional Venezuelan storyteller and her stories themselves, and *El plan infinito* (1991).

Isabel Allende is a major voice in Chilean and Latin American literature, but she is by no means the first. From the 1920s on, a significant development away from *criollismo* was the rise of the female voice. The first such novelist to achieve major recognition was **Marta Brunet** (1901-67), who brought a unique perspective to the rural themes she handled (including the need to value women), but who has also been described as a writer of the senses (by Nicomedes Guzmán). Her books include *Montaña adentro* (1923), *Aguas abajo* (1943), *Humo hacia el sur* (1946) and *María Nadie* (1957). Also born in 1901, **María Flora Yáñez** wrote about the alienation of women, too, with great emphasis on the imagination as an escape for her female protagonists from their routine, unfulfilled lives (*El abrazo de la tierra*, 1934; *Espejo sin imágen*, 1936; *Las cenizas*, 1942). **María Luisa Bombal** (1910-80) took the theme of alienated women even further (*La última niebla*, 1935; *La amortajada*, 1938, and various short stories): her narrative and her characters' worlds spring from the subconscious realm of female experience and are expressed through dreams, fantasies and journeys loaded with symbolic meaning.

Like her predecessors, Allende employs the marvellous and the imaginary to propose alternatives to the masculine view of social and sexual relations. The same is true of **Lucía Guerra** (born 1942), who published *Más allá de las máscaras* in exile in 1984. Another element in Chilean women's writing (again noted by Jara, page 236) is the flight from domestic space and the discovery of the body as a centre of experience. **Damiela Eltit** (born 1949, novelist, performance and video artist), did not leave Chile after 1973 and was actively involved in resistance movements. Her provocative, intense fiction confronts issues of exploitation, violence, the oppression of women and volatile mental states. In *Vaca sagrada* (1991) at least, the protagonist's body becomes the expression of her vulnerability, through her blood, her two lovers' effects upon it, the brutality inflicted upon it and her obsession with her heartbeat. The main characters live out their obsessions and fears in a city in which there are no jobs, no warmth. They wander from one end of it to another in a kind of perversion of the hallucinatory wanderings of María Luisa Bombal's unnamed heroine in *La última niebla*. But whereas the latter is drawn along by her dream of her lover, Eltit's heroine, alone, in the dark and the traffic, is followed by an unknown man. "There are no words for the terror I felt, and images were unleashed of death and blindness" (translated by Amanda Hopkinson, *Sacred Cow*, London: Serpent's Tail, 1995, page 69). Three earlier novels, *Lumpérica* (1983), *Por la patria* (1986) and *El cuarto mundo* (1988) maintain the same experimental, challenging approach to contemporary Chilean society.

20th century poetry

In the first half of the 20th century, four figures dominated Chilean poetry, Gabriela Mistral, Vicente Huidobro, Pablo Neruda and Pablo de Rokha. The three men were all socialists, but in their politics and the expression of their views, each followed a different trajectory. Neruda overshadows all other Chilean poets on an international level, and for this reason he is discussed in the accompanying box, but this should not hide the fact that Chile has had a very strong poetic tradition.

Gabriela Mistral (Lucila Godoy Alcayaga, 1889-1957; Nobel Prize 1945) wrote a poetry which rejected elaboration in favour of a simple style with traditional metre and verse forms. Her poetry derives from a limited number of personal roots: she fell in love with Romelio Ureta who, for a variety of reasons, blew his brains out in 1909. This inspired the *Sonetos de la muerte* (1914), which were not published at the time. She never lost the grief of this tragic love, which was coupled with her love of God and her 'immense martyrdom at not being a mother'. Frustrated motherhood did not deprive her of tenderness, nor of a deep love for children. The other main theme was her appreciation of nature and landscape, not just Chile, but also other parts of the world which she visited when her diplomatic career led to her representing Chile in North and South America and Europe. Her three principal collections are *Desolación* (1923, but re-edited and amplified frequently), *Tala* (1938) and *Lagar* (1954). She also wrote many poems for children.

If Gabriela Mistral relied on the traditions and her verse alone to present her unique view of a lone woman trying to find a place in a male-oriented world, **Vicente Huidobro** (1893-1948) wanted to break with all certainties and he made grand claims for the poet's role in this. His was nothing short of a quest for the infinite and for the language to liberate it (see David Guss' introduction to *The Selected Poetry of Vicente Huidobro*, New York: New Directions, 1981). From Santiago he moved to Buenos Aires, then Paris, where he joined the Cubists, collaborated with Apollinaire and others, began to write in French and got involved in radical politics. Between the 1920s and 1940s he moved from Europe to the USA to Chile, back to Spain during the Civil War, before retiring to Llolleo to confront time and death in his last poems, *Ultimos poemas*, 1948. Huidobro considered himself at the forefront of the avant-garde, formulating *creacionismo*, which basically says that the poet is not bound by the real world, but is free to create and invent new worlds through the complete freedom of the word (see *Manifestes*, 1925). Nevertheless, all the experimentation and imagery which 'unglued the moon' (*Tout à coup*, 1925, No 10), was insufficient to achieve the language of revelation. So in 1931 he composed *Altazor*, a seven-canto poem which describes simultaneously the poet's route to creation and the ultimate frustration imposed by time and the human condition.

Pablo de Rokha (Carlos Díaz Loyola, 1894-1968) was deeply concerned for the destiny of the Chilean people and the advance of international socialism. His output was an uncompromising, epic search for Chilean identity and through it, for all its political commitment, there runs a deep sense of tragedy and inner solitude (especially true in *Fuego negro*, 1951, written after the death of his wife). *Los gemidos* was his first major book (1922); others included *Escritura de Raimundo Contreras* (1929), a song of the Chilean peasant, *Jesucristo* (1933) and *La morfología del espanto* (1942).

These poets, and Neruda especially, furthered the Chilean poetic tradition, but those who came after Neruda in the 1950s were not necessarily keen to emulate his style or his politics. The new generation of poets was still critical of society but, taking their cue from Nicanor Parra, they did not elevate the writer's role in denouncing inhumanity, alienation and the depersonalization of modern life. Instead writer and reader are placed on the same level; rhetoric and exuberant language are replaced by a conversational, ironic tone. **Parra** (born 1914; see box on Violeta Parra and the Parra Family of Chillán, page 260), a scientist and teacher, called this attempt to overcome the influence of Neruda *antipoesía* (antipoetry). In the poem 'Advertencia al lector' in *Poemas y antipoemas* (1954), he writes:

> According to the doctors of the law this book should not be published:
> The word rainbow does not appear in it,
> Let alone the word grief,
> Chairs and tables, yes, there are aplenty,
> Coffins! Writing utensils!
> Which fills me with pride
> Because, as I see it, the sky is falling to bits.

Obra gruesa anthologizes his work to 1969, followed by *Emergency Poems* (1972, bilingual edition, New York), which contain a darker humour, found poems, satire, but remain compassionate, socially committed (see 'Manifiesto'), *Artefactos* (1972) and *Artefactos II* (1982), *Sermones y prédicas del Cristo de Elqui* (1979) and *Poesía política* (1983).

Pablo Neruda

Pablo Neruda was born in Parral, central Chile, on 12 June 1904. His real name was Ricardo Neftalí Reyes. Two months after his birth his mother died. His father and stepmother soon moved to Temuco and Neruda's childhood memories were dominated by nature and, above all, rain, "my only unforgettable companion", as he described it in Confieso que he vivido. Among his teachers in Temuco was Gabriela Mistral. In 1921 he went to study in Santiago, but already he had decided on a literary career. His first book of poems, Crepusculario (1923), was published under the pseudonym Neruda, borrowed from a Czech writer; it was postmodernist in style but did not yet reveal the poet's own voice. His next volume, Veinte poemas de amor y una canción desesperada (1924) catapulted him into the forefront of Latin American poetry. The freedom of the style and the natural, elemental imagery invoking the poet's two love affairs, with a girl from Temuco and another from the capital, made the collection an immediate success. Three books followed in 1926 before Neruda was sent to Rangoon as Chilean consul in 1927. His experiences in the Orient, including his first marriage, did not alleviate an intense period of solitude and anguish. This inspired one of his finest collections, Residencia en la tierra (covering the years 1925-35). The inherent sadness of the Veinte poemas becomes despair at the passage of time and human frailty. Reinforcing this overriding theme is a kaleidoscope of images, all seemingly jumbled together and yet deliberately placed to show the chaos and fragmentary nature of man's passage towards death (see particularly "Arte poética").

In the 1930s, Neruda moved to Spain, where he edited the review Caballo verde para la poesía and kept company with many poets. The Civil War, especially the death of Federico García Lorca, affected him deeply and his poetic vision changed radically, away from the subjectivity of his earlier work to a more direct poetry, with a strong political orientation. See "Explico algunas cosas" in Tercera residencia (1947, which included España en mi corazón of 1938), which explains the move towards militancy.

Between 1938 and the election of Gabriel González Videla to the Chilean presidency he worked with the Frente Popular, was consul general in Mexico and maintained his membership of the Communist Party. He also composed at this time his epic poem of Latin American and Chilean history, from a Marxist stance, Canto general (1950). It contains 15 cantos, chronicling the natural and human life of the Americas, the oppression of its peoples, from the conquered precolumbian inhabitants to the 20th century labourers. It celebrates Chile and its campesinos, its anonymous workers in the copper, coal and salt mines and ends with his own testament, "Yo soy". One of its most famous sections is "Alturas de Machu Picchu" which mirrors the tone of the whole and his own poetic development: from the universal to the "miniscule life", from his own introspection

The adherents of antipoesía continually sought new means of expression, so that the genre never became institutionalized. There are too many poets to list here, but Gonzalo Rojas (born 1917), Enríque Lihn (1929-88), Armando Uribe (born 1933) and Miguel Arteche (born 1926) are perhaps the best known. Another poetic development of the 1950s onwards was poesía lárica, or de lares, poetry of one's place of origin (literally, of the gods of the hearth). Its founder and promoter was **Jorge Teillier** (born 1935), whose poems describe a precarious rural existence, wooden houses, fencing, orchards, distant fires, beneath changing skies and rain. The city dweller is an exile in space and time who returns every-so-often to the place of origin. See especially "Notas sobre el último viaje del autor a su pueblo natal", which evokes the lost frontier of his youth, the changed countryside and his city life. As for to his new-found role as the voice of the oppressed. Everything now revolves not around futility, but hope and struggle.

Canto general defined Neruda's subsequent enormous output. The political commitment remained, but did not submerge his respect for, and evocation of nature: eg Odas elementales (1954), Nuevas odas elementales (1957) and Tercer libro de odas (1959), which begins with "El hombre invisible":

"for my life, give me all lives,
give me all the sorrow
of all the world
and I will transform it
into hope ...
give me
the daily
struggle,
because these things are my song
the song of the invisible man
who sings with all men."

(Translated by Margaret Sayers Peden, London: Libris 1991, pages 16-18).
Neruda remarried twice and never tired of writing lyric verse, eg Los versos del capitán (1950), Cien sonetos de amor (1959). He also wrote memoirs such as Memorial de Isla Negra (1964), Confieso que he vivido (1974).

Extravagaria (1958), whose title suggests extravagance, wandering, variety, vagaries, is full of memory, acceptance and a kind of world-weary joy; see "Aquellos días". Also compare "Walking around", the most pessimistic poem in Residencia en la tierra ("It happens that I am tired of being a man" ...) with "A certain weariness":

"I don't want to be tired alone,
I want you to be tired with me ..." I am tired of the hard sea and the mysterious earth, of the chickens (we never know what they are thinking) ... of getting up ... of going to bed without glory ... of statues, of remembering.

"I want you to grow tired with me
of everything that is well done.
Of everything that makes us grow old.
Of all that lies in wait to wear out other people
Let us tire of what kills
and of what does not want to die."

(Extravagaria has been translated by Alastair Reid, New York: Farrar, Straus and Giroux, 1974.)

Neruda, who was awarded the Nobel Prize in 1971, died of cancer on 23 September 1973, his death hastened by the Pinochet coup and the military's heartless treatment of him when they removed him from Isla Negra to Santiago. The poet's three properties (see pages 83, 124 and 137) were either ransacked or shut up by the dictatorship, but many of the thousands of Chileans to whom and for whom the poet spoke visited Isla Negra to leave their messsages of respect, love and hope until democracy returned. (See Ariel Dorfman's Afterword in The House in the Sand, translation of Una casa en la arena by Dennis Maloney and Clark M Zlotchew, Minneapolis: Milkweed, 1990.) For a bilingual anthology, see Selected Poems of Pablo Neruda, translated and edited by Ben Belitt (New York: Grove Press, 1961); there are many other translations of individual volumes.

the future, "if only it could be as beautiful as my mother spreading the sheets on my bed", but it is only an unpaid bill; "I wish the UFOs would arrive". In his later poems, the violence of the city and the dictatorship invade the lares. Among Teillier's books are Para angeles y gorriones (1956), Para un pueblo fantasma (1978), Cartas para reinas de otras primaveras (1985) and Los dominios perdidos (1992). Another poeta lárico, but also an antipoeta, is Floridor Pérez (born 1937). A variation on this type of poetry comes from **Clemente Riedemann** (born 1953), whose Karra Maw'n deals with the Mapuche lands and the German immigration in the area.

Many poets left Chile after 1973 (eg Oscar Hahn, Federico Schopf, Waldo Rojas, Gonzalo Millán), but others stayed to attack the dictatorship from within through provocative, experimental works. Several of these writers were members of the Grupo

Experimental de Artaud: Damiela Eltit (see above), Raúl Zurita, Eugenia Brito, Rodrigo Cánovas. Zurita's verse is a union of mathematics and poetry, logical, structured and psychological. *Purgatorio* (1979) had an immediate impact and was followed by *Anteparaíso* (1982), *El paraíso está vacío* (1984), *Canto a su amor desaparecido* (1986) and *El amor de Chile* (1987). 'Pastoral de Chile' in *Anteparaíso* reveals most of Zurita's obsessions: Chilean landscapes, love, Chile's distress, sin and religious terminology (perhaps not as overt in other poems). *La Tirana* (1985) by Diego Maquieira is a complex, multireferential work, dealing with a Mapuche virgin, surrounded by a culture which oppresses her and with which she disguises herself. It is irreverent, a 'black mass', threatening to the régime. Carmen Berenguer's *Bobby Sands desfallece en el muro* (1983) is a homage to the IRA prisoner and thus to all political prisoners. She also wrote *Huellas del siglo* (1986) and *A media asta* (1988). Carla Grandi published *Contraproyecto* in 1985, an example of feminine resistance to the coup.

Bibliographical note A great many sources have been consulted in the preparation of this section. Apart from those already mentioned, reference is made to: Cedomil Goic, *La novela chilena. Los mitos degradados* (Santiago: Universitaria, 1991); Kenneth Fleak, *The Chilean Short Story. Writers from the Generation of 1950* (New York: Peter Lang, 1989); René Jara, *El revés de la arpillera, perfil literario de Chile* (Madrid: Hiperión, 1988); Jean Franco, *Spanish American Literature since Independence* (London: Ernest Benn, 1973); Eugenia Brito, *Campos minados. Literatura post-golpe en Chile* (Santiago: Mujeres Cuarto Propio, 1990); *Poesía chilena de hoy. De Parra a nuestros días*, selected by Erwin Díaz (Santiago: Ediciones Documentas, 1989); Lautaro Silva, *Vida y obra de Gabriela Mistral* (Buenos Aires: Andina, 1967); Gordon Brotherston, *The Emergence of the Latin American Novel* (1977) and *Latin American Poetry. Origins and Presence* (Cambridge University Press, 1975); Darío Villanueva y José María Viña Liste, *Trayectoria de la novela hispanoamericano actual* (Madrid: Austral, 1991); Jason Wilson, *Traveller's Literary Companion: South and Central America* (Brighton: In Print, 1993); Gerald Martin, *Journeys through the Labyrinth* (London: Verso, 1989).

Cinema

Not many months after the first screening organized by the Lumière brothers in Paris in December 1895, moving pictures were exhibited in Chile on 25 August 1896. Initially all the films were imported, but some years later - from 1902 - local artists and entrepreneurs began to produce short documentaries and the first narrative movie, *Manual Rodríguez*, was screened in September 1910. Cinema took root in the developing cities of early 20th century Chile: speed, motorized transport, artificial light, electricity cables, radio aerials were all signs of the changing perceptions of modernity and the growth of a culture industry in which cinema would become central. But cinema would increasingly rely on advanced technologies that only the metropolitan centres could provide. The melodramas of French and in particular Italian cinema dominated the world market up to the 1910s, but from about 1915, with European production semi-paralysed by war, the pre-eminence of Hollywood cinema was established. North American films could achieve dominance in the world market because in general they were amortized in the home market (which contained about half of the world's movie theatres), and could thus be rented cheaply abroad. The modern dreams of Hollywood were often more complex, technologically superior and more entertaining than the products of rudimentary national cinemas. The historian of Chilean silent films, Eliana Jara Donoso, quotes a publicity handout for a local movie that read, 'it's so good that it doesn't seem Chilean'. But despite overwhelming presence of Hollywood, local film makers in the silent era could still establish a small presence in the market. In the main they made documentaries, for this was a niche that international competitors were not concerned with: regional topics, football competitions, civic ceremonies, military parades. Almost 100 feature films were also made, but these are the domain of the film historian, searching through newspaper articles, for only one such movie has survived (carefully restored by the University of Chile in the early sixties): *El húsar de la muerte* (The Hussar of Death), directed by Pedro Sienna in 1925. It was, like many movies in Latin America at the time, an historical melodrama, exploring the fight for Chilean independence from Spanish rule in the 1810s through the heroic exploits of the legendary Manual Rodríguez. It achieved a great box office success in a year when 16 Chilean films were screened. Never again would so many national movies be produced annually.

If, due to the relative simplicity of the technology, the silent era allowed some space for local directors with energy to draw on strong national traditions of popular culture, the coming of synchronized sound created a new situation in Latin America. In those countries with a large domestic market - in particular Mexico, Argentina and Brazil - investment was made in expensive machinery, installations and rudimentary studios and local production could develop in the shadow of Hollywood. Elsewhere, and Chile is a telling example, sound devastated local production due to its cost and complexity. Local entrepreneurs were not prepared to make the risky captial investment and the movie houses that converted to sound would screen Hollywood and later some Argentine and Mexican movies (in particular those based on song: tango films from Argentina and 'singing cowboys' from Mexico). An attempt was made in the 1940s to stimulate cinema through state investment. The state agency CORFO, set up to encourage Chile's economic modernization, saw cinema as an important growth industry and in 1942 gave 50 percent finance to set up Chile Films. Costly studios were erected, but the plan proved over ambitious and Argentine film makers ended up using most of the facilities. By 1947 Chile Films had collapsed and it would take the shift from studio-based film production to lower cost, more flexible, movie making, that occurred in the 1950s, for cinema to revive in Chile. In the mid-1950s, the Universidad de Chile set up a vigorous film club, which screened the movies of European 'new wave' directors and in 1959 a Centre for Experimental Cinema was formed under the direction of a young documentary film maker Sergio Bravo which trained aspirant directors from Chile and elsewhere in Latin America (notably the Bolivian Jorge Sanjinés).

Cinema became intricately involved in the wider political discussions of the 1960s. Under the Frei government (1964-1970) there was a flowering of oppositional activity in theatre, music and cinema and the years 1968-1969 saw the maturity of Chilean cinema. Five features came out: Raúl Ruiz's *Tres tristes tigres* (Three Sad Tigers); Helvio Soto's *Caliche sangriento* (Bloody Nitrate); Aldo Francia's *Valparaíso mi amor* (Valparaíso My Love); Miguel Littín's *El chacal de Nahueltoro* (The Jackal of Nahueltoro) and Carlos Elsesser's *Los testigos* (The Witnesses). These film makers came from different ideological and aesthetic tendencies, from the inventive maverick Raúl Ruiz to the sombre neo-realism of Francia, but they can be seen as a group, working with very scarce resources: the films by Ruiz, Elsesser, Francia and Littín were made, consecutively, with the same camera. Aldo Francia, a doctor by profession, also organized a famous 'Meeting of Latin American Film makers' at the Viña del Mar film festival in 1967. This would be one of the key events in the growing awareness of cineastes across the continent that they were working with similar ideas and methods, producing 'new cinemas'.

The narrow victory of the Popular Unity parties in the election of 1970 was greeted by film makers with an enthusiastic manifesto penned by Littín and Littín himself was put in charge of the revived state institution Chile Films. He lasted for only 10 months, tiring of bureaucratic opposition and inter-party feuding, as the different members of Popular Unity all demanded a share of very limited resources. Few films were made between 1970 and 1973 and the state bodies could do little to affect distribution and exhibition, which remained dominated by foreign interests. United States pressure on the Chilean government included the suspension by the MPEA of US films from June 1971 and Chile Films was forced into bilateral exchanges with countries from the Eastern bloc and from Cuba. Raúl Ruiz was the most productive film maker of the period, with a number of films in different styles. Littín was working on an historical feature *La tierra prometida* (The Promised Land) when the 1973 coup occurred and post production took place in Paris. The most ambitious film to trace the radicalization of Chile in 1972 and 1973 was Patricio Guzmán's three part documentary *La batalla de Chile* (The Battle of Chile) which was edited in exile in Cuba. In the first years of exile, this film became Chile's most evocative testimony abroad and received worldwide distribution. Paradoxically, Chilean cinema, which had little time to grow under Popular Unity, strengthened in exile.

Policies following the coup practically destroyed internal film production for several years. Chile Films was intervened by the military and irreplaceable film archives were destroyed. Film personnel were arrested, tortured and imprisoned and many escaped into exile. Severe censorship was established: even *Fiddler on the Roof* was banned for displaying Marxist tendencies. It is from the exile directors that we can see the first manifestations of a continuity of film culture. Miguel Littín took up residence in Mexico, supported by Mexican President, Echeverría, and became an explicit spokesman for political Latin American cinema, making the epic *Actas de Marusia* (Letters from Marusia) in 1975 and several other features in Mexico and later in Nicaragua. In the mid-1980s he returned clandestinely to Chile with several foreign film crews to make the documentary *Acta General de Chile* in 1986, a perilous mission documented by Gabriel García Márquez in his reportage *Clandestine in Chile* (1986). Raúl Ruiz took a less visible political role, but since his exile to France, he has produced a body of work that has earned him the reputation of being one of the most innovative directors in Europe, the subject in 1983 of France's distinguished journal *Cahiers du Cinéma*. Merely to list his titles to date would overrun the space of this article. He makes movies with great technical virtuosity and often a great speed: on a visit to Santiago to celebrate the return to civilian rule in 1990, he shot a film, entitled *La telenovela errante* (the Wandering Soap Opera), in less than a week for US$30,000. Other exile directors to make their mark include Ruiz's wife Valeria Sarmiento, Gastón Ancelovici and Carmen Castillo, all based in France, Patricio Guzmán in Spain, Marilú Mallet in Canada, Angelina Vásquez in Scandinavia, Sebastián Alarcón in the Soviet Union and Antonia Skármeta in Germany (whose novel and film *Ardiente paciencia* (Burning Patience, 1983) about the Chilean poet Pablo Neruda and a postman who befriends him, was remade in Italy with the title *Il postino*).

Under censorship, film production began tentatively inside Chile with Silvio Caiozzi's *Julion comienza en julio* (Julio begins in July, 1979), set carefully in a turn-of-the-century historical location and self-financed through Caiozzi's work in commercials. It would take him a further 10 years to produce a second feature, *La luna en el espejo* (The Moon in the Mirror), based on a script by José Donoso, Chile's leading contemporary novelist, which was screened in 1990. An example of increased critical debate within Chile in the last years of the Pinochet régime can be found in Pablo Perelman's *Imagen latente* (Latent Image, 1987) which tells of a photographer's search for a missing brother who disappeared after the coup. Although the film was not released in Chile until 1990, it was possible to film it in that country in the mid-1980s.

The election of a civilian government after 17 years of military rule had some benefits for film makers, most notably the easing of censorhip. The Viña del Mar Film Festival was symbolically reinstated after 20 years and saw the emotional return of many exiled directors, but that, in itself, could not solve the problems of intellectual community dispersed around the world and the chronic under funding and under representation of Chilean films in the home market, with shrinking cinema attendance (until the multiplex invasion of the mid-1990s sought to stabilize and increase cinema viewing). New names have emerged and some successful films have been made, most notably Ricardo Larraín's *La frontera* (The Frontier, 1991), which tells of a school teacher's internal exile in the spectacular scenery of southern Chile in the late 1980s and Gustavo Graef-Marino's *Johnny Cien Pesos* (1993). The latter was produced by Chile Films, a short lived production company made up of film directors and producers financed by a State Bank credit loan. The loan was withdrawn, however, when other productions failed at the box office. The last few years have seen the screening of one or two Chilean features a year, the best received being the political thriller *Amnesia* (1994), directed by Gonzalo Justiniano and Sergio Castillo's 1997 *Gringuito*, which focuses on the problems of children brought up in exile, returning as foreigners to Chile. This gentle comedy of reintegration has been made to seem somewhat tame by the demonstrations in Chile surrounding the Pinochet extradition process. Larraín's latest feature *El entusiasmo* (Enthusiams, 1999) has not lived up to its title among local audiences, but is garnering international recognition. In a world of increasing globalization of the culture industry, it seems that this pattern of scarce local production is likely to continue.

With grateful thanks to John King.

Music and dance

At the very heart of Chilean music is the Cueca, a courting dance for couples, both of whom make great play with a handkerchief waved aloft in the right hand. The man's knees are slightly bent and his body arches back. It is lively and vigorous, seen to best advantage when performed by a Huaso wearing spurs. Guitar and harp are the accompanying instruments, while handclapping and shouts of encouragement add to the atmosphere. The dance has a common origin with the Argentine Zamba and Peruvian Marinera via the early 19th century Zamacueca, in turn descended from the Spanish Fandango. For singing only is the Tonada, with its variants the Glosa, Parabienes, Romance, Villancico (Christmas carol) and Esquinazo (serenade) and the Canto a lo Poeta, which can be in the form of a Contrapunto or Controversia, a musical duel. Among the most celebrated groups are Los Huasos Quincheros, Silvia Infante with Los Condores and the Conjunto Millaray. Famous folk singers in this genre are the Parra family from Chillán, Hector Pávez and Margot Loyola. In the north of the country the music is Amerindian and closely related to that of Bolivia. Groups called 'Bailes' dance the Huayño, Taquirari, Cachimbo or Rueda at carnival and other festivities and pre-Columbian rites like the Cauzulor and Talatur. Instruments are largely wind and percussion, including *zampoñas* (pan pipes), *lichiguayos*, *pututos* (conch shells) and *clarines*. There are some notable religious festivals that attract large crowds of pilgrims and include numerous groups of costumed dancers. The most outstanding of these festivals are those of the Virgen de La Tirana near Iquique, San Pedro de Atacama, the Virgen de la Candelaria of Copiapó and the Virgen de Andacollo.

In the south the Mapuche nation, the once greatly feared and admired 'Araucanos', who kept the Spaniards and Republicans at bay for 400 years, have their own songs, dance-songs and magic and collective dances, accompanied by wind instruments like the great long *trutruca* horn, the shorter *pifilka* and the *kultrun* drum. Further south still, the island of Chiloé, which remained in the hands of pro-Spanish loyalists after the rest of the country had become independent, has its own unique musical expression. Wakes and other religious social occasions include collective singing, while the recreational dances, all of Spanish origin, such as the Vals, Pavo, Pericona and Nave have a heavier and less syncopated beat than in central Chile. Accompanying instruments here are the *rabel* (fiddle), guitar and accordion.

Wine

Chile is a major producer and exporter of fine wines. The wine-producing area stretches from the valley of the Río Aconcagua in the north to the Biobío valley in the south. Grapes are also produced outside this area, notably around Ovalle and in the Elqui valley near La Serena, which is the main production centre for *pisco*, a clear distilled spirit commonly drunk with lemon as *pisco sour*.

The great majority of Chilean wines come from the Central Valley which is generously irrigated by the melting Andean snows to the east. While rainfall is generally abundant in winter, irrigation is essential in summer in over half the wine regions. The hot, dry summers guarantee exceptionally healthy fruit. Chilean wine is famous for being free from diseases such as Downy Mildew and Phylloxera. As a result growers are spared the costs of spraying and of grafting young vines onto Phylloxera resistant rootstocks. Fertilizer is necessary in most regions, especially in Maipo, Aconcagua, Bio Bio and Maule.

Legislation in 1979 and 1985 established the current system of denominated regions and subregions. There are five denominated wine-growing regions, based around the valleys of the Ríos Aconcagua, Maipo, Rapel, Maule and Biobío. Each of these has several subregions. The heartland of Chilean wine production is the Maipo valley, just south of Santiago, which is home to many of the most prestigious names in Chilean wine. Although the Maipo produces far less wine than the regions to the south, it is considered by many experts to produce the best wines in Chile as a result of the lime content of its soils. For visits to vineyards in this area see page 105.

The main harvest period begins at the end of February, for early maturing varieties such as Chardonnay, and runs through to the end of April for Cabernet Sauvignon, though there are regional variations. Harvest celebrations are often accompanied by two drinks: *chicha*, a partly fermented grape juice and *vino pipeño*, an unfiltered young wine which contains residue from the grapes and dried yeast.

Although the vine was introduced to Chile in the mid-16th century by the Spanish, the greatest influence on Chilean vineyards and wine making has been exerted by the French. In the 1830s one prominent Frenchman, Claudio Gay, persuaded the Chilean government to establish the *Quinta Normal* in Santiago as a nursery for exotic botanical specimens including vines. In the 1970s domestic consumption of wine dropped and wine prices fell, leading to the destruction of many vineyards. In the last two decades, however, large-scale investment, much of it from the United States and Europe has led to

Demarcated wine regions

Wine Regions	3 Rapel
1 Aconcagua	4 Maule
2 Maipo	5 Biobío

0 km 100
0 miles 60

Chilean wine: an aristocratic tradition

The cultivation of grapes in Chile dates back almost to the Spanish conquest, the first recorded vineyard being established in 1551 in La Serena by Francisco de Aguirre. One of the major motives for early vine-growing was to supply wine for the celebration of mass. In the 18th century the efforts of Madrid to restrict the planting of new vines in order to prevent competition with Spanish wines were largely ignored and vineyards became common on haciendas and villages throughout the central valley as far south as the Biobío valley.

Some of the most famous Chilean wines are closely associated with major names in the Chilean élite of the 19th century among them the Errázuriz, Cousiño, Subercaseux and Undurraga families. With the introduction of direct steamship services to Europe, the heads of many of these families *travelled to France and returned with French and German grape varieties. New cultivation techniques were also introduced from France. French experts were employed to design the cellars, some of which, with their double walls designed to prevent temperature fluctuations, can be visited today. Some of the largest and most famous of these vineyards were situated just south of Santiago in the floodplains of the Ríos Pirque and Maipo, which were adapted for commercial agriculture by the building of a network of canals. Defended by natural frontiers, the Pacific, the Andes and the Atacama Desert, Chile also benefitted by being one of the very few wine-growing areas in the world not to suffer the devastation of the phylloxera louse which destroyed the vineyards of Europe after 1863.*

increases in wine production, increasingly of quality wines destined for export. In 1992, 152 million litres of wine were produced of which 73 million were exported.

There is a marked distinction between export wines and wines grown for domestic consumption. The most commonly planted grape variety is the dark-skinned *Pais*, found only in Chile, and thought to be a direct descendant of cuttings imported by Spanish colonists, but much of this is planted on poorly drained land in the southern Maule and Biobío regions. Many of the vines known in Chile as Sauvignon are not the familiar Sauvignon Blanc, but rather Sauvignon Vert or Sauvignon Gris. Although Chilean wines, especially those produced for export, are typically very clean and fruity, they have, until recently, rarely displayed much structure. Most export wines are of a varietal character, Cabernet and Chardonnay being the main red and white varietals respectively. In the opinion of most experts, Chile has yet to develop its own wine style, unlike other 'new world' producers such as California with its Zinfandel, Argentina with its Malbec and Torrontes and Uruguay with its Tannat. In recent years it has become easier to buy export-quality wines in shops in large cities such as Santiago, Valparaíso and Concepción.

Four large companies now account for 80 percent of all the wine sold inside Chile: Concha y Toro, Santa Rita, San Pedro and Santa Carolina. A few others, among them Errázuriz/Caliterra, Undurraga, Cánepa and Manquehue, supply most of the rest of the domestic market. Many of the smaller wineries, however, specialize in exports. Although a few wineries, including Cousiño-Macul, Los Vascos, Montes, Portal del Alto, Santa Monica and Santa Inés, use only their own grapes, this practice is rare and most companies buy in grapes from a range of buyers.

Among the interesting names given to wines, two stand out: '120' commemorates the 120 Patriot soldiers under O'Higgins who hid in the Santa Rita cellars in 1814 after their defeat at Rancagua. *Casillero del Diablo*, one of the best known red wines from Concha y Toro, was one of the favourite wines of the founder Don Melchor de Santiago Concha who kept intruders away by spreading the rumour that the corner of the cellar where he kept it was haunted by the devil.

With grateful thanks to Dereck Foster, *Buenos Aires Herald*.

Modern Chile

Economy

Structure of production Chile is endowed with a diversified environment, allowing the production of all temperate and Mediterranean products. Traditional crops, such as cereals, pulse, potatoes and industrial crops, such as sugarbeet, sunflowerseed and rapeseed, account for about a third of the value added of agriculture, and vegetables for a quarter. Fruit growing has grown rapidly and fresh fruit now accounts for over US$1 billion in exports a year, making fruit the second most important earner after copper. Another area of expansion is forestry; timber and wood products make up the third place in exports. More than 80 percent of the 1.6 million hectares of cultivated forest is planted with insignis radiata pine, a species which in Chile grows faster than in other countries. However, native forest has been declining rapidly, partly because of demand by wood chippers. Chile is the most important fishing nation in Latin America and the largest producer of fishmeal in the world. Industrial consumption absorbs about 93 percent of the fish catch; fresh fish and fish products contribute about 10 percent of merchandise exports. Salmon farming is being expanded.

The dominant sector of the economy is mining. Chile has been the world's largest producer of copper since 1982 and also produces molybdenum, iron ore, manganese, lead, gold, silver, zinc, sulphur and nitrates. Chile has a quarter of the world's known molybdenum ore reserves and is believed to have around 40 percent of the world's lithium reserves. Mineral ores, most of which is copper, account for half of total export revenue. Fluctuations in world prices for minerals can have a great impact on the balance of payments. Foreign investment is the driving force in mining, which has averaged almost US$900 million a year in the 1990s in exploration and mine development. By 2000 output of copper will be four million tonnes a year, over 40 percent of world production, of which 1.4 million tonnes will be produced by the state company, Codelco, from its five mines, Chuquicamata, El Teniente, Salvador, Andina and Radomiro Tomic (to come on stream in 1998). Privately owned, high-tech mines or joint ventures are responsible for most of the expected growth.

Chile is fortunate in possessing reserves of oil, natural gas and coal, and abundant hydroelectricity potential. Almost all the country's hydrocarbon reserves are in the extreme south, on Tierra del Fuego, in the Strait of Magellan and the province of Magallanes. Natural gas is likely to be piped across the Andes from Argentina from 1997. Two pipelines are planned and up to six new gas-fired power plants may be built in 1998-2002, reducing electricity costs and pollution around Santiago if coal-fired plants are closed.

Manufacturing activity is mostly food processing, metalworking, textiles, footwear and fish processing. The sector has been vulnerable to changes in economic policy: nationalization during the Allende administration in the early 1970s; recession brought about by anti-inflation policies in the mid-1970s; increased competition resulting from trade liberalization in the early 1980s and greater exports together with import substitution in the mid-1980s. The contribution of manufacturing to total gdp fell from 25 percent in 1970 to 20 percent in 1994, but its share of exports rose and the sector grew by over six percent a year in the 1990s.

Mercosur

In June 1996 Chile signed up to become an associate member of Mercosur, the Southern Cone Common Market. Founded in 1991 by Argentina, Brazil, Paraguay and Uruguay, Mercosur is the world's fourth largest integrated international market. Except in aspiration it is not, however, yet a common market. Most goods are tariff-free inside Mercosur, but there is, as yet, no common external tariff, though in December 1995 the four full member states agreed a five-year programme to establish one. Since, however, there is no freedom of movement for workers, a full common market remains a distant aspiration.

As a result of associate membership, Chile and the full members were due to reduce tariffs on trade by 30 percent with further reductions by the year 2005 eliminating them altogether. A small group of Chilean food and agricultural imports from Mercosur will not be covered by this: tariffs on most of these will be cut between 2006 and 2011, though wheat, flour and sugar will retain their existing tariffs until at least 2014. Within Chile the main opposition to associate membership came from farmers fearing competition from the large-scale meat and grain producers of Mercosur states: to placate their hostility the government offered US$500m of support for agriculture over the next five years as the Mercosur bill passed through Congress.

Recent trends

The policies used to bring inflation down from over 500 percent at the end of 1973 to less than 10 percent by the end of 1981 resulted in fiscal balance but an overvalued currency. Freeing the exchange rate in 1982 caused renewed inflation; this was restricted by tight monetary control and a lower public sector borrowing requirement which caused a severe recession and contraction in gdp. IMF help was sought following a sharp fall in international commercial lending in 1982 and a decline in Chile's terms of trade. In the 1980s Chile negotiated several debt refinancing packages and reduced its foreign debt through schemes which converted debt into equity in Chilean companies. Renewed growth in debt in the 1990s was offset by rising gdp and exports which meant that the debt: gdp ratio fell from 94 percent in 1985 to an estimated 40 percent in 1995, while the debt service ratio declined from 48 percent to about 15 percent in the same period.

The Government follows anti-inflationary policies, accompanied by structural adjustment and reform. Privatization has been widespread, although certain key companies such as Codelco remain in state hands. Privatizing the pension system and corporate savings have doubled domestic savings to 27 percent of gdp. Pension funds now manage assets of US$25 billion, about 40 percent of gdp. Rising investor confidence has brought economic growth every year since the mid-1980s and the Chile model has been held up as an example for other debtor countries to adapt to their own needs. Unemployment has fallen and progress is being made in reducing poverty with increased public spending on health and education. Infant mortality has dropped; the literacy rate has risen and the percentage of malnourished children fell from 8.8 percent in 1982 to 5.3 percent in 1993.

In early 1998 the central bank had to implement measures to restrict demand and stabilize the peso. The crisis in Asian markets (which take about a third of Chilean exports), falling copper prices and the delay caused by El Niño to export crop harvests were all negative influences. Gdp growth for 1998 was forecast to be at least one percentage point lower than the predicted 6.8 percent (compared with 5.8 percent in 1997), unemployment was expected to rise and the government would be hard-pressed to keep to its 4.5 percent inflation target.

Constitution and government

Chile is governed under the 1980 Constitution, introduced by the military government of General Pinochet and approved in a plebiscite on 11 September 1980, although important amendments were made during the transition to civilian rule in 1989-1990. The new constitution provided for an eight-year non-renewable term for the President of the Republic (although the first elected president was to serve only four years), a bicameral Congress and an independent judiciary and central bank. Although Pinochet was not mentioned by name, only one candidate, nominated by the military was to contest the 1981 and 1988 elections. Only after the rejection of Pinochet in the 1988 vote did most of the provisions of the constitution come into operation. In February 1994, the Congress cut the presidential term of office from eight years to six. A two-thirds majority in both houses of Congress is required to reform the constitution.

Congress is composed of a 120-seat Chamber of Deputies and a 47-seat Senate, eight of whose members are nominated rather than elected. Among the nominated senators are one former head of each of the armed forces. Former presidents who have completed a full six-year term are also eligible to join as Life Senators. In March 1998 Pinochet took up his seat under this provision. The existence of nominated senators has enabled the right-wing opposition parties to block constitutional reform. The abolition of nominated senators has been a major aim of civilian governments since 1990.

Since 1990 the dominant party in Chile has been the Christian Democrats. A centre party which grew rapidly after its foundation in 1957, the Christian Democrats welcomed the overthrow of Allende, but later became the focus of opposition to the dictatorship. Not strong enough on their own, since 1990 they have contested elections in an alliance known as the Concertación. The other members are the Socialists, a centre-left party traditionally split between different factions, the Radicals

Chile: regions

Regions
I Tarapacá
II Antofagasta
III Atacama
IV Coquimbo
V Valparaíso
VI Libertador General Bernardo O'Higgins

VII Maule
VIII Bío Bío
IX Araucanía
X Los Lagos
XI Aisén del General Carlos Ibañez del Campo
XII Magallanes y Antártica Chilena

Population (1995)

Region	Name	Population
I	*Tarapacá*	*410,343*
II	*Antofagasta*	*415,487*
III	*Atacama2*	*02,810*
IV	*Coquimbo*	*525,432*
V	*Valparaíso*	*1,478,281*
	Región Metropolitana de Santiago	*684,179*
VI	*Libertador General Bernardo O'Higgins*	*902,646*
VII	*Maule*	*1,753,662*
VIII	*Biobío*	*853,187*
IX	*Araucanía*	*957,212*
X	*Los Lagos*	*88,782*
XI	*Aisén del General Carlos Ibañaz del Campo*	*181,551*
	Metropolitana de Santiago	*5,783,703*

Source: Encyclopaedia Britannica

and the Partido por la Democracía, a new centre-left grouping led by ex-socialists. The main opposition to the Concertación has come from the right wing, which is divided into two main parties: Renovación Nacional and the Unión Democrática Independiente: for the 1993 elections they formed an alliance called the Unión por el Progreso. The Chilean Communist Party, which in the 1960s was the largest communist party in Latin America, lost support during the Pinochet years and is now of little importance.

Chile is divided into 13 regions, often referred to by Roman numerals although they also have names. The government of each region is headed by an Intendent who is appointed by the President. Although this system was introduced in 1974 to replace the old system of provinces, the 25 provinces still exist but their power has been reduced.

Background

Footnotes

17

Footnotes

17

Main routes: north of Santiago

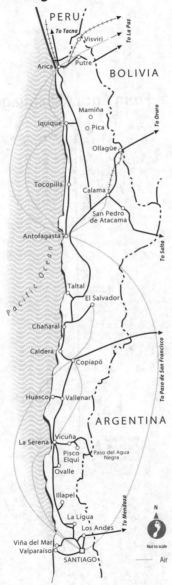

From Arica to Santiago

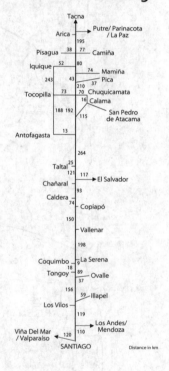

Tacna

Arica ⟶ Putre/ Parinacota / La Paz

195

Pisagua — 38 — 77 — Camiña

80

Iquique — 52

74 — Mamiña

43 — Pica

210 37

243 70 — Chuquicamata

Tocopilla — 73 16 — Calama

188 192 115 — San Pedro de Atacama

Antofagasta — 13

264

Taltal — 25

121 — 117 — El Salvador

Chañaral —

93

Caldera —

74 — Copiapó

150

Vallenar

198

Coquimbo — 5 — La Serena

Tongoy — 18 — 89 — Ovalle

37

156 59 — Illapel

Los Vilos —

119

Viña Del Mar / Valparaíso ⟶ 120 110 — Los Andes/ Mendoza

SANTIAGO

Distance in km

Main routes: Santiago - Puerto Montt

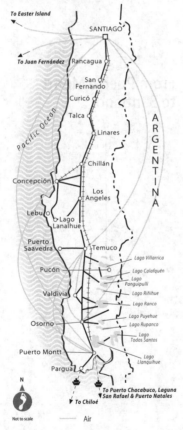

To Easter Island

SANTIAGO

To Juan Fernández   Rancagua

San Fernando

Curicó

Talca

Linares

Pacific Ocean

A R G E N T I N A

Chillán

Concepción

Los Angeles

Lebu

Lago Lanalhue

Puerto Saavedra   Temuco

Lago Villarrica

Pucón

Lago Calafquén

Lago Panguipulli

Lago Riñihue

Valdivia

Lago Ranco

Lago Puyehue

Osorno

Lago Rupanco

Lago Todos Santos

Puerto Montt

Lago Llanquihue

Pargua

N

To Puerto Chacabuco, Laguna San Rafael & Puerto Natales

To Chiloé

Not to scale

——— Air

From Puerto Montt to Santiago

Distance in km

Valparaíso & Viña Del Mar	120 — Santiago
	87
San Antonio	109 — Rancagua
	87 — San Fernando
Curicó	55
	62
	49 — Talca
	— Linares
	101
	— Chillán
Concepción	86
	105
	82 — Los Angeles
Victoria	114 — 56 — Curacautín
	71
	— Temuco
	17
	54 — 55 — Villarrica/ Pucón
Loncoche	33
	15 — Panguipulli
	42 — 49
Valdivia	34 — 140
	— Osorno — 35 — Entre Lagos
	67
	— Frutillar
	43
	— Puerto Montt
Pargua/ Chiloé	— Carretera Austral

Footnotes

Main routes: south of Puerto Montt

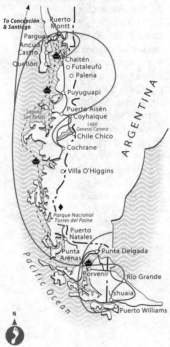

Advertisers

Colour Section
Aerolineas Argentinas, UK
Patagonia Connection, Chile
Transtour, Chile
Travellers, Chile

38	Asatej, Chile
36	Austral Tours, UK
104	Aventuras Nicole, Chile
104	Azimut 360, Chile
403	Azimut (Terra Luna Lodge), Chile
396	Baquedano Language School, Chile
235	Birding Alto Andino, Chile
333	Campo Aventura, Chile
427	Casa Cecilia, Chile
201	Desert Adventure, Chile
337, 423, 481	Discover Chile Tours, USA
102	Edward A Cahill, USA
102	Escuela de Idiomas Violeta Parra, Chile
274	Guesthouse 'El Rincon', Chile
297	Hosteria/Restaurant 'Ecole, Chile
105	Intijalsu Tour, Chile
39	Journey Latin America, UK
22	Ladatco Tours, USA
37	Last Frontiers, UK
30	Latin American Travel Advisor, Ecuador
23	Myths and Mountains Inc, USA
87	Santa Magdalena Apartments, Chile
66	Stanfords, UK

Shorts

Special interest pieces on and about Chile

Footnotes

Index

Note: grid references to the colour maps are shown in italics after place names. So
Algarrobo *M3B2* can be found on Map 3, grid B2.

Footnotes

Map index

Will you help us?

We try as hard as we can to make each Footprint Handbook as up-to-date and accurate as possible but, of course, things always change. Many people write to us - with corrections, new information, or simply comments.

If you want to let us know about an experience or adventure - hair-raising or mundane, good or bad, exciting or boring or simply something rather special - we would be delighted to hear from you. Please give us as precise information as possible, quoting the edition number (you'll find it on the front cover) and page number of the Handbook you are using.

Your help will be greatly appreciated, especially by other travellers. In return we will send you details about our special guidebook offer:

Write to Elizabeth Taylor
Footprint Handbooks
6 Riverside Court
Lower Bristol Road
Bath
BA2 3DZ
England
or email info@footprintbooks.com

TERMAS DE PUYUHUAPI HOTEL & SPA

South of Silence
The Spirit of Patagonia

Chile's Patagonia is a wonderous region of our planet wanting to preserve its privacy and purity

Located in an exclusive area of the exotic Chilean Patagonia, the TERMAS DE PUYUHUAPI HOTEL & SPA emerges in complete harmony with the landscape, surrounded by pristine nature. Its classy facilities provide the perfect conditions for an unforgettable stay.

The complete SPA and Thalassotherapy Center offer a wide variety of treatments, using the benefits of the thermal waters and the marine environment, such as seaweed and sea water.

Termas de Puyuhuapi Hotel & Spa is a place reserved only for those who are looking for something different.

PATAGONIA EXPRESS

The San Rafael Glacier is an enormous mass of ice which flows from the high peaks of the Andes Mountains west towards the sea, into the San Rafael Lagoon, offering a wonderful spectacle.

Our programs include a full day excursion to enjoy this beautiful experience by travelling through the patagonia fjords and channels on board the luxury PATAGONIA EXPRESS Catamaran.

Patagonia Connection S.A.
Termas de Puyuhuapi Hotel & Spa

Fidel Oteiza 1921 of. 1006, piso 10 • Santiago, Chile • Tel.: (56 - 2) 225 6489 - 223 5567
Fax: (56 - 2) 274 8111 • e-mail: info@patagoniaconnex.cl

Travellers

Altiplano

CHILE

Easter Is.

Litoral

Araucanía

Los Lagos

Chiloé

Careterra Austral

Travellers

Ph:+56-65-262099
Fax:+56-65-258555
info@Travellers.cl

Patagonia

www.Travellers.cl

Altitude in metres

4000
3000
2000
1000
500
200
0
Neighbouring
Country

Major roads
Unpaved or *ripio* roads
Railway
Ferry between Puerto Montt &
Puerto Natales (Puerto Edén)
Ferry between Puerto Montt &
Puerto Chacabuco/Laguna San Rafael
Ferry between Quellón & Chaltén
National Park
International Border
Regional Border
Salt plains

□ **CAPITAL**
□ **Regional Capital**

N

0 km   200
0 miles   125

PERU

❶

Iquique □   BOLIVIA

Antofagasta □
❷

Copiapó □

La Serena □

❸

Valparaíso □
□ SANTIAGO
Rancagua □

Talca □

Concepción □
❹

Temuco □   ARGENTINA

Puert Montt □

❺

Coyhaique □

❻   ❼

Punta
Arenas □

MAP 1

PERU

Pacific
Ocean

BOLIVIA

REGION I

REGION II

Tacora (5,988m) ▲
Visviri
Pomerape (6,282m) ▲
Putre
Parinacota
Parque Nacional Lauca
Parinacota (6,342m) ▲
Paso Tambo Quemado
Acotango (6,050m) ▲
Capurata (5,990m) ▲
Gualltiri (6,060m) ▲
Guallatiri ◆
Geoglifos de Lluta
Poconchile
Arica
Río Lluta
Geoglifos de Azapa
Belén ◆
Río Azapa
Tignamar
Tignamar Viejo
Reserva Nacional Las Vicuñas
Codpa
Salar de Surire
Monumental Natural Salar de Surire ◆
Surire
Río Camarones
Cuya
Geoglifos de Chiza
Camiña
Parque Nacional Volcán Isluga
Isluga (5,530m) ▲
Colchane
Isluga
Geoglifos de Tiliviche
British Cemetery
Cariquima
Pisagua
Reserva Nacional Pampa del Tamarugal
Alto Toroni (5,982m) ▲
Cta Buena
Giante del Atacama ◆
Chusmisa
Huara
Tarapacá
Humberstone
Mamiña
Iquique
Reserva Nacional Pampa del Tamarugal
Pozo Almonte
La Tirana ◆
Salar de Huasco
Salar de Pintados
Pica
Matilla
Geoglifos de Pintados
Salar de Coposa
Puerto Patillos
San Marcos
Salar de Llamara
Quillagua
Ollagüe
Buenaventura
Ollagüe (5,863m) ▲
Salar de Carcote
Cebollar
Salar de Ascotán
Ascotán
San Pedro
Conchi Viejo
Conchi
Inacaliri
Tocopilla
Baños de Turi
Línzor
Punta Blanca
Ayquina
Toconce
Mantos de la Luna
Chiu Chiu
Caspana
El Tatio Geysers
Gatico
Lasana
María Elena
Chuquicamata
Cobija
Pedro de Valdivia
Calama
Michilla
Salar Miraje
Río Grande
Catarpe
Puritama
Hornitos
Pukará Quitor
Lincancábur (6,916m) ▲
Zapaleri (5,653m) ▲
Sierra Gorda
San Pedro de Atacama
Mejillones
Tulor
Chacabuco
Salar de Atacama
Toconao
Baquedano
Carmen Alto
Camar
Talabre
Lascar (5,154m) ▲
Salar de Quisquiro
Bolsico
La Portada
Juan Lopez
La Chimba
Socaire
Peine
Laguna Miscanti
Antofagasta
Tilopozo
Tilomonte
Laco

N

0 km
0 miles

Map 2

MAP 6

Puerto Edén

Isla
Wellington

5

N

0 km   50
0 miles   31

A

ARGENTINA

Map 7

Parque Nacional
Bernardo O'Higgins

Parque Nacional
Torres del Paine

Cerro Castillo

Paso Cancha Carrera

REGION XII

Cueva del Milodón

Balmaceda
(2,035m)

Seno Ultima
Esperanza

Paso Dorotea

Puerto Edén
Ferry Route

Puerto Natales

Paso Casas Viejas

Pacific
Ocean

B

9

Villa Tehuelches

Río Verde

Parque
Nacional
Magallanes

Punta
Arenas

Parque Nacional
Laguna Parillar

Fuerte
Bulnes

Estrecho de Magallanes

C

1   2   3

MAP 7

ARGENTINA

Atlantic Ocean

Map 6

Punta Delgada

255

Ferry Crossing

Punta Espora

Cerro Sombrero

Otway Sound

Isla Isabel

Punta Arenas
Fuerte Bulnes

Ferry Crossing

Porvenir

San Sebastián

San Sebastián

Estrecho de Magallanes

Camerón

Río Grande

Isla Dawson

Lago Blanco

Tierra del Fuego

Lago Fagnano

Lago Escondido

ARGENTINA

Ushuaia

Harberton

Puerto Williams

Canal Beagle

Isla Navarino

Isla Wollaston

Cape Horn

N

0 km 50
0 miles 31

1   2   3

Complete listing

Latin America
Argentina Handbook 1st
1 900949 10 5 £11.99
Bolivia Handbook 1st
1 900949 09 1 £11.99
Bolivia Handbook 2nd
1 900949 49 0 £12.99
Brazil Handbook 1st
0 900751 84 3 £12.99
Brazil Handbook 2nd
1 900949 50 4 £13.99
Caribbean Islands Handbook 2000
1 900949 40 7 £14.99
Chile Handbook 2nd
1 900949 28 8 £11.99
Colombia Handbook 1st
1 900949 11 3 £10.99
Cuba Handbook 1st
1 900949 12 1 £10.99
Cuba Handbook 2nd
1 900949 54 7 £10.99
Ecuador & Galápagos Handbook 2nd
1 900949 29 6 £11.99
Mexico Handbook 1st
1 900949 53 9 £13.99
**Mexico & Central America
Handbook 2000**
1 900949 39 3 £15.99
Peru Handbook 2nd
1 900949 31 8 £11.99
South American Handbook 2000
1 900949 38 5 £19.99
Venezuela Handbook 1st
1 900949 13 X £10.99
Venezuela Handbook 2nd
1 900949 58 X £11.99

Africa
East Africa Handbook 2000
1 900949 42 3 £14.99
Morocco Handbook 2nd
1 900949 35 0 £11.99
Namibia Handbook 2nd
1 900949 30 X £10.99
South Africa Handbook 2000
1 900949 43 1 £14.99
Tunisia Handbook 2nd
1 900949 34 2 £10.99
Zimbabwe Handbook 1st
0 900751 93 2 £11.99

Wexas
Traveller's Handbook
0 905802 08 X £14.99
Traveller's Healthbook
0 905802 09 8 £9.99

Asia
Cambodia Handbook 2nd
1 900949 47 4 £9.99
Goa Handbook 1st
1 900949 17 2 £9.99
Goa Handbook 2nd
1 900949 45 8 £9.99
India Handbook 2000
1 900949 41 5 £15.99
Indonesia Handbook 2nd
1 900949 15 6 £14.99
Indonesia Handbook 3rd
1 900949 51 2 £15.99
Laos Handbook 2nd
1 900949 46 6 £9.99
Malaysia & Singapore Handbook 2nd
1 900949 16 4 £12.99
Malaysia Handbook 3rd
1 900949 52 0 £12.99
Myanmar (Burma) Handbook 1st
0 900751 87 8 £9.99
Nepal Handbook 2nd
1 900949 44 X £11.99
Pakistan Handbook 2nd
1 900949 37 7 £12.99
Singapore Handbook 1st
1 900949 19 9 £9.99
Sri Lanka Handbook 2nd
1 900949 18 0 £11.99
Sumatra Handbook 1st
1 900949 59 8 £9.99
Thailand Handbook 2nd
1 900949 32 6 £12.99
Tibet Handbook 2nd
1 900949 33 4 £12.99
Vietnam Handbook 2nd
1 900949 36 9 £10.99

Europe
Andalucía Handbook 2nd
1 900949 27 X £9.99
Ireland Handbook 1st
1 900949 55 5 £11.99
Scotland Handbook 1st
1 900949 56 3 £10.99

Middle East
Egypt Handbook 2nd
1 900949 20 2 £12.99
Israel Handbook 2nd
1 900949 48 2 £12.99
Jordan, Syria & Lebanon Handbook 1st
1 900949 14 8 £12.99

Sales & distribution

Footprint Handbooks
6 Riverside Court
Lower Bristol Road
Bath BA2 3DZ England
T 01225 469141
F 01225 469461
E Mail info@
footprintbooks.com

Australia
Peribo Pty
58 Beaumont Road
Mt Kuring-Gai
NSW 2080
T 02 9457 0011
F 02 9457 0022

Austria
Freytag-Berndt Artaria
Kohlmarkt 9
A-1010 Wien
T 01 533 2094
F 01 533 8685

Reiseladen
Dominikanerbastei 4
A-1010 Wien
T 0222 513 8936
F 0222 513 893619

Belgium
Craenen BVBA
Mechelsesteenweg 633
B-3020 Herent
T 016 23 90 90
F 016 23 97 11

Canada
Ulysses Travel Publications
4176 rue Saint-Denis
Montréal
Québec H2W 2M5
T 514 843 9882
F 514 843 9448

Caribbean
Kingston Publishers
10, LOJ Industrial Complex
7 Norman Road
Kingston CSO
Jamaica
T 001876 928 8898
F 001876 928 5719

Europe
Bill Bailey
16 Devon Square
Newton Abbott
Devon TQ12 2HR. UK
T 01626 331079
F 01626 331080

Denmark
Kilroy Travel
Skindergade 28
DK-1159 Copenhagen K
T 33 11 00 44
F 33 32 32 69

Nordisk Korthandel
Studiestraede 26-30 B
DK-1455 Copenhagen K
T 3338 2638
F 3338 2648

Scanvik Books
Esplanaden 8B
DK-1263 Copenhagen K
T 33 12 77 66
F 33 91 28 82

Finland
Akateeminen Kirjakauppa
Keskuskatu 1
FIN-00100 Helsinki
T 09 12141
F 09 121 4441

Suomalainen Kirjakauppa
Koivuvaarankuja 2
01640 Vantaa 64
F 08 52 78 88

France
L'Astrolabe
46 rue de Provence
F-75009 Paris 9e
T 1 42 85 42 95
F 1 45 75 92 51

VILO Diffusion
25 rue Ginoux
F-75015 Paris
T 01 45 77 08 05
F 01 45 79 97 15

Germany
GeoCenter ILH
Schockenriedstrasse 44
D-70565 Stuttgart
T 0711 781 94610
F 0711 781 94654

Brettschneider
Fernreisebedarf
Feldkirchnerstrasse 2
D-85551 Heimstetten
T 089 990 20330
F 089 990 20331

Geobuch Gmbh
Rosental 6
D-80331 München
T 089 265030
F 089 263713

Gleumes
Hohenstaufenring 47-51
D-50674 Köln
T 0221 215650

Globetrotter Ausrustungen
Wiesendamm 1
D-22305 Hamburg
F 040 679 66183

Dr Götze
Bleichenbrücke 9
D-2000 Hamburg 1
T 040 3031 1009-0

Hugendubel Buchhandlung
Nymphenburgerstrasse 25
D-80335 München
T 089 238 9412
F 089 550 1853

Kiepert Buchhandlung
Hardenbergstrasse 4-5
D-10623 Berlin 12
T 030 311880

Greece
GC Eleftheroudakis
17 Panepistemiou
Athens 105 64
T 01 331 4180-83
F 01 323 9821

India
Roli Books
M-75 GK II Market
New Delhi 110048
T (011) 646 0886
F (011) 646 7185

Israel
Geographical Tours
8 Tverya Street
Tel Aviv 63144
T 03 528 4113
F 03 629 9905

Italy
Librimport
Via Biondelli 9
I-20141 Milano
T 02 8950 1422
F 02 8950 2811

Kenya
Textbook Centre
Kijabe Street
PO Box 47540
Nairobi
T 2 330340
F 2 225779

Netherlands
Nilsson & Lamm bv
Postbus 195
Pampuslaan 212
N-1380 AD Weesp
T 0294 494949
F 0294 494455

Norway
Schibsteds Forlag A/S
Akersgata 32 - 5th Floor
Postboks 1178 Sentrum
N-0107 Oslo
T 22 86 30 00
F 22 42 54 92

Tanum
PO Box 1177 Sentrum
N-0107 Oslo 1
T 22 41 11 00
F 22 33 32 75

Olaf Norlis
Universitetsgt 24
N-1062 Oslo
T 22 00 43 00

Pakistan
Pak-American Commercial
Zaib-un Nisa Street
Saddar
PO Box 7359
Karachi
T 21 566 0418
F 21 568 3611

South Africa
Faradawn CC
PO Box 1903
Saxonwold 2132
T 011 885 1787
F 011 885 1829

South America
Humphrys Roberts
Associates
Caixa Postal 801-0
Ag. Jardim da Gloria
06700-970 Cotia SP
Brazil
T 011 492 4496
F 011 492 6896

Southeast Asia
APA Publications
38 Joo Koon Road
Singapore 628990
T 865 1600
F 861 6438

Spain
Altaïr
Balmes 69
08007 Barcelona
T 93 3233062
F 93 4512559

Bookworld España
Pje Las Palmeras 25
29670 San Pedro Alcántara
Málaga
T 95 278 6366
F 95 278 6452

Libros de Viaje
C/Serrano no 41
28001 Madrid
T 01 91 577 9899
F 01 91 577 5756

Sweden
Hedengrens Bokhandel
PO Box 5509
S-11485 Stockholm
T 8 6115132

Kart Centrum
Vasagatan 16
S-11120 Stockholm
T 8 111699

Lantmateriet Kartbutiken
Kungsgatan 74
S-11122 Stockholm
T 08 202 303
F 08 202 711

Switzerland
Artou
8 rue de Rive
CH-1204 Geneva
T 022 311 4544
F 022 781 3456

Office du Livre OLF SA
ZI 3, Corminboeuf
CH-1701 Fribourg
T 026 467 5111
F 026 467 5466

Schweizer Buchzentrum
Postfach
CH-4601 Olten
T 062 209 2525
F 062 209 2627

Travel Bookshop
Rindermarkt 20
Postfach 216
CH-8001 Zürich
T 01 252 3883
F 01 252 3832

USA
NTC/ Contemporary
4255 West Touhy Avenue
Lincolnwood
Illinois 60646-1975
T 847 679 5500
F 847 679 2494

What the papers say

"*I carried the South American Handbook in my bag from Cape Horn to Cartagena and consulted it every night for two and a half months. And I wouldn't do that for anything else except my hip flask.*"

Michael Palin

"*Footprint's India Handbook told me everything fr the history of the region to where to get the best cu*

Jennie Bond, BBC correspondent

"*Of all the main guidebook series this is genuinely only one we have never received a complaint abou*

The Bookseller

"*All in all, the Footprint Handbook series is the best thing that has happened to travel guidebooks in years. They are different and take you off the beaten track away from all the others clutching the competitors' guidebooks.*"

The Business Times, Singapore

Mail order
Available worldwide in good bookstores, Footprint Handbooks can also be ordered directly from us in Bath, via our website or from the address on the back cover.

Website
www.footprintbooks.com
Take a look for the latest news, to order a book or to join our mailing list.

Acknowledgements

Thanks are due to a large number of people for their help in the preparation of this book, including the many travellers who wrote, faxed and e-mailed corrections and additions to the first edition of the *Chile Handbook* and to its companion, the *South American Handbook*.

The author would like to thank the following for their contributions to this second edition:

Simon Watson-Taylor, writer, translator and veteran world traveller, who has contributed to other titles in the *Footprint* series. Simon's exhaustive reports on his travels from Santiago to Arica provided the basis for a thorough revision of the text on the northern part of the country.

Barbara Knapton, Alaskan biologist and ornithologist who runs the tour agency *Birding Alto Andino*, and who contributed extensively to the revison of the sections on the northern altiplano including the Parque Nacional Lauca.

Santiago de la Vega, Antarctic scientist and specialist writer on wildlife issues in Argentina, Chile and the Antarctic, who wrote the section on flora. Valuable additional advice and material on flora was provided by **Jane Norwich**, freelance garden designer, who visited Chile in 1997 and 1999. **Robert Terwilliger**, biologist from California, wrote sections on endangered fauna.

John King, Professor of Comparative American Studies, University of Warwick contributed the new section on Chilean cinema as well as material on Ariel Dorfman.

Special thanks for assistance are also due to the following: **Ms Gloria Dean**, Carshalton, UK, former resident and frequent visitor to Chile, corrected many of the errors in the first edition; **Maggie Wilkinson**, enthusiastic supporter of Universidad Católica, who offered many insights especially on Chilean football; **Naomi Peirce**, Hitchen, UK, geographer who provided much valued assistance on Chilean landforms; **Noëlle Durandin**, of the *Hostería école*, Pucón and **Hans Liechtiand** and **Verónica Araneda**, at *La Tetera*, also in Pucón, assisted in revising the material on Pucón and the surrounding area; **Carlos** and **Brian Grady**, of the *Hospedaje Esmeralda by the Sea*, Chonchi, provided updates and new material on Chiloé; **Werner** and **Cecilia Ruf-Chaura**, at the *Casa Cecilia*, Puerto Natales, provided valuable material on Puerto Natales; **Patricio Guzmán**, in Coyhaique, for information on the Coyhaique region and his brother **Luis Guzmán**, in Chillán, for material on traditional handicrafts; **Dereck Foster**, of the *Buenos Aires Herald*, provided comments and ideas on Chilean wines; assistance on this topic was also received from **Charlie Stephenson** (*Oddbins*, Cambridge UK); **Ben Box** editor of the *South American Handbook*, was, as ever, generous with his time, advice and support.

The author would like to thank the following for their kind hospitality and assistance during his visit to Chile in 1999: **Adrian Turner** of *Travellers*, Puerto Montt; **Rodda Thomas** in Osorno; **Carlos Grady** at the *Hospedaje Esmeralda by the Sea*, Chonchi; **Nicolas La Penna** of *Chaitur* in Chaitén; **Luis** and **Alicia Guzmán** in Chillán; **Marilú Cerda** in Santiago.